# THE GROWTH OF
# PAPAL GOVERNMENT
# IN THE MIDDLE AGES

RECONSTRUCTION OF MEDIEVAL ST. PETER'S, ROME

Originally drawn by H. W. Brewer in *The Builder*, vol. lxii (1892).
Drawing modified by M. Crostarosa (cf. H. Grisar, *Geschichte Roms und der Päpste*, Freiburg, 1901, pp. 239, 832)

# THE GROWTH OF
# PAPAL GOVERNMENT
# IN THE MIDDLE AGES

*A study in the ideological relation
of clerical to lay power*

by
## WALTER ULLMANN

METHUEN & CO. LTD LONDON
11 NEW FETTER LANE, EC4

*First published in* 1955
*Second edition* 1962
*Reprinted with minor corrections* 1965
*Third edition* 1970
*Printed in Great Britain by*
*John Dickens & Co Ltd, Northampton*
SBN 416 15890 0
3.1

*Distributed in the USA*
*by Barnes & Noble Inc*

# *Preface*

THERE are probably fewer topics in history which have attracted greater attention than the perennial problem of the relations between Church and State. For the medieval period, however, it is increasingly recognized that this modern dichotomy has little, if any, meaning. At the same time it is generally recognized that the medieval papacy, certainly after the late eleventh century, exercised considerable governmental authority over empires, kingdoms, princedoms, and so forth.

What this book attempts to do is to trace the development of papal governmental authority. Roughly speaking, the period which witnessed this evolution was that between Emperor Gratian and Master Gratian. By the time of Master Gratian the development was virtually concluded: the period from the mid-twelfth century onwards, beginning with Alexander III's pontificate, shows the papal government at work through the agency of the law—the canon law—the scientific elaboration of which owed so much to the monk of Bologna. In the last chapters I have found it advisable to indicate in the notes how the one or the other point developed in the later period.

This essay is not written from the papal, or imperial, or royal or any particular point of view; nor does it try to justify or to refute any standpoint or theory or ideology, past or present. It tries, with the limited resources accessible to a mere student of history, to find an answer to the question of how this papal government grew, what factors contributed to its growth, what obstacles it had to overcome, what were its essential features, and so forth. The problem of the secular power is most intimately linked with these central questions: what functions did papal doctrine attribute to a king or an emperor, and why was he to assume a position of inferiority—these and numerous other topics are so essential to the theory of papal government that they are part and parcel of the central theme. Therefore, this essay is not a history of the medieval papacy or of the medieval Church, but is concerned with the development of the basic principles upon which rested the governmental authority of the Roman Church in the medieval period. A very modest attempt is here made to explain this development

v

with the help of historical facts. I felt that one kind of modern historiography is too much concerned with the presentation of facts to the detrimental exclusion of ideas which, after all, are closely related to these facts, whilst another kind of historiography deals too much with the presentation of ideas and virtually excludes the historically relevant facts. This essay is a very humble attempt to build a bridge between these two extremes by the combination of the processes of re-thinking and therefore of re-assessing.

Considering the multitude of elements which went to make the governmental edifice of the medieval papacy, I am fully aware of the weaknesses and shortcomings of this essay. Perhaps not its least defect lies in its not taking into account St Augustine. I may perhaps be allowed to say that originally I had of course intended to give Augustinian thought its due, but I became convinced that its presentation would not only involve his "political" theories, but also his teleology of history, Platonism and Neo-Platonism no less than the other agencies which moulded the great African's mind. But this can no longer be done within a chapter or two. As it was, I had to deal with a great number of topics which—for inscrutable reasons—lie outside the historian's view, such as liturgy, symbolism, and so forth. I can only hope that I have not made too many blunders in these departments which I strongly feel are far too little the direct concern of medieval historians, although they are by no means the only ones which should at least be accorded the status of auxiliary sciences.[1]

The long period which this book covers, necessitated some care in the selection of literary sources. I preferred to rely on the actual texts and have therefore quoted at fairly great length from them, because so much depends on the actual (and usually carefully chosen) wording of the record. I have for this reason also preferred, if possible, not to translate. The pitfalls of translating medieval Latin, particularly of official records, and the consequential blurring of their meaning, are commonplace knowledge. I am fully conscious of the inadequacy of my modern literary apparatus, but if the footnotes were not to become too unwieldy, a severe pruning had to take place: even so, they are still very long and numerous. I have cited liberally modern authorities

---

[1] This applies also and to a very special degree to philology—"cette mère nourricière de l'histoire" (F. L. Ganshof in *Revue belge de philologie et d'histoire,* xxx (1952), p. 1275)—and the decline in the knowledge of Latin nowadays can, from the medievalist's standpoint, only be viewed with alarm. Medieval jurisprudence and a grounding in Roman law principles is one more such subject that should at least be raised to an auxiliary historical science.

in the language in which they were originally written. I believe that herewith a service to the reader is rendered who, indeed, is not helped when confronted with a string of references to authorities—original and secondary—which he is not usually in a position to check, unless he is permanently resident in some great library. The terminology adopted which at first sight may seem unfamiliar, is derived from the actual expressions, terms, phrases, etc., occurring in the historical documents. I am not unaware of a certain repetitiveness, but in mitigation I may plead that this is conditioned by the subject itself. Nor do I fail to see that some concepts and facts merited lengthier treatment, but again my plea is that if the study was not to become too unwieldy, it was advisable to indicate certain developments—pointing to further literature—rather than to try and attempt to write exhaustively. My main object was to concentrate on the fundamental principles.

A glance at the notes will show in fact better than I can do in words how much I owe to the modern pioneers of medieval historical scholarship. It is with a very deep sense of gratitude that I acknowledge my great debt to them: without them this book could never have been written. Some of those to whom I am so greatly indebted, are no longer *inter vivos*—may this essay not be unworthy of their pioneering works.

Immediate and personal help I have had from many quarters: to name them all would be tedious. But it would be ungracious on my part, were I not to say how much stimulus I have derived from my pupils, undergraduates and graduate research students alike.

There remains for me only to discharge a very pleasant duty and to thank two of my colleagues in the University who have had the kindness and patience to read through the typescript of the book and to criticize it to my very great profit. To both of them, to Mr R. F. Bennett, of Magdalene College, and to Mr C. N. L. Brooke, of Gonville and Caius College, I owe far more than the cold printed word can convey. I most gratefully acknowledge their valuable help so generously given. *Amicis fidelibus nulla est comparatio.*

Lastly, I must thank my wife for her constant forbearance and assistance.

Trinity College,                                        W.U.
Cambridge
21 August, 1953

# Preface to the Second Edition

A GOOD deal of new material has been made available since this volume was originally finished, and the need for a second edition should have provided an opportunity for not only incorporating this new material, but also for improving and clarifying the text where this might have appeared advisable. But apart from the fact that the work has already seen a revised and somewhat enlarged German edition (*Die Machtstellung des Papsttums im Mittelalter* (Graz-Cologne, 1960) ), this procedure would have entailed the resetting of the whole book and would thus have greatly increased the costs. The other alternative was to let the text stand and simply to reprint, but I could not bring myself to adopt this alternative. The new material did not on the whole seem to justify the adoption of the first alternative, because none of the essential points is in need of drastic revision or modification as a result of new publications or additional material. On the other hand, this new and additional material appeared to be both in quantity and quality sufficiently weighty and meritorious to be at least mentioned without however incurring the necessity of resetting the entire book. I have therefore adopted a compromise solution and have added in a few places that literature which would seem to be of use to those readers who would like to have up-to-date information. But I have by no means added every new article or book or source and have only appended the most appropriate and relevant literature, in so far as it has appeared since August 1953 or should have been originally included. Modifications and additions to many passages in the text have been added in Appendix B (page 461). My publishers have asked me to apologize on their behalf for this rather cumbersome solution, but they point out that without it the price of the book would have had to be even more significantly increased than it is.

My continued occupation with the records of papal history in the Middle Ages has further clarified a number of concepts and principles and has once again shown to me the consistency and coherency of papal thought in the Middle Ages. Since the papacy entered the historic scene in the fifth century, its inflexible adherence to the correctly understood monarchic principle through the centuries must indeed appear remarkable to the historian who is attuned to witness change on the plane of historical process. True enough, the papacy in these medieval centuries often lacked the means or the opportunities to translate its doctrines of government into practice, and often enough temporary shifts and accommodations to an already existing situation or even seemingly wholesale reversals of earlier steps can easily be observed, but—and this is the vital point—the stubbornness and resilience with which the papacy clung to its doctrinal programme, is indeed one of the most noteworthy features in the history of European institutions. When dealing with the papacy, the enquirer stands on very firm ground, because the material flows so richly from the papal pens. For this programme was derived, as the popes loudly, insistently and constantly proclaimed, from the Bible and was held by them and by contemporary Europe to be nothing less than the practical realization of biblical doctrine. The link with divinity was a most potent element that supplied—in the contemporary environs—the firmest possible base. Divinity spoke through the papacy, so it was held, and when due recognition is given to this fact, not only the constancy but also the appealing logicality of the papal programme becomes understandable.

It is therefore incomprehensible how some writers nowadays can maintain, amongst other things, that the programme and principles of the medieval papacy underwent radical changes: in particular it is asserted that after Innocent III the papacy changed its original dualist programme into an hierocratic standpoint. He who asserts a point of view such as this, stands convicted before the historic forum on a charge of ignorance of the sources or culpable lack of understanding of the papal theme.[1] For it was always one of the sources of strength

[1] These writers—they are less numerous than their vociferously publicized views would suggest—conveniently overlook that the very term and idea of a *dualitas* of government was the invention of the excommunicated and deposed King Henry IV to be used as an instrument *against* the papacy; and this dualist idea became the panacea of royal and imperial governments in opposition to the papacy from the Investiture Contest down to the Reformation. But these writers now wish to tell their unsuspecting and uninitiated readers that the dualism was the official papal programme from which only the thirteenth-century papacy deviated. For Henry IV see infra, pp. 345 ff., and see also my remarks in my Preface to *Machtstellung*, at pp. xxxiv ff. and in *Hist. Z.*, cxci (1960), pp. 620 ff. It is particularly teasing to read that Innocent III was a "dualist" and that the deviation was especially due to Innocent IV and Boniface VIII. One has but to look at the legislative output of Innocent III and at the commentaries and glosses on the *Compilationes Antiquae* (notably II, III, IV) which contained overwhelmingly Innocentian material, to realize the effects of this pontificate upon the crystallization of hierocratic thought.

of the papal government that it simply made known God's will through the vehicle of the law and continued the lines laid down by antecedent popes. They who would like to see such radical changes in the papal programme and attribute to the thirteenth-century papacy this deviationism, put—admittedly, unknowingly and unwittingly—the papacy on a level not different from a royal or a city or a village government, revive in a different form the long-demolished thesis of Rudolf Sohm and by implication deny that very element which was the hallmark of the papacy, that is, its being a specific organ of divinity instituted for particular purposes by Christ Himself. There is no need to dwell at any length on the logical consequences to which this falsification of history must necessarily lead. The secret of the papacy's success in the Middle Ages lay precisely in that it inflexibly adhered to its programme and principles and vital axioms because it held them to be of divine origin. Any other explanation or "view" comes dangerously close to asserting the changeability of divinity itself. It can, however, readily be conceded that this programme of the medieval papacy causes some discomfort to the historically untrained or uninformed, and it can furthermore be admitted that from a practical modern point of view this medieval papal programme appears disconcerting or even disagreeable, but historical truth as contained in the thousands of papal communications from the fifth to the fifteenth centuries cannot take into account modern requirements—with the inevitable result that history becomes tailored so as to fit a transient scheme.

Whilst the historic recognition of the programme itself does not constitute major difficulties, there are nevertheless a number of problems which are still in need of detailed examination. One of these concerns the extent to which the medieval papacy has relied on the Bible. This question does not focus attention on the correctness or incorrectness of biblical interpretation by the papacy, because this is not the business of the historian; nor does this question primarily refer to the invocation of the already well-known passages. What this question concerns is the less obvious, hidden and unacknowledged influence of the Bible upon, not only the programme, but also on the style, language and thought processes of the papacy. My occupation with papal history has convinced me that more often than not the papal writer himself was unaware of the biblical root of his views or expressions. I have collected a good deal of material on this point, but to have incorporated it in this book would probably have doubled its size. This dependence on the Bible is not at all startling—it equally applies to royal and imperial governments, with this difference, however, that by its very function the papacy had far more opportunities of being influenced by the Bible than the other forms of government. It is, after all, not so very difficult to understand how the Bible became part and parcel of the papal equipment, and this without the popes themselves becoming aware of the constant infusion of biblical terms, elements, views, allegories, etc., into their mental system.[1] It will be seen, however, that a number of preparatory studies has first to be undertaken and that the inclusion of this cluster of problems into the present volume would not only have been premature, but also inadvisable. But this is only one of the many problems still awaiting its treatment *ex professo*, though it is possibly the most urgent.

Only one or two of these other problems can here be mentioned. The detailed influence of the Roman law and of the Roman constitution upon the papacy and its principles of government is one such topic that needs to be examined and analysed. This is especially important in regard to the fifth and sixth centuries, those centuries in which the legal and constitutional bases of the papal government were laid and in which the papacy came to assume its own institutional personality. The challenge issued by the papacy to the imperial government would indeed show that the papacy felt itself strong enough to enter into a conflict with its adversary in Constantinople on grounds which were the latter's own—the law, which in its papal shape had received its characteristic Roman sustenance and complexion and had become Roman law applied and adjusted. As far as I can see at present, however, a satisfactory treatment of this problem of Roman law influence will have to distinguish between the influence of classical Roman law and that of the Justinianean codification. That a host of subsidiary questions will emerge in connexion with this basic problem, needs not specifically to be stated. Another problem is that of the concrete and provable influence of Western royal governments and other secular institutions upon the papacy, that is, how much were, institutionally, the popes the *famuli* and the kings the *magistri?*[2] Not far removed from this topic is the analysis of the relations between

---

[1] A good illustration is afforded by the very concept of "*positive* law" which seems foreshadowed in the Bible where the terminology is consistently *legem ponere* (or *dare* or *condere*), a terminology which clearly betrays legislative omnipotence. On this cf. my remarks in *Revue d'histoire du droit*, xxix (1961), pp. 118 ff.

[2] For a few remarks cf. my *Principles of Government and Politics in the Middle Ages* (London, 1961), pp. 108 ff.

the papacy and Eastern governments, such as Poland, Hungary, Russia, Lithuania, Estonia, and so forth; clearly, this group of problems must be seen in relation to the Byzantine empire on the one hand and to the West-Roman empire on the other hand. In what way did the capture of Constantinople affect the implementation of papal doctrine towards the other Eastern governments? How far did German and papal aspirations towards the East coincide, how far did they overlap and how far were they antagonistic to each other? It is high time that the influence of papal legislation upon what later came to be known as international law, were investigated in detail,[1] for a number of stipulations in present-day international law have indisputably their roots in the medieval papal legislation, because the pope as *speculator omnium* and *universalis monarcha*, thus standing above the inter-regal turmoil, claimed to regulate the relations between kingdoms. No less important a topic to be examined is the problem of the period of time which a number of papal principles took to come to full fruition. Why was it that some principles as soon as they were enunciated, became part and parcel of the papal mental equipment, whilst others had to wait a very long time before they could find favour? These latter lay, so to speak, dormant and were resuscitated only after a very long time. How is one to explain this feature? An obvious instance is the development of the concept of the pope's vicariate of Christ: Paul I in the eighth century had it pronounced as clearly as one might, and yet it took just about another four hundred years before the concept became operational. Further, how far did the dogmatic and patristic literature influence the papacy and how far was the latter instrumental in shaping dogma and doctrine? One more and rather urgent problem that awaits its historical and structural analysis is that of the relations between the papacy and the episcopacy. Episcopalism was a very serious—perhaps the most serious—obstacle to the full deployment of papal governmental principles; in fact, episcopalism constituted a far more obstinate impediment to the papal government than any royal or imperial opposition. How did the papacy, at least temporarily, overcome episcopalism, how was the latter, so to speak, driven underground, and how did it gather force again in the late Middle Ages? These are only a few of the problems which the opulent history of the medieval papacy poses. Much work has yet to be done, and it may perhaps not be presumptuous to express the hope that those who are so anxious to tailor medieval papal history to modern exigencies,

[1] Cf. infra, p. 450.

might one day profitably and constructively direct their energies to the one or the other problem here mentioned.

Once again I would like to thank the many friends and colleagues who have sent me offprints of their articles and papers and copies of their books: only he who knows how easily new publications may escape notice, will appreciate this generosity.

Cambridge,                                                                                          W.U.
15 November, 1961


Apart from some small additions and the correction of some misprints no substantial changes have been made in this printing. But in order to assist the reader, I have put asterisks (*) in the margin of the texts and footnotes to indicate that Appendix B has additional material or adjustments to the text.

Cambridge,                                                                                          W.U.
21 October, 1964


## *Preface to the Third Edition*

The amount of new material that has become available in recent years still does not warrant a revision of the work which in any case would have been, in present conditions, a very costly undertaking. I have therefore continued the method which I adopted on previous occasions and have added in a new Appendix C some of the new literature which appeared to me particularly relevant, but it should be borne in mind that in order to keep this Appendix as short as possible to save costs, the supplementation represents a mere fraction of the new material. Again, for the benefit of the reader I have indicated by a dagger (†) in the margin of text and notes that Appendix C contains new matter.

Cambridge,                                                                                          W.U.
17 April, 1969

# Contents

*Frontispiece*

Reconstruction of Medieval St. Peter's Rome
(*Reproduced by kind permission of Herder & Co., Freiburg*)

# Abbreviations

| | |
|---|---|
| CSEL. | *Corpus scriptorum ecclesiasticorum latinorum* |
| D. | Diploma |
| DA. | Dictate of Avranches |
| DAC. | *Dictionnaire d'archéologie chrétienne et de liturgie* |
| DHE. | *Dictionnaire d'histoire et de géographie ecclésiastiques* |
| DP. | Dictate of the Pope (Gregory VII) |
| EHR. | *English Historical Review* |
| Ep. | Epistola |
| Epp. | Epistolae |
| hist. | historical; historique; historisch |
| *Hist. Jb.* | *Historisches Jahrbuch der Görresgesellschaft* |
| *Hist. Z.* | *Historische Zeitschrift* |
| J. | Ph. Jaffé, *Regesta Pontificum Romanorum*, 2nd ed. |
| LdL. | *Libelli de Lite* |
| MA. | Middle Ages; Moyen Age; Mittelalter |
| Mansi | J. D. Mansi, *Sacrorum conciliorum nova et amplissima collectio* |
| MGH. *Const.* | *Monumenta Germaniae Historica: Constitutiones* |
| MGH. *Epp.* | *Monumenta Germaniae Historica: Epistolae* |
| MGH. *Leges* | *Monumenta Germaniae Historica: Leges* |
| MGH. *SS.* | *Monumenta Germaniae Historica: Scriptores* |
| MIOG. | *Mitteilungen des Instituts für oesterreichische Geschichtsforschung* |
| *Misc.* | *Miscellanea* |
| OR. | *Ordo Romanus* |
| PG. | J. P. Migne, *Patrologia Graeca* |
| PL. | J. P. Migne, *Patrologia Latina* |
| Potthast | A. Potthast, *Regesta Pontificum Romanorum* |
| *Reg.* | Register |
| RHE. | *Revue d'histoire ecclésiastique* |
| RNI. | *Regestum Innocentii III papae super negotio Romani imperii* |

| | |
|---|---|
| *Sav. Z. Kan. Abt.* | *Zeitschrift der Savigny Stiftung für Rechtsgeschichte Kanonistische Abteilung* |
| *Sav. Z. Roman. Abt.* | *Zeitschrift der Savigny Stiftung für Rechtsgeschichte Romanistische Abteilung* |
| *Sav. Z. Germ. Abt.* | *Zeitschrift der Savigny Stiftung für Rechtsgeschichte Germanistische Abteilung* |
| SB. | *Sitzungsberichte* |
| SB. *Vienna* | *Sitzungsberichte der Akademie der Wissenschaften, phil. hist. Klasse, Wien* |
| SB. *Munich* | *Sitzungsberichte der bayrischen Akademie d. Wissenschaften* |
| SB. *Berlin* | *Sitzungsberichte der preussischen Akademie d. Wissenschaften* |
| SB. *Heidelberg* | *Sitzungsberichte der Heidelberger Akademie d. Wissenschaften* |
| SS. RR. GG. | *Scriptores Rerum Germanicarum* |
| Z. | *Zeitschrift* |

(Biblical references are to the Vulgate.)

# CHAPTER I

# *Introduction*

THE manifestation of papal governmental authority in the Middle Ages illustrates the strength of an idea and its transformation into law. The government effected by the papacy was a potent factor in every sphere of medieval life. How did the papacy—and with it the priesthood—reach this position? To be more precise, what elements assisted, and what elements retarded, the growth of papal governmental authority in the Middle Ages? From small beginnings, from an insignificant community in the capital of the Roman empire, the Church of Rome developed into the most influential and important governmental institution in the medieval period. The whole of medieval Europe—Western Europe—from Iceland to the Mediterranean, from Ireland to Hungary, was in receipt of the decrees, mandates, rescripts and verdicts issuing forth in prolific quantities from the Church of Rome. Within these regions, within Latin Christendom, there was no emperor, no king, no prince; there was no bishop or abbot; no layman or cleric, however high or low, whose life in one way or another was not affected by the exercise of papal authority.

In studying this growth the historian cannot but be struck by its steady continuity. The papal theory of government rested upon certain principles and themes. Throughout the history of the medieval papacy there is observable a unity of themes and a consistency of principles which were detectable *in nuce* even before the name "pope" (*papa*) or the term "papacy" (*papatus*) were coined. And of these themes and principles none was more fundamental than that of the conception of the Church and the qualification of those of its members who were to govern it. Baptism secured membership of the Church, but membership as such did not entail the proper qualification for governing it. Another element, namely ordination, was needed to secure, according to papal views, the right to direct the Church. The distinction between ordained and unordained members of the Church, between clerics and laymen, was the distinction which was not only to give medieval society its peculiar imprint, but also to make the problems of this society, that is, of Latin Christendom, accessible to understanding. The distinction—not between Church and State, but between clergy and laity as parts of one and the same unit—is a thread that runs throughout the medieval period.

## I

In the realm of government the teleological principle upon which any society must needs rest, operates through the principle of functional qualification. For society and its government are two complementary concepts. The latter directs the former in accordance with its underlying purpose or aim, its "finis" or "telos". Only those who are qualified, claim to be entitled to govern; and the qualification depends upon the nature and purpose of society. The function of rulership presupposes the fulfilment of certain qualifications. He who is qualified to translate the purpose for which society exists, into concrete terms and measures, acts in the capacity of a ruler: he functions as a ruler, because he is appropriately qualified. This principle of functional qualification is operative in any society. The form of rulership or government, whether monarchic or oligarchic or aristocratic and so forth, may vary, but this does not affect the general principle.

When Pope Leo I spoke of himself as functioning on behalf of St Peter—"cuius vice *fungimur*"—he succinctly expressed the principle of functional qualification in monarchic form.[1] By virtue of succeeding to the chair of St Peter, Leo claimed that he alone was functionally qualified to rule the universal Church, that is, to rule it on the monarchic principle.[2] This designation by Leo of the pope as "vicar of St Peter" was new; the idea which it embodied was not. The formula chosen by Leo was the dress in which the idea of the *principatus* of the Roman Church was clothed.

The idea embodied in the term *principatus* belongs to the realm of government. And government concerned the direction and orientation of the body of Christians, that is, of the universal Church. The Church designates the corporate union of all believers in Christ, as it was so manifestly made clear in Pauline doctrine. But this doctrine also makes

---

[1] The term "fungimur" may be borrowed from II *Cor.* v. 20.

[2] *Sermo* 3, cap. 4 (we quote from the Ballerini edition in Migne, PL. liv). Cf. also *Sermo* 4, c. 2: "De toto mundo *unus* Petrus eligitur, qui et universarum gentium vocationi et omnibus apostolis cunctisque ecclesiae patribus praeponatur; ut quamvis in *populo Dei* multi sacerdotes sint multique pastores, omnes tamen proprie *regat Petrus*, quos principaliter *regit et Christus*."

it clear that this body, the *unum corpus*, is not merely a pneumatic or sacramental or spiritual body, but also an organic, concrete and earthy society. This dual nature of the *corpus Christi* is of fundamental importance:[1] the element, however, which brings this concrete body into existence, which makes the union a corporate entity, is the spiritual element of the Christian faith: this element alone gives this body its complexion. As a body the *corpus Christi* is in need of direction and orientation: although the many constitute this *unum corpus*, not all have the same functions within it. There are gradations of functions within this body; and one of these functions concerns the actual government of this Christian society, called the universal Church, so as to bring its underlying purpose, its "finis" or "telos" to fruition. The presupposition for this is unity of the body, and unity will be achieved by the dovetailing of the various functions or offices so as to make the body an integrated whole.

The government of this Christian body,[2] like that of any other society, necessitates authoritative guidance and recognition of this authority by the governed. As we have said, the constitutive element of this Christian *corpus* was the spiritual-sacramental one; being constitutive, it is also determinative for the selection of those of its members who are particularly fitted or qualified to lead or to guide it. The authoritative element manifesting itself in the direction and orientation of the *corpus* is the result of what came later to be called ordination.[3] And through ordination the most important distinction is drawn be-

[1] In early philosophic theory this dualism (spiritual—corporeal) is also applied to God Himself, cf., e.g., Tertullian, *Adversus Praxean*, c. vii: "Quis enim negaverit, Deum corpus esse, etsi Deus spiritus est? Spiritus enim corpus sui generis in sua effigie." (Quoted from Ueberweg-Geyer, *Grundriss der Geschichte der Philosophie*, 12th ed., Basel, 1951, p. 51.)

[2] The terminology which was applied to this body, varied: it was called "communio" or "koinonia" or "societas" or "unitas"; for this see L. Hertling, "Communio und Primat" in *Xenia Piana*, 1943, pp. 3 ff. But cf. also P. Batiffol, *Cathedra Petri: Etudes d'histoire ancienne de l'église*, Paris, 1938, p. 203, who speaks of a "fellowship." This *corpus* could be, and was, conceived as a juristic entity and as such it was to play in later hierocratic thought a crucial role. Cf., e.g., the second-century Roman jurist Pomponius distinguishing between three kinds of *corpora*: "Tertium (corpus) quod ex distantibus constat, ut corpora plura non soluta, sed uni nomini subjecta, veluti populus, legio, grex," *Dig.* 41.3.30 pr. On the juristic transformation of the Pauline idea of the *corpus* cf. M. Roberti, "Il corpus mysticum di S. Paolo nella storia della persona giuridica" in *Studi in onore di Enrico Besta*, Milan, 1939, iv. 37–82; here also further literature. Cf. now also A. Ehrhardt, "Das Corpus Christi und die Korporation im spät-röm. Recht" in *Sav. Z. Rom. Abt.*, lxx (1953), 299–347. The great work of O. Gierke is still fundamental.

[3] For this see especially L. Hertling, art. cit., pp. 24–6.

tween the members constituting the *unum corpus*, that between the lay
and sacerdotal members.[1] The members of the Church are divided into
categories according to their functions: there are certain functions—
and they are the important ones considering the nature of the *corpus*—
for the fulfilment of which unordained members are not qualified; they
do not possess the necessary functional qualifications. Although "we
are one body in Christ", "all members have not the same office". On
the model of the easily available Roman terminology, the ordained
members are said to form an *ordo*.[2] This designation of *ordo* will also
later be applied to the unordained members of the *corpus*, so that the
*ordo laicalis* and the *ordo sacerdotalis* will form the *ecclesia*.

The form of government was monarchic. Only in the monarchic
form could be found the guarantee of unity: only the leadership provided by one sole authority was considered adequate to prevent disunity and schism. Whilst there is sufficient evidence to warrant the
confident assertion that the bishop of Rome exercised an authoritative
position, that is, acted within the monarchic frame of government
from early times onwards, the theoretical exposition of his authoritative
function followed considerably later: the theoretical exposition presupposed the realization and clarification of the primatial position of St
Peter himself.[3] Since the Roman Church was held to be the "cathedra
Petri", the "primatus Petri" could then be applied to the pope as St
Peter's successor.

It may be recalled that towards the end of the second century,
Irenaeus wrote that the Roman Church had *principalitas* over the other
churches. This *principalitas* of the Roman Church in course of time

---

[1] The distinction is already referred to in the letter of (Pope) Clement to the
Corinthians: the hieroi and the laikoi (cap. 40: F. X. Funk, *Patres apostol.*, ed.
K. Bihlmayer, 1924, i. 47). It is not without significance that the distinction was
drawn on the occasion of a constitutional conflict, see E. Kohlmeyer, "Charisma
oder Recht" in *Sav. Z.*, *kan. Abt.*, xxxviii (1952), p. 31. This Clement letter is
usually taken as the first clear manifestation of Roman primatial authority. Against
this see Dom R. van Cauwelaert, "L'intervention de l'église de Rome à Corinthe"
in RHE., xxxi (1935), pp. 267 ff., especially pp. 282 ff. Cf. p. 305: "Analysant le
text luimême de la *Ia Clementis* nous n'y avons trouvé aucune affirmation explicite
des droits du siège romain. L'autorité sur laquelle elle déclare s'appuyer, et le
style de sa composition n'impliquent pas davantage un appel à la primauté." Cf.
also idem, ibid., pp. 765 f. But see now G. Bardy in DHE. xii. 1092.

[2] See Tertullian. *De exhortatione castitatis*, cap. 7 (C. Mirbt, *Quellen zur Geschichte des Papsttums*, Tübingen, 4th ed., 1924, no. 56, p. 25): "Differentiam
inter ordinem et plebem constituit ecclesiae auctoritas, et honor per ordinis concessum sanctificatus." Cf. also L. Eisenhofer, *Grundriss der Liturgik*, 5th ed. by
L. Lechner, Freiburg, 1950, pp. 277, 278; here also further literature.

[3] *Matt.* xvi. 18; *John*, xxi. 15.

gave way to the thoroughly Roman political formula of the *principatus apostolicae sedis*. The term "apostolica sedes" was applied to the Roman Church alone and excluded the other apostolic cities: this one Church claimed jurisdictional, that is, supreme governmental powers. Now the time and the occasion of the coining of the term "apostolica sedes" is not without significance.[1] It was used as a reply to Constantinople's pretensions expressed as they were in the third canon of Constantinople (381) according to which Constantinople, because it was New Rome, claimed to rank immediately after (Old) Rome.[2] The Roman synod held the year after (382) confronted this Eastern claim with the argument firstly, that the Roman Church was not founded by a synodal decree; secondly, that the Roman Church owed its primatial position to the commission given to St Peter by Christ; and thirdly, that, unique amongst all churches, the Roman Church was founded by two apostles, SS. Peter and Paul, whilst Constantinople had no warranty for claiming apostolic foundation.[3]

The important point is therefore the "double apostolicity" of the Roman Church which therefrom derives jurisdictional and magisterial primacy. Being founded by two apostles, the Roman Church was held to be the "exordium" of all Christian religion.[4] It was not merely the

---

[1] It was first coined by Pope Damasus in 378, see P. Batiffol, "Papa, sedes apostolica, apostolatus" in *Rivista di archeologia cristiana*, ii (1925), pp. 99–116; idem, op cit., pp. 151–68; and H. Rahner, "Navicula Petri" in *Z. f. kath. Theol.*, lxix (1947), pp. 28–9.

[2] Cf. now also V. Monachino, "Genesi storica del can. 28° di Calcedonia" in *Gregorianum*, xxxiii (1952), pp. 267 ff., and T. O. Martin in *Chalkedon*, ii (1953), 435 ff.

[3] The (third) canon was contained in the so-called *Decretum Gelasianum*: PL. xiii. 374 = Pseudo-Isidore, ed. P. Hinschius, p. 635; also edited by E. Dobschütz in *Texte und Untersuchungen zur altchristlichen Literatur*, xxxviii, no. 4, 1912, pp. 29–31. It runs: "Sancta tamen Romana ecclesia nullis synodicis constitutis ceteris ecclesiis praelata est, sed evangelica voce domini nostri primatum obtinuit: Tu es Petrus . . . Cui addita est etiam societas beatissimi Pauli apostoli vasis electionis, qui non diverso, sicut haeretici garriunt, sed uno tempore, uno eodemque die gloriosa morte cum Petro in urbe Roma sub Caesare Nerone agonizans coronatus est, *et pariter* supradictam sanctam Romanam ecclesiam Christo domino consecraverunt talesque omnibus urbibus in universo mundo sua praesentia atque venerando triumpho praetulerunt. Est ergo prima Petri apostoli sedes Romana ecclesia non habens maculam neque rugam nec aliquid huiusmodi." For the historical background cf. also E. Caspar, *Geschichte des Papsttums*, Tübingen, 1930, i. 241 ff., esp. 247 ff. For the *Decretum Gelasianum* idem, ibid., 598 and H. Leclercq in DAC. vi. 722–47.

[4] Cf., for example, the *Oratio* in the *Missale Romanum*, ad 29 June: "Deus, qui hodiernam diem apostolorum tuorum Petri et Pauli martyrio consecrasti . . . per quos religionis sumpsit exordium." In the first decretal issued by the papacy (385 by Siricius, cf. infra p. 7, 12) this double apostolicity is skillfully blended for

centre therefore, but also the epitome[1] of all Christianity: all Christianity and hence also all ecclesiastical life was in a concentrated, epitomized form in the Roman Church. From this doubly apostolic foundation,[2] from the Roman Church, all religious and ecclesiastical life emanated: Christianity was diffused throughout the world from that doubly apostolic city.[3] From the point of view of the corporate nature of the Christian body, of the universal Church, the fruitfulness of this idea can hardly be exaggerated: all Christian life was to flow downwards from the head of the body.[4] The corporate union was ruled monarchically by the head: the metaphorical application of the *caput-membra* relationship, suggested in Pauline doctrine, was to prove

---

legislative purposes. St Paul's statement (II *Cor.* xi. 28) that on him "the care of all the churches" rests, is applied to the pope ("nos ... quibus praecipue secundum Paulum instantia quotidiana et sollicitudo omnium ecclesiarum indesinenter incumbit" decr. cit.) in whom St Peter carries the burden of all: "Portamus onera omnium, qui graventur: quinimo haec portat in nobis beatus apostolus Petrus, qui nos in omnibus, ut confidimus, administrationis suae protegit et tuetur haeredes." It was for the first time that the two statements were made and they were made in the first decretal issued by the papacy. The Pauline statement together with *Matt.* xvi. 18 was from now on to form the backbone of the thousands of decretals coming forth from the Roman chancery. About the "heirs" cf. infra p. 8 n. 4.

[1] Due consideration should, in this context, be given to the terms used by second-century Roman jurists who operated with Ciceronian phraseology: Rome was the fatherland of all. Cf., e.g., Modestinus: "Roma communis nostra patria est" (*Dig.* 50.1.33; cf. idem, *Dig.* 27.1.6 (11)); cf. also Callistratus: "Roma omnium est patria" (*Dig.* 48.22.19). See Cicero, *De lege agraria*, ii. 86: "Contra hanc Romam, communem patriam omnium nostrum." Cf. also *De oratore*, i. 196: "Patria parens omnium nostrum."

[2] The late E. Eichmann, *Weihe und Krönung des Papstes im Mittelalter* (ed. Kl. Mörsdorf, in *Münchener Theologische Studien*, 1951), pp. 49–55, refers also to the designation of John VIII as "vicarius ipsorum" (i.e. Petri et Pauli) and to the fact that the pallium was worn "ad honorem b.apostolorum Petri et Pauli." The appeal of Gregory VII to the two apostles is too well known to need any comment. In later times this double apostolicity was, as Eichmann points out, also of great symbolic importance on the occasion of the pope's coronation. During the coronation ceremony the pope had to take physical possession of the two curule chairs which designated the chairs of St Peter and St Paul. According to OR. XII, the pope took physical possession of these two chairs by half sitting (or lying) on them. See OR. XII, PL. lxxviii. 1098, no. 79: "Qui siquidem electus in illis duabus sedibus sic sedere debet, ac si videatur inter duos lectulos jacere, id est, ut accumbat inter principis apostolorum primatum Petri, et Pauli doctoris gentium praedicationem."

[3] See again canon iii of the Roman synod of 382: "Universae per orbem catholicae *diffusae* ecclesiae." Cf. also Boniface I infra p. 7.

[4] A contemporary similar point of view can be found in the so-called "Ambrosiaster", cf. E. Caspar, op. cit., i. 243–4. On the work itself see the comprehensive study of C. Martini, *Ambrosiaster*, Rome, 1944. See also Leo himself, Ep. 78: "Ut ab ipso quodam capite dona sua velut in corpus omne *diffunderet*."

commission of powers will be understood to signify St Peter's vicariate of Christ.[1]

The sum total of jurisdictional powers entrusted to St Peter was conceived as a *principatus*.[2] Consequently, the pope too had the *principatus*. The Innocentian "*auctoritas*" appeared now in the Leonine *principatus*.[3] Because the pope occupies the "*apostolica sedes*" he inherits St Peter's *principatus*. The term is the political expression of the jurisdictional primacy of the Roman Church within the Christian *corpus*, the "*mundus*".[4]

Nevertheless, whilst Leo I was so anxious to establish the *principatus*, there is every indication that his contemporary emperors sensed the inherent danger that lay in the idea enshrined in the term *principatus*. The papal anxiety to apply the *principatus* to the "*apostolica sedes*" was paralleled by the imperial anxiety to withhold this meaningful designation from the Roman Church.[5] Indeed, the imperial and papal points of view are wholly understandable. The empire had become Christian in every respect: from the papal point of view this entity could very well be considered as the corporate union of Christians, as the *corpus* of Christians—who, because they were Christians, had to be ruled by the successor of St Peter; for from the "*apostolica sedes*" alone Christianity took its visible origin. On the other hand, quite apart from the prevalence of the old conception, namely that the emperor was also the

---

(Pomponius): "Haereditas domini loco habetur." All these jurists belonged to the second century A.D. The juristic contents of Leo's statements and conceptions have also struck Klinkenberg, art. cit., pp. 58, 59 ("juristische Denkweise des Papstes"): An Stelle der Spekulation setzt Leo in juristischer Methode die wie einen Gesetzestext behandelte heilige Schrift . . . römische Jurisprudenz gegen griechische Metaphysik."

[1] In this context the sagacious observations of Hertling concerning the evolution of a thesis should be heeded, art. cit., pp. 26, 39–42.

[2] Ep. 9, preface: "A domino acceperit *principatum*."

[3] Innocent I, PL. xx. 582, cap. i.

[4] Cf. P. Batiffol, op. cit., p. 86: "L'église romaine a un *principatus* sur toutes les églises du monde entier et elle tient ce *principatus* de Pierre prince des apôtres . . . nous venons de voir le mot principatus s'introduire dans le langue ecclésiastique au Vᵉ siècle, et servir à designer le primatus de Pierre entre les apôtres, mais là aussi la souveraineté qui s'attache à l'autorité du siège de Rome, et tout de suite ce *principatus* du siège de Rome s'avère analogue à celui de l'empereur."

[5] For instance, in the famous decree of Valentinian III (8 July 445) the term *principatus* is studiously avoided; instead, the decree speaks of the "primatus sedis apostolicae." Further examples in Batiffol, op. cit., pp. 86 ff., who remarks, p. 89: "Le style de la chancellerie impériale, soit à Ravenne, soit à Constantinople, se gardait de qualifier de *principatus* l'autorité de l'évêque de Rome. Le terme de *principatus* était apparemment reservé pour desig" la souveraineté impériale."

chief priest[1] and the *jus sacrum* part of public law the very idea of a papal *principatus* was to stir up the emperor's monarchic instincts. Again, Christianity had established itself as a most potent factor in cementing the empire since it had become the official religion of the empire.[2] It would be idle to ponder on the force of coherence which Christianity imparted to the empire. From the governmental point of view of the imperial monarch, the control of this force as well as of the sacerdotal body was essential. Hence the development of caesaro-papism in the second half of the fifth century, which reached its clear outward manifestation in the *Henoticon* of the Emperor Zeno.

On the other hand, the caesaropapist tendencies of the emperors were not hidden from the papacy. The signs of the times were unmistakable. The Council of Chalcedon (451) decreed for the see of Constantinople a rank equal to that of Rome,[3] the reason being that Constantinople was New Rome, because, in other words, it was the residence of the emperor. The year before Chalcedon the pope was addressed as "Patriarch" by the emperor, that is, he was considered an equal of the bishop of Constantinople.[4] The imperially decreed depositions of Flavian, the bishop of Constantinople, and of a number of other prominent bishops, were ominous warnings. The fixation of the Roman-Petrine governmental function of the pope by Leo was in the

---

[1] The Council of Chalcedon greeted the emperor (Marcian) as "sacerdos imperator" whilst Theodosius II was greeted at the Council of Constantinople (448) as ἀρχιερεὺς βασιλεύς cf. also Caspar, op. cit., i. 467–8, and infra p. 16.

[2] In this context particular importance should be attached to the edict of the emperors of 27 February 380 (*Cunctos populos: Cod. Theod.* XVI. i. 2 = *Cod. Just.* I. i. 1) that all the peoples must accept the religion "quam divinum Petrum apostolum tradidisse Romanis religio usque nunc ab ipso insinuata declarat . . . hanc legem sequentes Christianorum catholicorum nomen jubemus amplecti, reliquos vero dementes vesanosque judicantes, heretici dogmatis infamiam sustinere." Cf. the excellent characterization of this important document by H. Rahner, *Abendländische Kirchenfreiheit*, Einsiedeln, 1943, pp. 104–5: the document marks the beginning of a new period, that of the "imperiale Reichskirche, in der das letzte Wort der himmlisch erleuchtete Kaiser zu sprechen hat."

[3] For the historical background see Monachino, art. cit., pp. 261–91. E. Herman in *Chalkedon*, ii (1953), 463 ff; and A. Michel, ibid., 497 ff.

[4] Cf. in this context the letter of Theodosius II in Leo's correspondence (Ep. 62, col. 875). On the letter itself see Batiffol, op. cit., p. 251, note 2, and Caspar, op. cit., i. 500, ii. 747–8. In the same year the first imperial coronation by the patriarch was performed, see P. Charanis, "Coronation . . . in the later Roman empire" in *Byzantion*, xv (1941), p. 52. Against this see W. Ensslin, "Zur Frage nach der ersten Kaiserkrönung durch den Patriarchen" in *Byzantinische Z.*, xlii (1949), pp. 101–15, also 369–72, holding that the patriarch did not crown the emperor until 457 (Emperor Leo I). The coronation had no constitutive effects.

last resort aimed against the emperor.[1] Who—that was the basic problem—was to govern, that is, to direct and orientate the corporate union of Christians—the emperor, because he was emperor, or the pope because he was successor of St Peter? Who was to lay down faith and doctrine,[2] who was to make "statuta" for the Christian body corporate, who was to control the sacerdotal organism effectively? We must not, if we wish to be just, forget the overriding consideration of the papacy that the leadership of this union of Christians, of the universal Church,[3] ought to be in papal hands. The emperors, on the other hand, viewed this same entity as the Roman body politic, as a mere empire, within which Christianity was indeed of paramount importance and for this very reason demanded imperial control. If we keep in mind that Christianity seizes the whole of man and cannot, by its very nature, be confined to certain departmental limits; that Christianity is a force that makes man "a new creature"[4]—"catholica fides quae humanum genus sola vivificat" as Leo had it;[5] that Christianity demands the whole, and not part, of man, we shall perhaps grasp the intrinsic force of papal ideology and the strength of imperial resistance. In brief, who was functionally qualified to define the doctrine, purpose and aim underlying the corporate union of all Christians, to direct that body according to its underlying purpose and aim—emperor or pope?

The abstract principles of faith must be enunciated, and they can be enunciated only by those who are qualified.[6] And the translation of these

[1] See Klinkenberg, art. cit., p. 47: "In letzter Konsequenz Wendung gegen den die Kirche lenkenden Kaiser." Hence also Leo's opposition to councils, pp. 53, 88, 94, 107. The resemblance between papal and imperial aversions from councils is indeed striking. On the *Henoticon* see infra p. 15.

[2] We should not forget in this context the importance of imperial legislation (378) by Valentinian and Gratian: the imperial courts were to try heresy, but the important point is the criterion which makes conduct heretical and hence criminal. The distinction is that between adjective (procedural) law—the criminal trial—and substantive law, the crime itself. Cf. *Cod. Theod.* XVI. v, 5 = *Cod. Just.* I. v. 2: the criterion is deviation "a judicio catholicae religionis." In the same year the Roman synod under Damasus requested the emperor's help against those who had been condemned by Damasus, so that the emperor should receive his reward on the Day of Judgment, Mansi, iii. 626, c. 10.

[3] The "totum ecclesiae corpus": *Sermo* 4, c.2, also Ep. 14; the "universitas" which is the "populus Dei": *Sermo* 3, c. 2; who is to be the "rector" of this "corpus"? *Sermo* 4, c. 1. These Leonine expressions on the corporate wholeness of the Church (including priesthood and laity) could easily be multiplied.

[4] *Gal.* vi. 15.

[5] Leo, Ep. 162.

[6] Leo, Ep. 164: "verae fidei sufficit, *quis* doceat." The biblical basis of these views was Pauline; cf. *Rom.* i. 17: "Justus *ex* fide vivit"; cf. also *Gal.* iii. 11; *Hebr.* x. 38.

abstract principles into practice so as to shape the actual mode of living by Christians, into concrete measures and terms is government; this too can be undertaken only by those who are qualified by virtue of their functions. The presupposition for the formulation of doctrine and of its translation into practice is functional qualification: under this presupposition the "civitas Dei" which is built on the rock, will be erected.[1] We must bear in mind that the *corpus* of Christians is not merely a pneumatic or spiritual body, but at the same time also a concrete, visible, entity. Its organization is indispensable to the realization of its underlying purpose. Hence, in the Christian *corpus* the administration of the temporal things should be undertaken, *in order* to bring about the realization of the purpose of the *corpus*. For this *corpus* is a living entity made up of living and acting men: their actions must be controlled—they must be guided.[2] And guidance to be effective can be undertaken only within the limits and terms of the law which by its very nature relates to human actions and conduct: they must fulfil a certain purpose, hence must be guided.[3] But this is nothing else but government, hence the emphatic insistence of the papacy on the *principatus apostolicae sedis*[4] and on the binding character of its laws, that is, of its "statuta" or "canones" or "decretalia constituta".[5]

[1] Leo in Ep. 162: ". . . vivificat, sola sanctificat, in una confessione permaneat et dissensiones . . . a soliditate illius petrae supra quam civitas Dei aedificatur, abigantur." On the Augustinianism of this letter see Klinkenberg, art. cit., p. 104, note 149. A direct quotation from St Augustine is also in Ep. 165, c. 5.

[2] This is why the terms "gubernatio", "gubernator" and the like, come so readily to the pen of popes; cf. e.g., Leo I, *Sermo* 3, cap. 3 ("gubernacula") or Simplicius, Ep. 21 pr. (in A. Thiel, *Epp. Rom. pont. genuinae*, p. 213: "gubernator"); or Felix III, Ep. 2, c. 7 (Thiel, p. 237: "gubernatio"). For many other examples see H. Rahner in *Z. f. kath. Theol.*, lxix (1947), pp. 5 ff.; cf. also Innocent I, ibid., p. 29, and the passage quoted from the *Sacramentarium Leonianum* (p. 9): "gubernacula apostolicae sedis." In parenthesis we may note that the *Sacramentarium Rossianum*, sub no. 345, contains the same terminology as regards the prayer for a dead pope (p. 181, of the ed. by J. Brinktrine, in suppl. vol. xxv, 1930, of *Römische Quartalschrift*). On the emperors as "gubernatores" see infra p. 107 n. 1.

[3] Cf. Leo's *Sermo* 3, cap. 2. See also Siricius in his decretal, cap. 7: "Ubi poterit nisi in corporibus, sicut legimus, sanctis sanctus Dei spiritus habitare?"

[4] The juristic elements in the papal statements of this period would need close analysis, especially of Leo I and Gelasius I. For the latter cf. E. J. Jonkers, "Pope Gelasius and the civil law" in *Rev. d'hist. du droit*, xx (1952), pp. 335 ff.

[5] The important point of the first decretal of the papacy is that it resulted from the constitutionally influential pontificate of Damasus. Sent to Spain, this first decretal is a formidable document dealing with fifteen major items and is appropriately called a "decretale opusculum" by Isidore of Seville, *De viris illustribus*, cap. xvi (PL. lxxxiii. 1092). The species "decretal" is the form in which the monarchic-papal legislative will is expressed. It is true law and as such had a sanction

But precisely because law was the effluence of the papal claim to *principatus*, the emperors, from their monarchic point of view, were bound to oppose this claim. Their caesaropapism was a reaction: it was their emphatic insistence on the monarchic principle, to be executed even in a Christian body corporate. The entity under their rule was the Roman empire to be governed only by the emperors: it was *their* laws by which the human actions of their subjects were to be guided, not the papacy's.

What, then, according to papal theory, was the role, the function, of the emperor in this corporate union of Christians? How was he to fit into the scheme of things obtaining in the Christian world? Was there in fact still room for a monarch's rule on the model of olden times, on the model of the ἀρχιερεὺς βασιλεύς, on the pattern of the *Rex-Sacerdos*? In the preceding century St Ambrose had already pointed to the emperor's role: he was the son, not the master of the universal Church. "Imperator enim *intra* ecclesiam, non supra ecclesiam est."[1] Leo I himself was to give the cue to later papal generations when, with great and characteristically Roman pathos, he wrote to the emperor (Marcian): the Christian *corpus* was founded on the Petrine commission and as a member of this *corpus* the emperor's function is its protection.[2] The *regia potestas* was conferred on the emperor specially—"maxime"—for the sake of guarding the Church, for the sake of protecting the

---

attached to it (cap. 7 decr. cit.), quite apart from such expressions characteristic of a legislator, "We decide", "We judge", "We provide", etc. The decretal in general is a *responsum* or a rescript to queries submitted to the pope; cf. Siricius's decretal: "Ad tua consulta rescripsimus . . ." The pope answers these queries and thereby creates new law emanating from the *caput ecclesiae*, and for this reason generally valid for the universal Church. In the form, namely in that of a *responsum* or *rescriptum*, the decretal follows closely the *responsa* of earlier Roman times (*responsa pontificum*) and the rescripts of the emperors, on which see F. Schulz, *History of Roman legal science*, Oxford, 1946, pp. 16–17, 152, 154. The imperial rescript also took the form of an *epistola*. Many features are common to both the decretal (*decretalis epistola*) of the pope, and the rescript of the emperor. And just as later collections of decretals were made, so were collections of imperial rescripts made, for instance, the *Decretorum Libri Tres*, cf. Schulz, op. cit., pp. 144–5, 154, 240.

[1] Ep. 21, cap. 36 (PL. xvi. 1007).

[2] See Leo's Ep. 156, cc. 3–5. To all seeming Leo I was the first pope who introduced the figure of Melchisedek into papal literature, see his *Sermo* 3, cap. 2, *Sermo* 5, cap. 3, also *Sermo* 4, cap. 1. On other Augustinian influences see supra p. 12. Melchisedek was the prototype of the priestly king, combining regal and sacerdotal powers. Christ was Melchisedek, cf. Leo's *Sermones* cit.; on Gelasius infra p. 23. For the whole question see G. Martini, "Regale sacerdotium" in *Archivio della R. deputazione di storia patria*, lxi (1938), pp. 1–166. Cf. also *Jud.* 25: Christ alone had *imperium* and *potestas*.

corporate union of Christians.[1] What Leo does is to impress upon the emperor his *raison d'être* within the corporate union of Christians, the "finis" or "telos" of his rulership.[2] In the plan of salvation the *Christian* emperor is allotted a definite role.[3] For the sake of bringing the Christian principles of life to fruitful realization, God had granted the emperor the administration of mundane things,[4] and naturally the temporal things should be administered with this purpose of assisting the divine plan in view.[5] According to the papal point of view, then, the Christian *corpus* was to be directed and governed by those functionally qualified,[6] not by an emperor.

## II

The emergence, in the second half of the fifth century, of caesaropapism, the regal-sacerdotal system, understandable though it is, peremptorily demanded from the papacy a theoretical clarification of the function, the *raison d'être*, and the standing of the emperor *within*

[1] Ep. 156, cap. 3 (to the emperor): "Debes incunctanter advertere *regiam potestatem* tibi non solum mundi regimen, sed maxime ad ecclesiae praesidium esse collatam." Cf. also E. Herman, art. cit., pp. 459 ff.

[2] Cf. the same teleological argumentation in Ep. 104, in which the pope appreciatively speaks of the emperor's efforts to quell heresy, but at the same time underlines the emperor's function as an assistant in the pope's task: through your zeal, he writes to the emperor, the most pernicious error is quelled: "*ut* labor noster citius ad desideratum pervenisset effectum."

[3] See Ep. 156, c. 3.

[4] See Ep. 142, c. 2 to Emperor Marcian: ". . . fidei Christianae, ob quam justus et misericors Deus tribuit ut vobis sicut divina sunt chara, ita sint mundana subjecta." The idea of protection combined with the metaphor of the "mater-filius" relationship is the theme of Ep. 164, c. 1. That the teleological considerations expressed in this and in many other letters, were Augustinian, seems beyond doubt. Whether the first historical work written on a teleological basis, that of Orosius, was known to Leo, is doubtful. About St Augustine's teleological view on Rome and the empire, cf. e.g., E. Lewalter, "Eschatologie und Weltgeschichte in der Gedankenwelt Augustins" in *Z. f. Kirchengeschichte*, liii (1934), pp. 1–51; Kaarlo Jäntere, *Die römische Weltreichsidee*, Turku, 1936 (Annales Universitatis Turkuensis, series B, vol. xxi), pp. 128–42; W. Kamlah, *Christentum und Geschichtlichkeit*, 2nd ed., Stuttgart, 1951, pp. 302 ff.; but cf. also G. Combès, *La doctrine politique de saint Augustin*, Paris, 1927, pp. 207–28. About Orosius and his views on the empire, namely, that it was created by God in order to prepare the advent of Christ, see E. Frauenholz, "Imperator Octavianus Augustus in der Geschichte und Sage des MA." in *Hist. Jb.*, xlvi (1926), pp. 90–4, and I. W. Raymond, *Seven books of history against the pagans*, New York, 1936, pp. 9 ff. (here also a translation of Orosius).

[5] See Ep. 162, c. 1, and *Sermo* 82. For further details cf. K. Jäntere, op. cit., pp. 157–62.

[6] *Sermo* 3 c. 2: "rectores ecclesia accipit, quos sanctus spiritus praeparavit." (Ordination.)

the corporate union of Christians, that is, *within* the Church. This theoretical clarification was undertaken by Gelasius I, first as the draftsman of Felix III's letters, and then as pope.[1] Indeed, it was Gelasius "qui a consacré le mot *principatus*".[2]

Sedes apostolica, quae Christo domino delegante totius ecclesiae retinet principatum.[3]

The whole corporate body of Christians—"totum corpus ecclesiae"—has its *principatus* in the Roman Church.[4] Gelasius is convinced that every Christian, whether lay or clerical, knows this.[5] And yet, the Roman Church, despite its claim to the *principatus* over the whole Christian body, was expected to announce the election of a new pope —to the patriarch of Constantinople, for which omission Gelasius, newly elected, was taken to task by the Patriarch Euphemios[6] as well as by the emperor himself.[7] The Roman Church claimed the *principatus* over the *Christiana societas*;[8] the patriarch of Constantinople on the way to becoming imperial pope—it was precisely at this time that the patriarch adopted the title "ecumenical patriarch"[9]—and the emperor issuing his *Henoticon* in order to achieve religious unity in the empire:[10] indeed, a situation that could not remain static. Although out-

---

[1] For this see especially Hugo Koch, "Gelasius im kirchenpolitischen Dienst seiner Vorgänger Simplicius & Felix III" in *SB. Munich*, 1935, fasc. 6; and N. Ertl, "Dictatoren frühma. Papstbriefe" in *Arch. f. Urkundenforschung*, xv (1938), pp. 61–66.

[2] Batiffol, op. cit., p. 89.

[3] In the council of Rome, 495, see A. Thiel, *Epistolae pontificum Romanorum genuinae*, p. 441. All Gelasian statements will be quoted from this edition.

[4] Gelasius, Ep. 14, c. 9, p. 367: ". . . satisque conveniens sit, ut totum corpus ecclesiae in hac sibimet observatione concordet, quam illic vigere conspiciat ubi Dominus ecclesiae totius posuit principatum."

[5] Ep. 26, c. 3, p. 395: "ex paterna traditione perpensis confidimus, quod nullus jam veraciter Christianus ignoret . . . pro suo scilicet principatu quem beatus Petrus apostolus Domini voce perceptum, ecclesia nihilominus subsequente, et tenuit semper et retinet."

[6] Ep. 3, c. 1, p. 313 considers the patriarch's remonstration as mere arrogance: "quia nimis judicaretur arrogans, si de prima sede taliter existimasset."

[7] On this see F. Dvornik, "Pope Gelasius & Emperor Anastasius" in *Dölger Festschrift*, Munich, 1951 (= *Byzantinische Zeitschrift*, xliv), p. 112.

[8] Cf. Gelasius, *Tractatus II*, c. 8, p. 529.

[9] See E. Caspar, op. cit., ii. 747. Felix III had already written to the patriarch, Acacius, in 483, Thiel, p. 237, c. 8: "Mihi crede, nescio quemadmodum te ecclesiae totius asseras principem."

[10] The *Henoticon* was nothing else but a "kaiserliches Glaubensedikt," Caspar, ii. 35; its significance lies in that the emperor without a synod for the first time decrees the faith for the whole empire, and in so far it marks the beginning of caesaro-papism in the East, see Caspar, loc. cit.; this is strongly supported by

wardly the patriarch of Constantinople had to bear the brunt of the
papal attack, its real target was the imperial monarch, first Zeno[1] and
then his successor Anastasius.[2]

Aided as they were by oriental-hellenistic influences as well as by
the old Roman ideology of the emperor's representing divinity[3] on
earth and as a result of the combination of these ideas with a profound
sense that they were Christian emperors, the Byzantine emperors considered themselves as the personification of the *Rex-Sacerdos* idea: like
David or even like Christ Himself, the emperor was βασιλεὺς καὶ
ἱερεύς. He was ἰσόχριστος—Christ-like—and Autocrator: αὐτοκρά-
τωρ καῖσαρ. It was due to this deification of the emperor that not only
were the most difficult theological problems submitted to, and decided
by, him,[4] but also that his "divinitas"[5] showed itself in governmental

---

H. Rahner, *Abendländische Kirchenfreiheit*, p. 185. As a religious edict the *Henoticon*
was a patchwork and aimed at appeasing the monophysites and the Chalce-
donenians. Cf. also G. Ostrogorsky, *Gesch. d. byz. Staates*, Munich, 1940, p. 38f.

[1] "Eiusdem Acacii specialis fautor et amator" as Gelasius said: Ep. 26, c. 8,
p. 406.

[2] Who was "condemned", although not excommunicated by name: he was
"damnatus", see his own complaint as reported by Gelasius, Ep. 10, c. 2, p. 341:
"Quod dixerit imperator, a nobis se irreligiose damnatum." On the case see
Caspar, op. cit., ii. 54, 73, esp. note 4.

[3] The roots of this go back far into the Hellenistic times. It is known that ideas
of a saviour dominated the ancient world and these ideas became inseparably
bound up with the emperors themselves. Hence the acclamations of the new
emperor as the saviour, the "*adventus* Augusti"—and these acclamations had all
the sacral appurtenances. For this see A. Alföldi, "Die Ausgestaltung des monarchischen Zeremoniells am römischen Kaiserhof" in *Mitteilungen des deutschen
archaeologischen Instituts*, Rom. Abt., vol. xlix (1934), pp. 29, 30, 88 ff. These
acclamations greeting the emperor as the saviour of the world, continued in
Rome down to the late fourth century A.D. (ibid., pp. 92–3) and, of course, were
noticeable at Constantinople. For this cf., for example, *Liber de cerimoniis*, ed.
Bonn, i. 5, pp. 49–50: "Dicunt praecentores: 'Feliciter venit *divina majestas*.'
Clamat et populus ter: 'Feliciter venistis' . . . populus cursorie dicit: 'Salve
potentissime imperator, gaudium orbis, famule Dei, Romanorum felicitas . . . te
divinum numen centum annos populo suo praeesse sinat' . . . 'Gaudium hodie,
tranquillitas et quies ingens! Domini enim gaudium induti, ut phosphori . . .
gaudeant coelestes spirituum exercitus, gaudeant copiae Romanorum, Christiani
omnes, festum Deo celebraturi, simul gaudeant'." Cf. also infra p. 35, and *Lib.
de cerim.*, ii. 40, p. 638, according to which the patricians represent the apostles,
and the emperor God Himself: "Magistri enim et patricii referunt apostolos;
optimus autem imperator Deum, quatenus nempe homini Deum referre datum
est."

[4] H. Rahner, op. cit., p. 181. The consolidation of the Christian religion produced reinvigorating effects upon the imperial cult, see Alföldi, op. cit., p. 35.

[5] Soon after Chalcedon the Armenian bishops in their address to the emperor
applied the Petrine words to him: "Christ is the head of the Church, but you are
the strength and foundation of the Church"—"vos autem robur et fundamentum

actions: he was the true monarch ruling the cosmos.¹ From this point of view it was essential that the emperors stressed their direct divine appointment and selection: and it is surely no coincidence that precisely in the second half of the fifth century this direct divine derivation of imperial powers and functions came to be so emphatically stressed. In the reiteration of this theme the fifth-century emperors obviously saw the proof of their legitimate position,² sanctioned as it was by the patriarch crowning them.³

By virtue of being divinely appointed the emperors considered themselves entitled and bound, in their capacity as Christian monarchs, to rule their subjects upon the principles of Christianity, which by the second half of this century had become the most pronounced spiritual, mental and intellectual force of society. But just as unity within the empire was essential, so was unity of the faith essential for this empire which had indeed become the *imperium christianum*.⁴ And in order to

---

imitantes immobilem Christi *petram,*" quoted from Th. Schnitzler, "Im Kampf um Chalcedon" in *Analecta Gregoriana*, xvi (1938), pp. 111–12. Agapitus of Rhodes writes to the emperor: "Vere namque *sacerdos* et natura *imperator* existis," quoted ibid., p. 112. The emperor is "semen et radix et cultura et scintilla nobis salutis inextinguibilis," ibid. For other similar statements see Schnitzler, ibid., pp. 109 ff. Schnitzler pertinently remarks (p. 110) that these expressions might be read in a tract entitled "De infallibilitate imperatoris": they amount to a real *Kaisertheologie* (p. 104).

¹ γῆς ἁπάσης μονάρχος. For all details see L. R. Taylor, *The divinity of the Roman emperor*, New York, 1931; A. Alföldi, "Insignien & Tracht der römischen Kaiser" in *Mitteilungen des deutschen archaeologischen Instituts*, Rom. Abt., vol. l (1935), pp. 94–134; M. P. Charlesworth, "Some observations on Ruler-Cult" in *Harvard Theological Review*, xxviii (1935), pp. 28 f., 32, 35 (the emperor as "Dominus et Deus noster"); E. Eichmann, *Die Kaiserkrönung im Abendlande*, Würzburg, 1943, i. 12 ff.; cf. also P. Koschaker, *Europa & das römische Recht*, Munich, 1947, pp. 8 f. The book by Treitinger was not accessible to me.

² On this see W. Ensslin, "Gottkaiser & Kaiser von Gottes Gnaden" in *SB. Munich*, 1943, fasc. 6, pp. 83 ff.

³ The imperial coronation by the patriarch was declaratory, and not constitutive. Cf. Alföldi, op. cit. (1935), p. 56; F. Dölger, in *Gnomon*, xv (1938), pp. 209–10 (book review); Eichmann, op. cit., i. 17–18; Ensslin, art. cit., p. 113. Apparently against this Charanis, in *Byzantion*, art. cit., pp. 51–2. Actually, the earliest evidence of a "coronation" is shown on the golden medallion of Emperor Constantius II which depicts him festooned by the hand of God reaching down from the clouds, see Alföldi, table 6, p. 55, who remarks (p. 56) that the Christian interpretation of the scene cannot be doubted: it is the christianization of a pagan allegory.

⁴ According to N. Baynes, "Eusebius and the Christian empire" in *Annuaire de l'institute de philologie et d'histoire orientales*, ii (1934), p. 13, a good deal of Byzantine state philosophy was derived from Eusebius, who is said to have stated in his oration for the celebrations of the Tricennalia of Constantine I "the political philosophy of the Christian empire, that philosophy of the state which was

preserve this unity of the faith, Zeno issued his *Henoticon* in which he spoke of the Catholic-apostolic Church as the indestructible and perennial *mother of his rule*.[1] In a way, one might speak of a transmutation of the earlier Roman pagan emperor into a Christian emperor of whose governmental ideology the Christian-religious element had become an integral part. But government demanded not only the proclamation of the correct faith by the divine majesty of the emperor, but also effective intervention in organizational and disciplinary matters, to wit, the exercise of imperial jurisdiction over clerics and appointment of clerics. The deposition of Flavian and the numerous other bishops was only a beginning: later in the century the trials of John Talaja and Calendio, the Alexandrian and Antiochian bishops, for high treason, were manifestations of this governmental activity which aimed at the preservation of the unity of the faith.

Indeed, as we have said, the situation demanded from the papacy the clarification of the function of an emperor *within* the corporate union of Christians. And the clarification concerned the origin of the emperor's claim to fix faith and doctrine and to try and to appoint clerics. Was he functionally qualified—in a Christian society—to proceed as he did? By what authority did he proceed? Did not the whole conceptual framework of the emperor's position rest upon a profound misconception of his role, of his function, of his *raison d'être* within the *ecclesia*? Of course, it was undeniable that the emperor received his rulership from God—where else could power originate?—but is this sufficient justification for decreeing faith and for trying those who are the special bearers of divine sacraments and gifts, namely the priests? Surely the administration of divine things, entrusted only to the ordained members, is vital in a divine community such as the one founded by Christ, the *ecclesia*? Through the sacraments the body of Christ as the congregation of the faithful is alive, but the transmitters of the sacraments and hence of grace are the ordained members of the *corpus Christi*. Moreover, this society being divinely founded by Christ, must be directed in its outward actions: the actions of Christians must

---

consistently maintained throughout the millenium of Byzantine absolutism. The basis of that political philosophy is to be found in the conception of the imperial government as a terrestrial copy of the rule of God in heaven: there is one God and one divine law, therefore there must be on earth but one ruler and a single law. That ruler, the Roman emperor, is the vicegerent of the Christian God." Cf. also p. 17: "For the divine creation (which his source, Diotogenes, had maintained), Eusebius had but to substitute the kingdom of heaven."

[1] See Ensslin, art. cit., p. 93: "Reichseinheit und Kircheneinheit" were "eine wesentliche politische Forderung," referring to the *Henoticon*, ibid., note 2.

be Christian, that is, in consonance with the teaching of Christ which is entrusted to the priests. In short, public life in the Christian society must be Christian, and public life can effectively be regulated only by the laws which in themselves are only the crystallization of non-legal principles. A Christian society can be directed only by the law that is based upon Christian principles. But is the emperor qualified to lay down those principles and to make them into law?

His function in a Christian society is to learn, not to teach—the famous Gelasian antithesis of *discere-docere*—what is (and what is not) Christian. What is Christian, however, can be laid down only by those who are qualified to pronounce upon it. The *ecclesia*, indeed a divine foundation, hence a divine community,[1] cannot be directed by those who are not qualified: in this Christian *corpus* there is nothing more important or vital than those things which belong to religion,[2] for they cause prosperity of the society as such.[3] The Christian religion is the leaven of the *respublica* and the preservation of the true faith is therefore in the public interest.[4] Divine things and religious matters cannot be administered or decreed upon by the emperor; he must find out *what* is divine from him who is qualified,[5] to wit, from him who has the *principatus* over the *divina communitas*, the pope: he is responsible for those "quos *regendos* accepit (scil.Petrus)."[6] For the pope's powers are those of St Peter himself: according to Gelasius, the Petrine commission is all comprehensive and all embracing. The "Quodcumque" of the commission[7] comprises everything without exception: everything can be bound and loosed:

[1] Gelasius, Ep. 1, c. 29, p. 303.   [2] Ep. 1, c. 23, p. 299.
[3] "Nulla tamen major est necessitas quam divino cultui et religioni, unde omnia prosperantur."
[4] Cf. Ep. 1, c. 33, p. 305: "Si fides catholica et communio servetur, imperator laedatur, et illis violatis, imperator non laeditur? Absit, ut hoc Christianus et catholicus imperator dicat, vel aliquis catholicus Christianus dicat debere fieri." And before he says this: "Si fides communioque catholica servatur, dignitas sedis apostolicae minuitur, si illa violatur, sedis apostolicae dignitas manet? Absit, ut hoc Christianus catholicus depromat. Si fides catholica et communio laedatur, respublica juvatur, et si illa salva sit, respublica laeditur? Absit, ut hoc Christianus et catholicus profiteatur."
[5] Ep. 10, c. 9, p. 347: "Si quantum ad religionem pertinet, non nisi apostolicae sedi juxta canones debetur summa judicii totius; si quantum ad saeculi potestatem, illa a pontificibus et praecipue a beati Petri vicario *debet cognoscere, quae divina sunt*, non eadem ipsa judicare. Nec sibi hoc quisquam potentissimus saeculi, qui tamen Christianus est, vindicare praesumit, nisi religionem persequens."
[6] Ep. 3, c. 16, p. 320. Cf. already Gelasius through Felix III, Ep. 15, c. 3, p. 272: ". . . in me qualicumque vicario beatus Petrus apostolus, et haec in illo, qui ecclesiam suam discerpi non patitur, ipse etiam Christus exposcit."
[7] *Matt.* xvi. 18–19.

In "quibuscumque" omnia sunt quantacumque sint et qualiacumque sint.[1]

In so far this jurisdictional power creates a "humanum judicium".[2] Considering the nature of Christian society, this claim of Gelasius is rather self-evident, for in a Christian society all human actions have an essentially religious ingredient.

Since the pope alone has the *principatus* over the Christian body, the emperor, according to Gelasius, must be directed by the *sacerdotium*. The secular power has not only no right to issue decrees fixing the faith, since the emperor is no bishop, but he also must carry out his government according to the directions given to him by the priesthood. This is what Gelasius says:

Porro regia dignitas a sacerdotio directa diu manet.[3]

Again, considering the nature and character of this Christian corpus, Gelasius's claim that the priesthood must direct royal power, is self-evident: and if the *sacerdotium* is disregarded, it will sap the very foundations upon which this society is built.[4]

Consequently, in this Christian world, in the "mundus",[5] the secular power has a mere "potestas", whilst the *principatus* of the pope

---

[1] *Tractatus IV*, c. 5, p. 562. Cf. also Gelasius through Felix III, Ep. 2, c. 7, p. 237: "Omnia, quae per apostolicae scita doctrinae ligarentur in terris, nec in coelestibus memoravit (scil. Salvator) absolvi." See also Gelasius himself again, Ep. 30, c. 12, p. 445: "Sicut et his verbis (scil. Quodcumque ligaveris . . .) nihil constat exceptum, sic per apostolicae dispensationis officium et totum possit generaliter alligari, et totum consequenter absolvi." This all comprehensive power to bind and to loose was the hallmark of hierocratic ideology. The terms used hardly varied, cf. infra p. 209, 221 n. 4; Gregory VII infra p. 277; also Innocent III: "Nihil excipiens, qui dixit 'Quodcumque' " (*Extra:* I. xxxiii. 6), and so forth. Anti-hierocratic writers, especially those who propagated a dual form of government, made this claim to an all-embracing power to bind and to loose the main target of their attacks; cf. infra 406. Dante's protests against it are too well known to need any comment, cf. *Monarchia*, iii. 3 and 8. Viewing society as the *corpus Christi*, this claim is nothing else but the principle of monarchic government expressed in religious terms. About the *claves juris* (the juristic transformation of the *claves regni coelorum*) cf. infra 437; the papal point of view was that in a Christian society every human action must needs have an essentially religious ingredient.

[2] Ep. 30, c. 13, p. 446.

[3] Ep. 43, c. 6, p. 478: "Etiamsi enim hic rex processit, non tamen episcopus est ordinatus. Porro . . ." as text. It is no doubt interesting that the emperor who had issued the *Henoticon*, was qualified as "rex".

[4] Ibid., continuing: "Sacerdotium vicissim a rege honoratum, purpuram laetificat, sceptrum illustrat, dignitatem sanctificat; si vero injuriis afficitur, *fundamenta convellit.*"

[5] To a Roman the term "mundus" was co-terminous with Roman empire.

expresses itself in the pontifical *auctoritas*.[1] And this *auctoritas* being divinely conferred for the purpose of governing the Christian body corporate, is logically enough *sacrata*, whilst the emperor's power is a simple "regalis potestas". This is a thoroughly juristic terminology employed by Gelasius. *Auctoritas* is the faculty of shaping things creatively and in a binding manner,[2] whilst *potestas* is the power to execute what the *auctoritas* has laid down. The Roman senate had *auctoritas*, the Roman magistrate had *potestas*.[3] The antithesis between *auctoritas* and *potestas* stated already by Augustus himself,[4] shows the "outstanding charismatic political authority" which his *auctoritas* contained.[5] It was sacred, since everything connected with Roman emperorship was sacred[6] emanating as it did from his divinity.[7] It was therefore all the easier to transfer these characteristically Roman ideas to the function of the pope and to his *auctoritas*. Whilst, however, this fundamental difference between the pontifical *auctoritas* and the imperial *potestas* was clear to anyone versed in Roman juristic terminology and ideology, Gelasius superimposed a typical Christian argument upon it: in a Roman-Christian world, the sacred pontifical *auctoritas* is all the

---

[1] Ep. 12, c. 2, p. 351, which is the famous *Duo quippe* passage. The letter of Pope Symmachus to the emperor (Ep. 10, in Thiel, pp. 700–708) reads like a pointed paraphrase of Gelasius's Ep. 12.

[2] One should not forget in this context the etymology: *auctor* and *auctoritas*.

[3] Cf. Paulus in *Dig.* l, xvi. 215: "Potestatis verbo plura significantur, in persona *magistratuum imperium.*" See also Cicero, *De Leg.*, iii. 3, and Ulpian, in *Dig.* xiv. 4. 1. 4: "Potestatis verbum ad omnem sexum, item ad omnes, qui sunt alieno juri subjecti, porrigendum erit." Originally, the emperor title of Augustus indicates that he has received his *potestas* from the "senatus populusque Romanus," see V. Ehrenberg, "Monumentum Antiochenum" in *Klio*, xix (1925), pp. 203, 210.

[4] "Post id tempus *auctoritate* omnibus praestiti, *potestatis* autem nihil amplius habui quam qui fuerunt mihi quoque in magistratu conlegae," *Monumentum Ancyranum*, c. 34, quoted by F. Schulz, *Principles of Roman Law*, Oxford, 1936, p. 182; also by A. Alföldi, op. cit., p. 74; and by E. Schönbauer, "Untersuchungen zur römischen Staats- und Wirtschaftsrecht" in *Sav. Z., Rom. Abt.*, xlvii (1927), pp. 264–5.

[5] See Schulz, op. cit., p. 182: "By virtue of his outstanding charismatic political authority Augustus directed the popular assembly, the senate, the magistrates and finally all social life." See also E. Schönbauer, "Studien zum Personalitätsprincip im antiken Recht," in *Sav. Z., Rom. Abt.*, xlix (1929), p. 400: by virtue of his *auctoritas* the emperor becomes a πολιτικός or a "Staatsführer."

[6] Cf. Alföldi, op. cit., pp. 70 f., and Taylor, op. cit., pp. 149 ff.; 158 ff.

[7] See Schönbauer, art. cit. (note 4), p. 292. From here the way lay open to the Roman *crimen laesae majestatis* which was essentially a religious crime (*impietas*) and blasphemy, see Alföldi, op. cit., p. 76; also Charlesworth, art. cit., p. 33. The offence concerned a super human being, for which see Schönbauer, pp. 288 ff.

greater, as it has to render an account even for the doings of the kings themselves on the Day of Judgment.[1]

Of course, the emperor has his rulership from God,[2] but it is a divine *beneficium* which he has received, and because it is a divine *beneficium*, the pontiffs have to render an account of how the emperor has administered his divine *beneficium*. He should not therefore show himself ungrateful for these divine favours which he received in the shape of "*privilegia* potestatis suae": these are indeed privileges divinely conferred. And since rulership comes from God—an axiom which the emperors themselves were ever more anxious to stress just in that period[3]—God's priests are particularly concerned with the emperor's exercise of the (divinely conferred) rulership: and since in a Christian society, of which the emperor through baptism is a member, every human action has a definite purpose and in so far has an essential religious ingredient, the emperors should submit their governmental actions to the ecclesiastical superiors and should not order the latter about, since they alone know what is, and what is not, divine and therefore Christian: they alone have *auctoritas* within a Christian body corporate:

Imperatores christiani subdere debent exsecutiones suas ecclesiasticis praesulibus, non praeferre.[4]

The view behind these statements is that of the mediatory role of the priesthood and in particular of the pope. It was in this period that the emperor was first addressed by the popes themselves as "Son,"[5] which designation is suggestive of the role of the Roman Church as the "Mother" of the emperor and the pope as the "Father."[6] And since

\*
†
[1] Ep. 12, c. 2: "Duo quippe sunt, imperator auguste, quibus principaliter mundus hic regitur, auctoritas sacrata pontificum et regalis potestas. In quibus tanto gravius est pondus sacerdotum, quanto etiam pro ipsis regibus hominum in divino reddituri sunt examine rationem."

\*
[2] See already Gelasius through Felix III to Zeno, Ep. 1, c. 1, p. 223: the emperor should bear in mind "et temporalis culminis et aeternae vitae commercia de superna propitiatione pendere."

[3] See supra p. 16 f. and Ensslin's numerous quotations from official titles and documents. About Eastern episcopal statements see Th. Schnitzler, op. cit., pp. 104 ff.; 109 ff. Cf. also supra p. 17.

[4] Which is exactly the same thought as he expressed in Ep. 43, quoted supra p. 20.

[5] Gelasius through Simplicius, Ep. 3, c. 2, p. 180: "Gloriosissime et clementissime fili imperator." Gelasius through Felix III, Ep. 1, c. 3, p. 224: "Fili piissime." About St Ambrose see supra p. 13 and Leo I supra p. 14.

[6] The designation of the pope alone as "Papa" becomes usual in the fifth century. For the history of the term and its Homeric origins see E. Dobschütz, *Texte*, cit. (supra 5 n. 3), pp. 226–32; P. Labriolle, "Une esquisse de l'histoire du mot 'Papa'" in *Bulletin d'ancienne littérature et d'archéologie chrétienne*, i (1911),

rulership, including emperorship, is a benefice divinely conferred, the function of the pope as the one who has to render an account, is unquestionable. That emperor who recognizes this state of affairs, is entitled to call himself a "Catholic emperor": the significance of the term "Catholic emperor" is that he subordinates himself to the rulings of the priests of Christ;[1] then, he tells the emperor, "possis regnare cum Christo."[2]

We need not dwell on the ingenuity with which Gelasius turned the imperial argument of the divine derivation of imperial powers into an argument with which to establish control over the emperor. It was in fact the same imperial argument which Gelasius wished to destroy in his *Tractatus IV* and which gave him a further opportunity to indicate, at least in embryonic form, some other very important principles. When the contemporary emperors asserted, in practical terms, true monarchical power manifesting itself in the combination of regal and sacerdotal functions, for which Melchisedek of the Old Testament stood as a prototype,[3] this was a conception, according to Gelasius, which could not prevail within a Christian society.

---

pp. 215–20; idem, "Papa" in *Bulletin Du Cange*, iv (1928), pp. 65–75; P. Batiffol, in *Rivista di archeologia cristiana*, cit., i (1924), pp. 99–103; and H. Leclercq in *DAC.* xiii. 1097–1101. Batiffol, op. cit., pp. 263–4, draws attention to the designation of "pater patrum" which was applied to the popes only in the sixth century. In parenthesis we may note that second-century jurists styled the emperor "pater patriae," cf. Callistratus in *Dig.* 48, 22, 19. The formula is still used by Gelasius's contemporary emperor (Anastasius), see infra p. 24. It seems that Caesar himself was the first who was thus hailed by M. Cato and Q. Catulus, see Th. Mommsen, *History of Rome*, London, 1901, iv. 483. It is curious to note that Edward Coke in *Calvin's Case* (1608) declared the king to be "Pater patriae," see 7 Co. Rep. la, at 13b (*Engl. Rep.*, lxxvii. 393).

[1] Ep. 1, c. 10, p. 292: "Quod si dixeris 'Sed imperator catholicus est,' salva pace ipsius dixerimus, *filius est, non praesul ecclesiae*, quod ad religionem competit, discere ei convenit, non docere; habet privilegia potestatis suae, quae administrandis publicis rebus divinitus consecutus est; et eius beneficiis non ingratus contra dispositionem coelestis ordinis nil usurpet. Ad sacerdotes enim Deus voluit, quae ecclesiae disponenda sunt, pertinere, non ad saeculi potestates, *quas, si fideles sunt*, ecclesiae suae et sacerdotibus voluit esse *subjectas*. Non sibi vindicet alienum jus, et ministerium, quod alteri deputatum est, et contra illius beneficia pugnare videatur, a quo propriam consecutus est potestatem. Non legibus publicis, non a potestatibus saeculi, sed a pontificibus et sacerdotibus omnipotens Deus Christianae religionis dominos et sacerdotes voluit ordinari, et discuti recipique de errore remeantes. Imperatores christiani . . ." (as text).

[2] Ep. cit., c. 4, p. 352. Cf. also Ep. 27, c. 8, p. 430: "Obsequi solere principes christianos decretis ecclesiae, non suam praeponere potestatem, episcopis caput subdere principem solitum, non de eorum capitibus judicare."

[3] Cf. *Gen.* xiv. 18: Melchisedek *king* of Salem and *priest* of the most high God. See also *Ps.* cix. 4; *Hebr.* vii. 1–2, 10, 11, 15, 21. Cf. also *Jud.* 25: Christ alone has *imperium* and *potestas.*

According to Gelasius, Christian emperorship originates in Christ Himself. Christ was the last *Rex et Pontifex*, the last Melchisedek, and by "a marvellous dispensation" He had discerned between the functions of the royal and of the sacerdotal power. Since the time of Christ no emperor had arrogated to himself the title of a pontiff[1] and no pontiff had claimed the height of royal power, although the pontiffs were actually, through Christ's generosity and in a very special sense, both royal and priestly.[2] But Christ, "mindful of human fragility"[3] had discerned between the functions of each power: "discrevit officia potestatis utriusque." His reason for so doing was twofold. On the one hand, it is written that no one warring for God should be entangled with secular things.[4] The *raison d'être* of the royal power was to relieve the clerics of the burden of having to care for their carnal and material wants. For the temporal necessities the pontiffs indeed need the emperors, so that they can devote themselves to their functions properly and are not distracted by the pursuit of these carnal matters, but the emperors, Christian as they are, need the pontiffs for the achievement of eternal salvation.

[1] This is historically not true, quite apart from the pre-Constantinean emperors. Constantine himself was ἰσαπόστολος, who addressed the bishops as his "dearest brothers" (Mansi, ii. 477). The title "pontifex" was also kept by other Christian emperors; and, as we have seen, in the fifth century the emperors were "divine" (cf. Ensslin, op. cit., pp. 53 ff.), and were greeted as ἀρχιερεὺς βασιλεύς. And, significantly enough, in the edict of the Emperors Valentinian III and Marcian concerning disputations about the faith "coram vulgo," each of the two emperors is styled "pontifex inclytus," cf. Hardouin, *Conc. coll.*, ii. 659 (sub anno 452): "Edictum Valentiniani et Marciani imperatorum quo prohibentur disputationes de fide coram vulgo: Imperatores Caesares, Flavius Valentinianus, *pontifex inclytus* . . . et Flavius Marcianus, *pontifex inclytus* . . ." (the designations are omitted in Mansi, vii. 475; the edict is partly in *Cod. Just.* I. i. 3). It was against the alarmingly increasing regal-sacerdotal manifestations of the emperors that *Tractatus IV* was written by Gelasius. Moreover, in one of the few letters preserved by Emperor Anastasius, Gelasius's contemporary emperor, we read the following address: "Imperator Caesar Flavius Anastasius *Pontifex inclytus*, Germanicus inclytus, Alamannicus inclytus, Francicus inclytus, Sarmaticus inclytus, tribuniciae potestatis XXV, consul III, Pius Felix Victor semper Augustus, Pater Patriae proconsulibus, consulibus, praetoribus, tribunis plebis senatuique suo salutem dicit," Thiel, ed. cit., p. 765; also in F. Maassen, *Geschichte der Quellen und Literatur des kanonischen Rechts*, Graz, 1870, i. 334 (sub no. 5). For the meaning of "felix" and "pius" etc., see Alföldi, op. cit., pp. 88–90.

[2] *Hebr.* cit., with I *Pet.* ii. 9. On this see G. Martini, art. cit. According to Leo I, Rome was a royal and sacerdotal city, see *Sermo* 82. Leo also coined the term "discretio potestatis," see supra p. 8.

[3] The argument of the "humana fragilitas" appears also in a different context, Gelasius, Ep. 14, c. 22, p. 375.

[4] II. *Tim.* ii. 4. But cf. Gelasius's "carnales incursus" with the biblical "negotia saecularia."

On the other hand, Gelasius introduces the very important and fruit-ful principle of functional order operating within society. To each part of an organic whole is assigned a special function and each member should adhere to the scope of functions allotted to him: then there will be order, or as Gelasius put it, human haughtiness—humana superbia —will be prevented from coming into its own again. This principle of functional order is a principle which is necessitated by the manifold functions which a body has to perform in order to be an integrated whole: it is a principle which will play a major part in the fully developed hierocratic ideology.[1] It is a principle that is based as much upon interpretation of history as upon the teleological view of society as a *corpus*.[2]

The pontiffs have unrestricted power to bind and to loose, that is the "*potestas* ligandi et solvendi," given to them by Christ, but this *potestas* is within the framework of government an *auctoritas*,[3] which is the essence of the pope's *principatus*, to be displayed within Christian society. That is why the pope's jurisdictional primacy appears so much in the foreground in the communications and tracts of Gelasius. What

[1] See infra 41, 435 on Gregory I and VII and especially Bernard. This principle of order was of course first applied to the purely sacerdotal organism, so for instance by Leo I, Ep. 16, cap. 2 (to the Sicilian bishops): the various functions were dis-tributed, "ut in Christiana observantia nihil *inordinatum*, nihil pateretur esse *confusum*; *discernendae* sunt causae solemnitatum, et in omnibus institutis patrum principumque nostrorum rationabilis servanda *discretio*." Hence the often re-peated insistence on the delineations of the functions to be performed by ecclesias-tical officers. The biblical basis of this principle of functional order may be I *Cor*. xxi. 6: "divisiones operationum."

[2] The passage runs, *Tract. IV*, cap. 11, p. 567: "Fuerint haec ante adventum Christi, ut quidam figuraliter, adhuc tamen in carnalibus actionibus constituti, pariter reges exsisterent et pariter sacerdotes, quod sanctum Melchisedek fuisse sacra prodit historia . . . Sed cum ad verum ventum est eundem regem atque pontificem, ultra sibi nec imperator pontificis nomen imposuit, nec pontifex regale fastigium vindicavit: (quamvis enim membra ipsius, id est, veri regis atque pontificis, secundum participationem naturae magnificae utrumque in sacra generositate sumpsisse dicantur, ut simul regale genus et sacerdotale subsistant:) quoniam Christus memor fragilitatis memor humanae, quod suorum saluti con-grueret, dispensatione magnifica temperavit, sic actionibus propriis dignitati-busque distinctis officia potestatis utriusque discrevit, suos volens medicinali humilitate salvari, non humana superbia rursus intercipi: ut et Christiani impera-tores pro aeterna vita pontificibus indigerent, et pontifices pro temporalium cursu rerum imperialibus dispositionibus uterentur; quatenus spiritalis actio a carnalibus distaret incursibus, et 'Deo militans minime se negotiis saecularibus impli-caret' . . ."

[3] Gelasius could not very well have said that Christ had given to St Peter "auctoritas ligandi," hence we think that it is erroneous to speak of Gelasius's "dangerous attempt at equalizing the two potestates," so F. Dvornik, art. cit., p. 114.

matters in this Christian society, is the preparation for eternal life, and for this the pontiffs alone are the key bearers. "Inferior quippe potiorem absolvere non potest,"[1] as Gelasius says in the same *Tractatus IV*.

In view of this influential Gelasian thesis it seems appropriate to direct attention to his theme that Christian imperial power originated in Christ: the pontifical *auctoritas* and the royal *potestas* are united in Christ, the true *Rex et Pontifex*.[2] The pope functioning as the vicar of St Peter does not, according to Gelasius, combine, like Christ, the two powers in his person and office. It was not until the Petrine commission was considered to constitute a vicariate of Christ that the pope could be said to combine both powers: then as the vicar of Christ he was, like Christ Himself, "rex et sacerdos secundum ordinem Melchisedek" —with the further consequence that Christian imperial power "originated" in the pope.[3] Until then, as Gelasius said, "Deus est summus et verus imperator."[4]

In short, then, the Petrine *principatus* over the Christian body corporate is in papal hands. It is the *gubernatio principalis* which is committed to the pope[5] over all Christians, whether or not they are kings or emperors. "An nescis et te membrum esse pontificis?"[6] All Christians form one closely knit organic union, a body corporate,[7] that because it is Christian, must be directed according to Christian principles; and to define these is the proper function of the pope. Hence the exclusion of certain members from this society is necessary, if

---

[1] *Tract.* cit., cap. 13, p. 569.

[2] Cf. *Jud.* 25: Christ having *imperium* and *potestas*.

[3] This step was not formally taken until Innocent III.

[4] *Ep.* 26, cap. 12, p. 410. The conception of the vicariate of Christ enabled later writers and popes to apply to the pontiffs what applied to Christ, Whose vicars they were. Then also *Matt.* xxviii. 18 ("All power is given unto me in heaven and on earth") could be applied to the pope. It is true that at the conclusion of the Roman synod of 495, the episcopal participants hailed Gelasius eleven times "Vicarium Christi te videmus" (p. 447), but, on the other hand, Gelasius's immediate successor, Anastasius, wrote in 497 to the emperor that he (the emperor) was "vicarius Dei" (Thiel, p. 620) and in the same letter the pope said of himself: "Legatione *fungimur* pro Christo," p. 616. These designations were quite untechnical and well into the medieval period all bishops were called "vicarii Christi" and most of the emperors too.

[5] *Ep.* 19, c. 1, p. 386: "Quanto enim totius ovilis curam Christo Domino delegante susceptam beati Petri apostoli gubernatio principalis universo gregi debet in orbe terrarum."

[6] *Tract. VI*, c. 4, p. 600 (to the senator Andromachus and other non-clerical Romans).

[7] Cf. also *Tract II*, c. 8, p. 529: "Una monstraretur *compago corporis Christi*, quae ad unum caput gloriossissima dilectionis *societate* concurreret et *una* esset *ecclesia*."

through them the whole body may be infected or affected. A healthy unity of this body demands this.[1] Excommunication, in other words, is an effluence of the close organic nature of this society.[2] This exclusion, too, is reserved to those who are functionally qualified to judge what affects the health of this body. At the same time judgment on clerics, because they are the administrators of the divine mysteries, is necessarily reserved to superior ecclesiastical officers: the emperor is not qualified to judge clerics, since the disciple is not above the master.[3]

The imperial judgments on John Talaja and Calendio were therefore quite unjustifiable: true, they were condemned for high treason, but however badly the two bishops may have failed "out of worldly error," and of whatever quality they might have been, as priests they were not subjected to laical jurisdiction.[4] The *privilegium fori* is not a privilege at all, but a right, since in the corporate union of Christians the standing of the priests is radically different from that of lay persons.[5] The *principatus* of the Roman Church entails that it is the supreme tribunal in the *ecclesia*, that is, within the congregation of the faithful. There is nobody who can sit in judgment on a verdict of the Roman Church,[6] because it has the right to judge the whole Church, the whole body of Christians.[7] In brief,

---

[1] With particular reference to I *Cor.* xii. 26 this theme is very pronounced in Gelasius's letters; cf. also Ep. 9, c. 4, p. 341.

[2] Gelasius through Felix III, Ep. 12, c. 2, p. 258: "A probatorum consortio contagia repellenda sunt perditorum, quoniam mores bonos colloquia perversa corrumpunt"; Ep. 11, c. 3, p. 254: "inter episcopos sanctos et inter Christianos judicavimus non haberi." Gelasius's Ep. 26, c. 5, p. 399: "Contagio haereticorum." The biblical foundation is *Matt.* xviii. 18; I *Cor.* xii. 26 and 27; xv. 33.

[3] Gelasius, Ep. 1, c. 8, p. 291. The biblical foundation is *Matt.* x. 24; *Luke*, vi. 40.

[4] Ep. 26, c. 11, p. 407: "qualescumque pontifices, etsi errore humanitus accedente, non tamen religionem ullatenus excedentes."

[5] Cf. in this context also his argumentation about the contrast between clerics and lay in Frag. 49, pp. 509–10.

[6] Ep. 26, c. 5, p. 399: "Neque cuiquam de eius liceat judicare judicio . . . ab illa autem nemo sit appellare permissus." This is a characteristic example of how unnecessary certain forgeries were: the Symmachan forger working two or three years after this was written, concocted the so-called *Constitutum Silvestri*, in which he coined the famous phrase "Prima sedes a nemine judicatur," with which he credited Silvester. The forger had at his disposal a perfectly genuine statement by Gelasius, which would have suited his purpose.

[7] Ep. 10, c. 5, p. 344: "Ipsi sunt canones, qui appellationes totius ecclesiae ad huius sedis examen voluere deferri, ab ipsa vero nusquam prorsus appellari debere sanxerunt. Ac per hoc illam de tota ecclesia judicare, ipsam ad nullius commeare judicium, nec de eius unquam praeceperunt judicio judicari, sententiamque illius constituerunt non oportere dissolvi, cuius potius sequenda decreta mandarunt."

Nobody at any time and for whatever human pretext may haughtily set himself above the office of him who by Christ's order was set above all and everyone and whom the universal Church had always recognized as its head.[1]

In sum, then, the Gelasian thesis culminates in the monarchic conception of the *principatus*: the pope as successor of St Peter has sole *auctoritas* over the corporate body of Christians, amongst whom the emperor takes indeed a vital place, but one of an assistant nature: his function is reduced from that of a monarch to that of a mere "saecularis" or "regia potestas." The direction of this royal power by those who are, within the corporate union of Christians, qualified to do so, is as necessary as the direction of the whole body corporate. In this way this body will fulfil the purpose for which it was founded. The material or corporeal or temporal element in this body demands the guidance, that is orientation and government, by the spiritual or sacramental element of this self-same body. Gelasius bequeathed to all papal generations a set of ideas based upon an interpretation of history in the light of Christian teleology.[2]

Isidore of Seville furnished the most perfect ideological complement to the Gelasian thesis. And it is perhaps not without deeper significance that the Roman was to find his literary complement in a Spaniard who, to all seeming, was unaware of the great author-pope's views. Isidore might well serve as an example which demonstrates the multifarious and variegated roots from which the later imposing hierocratic system developed. Moreover, Isidore was a true bridge-builder between the early and late medieval times; a bridge-builder also between the

[1] Ep. 12, c. 3, p. 352.

[2] The invigorating effect of the Gelasian pontificate can be seen in his immediate successor, Anastasius II, who, as far as we can see, was the first to apply *Luke* x. 16, when he wrote to the emperor: "Haec me suggerentem frequentius non spernat pietas tua, ante oculos tuos habens Domini in evangelio verba: 'Qui audit vos, me audit; et qui vos spernit, me spernit etc.' Nam et apostolos concinens salvatori nostro, ita loquitur: 'Quapropter qui haec spernit non hominem spernit sed Deum, qui dedit spiritum suum sanctum in nobis,' " (the last reference is to I *Thess.* iv. 8). Ep. 1, p. 620. Anastasius's letter to Clovis, the newly converted Frankish king, has something of a prophetic ring when he writes: "Tuum, gloriose fili, in Christiana fide cum exordio nostro in pontificatu contigisse gratulamur. Quippe sedes Petri in tanta occasione non potest non laetari, cum *plenitudinem gentium* intuetur ad eam veloci gradu concurrere, . . . (Dominus) qui eruit te de potestate tenebrarum et *in tanto principe providit ecclesiae, qui possit eam tueri et contra* occurrentes pestiferorum *conatus galeam salutis induere*," Ep. 2, Thiel, p. 624. The authenticity of this letter is disputed.

Germanic and Roman nations.[1] And from the ideological point of view
he fully deserves the title "Doctor ecclesiae."

The theme of Isidore was the teleological one of the functions of the
prince as a member of the Church. To Isidore the Church is the
"Corpus Jesu Christi."[2] This *corpus* is made up of a plurality of nations
within which the princes function. There is but one *corpus*, held together by one faith, and consequently there is but one *regnum*:[3] "unus
Dei populus unumque regnum."[4] The congregation of all the nations
is the Church:

Huius populi congregatio ex gentibus ipsa est ecclesia.[5]

It is the "universitas gentium"[6] which forms the Church. In a word,
Christendom or the Church is a *civitas regis magni*.[7]

Isidore's views on the function of the prince might be described as a
paraphrastic elaboration of Pauline doctrine.[8] The function of the king
standing as he does within the Church is the strengthening of sacerdotal directives: his function is the support of the sacerdotal word by
the princely "terror." This is his *raison d'être*.[9] But since this *corpus*
lives by the rulings given by the ordained members, the support of
"ecclesiastical discipline" by the Christian prince and his sword is his
duty: in fulfilling this duty, he thereby justifies his existence, for Christ
gave him rulership in order to protect and guard the body of believers

[1] K. Vossler, in *Hochland*, xxxix (1947), p. 420 f. Cf. also E. Anspach, "Isidor
vom 7. bis 9. Jahrhundert" in *Miscellanea Isidoriana*, 1936, pp. 323–56.

[2] Isidore, *Quaestiones in Vet. Test.* ("In Esdram"), c. i. no. 2 (Migne, PL.
lxxxiii. 423).

[3] The *regnum* and the *sacerdotium* of Christ were pre-portrayed by Melchisedek
"cuius origo secreta est," *De ortu et obitu patrum*, c.v. PL. cit., col. 132. Cf. also
his *Allegoriae quaedam Scripturae sacrae*, no. 19, PL. cit., col. 104: "Melchisedek
. . . regnum Christi, qui est verus rex justitiae, et sacerdotium figuravit"; see also
his *Quaestiones in Vet. Testam.* ("In Genesin"), c. xi. nos. 4–5, cols. 239–40.

[4] *De fide catholica*, ii. 1, no. 3, PL. cit., col. 499.

[5] *De fide catholica*, no. 4.

[6] *De fide catholica*, ii. 7, no. 3, col. 513: "cuius universitas nunc per totum
orbem terrarum exsultans dicit . . ."

[7] *Quaest. in Vet. Testam.* ("In Regum Primum"), c. i. no. 7, col. 393, obviously borrowing the Augustinian idea of the universal Church.

[8] Especially of *Rom.* xiii. 4.

[9] See *Sententiae*, iii. 51, no. 4, PL. cit., col. 723: "Principes saeculi nonnum-
quam intra ecclesiam potestatis adeptae culmina tenent, *ut* per eandem potestatem
disciplinam ecclesiasticam muniant. Ceterum intra ecclesiam potestates neces-
sariae non essent, *nisi ut*, quod non praevalet sacerdos efficere per doctrinae
sermonem, potestas hoc imperet per disciplinae terrorem." For a characteristic
application of this Isidorian view cf., for example, Humbert, infra 269. Almost
the same words in Hugh of Fleury's *Tractatus de regia potestate*, LdL. ii. 469 and
in Placidus of Nonantula, *De honore ecclesiae*, LdL. ii. 573.

in Him.[1] For rulership, which Isidore calls *principatus*, is given to the king as a "donum Dei"—the ideological kinship with Gelasius's *beneficium* will be noted—and it is given for a particular purpose, namely for the protection of the members of Christ who are the "fideles populi."

Dono Dei pro tuitione utantur membrorum Christi.[2]

In this way the king will prove himself useful: "*Prodesse* ergo debet populis principatus, non nocere."[3] Naturally, usefulness is not an *a priori* notion: usefulness of rulership depends upon the character of society, and the character of this *corpus* was Christian, and hence usefulness can be determined only by Christian principles and to lay these down is the sole prerogative of the ordained members of this *corpus*. They are the "sors Domini," the "lot of the Lord."[4]

The criterion of Isidore's idea of rulership, namely the "*bene regere*"[5] cannot have universal validity: it is applicable only to a Christian society. "Good government" according to Isidore, is useful government. Useful government is government that realizes the purpose and aim of society that is governed.

Non statim *utile* est omne *potestatis insigne*, sed tunc vere *utile* est, si bene geratur. Tunc autem bene geritur, quando subjectis *prodest*.[6]

Accordingly, the implementation of justice is one of the principal avenues by which the king will prove himself useful to his people: but the contents of justice can be determined only by a recourse to the principles, purpose and aim of the society within which justice is to

---

[1] *Sent.*, no. 6: "Cognoscant principes saeculi Deo debere se rationem reddere propter ecclesiam, quam a Christo tuendam suscipiunt." We note that, in contrast to Gelasius, it is the princes themselves who have to render an account, and not the pontiffs.

[2] *Sent.*, iii. 49, no. 3, col. 721.

[3] *Sent.*, no. 3, and: "ut vere sit *utile* hoc potestatis insigne."

[4] We think that the earliest designation of the clerics as "sors Domini" a term which later will assume so much importance, was by St Jerome, CSEL. liv. 421. Cf. also Isidore's *Quaestiones de veteri et novo Testam.*, qu. x: "Dic mihi, clerus in cuius lingua dicitur? Respondit: in Graeca; in Latina sors Domini interpretatur." (PL. cit. col. 203.)

[5] *Sent.*, iii. 48. col. 718.

[6] *Sent.*, no. 5, col. 718. In his *Etymologies*, IX. iii. 4 (ed. W. M. Lindsay, Oxford, 1911), Isidore says: "*Recte igitur faciendo regis nomen tenetur, peccando amittitur.*" The determination of what constitutes "peccare" must be left to those who are qualified to pronounce upon it. For some very interesting observations about how these "apparently harmless linguistic remarks" were transformed into legal or political principles, see F. Schulz, "Bracton on Kingship" in EHR., lx (1945), p. 152.

be executed. Again, this being a Christian society, justice will derive its substance from Christian principles: in doing justice, "the prince's heart will not depart from God."[1] In short, by virtue of being Christians themselves, the princes will impart into their laws "the faith of Christ."[2] Naturally, what this faith is, does not depend upon the princes, but upon the "sors Domini." The princes are subjected to "the discipline of religion":

Sub religionis disciplina saeculi potestates subjectae sunt.[3]

The function of the king is therefore auxiliary: he assists where the priestly word proves itself inadequate. And he assists by inculcating fear into his subjects. Without fear, Isidore holds, no government can exist.[4] Fear appears to him a wholesome stimulus to the people to keep the laws. The coercion exercised by the king is therefore purely negative: to prevent evil doing—"ut terrore suo populos a malo coercerent"[5]—and thereby he will induce the subjects to "a right way of living."[6]

The fusion of the Gelasian thesis with the Isidorian theme of the function of the prince in a Christian society will in course of time yield the properly medieval hierocratic doctrine. All the basic elements were there: they needed only to be developed.

### III

It is perhaps not without a certain historical irony that within the century which lay between the two principal architects of hierocratic ideology, Gelasius and Isidore, the exact opposite ideology came to be applied in legislation and in practice. The at least latent regal-sacerdotal tendencies of the (Eastern) emperors were given their permanent complexion through Justinian. Indeed, Justinian was the proto-

---

[1] *Sent.*, iii. 49, no. 2, col. 720: "Qui recte utitur regni potestate formam justitiae factis magis quam verbis instituit . . . nec a Domino recedit cor eius."

[2] Cf. *Rom.* i. 17.

[3] *Sent.* iii. 51, no. 3, col. 723, continuing: "Et quamvis culmine regni sunt praediti, vinculo tamen fidei tenentur astricti, ut et fidem Christi suis legibus praedicent, et ipsam fidei praedicationem moribus bonis conservent." The passage quoted in the text will be quoted as late as the outgoing eleventh century, by Hugh of Fleury, *Tractatus de regia potestate*, LdL. ii. 475.

[4] *Sent.* iii. 47, no. 1, col. 717: "Nam si omnes sine metu fuissent, quis esset qui a malis quempiam prohiberet? Inde et in gentibus principes, regesque electi sunt, ut terrore suo populos a malo coercerent, atque ad recte vivendum legibus subderent."

[5] *Sent.*, see quotation in preceding note. Cf. also *Rom.* xiii. 4.

[6] Ibid.

type of the Roman monarch: inheriting the paganism of Hellenistic conceptions and Roman rulership, tinged with a good deal of Eastern mysticism and sublimated by the deep Christianity of the emperor, the Eastern monarch appeared as the earthly representation of divine power: the *Sol invictus*. He is divinity on earth.[1]

As a divinely appointed monarch (the autokrator and kosmokrator) the emperor necessarily rules solely over the entity that is divinely entrusted to him:[2] he rules it in every respect and since this empire is wholly Christian, it is he alone who directs it according to Christian principles emanating from the fount of all Christianity, the divine majesty of the emperor himself. His laws are divine and sacred.[3] Justinian's government is the classic example of the Christian monarch at work in a Christian society. Hence he not only lays down the faith for his subjects,[4] but also must necessarily legislate upon the functions and organic structure of the priesthood itself; hence it is also that, in his capacity as the monarch, he extends his special protection to the priesthood. For, as he laid down in one of his best-known decrees, since both the *imperium* and the *sacerdotium* proceed from one and the same source, there is nothing of greater concern to the emperor than the "probity and reputation" of the priesthood: it is the priests who intercede with God.[5] The "honestas sacerdotum," however, is, from the governmental point of view, nothing else but the suitability of the priests for their office: hence the imperial "care" for the priests no less than for the true dogmas of God.[6] What however the true dogmas of God were, it was the business of the monarch to fix, as the history of

[1] Cf. A. Alföldi, "Insignien & Trachten etc." in *Mitteilungen des deutschen archaeolog. Instituts*, Rom. Abt., vol. l (1935), tables 9 and 18, pp. 108, 141.

[2] Cf. F. Dölger, "Die Kaiserurkunde der Byzantiner" in *Hist. Z.*, 1939, p. 246: the emperor is the shepherd of the Christians divinely entrusted to him; see also p. 239.

[3] Cf. again W. Ensslin's numerous examples, op. cit., pp. 63 ff.; see also *Cod. Just.* V. xxvii. 7 (1): "divinis jussionibus"; VII. lxiii. 4: "divina sanctio"; X. xxxv. 2: "Lex divalis"; etc.

[4] The whole of the title "De summa trinitate et fide catholica" in Justinian's *Codex* can be adduced to show doctrinal legislation. Cf. also *Cod. Just.*, I. i. 6 pr: "We have hastened to instruct (our subjects) what is the true Christian faith."

[5] *Nov.* vi. pr.: "Maxima quidem in hominibus sunt dona Dei a superna collata clementia, sacerdotium et imperium: et illud quidem divinis ministrans, hoc autem humanis praesidens ac diligentiam exhibens: ex uno eodemque principio utraque procedentia, humanam exornant vitam. Ideoque nihil sic erit *studiosum imperatoribus*, sicut sacerdotum honestas, cum utique et pro illis ipsi semper Deo supplicent." Cf. also *Cod. Just.* I. iv. 34.

[6] *Nov.* cit.: "Nos igitur maximam habemus solicitudinem circa vera Dei dogmata et circa sacerdotum honestatem quam illis obtinentibus credimus . . ."

Justinian's government only too plainly revealed.[1] In all this we will no doubt detect the gentle, but effective reversal of the Gelasian thesis: Justinian's thesis is modelled on that of Gelasius, and is Gelasianism turned upside down.[2]

The character of the empire as Roman on the one hand and as Christian on the other hand, together with the exercise of true monarchical power by the emperor, explains the quite unprecedented legislation on matters touching the essence of this empire. Roman spirit and Roman rule had always been characterized by the supremacy of law, hence Justinian's predilection for legislation on all sorts of matters which basically violated papal-hierocratic principles. It is, of course, no coincidence that the Roman character of Justinian's empire is so much stressed.[3] Since the empire was Roman and Christian, the honorary rank allotted to the "patriarch of Rome" by the monarch is understandable. As the bishop of that city which in fact gave the empire its Roman complexion, the pope quite naturally was given an honorary rank above the other patriarchs. But this should not mislead us into thinking that the pope played any other role but that of a patriarch in the scheme of things devised by Justinian.[4] As a monarch the emperor

---

[1] In fact, specific occasions apart, none of the emperors considered it necessary to submit ecclesiastical legislation to a council. Cf. also C. Silva-Tarouca, *Institutiones historiae ecclesiasticae* ii. 1 (1933), p. 31: "Imperatoris legibus episcopi, clerici, monachi, fideles reguntur."

[2] This is very rightly pointed out by H. Rahner, op. cit., p. 237: "eine stillschweigende Korrektur der Gelasianischen Gedanken."

[3] For this see especially F. Dölger, "Rom in der Gedankenwelt der Byzantiner" in *Z. f. Kirchengeschichte*, liv (1937), pp. 4 ff.; cf. Justinian's *Nov.* xxii. c. 2; xxv. pr. and c. 2; xlvii. pr. and c. 1, etc., and Ostrogorsky, pp. 42 ff.

[4] Cf. Silva-Tarouca, op. cit., ii. 32: "Papa fit unus ex quinque patriarchis imperii, quem imperator ita regere intendit ac suum patriarchum aulicum regit." Cf. also L. Duchesne, *L'église au VI siècle*, p. 266; L. Brehier, in Fliche-Martin, *Histoire de l'église*, iv. 441; H. Rahner, op. cit., p. 237. We are not unaware of the modern fashion which denies the caesaropapism of the Eastern emperors. G. Vernadsky even spoke of a diarchy between emperor and patriarch, see P. Charanis, art. cit., p. 59, note 51. The term caesaropapism may well be unaesthetic or inadequate, but what matters is the thing itself, not the term. Cf. especially K. Voigt, *Staat & Kirche*, 1936, pp. 27, note 28, 53–5, 81, 109. There can be no doubt about the true monarchic functions in every sphere, including the ecclesiastical one, as they were effectively exercised by the emperor. Cf. Th. Schnitzler in *Anal. Greg.* xvi (1938), pp. 113–17 (here also the long quotation from A. Gasquet *De l'autorité impériale*, etc., p. 266, at p. 115 note 6) and now C. Toumanoff, in *Traditio*, vii (1952), p. 489 (book review): "In the course of history, from the first Constantine to the last, Caesars enjoyed *de facto* the position of popes in Byzantine Christianity. Few will deny that the masters of the surviving Roman empire arrogated to themselves both the apostolic see's supreme power of jurisdiction and its teaching authority when, e.g. they convoked councils of the Church

could not concede a *principatus* to the Roman Church in precisely those matters which were vital and basic to the conceptual framework of the empire itself. From his own point of view Justinian may well say that there is little difference between the *sacerdotium* and the *imperium*.[1] In his statement that his laws, the *leges*, imitated the canons, Justinian reveals his ideology all too plainly.

This Byzantine regal-sacerdotal scheme presents itself as the translation of the Christian faith into an essential ingredient of the government. Hence not only the religious and ecclesiastical legislation of Justinian,[2] but also, since there was little difference between the Roman and the Christian empire, the direction of that whole body must needs lie in the hands of the one monarch. The empire is the divinely instituted guardian of peace and order: outside its frontiers there is darkness and faithlessness. Only the autokrator, the emperor, he who virtually represents divinity on earth, can effectively provide for unity, peace and order.[3] Just as in the celestial cosmos there was only one who combined all power—Christ as the Pantocrator—so there was in the terrestrial cosmos only one monarch.[4]

---

\*   or issued dogmatic pronouncements. But, more than that, they finally became also, in the eyes of their subjects, endued with the papal function of the centre of unity, of the point of concentration, in the Church. It was already by the time of Justinian . . . that the cesaropapist confusion of these two unities had given birth to the idea of the Church as an imperial Church. This was the root of the frictions between the apostolic see and the imperial throne . . ." In the troubled days of Martin I, the imperial messenger at Rome, Georgios, justified the emperor's *Typos* by saying to Maximus the Confessor: "The emperor is also a priest," (Migne, PG. xc. 115) and by arguing that scriptural evidence shows clearly Melchisedek having been king and priest. Maximus retorted that Melchisedek was the prototype of Christ, but "the emperor is a layman, for at mass we think of him in connexion with laymen, at the *memento* and *after* the bishops, priests and deacons." (PG. ibid.)

\*   [1] *Nov.* vii. c. 2: "Neque multum differant ab alterutro sacerdotium et imperium."
[2] Orthodoxy of faith to be preserved only by imperial legislation, *Nov.* cxxxi; legislation against heretics (*Cod.* I. i. 6), against monophysites (*Nov.* xlii), Manichaeans (*Cod.* I. v. 11); only orthodox Christians suitable for military service, *Cod.* I. iv. 20 and I. v. 12; no practising of religion by Manichaeans etc., *Cod.* I. v. 14 and 20, no propagating or teaching of their faith, *Cod.* I. xi. 10, their books to be burned, I. v. 16; only Christians are citizens, *Cod.* I. xi. 10; clergy not to attend theatres, racing tracks or circus nor partake in games, *Cod.* I. iv. 34; *Nov.* cxxii. c. 12; no absenteeism of clerics, *Nov.* lvii, no military service, *Cod.* I. iii. 53; liturgical duties, *Cod.* I. iii. 42, and *Nov.* cxxxi; no private oratories, *Nov.* lviii; cf. also *Nov.* viii and lxxxvi, cc. 1, 6, 7, *Cod.* I. iv. 21, 23, 26.
[3] For this see F. Dölger, *Hist. Z.*, cit., p. 232: "buchstäblich gottähnliche Erhabenheit und Machtfülle"; see also idem in *Der Vertrag von Verdun*, p. 210.
[4] Speaking of Justinian as the most pronounced representative of Caesaropapism, K. Jäntere, op. cit., p. 167, says that his governmental principles were the

The sacredness and divinity of the emperor showed itself also in concrete stone and masonry and in the appropriate ceremonial symbolism. All the buildings constituting the imperial palace were sacred, and this sacred character was derived from that part which formed the centre of the whole, the hall of the throne: this had all the appearances of a church.[1] The building which housed this hall was called the Chrysotriklinos. In the conch of the central hall there was a mosaic depicting Christ as God and Man and underneath the mosaic stood the throne of the emperor. The adoration of the emperor on certain feast days had all the appearances of a divine service.[2] The emperor himself after having said his own prayers, was greeted and acclaimed by his dignitaries and subjects, whereupon he turned towards the mosaic in the conch and said a thanksgiving prayer: the acclamations of his subjects were, so to speak, forwarded to Christ, the real Ruler of the kosmos whose vicar the emperor considered himself.[3] On other occasions the emperor feasted his patriarch and patricians in the Chrysotriklinos, a ceremony that no doubt was an imitation of the Lord's Supper.[4] Here in the hall of the throne the kosmokrator and vicar of divinity also

---

same as those of his predecessors. "Ein Staat, ein Gesetz, eine Kirche." The true monarchic conception of the emperor found legal expression in the famous "Princeps legibus solutus." This was not of Roman, but of Greek origin and unknown to the classical jurists, e.g., Ulpian (*Dig.* 1. 3. 31), see F. Schulz, in EHR., lx, 1945, pp. 157–60.

[1] See J. Ebersolt, *Le grand palais de Constantinople*, p. 169: "Les personnages religieux disséminés dans toute la salle, le Christ trônant dans l'abside, conservèrent au Chrysotriklinos l'aspect qu'il avait au début, celui d'une église," quoted by H. Fichtenau, "Byzanz und die Pfalz zu Aachen" in MIOG., lix (1951), p. 8. See also A. Alföldi, "Die Ausgestaltung des monarchischen Zeremoniells" in *Mitt. des deutschen archaeolog. Inst.*, Rom. Abt., xlix (1934), p. 33. The hall was finished during Justin II's reign, 565–78, see J. B. Bury, *History of the later Roman empire*, ii. 73, note 1. For early Roman basilicas which were "Thronsäle Gottes, nicht Christi, nach dem Modell der Thronsäle eines Kaisers, der sich als 'vicarius' Gottes auf Erden fühlte," see A. Stange, *Das frühmittelalterliche Kirchengebäude als Bild des Himmels*, Cologne, 1950, pp. 87, 88–91; about the church of Trier and its innovation, see ibid., pp. 114–20. For symbolic Byzantine details see A. Grabar, *L'empereur dans l'art Byzantin*, Paris (1936), esp. ch. 4: "L'empereur et le Christ," pp. 98–122; also tables 18, 19, 21, 25, etc.

[2] See Fichtenau, art. cit., pp. 9 ff.

[3] Fichtenau, p. 12; cf. *Liber de cerimoniis*, ed. Bonn, i. 1, p. 22; for the acclamation of the emperor see also the passage quoted supra p.16, and *Lib de cerim.*, ii. 43, p. 222: "Cantores accinunt: 'appareat divina majestas.' Populus ter: 'appareat.' " Cf. also the description of the procession in the imperial palace, ibid., ii. 1, p. 518 ff., esp. p. 519: "Indutus imperator egreditur in chrysotriklinium et stat erectus, in concha orientali, in qua imago Dei et Domini nostri, sub humana specie Deum exhibens depicta conspicitur, precesque Deo consuetas exsolvit, et metanoeam induit." See also ibid., ii. 52, p. 705.

[4] Cf. Fichtenau, loc. cit. Cf. also infra p.342 n. 5.

received foreign diplomats.[1] To a casual observer it may not always have been easy to decide whether he witnessed an imperial or a divine service. The documents which issued from the imperial chancery exhibited the same symbolic traits. The "divine right hand of the emperor" used red ink for the imperial signature,[2] whilst the profile of his divine majesty denoted his "omnipresence."[3] The elaborate ornamentation and miniatures on the documents served the same purpose, namely, to show them to the world as the products of the divine emperor. The subject on receiving the imperial document deeply bowed and kissed the roll reverently, before he took actual possession of it.[4]

Despite the temporary unification achieved by Justinian in 553 and despite the incessant proclamation by him and his successors of the Roman fibre of the empire, this empire in reality assumed an ever stronger Greek complexion. In fact, the re-union of Italy with the empire made contemporaries realize the cultural, social and religious chasm that lay between them and the imperial regime. Though nominally Roman, the empire was to all intents and purposes Greek.[5] The mishandling of Pope Vigilius by Justinian showed the overpowering influence of the divine majesty on the first of the five patriarchs. The guardian of Roman rule, tradition, and spirit was not the Graecized Roman empire, but the Roman papacy itself constitutionally an integral part of the empire. The physiognomy of the papacy was thoroughly Roman—we have only to recall Gelasius's statements to realize this, and by the end of the following century this impregnation appeared all the more pronounced by contrast with the "alien" Greek regime.

The true significance of Gregory I's quarrel with the Eastern patriarch over the title of "universal patriarch" emerges when this quarrel is set against the background of the English mission. The assumption of this title by the patriarch, John IV (the Faster), was neither new[6] nor unknown to Gregory before 595, and yet he did not

[1] Into this category of symbolism belong also the veiled hands of the emperor ("manus velatae") and the use of curtains hiding him from the view of his subjects, about which see A. Alföldi, op. cit. (1934), pp. 33–8.

[2] For this see F. Dölger, "Die Kaiserurkunde der Byzantiner" in *Hist. Z.*, 1939, pp. 229 ff., esp. 233 ff.

[3] Dölger, art. cit., p. 235, note 2.        [4] Dölger, art. cit., pp. 234, 239.

[5] Gregory I's complaint that there was hardly anyone in Constantinople who was able to translate Latin letters into Greek, is significant.

[6] See supra p. 15. Justinian had also used it in 539, see his *Nov.* lxxxiii pr.: "Petiti sumus a Menna Deo amabili archiepiscopo huius felicissimae civitatis et *universali patriarcha*."

protest until the June of that year, barely three months before the advance party left for the Frankish kingdom to prepare the way for the English mission.[1] The mission to England occasioned Gregory's protest. What the title meant was that the patriarch claimed universal jurisdictional power, the same claim that was enshrined in the *principatus* of the Roman Church.[2] The envisaged extension of Christianity and the consequential exercise of the *principatus* of the Roman Church necessitated a sharp remonstration against the title claimed by the patriarch. In order to safeguard the claim of the Roman *principatus* towards the West, Gregory I was bound to protest vigorously to the East.[3] And the very choice of the term *principatus* in this June 595 protest[4] reveals the underlying motive. *Principatus* over the "populus Dei" belongs solely to the Roman Church,[5] epitomizing as it does the "corpus Christi, quod est sancta universalis ecclesia."[6]

Gregory I's *societas reipublicae christianae*[7] over which the Roman Church exercises its *principatus* unimpeded by considerations of a constitutional nature, is the prophetic vision of medieval Europe. This *societas* was made up of the nations and kingdoms outside the

[1] For this see *Reg.* v. 31; vi. 5, 6 and 10. We quote from the Register edition in MGH. *Epp.* i and ii.

[2] The patriarch's claim was of course linked with Constantinople as the *urbs regia*, cf. Gregory himself, *Reg.* vii. 37, p. 485; also vi. 58.

[3] Gregory was on friendly terms with the patriarch, John IV, during his sojourn in Constantinople as apocrisiary; the friendship continued into Gregory's pontificate; the *Regula pastoralis* was dedicated to John; one of the first letters was written to John, *Reg.* i. 3, October 590; there is no protest in the *Synodica* of February 591, *Reg.* i. 24; although according to Gregory there had already been a dispute between Pelagius II and John on the title question (*Reg.* v. 41, p. 332, lines 6–15; v. 39, p. 327, lines 10–12; v. 44, p. 339, lines 4–10; ix. 156), he did not protest until June 595: *Reg.* v. 37. This letter stands in sharp contrast to all previous letters written by Gregory, cf. also its characterization by E. H. Fischer, "Gregor d. Gr. und Byzanz" in *Sav. Z. Kan. Abt.* xxxvi (1950), p. 109: "Schroffheit"; see also Holmes Dudden, *Gregory the Great*, London, 1905, ii. 250: "insolent."

[4] *Reg.* v. 37. The possibility that the Irish-Celtic Church (which had its headquarters in Iona and by Gregory's time had made a considerable advance into the North of England) was strongly influenced by the Eastern Church, should not be ruled out altogether. Cf. also Caspar, op. cit., ii. 506, 677. See also G. S. M. Walker, "On the use of Greek words in the writings of St Columbanus of Luxeuil" in *Bulletin du Cange*, xxi (1950), pp. 117 ff., who points out (p. 131) the wide interests in Greek studies in sixth-century Ireland and who also refers to the use of the vernacular Greek language at that time in Ireland.

[5] The assumption by Gregory I of the title "servus servorum Dei" is an inverted exaltation of his office; cf. also "cunctorum sacerdotum servus," p. 323, line 10; p. 322, line 24—*Luke* xiv. 11. The term "principatus" had been used by Gregory only once before: *Reg.* i. 24 to the Eastern patriarchs.

[6] *Reg.* iv. 3, p. 235, line 26.          [7] *Reg.* ix. 67, p. 88, lines 5–6.

imperial framework, that is, outside the legitimate sphere of imperial jurisdiction. No less prophetic is the exaltation of the Frankish king (Childebert II) and of the Frankish people. "Just as royal dignity surpasses all individual men, in the same way the Frankish kingdom excels all other peoples."[1] And most significantly, this communication was despatched in that historic month of September 595 when the advance party left for the West. The Franks excel the other nations because of their orthodoxy: the theme of St Peter which formed the keynote of this letter, heralds another age which was to translate the prophetic vision of Gregory I into political reality.[2]

There is in Gregory's letters a remarkable difference in tone between those addressed to the emperor and those to Western potentates. Whilst the emperor is invariably the "dominus," Western rulers are the pope's "filii."[3] Towards the West the pope adopts language of commanding authority.[4] And it was in the West that the *principatus* of the Roman Church was effectively realized: from the farthest corner of Europe came the enduring stimulus for the unification of all the "Romani." In more than one respect Gregory I can be called, not only "Consul Dei," but also "pater Europae."

It is nevertheless true that Gregory I did not materially contribute to the development of the hierocratic theme, although by virtue of his writings and his Registers[5] so widely used in the later papal chancery, a great number of his statements and expressions found their way into later papal communications. The teleological view on royal power is strongly endorsed by Gregory: the earthly power is at the service of the celestial power. The former is modelled on the latter.[6] Not only

---

[1] *Reg.* vi. 6, p. 384 to Childebert II: "Quanto ceteros homines regia dignitas antecedit, tanto ceterarum gentium regna regni vestri (scil. Francorum) culmen excellit."

[2] Gregory also sent the keys of the Confession of St Peter to Childebert: "Claves sancti Petri, in quibus de vinculis catenarum eius inclausum est excellentiae vestrae direximus," ibid., p. 385. Cf. also ibid.: "Esse autem regem, quia sunt et alii, non mirum est, sed esse catholicum, quod alii non merentur, hoc satis est." This comparison with "aliae gentes" or "ceterae gentes" might possibly be an echo of the anonymous tract *De vocatione omnium gentium*, written in the late fifth century, cf. infra p. 76 n. 4.

[3] Only once Gregory spoke of the emperor as "piissimus dominus filius noster" (*Reg.* vii. 24, p. 469, line 19), but this was addressed to Anastasius of Antioch, and not to the emperor himself.

[4] Cf., e.g., *Reg.* ix. 47, p. 320, lines 5–9; ix. 213, p. 199; ix. 215, pp. 201–3, etc.

[5] About Gregory's Registers see especially W. Peitz, "Das Register Gregors I" in *Stimmen der Zeit*, suppl. vol. ii (1917), particularly pp. 69 ff. Cf. also E. Posner, "Das Registers Gregors I" in *Neues Archiv*, xliii (1922), pp. 243–315.

[6] *Reg.* iii. 61, p. 221, lines 9–13: "Ad hoc enim potestas super omnes homines

in this is implied the view of the pope's mediatory role, but also logically arising out of it, is the sanction for violating a papal decree, namely excommunication. And this threat concerns kings as well as clerics.[1] Gregory emphasizes equally the role of the *sacerdotium* in a Christian society as a vehicle for transmitting papal decrees.[2] The "sacerdotes" are the cultivators of the "ecclesia Dei."[3] The "sacerdotes Christi vice *in ecclesia* legatione *funguntur*,"[4] a view and a sentence that gained wide currency in later times. And not the least interesting facet of Gregory's view on the relation between the priests and the emperor is that Emperor Constantine is held up to Emperor Maurice as an example to be followed—and this was written to the emperor in the same month of June 595 in which the pope for the first time protested against the patriarchical title.[5] In this communication Gregory I—as far as can be seen he was the first to do so —quotes from the ecclesiastical history of Rufinus which puts into the mouth of Constantine the—later—famous address to the bishops assembled at Nicaea: "You are gods, constituted by the true God; it is not right that we sit in judgment over gods."[6] This state-

---

pietati dominorum meorum coelitus data est, ut qui bona appetunt adjuventur, ut coelorum via largius pateat, ut terrestre regnum coelesti regno famuletur." Cf. in this context St Augustine, *De civ. Dei*, v. 24; against this interpretation E. Caspar, op. cit., ii. 469, note 3; cf. also P. Batiffol, *Gregoire le Grand*, p. 241, and Fischer, art. cit., p. 138; but see H. X. Arquillière, *L'augustinisme politique*, Paris, 1932, p. 81, who rightly points out that this Gregorian passage contains "la conception ministérielle" of kingship.

[1] See the two *privilegia* in *Reg.* xiii. 11 and 12, pp. 376–80: "Si quis vero regum, sacerdotum, judicum atque saecularium personarum hanc constitutionem nostrae paginam agnoscens contra eam venire temptaverit, potestatis honorisque sui dignitate careat reumque se divino judicio existere de perpetrata iniquitate cognoscat et, nisi vel ea quae ab illo sunt male ablata restituerit vel digna poenitentia inlicite acta defleverit, a sacratissimo corpore ac sanguine Dei Domini redemptoris nostri Iesu Christi alienus fiet atque in aeterno examine districtae ultioni subjaceat" (p. 378). It is known that Gregory VII was to fall back on this, see his *Reg.* viii. 21, though with a characteristically Hildebrandine accentuation: "Non modo deponi, sed etiam excommunicari . . . decrevit." The *Liber Diurnus*, form. 32, p. 86, 89, has a similar penal sanction, but it does not include kings.

[2] Cf. *Reg.* xi. 56a, p. 333, lines 8–9; see also *Reg.* i. 32, p. 45, lines 1–2.

[3] See *Reg.* i. 75, p. 95, lines 9–12.

[4] *Reg.* ix. 64. Cf. II *Cor.* v. 20.

[5] *Reg.* v. 36, p. 318 f.; *Reg.* v. 37 contains the protest about the title.

[6] *Reg. cit.*, p. 318; Rufinus, *Hist. eccl.*, i. 2, in PL. xxi. 468–9. On Rufinus see M. Villain, "Rufin d'Aquilée et l'histoire ecclésiastique" in *Recherches de science religieuse*, xxxiii (1946), pp. 188–91 ("l'image que notre historien se faisait de l'empereur était tout idéalisée . . ." p. 189). Cf. also J. E. L. Oulton, "Rufinus's translation of the Church History of Eusebius" in *Journal of theological studies*, xxx (1929), pp. 164–8, and G. Bardy, "Faux et fraudes littéraires" in RHE.,

ment of Gregory culled from Rufinus will also gain a very wide currency.[1]

The monastic outlook of Gregory I is faithfully mirrored in the stamp which he impresses upon the *sacerdotium*. Authority, submission and subordination to superior orders characterized the Benedictine Rule, itself so largely inspired by these characteristic Roman features,[2] which as a result of the wide dissemination of Benedictine monachism was a very powerful agent in the impregnation of the fallow Western soil.[3] On the model of the Benedictine Rule the bishop becomes the "pater familias" of his diocese which is likened to a "regnum,"[4] and over which he exercises a "sacrum regimen."[5] In general, the priesthood is a "religiosa militia" whose "exercitus" is entrusted to suitable leaders.[6] The coercion of obstreperous lay people by a subdeacon is not an action against the law, but one in its support.[7] Priests are superior to

---

*  xxxii (1936), pp. 282–6. For Eusebius cf. D. Ireneio, "I documenti Constantiniani della Vita Constantini di Eusebio" in *Analecta Gregoriana*, xiii (1938); and W. Völker, "Tendenzen in Eusebius's Kirchengeschichte" in *Vigiliae Christianae*, iv (1950), pp. 164–6. Also F. E. Cranz in *Harvard Theol. Rev.*, xlv (1952), pp. 47 ff.

[1] According to Gregory, Constantine merely applied relevant expressions of the Old Testament. When Moses said. "Thou shalt not revile the gods" (*Ex.* xxii. 28) he wished to say "Thou shalt not revile the priests"; the same interpretation of *Ex.* xxiii. 8: "Applica illum (scilicet furem) ad deos, videlicet sacerdotes." In Scripture, according to Gregory, the priests are sometimes called gods, sometimes angels, see *Reg.* cit.: "Nam in divinis eloquiis sacerdotes aliquando dii, aliquando angeli vocantur." Cf. *Mal.* ii. 7.

[2] For a brilliant characterization of the Rule, see D. Knowles, *The Monastic Order in England*, Cambridge, repr. 1950, pp. 5–15; cf. especially pp. 8–9 referring to the governmental principles obtaining in the Roman Church as a source on which St Benedict drew.

*  [3] On these Roman features and especially the spirit of, and the borrowings from, Roman law in the *Regula*, see Ildephons Herwegen, "Vom Geist des Römischen Rechts in der Benediktiner Regel" in *Festschrift f. R. Guardini*, Rothenfels am Main, 1935, pp. 184 ff., pointing out that St Benedict's instructions resemble Roman imperial decrees: the influence of Roman law in the Rule is particularly noticeable in the penal part of the Rule (cc. 23–30), in the parallelism between "publica disciplina" and "domestica disciplina," and so forth. Cf. also K. Gross, "Auctoritas-Majorum exempla" in *Studien & Mitteilungen ur Geschichte des Benediktiner Ordens*, lviii (1940), pp.102–38. For some observations on this topic see also O. Gradenwitz, "Zur Regula sancti Benedicti" in *Studi in onore di Salvatore Riccobono*, Palermo, 1936, i. 573–84. The problem of the *Regula Magistri* is of no concern to us.

[4] *Reg.* ii. 52, p. 156, line 30; cf. also *Reg.* vi. 50, p. 427, line 2; and ix. 218, p. 207, line 31.

[5] *Reg.* ix. 210, p. 218, lines 3–4.

[6] *Reg.* v. 60, p. 374, lines 19–25; "clericatus militia" in *Reg.* iv. 11, p. 244.

[7] *Reg.* iii. 5, p. 163, lines 3–5: "Violentos namque laicos coercere non contra leges est agere, sed ferre subsidium."

laymen: inequality of functions is essential to the proper ordering of Christendom. The principle of functional order which we have already met in Gelasius I, appears here in a memorable passage:

Neque enim universitas alia poterat ratione subsistere nisi huiusmodi magnus eam differentiae ordo servaret.[1]

For terrestrial society is modelled on celestial society—the Augus-. tinian background of Gregory I—and just as here there is no equality, so there is none in the former.[2] Strict hierarchical ordering is the condition for the proper working of the *Societas reipublicae Christianae*.[3] In brief, then, since the body corporate of the Christians is held together by the spiritual element of the faith, those who function as its leaders must be suitable. The cause of a people's ruin lies in bad priests.[4] This, according to Gregory I, is the crucial importance of the priesthood in a Christian society.

The century that followed Gregory I witnessed an ever-growing gulf amounting to open hostility between the "Roman" empire and its Western provinces; this same century also saw the quite unprecedented mishandling of the papacy by the imperial government;[5] it was also in this century that the Western soil was so strongly permeated

---

[1] *Reg.* v. 59, p. 371, lines 15–16. About the application of this important statement by Gregory VII see infra 289. Cf. also St Augustine, *Civ. Dei*, xix. 13: "Pax omnium rerum tranquillitas ordinis. Ordo est parium dispariumque rerum sua cuique loca tribuens dispositio." The principle of functional order could not be better expressed.

[2] *Reg.* cit., lines 16–20: "Quia vero creatura in una eademque equalitate gubernari vel vivere non potest, coelestium militiarum exemplar nos instruit, quia, dum sint angeli, sint archarchangeli, liquet, quia non aequales sunt, sed in potestate et ordine, sicut nostis, differt alter ab altero."

[3] The tendency to centralization is clearly noticeable as also the attempt to weaken episcopal power: the monasteries were encouraged to get into direct contact with the pope, cf. e.g., *Reg.* v. 47; 49; vi. 44; vii. 12; 40; viii. 17; xiii. 11; 12 and 13. On this see also H. Dudden, op. cit., ii. 188. Cf. also the reason for the despatch of the Defensor John to Spain, *Reg.* xiii. 50, pp. 414–18. The papal instruction to his legate is a juristic masterpiece. The legalism of Gregory I was very pronounced and not one of the least important features bequeathed to later generations, cf. also M. Conrat, *Geschichte der Quellen & Literatur des römischen Rechts im MA.*, Leipzig, 1906, p. 36: Gregory's letters show "eine Fülle juristischer Weisheit." On the canonistic importance of Gregory's Register see now G. Damizia, *Lineamenti di diritto canonico nel Registrum Epistolarum di s. Gregorio*, Rome, 1949.

[4] *Reg.* xi. 46, p. 319, lines 4–5: "Nam causa sunt ruinae populi sacerdotes mali."

[5] For this see E. Caspar, op. cit., ii. 515–619; cf. also the excellent selection of documents by H. Rahner, op. cit., pp. 283–346; also Th. Schnitzler in *Analecta Gregoriana*, xvi (1938), pp. 78 ff.

3

with the characteristic Roman features, through all sorts of agencies which eventually emanated from, or were promoted by, the Roman papacy. And not the least significant aspect of this century was the strong tie which the Church of Rome had established with the farthest outpost of Latin Christendom, England.

Set against this background of the seventh century, the firm stand which Pope Sergius I took against the imperially convoked *Quinisexta* (692) is understandable. Western temper had reached a point which enabled this pope to go into open rebellion against the regal-sacerdotal scheme of the empire, personified as this was in the second Justinian. The significance of the *Quinisexta* lies in that its decisions were to have universal validity, although the West was not even invited to partake in the deliberations. They resulted in the passing of a number of decrees provocatively directed against the *principatus* of the Roman Church.[1] Asked by the emperor to sign these decrees, Sergius I flatly refused,[2] because they were invalid.[3] Although, by order of the emperor, two of the trusted papal advisers—the bishop of Porto, Peter, and the papal counsellor, Boniface—were arrested and taken to Constantinople for trial, the imperial warrant of arrest against the pope himself could not be executed because of the hostility of the crowd.[4]

The impossibility of executing an imperial warrant of arrest was significant. No less significant was the intimate connexion between the Roman Church and England during the pontificate of Sergius I. The seed which Gregory had planted at the beginning of this century, had come to fruition. Not only had the Romanization of Western regions advanced, but also throughout this century the links between Rome and England had been of a very special and personal kind: links which were forged through papal legations, conferment of specific monastic privileges and above all by pilgrimages to Rome—not primarily because Rome was *Roma aurea*, but because Rome was the

---

[1] *Constantinople*, c. iii, and *Chalcedon*, c. xxviii were re-issued (cap. xxxvi); the change in the civil status of a city entailed a change in its ecclesiastical status (cap. xxxviii); no celibacy for deacons and presbyters (cap. xiii)—this chapter created the legal basis of the Eastern difference as regards celibacy. The emperor was the first to sign the decrees, Mansi, xi. 988. For details see Caspar, op. cit., ii. 632 ff.; G. Fritz, *Dict. Théol. Cath.* xiii, s.v., cols. 1581–97.

[2] Cf. *Liber Pontificalis*, ed. L. Duchesne, i. 372.

[3] *Lib. Pont.*: "eos ut invalidos respuit."

[4] The *Lib. Pont.* loc. cit., has a long description of these events. The imperial officer, Zacharias, who was to have executed the warrant, fled before the wildly excited crowd into the room of the pope himself, and hid himself under the papal bed. Afterwards he was chased out of the town.

burial place of St Peter.[1] Rome and St Peter became inextricably bound up in Western minds, hence the numerous church dedications to St Peter, St Paul, and so forth, which all bore an overwhelmingly Roman character.[2] On the other hand, the Roman Church could not but feel a sense of security as a result of these strong ties existing between it and the Western outposts of Latin Christianity. And most significantly, it was just in Sergius's pontificate that these Western manifestations of Petrine-Roman veneration became most pronounced. The king of the West Saxons, Caedwalla, resigned his throne in 689 to go to Rome, in order to be baptized "Peter" by Sergius.[3] In 690 Willibrord went to Rome to ask permission of Sergius to carry out his missionary work amongst the Frisians,[4] and to obtain relics "to put into the newly erected churches."[5] Five years later Willibrord was consecrated archbishop of the Frisians and received the pallium from Sergius: the new archbishop received the Roman name of Clement.[6]

It was precisely in these years of the outgoing seventh century which witnessed these unmistakable symptoms of Western devotion and orientation to Rome, that Pope Sergius took his firm stand against the demands of Emperor Justinian II.[7] Indeed, the purely theoretical protest of Gregory I, prompted by the envisaged expansion of Christianity exactly a hundred years earlier, had produced practical effects now that the Roman Church, as a result of the Western orientation towards Rome, felt strong enough to exercise its *principatus*, albeit in a negative manner, by condemning the decrees of the *Quinisexta* and by openly revolting against imperial orders. In this we might well see the heraldings of a new age.

[1] For all details see W. Levison, *England & the Continent*, Oxford, 1946, pp. 15–44, and Jäntere, op. cit., 249–51. The works of Th. Zwölfer and E. Pfeil were not accessible to me. [2] Levison, op. cit., p. 34.

[3] See Bede, *Hist. eccl.*, V. vii; here also the epitaph "written on the pope's command on his tomb." Before Caedwalla Oswiu of Northumbria desired to go to Rome for the same purpose, but died before he could go, see Levison, op. cit., p. 37; cf. also Caspar, op. cit., ii. 679 f. After Caedwalla Coenred of Mercia and Offa of Essex went the road to Rome, Levison, p. 38.

[4] See Bede, V. xi. [5] Bede, V. xi.

[6] Bede, V. xi, and Levison, p. 60, note 1, drawing attention to the mass of St Clement in the *Sacramentarium Leonianum*, p. 152, ed. Ch. Feltoe. Twenty years later Wynfrid was given the Roman name of Boniface. Cf. also Levison, p. 57: "The English Church was conscious of its Roman origin; now its first continental offspring (i.e. the Frisian Church) entered into the same relation at once, an attitude which also became the distinctive mark of Boniface and of the German Church created by him."

[7] The intitulation of this emperor in a recently discovered edict of his throws significant light on imperial ideology, cf. the transcription by A. Vasiliev, "An edict of Emperor Justinian II, 688" in *Speculum*, xviii (1943), pp. 5–6.

# CHAPTER II

# The Emancipation
# of the Papacy from the Empire

THERE can have been few decades in European history which were of so decisive moment for Europe as those between the third and fifth decades of the eighth century. Battered, in the literal and metaphorical sense, the papacy had emerged from the many vicissitudes of the previous age: Martin I's martyrdom; Maximus the Confessor's dignified stand; the subsequent trials besetting the papacy in the christological disputes; the Trullanum and its consequences—indeed all these, to mention only the gravest issues, had tested the papacy to a point at which ordinary human endurance would have failed. The seventh century can indeed be called the heroic age of the papacy. And yet, the underlying causes of the virtually inexhaustible disputes and battles were simple. The papal claim to magisterial and jurisdictional primacy (the *principatus*) was severely attacked by the emperor acting as a true monarch (autokrator): in this function he could not permit papal intervention in spheres directly affecting the working of his (Christian) body politic. The papacy, on the other hand, insisted on the proper qualification for determining doctrinal matters and for controlling the sacerdotal organism. Papal insistence on these vital points led to resistance.

But, from the constitutional point of view, resistance on the part of the papacy to the imperial claims was made much more difficult, since the Roman Church was within the constitutional framework of the Roman empire. The empire as such had not changed; what had changed was merely the capital. Again from the constitutional point of view, resistance to the decrees issued by the Eastern emperor, the *Rex-Sacerdos*, was a very serious matter, since resistance took the form of rebellion which was nothing else but high-treason. This was really the crux of the matter. As long as the Roman Church formed an integral part of the Christian Roman empire—and we must take note that the empire in its turn was highly concerned with this, for it would have been most incongruous if the Church of Rome were outside the nexus of the Roman empire—there was no means by which it could offer effective resistance to the imperial government. The only way open to the papacy was to extricate itself from the imperial framework, a step that was to entail freedom of movement for the papacy and a good deal of loss of prestige for the Roman empire.

There is no gainsaying the lesson which the papacy had learnt in the preceding two centuries. Perhaps the chief lesson which they taught was that the papacy as an institution was powerless, if it did not have at its disposal a protector and defender, when protection and defence were called for. The papacy had, so to speak, grown into the texture of the already existing Roman empire, precisely because the papal church was the Church of Rome, when Rome was still the capital of the empire. Considered from this historical point of view, there was indeed no possibility for the Roman Church as a Roman institution to create a defender and protector in the shape of the Roman empire which had turned out to be its oppressor. But there was no secular power which could have been made a protector and defender of the Roman Church. In short, then, by virtue of the papacy's being part and parcel of the Roman empire, it could not only not offer effective resistance to the Roman emperor, but there was also no possibility of obtaining an effective protector and defender. In order to attain these two objectives emancipation from the imperial framework was essential. The pontificate of Gregory II began this process of emancipation.

## I

It was a matter of taxation that brought the issue to a head. Gregory II refused to execute the taxation decrees of the emperor, Leo III; the pope caused open obstruction,[1] although theoretically and constitutionally he was bound to obey. The imperial oppressions of Italy which took the form of levying heavy taxes acted as a further stimulus to the resistance to the "alien" Greek regime. What Gregory II did was to endorse the already considerable resistance to the imperial government. No doubt this was a bold and courageous move on the part of the pope who, after all, was virtually the viceroy of the emperor in Italy. The imperial threat to prosecute the pope for high treason did not apparently produce the desired papal reaction.[2] The emperor, how-

---

[1] See E. Caspar, *Geschichte des Papsttums*, Tübingen, 1933, ii. 645.

[2] About the attempt to murder the pope cf. *Liber Pontificalis*, i. 403: "Paulus vero exarchus imperatorum jussione eundem pontificem conabatur interficere, eo quod censum in provincia ponere praepediebat."

ever, anxious to secure the co-operation of the pope, offered to abstain from prosecuting the pope for high treason,[1] if the pope would agree to the imperial decree[2] prohibiting the veneration of images.[3]

The letters written by Gregory II in 729,[4] deserve some fuller quotation. They mark the end of an epoch. Their language is firm and frank. They reveal an utter contempt for the emperor.

We derive our power and authority from the prince of the apostles, Peter, and we could, if we wished, pronounce judgment upon you, but you have already pronounced judgment on yourself and on your counsellors: and you and they may just as well remain accursed.[5]

As an emperor of Christians he would have the duty of consulting those who have knowledge and experience in matters of doctrine, who in fact are qualified to teach him:

Listen to us, emperor, cease behaving like a priest, and follow the sacred churches, as you ought to. Dogmas are not the business of emperors, but of pontiffs, because *we have the sense and mind of Christ.*[6] . . . you, emperor, cannot have the right mind for dogmas; your mind is too coarse and martial.

Gregory reiterates the old theme that the emperor has no right to supervise the churches, to judge clerics, to consecrate symbols of the

---

[1] About this point see E. Caspar, "Papst Gregor II und der Bilderstreit" in *Z. f. Kirchengeschichte*, lii (1933), p. 54, note 64.

[2] About this "jussio" see F. Dölger, *Regesten der Kaiserurkunden*, No. 291, of 728. See also No. 294.

[3] *Lib. Pont.*, i. 404: "Si adquiesceret pontifex, gratiam imperatoris haberet; si et hoc fieri praepediret, a suo gradu decideret."

[4] J. 2180 and 2182; both these letters were edited by Caspar, art. cit. (supra note 1), from which edition we quote. The authenticity of these two letters was established by Caspar with convincing reasons which are not invalidated by the argument of H. Grégoire, in *Byzantion*, viii (1933), pp. 762–3 (book review).

[5] Ed. cit., p. 78, lines 194 ff.: " ἠθελήσαμεν καὶ ἡμεῖς ὡς ἔχοντες τὸ κῦρος καὶ τὴν ἐξουσίαν καὶ αὐθεντίαν ἐκ τοῦ ἁγίου Πέτρου τοῦ κορυφαίου, δοῦναί σοι ἐπιτίμια. Ἀλλ᾽ ἔνθα ἑαυτὸν τὴν κατάραν δέδωκας μένε ἔχων αὐτήν, μετὰ οὓς περιπλέκῃ τοῦς συμβουλεύοντάς σοι."

This is no doubt intended to be a sharp reminder to the emperor that, theoretically, he is subjected to the priestly power, even if the pope evades the personal and actual excommunication of the emperor by the skilful device of maintaining that the emperor has excluded himself from the community of Christians, cf. also Caspar, art. cit., p. 58. The same theme returns in the second letter where, however, the power to bind and to loose was said to have been directly transmitted to the pope by Christ, without the intermediary of St Peter. "ὡς λαβόντες παρὰ κυρίου τὴν ἐξουσίαν καὶ αὐθεντίαν λύειν καὶ δένειν τὰ ἐπίγεια καὶ τὰ ἐπουράνια." The pope has therefore power and authority—"potestas et auctoritas"—to bind and to loose the terrestrial as well as the celestial.

[6] "νοῦν χριστοῦ ἔχομεν"—"Christi sensum nos habemus" in the Latin translation. For the original Greek text see ed. cit., p. 86, lines 411 ff.: "οὔκ εἰσι τὰ δόγματα τῶν βασιλέων, ἀλλὰ τῶν ἀρχιερέων, ὅτι ἡμεῖς νοῦν Χριστοῦ ἔχομεν."

holy sacraments and to handle them or even to receive them without
the participation of the priests.[1] Indeed, these are very weighty pronouncements summing up, so to speak, the reason for the papacy's
resistance. We have the sense and mind of Christ: only the ordained
members of the Church—the ἱεροί—have this privilege; they alone
are functionally qualified in a Christian society to pronounce what is,
and what is not, Christian, and to shape the pronouncements into a
rule binding upon all Christians.

The further threat of the emperor that the same fate would be in
store for the pope which had been visited upon Martin I, made little
impression on Gregory II. On the contrary, it apparently gave him a
welcome pretext to boast of the security which he could enjoy in
regions outside the imperial clutches: these regions were a mere three
miles away, as the pope symbolically expressed it. There a new future
lay—there the power and authority of the pope was not apparently
subjected to the sacerdotal rulings of the emperor.

If you swagger and threaten us with the fate of Martin, we do not wish to
enter into a quarrel with you. Three miles away the pope will escape into
Campania, and then good luck to you—you might just as well chase the
wind.[2]

And so as to leave no doubt in the mind of his imperial reader, the pope
a few lines later returns to the same theme:

You know very well that your empire cannot even be sure of Roman Italy,
except the city of Rome and this only because of the nearness of the sea. But,
as I have said, the pope has to move only three miles and he is outside your
empire. It is regrettable that the savages and barbarians have become cultured,
whilst you as a cultured individual have degraded yourself to the level
of the barbarians . . . the whole occident offers the prince of the apostles
proofs of faith, and if you should send men to destroy holy images (in the
occident) then I had better warn you: we prophesy to you beforehand that
we shall be innocent of the blood that will then flow; this blood may recoil
upon you.[3]

And furthermore:

The whole occident looks to us, and even if we do not deserve it, the occi-
dental peoples have great confidence in us and in him whose images you

---

[1] Ed. cit., p. 86, lines 425 ff.: "οὔτε βασιλεὺς ἐγκύψαι εἰς τὰς ἐκκλησίας καὶ
ψήφους ποιήσασθαι εἰς τὸν κληρὸν οὔτε ἁγιάζειν καὶ χειρίξειν τὰ σύμβολα τῶν ἁγίων
μυστηρίων ἀλλ' οὔτε μεταλαμβάνειν χωρὶς ἱερέως."

[2] Ed. cit., p. 82, lines 315–16: "Τρεῖς μιλίους ὑποχωρήσει ὁ ἀρχιερεὺς 'Ρώμης
εἰς τὴν χώραν Καππανίας καὶ ὕπαγε, δίωξον τοὺς ἀνέμους."

[3] Ed. cit., p. 83, lines 343–8.

wish to destroy, that is, St Peter, whom all kingdoms of the West venerate like God on earth: if you wish to test this, verily, the peoples of the West are ready.[1]

These manly words of the pope threatened with the fate of Martin and with a prosecution for high treason, produced a reply from the emperor which sounds as stale, hollow and stereotyped as it was unconvincing:

βασιλεὺς καὶ ἱερεὺς εἰμι.
I am king and priest.[2]

In historic significance the second Gregory stands on no lower a level than the first. He reaped the fruits of the great Gregory. He attempted physically to tread the avenue which the great Gregory had opened up ideologically. It was indeed a historic decision to leave the city that gave the Church whose head he was, its historic name; to leave that political entity, in whose bosom the Church of Rome had grown; to journey to those distant and wild regions—free as they were from imperial control—which acknowledged the pope as vicar of St Peter.[3]

You have followed the treacherous doctrines of perverse teachers: may you well continue with them. We however as we have already written to you, have decided to undertake a journey with God's help, into the innermost parts of the Western countries to give baptism to those who demand it. First I had sent bishops and clerics of our holy church, but their chieftains would not bow their heads to them, but demanded that I personally come to baptize them. Thereupon we decided upon the journey.[4]

The journey was not undertaken by Gregory II who died shortly after these letters were written, but the idea of this journey lived on and was realized twenty years later, in 754, by Stephen II. A new chapter in the history of the papacy and of Europe was to open.

By initiating the process of emancipation, Gregory II in fact inflicted an irreparable loss of prestige upon the empire. The main constitutional problem created was indeed serious, for a constitutional vacuum was created in Italy: as a consequence of the ineffective rule exercised by imperial authority in Italy, the pope had become the

---

[1] Ed. cit., p. 83, lines 335 ff.

[2] Ed. cit., p. 85, line 382; also p. 88, line 484: "παρακαλοῦμεν σε, γενοῦ ἀρχιερεὺς καὶ βασιλεύς, καθὼς προέγραψας." *Reg.* No. 298.

[3] In view of later history it should be mentioned that in 724, hence five years before these letters were written, Gregory II in a letter to St Boniface, referred to Charles Martel as "patricius," see Migne, PL. lxxxix. 504.

[4] Ed. cit., p. 88, lines 496–505.

viceroy, upon whom fell a large amount of administrative and political business. The emancipation of the papacy from the imperial framework amounted therefore to the annulment of imperial rule in Italy.

The first Gregory's vision had borne fruit: the English mission produced all the effects on the continent which had lain dormant in Gregory's idea. From England came the impetus for the conversion of large parts of Europe, carried out notably by Willibrord and Boniface.[1] As far as the second Gregory was concerned, the vital result of the Bonifacian activity in Frankish lands was the structural organization of the Church and its close link with the Roman Church;[2] of no lesser significance was the undoubted veneration of St Peter by the virile and youthful Western nations; of equal importance was the effect which this "Roman" orientation produced: for the Western mind became from now onwards soaked with characteristic Roman features, that is, features which in themselves had nothing to do with the papacy itself, since they were of much older provenance, but these features—authority, law, order, subordination, intellectual tidiness, a practical and sober approach, and so forth[3]—with which the Western

---

[1] For this see especially, W. Levison, *England & the Continent*, Oxford, 1946, pp. 53 ff., 70 ff.

[2] Upon his appointment as missionary bishop of the whole of "Germania," on 30 November 722, Boniface took the same oath of obedience and fidelity which every other bishop of the Roman province had taken, cf. Levison, op. cit., pp. 72–3. The appointment by Gregory III of Boniface as the papal vicar was of great importance: MGH. *Epp.* iii. no. 44, p. 292: "... praesentem Bonifatium nostram agentem vicem cum digno et debito honore pro Christi nomine suscipere." For details see H. v. Schubert, *Geschichte der christl. Kirche im Frühmittelalter*, Tübingen, 1923, pp. 303 ff.; Caspar, op. cit., ii. 701 ff.; Levison, op. cit., pp. 73 ff. The effect of all this could be seen in the council of 747 (MGH. *Concilia* ii. no. 6, p. 47): "Decrevimus autem in nostro sinodali conventu et confessi sumus fidem catholicam et unitatem et subjectionem Romanae ecclesiae fine tenus vitae nostrae velle servare; sancto Petro et vicario eius velle subjici." Thrown against this background Pope Zacharias's letter addressed to the clerics and counts and dukes in the Frankish kingdom is a clear signpost: he lays stress on the "differentia inter laicos et sacerdotes," and asserts that the priests are the salt of the earth (*Matt.* v. 13): MGH. *Epp.* iii. no. 61, p. 326; see also no. 83, p. 365, lines 40–1 (anno 748): "apostolicum praeceptum vobis mando, ut nullus saecularis clericum in suum obsequium habeat."

[3] Of course the earlier Roman (imperial) administration had left traces in Western Europe; but one must not underestimate the difficulties with which this Romanism had to contend: even leaving out of account the tenacious tradition of a backward civilization, the most effective incubator of Romanism, the Latin language, had, to all intents and purposes, vanished entirely as a living language in Gaul, certainly since the end of the sixth century; cf. on this the penetrating study by the late F. Lot, "A quelle époque a-t-on cessé de parler latin?" in *Bulletin du Cange*, vi (1931), pp. 97–152.

3*

mind had become impregnated, were inculcated into it by the very bearers and propagators of the Christian faith—the educated clergy. Western Europe, that is, the so-called imperial-free regions, were now drawn more and more into the Roman orbit in its religious and secular aspects. The Roman empire was to remain Greek.

Nevertheless, the Frankish king *qua* king was not yet brought into that close Roman-papal nexus which, from the papal point of view, would have been desirable. To take an obvious example. In old Merovingian times the validity of synodal decrees was not dependent upon royal approval: on the other hand, the Merovingian monarchy did not lend its hand to the execution of these decrees. But in the later Frankish kingdom these synodal decrees were promulgated as royal decrees—as *capitularia*—and these decrees concerned all sorts of ecclesiastical matters, such as visitation, discipline, monastic rules, clerical dress, deposition, degradation, and so forth.[1] What was of equal importance was that the participants of these Frankish councils were lay as well as clerical: in a way one might say that these Frankish synods constituted the organs of a territorially conceived Christian people: it was, so to speak, a territorial union of Christians which through the medium of bishops and counts deliberated in the synods upon all matters affecting the Frankish "populus christianus." The king himself convoked the synods in the interest of the people.[2] In a way, furthermore, one might say, paradoxically enough, that the universal Church —the congregation of all the faithful—was conceived on a territorial plane: it was the universal Church *en miniature*.[3]

Moreover, the strong hold which Christianity had obtained over the Franks explains the assertion of monarchic functions on the part of the king. As soon as the monarch perceived the strength which Christi-

---

[1] These examples are taken from the so-called *Concilium Germanicum*, held in 742 under Carlomann: MGH. *Conc.*, ii. no. 1, pp. 3–5. On this council see Levison, op. cit., pp. 83 f., who points out that the decrees were merely "proposals submitted to the ruler . . . he reserved the final decisions to himself."

[2] Cf. the prologue of the *Concilium Germanicum*, p. 2, lines 20 ff.: Carlomann had summoned that synod "qualiter populus Christianus ad salutem animae pervenire possit et per falsos sacerdotes deceptus non pereat." Cf. also his decree, p. 3, lines 1 ff.: "Per consilium sacerdotum et optimatum meorum ordinavimus per civitates episcopos et constituimus super eos archiepiscopum Bonifatium qui est missus sancti Petri." H. Schubert, op. cit., 308, points out that the prologue and canon 1 are reminiscent of the law of the Wessex king Ine issued earlier on.

[3] We think that this territorial conception of Christianity was also Charlemagne's own, in which case it would help us considerably in understanding his "imperial" policy. See infra pp. 112, 116.

anity had obtained, his monarchic "instinct" came to the fore: Christian principles were to constitute the subject-matter of his decrees; these principles were to be built into the royal laws. This applied to organizational as well as doctrinal matters. As monarchs the Frankish kings, including Charlemagne, naturally had to take the liveliest interest in the Roman-directed Christianity; but which Christian principles expounded by the Roman Church, were to become generally binding rules of conduct within the Frankish domain, was to be left—on the basis of the monarchic idea—to the king himself. Hence the royal control of the synods; hence also the *capitularia* which, as we have said, were royal decrees that made the resolutions of the synods into laws of the kingdom.

There can be little doubt that the papacy was vitally interested in these assertions of full monarchic powers. Although basically there was no difference between the emperor and the Frankish king—both were monarchs of their respective realms—as far as the papacy was concerned, however, there was a very considerable difference: the emperor demonstrably flouted the papal claim to magisterial and jurisdictional primacy; he made the denial of the Roman primacy a specific doctrinal point and thus openly attacked the most vital papal principle. The Frankish kings, on the other hand, did not openly obstruct the pope, and thus made the task of the papacy considerably easier. The Frankish kings bore a genuine veneration for St Peter and his vicar, that is, they paid due regard to the magisterial primacy. In actual fact the monarchic idea militated against their recognizing the latent papal claim to jurisdictional primacy. Furthermore, the papacy had been constitutionally part and parcel of the empire; constitutionally it was independent of the Frankish kingdom. But, seen from a wider viewpoint, the development in the Frankish kingdom, particularly later under Charlemagne, showed signs which pointed to the possibility of a most uncomfortable repetition: there were ominous signs that the East was going to be transplanted to the West.[1] That this repetition so dreaded by the papacy, did not come about, was exclusively due to the initiative which the popes kept firmly in their hands throughout the eighth century.

The presupposition for a fruitful deployment of papal authority was the extrication of the papacy from the imperial nexus, a process that had so dramatically begun with Gregory II. Papal initiative was guaranteed, as long as the papacy was engaged upon the execution of the emancipation plan. The creation of a dominion recognized in public

[1] See infra 95 concerning the *secunda Roma*.

law, pontifically controlled on the monarchic model, and protected and defended by a strong secular power, was the means by which the papacy carried out the extrication in practice, with the consequence that it emerged as a power with an independent status. The device employed by the papacy for bringing about this extrication—and could extrication take a more convincing form than the shape of a dominion (loosely called the pontifical or papal state) that was independent in its status by all standards of public law?—was the harnessing of the Frankish king in the function of the "patrician of the Romans." This flexible and adaptable device was perhaps the most useful instrument which the papacy had ever wielded, for the Frankish king as a "patrician of the Romans" enabled the papacy to carry out and bring to a close the process of emancipation; but there was much more to it: the idea of the "patrician of the Romans" crystallized the papal conception of a Ruler's function: which was to be a protector and defender of the Roman Church. The idea embodied in the papally created patrician of the Romans was to prove fundamentally hostile to, and destructive of, the idea of royal monarchy in a Christian society.

## II

The execution of the emancipation plan was considerably facilitated by the actual conditions prevailing in Northern and Central Italy.[1] The Lombards in particular were a source of continual trouble: their forces had made considerable advances and clearly threatened Rome itself. In the process of emancipation the Lombards begin to play an integral part. Their oppressions, real or exaggerated, were made to serve as the basis of papal demands put to the Franks. The theme of liberating the Roman Church from the clutches of the Lombards becomes now the predominant subject of communications between the popes and the Franks. But behind this apparent theme there stands the real object of papal policy, namely, the extrication of the papacy from the imperial framework. Gregory III's appeal to Charles Martel makes the apparent and the real motives quite plain. He appealed to Charles "who ruled the kingdom of the Franks"[2] for the liberation of the

[1] Administratively, since the early seventh century Italy was divided into several districts at the head of which stood a "dux" also called "consul." Cf. also infra p. 58 n. 3.

[2] *Liber Pontificalis*, ed. L. Duchesne, i. 420, lines 16 ff.: "Concussaque est provincia Romanae dicionis subjecta a nefandis Langobardis seu et rege eorum Liutprando . . . vir Dei (papa) undique dolore constrictus sacras claves ex confessione beati Petri apostoli, navali itinere per missos suos direxit, id est . . .

papacy from Lombard oppression, and in this same appeal he seems to have proposed to make the Frank the "Consul" (Duke) of the Roman duchy.[1] Charles Martel was not tempted.

On the other hand, the very deep veneration which the Franks entertained towards St Peter and hence towards the pope as his vicar, makes it understandable that Pippin, the new Frankish king, sought papal approval of his *coup d'état* against the Merovingian king, Childeric III; the pope's favourable verdict compensated for Pippin's lack of legitimate succession to the Austrasian dynasty.[2] What the appeal of Pippin for papal sanction made plain[3] was that the pope in Frankish eyes was the supreme moral authority in Western Europe: indeed, the nature of Pippin's step, taken in no lesser cause than that of substituting one reigning house for another, was no doubt properly appreciated by the papacy.[4]

The Frankish monarchy appeared to the papacy as the instrument by which the plan of emancipation could be brought to a successful

---

postulandum a (ad?) praefato excellentissimo Carolo ut eos a tanta oppressione Langobardorum liberaret." This passage was actually inserted in the *Lib. Pont.* during Stephen's pontificate, see editorial note no. 34, ibid., and Introduction, p. ccxxiii.

[1] This is naturally omitted in the papal account, but reported by the *Contin. Fredegarii* (MGH. SS. RR. *Merovingicarum*, ed. B. Krusch, ii. 178–9, cap. 22 (110)): "Eo etenim tempore bis a Romana sede sancti Petri apostoli beatus Gregorius claves venerandi sepulchri cum vinculis sancti Petri et muneribus magnis et infinitis legationem, quod antea nullis auditis aut visis temporibus fuit, memorato principi destinavit, eo pacto patrato, ut a partibus imperatoris recederet et Romano consulto praefato principi Carlo sanciret." About possible other readings see B. Krusch, ibid., p. 179, note 1, and K. Jäntere, *Die römische Weltreichsidee*, 1936, pp. 231–6.

[2] For details of fact see L. Halphen, *Charlemagne & l'empire carolingien*, 2nd ed., Paris, 1949, pp. 21 ff.

[3] It should be noted that Pippin sent the highest available ecclesiastics to Rome, Bishop Burchard of Wurzburg and Abbot Fulrad of St Denis, see *Annales Regni Francorum*, ed. F. Kurze, p. 8, ad 749: "Burghardus Wirzeburgensis episcopus et Folradus capellanus missi fuerunt ad Zachariam papam, interrogando de regibus in Francia, qui illis temporibus non habentes regalem potestatem, si bene fuisset an non. Et Zacharias papa mandavit Pippino, ut melius esset illum regem vocari, qui potestatem haberet, quam illum, qui sine regali potestate manebat; ut non conturbaretur ordo, *per auctoritatem apostolicam jussit Pippinum regem fieri.*" The unction of Pippin by St Boniface, ibid., ad 750.

[4] Although later much distorted, especially by Gregory VII, the sanction which Zacharias gave, was perfectly justifiable from the point of view of papal ideology. Childeric was useless and according to papal ideology, usefulness (or uselessness) could be judged only by the criterion which papal ideology itself supplied. Modern absolute criteria in judging Zacharias will only blur the issue. Cf. now also H. Büttner, "Aus den Anfängen des abendländischen Staatsgedankens" in *Hist. Jb.*, lxxi (1952), pp. 77–90.

conclusion.[1] It is in this context that the Lombards assumed the historic role of serving as a basis for the appeals of liberation, so urgently sent to the Frank who, on his part, had so recently received a favourable papal verdict. The Lombards under Aistulph conquered Ravenna (751), and the whole surrounding district, and directed their army to the south, to Rome. It was no doubt an alarming situation for the empire; there was no doubt also that the papacy now under Stephen II viewed the approach of the Lombard forces with dismay. Gregory III's appeal to Charles Martel served as a precedent for soliciting Frankish help; Gregory II's plan of going personally to the innermost parts of Western Europe, was not forgotten either. Both Gregory II and III make Stephen II's journey across the Alps understandable, and the second Stephen's journey was to serve as another precedent for the fourth Stephen's journey across the Alps some sixty years later. Pippin's request in the question of succession had demonstrated "the majesty of the position held by the Roman pontiff in relation to the Franks."[2] The stage was set.

In 752 Stephen II despatched messengers to Pippin with the request that he would send an escort for the pope so as to enable him to go to the Frankish kingdom. Pippin acceded to the papal request. His messengers arrived in Rome "where they found Stephen quite ready to set out."[3] But in Rome there had also arrived the emperor's messenger, John the Silentiary, with the imperial order (*jussio*) to Stephen to proceed to Aistulph at Pavia with the imperial messenger and to ask the Lombard king for the return of the Ravenna district. The whole party set out from Rome on 14 October 753.[4] It is therefore important to keep in mind that Stephen had already resolved to go to Pippin when John, the Silentiary, arrived; it is also clear that the pope was imperially ordered to support John's demands to Aistulph. Considering therefore Stephen's aims, he travelled from Rome to Pavia (Aistulph's Headquarters) in a twofold capacity. On the one hand, he appeared as the supporter of the imperial legate John;[5] on the other hand, he pursued an aim that was diametrically opposed to his function as a supporter of imperial demands, for nothing could be further from his intention than

---

[1] Had not the first Gregory indicated that way? Did not he extol the Franks at the historic moment of initiating the English mission? Cf. supra p. 38.

[2] L. Duchesne, *Les premiers temps de l'état pontifical*, Engl. translation, p. 31.

[3] Duchesne, op. cit., p. 33.          [4] *Lib. Pont.*, i. 445, line 10.

[5] *Lib. Pont.*, ibid., lines 2–4: "(jussio) in qua inerat insertum ad Langobardorum regem eundem sanctissimum papam esse properaturum, ob recipiendum Ravennantium urbem et civitates ei pertinentes."

the "return" of the "exarchate of Ravenna" and the "people of the whole Italian province" to imperial rule, which was the purpose of the imperial legate's embassy to Aistulph.[1] The imperial-papal mission was fruitless.[2] But we must keep in mind that the pope asked Aistulph for the "return of the lost sheep of the Lord" and for "restitution of the property to the owners."[3]

"Gnashing his teeth like a lion"[4] Aistulph permitted the papal party to proceed to the Frankish kingdom. Pippin and Stephen met at Ponthion, Epiphany 754.[5] The pope, according to his biographer, requested Pippin to "order the cause of St Peter (and) of the commonwealth of the Romans."[6] Moreover, as a symbolic detail the biographer tells us that Pippin, after dismounting from his horse, threw himself

---

[1] The author of the papal biography says this, *Lib. Pont.*, i. 444, lines 3 ff.: "Serenissimus vir jamfatum pestiferum Langobardorum regem immensis vicibus, innumerabilia tribuens munera, deprecaretur pro gregibus sibi a Deo commissis et perditis ovibus, scilicet pro universo exarchato Ravennae atque cunctae istius Italiae provinciae populo, quos diabolica fraude ipse impius deceperat rex et possidebat." The biographical account would almost make us believe that after Aistulph's refusal, the pope continued the journey in the interest of the emperor, for the author goes on to say: "et dum ab eo nihil hac de re optineret, cernens praesertim et ab imperiali potentia nullum esse subveniendi auxilium; tunc quemadmodum predecessores eius b.m.domni Gregorius et Gregorius atque domnus Zacharias beatissimi pontifices Carolo excellentissimae memoriae regi Francorum direxerunt, petentes sibi subveniri propter oppressiones ac invasiones . . ."

[2] *Lib. Pont.*, i. 446, lines 7 ff: "Sed nullo modo apud eum impetrare valuit. Nam et imperialis missus et ille *simili modo* petiit et imperiales litteras illi tribuit et nihil obtinere potuit." It is clear from this account that both pope and imperial legate presented the same demand to Aistulph.

[3] "Eum petiit, ut dominicas quas abstulerat *redderet* oves et propria propriis *restitueret*." One might almost think that the Lombards were pagans. Who really was the proprietor to whom the "propria" were to be given back? There can be few historical sources which are so deliberately vague as the "Vita Stephani," our only contemporary account of these highly important doings. For a characterization of this biographer's work, see Duchesne in his Introduction to his edition, p. ccxliii: "Quant à l'hypothèse d'un mensonge, elle ne saurait être admise en aucune façon. Les biographes pontificaux ont une manière de cacher les choses qui leur paraissent dèsagréeables, c'est de s'en taire." The "lost sheep" may be an allusion to *Matt.* xv. 24.

[4] So the author of the "Vita," ibid., p. 446, line 12: "ut leo dentibus frenebat." Cf. *Mk.* ix. 17 (18).

[5] The best account and the most satisfactory reconstruction is that by E. Caspar, *Pippin und die römische Kirche*, 1914; cf. of more recent studies on this question, L. Levillain, "L'avènement de la dynastie carolingienne et les origines de l'état pontifical" in *Bibl. de l'école des chartes*, xciv (1933), pp. 225–95. Before setting out for his journey, Stephen is said to have furnished himself with a map of Italy, see A. Dove, "Corsica & Sardinien in den Schenkungen an die Päpste" in *SB. Munich*, 1894, p. 202.

[6] *Lib. Pont.*, i. 447, lines 19 ff.–p. 448: "(papa) regem lacrimabiliter deprecatus est, ut per pacis foedera causam beati Petri (et) reipublicae Romanorum dispon-

on the ground and then performed the service of a "strator" to the pope, that is, he held the bridles of the papal horse and led it along a little distance. These ceremonies over, Pippin, according to the biographer, at once took an oath: "he would obey the pope's orders and admonitions with all the power at his disposal; he would *return* the exarchate of Ravenna; he would *restore* as far as possible the localities and the (violated) rights of the commonwealth."[1] Pippin's promise at Ponthion was solemnized at Easter (14 April 754), ratified at Kierzy[2] and very shortly afterwards at the monastery of St Denis the pope anointed Pippin, his wife and sons; at the same time Pippin was created a "patricius Romanorum."[3] Moreover, under pain of excommunication, Stephen prohibited the choice of a king who did not belong to the family of those whom divine foresight had deigned to exalt and "through the intercession of the blessed apostles to confirm and to consecrate through the medium of their vicar, the pope."[4]

According to the papal biographer, Pippin promised to "restitute" the stolen property to its rightful owner. He therefore despatched emissaries to Aistulph who put this demand to him,[5] although without

eret." The *Annales Mettenses Priores* (ed. B. Simson), p. 44–5, give a somewhat different picture of the reception by Pippin, but this is of little importance to us.

[1] So according to the *Lib. Pont.*, i. 448, lines 1–3: " Qui (Pippinus) de praesenti jurejurando eundem beatissimum papam satisfecit omnibus eius mandatis et ammonitionibus sese totis nisibus obedire, et ut illi placitum fuerit exarchatum Ravennae et reipublicae jura et loca *reddere* omnibus modis."

[2] This is the famous "promissio Carisiaca" which is lost but reconstructed by E. Caspar, op. cit., pp. 99–153. Against the "promissio" being a formal act of Pippin see L. Saltet, "La lecture d'un texte et la critique contemporaine: les pretendues promesses de Quierzy (754) et de Rome (774) dans le 'Liber Pontificalis'" in *Bulletin de la littérature ecclésiastique*, 1940, pp. 176–206; also 1941, pp. 61–85.

[3] For this see the account in the "Clausula de unctione Pippini" in MGH. SS. RR. *Merovingicarum*, i. 465; cf. also *Chronicon Moissiacense*, in MGH. SS. i. 293. On the authenticity of the "Clausula" see L. Levillain, "De l'autenticité de la Clausula" in *Bibliothèque de l'école des chartes*, lxxxviii (1927), pp. 20–42; also H. Leclercq in DAC. xiv. 282–90. We adopt the chronology as reconstructed by Levillain, art. cit., pp. 243–70.　　　　[4] Thus in the "Clausula."

[5] *Lib. Pont.*, i. 449, lines 6 ff.: "Porro christianissimus Pippinus Francorum rex ut vere beati Petri fidelis atque jamfati sanctissimi pontificis salutiferis obtemperans monitis direxit suos missos Aistulfo nequissimo Langobardorum regi propter pacis foedera et proprietatis sanctae Dei ecclesiae reipublicae *restituenda* jura." On the meaning of "Porro" see Levillain, art. cit., p. 271, note 1. With this account should be compared the account in the *Cont. Fredegarii*, loc. cit. cap. 119 which says of this legation: "Legationem ad Aistulphum regem Langobardorum mittens, petens ut propter reverentiam b. apostolorum Petri et Pauli in partibus Romae hostiliter non ambularet, et superstitiones ac impias vel contra legis ordinem causas, quod antea Romani numquam fecerant, propter eius petitionem facere non deberet."

avail. We take note, at this stage, that "rights and properties" were to be "restored to the Church of the commonwealth of the Romans." In the papal letters sent to Pippin entreating the king to implement his promise, the same curious phrase occurs: not an inch of territory had Aistulph restored: "nec unius enim palmi terrae spatium beato Petro sanctaeque Dei ecclesiae reipublicae Romanorum *reddere* passus est."[1] Pippin is reminded of his promise[2] because Aistulph "non reddere propria beati Petri voluit."[3] Pippin is entreated to hasten and to "return and hand over to St Peter" what he had promised.[4]

There is no need for our purposes to go into details of the Pavia convention of 754[5] and of the much more important Pavia Treaty of 756[6] which formed the basis of the "Donation" of Pippin to the Roman Church: deposited at the Tomb of St Peter, the document constitutionally established a dominion of the pope that was recognized in public law and enjoyed an independent status. This dominion, not quite correctly called the pontifical or papal State,[7] embraced the exarchate of Ravenna, the pentapolis and the districts reaching from Comacchio down south to Ancona-Jesi-Gubbio.

<h1 style="text-align:center">III</h1>

We have so far abstained from interpreting some of those curious phrases and terms which the papal biographer and papal letters employ and which seem, particularly in translation, to make little or no sense. In order to appreciate these newly coined phrases we should bear in mind that the papacy had to grapple with an altogether new situation, for which past history and terminology gave no warrant: these new

---

[1] *Codex Carolinus*, in MGH. *Epp.*, iii. no. 6, p. 489, lines 17–19. Through the foresight of Charlemagne the papal letters were collected in this *Codex* which contains all papal communications from the time of Gregory III down to the end of Adrian I's pontificate.

[2] *Cod. Car.*, no. 6, p. 489, lines 32–4: "Propria vestra voluntate per donationis paginam b. Petri sanctaeque Dei ecclesiae reipublicae civitates et loca *restituenda* confirmastis."

[3] *Cod. Car.*, no. 7, p. 492, lines 14–15.

[4] Cf. also *Cod. Car.*, no. 6, p. 490, lines 5–7: "Quod semel b. Petro polliciti estis, et per donationem vestram manu firmatam pro mercede animae vestrae beato Petro *reddere et contradere* festinate."

[5] According to Caspar, op. cit., pp. 76–80, no document was drawn up at Pavia in 754, which would have conferred property on the pope; only an oath was taken by Aistulph.

[6] Caspar, op. cit., pp. 85–9.

[7] In medieval times this dominion was called "Patrimonium beati Petri" or the "Regalia beati Petri," cf. also Caspar, op. cit., p. 155.

terms presented themselves as adaptations of old terminology to a new situation.

We have seen that the pope spoke on behalf of the "whole exarchate of Ravenna and of the people of this whole of Italy" (the lost sheep) and demanded the return of property to the rightful owner. The "exarchate of Ravenna" is one such new term which we meet in the fifties of the eighth century: it had never existed before, since the Ravenna district had not been styled "exarchatus."[1] No doubt, the new term was modelled on "exarcha" and on "ducatus (Romanus)"[2] and at least a partial explanation may be that in comparatively recent times the duchy of Rome was carved out of the larger administrative province of Ravenna, so that the central Italian administration was divided into the duchy of Rome (virtually governed by the pope) and the remaining Ravenna district (governed by the exarch).[3] What is of interest to us is that the papal biographer consistently brackets the exarchate of Ravenna and the duchy of Rome and in fact is obviously anxious to wipe out all difference between these two districts. What is furthermore important is that the "whole exarchate and the people of Italy" belong to the lost sheep of the Lord; and because they are "lost," the pope demands their return to the owner.

Pippin had promised the return—to the Roman Church. There can be no doubt that the basis of Stephen's demands was the Donation of

† Constantine. If this document is left out of account, it is not possible to explain the ever-recurring phrases of "reddere" and "restituere" which refer to districts which on no account could be said to "belong" to the Roman Church; without the Donation it is not possible to explain Pippin's promise of return and his conduct; it is furthermore not possible to explain the conduct of the imperial legate Gregory at his meeting with Pippin in 756; it is not possible to explain certain phrases in the papal biography or in papal letters. The Donation was fabri-

[1] See Caspar, op. cit., pp. 127–9.
[2] Caspar holds that the term was first coined by the pope at Kierzy and that the biographer, when composing his "Vita" afterwards, adopted it, see pp. 123, 130–3, 154, note 4.
[3] By about 710 this division seems to have been established. The *Lib. Pont.* reflects the stages of the development. The "Vita Constantini" seems the first to refer to a separate Roman district, i. 392, line 5, cf. Duchesne's note 28, p. 395 ("la première mention du duc de Rome"); "Vita Gregorii II," p. 403, line 13 ("Romanus ducatus"); and the "Vita Zachariae," p. 428, line 6, p. 429, line 10, and p. 431, line 1, where the "provincia Ravennantium" is juxtaposed to the "ducatus Romanus" or "provincia Romanorum." The next step was the "exarchatus Ravennae" in the "Vita Stephani."

cated before Stephen set out on his journey to the Frankish kingdom.[1]
Each of these points deserves a few observations.

Firstly, Pippin's conduct. The service of a "strator" performed by
him can be satisfactorily explained only by a recourse to the Donation,
for how was the Frank to know of this manifestation of servility shown
by Constantine?[2] Pippin's promise of virtually unlimited help can be
understood only if one takes into account that according to papal
protestations the Lombards had stolen territory which the Emperor
Constantine had given to St Peter through Pope Silvester. It was in
any case a disgraceful act to take territory that was given to a church;
but it was worse to steal territory whose lawful owner was St Peter.
And the genuine veneration which the Franks had for St Peter,
prompted Pippin to aid Stephen in the recovery of the stolen territory.

Secondly, after defeating Aistulph Pippin made out the document
to which we have already referred. When at Pavia in 756, he was
approached by the imperial legate Gregory who urged Pippin "to
*concede* to the imperial jurisdiction" precisely those districts for which
the pope himself claimed a "return."[3] Pippin refused. This meek request
made on behalf of the rightful owner of the districts, the emperor, can
be explained only by recourse to the Donation; what the request really
meant was that Pippin should disregard the Constantinean enactment
and should therefore "concede" the territories to the emperor. Under
this presupposition the biographer's account makes perfect sense. On
the other hand, Pippin had taken the oath to defend and protect the
Roman Church and his campaigns were the execution of this oath:
he acted as a defender of the Roman Church, or rather of St Peter who
was robbed of his territories, but on whose behalf Pippin had undertaken the campaign: in this capacity he could not possibly accede to

---

[1] L. Levillain, art. cit., p. 234: "Le Constitutum Constantini est la charte qui
a réglé les rapports du pape et du roi." See also L. Halphen, op. cit., pp. 30–4:
this document "explique et pretend justifier les revendications territoriales
d'Etienne II"; idem, in *A travers d'histoire du moyen âge*, Paris, 1950, p. 49, note 1.
This is also accepted by Bihlmeyer-Tüchle, *Kirchengeschichte*, 12th ed., Paderborn, 1948, ii. 42, but denied by O. Bertolini, "Il problema delle origini del
potere temporale dei papi" in *Miscellanea Pio Paschini*, Rome, 1949, i. 167–9.

[2] Cf. also Levillain, art. cit., p. 235, note 3, and text ibid. See also F. Kampers,
"Roma aeterna" in *Hist. Jb.*, 1924, p. 248: "Dem halb-barbarischen Pippin
waren die Dienste eines Strators in der feierlichen Prozession . . . sicherlich ganz
unbekannt." Cf. also Halphen, op. cit., p. 29: "Protocole jusqu' alors inusité,"
and H. Leclercq in DAC. xiv. 291–2.

[3] *Lib. Pont.*, i. 453, lines 1–3: "Nimis eum (Pippinum) deprecans atque plura
spondens tribui imperialia munera ut Ravennantium urbem vel cetera eiusdem
exarcatus civitates et castra imperiali tribuens *concederet* ditioni."

Gregory's request.[1] Pippin had conquered the districts on behalf of St Peter, hence strictly and legally speaking Pippin was a trustee and as such handed the territories to the pope.

Thirdly, the document handing over the territory was deposited at the Confession of St Peter. There is a remarkable similarity in phraseology between the Donation and the papal biographer's account. It was also the same place, the Confession, at which the Emperor Constantine had decreed that his document should be deposited. And the papal biographer in narrating the deposition chooses a phraseology which is reminiscent of the Donation:

| Donation: | Biographer: |
|---|---|
| Patri nostro . . . *tradimus perenniter atque* feliciter *possidenda.* | Apostolo . . . *perenniter possidendas adque* disponendas *tradidit.* |

To this context belong also the deliberately vague expressions in the papal letters which would tally with the no less vague statements in the Donation: both speak of the "civitates et loca."[2]

Fourthly, the aim of Stephen's journey was to obtain an overt confirmation of the Constantinean act by Pippin.[3] The confirmation served

---

[1] *Lib. Pont.*, i. 453, lines 3 ff.: "Et nequaquam valuit firmissimum jamfati christianissimi atque benignissimi, fidelis Dei et amatoris b. Petri, scilicet antelati Pippini Francorum regis, inclinare cor, ut easdem civitates et loca imperiali tribueret ditioni; asserens idem Dei cultor mitissimus rex nulla penitus ratione easdem civitates *a potestate beati Petri et jure ecclesiae Romanae* vel pontifici apostolicae sedis quoquo modo *alienari.*"

[2] According to the Donation, apart from the imperial palace and the city of Rome, Constantine had transferred "omnes Italiae seu occidentalium regionum provincias, *loca et civitates.*" Cf. the pope's letter to Pippin, *Cod. Car.* no. 6, p. 489, line 33: "Civitates et loca restituenda"; ibid., p. 490, lines 9–10: "Decertaveritis pro causa eiusdem principis apostolorum et restituendis eius civitatibus et locis"; ibid., no. 7, p. 493, line 9: "Beato Petro promisistis per donationem vestram civitates et loca." These examples could easily be multiplied. L. Levillain, art. cit., p. 233, note 1, draws attention to the phraseology in Stephen's letter to Pippin, *Cod. Car.*, no. 11, p. 506: "Omnia proprietatis suae percipiat, unde . . . *luminariorum concinnatio* Dei ecclesiis permaneat" which is reminiscent of the Donation, cap. 13: "Pro *concinnatione luminariorum* possessionum praedia contulimus." For another instance of borrowing from the Donation, in fact a literal copying, see infra 73. n. 2. It is not apparently possible to fix the dictator of these papal letters: he remains anonymous, cf. N. Ertl, "Die Dictatoren frühmittelalterlicher Papstbriefe" in *Archiv f. Urkundenforschung*, xv (1938), p. 81, note 201.

[3] See, for instance, his letters, *Cod. Car.* nos. 6 & 7, p. 489, lines 12–14: "Justitiam beati Petri . . . exigere studuistis et per donationis paginam restituendum *confirmavit* bonitas vestra"; ibid., line 34: "Vestra voluntate per donationis paginam b. Petri sanctaeque Dei ecclesiae reipublicae civitates et loca restituenda *confirmastis*"; ibid., p. 492, line 33: "(Quae) *confirmastis,* protectori vestro, beato Petro, reddere festinate." The oldest copy of the Donation is in the St Denis formulary infra pp. 74 n. 2, 199 n. 2 at end.

as the basis for the restitution of the districts claimed and hence of the dominion itself. From this point of view it becomes understandable why the biographer and the pope consistently speak of "reddere" and "restituere." The restitutions of territory gave the pope a status in public law: the papacy had virtually extricated itself from the imperial nexus. A district was created in public law which, constitutionally, was carved out of the empire.

We have already alluded to curious phrases adopted by the biographer and the pope. We have tried to give a partial explanation for the "exarchatus" and its close connexion with the Duchy of Rome. Whilst this term concerns the territorial claims, the curious term "sancta Dei ecclesia reipublicae Romanorum" is of far greater ideological significance. In close proximity to this term stands the other term "populus Romanus."

The term "respublica Romanorum" must on no account be confused with a very similar one—the "respublica Romana." This latter term was always synonymous with the empire. The former was no doubt modelled on the old term and yet conveyed an entirely different meaning. The change concerns the qualification of the "respublica." The new term designates the notion of a "commonwealth" composed of Romans, not of Greeks; a commonwealth or a society composed of those who live according to the Roman faith, not the Greek one; a society composed of those Christians who follow the teachings of the Church of Rome, not of Byzantium. The *Romani* in this sense are all Christians who accept the position of the pope as vicar of St Peter and follow his exposition of the faith. The Romans, in a word, are synonymous with Latin Christians.[1] This is indeed the fruit of St Boniface's work[2] and in a wider sense of Gregory I: it is the ideological conflation of *Romanitas* and *Christianitas*. Pippin's own purposeful introduction of the Roman liturgy[3] naturally promoted this process of exchanging

---

[1] If the two terms are not distinguished, confusion will arise, and Stephen would then make a demand for a return of territories on behalf of the emperor. It is well known that Ch. Diehl, *Etudes sur l'administration byzantine dans l'exarchate de Ravenna*, p. 221 ff., made this mistake. Of more recent date is T. G. Jalland, *The Church and the Papacy*, London, 1944, p. 371: "Stephen II felt obliged to undertake the task of ambassador on behalf of the Byzantine emperor Constantine V to the Frankish court. Yet actually it was a happy misfortune. The king who received him, was Pepin."

[2] On Pippin's share in the reform movement see especially W. Levison, *England & the Continent*, pp. 87–91. See now also Th. Schieffer, *Angelsachsen und Franken* (Abhandlungen d. Akademie d. Wissenschaften, Mainz, 1950), pp. 1435 ff.

[3] The effect of this was a unification of the Frankish services, about which see H. Netzer, *L'introduction de la messe Romaine en France sous les Carolingiens*,

*Romani* for *Christiani*. In this context due importance must be attributed to the sacramentaries and prayer texts.[1] In this eighth century the contrast between the "Romani" and the "Graeci" was clearly felt by contemporaries.[2] Nor should the significance of the second prologue to the *Lex Salica*, written in the reign of Pippin, be forgotten: the Franks alone were the chosen Christian people: "Vivat qui Francos diligit Christus."[3] In brief, a Christian was a Roman.

---

Paris, 1910; and Th. Klauser, "Die liturgischen Austauschbeziehungen zwischen der römischen und fränkischen Kirche" in *Hist. Jb.* liii (1933), pp. 169 ff. Later Charlemagne requested a copy of the *Sacramentarium Gregorianum*.

[1] See also infra p. 89 and especially G. Tellenbach, "Christlicher und römischer Reichsgedanke" in *SB. Heidelberg, 1934–5*. Here also due importance must be attached to the effects which the *Ordines Romani* exercised, even if these were confined to liturgy only. They too considerably contributed to the conflation of "Romanitas" and "Christianitas." After the Lateran synod of 680 Pope Agatho despatched Benedict Biscop and Johannes Archicantor to England with an OR., where it was at once introduced, see Bede, *Hist. Eccl.* iv. 18; cf. also Giles's remarks in the Bohn library translation, p. ix. This Johannes was probably the author of the OR. which preceded OR. I, see C. Silva-Tarouca, "Giovanni Archicantor di S. Pietro a Roma e l'Ordo Romanus da lui composta" in *Atti della pontificia accademia Romana di archeologia*, 1923, pp. 194–207, and A. Baumstark, in K. Mohlberg & A. Baumstark, *Die aelteste erreichbare Gestalt des Liber Sacramentorum anni circuli der römischen Kirche* (in Liturgiegeschichtliche Quellen, xi–xii, 1927), pp. 44*, 64* (I owe the reference to this work to Dr C. H. Talbot). Together with the Sacramentaries the ORi. were powerful agents in orientating the Western mind towards Rome. Migne (PL. lxxviii. 937–1368) printed the 15 ORi.; see M. Andrieu, *Les Ordines Romani du haut Moyen Age*, vol. i (1931) and esp. vol. ii (1949) and vol. iii (1951), with numerous additional *Ordines* of earlier times. Our numeration follows Mabillon's. The place of the *Ordines* in monasteries was partly taken by the monastic *Consuetudines*. About the introduction of certain feast days, e.g. ember days, Candlemasday, etc., cf. L. Eisenhofer, *Liturgik*, 5th ed. by J. Lechner, 1950, pp. 117, 150. Liturgical garments were of Roman provenance. For monastic dress see Ph. Oppenheim, *Das Mönchskleid im christl. Altertum*, suppl. vol. xxviii, 1931 of *Röm. Quartalschrift*.

[2] For a characteristic contemporary example see the *Historia Langobardorum* by Paulus Diaconus, MGH. SS. RR. Langobardorum, ii. 75, cap. 5: "Expedierat *Romanis* Gothis potius servire quam *Graecis*"; cf. Caspar, op. cit., p. 161. See also the contemporary Penitential of Theodore of Canterbury, where the same antithesis of Romans and Greeks will be found, iii. 8: "secundum *Graecos* . . . secundum *Romanos* (ed. H. I. Schmitz, *Die Bussbücher und das kanonische Bussverfahren*, ii. 568); cf. also ibid., p. 573, Rubrica: "De moribus Graecorum et Romanorum"; c. 4: "Graecorum monachi servos non habent, Romanorum habent." Roman liturgy was prescribed for all English churches by the synod of Cloveshoe in 747, see Haddan & Stubbs, *Councils & eccles. documents*, iii. 367, cap. 13.

[3] *Lex Salica*, ed. K. A. Eckhardt, Weimar, 1953, p. 88. In two assertive articles S. Stein tries to prove that the *Lex Salica* was a forgery made in the mid-ninth century, see his second article, "Lex Salica II" in *Speculum*, xxii (1947), especially pp. 406 ff. But cf. now J. M. Wallace-Hadrill in *Rev. d'hist. du droit*, xxi (1953), pp. 12–27.

But apart from this purely religious meaning of "Romani,"[1] the term[2] could be, and was, taken in a mere geographical sense denoting the inhabitants of Rome and in a wider sense the Italians. Just as the Church of Rome epitomized the whole of (Latin) Christianity, in the same way the geographical Romans—the *populus Romanus*—epitomized the Romans wherever they lived. In this sense the "Roman people" is, according to papal conceptions, the "peculiaris populus" of St Peter[3] who "himself" writes a letter to Pippin emploring his help. St Peter and Rome coalesce into one notion, into St Peter's Rome.[4] The city that holds the body of St Peter demands special protection: the city of Rome is the geographical expression of "Christianitas."[5]

In a transitional period such as the one with which we are dealing one cannot expect a fully matured terminology: so much was in the making and in a state of flux for which there was no terminological precedent.[6] This, we think, applies with particular force to the phrase from which we started: "Sancta Dei ecclesia reipublicae Romanorum." The "respublica Romanorum" was Christian society whose leaven

---

[1] Apart from the purely religious connotation there were also cultural and social implications in the term.

[2] Caspar, op. cit., pp. 147, 163–4, etc., takes the term only in the geographical sense and considers that it embodies a "national-Italian programme of the papacy."

[3] It is not without significance that the first pope who appealed to the Franks, Gregory III, also employed this term in his offer to Charles Martel, see *Cod. Car.*, No. 1, p. 477, lines 1–2: "Pro eius reverentia (Petri) nostris obedias mandatis ad defendendam ecclesiam Dei et peculiarem populum." The expression itself seems to be of biblical origin, *Deut.* vii. 6; xxvi. 18.

[4] St Peter's letter, *Cod. Car.*, no. 10, p. 501, lines 37 ff.: "Ego, apostolus Dei Petrus, qui vos adoptivos habeo filios ad defendendum de manibus adversariorum hanc Romanam civitatem et populum mihi a Deo commissum seu et domum, ubi secundum carnem requiesco . . ." See also ibid., p. 503, line 3: "Non separer a populo meo Romano"; and line 5: "Subvenite populo meo Romano."

[5] Cf. again St Peter's letter, cit., lines 22–5: "Defendite adque liberate . . . ne, quod absit, corpus meum, quod pro domino Jesu Christo tormenta perpessum est, et domus mea, ubi per Dei preceptionem requiescit, ab eis contaminentur." Cf. also p. 503, line 23: ". . . quatenus doleat vobis pro civitate ipsa Romana nobis a Domino commissa et ovibus dominicis in ea commorantibus necnon et pro sancta Dei ecclesia mihi a Domino commendata"; p. 502, lines 20 ff.: ". . . ad liberandam hanc meam civitatem Romanam nimis velociter occurreritis."

[6] It should be pointed out that a number of these new terms was dropped in this same century. For instance, the "sancta Dei ecclesia reipublicae Romanorum" does not appear after 774 in the *Lib. Pont.* or the papal letters. Precisely because these terms were coined during a period of transition, it is so very difficult to determine their exact ideological contents. Gregory I's expression may possibly have been a model, cf. supra p. 37.

was the faith as expounded by the Roman Church. This society was composed of the "Romani." Their epitome is the *populus Romanus*, the inhabitants of Rome.[1] The theme of those many letters of the popes written to the Franks, was that the "Roman people" had been committed to the pope's care.[2]

These considerations may help us to detect the meaning of that curious phrase. It is a terminology which can have meaning only within the scope of public law. It attempts to express the governance of the Romans by the Church of Rome. Again, this governance can be applied to the "respublica Romanorum" in the wider (religious) sense as well as in the narrow (geographical-territorial) sense. Considered from the point of view of the "restitutions" demanded by the pope, the term "Church of the commonwealth of the Romans" had a merely geographical and territorial meaning and denoted that entity which came loosely to be called pontifical or papal state[3] inhabited by the "populus Romanus."[4]

Now, by virtue of the Constantinean enactment St Peter was given through the medium of the pope a (more or less specified) territory, which Pippin as a Roman (= Christian) considered it his duty to protect and to defend against Lombard depredations. This, we think, is the meaning of the title conferred on him, "patricius Romanorum." The term meant "patrician" of those Christians who lived according to the Roman faith. Naturally, this term included the epitome of the Romans, the "populus Romanus," the city of Rome: protection and

---

[1] Cf. for instance, *Cod. Car.* no. 8, p. 496, line 40: "sanctam Dei *ecclesiam et eius populum* de inimicorum impugnatione debueratis liberare." See also p. 497, line 13.

[2] For instance, *Cod. Car.*, no. 6, p. 489, line 25: "(ad) populum nobis commissum sumus reversi."

[3] But whose actual territorial frontiers, as the letters of Stephen and his successors make so abundantly clear, were not clearly defined: the popes demanded more and more territory, that is to say, more restitutions. Despite our fundamental opposition to J. Haller's famous thesis we agree with him when he says that the popes were by no means satisfied with the frontiers as laid down in 756. "Der junge Staat tat eben, was alle Wesen in der ersten Jugend tun: er wollte wachsen," *Abhandlungen z. Geschichte des MA*, Stuttgart, 1944, p. 10.

[4] That these conceptions of the "Romani" were still current in the twelfth century is shown by the author of the *Summa Lipsiensis* (see the passage in J. F. Schulte, *Geschichte der Quellen & Literatur des kanonischen Rechts*, Stuttgart, 1876, i. 105, note 9); by Huguccio (cf. EHR. lvii, 1952, p. 435, note 1); by the *Summa Reginensis* (cf. A. M. Stickler, "Vergessene Bologneser Dekretisten" in *Salesianum* xiv, 1952, p. 488) and so forth. Cf. also the *Summa Coloniensis* ("populus Romanus" applicable to the city of Rome only) in Schulte, *SB. Vienna*, lxiv, 1870, p. 112.

defence of these latter Romans was the effluence of his protection and defence of all the Romans = Christians.

The protection of St Peter—that is the ever-recurring theme of those numerous papal letters beseeching Pippin's and later Charlemagne's help. And, as we have seen, in one case St Peter himself writes a letter to Pippin to ensure his help. The Roman Church, St Peter's Church, is threatened, the Petrine veneration of Pippin is to be translated into the tangible terms of military help to St Peter's Church. As a patrician of the Romans he is to be a fighter for St Peter, and in fighting for St Peter's Church he fights at the same time for the whole of Christendom, since the Roman Church is the "head and mother of all other churches."[1] By defending the Roman Church Christendom will be saved—Pippin is to exalt the Roman Church "per quam et salus Christianorum existit."[2] For St Peter, as he himself testifies, is the "preacher and illuminator of the whole world."[3] No other church has been committed to St Peter but the Roman one, and defence of this one church redounds to the good of all Christianity.[4] In short, the Roman Church is the "fons vivus," the "fundamentum fidei" of all Christianity.[5] If the Roman Church is endangered, the whole of Christendom will be endangered. According to papal conceptions, the proper functioning of the Roman Church which is in

---

[1] This is precisely one of the subjects in Stephen's letter to Pippin, *Cod. Car.* no. 11, p. 504: "Sancta omnium ecclesiarum Dei mater et caput." See also ibid., no. 6., pp. 488–9: ". . . valde studendum est, ut, unde gloriosiores ceteris gentibus in servitio b. Petri vos omnes christiani asserunt, inde omnipotenti Domino, qui dat salutem regibus, pro defensione sanctae suae ecclesiae perfectius placeatis." See also ibid., no. 8, p. 496, lines 37–41 and lines 17–19: "Peto te, ne pereamus, ne quando dicant gentes, quae in cuncto orbe terrarum sunt, ubi est fidutia Romanorum, quam post Deum in regibus et gente Francorum habebant?"

[2] *Cod. Car.*, no. 7, p. 491, lines 7–8.

[3] *Cod. Car.*, no. 10, p. 503, lines 37–9: "Deus et Dominus noster . . . nosque praedicatores et inluminatores totius mundi constituit." The "inluminator" may be reminiscent of the Donation of Constantine, cap. 8. The same term in Paul I's letter, ibid., no. 42, p. 556, lines 10–11: "beatus Silvester Christianorum inluminator fidei." J. Haller, op. cit., p. 22, note 3, draws attention to the intitulation of St Peter: "Petrus vocatus apostolus," a phrase which was not of Roman, but of Frankish, origin, hence there is some justification for saying that some Franks must have co-operated in the drafting of this letter of St Peter.

[4] Cf. *Cod. Car.*, no. 10, p. 501, lines 36–7.

[5] *Cod. Car.*, no. 10, p. 502, lines 35 ff.: "Currite, currite—per Deum vivum et verum vos adhortor et protestor—currite et subvenite, antequam fons vivus, unde satiati et renati estis, arescat; antequam ipsa modica stilla de flagrantissima flamma remanens, ex qua vestram lucem cognovistis, extinguatur; antequam mater vestra spiritalis, sancta Dei ecclesia, in qua vitam speratis percipere aeternam, humilietur, invadatur et ab impiis violetur atque contaminetur."

the interests of all the "Romani"—the whole "respublica Romanorum," the community of the Latin Christians—presupposes its freedom which only an independent territorial status of the Roman Church— the territorial "respublica Romanorum"—can guarantee.

Protector of the Romans = Christians; defender therefore of the mother church of all Romans = Christians; exaltation of the universal Church through the protection and defence of St Peter's Rome—this was the function which Pippin was to fulfil; this was the function which he also largely did fulfil. Pippin's service to St Peter was wholly conditioned by religious motives.[1] As a Roman = Christian he was bound to be moved by the insistent papal appeals; moved also by the—at times —picturesque papal descriptions of the rewards awaiting him in the next life. It is to these motives that the popes continually appeal; it is on the basis of these motives that Pippin acts. But we must not confuse the motives prompting Pippin with the function or office which he was supposed to perform. For the pope had clothed him in the garb of an officer, that of the "patrician of the Romans": this term too belonged to public law and designated an office and was one more new coinage, modelled on earlier terminology.

The imperial officer at Ravenna was known as the exarch or "patricius" without any qualification.[2] He was appointed by the emperor in Constantinople and acted on his behalf as a defender of Italy. The

---

[1] In so far we agree with Haller, op. cit., pp. 24–5.

[2] A. Hauck, *Kirchengeschichte Deutschlands,* 3rd & 4th ed., ii. 21, note 2; E. Caspar, op. cit., p. 182, note 1. The late Stein, "La période byzantine de la papauté" in *Cath. Hist. Rev.,* xxi (1935), pp. 161–2, considered that this title was not a novelty, because the Eastern patrician was acclaimed as πατρίκιε τῶν 'Ρωμαίων according to the *Liber de cerimoniis* (see ed. Bonn, 1832, i. 48, p. 253, line 9); but this was compiled by Constantine Porphyrogenitos in the tenth century, see also editorial note ad line 9. Stein's further reference (note 34) to Paulus Diaconus, *Hist. Langobardorum,* iv. 38 (MGH. SS. RR. *Lang.,* ed. G. Waitz) does not apply because this was written in the second half of the eighth century. Fredegar in his *Chronicon,* iv. 69, p. 155 (MGH. SS. RR. *Merov.,* ed. B. Krusch) uses the term "patricius" and "patricius Romanorum" indifferently and in no technical sense. Isidore of Seville speaks of a "Romanus patricius" in his *Chronicon,* cap. 115 (PL. lxxxiii. 1054). The "Clausula" itself, again quite untechnically, speaks of Pippin as "patricius." On the other hand, one might perhaps have expected official use of the title "patricius Romanorum" later, but it does not occur; for instance, in Constantine's *De administrando imperio* the title is throughout the simple "patricius" while the emperor is always βασιλεὺς τῶν 'Ρωμαίων, see the Greek edition with English translation by Gy. Moravcsik and R. J. H. Jenkins, Budapest, 1949. Treating of the "patricius Romanorum" conferred by Pope Stephen II on Pippin, H. Leclercq in DAC. xiii (1938), col. 1327 says: "Un titre nouveau, distinct du patriciat byzantin"; also col. 2494: "Ce patriciat est un inconnu jusqu'alors." Here also further literature.

Frankish patrician of the Romans was a novelty, not only because the pope had created him, but also because this specific officer had not existed before. Nevertheless, the term "Romans" whose patrician Pippin had become, had exactly the same meaning which we have tried to show in regard to that clumsy phrase "Church of the commonwealth of the Romans." Both terms in fact appear at exactly the same time, on the occasion of Stephen's journey to Ponthion. Since 751 when the last exarch of Ravenna was driven out by the Lombards, there had been no patrician, hence in a way one might say that the vacancy was filled by the appointment of the Frankish king as patrician.[1]

Now the manner of, and the purpose for, creating Pippin "patricius Romanorum" warrant a few observations. Little more than two years before the pope anointed him, he had already been anointed king by St. Boniface.[2] The significance of the papal unction lies not only in that the Carolingian dynasty was raised above any ruling family in Western or Eastern Europe by the action of St Peter's vicar, but also in that this act conferred the office of a patrician of the Romans: this is the form of address used by Stephen II and his successors when writing to Pippin. The significance of the papal act is only heightened when one realizes that in Rome the ceremony of anointing was not yet known.[3] The Frank was now the papally created and anointed king and at the same time was made an officer. Through this a most intimate religious connexion was established between king and pope, a connexion which was a distinction for the king, but also entailed service in his function as an officer.

Stephen II did not omit to drive this last point home. He wrote to Pippin that God Himself through the mediation of St Peter had anointed him[4] but with a definite purpose, namely, defence and protection and consequently exaltation of the Roman Church. Through

---

[1] Cf. also K. Jäntere, *Die römische Weltreichsidee*, p. 273.

[2] See *Annales Regni Francorum*, ed. cit., p. 8. On the date itself see L. Levillain, art. cit., pp. 228–9 (between 31 October 751 and 23 January 752). The parallelism between Saul-Childeric and David-Pippin should be noted, cf. E. Eichmann in *Hist. Jb.*, lxix (1949), p. 610.

[3] See G. Ellard, *Ordination Anointings in the Western Church*, Cambridge, Mass., 1933, p. 31; and H. Leclercq in DAC. xiii. 2136. Anointing as part of the priestly ordination became known only in the first half of the tenth century, see Ellard, op. cit., p. 77: "The anointing went to Rome by way of Ravenna. I think the subjugation of Rome at the hands of the woman (Marozia) extended farther than has been hitherto estimated. In appointing her relative John to the papacy (John X), did she not introduce the pontifical ritual from beyond the Alps that for all time should hold Rome captive?" Cf. also infra p. 150.

[4] *Cod. Car.*, no. 7, p. 493, lines 11–12; no. 8, p. 496, lines 15–16.

the unction Pippin became the specific defender of the Roman Church;[1] through the unction he was consecrated to service to the Roman Church[2] in his capacity as patrician of the Romans. The function of the "patrician of the Romans" was indissolubly linked with Pippin's kingship, but his kingship had no duties that were not purely Frankish; hence the need to create the king an officer. The anointing of Pippin as king by the pope presented itself as the medium through which the office could be conferred. This office provided the link in public law between the king and the pope, an all the stronger link as it was so powerfully and solemnly forged by anointing him king.

We should take note that whenever the pope referred to the unction in his letters, he invariably employed a phrasing which revealed the purpose, the telos, the finis, of the papal unction: the employment of conjunctive terms, such as the final "that," "in order to" ("ut") or "for the sake of" ("ad") are expressions characteristic of papal phraseology as well as of papal ideology: Pippin was anointed "*in order to* defend the Roman Church" or "for the sake of defence" or of liberation—these are standing phrases in the papal letters.[3] And in at least three letters this purposeful anointing is stated to have made Pippin the "arm," the "brachium," that would see that justice was done to St Peter.[4] And we obtain still more of a glimpse into the future when St Peter in his own letter declares:

Ideoque ego, apostolus Dei Petrus, qui vos adoptivos habeo filios ad defendendum de manibus adversariorum hanc Romanam civitatem et populum mihi a Deo commissum.[5]

[1] *Cod. Car.*, no. 7, p. 493, line 10: "Ideo vos Dominus per humilitatem meam mediante beato Petro unxit in reges, *ut* per vos sancta sua ecclesia exaltetur et princeps apostolorum suam suscipiat justitiam."

[2] Cf. also E. Eichmann, *Kaiserkrönung*, ii. 168, referring to W. Sickel, "Die Verträge der Päpste mit den Karolingern" in *Deutsche Z. f. Geschichtswissenschaft*, 1894, p. 335: "Die Salbung bedeutet die Weihe zu Dienst für die römische Kirche."

[3] Cf. the many passages which we have quoted; they could easily be multiplied.

[4] *Cod. Car.*, no. 6, p. 489, lines 27–8: "Omnes denique Christiani ita firmiter credebant, quod beatus Petrus princeps apostolorum nunc *per* vestrum fortissimum brachium suam percepisset justitiam." An almost identical wording in no. 7, p. 493, lines 28–30; see furthermore no. 13, p. 510, lines 19–20: "Quoniam maximam post Deum et b. Petrum in vestri fortissimi regni brachio possidemus spem . . ." E. Caspar, op. cit., p. 182, note 4, draws attention to the expression used by Martin I who also identified "brachium" with "patricius," see Mansi, x. 856: "Quomodo habebam ego tali viro adversus stare, habenti praecipue brachium universae militiae Italicae? An potius ego illum feci exarchum?"

[5] *Cod. Car.*, no. 10, p. 501, lines 38–9. About the adoption and its meaning, see infra p. 257. In 758 Paul I sent a big sword to Pippin, *Cod. Car.* no. 17, p. 517.

In short, then, the Frankish king, by virtue of the papally conferred office of the "patrician of the Romans" was to be the defender and protector of the Roman Church.

At this vital stage we should be clear about the nature of the papally conferred office. The office is the garb in which Pauline-Gelasian-Isidorian views were clothed. It was a characteristically Roman nomenclature. In its contents the office showed kinship with an older office, also of Roman provenance. The essence of the new patrician's duty was the (military) defence of the "Romani"; and in so far as this defensive aspect of his duty was concerned, there seems to be great kinship between him and the earlier *defensor civitatis*. This officer was created in 364[1] and his duty was the civil protection of those classes which were in need of his protection from oppression by powerful citizens in a municipality or other corporate entity.[2] These *defensores* were also called "patrons"[3] or "defensores reipublicae" or *advocati reipublicae* or "defensores disciplinae."[4] Their functions were greatly developed as time went on[5] and Justinian allocated to them a whole title in his Code.[6] Moreover, if they were to sue or to be sued, ecclesiastical bodies, such as individual churches, adopted this device of a *defensor* and appointed a layman who was to act and to represent them in the imperial courts. Upon conciliar request in 407 an imperial decree made the appointment of this *defensor ecclesiae* who was to be taken from the ranks of the *advocati*, a duty for ecclesiastical corporations.[7]

---

[1] For details of this office see A. M. Bethmann-Hollweg, *Der Civilprocess des gemeinen Rechts*, Bonn, 1866, iii. 107 f.; Pauly-Wissowa, *Realencyclopädie der klassischen Altertumswissenschaft*, iv. 2365 ff.; *Cod. Theod.*, I. xxix.: "De defensoribus civitatum."

[2] Pauly-Wissowa, iv. 2367.

[3] Cf. *Cod. Theod.* I. xxix. 1: "Edimus ut plebs omnis Illyrici officiis patronorum contra potentiorum defendatur injurias."

[4] Cf. *Cod. Just.*, I. lv. 6.

[5] The historical development of the *Defensores* is presented by E. Chénon, "Étude historique sur le Defensor civitatis" in *Nouvelle Revue hist. de droit français et étranger*, xiii (1889), pp. 321–62; 515–61.

[6] See *Cod. Just.*, I, lv; cf. also *Nov.* xv and xxv.

[7] It was of these *defensores* that Cassiodorus spoke, *Variae*, ix. 16 and ii. 30. For this see O. J. Zimmermann, *The late Latin Vocabulary of the Variae of Cassiodorus*, Washington, 1944, pp. 206, 219–20. From these must be distinguished their offshoot, also called *Defensores ecclesiae* (*Romanae*) who were particularly concerned with the administration of the papal patrimony, about which see F. Martroye, "Les defensores ecclesiae aux v<sup>e</sup> et vi<sup>e</sup> siècles" in *Revue hist. de droit français et étranger*, 4th ser., ii (1923), pp. 597–622; cf. also B. Fischer, "Die Entwicklung des Instituts der Defensoren in der römischen Kirche" in

The essential point is that this *defensor civitatis* was an officer in public law who derived his position from either an imperial appointment or popular election with subsequent imperial confirmation. There was no independence attached to the office—this functionary was created for a specific and limited purpose.[1] He was, so to speak, a police organ.[2] If he was a *defensor ecclesiae*, he had to be taken from laymen, as Pope Pelagius I had enjoined.[3] The *defensor* is a public officer whose duty consists in giving help, protection and defence when requested by those who ask for his intervention. The scope of his office is circumscribed; he acts upon instructions. The idea underlying this *defensor* or *advocatus* or *patronus* is that his power is derivative and that he acts when his services are invoked by those for whose protection he was appointed or elected.[4]

If we keep in mind the nature of this office and its practical application by the Roman Church, it will not be too difficult to see that what Stephen II did was to mould that officer into the patrician of the Romans: he was the military defender and protector of the Romans, and the pope had indeed an old model for this—the *defensor ecclesiae*. The patrician of the Romans was the *defensor ecclesiae* writ large. All this brings us back to the purpose of the unction. The religious-liturgical act provided the framework for the creation of this officer and his intimate link with the pope who performed the unction on behalf of God.

The significance of this would not be brought out clearly if Pippin's idea of defence and protection were not set against it. One might indeed be tempted to say that later medieval European history was telescoped into the spring months of 754. An appeal to Pippin for defence of the Roman Church was bound to fall on fertile soil. For quite apart from the very deep Petrine veneration of the Frank, the protection and

---

*Ephemerides Liturgicae*, xlviii (1934), pp. 443–54; and H. Leclercq in DAC. iv. 412, 418, 422. OR. I has "defensores" taking part in the public processions; this OR. is of eighth-century origin, see M. Andrieu, *Les ordines Romani du haut moyen age*, i, 1931, pp. 3,344; and ii, 1949, p. 38.

[1] See especially *Cod. Just.* cit., lex 5.

[2] Cf. also E. Chénon, art. cit., p. 337: "Un véritable commissaire de police et à ce titre l'auxiliaire du gouverneur de la province."

[3] J.986 (558–60), partly incorporated in Gratian, XVI. i. 20. The pope exemplifies the tasks of the "defensor" thus: "causarum cognitio, conventiones, actus, publicae litigiae et quaecumque vel ecclesiastica instituta vel supplicantium *necessitas poscit.*"

[4] He was, for instance, not free to renounce his office without imperial permission, *Cod. Just.* cit., lex 10.

defence of the defenceless and weak was precisely one of the chief functions of a monarch; and when it was St Peter's Church that was in need
of protective help from him who showed by words and deeds his
veneration for St Peter, the duty of the Frank was clear. And yet, did
his view on defence and protection tally with the Roman-papal idea
of defence and protection?

The function of Pippin, the monarch, was autonomous; it was the
old Germanic-royal idea that as a monarch he has the duty to protect
and to defend when he considers that defence and protection are needed.
As the monarch of the kingdom ruled by him, it was his prime function
to see that weak and defenceless individuals and corporate bodies must
be royally protected against injustice from whatever quarter it may
come. The judgment as to when injustice is committed, as to when in
other words, protection is called for, must be left to the monarch.
The judgment of how and when to act, to defend and to protect, is
the monarch's sole prerogative. He alone knows when the interests of
his kingdom and of his monarchy demand that his sword be drawn or
that new laws are necessary; he alone is the final and autonomous
judge who bases his decision to act upon criteria emanating from his
function as monarchic ruler. The protection and defence given by the
monarch are the effluence of his monarchic position.[1] Monarchic rule
incorporates the function of a protector and defender.

Put thus side by side, there is little difficulty in seeing the fundamental gulf separating the Roman-papal idea of protection and defence
and the corresponding monarchic idea. The former protector acts in
the capacity of an assistant, of a lieutenant, of an organ who is specially
appointed for this very purpose of defence and protection; this is his
*raison d'être*; he acts when ordered to act—he is literally speaking *ad*

---

[1] It was the great merit of A. Waas, *Vogtei und Bede*, Berlin, 1919, to have
drawn attention to the idea of the *Munt* (*mundeburdium*) as an essential element
in the conception of monarchy. See especially pp. 24, 25, 110. The conception of
the *Vogt*—linguistically derived from *vocatus*; see also *advowson* which is directly
based on *advocatus* (cf. O.E.D.)—has the same duplicity of meaning in the
medieval period as so many other terms in daily use. This is of great importance
in assessing the function of the monastic *Vogt*, cf. Waas, pp. 33–52, 99–118; also
H. Planitz in *Sav. Z., Germ. Abt.*, xli (1920), p. 424: "Klostervogtei ist ihrem
Wesen nach Muntherrschaft." It may, however, be open to doubt whether there
was a development from the Roman *advocacia* to the Frankish *Vogt*, as Waas
seems to suggest, cf. p. 52: "Aus dem Beamten ist ein Herr geworden." Cf. also
Planitz, loc. cit.: here is one of the many cases in which "ein dem Römischen
Recht entlehntes Rechtsinstitut im MA. seinen alten Namen beibehalten, sich
aber innerlich völlig gewandelt hat." We would hold that one and the same term
served to express two different things.

*vocatus.* The latter, also in a literal sense, is autonomous[1] and acts independently and on his own initiative; he is the monarch upon whom alone rests the decision when and how and where and whom to defend and to protect. The former conception denotes control of the protector; the latter denotes control of the protected.[2] The latter's protection and defence emanate from his being the monarch (and not from his being a public officer). *Protectio trahit subjectionem* might not be an inadequate summary of the Teutonic-royal idea. A good deal of medieval history revolves round the different interpretations of the one concept of protection.[3] The office of the "patrician of the Romans" signalled the first serious ideological breach in the monarch's fortifications.[4]

It is thus hardly possible to overestimate the ideological significance of Stephen II's step. In a symbolic nutshell, so to speak, the papal theme is presented to us, the theme according to which the king in a Christian society fulfils a certain function allotted to him: the king, in papal terms, is not a monarch: he is not autonomous; he is an assistant, *adjutor*, defender, *advocatus*. We can perhaps now understand why the papal letters issuing forth from the papal chancery in such prolific quantities during the second half of this century, consistently dis-

---

[1] αὐτός and νόμος.

[2] On no account do we suggest that Pippin exercised any control over the Roman Church; but we maintain that, as the Frankish monarch, he controlled the Frankish clergy and its legislation. But later there will ensue also control of the Roman Church on the basis of the monarchic protection exercised by the emperor of the Romans. For some very suggestive observations see P. E. Schramm, *Kaiser, Rom und Renovatio*, Leipzig, 1929, i. 175, note 5, although we are unable —as it is hoped the text makes clear—to follow the same savant in his "Das Versprechen Pippins und Karls d. Gr. für die römische Kirche" in *Sav. Z., Kan. Abt.*, xxvii (1938), pp. 193–217. Whilst protection is the generic idea, defence relates to a specific and concrete situation. Cf. *Cap.* i. 93, no. 33.

[3] Even the prototype of a medieval monarch, Charlemagne, used the terms in a way which may easily give rise to erroneous views. In his first "Capitulare" of 769 he said that he was "devotus sanctae ecclesiae *defensor* atque *adjutor* in omnibus." What he thought when using these terms was assuredly quite different from what the (Roman) papacy attributed to these characteristically Roman expressions.

[4] We have also to refer to Pippin's refusal to style himself "patrician of the Romans." Whether he sensed the implications of title and office, it is not possible to say. It is not, however, without significance that according to Einhard's report there was considerable resistance on the part of the Frankish barons to the projected implementation of the duties assumed by Pippin, see Einhard, *Vita Karoli*, ed. G. Waitz, cap. 6, p. 7. It would be idle to assert that Pippin threw himself with enthusiasm and zeal into the war against Aistulph. For a survey of some modern estimates of Pippin, cf. K. Jäntere, op. cit., pp. 276–9.

regard Pippin as a king before the papal intervention: St Boniface's unction of Pippin as a king was not mentioned once. What the papal letters stressed was that the pope anointed Pippin a king for the particular purpose of defence. A perusal of the papal communications may easily lead to the assumption that Pippin was not king before the papal act.

That Stephen II did not act upon this assumption is obvious. But it is also obvious that the unction of Boniface was tacitly set aside: into its place stepped the papal unction. Thereby kingship was given a new meaning altogether, a meaning that was expressed in the newly coined term of public law—the "patrician of the Romans." Pippin was created king by the papal unction; he was created a king for a specific purpose, that of protecting and defending the Roman Church. This was his task with which he was entrusted by the pope[1] and this was to be his function as a king. Indeed, this is very far removed from the function of the king who is a monarch. It is understandable why the letters lay so much stress on the fact that Pippin was anointed by God Himself (or St Peter) through the instrumentality of the pope: thereby the function of the king in a Roman (= Christian) society was made manifestly clear: Christ Himself, "King of kings and Lord of lords" had *instituted* Pippin as a king for the purpose of exalting His Church.[2] Papal unction was given a constitutive meaning.[3] In brief, the function

---

[1] This, we think, is the meaning of the term *commendare* frequently used in the papal letters to Pippin. There is no technical connotation attached to the term.

[2] Cf. *Cod. Car.*, no. 7, p. 491, line 15: "Rex regum et Dominus dominantium salvos vos instituit, ut per vos sancta Dei ecclesia exaltetur." Cf. also no. 6, p. 489, lines 41–2: "Conjuro vos . . . per beatum Petrum, principem apostolorum, qui *vos in reges unxit, ut* doleat vobis pro sancta Dei ecclesia." No. 7, p. 493, lines 11–12: "Ideo vos *Dominus* per humilitatem meam, mediante beato Petro, *unxit in reges, ut* per vos sancta sua exaltetur ecclesia et princeps apostolorum suam suscipiat justitiam." No. 8, p. 496, lines 15–16: "Sic *adjutorium sumas* a Deo omnipotente, qui *te unxit* super turbas populorum per institutionem beati Petri *in regem.*" These examples could be multiplied. Cf. Paul I, Stephen's successor, in *Cod. Car.* no. 13, p. 510, lines 15–16: "Coram Deo vivo, qui vos in regem per suum apostolum beatum Petrum ungui praecepit." Idem, ibid., no. 36, p. 544, lines 32–33: "Vester Dominus Deus noster, qui vos regnare jussit." Stephen III, ibid., no. 44, p. 559, lines 31–3: "Coram Deo vivo, qui vos regnare praecepit." With this should again be compared the Donation of Constantine, cap. 19, where Constantine says of himself: "Coram Deo vivo, qui nos regnare praecepit."

[3] But for Pippin the papal unction was a mere formality, since he had already been anointed by St Boniface. We cannot refrain from mentioning the very significant entries of Baronius in his *Ann. Eccles.*, ed. Lucca, 1744, xii. 589 (ad 754): after quoting the *Lib. Pont.* account of Pippin's unction by Stephen, the learned cardinal says: "Haud dubium est adversantes habere Latinos omnes historicos,

4

of the king, that of the patrician of the Romans, is the king's *raison d'être*. As yet, it is still attached to kingship, but the time is not so far distant when the "patricius Romanorum" will give way to the "imperator Romanorum."[1] And on the distant horizon there appears the problem of legitimate rulership in a Christian society.

## IV

A brief examination of the ideological significance and the genesis of the Donation of Constantine appears advisable. The forgery was made not later than the early fifties of the eighth century, at any rate before Stephen II set out on his journey to Pippin.[2]

---

qui unctionem Pipini factam jussione Zachariae pontificis per s. Bonifacium tradunt." Two pages later, we read (p. 591): "At licet litteris Zachariae pontificis Pipinus in regem ante provectus fuerit, et s. Bonifacii unctione initiatus, tamen non ab eo tempore, sed ab hoc anno (754) coepti sunt numerari anni ipsius regni, ut docent vetera monumenta Francorum." For the latter assertion there is no warrant as a glance at the DD. of Pippin proves.

[1] The actions of the second and the fourth Stephen were so similar that, as we have said, the former's intervention must have served as the precedent for the latter's. Pippin was king before the papal intervention, but the pope nevertheless made him king once more; Louis I was emperor before the papal intervention at Rheims (816), but he was made emperor again by Stephen IV who put the crown of Constantine on Louis's head. In each case papal intervention secured the course of events. On Louis see infra pp. 143 ff.

[2] See supra p. 59; furthermore, G. Lähr, *Die konstantinische Schenkung*, Berlin, 1926, p. 11, and the Paris MS (BN. 2777) written before 792 containing the forgery (cf. MGH. *Formulae*, no. 11, p. 503; F. Kampers, "Roma Aeterna" in *Hist. Jb.*, 1924, p. 245 f. (beginning of Stephen's pontificate). That the place of the forgery was the papal chancery is indisputable, cf. supra p. 60, and the arguments of K. Hartmann, "Grundherrschaft & Burokratie im Kirchenstaat" in *Vierteljahrsschrift f. Social & Wirtschafts geschichte*, 1909, pp. 146 f. and of H. v. Schubert, *Geschichte der christl. Kirche im Frühmittelalter*, Tübingen, 1923, p. 320, who points to the primicerius Christophorus as a possible author, a suggestion that has a good deal to recommend itself in view of the diction of the *Lib. Pont.* which we have pointed out, supra p. 60. Schubert held 756 as the most likely date, however. Scheffer-Boichorst, in MIOG., xi (1892), pp. 128 ff., L. M. Hartmann, *Geschichte Italiens im Mittelalter*, Gotha, 1910, ii–2, pp. 220 ff., and Caspar, op. cit., p. 183, assumed the pontificate of Paul I as the most likely time of the composition. Some have maintained that the forgery was made at Rheims and after the turn of the century, but before 816, so, for instance, M. Buchner, "Rom oder Reims, die Heimat des CC" in *Hist. Jb.*, 1933, pp. 137 ff., W. Neuss, *Die Kirche des Mittelalters*, Bonn, 2nd ed., 1950, p. 79, and E. Eichmann, *Kaiserkrönung*, i. 28, idem, *Weihe & Krönung des Papstes im MA.*, Munich, 1951, p. 24. Most recently, W. Ohnsorge, "Konstantinische Schenkung, Leo III und die Anfänge der kurialen römischen Kaiseridee" in *Sav. Z., Germ. Abt.*, lxviii (1951), pp. 78 ff., suggested as the date the year 804, but see infra p. 82. Here also a useful survey of recent views will be found, pp. 78–81. There is also select bibliography in Levillain, art. cit., p. 231, note 3. The text of the Donation

Since its detection as a forgery, the fabrication has not escaped very severe strictures on the part of some historians. But it would seem appropriate to keep apart the external trappings of the document and its substance. The document must be judged by contemporary standards: it elaborated an earlier product, and unless this is taken into account, the Donation is not understandable. That this detracts a good deal from the supposed originality of the forger, goes without saying. Moreover, some of the details, such as those relating to clothing, were not invented at all—the forger had perfectly genuine models—but in common with so many medieval forgeries, the author antedated everything in his document, so that everything was a gift to the pope from the great Constantine. Lastly, the ideology embodied in this document, is no invention either.

The basis upon which the eighth-century forger worked, was the *Legenda sancti Silvestri*, a somewhat romantic version of Constantine's conversion[1] made towards the end·of the fifth century. This *Legenda* was born of true Roman parentage.[2] The time of its composition is very significant: it was made during the years which witnessed the first serious clash between the papacy and the Roman empire situated in the East. The clash concerned nothing less than the authority of the emperor and the authority of the Roman Church in matters vital to both of them, in matters in faith, doctrine and jurisdiction over clerics. The emperor's *Henoticon* (482), the significance of which lies in that the emperor alone and without a synod for the first time decrees by law the faith for the empire,[3] was the prelude to this first serious clash,

is in P. Hinschius, *Decretales Pseudo-Isidorianae*, pp. 249–54, and the best modern edition is that by K. Zeumer, in *Festgabe f.R.v. Gneist*, 1888, pp. 47–59, which is also in C. Mirbt, *Quellen zur Geschichte des Papsttums*, 4th ed., 1924, no. 228, pp. 107–112.

[1] This was established by W. Levison, "Konstantinische Schenkung & Silvesterlegende" in *Miscellanea Fr. Ehrle*, Rome, 1924, ii. 181 ff., 239 ff. Levison also showed how well known the story was, not only in Rome, but also in England and the Frankish kingdom during the eighth century, see pp. 206–14. But cf. already C. B. Coleman, *Constantine the Great and Christianity* (in Columbia Studies in History, etc.), New York, 1914, pp. 161 ff., esp. 164 ff.

[2] Whilst there is every justification for saying that the papal chancery was the birthplace of the Donation, there is no shred of evidence that its source, the *Legenda*, was made there: on the contrary, everything points to its composition outside the chancery, see F. Di Capua, *Il Rituo prosaico nelle lettere dei papi*, Rome, 1948, iii. 171 ff. (Lateranum, n.s., xi–xii): all the Symmachan forgeries stand in sharp contrast to the style of the chancery. But cf. Peitz, p. 3 (of the work quoted infra 76 n. 3).

[3] Caspar, *Geschichte des Papsttums*, ii. 35, characterized it as a "kaiserliches Glaubensedikt": tacitly the Council of Chalcedon was set aside by it—the real

the Acacian schism lasting thirty-five years. It was just then that under Felix III in 485 historically unwarranted declarations were made in the Roman synod to the effect that the Council of Nicaea had submitted its decisions to Pope Silvester for confirmation;[1] and this synod of Rome that actually ratified the Nicaean decisions, was duly invented shortly afterwards.[2] It was just then also that Felix III and his draftsman who later became Pope Gelasius I, made the classic pronouncements on precisely those matters considered vital by both emperor and pope. They concerned the standing and function of the emperor in the Roman-Christian world. In this world there was no room for imperial decrees fixing dogma and faith and the exercise of jurisdiction over clerics; on the contrary, the emperor's role was to learn, not to teach, was to subject his decisions to priestly judgment.

Behind these vigorous assertions of the papal point of view[3] there is the basic assumption that the emperor has the duty to fulfil certain functions. The question engaging the papal mind was the *raison d'être* of the emperor: it was the same question which engaged even popular thought. Had not the Roman empire a providential mission? Was it not created providentially *for the sake* of preparing the ground for the union of all the nations in the one *corpus Christi*?[4] If the popular clerical

---

beginnings of Cesaropapism. This is strongly endorsed by H. Rahner, *Abendländische Kirchenfreiheit*, 1943, pp. 190, 192.

[1] Cf. Mansi, vii. 1140; E. Caspar, op. cit., i. 121; ii. 109.

[2] Cf. E. Caspar, op. cit., loc. cit. There were said to have been present 267 bishops at this (invented) Roman synod. This invention stands at the doorstep of the Symmachan forgeries of 501. The *Liber Pontificalis* in the "Vita Silvestri" contains this invented synod, but takes one more step by declaring that the Council of Nicaea was convoked by the order of Pope Silvester, see *Lib. Pont.* i. 171. About the initiation of the *Lib. Pont.* in the twenties of the sixth century, cf. Caspar, op. cit., ii. 314 ff., and H. Leclercq, DAC. ix. 354–460. From then onwards the papal biographies are contemporary entries and therefore so valuable.

[3] Indeed, the revolutionary thesis of W. Peitz, *Dionysius Exiguus als Kanonist* ("Schweizer Rundschau," Einsiedeln, 1945) concerning the summons of Dionysius by Gelasius to Rome (pp. 2, 6, 12–13) and the work of the monk would entirely fit into the framework of Gelasius who must have keenly felt the lack of an easily available collection of decrees: the whole pontificate of Gelasius was "rigorous traditionalism" (Caspar, op. cit., ii. 47) and for a traditionalist there can be no better support than the law emanating from Petrine Rome. Cf. already L. Duchesne in *Lib. Pont.* i, pp. xciii ff., concerning Dionysius and the *Legenda*, and Peitz, p. 3. On the importance of the Gelasian pontificate for canon law see especially G. Le Bras, "Un moment decisif" in *Revue historique de droit français et étranger*, ix (1930), pp. 506–18; idem, ibid., xxx (1952), pp. 497–8; and P. Fournier & G. Le Bras, *Histoire des collections canoniques*, Paris, 1932, i. 23 ff. Reckoning of years by the years of Grace was introduced by Dionysius.

[4] Cf. the contemporary anonymous tract *De vocatione omnium gentium* (PL. li. 704): "Ad cuius rei effectum credimus providentia Dei Romani regni latitu-

mind of Rome was moving within this historical-teleological framework, how much more was the papal mind enraptured by these teleological views. Did not Leo I shortly before expostulate on the function
of the (Roman) Church?[1] Did not the same Leo dwell on the theme of
Roma, formerly the teacher of error, now the mistress of truth, being
a royal and sacerdotal city, and therefore the mistress of the world?[2]
And, above all, was it not just then also that Constantinople ominously
struck up the theme of New Rome and raised claims by virtue of its
being the *urbs regia*, the residence of the emperor? Was not the twenty-
eighth chapter of Chalcedon a clear pointer? Constantinople was
assigned equal rank to Rome, because it was the seat of the imperial
government and senate.[3] Was this exclusively political argument a
sufficient justification for Constantinople's claims?[4] Moreover, did not
also from 451 (or 457) onwards the imperial crown play a ceremonial-
religious role by virtue of the patriarch's crowning the emperor?[5]
Rome was the mistress of the world, Pope Leo I had said, because
St Peter had resided there.[6] Surely, the physical presence of the emperor

---

dinem praeparatam: ut nationes vocandae ad unitatem corporis Christi prius jure
unius consociarentur imperii" (ii. 16). In this context the prayers for the Roman
empire in the *Sacramentaria* are worthy of note. About Orosius cf. supra p. 14 n. 4.

[1] See especially Leo's Ep. 104 and 156, cc. 3–5; Caspar, op. cit., i. 551, and
H. M. Klinkenberg, "Papsttum und Reichskirche bei Leo d. Gr." in *Sav. Z.,
kan. Abt.* xxxviii (1952), pp. 90, 100, 101, 109.

[2] Cf. Leo's *Sermo* 82, c. 1. In c. 2 he propounds the theme of the empire's providential mission which may have inspired that popular tract already referred to
(p. 76 n. 4). Cf. also the phrase "universarum gentium vocationi" in *Sermo* 4, c. 2
(cited supra p. 11). In parentheses we should note that the second-century Roman
jurists had apostrophized the city of Rome as "urbs regia"; cf. e.g., Modestinus,
in *Dig.* 27, 1, 6 (11): "In urbe regia, quae et habetur et est communis patria."
It is difficult to say whether Leo knew of this; about Leo's juristic sense cf. supra
p. 12. But he certainly seems to be the first pope who called Rome a royal *and*
sacerdotal city, *Sermo* 82.

[3] In this context reference must be made to c. 17 of Chalcedon according to
which the changed civil status of a city entails a change in its ecclesiastical status.
Cf. also Leo's statement with particular reference to the reasons of New Rome's
claims, in Ep. 104, c. 3.

[4] The weakness of this argument was clearly felt by Constantinople, hence the
attempt to make Constantinople an apostolic city next to Rome by inventing the
story of its foundation by the apostle, St Andrew, St Peter's brother. The story
was current between 476 and 525 but was fixed in writing later, see Caspar, ii. 748.

[5] See supra p. 10 n. 4.

[6] Leo's *Sermo* 82, cc. 3 and 7. Cf. also Ep. 14, c. 11, where Rome and the see
of Peter (the "una sedes Petri") are held to be identical: in a Roman-Christian
world, Rome alone can be the head, not that upstart city of Constantinople.
See now Klinkenberg, art. cit., pp. 44, 46, and his comments on that letter, ibid.,
note 19.

in Constantinople cannot make all this difference.[1] Anyway, how was it that Constantinople became the residence of the emperors? How did this change of capital come about? If Constantinople raised these claims by virtue of being the *urbs regia*,[2] how and why did it become an *urbs regia*?[3] Did not the great benefactor of the Roman Church, Constantine, remove his capital from Rome to Constantinople? Could there not be established a connexion between Constantine and the Church of Rome on the one hand, and the transfer of the capital on the other hand?

Set thus against the climate of the time[4] the *Legenda* assumes some ideological importance. It is no doubt true that it was a "tendentious novel"[5] written in hagiographic style, depicting Constantine's conversion in not always very attractive terms, and enumerating in some detail his activities during the first eight days as a Christian. The author was certainly not very skilled or particularly gifted, and yet the very choice of his theme, Constantine's conversion, points to his wishing to pursue a definite aim. And it was this underlying aim of the *Legenda* which was clearly grasped by the author of the Donation in the eighth century. In order to understand this, we must briefly review both documents.

According to the *Legenda*, Constantine had conferred on the Roman Church the privilege whereby it was the head of all the priests within the Roman world, just as the judges had their head in the person of

---

[1] Cf. Gelasius, Ep. 26, c. 10, p. 406; quoting the Leonine argument of Ep. 104, c. 3 about the *regia civitas*, Gelasius says: "*imperialis praesentia* mensuram dispensationis religiosae non mutat . . . de *imperatoris praesentia* blandiuntur . . ."

[2] Cf. the Eastern objections to the condemnation by Felix III of the Patriarch Acacius: the pope had no right to proceeed without a synod against the "pontifex" of the "regia civitas," see Gelasius in his Ep. 26, p. 393: the Easterners "pueriliter adjicientes: 'precipue pontificem regiae civitatis.' "

[3] One should not forget in this context the great cultural gulf between Orient and Occident. With true Roman superiority Gelasius contemptuously refers to the "Greeks" who are unable to separate the true and the false and with whom a hotchpotch of orthodoxy and heresy is excusable, Ep. 27, p. 435. Cf. also Ep. 7, p. 335, cap. 2, also cap. 3, p. 336. Nor should one leave out of account the change of the situation in Italy since 476 when the empire was again under the rule of one emperor residing in Constantinople, and when from the Eastern point of view Rome had sunk to the rank of a merely historic site. The 28th chapter of Chalcedon must have appeared still more ominous in the 70's and 80's of the fifth century.

[4] It appears that the contrast of "gold" and "lead," later to be so much exploited, was also coined at that time in the tract wrongly ascribed to Ambrose, *De sacerdotali dignitate*, cap. 2 (PL. xvii. 569); cf. on this point H. Rahner, op. cit., p. 175, note 5.

[5] So Levison, art. cit., pp. 186, 201, 214.

the king.[1] The blunder committed by the author need not detain us.[2] That the quotation of the alleged enactment of the first Roman-Christian emperor was aimed at Byzantium, there can be no legitimate doubt. The author also reports that on the eighth day after his conversion, Constantine as a sign of his contrition, had prostrated himself, had put his crown down and wetted his purple mantle with his tears.[3] This episode is very suggestive. Who conferred the crown on Constantine after this incident? That he was emperor after the eighth day, nobody ever doubted. In whose custody, so to speak, was the crown and the imperial insignia while the emperor lay prostrate? The answer to these questions was at least indicated: the trustee was the pope.[4]

What was only symbolically hinted at by the author of the *Legenda*, was fully expressed by the author of the Donation. In it he made Emperor Constantine hand over all the imperial garments, insignia and symbols, including the sceptre, the lance, the orb, the standards "et diversa ornamenta imperialia" to Pope Silvester.[5] Amongst the imperial garments the pope also received the "chlamys purpurea," the "lorum" and the "tunica coccinea."[6] And so as to emphasize the

---

[1] The text of the *Legenda* is in B. Mombritius (ed. H. Quentin and A. Brunet), *Sanctuarium seu vitae sanctorum*, Paris, 1910, ii. 508–31. The reference in the text is to p. 512: "Privilegium Romanae ecclesiae pontifici contulit, ut in toto orbe Romano sacerdotes hunc caput habeant, sicut judices regem." There is another edition of the text in Coleman, op. cit., pp. 217–27.

[2] We should note that the Donation did not contain this blunder.

[3] Mombritius, ed. cit., p. 513: "Octava die preressit albis depositis totus mundus et salvus: et veniens ad confessionem apostoli Petri ablato diademate capitis totum se planum projiciens in faciem tantam illic lachrymarum effudit multitudinem: ut omnia illa insignia vestimenta purpurea infunderentur: dans vocem inter amaras lachrymas quibus se errasse, se pecasse . . ."

[4] G. Lähr, op. cit., p. 3, has already drawn attention to this.

[5] The pope kept only the sceptre; this was the "ferula," the straight staff, a direct copy of the Byzantine imperial staff whose eagle on its top was exchanged with a cross. It was an extraliturgical papal symbol, cf. Eisenhofer, *Liturgik*, p. 109, and now also Eichmann, *Weihe & Krönung des Papstes*, p. 32. The episcopal staff is curved, but did not come into Roman usage before the eleventh century.

[6] The "chlamys" was the purple mantle worn by the emperor, open on its right side and held together by a clasp on the right shoulder, see Eichmann, op. cit., 33–5. The "tunica coccinea" was an outer garment of purple silk reaching down to the knees, cf. L. Duchesne, *Origines du culte chrétien*, Engl. transl. of the 5th ed., pp. 380–81. The "lorum" was a broad scarf embroidered and ornamented, the one end hanging down, the other was slung across the left arm. In fact, this "lorum" was the pallium which had already been in use in early sixth century and had developed out of the oriental omiphorion, cf. Duchesne op. cit., pp. 385–6, Eisenhofer, op. cit., p. 108, and Eichmann, op. cit., pp. 19–21. Cf. also the quotation from the *Lib. de cerim.*, infra, p. 80 n. 3.

totality of Constantine's gifts, the author then collectively mentions "omnia imperialia indumenta" as being given into the possession of the pope.[1] And as a further outward symbol of the emperor's servility to the pope, he performs the office of a papal "strator."[2]

The author of the Donation makes the emperor express the wish to place the imperial crown on Silvester's head as a sign of true imperial power. But Silvester refused to wear the imperial crown above his clerical tonsure, whereupon Constantine put the "phrygium" on the papal head: this "phrygium" was brilliantly white and designated the Lord's resurrection.[3] At the same time Constantine decreed that the pope alone should use the "phrygium" in public processions.[4] "Ad imitationem[5] imperii," as the author made Constantine say, he also gave to Silvester the imperial residence—"palatium nostrum"—as well as the city of Rome, all provinces of Italy and the occident, the "loca et civitates."[6] In short, the characteristic external symbols of emperorship and the "potestas" over the territories including the islands,[7] are handed to the pope.

It is of course a truism to say that the Donation made the pope a real

---

[1] Later papal attire was modelled largely on these imperial grants, see Eichmann, *Kaiserkrönung*, ii. 131 ff., and op. cit., pp. 22 ff.; cf. also P. E. Schramm, in *Studi Gregoriani*, ii. 413 ff.

[2] See cap. 16: "Tenentes frenum equi ipsius pro reverentia b. Petri stratoris officium illi exhibuimus."

[3] Cap. 16: "Decrevimus itaque et hoc, ut isdem venerabilis pater noster Silvester, summus pontifex, vel omnes eius successores pontifices diadema, videlicet coronam, quam ex capiti nostro illi concessimus, ex auro purissimo et gemmis pretiosis uti debeant et eorum capite ad laudem Dei pro honore b. Petri gestare; ipse vero sanctissimus papa super coronam clericatus quam gerit ad gloriam b. Petri, omnino ipsa ex auro non est passus uti corona, phrygium vero candido nitore splendidam resurrectionem dominicam designans eius sacratissimo vertici manibus nostris posuimus . . ." In this context attention should be drawn to the following passage in the *Lib. de cerim.*, ed. Bonn, ii. 40, pp. 637–8: "Credimus nempe loros, quos magistri et patricii die festo resurrectionis Christi Dei nostri gerunt, representare tumulationem eius. Quod autem loros auro conspicuos gestant, id interpretamur imaginem splendoris resurrectionis Christi esse; tamquam si a Christo, velut sole, per eius resurrectionem radiis solaribus circumcollustrati splenderent." Then follows the passage about the patricians representing the apostles, see the quotation supra p. 16 and also infra p. 254 on Henry VI.

[4] Cap. 16: "Statuentes eundem phrygium omnes eius successores pontifices singulariter *uti* in processionibus."

[5] The medieval meaning of the word "imitatio" is identical to the modern meaning, see J. de Ghellinck, "Imitatio" in *Bulletin du Cange*, xvi (1941), p. 153.

[6] See cap. 17.

[7] See cap. 13. On this claim to possess all the islands see A. Dove, loc. cit., and especially L. Weckmann, *Las Bullas Alexandrinas*, Mexico City, 1949, pp. 40–3, 65–6 ("omni-insular doctrine").

emperor, a *Rex-Sacerdos*, a *Papstkaiser*,[1] and that in this way the pope
became the very copy of the Eastern basileus-hiereus. The author of
the Donation took great care to make this point clear: the pope may
use the imperial insignia—"papa uti possit imperialibus insigniis" and
from here to Gregory VII is only a small step.[2] But, as we have said,
we should not assume that these external trappings, important though
they are, fully exhaust the significance of the document. For behind
these trappings there is hidden a very profound ideology.

In the first place, considering the time of the composition of this
document and its progenitor, it could have meaning only as regards
the Eastern empire. It was a document that was conceived entirely
within the mental climate and thought pattern of the Roman Empire.
In order to prove to Pippin the territorial claims, the Donation was
made, but the real object of Stephen's obtaining Pippin's confirmation
was the emancipation of the papacy from the imperial framework.

This brings us to the second and far more important point, which
concerns the very function of the Roman emperor as seen by the author
of the Donation. An answer had to be found to the question of how
this Roman empire that derived its very name from Rome, came to
have its capital in Constantinople. How did this transfer of the capital
come about? It is a very vital question. It was, we think, this problem
that engaged the author of the *Legenda*, the significance of which the
author of the Donation clearly and fully grasped. Although his source
only suggested an answer, he gave it explicitly. And in giving his
answer, he at the same time contributed a good deal to the fixation and
development of papal doctrine.

The change effected by Constantine's transfer to the East did not
concern the political institution of the Roman empire as such, but
merely affected the seat of the emperor, that is, the actual place where
the imperial crown was worn. The author of the Donation, like his
source, realized this vital point. That is why he offers an explanation
for the transfer of the capital by Constantine: he makes the emperor

---

[1] Eichmann's terminology.

[2] *Dictatus Papae*, cap. viii: "Quod *solus* papa uti possit imperialibus insigniis."
See on this especially Schramm, art. cit., p. 413 f. We should also note that the
imperial prerogative of a solemn public procession was now to be a papal prerogative "ad imitationem imperii nostri." There were perfectly genuine models
for the forger, if he had known history a little better. The Roman acclamations
on first receiving the picture of the new emperor were transferred to the person
of the pope, certainly by 686 when the *Lib. Pont.* reports, i. 368: "in eius laude
omnes simul acclamaverunt"; cf. Schramm, *Die Anerkennung Karls d. Gr.*,
Munich, 1952, pp. 19–20.

4*

declare that it would be inappropriate for an emperor to reside in the same place in which the divinely instituted head of the Christian religion has his seat, hence his decision to transfer his capital and to build a new city in the East.[1]

When we now link this explanation of the transfer with the refusal of the pope to wear the imperial crown, it will be seen that Constantine removed the crown from Rome to Constantinople with papal connivance. If the pope so wished, he could have worn the crown himself: the crown was his, but out of his own volition he refused to wear, that is, to *use* it.[2] Since Constantine had worn a crown after the removal to Byzantium, he wore it—we merely try to follow the author's thought—because the pope had acquiesced in Constantine's wearing it: Silvester had acquiesced in Constantine's transferring the crown from Rome to Byzantium, which city then became the capital of the Roman empire as a consequence of the emperor's residence. Moreover, Constantine bound all his successors to respect the constitutional arrangements which he had made with the pope, hence all post-Constantinean emperors, including the present one, must adhere to the enactments—which meant that their crown was there by papal acquiescence. The crown of the *Roman* empire was in Constantinople on sufferance by the pope: this is how Constantinople became an *urbs regia*. But this right to wear the crown in Constantinople could be withdrawn. In short, the historical fact of the capital's transfer was utilized for ideological purposes: it was presented as the effluence of papal volition.

All this marks a complete reversal of the state of things. Instead of the papacy, constitutionally, being subjected to the Roman emperor,

---

[1] See cap. 18: "Unde congruum prospeximus, nostrum imperium et regni potestatem orientalibus transferri ac transmutari regionibus et in Byzantiae provincia in optimo loco nomini nostro civitatem aedificari et nostrum illic constitui imperium; quoniam, ubi principatus sacerdotum et christianae religionis caput ab imperatore coelesti constitutum est, justum non est, ut illic imperator terrenus habeat potestatem."

[2] "quam (coronam) ex capite nostro illi *concessimus* . . . non est passus *uti* corona," cap. 16, quoted supra 80 n. 3. W. Ohnsorge, art. cit., p. 82, maintains that the Donation presupposes two real crowns, the one which Constantine left to the pope, and the other which he took with himself to Byzantium. This is precisely the mistake which Ohnsorge makes and which leads him to see in the Donation the papal expression of the Two-Emperor problem and a subsequent legitimation of the act of 800 (p. 86). But there is no warrant in the document for the statement that there were two crowns, see cap. 16 and cap. 18 (quoted supra, note 1). Cf. now also the observations of H. Löwe in *Deutsches Archiv*, ix (1952), p. 579.

it now turns out that the Roman emperor derives his right to wear the crown from papal acquiescence. But thereby also the whole Eastern regal-sacerdotal ideology was thrown overboard, or at least an attempt was made to do so—no wonder the East never recognized the Donation. The Roman emperor had no right, according to the Donation, to dictate to the papacy, because he wore the crown, that most conspicuous symbol that showed him to the world as the emperor, by virtue of papal acquiescence in Constantine's taking it to Constantinople. The crown was the pope's as a result of Constantine's grant, but he allowed its use to Constantine and his successors. In brief, the "true" state of things was the exact reverse of what the Eastern emperors had held it to be.

In order to explain the change of capital, the author takes recourse to ideology. Ideology furnishes him with the tools by means of which he gives the answer to that vital question of how Constantinople became the capital of the Roman empire.[1] But as regards the purpose of the Donation, its inherent ideology also concerns the function, the finis, the *raison d'être* of the Roman emperor. For what the author tries to express in these fact- and time-tied terms was the right order of things in the Roman-Christian world. The Roman empire pretended to be Christian. But past history had all too clearly shown that the Christianity of the emperor was more than questionable, since he had continually remonstrated against the Roman-papal exposition of the faith—we recall Leo III's stereotyped "I am king and priest"—and even openly attacked the position of the Roman Church. Again, our mind turns back to the fifth century when the Roman emperor was said to be "filius," not "praesul ecclesiae." He should follow, it was then said, the doctrinal and jurisdictional rulings of the Roman Church, not rebel against it, and not set himself above the priests: "exsecutiones suas ecclesiasticis praesulibus subdere debet," for this is the proper way of governing a Christian society as the Roman empire wishes to be considered. It is the function of the Roman-Christian

---

[1] This ideology which the author of the *Legenda* already had wished to express, might well have been suggested to him by the private letter of Emperor Honorius to Theodosius II in 421. In this letter the emperor said: "Procul dubio illius urbis ecclesia speciali nobis cultu veneranda est, *ex qua et Romanum principatum accepimus* et principium sacerdotium accepit," P. Coustant, *Epp. Rom. Pont.*, p. 1029 (PL. l. 769 f., in Boniface I's letters). Cf. with this also the stipulation of the *Legenda* itself, supra p. 79 and Nicholas I's statement to the Eastern emperor, infra p. 200. On the dossier in which this private letter was contained, see E. Caspar, op. cit., i. 601, 608. The new edition by C. Silva-Tarouca of this dossier, the *Collectio Thessalonicensis*, Rome, 1937, was not accessible to me.

emperor to subordinate himself to the rulings of the priests who alone know what is, and what is not, Christian, and who accordingly expound the dogma. "Nos habemus sensum Christi" Gregory II had declared shortly before.

A Roman emperor follows the Roman Church: if he does not, he ceases to be a Roman emperor; and becomes a Greek emperor. The prototype of all Roman-Christian emperors was Constantine. What Gelasius had so tenderly and subtly expressed, was now brought down to symbolic earthiness. Gelasius's idea of the emperor's holding his empire as a "beneficium" conferred by God, as a divine favour, not as a right, was now in the mid-eighth century contained in the view that the Byzantine emperor held his crown by papal connivance, that is, by papal favour. The divine favour appears in the cloak of a papal favour.[1] A favour can be withdrawn. As regards the idea itself, there is no difference between Gelasius and the Donation. In a Roman-Christian world there is no room for autonomous rulership: rulership is a favour, a "beneficium": it is not *sui juris*.

Thus seen, the Donation is not as inept as it is nowadays the fashion to denounce it. Credit must be given where credit is due. True, we must look beneath the trappings, if we wish to detect its contents which culminate in the representation of the function of a Ruler in a Christian society. What in the last resort the author of the Donation is concerned with is the problem of legitimate rulership in a Roman-Christian world: born and bred in the milieu of the Roman empire, it could not express this problem in any other terms but those of its surroundings, the Roman empire. The ideology, or the substance of the product, is not an invention: history is harnessed to the service of an ideological programme. Later medieval thought will develop the theory of the Ruler's function in a Christian society, within the *corpus Christi*, and most of this later theory will be quite independent of the Donation: and in so far papal doctrine was permanent. The Donation marks a transitory stage in the development of the papal theme.[2]

[1] It is at this point that the fundamental idea of the pope's mediatory role assumes its true importance. We recall the statement of Stephen II, *Cod. Car.*, no. 7, p. 493: "Vos Dominus *per* humilitatem meam *mediante* Petro unxit in reges . . ."

[2] Although primarily intended against the East, the Donation by virtue of its underlying ideology (which was no invention) was easily adaptable to Western conditions, too. This, we believe, explains its usefulness to later papal generations. Its original purpose, however, was never quite forgotten, as Leo IX's full quotation of the Donation in the troubles with Michael Kerrularios proved, cf. also infra p. 268. But there can be no doubt about the weakness of the document which derived the *Papstkaiser's* position from an imperial act. As long as the pope's

There is, however, an important observation which must be made. We have tried to show the meaning that could be attached to "Roman," namely, a purely religious one. Through the efficacy of the Donation a second meaning of "Roman" begins to emerge which in course of time will take its place next to the religious connotation of the term. This second meaning of "Roman" was historical-political. It belongs to a category of thinking entirely different from that implied by the other meaning. The notion of "Roman emperor" was political and denoted rulership: it denoted universality of dominion, at least conceptually. Now the empire whose capital was in the East, was Roman, because it directly continued that entity that had formerly arisen from *Roma antiqua*; in its genesis that empire and that emperor had nothing to do with the Church of Rome; the continuation of the Roman empire in the East, too, had (historically) nothing to do with the Church of Rome. By turning fact into fiction, namely by "explaining" the transfer of the capital, the Donation interlocked this historical-political Romanism and papal ideology. The ideational universality of the Roman Church and the ideational universality of the Roman emperor's function from now onwards are inextricably associated. The political repercussions on East and West were unforeseeable.

The crown symbolized rulership. The papal disposal of the Roman crown[1] signified the true monarchic position of the pope in the Roman-Christian world: the Roman Church as the epitome of a universal entity, Christianity, can through the pope confer only universal rulership, and the only such rulership available and understandable was that of Roman emperorship. The pope confers the crown in order to be in a position to govern Christian society, the *corpus Christi*.[2] The papal creation of the universal Ruler, the Roman emperor, has a definite purpose: the Roman emperor is not created a monarch, but a *defensor*

---

vicariate of Christ (Who was both king and priest; and Who had *imperium* and *potestas*) was not developed, this construction was indeed necessary. It was not until Innocent III that the vicariate of Christ was fully developed—but then the Donation was also "devalued" by him, cf. *Sermo in festo b. Silvestri*, PL. ccxvii. 481–2.

[1] We take note that after the abortive attempt of 800 the pope travelled to Rheims with Constantine's crown, in order to crown Louis I; cf. infra p. 143 ff.

[2] If we understand the late Eichmann correctly, he too seems to have sensed this, when he explained Silvester's refusal to wear the crown: "In Wirklichkeit lag in der Ablehnung des Gebrauchs das Eingeständnis, dass das Papsttum die ihm zugedachte Rolle nicht selbst übernehmen konnte, weil die militärischen Kräfte fehlten . . . es war indirekt doch gesagt, dass der Papst sie (the crown) eigentlich tragen konnte und durfte, dass er über sie verfügen und sie weitergeben kann," *Weihe . . . des Papstes im MA*, pp. 28–9.

or *advocatus* of the Roman Church. This is his function, his *raison d'être*, whilst the dignity of his rulership ascends to the highest available degree, to that of Roman emperorship. That is the reason why the political concept of universal rulership, of Roman emperorship, becomes henceforth an integral part of papal theory. The emancipation of the papacy from the Eastern imperial nexus is the prelude to the papal nexus of the Western Roman emperor, soon to be the "specialis filius" of the Roman Church. In other words, the teleology of functions has led to a teleology of history.[1] The Roman emperor's function is that of an *adjutor* of the Roman Church: a Byzantine cannot perform this function, only a Roman can. The religious Romanism of the king was the presupposition for his political role as a Roman emperor, as the "unicus filius ecclesiae Romanae."

[1] From a contemporary point of view the Donation seems to have fulfilled Isidore's criterion, namely, that "argumentum est ficta res, quae tamen fieri potuit," quotation by K. Pivec, in MIOG. lx (1952), p. 416 (book review). This teleology of history was not of course invented by the forger: it was at least as old as St Ambrose and St Augustine, and could be seen at work in a number of purely doctrinal topics, cf. supra p. 14. In this context attention might be drawn to the teleological interpretation of the Old Testament, for instance, by Isidore of Seville who relies heavily on St Augustine's teleology, cf. *Quaestiones in Vetus Testamentum*, PL. lxxxiii. 209 ff.

# CHAPTER III

# *Charlemagne*

## I

ALTHOUGH it had emancipated itself from the constitutional framework of the Eastern empire, the papacy had little cause to rejoice in its newly won "freedom." The position of the pope as the lord of the Duchy of Rome drew the Roman nobility conspicuously to the fore: it now demanded a share in the making of the pope and the "election" of Constantine (II), himself a soldier, and the subsequent tumultuous scenes brought forth a vigorous opposition party under the able leadership of Christophorus.[1] The Council held at Rome in April 769 in which many Frankish bishops[2] as well as of course still more Italian bishops participated, proceeded to the condemnation of Constantine (II)[3] and, what is more important for us, to the promulgation of an election decree. This election decree was later to serve as the model on which a better known papal election decree was built. The synodists of 769 laid down that no layman must partake in the election of a pope—only clerics were allowed to vote, whilst all the laymen were permitted to do was to salute the thus elected pope as the "lord of all."[4]

This election decree, however, lacked proper backing. And the subsequent history of papal elections and consecrations and the ever-

---

[1] Whom we have already met as a possible author of the Donation of Constantine.

[2] Those of Sens, Mainz, Tours, Lyons, Bourges, Narbonne, Rheims, Amiens, Langres, Worms, Wurzburg, and so forth.

[3] The treatment which Constantine received at the episcopal hands of the synodists was very cruel indeed, even by contemporary standards.

[4] MGH. *Concilia*, ii. no. 14, p. 86: "Decernimus, ut nulli unquam laicorum sive ex manu armata vel ex aliis ordinibus praesumant inveniri in electione pontificis, set a cunctis sacerdotibus atque proceribus ecclesiae et cuncto clero ipsa pontificalis electio proveniat. Et postquam pontifex electus fuerit et in patriarchium deductus, tunc optimates militiae vel cunctus exercitus et cives honesti atque universa generalitas populi huius Romanae urbis ad salutandum eum sicut omnium dominum properare debent." This is also in the *Coll. canon.* of Deusdedit, ii. 161, cf. also Gratian, *Dist.* lxxix, cap. 4.

increasing military influence of the Roman nobility made it imperative for the papacy to appoint an effective protector, a protector who was to guarantee the "freedom" of papal elections and thereby also to guarantee the authority of the newly elected pope. In course of time this need for protection was to lead to a number of special arrangements made in the ninth century which were to enshrine in documentary form the defence and protection of the Roman Church and herewith of the pope himself.

None was better qualified for this office than the Frankish "patricius Romanorum." Whilst the father had refused to bear the title, the son adopted it, certainly from 774 onwards. The intimate connexion between the Roman Church and the Frankish Church no less than the strengthening of the bonds between it and the Frankish monarchy in the two decades since Ponthion, were not without effects upon the mind of Charlemagne. The acceptance of the title and office of "patricius Romanorum" by Charlemagne is, we think, the effect, not of any political consideration on his part, but of his purely religious views. To him "Romanitas" and "Christianitas" were tautological expressions. Romanism for Charlemagne was not a historical-political term, but had an exclusively religious connotation: it signified the contrast to "Grecism," to that kind of faith which was not Roman-directed. Romanism simply meant Latin Christianity—that Christian faith which was directed and orientated by the Roman Church. The Bonifacian work, its concomitant close association with Roman-papal organization, the spreading of the characteristically Roman liturgies and their prayers, the religious orientation of the Frankish domains towards Rome, led to a complete amalgamation of Christian and Roman elements. This Roman ferment in that eighth-century Christianity of the Franks was of decisive importance, because "Christianitas" and "Romanitas" became virtually indistinguishable.[1] It is assuredly no coincidence that Charlemagne requested Adrian I for an "authentic" copy of the sacramentary which the great Gregory had created.[2] It is furthermore significant that at this time also the Benedictine Rule

[1] Cf. also the observations of G. Ermini, "Tradizione di Roma e unità giuridica europea" in *Archivio della R. Dep. Romana di storia patria*, lxvii, 1944, especially pp. 46–51. A number of new *Ordines* were composed in this eighth century by the Franks, cf. (Andrieu's) nos. xv–xviii, xxii, xxv, xxvii–xxxB.

[2] On this see G. Tellenbach, *SB. Heidelberg*, 1935, p. 24: "Es scheint im ganzen Frankenreich grosser Eifer geherrscht zu haben, sich eine Abschrift von diesem echten römischen Ritus darstellenden Buch zu verschaffen." Cf. furthermore Th. Klauser, "Die liturgischen Austauschbeziehungen, etc." in *Hist. Jb.*, liii (1933), p. 178, and P. E. Schramm, *Die Anerkennung Karls d. Grossen*, p. 21.

with its typically Roman features spread so rapidly through Frankish and newly conquered lands. Not less significant is it that a copy of the canonical collection of Dionysius Exiguus in the expanded and modified form given by Adrian I was personally handed to Charlemagne by the pope in 774.[1]

All these vehicles of Romanist transmission effected the imperceptible, though significant orientation towards Rome in all things that mattered most, namely, in those of religion and its cult. The old Roman formulae were repeated, the old Roman liturgical prayers were said and spoken by the Franks who might not always have fully grasped the intrinsic meaning of these prayers. The prayer that was originally in the Leonine Sacramentary[2] went in its original form and with the entreaty for the *Roman* security into the Frankish sacramentaries.[3] In other prayers the amalgamation of "Christianitas" and "Romanitas" went so far that the original term "Romanus" was exchanged for "Christianus." Thus, for example, in the Gelasian sacramentary[4] the reference to the "Romani" was altered in the Frankish sacramentaries to "Christiani."[5] In yet another of the prayer texts, contained in the Gelasian Sacramentary of the eighth century[6] for a copy of which

---

[1] See F. Maassen, *Geschichte der Quellen,* i. 441 ff.; Fournier-Le Bras, *Histoire des collections canoniques,* i. 95–6. The *Dionysio-Hadriana* also spread quickly, see Maassen, op. cit., pp. 465 ff.; Fournier-Le Bras, op. cit., i. 97. The acrostic and dedicatory poem offering the collection to Charlemagne renders the words: "Domino excell. filio Carulo magno regi Hadrianus papa." The poem is printed also by Duchesne in his edition of the *Liber Pontificalis,* i. 516 and by Maassen, pp. 965–7. On the other canonical collection, the *Quesnelliana,* also copied several times in Frankish lands (PL. lvi. 358–747), cf. W. Levison, "Neue Bruchstücke der Quesnellschen Sammlung" in *Papsttum & Kaisertum* (Festschrift Paul Kehr), pp. 138–45 and Fournier and Le Bras, i. 27.·It was used by Pippin in his *Capitulare* of 755, see Maassen, p. 494, and M. Andrieu, op. cit., iii. pp. xxxvii f.

[2] *Sacramentarium Leonianum,* ed. C. Feltoe, no. 375, p. 77; see Tellenbach, Texts, no. 13: "Omnipotens semper Deus *Romanis* auxiliare principibus ut tua virtute roboratis, omnis hostilitas nec viribus possit praevalere nec fraude. Nostris quaesumus, domine, propitiare temporibus, ut tuo munere dirigantur et *Romana* securitas et devotio *Christiana.*" On the Good Friday prayer for the "imperium Romanum" see Tellenbach, loc. cit., and W. Levison, *England & the Continent,* Oxford, 1946, pp. 122–3.

[3] See especially Tellenbach, loc. cit., at text 13, p. 59, where the Frankish sources will be found.

[4] *Sacramentarium Gelasianum,* ed. H. A. Wilson, no. 729, and no. 275; Tellenbach, Text no. 7.

[5] "Deus, servientium tibi fortitudo regnorum, propitius *Romani* (in Frankish sources: Christianorum) nominis esto principibus, ut quorum tibi subjecta est humilitas eorum ubique excellentior sit potestas."

[6] *Sacramentarium Gelasianum saeculi octavi:* cf. P. de Puniet, "Le sacramentaire Gelasien de la collection Phillips" in *Ephemerides Liturgicae,* xliii (1929), pp. 91 ff.; 281 ff.; Tellenbach, loc. cit., p. 19.

Pippin had already asked the pope, we find the amalgamation still more pronounced. The original prayer for security of the "Romani fines" was changed into one for security of the "Christianorum Romani fines."

Deus . . . pax a tua pietate concessa Romanos fines—Christianorum Romanos fines—ab omni hoste faciat esse securos.

In short, the Romanization of the Western mind by virtue of these diverse channels, led to the ideological conflation of Romans and Christians.

Set against this background it is perhaps understandable that Charlemagne should have had no hesitation in adopting the title and in playing the role of the "patricius Romanorum." When "Romanus" equalled "Christianus," there was indeed no obstacle to prevent his assuming that role which virtually meant no more than that of a military defender of the "Romans," that is the "Christians," a role which in fact he was accustomed to play in any case. What the title meant to him was that his protective function naturally embraced also those Romans who were the epitome of all the Romans in the world, that is, the geographical Romans: they were merely the Christians, as it were, in a condensed and crystallized form. And it was in his function as "patricius Romanorum," in his function as a protector of the Church of Rome, that he not only confirmed the "donation" of his father, but also added a considerable part of Italy to the territories which his father had "restored" to their rightful owner, the Church of Rome.

The biography of Adrian I informs us of the details of this "donation" as well as of the solemn reception given by the pope: Charlemagne[1] was received with all the honours due to the former exarch, now transformed into the "patricius Romanorum."[2] According to Adrian's biographer,[3] on the Wednesday following Easter, 6 April 774, Charlemagne ordered his chaplain and notary Etherius to draw up two copies of the "donation," the one to be handed to the pope, the other

---

[1] *Liber Pontificalis*, i. 497, lines 6–7: "Ipse vero a Deo institutus benignissimus Carolus magnus Francorum rex et *patricius Romanorum*."

[2] *Lib. Pont.*, loc. cit., lines 8 ff. According to E. Kantorowicz, *Laudes regiae*, Berkeley, 1946, p. 75–6, Charlemagne's entry into Rome "had a decidedly messianic note"; it may have been that the antiphon which was customary on such occasions, the *Ecce mitto angelum meum* greeted Charlemagne also: the symbolic meaning of this antiphon is that as the Lord at His coming is preceded by a messenger, so shall the emperor at his advent be preceded by an angel, see Kantorowicz, loc. cit. For the antiphon see *Consuetudines Farfenses*, quoted by Kantorowicz, op. cit., p. 72, note 27 (MGH. SS. xi. 547).

[3] *Lib. Pont.* i. 498.

to be deposited at the Confession of St Peter. This instrument was drawn up and modelled on that made twenty years earlier.[1] Charlemagne conceded to St Peter, and vowed that he would hand over to the pontiff, the territories enumerated, that is, Luna (near Specia), Parma, Reggio, Mantua, Monteselice, the "exarchate of Ravenna," the whole of Venetia and Istria; Corsica, the duchies of Spoleto and Benevento.[2] Although the biographer does not speak of a restitution but of a concession of territory, Einhard, on the other hand, considered the transaction as a "restitution" of stolen territory. This witness tells us that Charlemagne would not rest before he had subdued Desiderius and expelled him, nor before all the robbed territories were restored to the Romans.[3]

It seems clear that the Easter transaction of 774 had the same character as its precursor of twenty years earlier: in each case the transaction concerned "restoration" of property, stolen by the Lombards from its legitimate owner, the Roman Church. The test here as there lies in the transfer of property that was not in the hands of the Lombards—in our case, Venetia and Istria, to mention only the two most conspicuous examples. For both Venetia and Istria were still Byzantine and therefore belonged to the empire. The insistent demands of the pope put to Charlemagne for the implementation of the "donation"

---

[1] *Lib. Pont.* i. 498, lines 13–17: "Cumque ipsam promissionem, quae Franca in loco qui vocatur Carisiaco fact est, sibi relegi fecisset, conplacuerunt illi et eius judicibus omnia quae ibidem erant adnexa. Et propria voluntate, bono ac libenti animo, aliam donationis promissionem ad instar anterioris ipse antedictus precellentissimus et revera christianissimus Carulus Francorum rex adscribi jussit per Etherium, religiosum ac prudentissimum capellanum et notarium suum."

[2] *Lib. Pont.* i. 498, lines 17–22: "Ubi concessit easdem civitates et territoria b. Petro easque prefato pontifici contradi spopondit per designatum confinium, sicut in eadem donatione continere monstratur, id est: a Lunis cum insula Corsica, deinde in Suriano, deinde in monte Bardone, id est, in Verceto, deinde in Parma, deinde in Regio; et exinde in Mantua atque Monte Silicis, simulque et universum exarchatum Ravennantium, sicut antiquitus erat, atque provincias Venetiarum et Istria; necnon et cunctum ducatum Spolitinum seu Beneventanum." On the interpretation of this most important passage see Duchesne, *Lib. Pont.*, Introduction, pp. ccxxxiv–ccxli; Th. Sickel, *Das Privilegium Ottos I*, pp. 132–7 (who denies the veracity of this statement); A. Dove, "Corsica und Sardinien etc." in *SB. Munich*, 1894, pp. 230 ff.; E. Caspar, *Pippin und die Römische Kirche*, pp. 82 ff.; A. Brackmann, *Gött. Gel. Anz.*, 1918, pp. 419 ff.; E. E. Stengel, "Die Entwicklung des Kaiserprivilegs für die römische Kirche" in *Hist. Z.*, cxxxiv (1926), pp. 231 ff.; L. Halphen, op. cit., pp. 108–10. The literature about this passage is abundant and not of direct concern to us.

[3] Einhard, *Vita Karoli*, cap. 6, p. 7 (ed. Holder-Egger): "Karolus . . . non prius destitit quam et Desiderium regem . . . in deditionem susciperet . . . omnia Romanis erepta *restitueret*." A few lines later, p. 8: "Res a Langobardorum regibus ereptae Adriano Romanae ecclesiae rectori *restitutae*."

of 6 April 774, show us the rift between the pope's intentions and the king's actions, a rift that seems to have become particularly clear after Charlemagne's assumption of the title "Rex Langobardorum" on 5 June 774.[1] What is, moreover, very characteristic of these many letters sent by the pope, is the emphasis on the function of the Roman Church as the "spiritualis mater" of the king and the emphasis on his duty of protecting his spiritual mother—for this reason, if for no other, he ought to be a fighter "pro justitiis beati Petri exigendis."[2] The prospect of appropriate reward is not omitted in these papal letters: if he fulfilled his promises the king would exalt the Roman Church and herewith the universal Church, and thereby the orthodox Christian faith would be preserved.[3]

The exaltation by Charlemagne of the Roman Church is in fact the dominant theme in all these numerous papal appeals to the Frankish king. In one of his communications the pope goes even so far as to remind Charlemagne of the exaltation of the Roman Church by the Emperor Constantine: he is held up to the Frank as the model, for he had exalted the Church through his grant and had bestowed upon the pope these parts of the West, so that the "sancta Dei ecclesia" might flourish and blossom forth. "Et pro hoc petimus eximiam precellentiam vestram, ut in integro ipsa patrimonia beato Petro et nobis *restituere* jubeatis."[4] Divers emperors, Adrian I claims, patricians and other God-fearing men had conceded to St Peter and the apostolic Roman Church territories, such as Tuscany, Spoleto, Corsica, and so forth, and "of these transactions we have the documents in our Lateran archives."[5]

---

[1] See, for instance, the bitter and ironical tone in the pope's letter, *Codex Carolinus*, no. 49, p. 568, lines 25 ff. (exeunte 774), and also no. 53, p. 575 (anno 775). On the interpretation of Charlemagne's conduct after 774, see Dove, loc. cit., pp. 187 ff.

[2] *Codex Carolinus*, no. 56, p. 581, lines 25–6.

[3] *Codex Carolinus*, no. 55, p. 579, lines 9 ff.: "Unde et copiosum a vobis suscipi prestolamus fructum, ut, sicut coepisti, bonum opus perficias tuisque temporibus sancta Dei ecclesia multo amplius exaltata permaneat, quatenus omnipotens Dominus, intercedente b. Petro principe apostolorum, dignam vobis remunerationem tribuat et in coelestibus regnis cum sanctis et electis post huius vitae longevitatem perenniter exaltandum vos recipiat. Per te enim, bone, victoriosissime rex, praefata sancta universalis Dei ecclesia de inimicorum impugnationibus erepta magno, ut dictum est, triumphat gaudio et orthodoxa Christianorum fides vestro praesidio in pristino venerationis statu permanet inmutilata." In *Cod. Car.*, no. 56, p. 581, lines 32–3 Adrian says Charlemagne had "offered" the Duchy of Spoleto "protectori vestro b. Petro principi apostolorum per nostram mediocritatem pro animae vestrae mercede."

[4] *Cod. Car.*, no. 60, p. 587, lines 27–8 (anno 778).

[5] *Cod. Car.*, no. 60, p. 587, lines 18 ff.: "Sed et cuncta alia, quae per diversos

Hence Charlemagne should imitate the great emperor Constantine who had exalted the Church under Silvester so enormously and who had given the Roman Church the "potestas" over these Western parts of the world.[1]

Even though the pope's territorial ambitions remained largely unfulfilled,[2] the papal creations of Pippin, Charles's son, as "King of Italy," and of Louis as "King of Aquitaine," when there was no precedent for these offices and for papal conferments of royal dignity and function, should be appraised adequately as regards their symbolic significance.[3] Taken in conjunction with the creation of the Carolingian "patricius Romanorum" by Stephen II, these actions throw into clear relief the steady continuity of papal doctrine and plainly herald the much more significant act on Christmasday 800. Ponthion, Kierzy, Pavia, the creation of the "patricius Romanorum," Charlemagne's donation, the creation of the Italian and Aquitanian kings—these are powerful preparatory steps culminating in the creation of Charlemagne as "Imperator Romanorum." It is as if the papal theme gained momentum towards the closing years of the eighth century.[4]

---

imperatores, patricios etiam et alios Deum timentes pro eorum animae mercede et venia delictorum in partibus Tusciae, Spoletio seu Benevento atque Corsica simul Savinense patrimonio b. Petro . . . concessa sunt . . . vestris temporibus *restituantur.*"

[1] *Cod. Car.*, no. 60: "Et sicut temporibus b. Silvestri Romani pontificis a sanctae recordationis piissimo Constantino, magno imperatore, per eius largitatem sancta Dei catholica et apostolica Romana ecclesia elevata atque exaltata est et in potestatem in his Hesperiae partibus largiri dignatus, ita et in his vestris felicissimis temporibus atque nostris sancta Dei ecclesia, id est, b. Petri apostoli, germinet atque exultet et amplius quam amplius exaltata permaneat, ut omnes gentes, quae haec audierint, edicere valeant 'Domine, salvum fac regem, et exaudi nos in die, in qua invocaverimus'; quia ecce *novus* Christianissimus Dei *Constantinus* imperator *his temporibus* surrexit, per quem omnia Deus sanctae suae ecclesiae beati apostolorum principis Petri largiri dignatus est."

[2] It is not our task to go into the details of Charlemagne's refusal to meet all the papal requests; suffice it to say that he demanded production of the documents to which the pope had referred and which were supposed to contain the "donations." His request was refused. For details see E. Caspar, "Das Papsttum unter fränkischer Herrschaft" in *Z. f. Kirchengeschichte*, 1935, p. 158.

[3] Both were anointed by the pope, see *Annales Regni Francorum*, ed. G. Waitz, ad a. 781, p. 56: "Et duo filii supradicti domini Caroli regis uncti sunt in regem a supradicto pontifice, hi sunt domnus Pippinus et domnus Hludowicus reges, domnus Pippinus rex in Italiam, et domnus Hludowicus rex in Aquitaniam."

[4] Cf. also the observation of K. Hampe, "Italien u. Deutschland im Wandel der Zeiten" in *Hist. Z.*, cxxxiv (1926), p. 202: "Der Papst war es, der zur Vollendung seiner eigenen Ablösung von Byzanz den römischen Kaisertitel darauf propfte. Damit wurde das eigentümlich antiquierte, auf einer Fiktion beruhende Gebilde des mittelalterlich-römischen Kaisertums geschaffen."

For we must bear in mind that during the pontificate of Leo III there were some very specific signs pointing to great changes. It will be recalled that, according to the *Liber Diurnus*, the newly elected pope was to announce his election to the emperor or, in order to save time, to the exarch at Ravenna, so as to obtain imperial confirmation of the election. But when Leo III became pope, there was no longer an exarch nor did the papacy consider itself as part of the Roman empire. Yet Leo III sent a "decretalis cartula" to Charlemagne immediately after his election. We hold that the reason why the deed of the election was despatched, was not indeed to adhere to an obnoxious system—the requirement of imperial confirmation was of course fundamentally inimical to the papal point of view—but in order to utilize this old rule for quite a different purpose: the papacy thereby implied clearly the role for which the Frankish king was destined—that of an emperor, for it was the emperor (or on his behalf the exarch) who had to give imperial confirmation to the papal election. But whilst the purpose of notification was previously to obtain imperial confirmation, the purpose now was, we consider, to implement the duty of the protector of the Roman Church and of the pope. The notification was to serve as the signal to the "patricius Romanorum" that a new pope had assumed his office, who is now to be protected by the patrician.[1]

Furthermore, Adrian I had disregarded the rule laid down by Justinian[2] that all documents, including therefore papal ones, must be dated according to imperial years.[3] Leo III definitely abandoned this prescription of Justinian, but substituted in a document issued on 20 April 798, the regnal years of Charlemagne's rule in Italy for the imperial years (of the Eastern emperor).[4] The idea behind this innovation was the same as in the case of notification: it was to indicate the role for which the Frankish king was destined.[5]

---

[1] In view of the events in his pontificate this notification seems particularly significant. But Leo was not the first pope who announced his election to a Frankish king; the first to do so was Paul I in 757, see *Codex Carolinus*, no. 12; for Constantine (II) see *Cod. Car.*, no. 44. For details see *Cambridge Hist. J.*, xi (1953), pp. 114 ff., and F. Gutmann, *Die Wahlanzeigen der Päpste*, Marburg, 1931, p. 19.                    [2] *Nov.* xlvii, cap. 1.

[3] See R. L. Poole, "Imperial influences on papal documents" in *Proc. Brit. Acad.*, viii (1917), p. 240; idem, *Lectures on the history of the papal chancery*, p. 38; A. Menzer, "Die Jahresmerkmale in den Datierungen der Papsturkunden" in *Römische Quartalschrift*, xl (1932), pp. 27 ff. Adrian I was "a bold innovator" (p. 62), because he introduced the dating according to pontifical years.

[4] See A. Brackmann, *Germania Pontificia*, i. no. 7, p. 8; Poole, loc. cit., p. 241; Menzer, art. cit., pp. 48–51.

[5] In this context mention must be made of Adrian I's striking his own coins

The plan of Charlemagne to erect a Second Rome at Aix-la-Chapelle was an additional motive for Leo III to expedite matters in the direction in which they had already been moving. This plan of Charlemagne was revealed to him on the occasion of his visit to Paderborn in the summer of 799. Expelled by the Romans Leo sought to implore the help of the protector, the "patricius Romanorum." We shall have an opportunity to make some observations on what may be called Charlemagne's imitative rivalry with the Eastern emperor, but for the moment it must suffice to state that the residence of the Frank at Aix was largely modelled on the residence of the Eastern emperor, who lived in "New Rome" and, moreover, had at hand his chief priest, the patriarch. According to Charlemagne, the "Old Rome" was to be transplanted to Aix: next to the minster and the "*sacrum* palatium" which was the residence of the Frankish king, there was a third building, the "Lateran."[1] Like Constantinople, Aix was to be the Second Rome: the Lateran is in fact the "house of the pontiff" in Einhard's description.[2] And the court poet tells us of the "coming Rome"—"ventura Roma"—which Charlemagne is about to erect at Aix.[3] It was the *secunda Roma*.[4]

which showed his effigy instead of the emperor's: the old imperial coins were discarded; on this see W. Ohnsorge, *Das Zweikaiserproblem*, p. 20, and P. E. Schramm, *Anerkennung*, p. 14. A portentous sign post was also the famous Lateran mosaic in the triclinium, the great ceremonial hall, which was made in the first years of Leo's pontificate; the picture showed St Peter handing the standard to Charlemagne, and the pallium to Leo; on the picture see Duchesne in *Lib. Pont.* ii. p. 34, note 14; Tellenbach, loc. cit., p. 32, note 5; S. Heldmann, *Kaisertum Karls d. Gr.*, 184–5; G. Lähr, *Die konstantinische Schenkung*, p. 11; Schramm, *Anerkennung*, p. 26; and H. Fichtenau, art. cit. (infra, note 2), p. 41, note 207. The picture is in Schramm, *Die deutschen Kaiser und Könige in Bildern*, Table 4a–b; a description will be found ibid., vol. i, pp. 27–9. Cf. also infra p. 101 n. 4.
   [1] See especially C. Erdmann, "Das ottonische Reich" in *Deutsches Archiv*, iv (1943), p. 418; idem, *Forschungen zur Ideenwelt des Frühmittelalters*, Berlin, 1951, p. 23; cf. also *Chron. Moissiacense*, MGH. SS. i. 303: "Fecit ibi et palatium, quod nominavit Lateranis"; see also "Capitulare monasticum" in MGH. *Capit.* i. 344: "in domo Aquisgrani palatii, quae Lateranis dicitur"; cf. furthermore MGH. *Concilia*, ii. no. 40, p. 464, note 1, and no. 56, p. 705.
   [2] Einhard, *Vita*, cap. 32, p. 32: "domus pontificis." Cf. Erdmann, art. cit., pp. 418 ff., and op. cit., p. 24; also H. Fichtenau, "Byzanz und die Pfalz" in MIOG., lix, 1951, pp. 13, 43–4.  †
   [3] The poem (MGH. *Poetae Lat.*, i. 366 ff.) was written (see Erdmann, op. cit., p. 21) in 799: "Stat pius arce procul Karolus loca singula signans, altaque disponens *venturae* moenia *Romae*." Charlemagne was to be the father of Europe and Leo the pastor: "Rex pater Europae et summus Leo pastor in orbe." (vv. 97, 504).  *
   [4] "Rex Karolus, caput orbis, amor populique decusque Europae venerandus apex, pater optimus, heros, augustus (!), sed et urbe potens, ubi *Roma secunda* flore novo, ingenti, magna consurgit ad alta mole, tholis muro precelsis sidera

When Leo III implored the help of Charlemagne, the latter's intentions cannot have remained hidden from the pope. Did not in fact everything point to a most uncomfortable exchange of Byzantium for Aix? Was this exchange not a repetition of the set-up which the papacy had hoped to relegate to the past? Did not Charlemagne's exhortation to the pope have an ominous ring: he should lead an honest life, respect the canons, guide the Church religiously and diligently and fight simony—when this is compared with Justinian's view on the functions of the priesthood?[1] What other role but that of an archpriest was the pope to play in the scheme of things devised by the Frank? For the king's task was the effective strengthening, consolidating, propagating and preserving the faith—the pope's task was to support the king in this duty by praying for him like Moses did with elevated hands.

The Carolingian idea of a Second Rome at Aix, we hold, was one of the most severe challenges which the papal programme had to meet. For if this scheme of things had gone through, the foundations of the papal theme would have been sapped. European Christianity drawing its life blood from Romanism and nurtured by the Church of Rome, would have been deprived of its strongest and most attractive foundations. To have acquiesced in this plan of Charlemagne would have been a betrayal of all the Church of *Rome* stood for.[2] And had not the instrument been carefully prepared, though primarily as a weapon against the East? The Donation of Constantine was precisely the handle by which the emancipation of the papacy from the clutches of the Eastern emperor could be effected: and the threatening clutches of the Frankish king were a sufficient justification for employing the same

---

tangens," quoted by Erdmann, op. cit., p. 22, who drew attention to the significance of this poem. Cf. also Fichtenau, art. cit., p. 39 and note 198; P. E. Schramm, *Anerkennung Karls d. Gr.*, pp. 33–4; and W. Hammer, "The New or Second Rome in the Middle Ages" in *Speculum*, xix (1944), p. 56, who also refers to, and quotes part of, another's poem which depicts the important position of the new capital, the New Rome. Never again was Aix-la-Chapelle praised in this manner (p. 57). Alcuin referred "Secunda Roma" to Constantinople, see Erdmann, op. cit., p. 22, note 9.

[1] MGH. *Epp.* iv. no. 92, p. 135 f.; cf. also ibid., no. 93, p. 138, and Justinian's *Nov.* vi. pr.

[2] We can but subscribe to the brilliant thesis of Erdmann, op. cit., p. 26: "Aber dieser Aachener Lateran war für Leo ein schlechter Trost. Ihm musste es auf den Sitz in Rom selbst ankommen, weil er sonst die geistigen Grundlagen seiner Stellung aufs schwerste kompromittierte; das hat sich noch ein halbes Jahrtausend später zu Avignon aureichend erwiesen." Cf. also Fichtenau, *Das karolingische Imperium*, Zürich, 1949, p. 79. Cf. also G. Ladner in *Die Welt als Geschichte*, xi (1951), p. 145.

weapon against him. The "vacancy" in the empire provided the pretext; Leo's trial by Charlemagne two days before Christmas provided the additional stimulus for the momentous action on Christmas Day—for the transfer of the empire from the Bosphorus to the Tiber, by making the Frank the *Imperator Romanorum*. The historic significance of the act is only heightened when this twofold objective is appraised: the coronation was aimed against the empire as well as against the Frankish king. The seat of the empire was where the pope wished it to be—the seat of the *Roman* empire was *Rome*, not Constantinople, not Aix-la-Chapelle.[1]

It was a magnificent political and symbolic device which Leo adopted.[2] There can be no doubt that the initiative lay in papal hands: the act was well prepared—the Romans knew exactly what they had to shout,[3] although no pope had ever crowned an emperor in Rome.[4] The accounts in the official papal book[5] and in the Frankish

[1] The bold, not to say, fantastic plan of Leo III to arrange a marriage between the recently widowed Charlemagne and the widow Irene, should not be dismissed as a piece of fabulous invention, cf. P. E. Schramm, *Anerkennung*, p. 59; also F. L. Ganshof in *Moyen Age*, lv (1949), p. 166, note 3. For the plan itself see Theophanes, *Chronographia*, ed. C. de Boor, i. 475, who mentions the plan twice (800 and 802); Heldmann, op. cit., 376 f.; F. Dölger, in *Der Vertrag von Verdun*, p. 217; W. Ohnsorge, op. cit., pp. 20, 26; idem, "Renovatio Regni Francorum" in *Festschrift zur Feier des 200 jährigen Bestandes des Staatsarchivs*, ed. L. Santifaller, Vienna, 1952, ii. 308, note 4: this plan originated "natürlich" in the head of the pope; H. Fichtenau, op. cit., pp. 85–6, and H. Beumann in *Stengel Festschrift*, Munster, 1952, p. 160. Had this marriage succeeded, East and West would have been united and by virtue of this union the claim to papal primacy over the Eastern Church would have come nearer to its realization, provided always that Charlemagne was the emperor of the Romans. In a way, Leo's plan might well be considered a peaceful forerunner of Gregory VII's plan to bring about the realization of the Roman primatial claim over the Eastern Church; cf. infra p. 306.

[2] We entirely agree with W. Ohnsorge's characterization of Leo III as "ein Mann von überragender Geistesbedeutung," see "Die Konstantinische Schenkung, Leo III und die Anfänge der kurialen Kaiseridee" in *Sav. Z. Germ. Abt.*, lxviii (1951), p. 98.

[3] E. Eichmann, *Kaiserkrönung*, i. 26: "Die Römer wussten genau, was sie zu rufen hatten"; also p. 28. Cf. also A. Dumas in DHE. xii. 439: "Evidemment cette cérémonie avait été preparée à l'avance, car chacun des participants connaissait le rôle qu'il devait jouer. Tous les actes s'en déroulèrent conformément au rituel qui était en usage à Byzance pour le couronnement de l'empereur."

[4] Duchesne, *Lib. Pont.* ii. 38, note 34: "Les anciens empereurs d'Occident n'ont jamais été couronnés par le pape."

[5] *Lib. Pont.* ii. 7: "Post haec, advenientem diem Natalis domini nostri Iesu Christi in jamdicta basilica b. Petri apostoli, omnes iterum congregati sunt. Et tunc venerabilis et almificus praesul manibus suis propriis pretiosissima corona coronavit eum. Tunc universi fideles Romani videntes tanta defensione et dilectione quam erga s. Romanam ecclesiam et eius vicarium habuit, unanimiter altisona voce, Dei nutu atque b. Petri clavigeri regni coelorum, exclamaverunt:

annals¹ are substantially the same: because the pope had put the crown on Charlemagne's head, the Romans acclaimed him, in accordance with the previous arrangements, "imperator Romanorum." This acclamation by the Romans was to announce publicly the meaning of the papal act. Charlemagne became, by virtue of the pope's action, "imperator Romanorum"; but he also had to be designated and named as such in a public manner by the Romans present. That all this must have been carefully arranged, goes without saying: these previous arrangements, however, appear in the official papal accounts as the spontaneous inspiration of the Romans. Because the Romans—we follow the account—saw how much Charlemagne defended and loved the Roman Church and its vicar, they unanimously in a raised voice exclaimed, at the bidding of God and of St Peter: "To Charles, the most pious Augustus crowned by God, the great and peace loving emperor, life and victory." It is plain that the "spontaneous inspiration" was well planned and need not detain us.

It is not, however, without significance that the Romans witnessing the act with their own eyes, acclaim Charlemagne as "a Deo coronatus." And it is as a result of divine and Petrine inspiration that they shout thus. The significance of this lies in that the whole ceremony is presented as the working of the divine will—it is not the pope who crowned the Frank, but God Himself: "a Deo coronatus."

If we wish to understand this, we must keep in mind that, according to the papal standpoint, there was no difference at all between the function of the newly created emperor and that of the patrician of the Romans: he was the protector and defender of the Roman Church. In both of our sources this vital point breaks through. The *Liber Pontificalis* declares that out of recognition for Charlemagne's *defence* of the Roman Church the Romans had acclaimed him emperor; according to the Frankish annals the patrician became absorbed in the emperor.² And this is exactly what the papal book also says: "et

---

'Karolo, piissimo Augusto a Deo coronato, magno et pacifico imperatori, vita et victoria.' Ante sacram confessionem b. Petri apostoli, plures sanctos invocantes, ter dictum est; et ab omnibus constitutus est imperator Romanorum."

¹ *Annales Regni Francorum*, ed. cit., p. 112: "Ipsa die sacratissima natalis Domini, cum rex ad missam ante confessionem b. Petri apostoli ab oratione surgeret, Leo Papa coronam capiti eius imposuit et a cuncto Romanorum populo adclamatum est: *Carolo augusto, a Deo coronato magno et pacifico* imperatori Romanorum, *victoria et vita*. Et post laudes ab apostolico more antiquorum principum adoratus est atque ablato patricii nomine imperator et augustus est appellatus." Italicized words are from the Frankish *laudes*.

² "Ablato patricii nomine imperator et augustus appellatus." This is also the

ab omnibus constitutus est imperator Romanorum." This means that the patrician was now acclaimed or called—as the Frankish annals have it—or was "set up" as "emperor of the Romans" because the pope had crowned him: papal action preceded the acclamation—the Romans acclaimed the thus crowned Frank an "imperator" who had as a consequence of the papal coronation been raised from the office of patrician of the Romans to the dignity of the emperor of the Romans. The constitutive act was that of the pope: the acclamation derives its meaning from the papal act: the papal act is announced to the world. The patrician wears no crown; the emperor does, and he wears it because the pope has imposed it: the crowned emperor is acclaimed.

The "vacancy" on the imperial throne—and we take note that the increase of the indications pointing to fundamental changes coincides with Irene's rule as empress—provided the pretext for transforming an office into a dignity:[1] the office of the patrician was transformed into the dignity of Roman emperorship. Functionally, however, nothing changed, as far as papal intentions went: whether patrician or emperor his function was defence and protection of the Roman Church. Constitutionally, however, there was a radical change for there was now an emperor of the Romans where previously there had been none —the consequence was the emergence of the "problem of the two (Roman) emperors."[2] Charlemagne's coronation was, so to speak, the final and solemn and public act by which the papacy emancipated itself from the constitutional framework of the Eastern empire.[3] There remains to be answered the question, By what authority did the pope proceed in the manner in which he did?

---

opinion of F. Dölger, "Europas Gestaltung im Spiegel der fränkisch-byzantinischen Auseinandersetzung" in *Der Vertrag von Verdun*, ed. Th. Mayer, 1943, p. 215–16: "eine Verwandlung des 'patricius Romanorum' in einen 'imperator Romanorum'."

[1] One might be tempted to find a parallel between the vacant exarchy of Ravenna (leading to the creation of the "patricius Romanorum" in 754) and the vacant imperial throne (leading to the creation of the "imperator Romanorum").

[2] It is the great merit of W. Ohnsorge to have drawn attention to this problem which he presents in his work *Das Zweikaiserproblem*, Hildesheim, 1947. The forces at work are not quite adequately assessed by K. Jäntere, *Die römische Weltreichsidee*, pp. 332 ff. Cf. now for an excellent characterization of the period the study of H. Löwe, "Von Theoderich dem Grossen zu Karl dem Grossen" in *Deutsches Archiv*, ix (1952), pp. 353 ff., especially pp. 379 ff.

[3] Cf. already Fustel de Coulanges, *Histoire des institutions politiques* (vol. vi: *Les transformations*), Paris, 1892, p. 312: "Le couronnement de Charles comme empereur est, de la part du pape, une rupture avec Constantinople."

If we keep in mind that according to the accepted doctrine all power comes from God; if we recall that ideologically there was no difference between the famous Gelasian statement and the Donation of Constantine; if we consider the function which, in the papal view, the (secular) Ruler was to play—if we duly appraise all this, it will not be too difficult to realize that the pope acted not only as the mediator between God and man in imposing the crown—hence Charlemagne is "a Deo coronatus"—but also as the dispenser of the highest available dignity and power (*potestas*), of Roman emperorship. In fact, the dignity and power conferred by the pope could be no other but a conceptually universal one: the Roman Church being the epitome of universal Christianity, can confer through the pope only a universal Christian power: and the only universal power that was available at the time was that designated by the title "emperor of the Romans." Moreover, although the imperial crown was in Constantinople, it was there on sufferance by the pope (Silvester): not only was there no emperor now, but those emperors who had been there before, were not worthy being called *Roman-Christian* emperors. For—we try to follow papal reasonings —these emperors had in fact constantly infringed the—for the papacy —most vital principle, that of the *principatus* of the Roman Church. With particular reference to this point Gelasius had declared that the emperor held his empire as a trust, as a *beneficium*, from God: but by demonstrably setting aside the divinely instituted papacy, the Eastern emperors had misused their trust—hence the pope considered himself entitled to withdraw his consent which by implication he had given to Constantine's taking his crown to Constantinople.

The emperors in the East, although ostentatiously styling themselves *Roman* emperors, had, by virtue of their opposition to the *Roman* Church, forfeited their claim to be *Christian* emperors. They were considered—as later terminology will have it—unsuitable emperors, and the papacy therefore was, always provided that the Donation was efficacious, entitled to transfer Roman emperorship from Constantinople to Rome: the Donation was the basis upon which Leo could proceed. This is nothing extraordinary, for, as we pointed out, the Donation was originally intended to be employed as a weapon against the East, so as to effect the emancipation of the papacy from the Eastern constitutional framework. And the possibility of a withdrawal of Roman emperorship from the East was as much inherent in the document as the papal consent to Constantine's taking the crown thither.[1]

[1] It is interesting to note that Ansgar in his *Vita Willehadi* (archbishop of

Gelasius had maintained that Christ was "Rex" and "Sacerdos"[1] the "potestas regalis"—signifying the "Rex"—and the "auctoritas sacrata pontificum"—signifying the "Sacerdos"[2]—were united in Him, but "by a marvellous dispensation" He had distinguished between the function of the priest and that of the king. It was Christ's own act: Christian imperial power therefore originated in Christ. There was no possibility of asserting that the pope conferred imperial power: until his position as the vicar of Christ was fully developed there was indeed no possibility for him to combine—like Christ— "potestas regalis" and "auctoritas sacrata"; therefore, there was also no possibility of conferring imperial power or of withdrawing it.[3] This defect was made good by the Donation: as a consequence of Constantine's grant, the pope disposed of the crown, the external symbol of imperial power. And in this capacity Leo III acted on Christmas Day 800.[4] Had not his predecessor, Adrian I, declared that the Roman Church was the "caput totius mundi,"[5] an obvious allusion to Gelasius's "mundus"—and was it not the same Adrian who quoted the Donation?[6] The "mundus" could be nothing else but Christen-

---

Bremen, *ob.* 789) speaks of a translation of dominion from East to West, although this translation was effected by the Romans: "Temporibus ipsius (Karoli) per electionem Romani populi in maximo . . . concilio ad Francorum *translatum est dominium*," MGH. SS. ii. 381, lines 39 ff.

[1] *Tract. IV*, quoted supra p. 25 n. 2.

[2] Ep. 12, c. 2.

[3] For Innocent III cf. infra p. 343 n. 2, 443 n. 5, RNI. 62.

[4] The mosaic in the Lateran's triclinium might be adduced to support this view, if it were possible to ascertain with certainty that the right-side picture did in fact show how Christ handed the imperial standard to Constantine and the keys to Silvester. This right-hand picture was reconstructed in 1625 (see Schramm's Table 4b, op. cit., supra p. 95 ) but although it is very likely that the reconstructed picture corresponds to the original, there is no certainty about it. The left-hand picture shows St Peter handing the pallium to Leo and the standard to Charlemagne. It may be that this standard is the one which Leo despatched to Charlemagne with his "decretalis cartula," reported in the *Annales Regni Francorum*, ed. cit., p. 98. For a possible, though not entirely convincing explanation, see C. Erdmann, "Kaiserliche und päpstliche Fahnen im hohen MA" in *Quellen und Forschungen aus italienischen Archiven*, xxv (1934), pp. 11 ff.; and Schramm, *Anerkennung*, pp. 26–7. The book by G. Ladner, *Die Papstbildnisse des Altertums und Mittelalters*, Città del Vaticana, 1941, was not accessible to me. The attractive suggestion of H. Beumann in *Stengel Festschrift*, p. 159, that the mosaic, like the Donation itself, looks towards the East, has very much in its favour. Cf. also Cl. Schwerin in *Koschaker Festschrift*, Weimar (1939), iii. 332, note 41.

[5] *Cod. Car.*, no. 94, p. 636, line 5.

[6] See the quotation supra p. 93. He had also written to Charlemagne, *Cod. Car.* no. 68, p. 597, lines 23 ff.: "Spiritalis mater vestra, s. apostolica et catholica Romana ecclesia, per vestra a Deo protecta laboriosa certamina relevata exultat,

dom, of which the Roman Church was the epitome and head: Charlemagne should conquer the barbaric nations;[1] he in fact was already
hailed as *the* Christian Ruler,[2] Christian, because the spiritual son of
the *Roman* Church. The empire in the East, though so ostentatiously
calling itself Roman and Christian, could not justify these appellations
—Leo took the step which was, from the point of view of papal doctrine, wholly understandable. The Roman Church being the "caput"
of the (Christian) universe ("Mundus") creates through the pope a
universal (Christian) protector who alone deserves the dignity of an
"emperor of the Romans." This is his dignity—his function is that of
a protector and defender, in the Roman-papal sense: the *principatus*
of the Roman Church over the ideational universal entity, the *corpus
Christi* (the universal Church), can be exercised through the agency of
an ideational universal *potestas*, the emperor of the Romans.

## II

The reaction of Charlemagne to this event was spontaneous, natural
and as understandable as the pope's action was. If he had known of the
papal plan, he would not have entered the church, although it was so
high a feast day, his biographer Einhard reports.[3] Charles's whole

---

a templo sancto b. Petri fautoris vestri: 'Confirma hoc, Deus, quod operatus es in
nobis' crebro orantibus in vobis triumphum; et mandat cotidie virtutem suam per
b. Petrum apostolorum principem, vobis subjiciens omnes barbaras nationes,
dilatans atque amplius exaltans *in toto orbe terrarum* vestrum splendidissimum
regnum."

[1] *Cod. Car.* no. 94, p. 636, and no. 72, p. 603, lines 1 ff.: "Et pro hoc nempe
certe facti estote: quia, quantum *caput totius mundi*, eandem sanctam Romanam
ecclesiam eiusque rectorem simulque pontificem amplectendo seu fovendo honor-
abiliterque glorificando diligitis, tantum vos b. Petrus apostolorum princeps
inconcussos facit triumphos hic et in futuro victores *super omnes regnare reges*."

[2] Cf. also Notker, quoted infra note 3 at end.

[3] Einhard, *Vita Karoli*, ed. Holder-Egger, cap. 28, p. 28: "Quo tempore
imperatoris et augusti nomen accepit. Quod primo in tantum aversatus est, ut
adfirmaret se eo die, quamvis praecipua festivitas esset, ecclesiam non intraturum,
si pontificis consilium praescire potuisset." As is well known, the passage has
aroused a good deal of controversy, but we might recall the statement of Dove,
*Ausgewählte Aufsätze*, Leipzig, 1925, i. 19: "Demgegenüber muss man mit Einhard's Zeugnis doch endlich einmal vollen Ernst machen und herauslesen, was
drin steht, nämlich dass Karl nicht bloss aus irgendeinem Grunde durch die
Form dieser Weihnachtsüberraschung unangenehm betroffen war, sondern dass
er die Sache selbst, die sich freilich nicht rückgängig machen liess, eine Zeitlang
unwillig ertragen hat." Despite the eloquent pleading of F. L. Ganshof, *The
imperial coronation of Charlemagne*, Glasgow, 1949, p. 22, for the historical
veracity of the *Annales Laureshamenses* (MGH. SS. i. 38, cap. 24), their full
trustworthiness cannot be accepted; they contain, however, a grain of truth, see

political programme was based upon the conception that the Roman empire was in the East: Leo's action cut right across all Charles had stood for: according to papal intentions Charles was the "imperator Romanorum." Against the papal idea of an exclusive and universal Roman emperor—and only a Roman emperor could be considered universal—there stood Charlemagne's idea of a co-existence of the two empires, there stood his idea of parity and equality with the Eastern emperor, who was the legitimate Roman emperor.[1] Thoroughly Frankish orientated as he was, the historical-political concept of a Roman empire meant nothing to him: that empire in the East was the legal and constitutional Roman empire, the disposal of which could not lie in papal hands. Objection to emperorship Charlemagne did not and could not raise—but objections to Roman emperorship he did raise.

Charlemagne's basic theme and intention was to live on a footing of equality and parity with the Eastern emperor. What the latter was in the East, he desired to be in the West. His reaction to Leo's action was wholly political. The ideology of Roman emperorship never appealed to him; the historic, cultural and political appeal made no impression on him;[2] realistically inclined as he was he envisaged a partition of the world into two equal empires, of which the Eastern one was the Roman

infra p. 116. Cf. also the characterization of this source by L. Halphen, op. cit., p. 132: "Il y aurait, pensons nous, quelque naïveté à tenir pour exacte dans son ensemble la thèse qui vient d'être rapportée. Elle réponde visiblement à un souci d'apologie, qu'explique sans doute le désir de menager les susceptibilités du gouvernement byzantin"; E. Amann, *L'époque carolingienne*, Paris, 1947, p. 162, and S. Heldmann, op. cit., p. 15. Above all, the report is not borne out by the subsequent conduct of Charlemagne, whilst Einhard's is fully supported by Charlemagne's actions and conduct after 800. Even so, the account in the *Ann. Laur.* leaves no doubt about the papal initiative: "Quia tunc cessabat a parte *Graecorum* nomen imperatoris, et femineum imperium apud se abebant, *tunc visum est ipso apostolico Leoni* et universis sanctis patribus qui in ipso concilio aderant, seu reliquo christiano populo, ut ipsum Carolum regem Franchorum imperatorem nominare *debuissent* . . . ideo justum eis esse videbatur, ut ipse cum Dei adjutorio et universo christiano populo petente ipsum nomen aberet. Quorum petitionem ipse rex Karolus denegare noluit, sed . . . ipsum nomen imperatoris cum consecratione (?) domni Leonis papae suscepit." Cf. also Notker (the monk of St Gall) in his *Gesta Karoli*, i. cap. 26 (MGH. SS. ii. 743, lines 12 ff.): "Tunc *sanctus* ille (Leo), divinam constitutionem secutus, ut qui jam re ipsa rector et imperator plurimarum erat nationum, nomen quoque imperatoris Caesaris et Augusti apostolica auctoritate gloriosius assequeretur, invictum Karolum Romam venire *postulavit.*"

[1] This is convincingly shown by W. Ohnsorge, in the work already quoted. Cf. also G. Ostrogorsky, *Gesch. d. byz. Staates*, pp. 127–8.

[2] Ohnsorge, op. cit., p. 23: "Karl fühlte sich als Frankenkönig und wollte die Grösse seines Frankenreiches; alles Römische war ihm gleichgültig, wenn nicht verhasst." Against this thesis is H. Beumann, "Romkaiser und fränkisches

empire, and his was the Christian empire or, as some of his contemporaries called it, *Europa*.[1] But apart from this purely political objection, there was also the strong religious objection which made Charlemagne view the Eastern empire as not orthodox, as not properly Christian. The book composed under his supervision contains some very caustic observations on the subject[2] and the whole pompous Eastern ceremonial was as intensely disliked by the Frank as was the artificial Eastern Roman empire ideology: unburdened by Roman tradition Charlemagne viewed the whole Eastern set-up as the result of a moribund, degenerated megalomania.[3]

Yet despite Charlemagne's aversion from the oppressive and unreal superstructure that overlaid the Roman empire (in the East), there were very many features in his government which showed his imitative rivalry with the East: an imitative rivalry that was prompted by his desire to be an equal of the Eastern basileus. In a way one might indeed speak of Charlemagne as an ἰσοβασιλεύς,[4] a Ruler who was

---

Reichsvolk" in *Festschrift E. E. Stengel*, pp. 164 ff. It is perhaps an oversimplification to say that Charlemagne "never really understood the full significance of the imperial dignity," F. L. Ganshof, "Charlemagne" in *Speculum*, xxiv (1949), p. 526. Cf. also the pertinent observations of E. Rota, "La consacrazione imperiale di Carlo Magno" in *Studi in onore di Enrico Besta*, Milan, 1939, iv. 178 ff.

[1] C. Erdmann, *Forschungen zur politischen Ideenwelt des Frühmittelalters*, p. 25, refers to Charlemagne's letter to the emperor (MGH. *Epp.* iv. 556), according to which there was to be a grouping of two empires, an "orientale et occidentale imperium." See above all the comprehensive study of F. Dölger, "Europas Gestaltung im Spiegel der fränkisch-byzantinischen Auseinandersetzung" in *Der Vertrag von Verdun*, ed. Th. Meyer, Leipzig, 1943, pp. 203–73. Cf. also P. E. Schramm, *Anerkennung*, p. 62; H. E. Feine, *Kirchliche Rechtsgeschichte*, Weimar, 1951, i. 200: "Parität des fränkischen mit dem byzantinischen Kaisertum."

[2] Obviously alluding to the Eastern emperor's claim that he was like an apostle (ἰσαπόστολος) Charlemagne says that between the emperor and the apostle there is as much distance as between saints and sinners, see his *Libri Carolini* (*Capitulare de imaginibus*), ed. H. Bastgen, iv. 20, p. 212, lines 12–15. It was Eastern arrogance to say "quo et Deum sibi conregnare et se divos (!) nuncupare praesumunt . . . insania est . . . Quis sanae mentis tale quid protulerit," p. 142, lines 40 ff.; cf. also i. l, p. 8, and preface, p. 5: "Contra cuius errores ideo scribere compulsi sumus." Cf. also i. 2, p. 14; iv. 5, p. 180, lines 23 ff. The Vatican MS of this book was in fact used by Charles, see W. von den Steinen, "Karl d. Gr. und die Libri Carolini" in *Neues Archiv*, xlix (1932), pp. 207–80 and D. de Bruyne, "La composition des Libri Carolini" in *Revue Bénédictine*, xliv (1932), pp. 217 ff. The *Libri* were never published, see L. Wallach, "Charlemagne's 'De litteris colendis' and Alcuin" in *Speculum*, xxvi (1951), p. 301 and note 70.

[3] Cf. also the observations of H. Fichtenau, "Byzanz und die Pfalz" in MIOG. lix (1951), p. 13.

[4] So Schramm, *Anerkennung*, p. 32.

basileus-like.[1] But the policy of parity and equality pursued by Charlemagne would have been thrown overboard, had he accepted the papal
action with all its implications. For by so doing he would have stepped
into the place of the—according to him—legitimately constituted
"emperor of the Romans" who was in the East: acceptance of the
papal plan would have entailed an entire re-orientation of his aims and
policy. And it may even have been that the various manifestations of
Charlemagne's imitative rivalry confirmed the papacy in its belief that
he might not be averse to the rise in his status: indeed a serious mis-
calculation on the part of Pope Leo III.

There was thus no desire on the part of Charlemagne to play the
role of the one "emperor of the Romans." This refusal explains otherwise inexplicable formulae and titles adopted by the Frank after his
coronation. These formulae stand in closest proximity to the role
which he did play. This role was none other than that of the true
monarch in the West, of the monarch ruling over that entity which was
called *Europa* by some, and the *imperium christianum* by others, and
also *imperium Romanum* by still others: they are all tautological expressions meaning one thing only—the empire under Charlemagne's rule
was that entity which was held together by the Christian faith as
expounded by the Roman Church.[2] It was this element that was meant

---

[1] Ohnsorge, op. cit., p. 21: the Greek court was, despite all his fundamental
aversion, always an object of comparison, example and stimulus to Charles. Only
a few of such imitative manifestations can here be mentioned. On the model of
the Eastern chancery practice Charles introduced the golden seal next to the
earlier waxen seal, Schramm, loc. cit.; in imitation of the Eastern practice the
appellation of "sacer" for the court emerged, Schramm, ibid., with further
literature; the manner of dating documents would also point to an imitation of
Eastern practices, see F. Dölger in *Byzantinische Zeitschrift*, 1936, pp. 123 ff.;
on the Eastern model the chancellor signs on behalf of Charles and uses red ink,
see Dölger, "Rom in der Gedankenwelt der Byzantiner" in *Z. f. Kirchengeschichte*, lvi (1937), pp. 6 ff.; the introduction of the Trinity invocation in his
documents also belongs to the category of imitation, see Dölger, "Die Kaiserurkunde der Byzantiner" in *Hist. Z.*, clix (1939), p. 250, note 1; perhaps the most
telling manifestation of this imitative rivalry was Charles's plan of his residence at
Aachen, the "*sacrum* Palatium." The term itself was borrowed from the East,
see Fichtenau, art. cit., p. 13; there is every indication that the Byzantine palace,
the Chrysotriklinos, served as a model for Charles's residence as planned, about
which see especially Fichtenau, art. cit., pp. 7–25, here also a description of the
Chrysotriklinos on the basis of the available material. The appointment of Louis
as emperor in 813 by the father was one more sign of this imitative rivalry. This
politically conditioned rivalry found a counterpart in the cultural imitation of
Greek elements, about which see B. Bischoff "Das griechische Element in der
abendländischen Bildung des MA" in *Festschrift f. F. Dölger*, 1951, pp. 27–55.

[2] Cf. also Rota, art. cit., p. 206: "Il concetto politico si fonde in perfetta
identità con il concetto religioso."

5

to give that vast empire its coherence; it was this element that makes Charlemagne's adoption of those inexplicable formulae and titles understandable.

To Charlemagne the Christian-Roman faith was of paramount governmental importance. His empire was, so to speak, the concrete realization of the Christian idea. He was indeed hailed as the one whom God Himself had raised to the government of the *regnum Europae*.[1] In poetic transfiguration the Frank is made "rex pater Europae" or the "apex Europae."[2] And it seems that, because he was the true monarch of *Europa*, he was credited with the vicariate of Christ,[3] or with that of St Peter who possesses the keys of heaven.[4] It is not therefore surprising that the official book to which we already have referred, the *Libri Carolini*, speak of Charlemagne exercising government over the "regnum sanctae ecclesiae":[5] the "kingdom of the Church" was Europe. The importance of this concept lies in its negative aspects: the Eastern empire does not belong to the Europe governed by Charlemagne.[6] We repeat therefore that this entity which was called *Europa* was that body politic which received its cementing bond from the Christian faith as expounded by the Roman Church. *Europa* and *ecclesia* are, within this conceptual framework, identical: they constitute the political expression of the union of all Latin Christians, that is, the union of all "Romani."

Over this *Europa* the Frank rules as the monarch: he was the "rector of the Christian people" as the Council of 794 made so perfectly plain. He was to be the "lord and father, king and priest, the governor of all

---

[1] Cathwulf, soon after the Lombard conquest, in MGH. *Epp.* iv. 503: "Ipse (scil. Deus) te exaltavit in honorem gloriae regni Europae."

[2] See the quotations by Erdmann, op. cit., p. 21; there is some possibility that Einhard himself was the author of these expressions, see Erdmann's note 5, p. 21; Cf. also *Vita Willehadi*, MGH. SS. ii. 381, lines 39 ff.: "Quem . . . catholica Europae . . . suscepit ecclesia."

[3] Cathwulf, loc. cit., p. 502: "Memor esto, ergo semper, rex mi, Dei regis tui cum timore et amore, quod tu es in vice illius: super omnia membra eius custodire et regere, et rationem reddere in die judicii, etiam per te. Et episcopus est in secundo loco, in vice Christi tantum est."

[4] Theodulf of Orleans, *Carmina*, no. 32, in MGH. *Poetae Lat.*, i. 524: "Teque sua voluit fungire ille vice / coeli habet hic claves, proprias te jussit habere / Tu regis ecclesiae, nam regit ille poli / Tu regis eius opes clerum populumque gubernans / hic te coelicolas ducet ad usque choros." With this should be compared some of the Eastern episcopal expressions coined for the Eastern emperors, supra p. 16 n. 5.

[5] Ed. cit., p. 3, preface.

[6] See also F. Dölger, in *Der Vertrag von Verdun*, p. 203: there was an "Europabegriff jedoch immer unter Ausschluss des byzantinischen Balkangebietes."

Christians."¹ The aggregate of all (Latin) Christians formed a "city," a "civitas," which appears to have been the concrete manifestation of St Augustine's *City of God*.² The universal Church was the union of all (Latin) Christians and governed by the Frank.³ The appearance of fullness of royal power as reflected in Charlemagne's government prompted Alcuin to state that "divine power had armed the king with two swords and placed one in the right, and the other in the left hand."⁴ It was this appearance of true monarchic power, we hold, which gave rise to statements according to which Charlemagne held the vicariate of Christ or functioned as the vice-gerent of Christ,⁵ who also himself sometimes identified his decisions with the will of God.⁶

¹ MGH. *Concilia*, ii. no. 19, p. 142, lines 13–14: "Sit dominus et *pater*, sit rex et sacerdos. Sit omnium Christianorum moderantissimus *gubernator*." The Eastern emperors termed themselves and were termed "Romanorum gubernatores," see Beumann, art. cit., p. 168, note 1; here also the instance in which St Boniface (745–6) used the verb "gubernare" in the address: "inclita Anglorum imperii sceptra gubernanti Aethilbaldo regi." (MGH. *Epp.* iii. no. 73, p. 340). Cf. also the following note, and Bishop Waldheri's (of London) designation of Theodore's successor, in 705: "Berctvaldo totius Brettaniae gubernacula regenti," quoted by W. Levison, *England & the Continent*, p. 248, note 6 (Haddan & Stubbs, *Councils & eccles. documents*, iii. 274). I have not seen Ganshof's contribution to the *Misc. A. de Meyer*, 1946. About the popes using the term, see supra p. 12. n. 2.

² Alcuin, MGH. *Epp.* iv. 327: ". . . civitatem pretioso sanguine Christi constructam regere atque *gubernare*."

³ Alcuin, MGH. *Epp.* iv. 242: "Universalis ecclesia, quae sub . . . dominationis vestrae imperio conversatur."

⁴ Alcuin, MGH. *Epp.* iv. 171, pp. 281–2: "His duobus gladiis vestram venerandam excellentiam dextra levaque divina armavit potestas, in quibus victor laudabilis et triumphator gloriosus existis." Cf. also no. 136, pp. 205–10. It is rather doubtful whether Alcuin understood the symbol of the two swords in the manner in which it was understood later. Cf. also infra 117 and L. Lecler, "L'argument des deux glaives" in *Recherches de science religieuse*, xxi (1931), pp. 299–300; here also the purely scriptural interpretation of earlier times, pp. 300–5. See now also W. Levison, "Die mittelalterliche Lehre von den beiden Schwertern" in *Deutsches Archiv*, ix (1952), pp. 14–42.

⁵ Smaragdus, *Via regia*, c. 18 (PL. cii. 958): "Fac quicquid potes pro persona quam gestas, pro ministerio regali quod portas, pro nomine Christiani, quod habes, pro *vice Christi, qua fungeris*." Cf. also ibid., col. 933: "Deus omnipotens te, o clarissime rex . . . dignanter in filium adoptavit (!): constituit te regem populi terrae, et proprii filii sui in coelo fieri jussit haeredem." See also Sedulius Scotus, *De rectoribus christianis*, c. 1 (ed. S. Hellmann, p. 22): "Quid enim sunt christiani populi rectores nisi ministri omnipotentis?" and c. 19, p. 86: "Oportet enim Deo amabilem regnatorem quem divina ordinatio *tamquam vicarium suum* in regimine ecclesiae esse voluit, et potestatem ei super utrumque ordinem praelatorum et subditorum tribuit, ut singulis personis ea quae justa sunt, decernat."

⁶ Cf. Charlemagne's letter discovered in a Munich palimpsest and quoted by W. Levison, op. cit., p. 95, note 1; the letter is written to Adrian I: "Cor enim regis in manu Dei consistere credimus nutuque illius huc illucque verti. Ideoque non nostro arbitrio, sed Dei credimus esse pastorale illi culmen concessum."

Considering *Europa* as a body politic whose constituent element was the Christian faith as expounded by the Roman Church, it was not consequently surprising that Charlemagne was hailed as the "rector of true religion," as the archiepiscopal and episcopal synodists of the council of 813 declared.[1] What all these expressions amounted to was that contemporaries saw in the Frank the embodiment of the true monarch who autonomously governs *Europa* which as we know, was nothing else but the Latin Christian body politic. The government of the monarch—and not merely that of a king—affects all spheres of political and social—and religious life: monarchic government means that every aspect which is politically or socially or religiously important for the well-being of the body politic under the monarch's rule, must be an item of the monarch's government. In practical terms, therefore, it was Charlemagne's function as monarch—as the "rector populi Christiani"—that made him function as legislator on all sorts of matters, such as liturgy, religious instruction, baptism, ecclesiastical and monastic discipline, feast days, sacraments, and so forth.[2] And for the government of a professedly Christian body politic it was, moreover, essential that only suitable ecclesiastical officers, that is bishops and archbishops, were appointed by the monarch; nor was it of any lesser importance for the proper working of this *Europa* that its monarch convoked, or presided over, councils composed of the high ecclesiastics, although the councils themselves were merely consultative organs.[3] Whatever decrees were passed by a synod had to be submitted to the monarch for approval.[4] In short, monarchic government expressed itself in the effective shaping, through the medium of the law, of all items which concerned the proper functioning of the body politic: and none was of greater importance than the religious item which was the foundation and the cementing element of that vast body politic.

---

The reference is to the bishopric of Pavia conferred on Abbot Waldo of Reichenau, Levison, loc. cit. The biblical reference is to *Prov.* xxi. 1.

[1] Council of Mainz, MGH. *Conc.* ii, no. 36, p. 259.

[2] For details see L. Halphen, op. cit., pp. 213 ff. For liturgical "reforms" cf. also E. Bishop, "The liturgical reforms of Charlemagne" in *Downside Review*, 1919, pp. 1–16; and for all general aspects see Carlo de Clercq, *La législation religieuse de Clovis à Charlemagne*, Louvain, 1936, pp. 158 ff.

[3] Cf. P. Hinschius, *Kirchenrecht*, iii. 549.

[4] There is a striking resemblance between Justinian and Charlemagne's legislation, about which see also J. de Ghellinck, *Mouvement théologique*, 2nd ed., Paris, 1948, p. 19. H. Rahner, *Abendländische Kirchenfreiheit*, p. 238, calls Charlemagne the Frankish Justinian.

Hence the imperative need for the monarch to focus his legislative attention on this aspect.[1]

The significance of this legislative activity on the part of Charlemagne lies in that certain doctrinal matters which appeared to the "rector populi christiani" as sufficiently important, were given the halo of an enforceable decree, the halo of law, of a binding rule. This is in fact the effluence of the true monarch's function, namely, to govern, and to govern by law: but what items are to be made the subject of the law, must be left to him. In other words, as true monarch Charlemagne could not and did not concede to the pope what was technically called jurisdictional primacy. Since it included legislation, the concession of jurisdictional primacy would have meant that Latin Christianity, that *Europa*, was governed by two heads: that there was not a monarchy but a diarchy.[2] What Charlemagne did concede was what was technically called magisterial primacy. The exposition of the Christian faith was the task of the pope—but what items of this Roman-expounded faith were to become a binding rule, a law, that was an issue that fell into the competency of him who actually governed, into the competency of the monarch. Charlemagne was convinced that true apostolic doctrine came from the Church of Rome—and not from that in Constantinople—but by doctrine alone it was not possible to govern: what was necessary for governmental purposes was that doctrine became an essential part of governmental machinery, that is, became the subject of law. And the conception of monarchic government precluded legislation by anyone else but by the monarch, by Charlemagne. Not each and every doctrine propounded by the Roman Church needed to be raised to the level of a law; only those which the monarch of the Christian people considered suitable and necessary for the proper functioning of the body politic that was, according to his conception, entrusted to his care. The pope's function in this scheme of things was that of a metropolitan within the empire.[3]

Only a few of the instances in which Charlemagne shows his acknowledgement of the magisterial primacy of the Roman Church can

[1] Cf. also H. Brunner, *Deutsche Rechtsgeschichte*, Leipzig, 1892, ii. 318: "Die kirchliche Gesetzgebung ist Königsrecht" (my italics). See also Hinschius, iii. 712.

[2] Cf. also U. Stutz, in H. E. Feine, *Kirchliche Rechtsgeschichte*, i. 199: there was no room for a "Rechtsprimat" of the pope.

[3] See the last will of Charlemagne of 811, in Einhard, *Vita*, cap. 33, p. 33, where Rome ranks as the first metropolitan church followed by that of Ravenna and Milan: "Nomina metropoleorum ad quas eadem eleimosina sive largitio facienda est, haec sunt: Roma, Ravenna, Mediolanum, Forum Julii, Gradus, Colonia, Mogontiacus . . ." Cf. also F. L. Ganshof, "Charlemagne" in *Speculum*, xxiv

here be given. The *Libri Carolini* stress the supremacy of the Roman Church over all other churches; its superiority is not founded on conciliar decrees, but on Christ Himself; only those Church fathers should be followed whose writings the Roman Church had approved, hence its advice should be adhered to by all the faithful. To Adrian I Charlemagne wrote that the exposition of dogma should be the guiding principle of the pope's office.[1] It is Roman liturgy which is firmly established by Charlemagne, not because of its inherent superiority, but because of its Roman origin.[2] The clerics should be dressed according to "Roman custom."[3] It was the Roman rite of baptism which was to become the rule.[4] These examples could be multiplied; what they all make clear is that Charlemagne emphasizes the Roman substance of his "ecclesiastical" legislation, but at the same time they make abundantly clear that the term "Roman" had no historical-political meaning; "Roman" indicated nothing else than the connexion with the Church of Rome. The term had a purely religious connotation and denoted, in its negative aspect, the antithesis to "Greek."[5]

The Frankish Ruler, then, was the embodiment of the monarchic idea, namely, that one only governed the body politic which was in its

---

(1949), p. 524: the pope "became more or less the first of his bishops." The preamble of his first "Capitulare" (which, amongst other things, forbade the bearing of arms by clerics) is quite characteristic: "Apostolicae sedis *hortatu*, omniumque fidelium nostrorum et maxime episcoporum ac reliquorum sacerdotum, consultu servis Dei per omnia omnibus armaturam portare vel pugnare . . . omnino *prohibemus*," MGH. *Capit.* i. 44, no. 19.

[1] MGH. *Poet. Lat.*, i. 92, verse 20: "Ecclesiamque Dei *dogmatis arte* regas." This was written in the dedication of the ornamental copy of the Psalter which Charlemagne had sent to Adrian I.

[2] See the Capitulare of 789, MGH. *Capit.* i. 61; cf. also ibid. 235 and MGH. *Epp.* iv. 542 f., no. 30. The *Sacramentarium Gregorianum* was sent to Charlemagne by Adrian I and was kept in the palace at Aix; it was supplemented by Alcuin, for details see H. A. Wilson, *The Gregorian Sacramentary under Charles the Great*, Cambridge, 1918.

[3] MGH. *Capit.*, i. 64, no. 23, cap. 24: "De calciamentis secundum Romanum usum." Prayers were to be said "secundum Romanum usum," ibid., p. 109, cap. 2. Candidates for the priesthood must know the "divinum officium secundum ritum Romanum," ibid., p. 234, cap. 7; etc. About the pronunciation of Latin see F. Lot in *Bulletin du Cange*, vi (1931), pp. 144 ff.

[4] Council of Mainz, MGH. *Concilia*, ii. 261, No. 36, cap. 4: "Sacramenta itaque baptismatis volumus . . . ita concorditer atque uniformiter in singulis parochiis secundum Romanum ordinem inter nos celebretur." Cf. also the questionnaire sent to the archbishop of Milan, Odilbert, concerning baptism: Odilbert should inform Charlemagne "de symbolo quae sit eius interpretatio *secundum Latinos*," MGH. *Capit.* i. 247, no. 125.

[5] We think that this may also explain Charlemagne's attitude in the vexed iconoclastic question. The proposed solution of this problem, so it appears to us,

substance Christian. And in this capacity he also functioned as the supreme autonomous protector of the "populus Christianus." It was his function as protector to see that the Christian people were guided and ruled according to the "orthodox" faith; that they were spared heretical infections; that the Christian faith, in short, was protected effectively. Viewing protection from this aspect, it is understandable how Charlemagne considered the conquest of the "barbarian" nations as an item of protection, for thereby he exalted the Church universal and herewith consolidated Latin Christianity. But, again, just as he was autonomous in his function as the monarch, so was he autonomous in his complementary function as a protector. That is to say, the decision as to when, and how, and where to act as a protector was to be left to him as the supreme "rector populi christiani." Charlemagne, by virtue of personifying the monarchic idea, was the protector in the Germanic-royal sense *par excellence.*[1]

The Old Testament, the mastery of which was perhaps the hallmark of the Frankish theologians surrounding Charlemagne, may help us in finding the key to those formulae and titles to which we have already alluded. If we keep in mind the role papally allocated to Charlemagne, namely, that of the "imperator Romanorum"—a role which we must always bear in mind was exclusively political—and if we set this

---

was too much tainted with "Greek" (i.e. Nicaean) ideology to be palatable to Charlemagne and his theologians. And it is not without significance that the most vituperative observations on the Eastern-Greek ideology appeared in the *Libri Carolini* which dealt with the iconoclastic problem.

[1] In a way one might indeed speak of Charlemagne as "a king who had almost directly descended from the Old Testament," E. Kantorowicz, *Laudes regiae,* Berkeley, 1946, p. 56. In the intimacy of his circle he was apostrophized "David," and the "regnum Davidicum" was the political expression of supreme monarchy modelled on the Old Testament, Kantorowicz, p. 57. And in this sense he could indeed be spoken of as the "New Moses," the "New David," the priestly king, see Kantorowicz, pp. 56-7. We should bear in mind, however, that the Eastern emperor was also addressed as "David," see Th. Schnitzler, in *Analecta Gregoriana,* xvi (1938), p. 109. On the meaning of the term "Rex-Sacerdos" see infra 156. H. Fichtenau, art. cit., p. 29, note 144, draws attention to the rebus in the poem of Paulus Diaconus: MGH. *Poet. Lat.* i. 52, no. 14: the DD was the usual abbreviation for David. Cf. also the letter of Alcuin (referred to by Fichtenau, loc. cit.) MGH. *Epp.* iv. 84, no. 41, where David, Christ and Charlemagne and the government of the "populus christianus" are brought into close relationship. For further examples of Alcuin addressing Charlemagne as David, see e.g., no. 25, p. 67, line 3; no. 72, p. 115, line 7 ("Domnus meus David"); no. 118, p. 173, line 21 ("mi David"); no. 145, p. 231, line 23 ("Davidica gloria" and "Davidica sapientia"); no. 229, p. 372, line 15 ("dulcissime David"); etc. Cf. also editorial note at p. 67, note 3. On the earlier cryptographic influences exercised by St Boniface on the continent, esp. Fulda, see W. Levison, op. cit., pp. 137-8, 290-4.

allocated role against Charlemagne's policy and aims concerning the East and his function in the West, namely, that of the true monarch, it will become clear that the inscription chosen for Charlemagne's seal after his coronation—*Renovatio Romani imperii*—was an exquisitely selected way out of the impasse created by the papal action on Christmas Day 800. One can but marvel at the ingenuity of the Frankish theologians in their attempt to devise a formula which, on the one hand, was not to affront the pope and, on the other hand, was to assuage the suspicions of the East, and yet do justice to Charlemagne's own conceptions. This formula had nothing to do with a "renovation" or "restoration" of the Roman empire, if "Roman empire" was to designate a political concept. But we know that Charlemagne considered the Roman empire (in the political sense) to be legitimately and constitutionally situated in the East.

The formula was taken from the Old Testament, where we read that Samuel *renovavit imperium*.[1] Here as there the term has a religious connotation. In Charlemagne's inscription on his seal[2] the *imperium* is qualified as *Romanum*: it is the Christian empire, the *imperium christianum*, of which Alcuin had written before and was to write afterwards.[3] The papal action was interpreted in a purely religious sense. Charlemagne attributed to the coronation the meaning of a "renovation" or "restoration" of the true Roman-Christian empire by the pope. The empire in the East was Roman in the political sense; the empire in the West was Roman in the religious sense. This interpretation of the coronation by Charlemagne tallied of course with his political programme of a parity between the *orientale* and the *occidentale imperium*.[4] This latter empire is that entity, the cementing bond of which is the Christian faith as expounded by the Church of Rome. That entity, and some, as we have seen, called it *Europa*, formed the effective and concrete union of all Latin Christians: it was the *regnum*

---

[1] *Eccl. us*, xlvi. 16. The late E. Eichmann, *Kaiserkrönung*, i. 113, note 15, was the first to draw attention to this biblical origin of the phrase; cf. also H. Fichtenau, *Das karolingische Imperium*, p. 308, note 88.

[2] Cf. the facsimile in P. E. Schramm, op. cit., ii. Table 7a–e.

[3] See also the pertinent observations of Ganshof, op. cit., p. 14: "That 'christian empire' is the whole of the territories submitted to Charlemagne's authority and inhabited by the 'populus christianus' which is the community spiritually dependent on Rome." Here also the references to Alcuin's *geographical* limitations of the *imperium christianum*, MGH. *Epp.* iv, nos. 174, 177, 178, 185, 202, 217, 234. Cf. also E. Caspar, art. cit., p. 218 f.; and W. Levison, op. cit., pp. 121–2, 124–5.

[4] About the two empires see supra p. 104 and see also *Eccl. us*, xlvii. 23: "Faceres imperium *bipartitum*."

*Europae,* now reborn as *imperium Romanum.* The term "Roman empire" in Charles's inscription is therefore purely religious and has nothing in common with the political term, except its name.[1] It was conceived by him as the empire of the Romans (= Latin Christians) and adopted in order to meet the pope half-way. But in so doing he rendered the coronation harmless and adjusted it to his own conceptual framework.

In the centre of the seal we find the picture of a city gate and underneath written the word ROMA. This, we think, bears out the interpretation of the inscription *Renovatio Romani imperii.* The city gate is overshadowed by a large cross in the background which can mean one thing only, the *Church* of *Rome.* The city gate leads into the City of God.[2] Here again, Charlemagne gave the coronation the meaning which harmonized with his own conceptions of his empire, namely, an entity which derives its cementing substance from the Church of Rome: in this sense indeed he could speak of an *imperium Romanum,* because this empire had no connection at all with the historical-political concept of the Roman empire. But he was not an emperor of the Romans, and he never styled himself thus, because this was considered by him a purely technical and political term which he refused to accept.[3] His empire was still the *regnum Europae,* that entity which stood, precisely because of its religious substance, in contrast to the Roman empire in the East.

The situation created by the pope's action was no doubt one that required some adroitness in adjusting Charlemagne's official title. This title was to bring out, on the one hand, his equality with the East,

---

[1] The usual interpretation is that the (political) Roman empire is restored by Charlemagne, e.g. L. Levillain, "Le couronnement imperial de Charlemagne" in *Revue d'histoire de l'église de France,* xviii (1932), pp. 13 ff.; G. Tellenbach, "Germanentum & Reichsgedanke" in *Hist. J.B.,* lxix, 1949, pp. 129–33; also H. Beumann, art. cit., pp. 168, 172: "Bekenntnis zur Tradition des antiken Römerreiches."

[2] Cf. Einhard's famous passage, in his *Vita,* cap. 24, p. 25: "Legebantur ei historiae et antiquorum res gestae. Delectabatur et in libris sancti Augustini, praecipueque his qui de civitate Dei praetitulati sunt." Cf. also H. X. Arquillière, *L'augustinisme politique,* p. 116 and also L. Halphen, op. cit., p. 214.

[3] Cf. again Einhard, cap. 28, p. 28. The East became so suspicious that they considered military steps against Charlemagne, but he addressed them as "Brothers" (and not as "sons" which would have been the address, if he had acquiesced in the papally allocated role of an "emperor of the Romans"). See Einhard: "Vicitque eorum (scil. 'Romanorum imperatorum') contumaciam magnaminitate, qua eis procul dubio longe praestantior, erat mittendo ad eos crebras legationes et in epistolis fratres eos appellando." Cf. also F. Dölger in *Der Vertrag von Verdun,* p. 220, and W. Ohnsorge, op. cit., pp. 28–9.

and on the other hand, his function as the monarch of the Roman-Christian empire. Had he accepted the pope's plan, he would have called himself *imperator Romanorum*, for as such he was acclaimed and as such the pope wished him to appear. But this designation had to be avoided, because it was the title used by the Eastern emperors.[1]

The title which appeared on 29 May 801 for the first time (in a document issued near Bologna)[2] and which he kept for the rest of his reign was:

Karolus serenissimus augustus a Deo coronatus magnus pacificus imperator Romanum gubernans imperium, qui et per misericordiam Dei rex Francorum et Langobardorum.

It is clear that this title evades the designation of Charles as "imperator Romanorum" and instead has "imperator Romanum gubernans imperium." The "Roman empire" in this title is of course nothing else but Latin Christendom, that entity which, although, according to Charlemagne, renovated by Leo's action, he alone governed: he governed it in the same manner in which his Eastern colleague did, namely on the monarchic level. The designations of earlier emperors upon which indeed he might have alighted on the occasion of his visit to Ravenna in May 801[3] may very well have stood as models, as their terminology fitted exactly the meaning which Charlemagne wished them to have.[4]

In short, the action on Christmas Day 800 could not be undone. It had to be given a meaning which could not possibly offend the pope, was designed to assuage the East, and yet did full justice to Charlemagne's own conceptions. Distinguished as "emperor crowned by God" it was he who governed (*gubernans*),[5] but the formula of the title does not omit to drive home that his position as a monarch, as

---

[1] For this see especially P. Classen, "Romanum gubernans imperium" in *Deutsches Archiv*, ix (1952), pp. 113–17. The work of V. Laurent was not accessible to me. The Eastern emperors stressed from now on the title Basileus ton Romaion, giving the Frank the title Basileus ton Fraggon.

[2] DK. 197.

[3] See the important article by P. Classen, loc. cit., pp. 105–12. Classen also refers to Justinian's wording in the arenga of his decree, in *Cod*. I. xvii. 1: "Deo auctore nostrum gubernantes imperium, quod nobis a coelesti majestate traditum est, et bella feliciter peragimus . . ." Cf. also Theodosius in *Cod. Just.*, I. i. 1: ". . . populos, quos clementiae nostrae regit imperium."

[4] Cf. also Schramm, *Anerkennung*, p. 56.

[5] The verb "gubernare" in the title was extremely well chosen to convey what Charlemagne wished to convey. We recall that the Eastern emperors were styled and styled themselves "Romanorum gubernatores" and on the other hand

one who actually governed, was due to his being king of the Franks and the Lombards "per misericordiam Dei." This kingship was the real source and basis of his power.[1] Negatively expressed, his position as European monarch was not derived from the coronation, but from the undeniable fact that he was the king of the Franks and of the Lombards. This, in our opinion, is the meaning of the somewhat tortuous and cumbersome imperial title.

Let us briefly sum up, so as to bring the differences between Leonine and Caroline conceptions into clear relief. For Leo III the overriding idea was to complete the papacy's emancipation from the Eastern constitutional framework by creating the Frankish king the "emperor of the Romans." Technically, the "imperator Romanorum" was universal, at least conceptually: the "imperator Romanorum" was the only available designation of rulership which denoted universality of dominion in an ideational sense.[2] The papacy, by virtue of the Roman Church being the epitome of universal Christianity, cannot confer any other dignity but a universal one. The conceptions and actions of the eighth-century papacy were entirely logical and consistent. The Eastern emperors, on their part, assuming Charles's role to be that of an "imperator Romanorum"—from their point of view they could not imagine any other emperor but one of the Romans—gave the coronation the same meaning which Leo wished it to have; hence to them Charles was an usurper who tried to take away their empire.[3]

---

Charlemagne himself had been styled a "gubernator" of all Christians (= Romans), see supra p. 107, so that here again the aim at parity and equality is detectable. In parenthesis it should be remarked that the title "augustus imperator" and the following "Romanum gubernans imperium" are not tautological. "Imperator" means the dignity conferred upon him by the pope—an event that could not be wiped out—whilst the subsequent "Romanum gubernans imperium" refers to the territory over which he as monarch rules.

[1] In so far Beumann, art. cit., p. 168, is right when he says that this formula "enthält also eine Spitze gegenüber dem päpstlichen Krönungsanspruch"; cf. also E. Caspar, art. cit., p. 262.

[2] For this see especially C. Erdmann, *Forschungen*, cit., pp. 1–2, pointing to the Rome-free emperors, such as the Russian Czar, the emperador of Brazil, the German Kaiser, the emperor of Mexico, the emperor of India, etc. None of them was a Roman emperor, hence none of them claimed universality of dominion, such as was inherent only in the Roman emperor.

[3] Cf. Einhard, cap. 16, p. 17: "Imperatores etiam Constantinopolitani (!) Niciforus, Michahel et Leo, ultro amicitiam et societatem eius (scil. Caroli) expetentes, conplures ad eum misere legatos. Cum quibus tamen propter susceptum a se *imperatoris nomen* et *ob hoc* eis, quasi qui imperium eis eripere vellet, valde suspectum foedus firmissimum statuit . . ." Of a little later date is Notker in his *Gesta Karoli*, i. cap. 26 (MGH. SS. ii. 743, lines 26 ff.): ". . . ne, sicut tunc fama ferebat, Karolus insperato veniens regnum illorum suo subjugaret imperio."

For this way of thinking Charlemagne had no understanding. He was a *Realpolitiker*. To him an ideational universal rulership meant nothing: as a monarch he governed, and he governed a concrete, clearly definable and defined entity. His conceptions were firmly rooted in the realities of political life: his conceptions were based upon territory, that is, on territory over which his government exercised real, as distinct from imaginary, control. Universal emperorship, such as was contained in the dignity of the "imperator Romanorum" was a conception entirely alien to him. He therefore conceived—ideologically not quite correctly—the government of the "imperator Romanorum" to be just as much territorially confined as his own government was. His "imperium Romanum" was a territorial conception: it was Europe, ideologically and religiously nurtured by the Church of Rome, but monarchically governed by him. He was indeed "imperator Romanum gubernans imperium." The difference between Leo's and Charles's conceptions therefore lies in that the former considered the Roman emperor on the political plane of an ideational universality, as a means of translating the *principatus* of the Roman Church into reality. The latter thought of the Roman empire on the religious plane of a strictly limited territorial confine, limited by the extent of Latin Christendom. Charlemagne's *imperium Romanum* pre-portrayed the later medieval *societas christiana*: it was the *imperium christianum*.

Charlemagne's assumption of the title "imperator" can be understood only in regard to his overriding ambition to be on a footing of equality and parity with the Eastern emperor. As we have said in the beginning of this section, objection to emperorship as such he did not have; he objected to Roman emperorship, as his somewhat lengthy title reveals all too plainly.[1] Indeed, the suggestion of his assuming emperorship might well have originated in Alcuin who must have been perfectly familiar with the Anglo-Saxon usage of the title and who

---

[1] This, we believe, is the kernel of truth in the account of the *Annales Laureshamenses* when their author speaks of the "emperor" without any qualification and in the absolute sense. In so far there is no discrepancy between the *Annales* and Einhard. The discrepancy concerns the qualifications of emperorship and here Einhard's straightforward testimony is entirely supported by Charles's own conduct. What Charles objected to, according to Einhard, was the "name" of the emperor conferred upon him by the pope, see the passage quoted supra p. 102 and immediately continuing Einhard says that the *Roman* emperors were indignant about the supposed role of Charlemagne (cf. also cap. 16, supra p. 115), although he bore their ill-will with patience: "Invidiam tamen suscepti nominis, Romanis (!) imperatoribus super hoc indignantibus, magna tulit patientia," cap. 28, p. 28; then follows Einhard's statement about Charles's addressing the Eastern emperors as "Brothers."

might well have transported the title to the court of Charlemagne.[1] Charlemagne's "imperator" did not denote universality of dominion.[2]

A chapter on Charlemagne would not give a faithful picture if it did not at least allude to the one or the other symptom which heralded a time radically different from his own. It is Alcuin who invites our attention. We have already cast doubt upon the interpretation which at first sight might be put on his addressing Charlemagne as the possessor of the two swords. There is, as far as this statement of Alcuin goes, really nothing to suggest that he expressed with it anything more than fullness of royal power. On the other hand, it seems that Alcuin was quite clear in his mind about the true function of a king in a Christian society, although his views are expressed rather cautiously. In one of his letters he adopts the Isidorian point of view according to which the king wields the sword merely for the sake of suppressing evil: his function is, so to speak, negative. Sacerdotal power, on the other hand, symbolizes life, and not, as its counterpart, death: for sacerdotal power has the key to eternal beatitude.[3] It is a weighty statement on the part of one who was so intimately connected with him who was hailed as the "rector of Christian religion" and addressed as the *Rex-Sacerdos*.

No less significant is Alcuin's view on the pending trial of Leo III. It will be recalled that the great forgery made during the pontificate of Symmachus (*ca.* 501) contained the stipulation that the supreme pontiff could not be tried, since the pupil was not above the master.[4] Before Charlemagne sat in judgment over Leo in December 800, Alcuin had written to his friend Arn of Salzburg pointing out the inadmissibility of trying a pope: he protested against the trial and said:[5]

If I remember rightly I have read in the canons of St Silvester that a bishop can be accused only on the testimony of 72 witnesses . . . and I also read in

---

[1] For this see E. E. Stengel, "Kaisertitel und Souveränitätsidee" in *Deutsches Archiv*, iii (1939), pp. 16 ff., 25 ff., also Levison, op. cit., pp. 121–2, 124–5.

[2] All the evidence goes to show "dass er kein römischer Kaiser sein wollte," C. Erdmann, op. cit., p. 27.

[3] See the letter written in 802, MGH. *Epp.* iv. no. 255, p. 413: "Divisa est sacerdotalis atque regalis potentia. Illa portat clavem in lingua coelestis regni, ista gladium ad vindictam reorum. Sed multo praestantior potestas, quae vivificat quam illa, quae occidit, quia melior est vita quam mors, melior est eterna beatitudo quam jocunditas."

[4] The reference is to the *Constitutum Silvestri*, cap. iii: Mansi, ii. 623: "Non damnabitur praesul nisi in LXXII. Neque praesul summus judicabitur a quoquam, quoniam scriptum est: Non est discipulus super magistrum." The *Constitutum Silvestri* purported to originate in Silvester's pontificate. On the Gelasian influence see supra p. 27 n. 6.

[5] MGH. *Epp.* iv. 296. Cf. also E. Caspar, art. cit., pp. 223–4.

other canons that the apostolic see must not be judged but that it judges everyone.

When then in actual fact Charlemagne did sit in judgment over Leo at Christmastide 800, the episcopal participants of the synod—the trial was conducted in the manner of a synod[1]—declared, obviously paraphrasing the forged canon:

We do not venture to judge the apostolic see, which is the head of all churches, for by it and its vicar we all are judged; this see, however, is not judged by anyone as it also is the old custom.[2]

These are indeed weighty words and warnings which as so much else in this period, had purely theoretical value, but which nevertheless constituted the very faint heraldings of another time, a time which Charlemagne had so materially and powerfully assisted in bringing about.

---

[1] Caspar, art. cit., p. 226.
[2] *Liber Pontificalis*, ii. 7: "Nos sedem apostolicam, quae est caput omnium ecclesiarum, judicare non audemus. Nam ab ipsa nos omnes et vicario suo judicamur, ipsa autem a nemine judicatur quemadmodum et antiquitus mos fuit." In his oath of purgation Leo himself said this: "Ego Leo pontifex sanctae Romanae ecclesiae, a nemine judicatus neque coactus, sed spontanea mea voluntate purifico et purgo me in conspectu vestro coram Deo et angelis eius . . . non quasi in canonibus inventum sit, aut quasi ego hanc consuetudinem aut decretum in sancta ecclesia successoribus meis necnon et fratribus et coepiscopis nostris inponam," MGH. *Epp.* v. no. 6, p. 64. There is now a somewhat lengthy account by H. Adelson and R. Baker, on "The Oath of Purgation of Leo III in 800" in *Traditio*, viii (1952), especially pp. 57 ff., 67–76.

# CHAPTER IV

# The Frankish Ethos after Charlemagne

## I

THE debt which medieval Europe owed to Charlemagne's conceptions is a memorial to his statecraft, political acumen and deep religiosity. His empire was the political expression of Latin Christendom. His empire was the apotheosis of the idea that all Latin Christians form one body politic: it was the *imperium christianum*, and since to him Christianity was equivalent with Latin or Roman Christianity, this empire could legitimately be called *imperium Romanum*. But, and this is the vital point, the government of this body lies in the hands of the monarch. The element that gave that empire its unitary complexion was that of the Christian faith as expounded by the Roman Church: this element is as essential to Charlemagne's imperial ideas as it is to the later form of the *societas christiana*. On the other hand, however fundamental was the emphasis of Charlemagne on the magisterial primacy of the Roman Church, it was of equally fundamental importance to his system of government that the jurisdictional-legislative primacy of the Roman Church was implicitly denied. In its origin this empire was thoroughly Frankish-Germanic; in its substance it was thoroughly religious and therefore in this sense Roman.

To insist on the magisterial primacy of the Roman Church and at the same time to deny its jurisdictional primacy, is certainly possible as a temporary expedient: but there is little doubt that this arrangement bore all the germs of its inner destruction in itself.[1] The same observation can be made as regards the conception of the empire: its Frankish-Germanic origins, roots and bases were bound to come into conflict

---

[1] It is from a different angle that Fustel de Coulanges viewed the situation: "Les Carolingiens furent écrasés par la haute idée qu'ils se firent de leur pouvoir. Commander au nom de Dieu, vouloir régner par lui et pour lui quand on n'est qu'un homme, c'est s'envelopper d'un réseau d'inextricables difficultés. L'ideal en politique est toujours dangereux. Compliquer la gestion des intérêts humains par des théories surhumaines, c'est rendre le gouvernement presque impossible," *Histoire des institutions politiques*, cit., p. 233.

with its Roman substance. In fact, the Frankish-Germanic origin of the empire accounts for the denial of the Roman jurisdictional primacy: Charlemagne's government was the prototype of *monarchic* rule, the very natural continuation of the old Teutonic monarchy. It was this Teutonic and monarchic form of government which militated against the acknowledgment of Rome's jurisdictional and legislative primacy, for there cannot be two monarchs, i.e. a diarchy, ruling one and the same entity. But the infusion into this body, of the Roman substance, even if only in the form of a religious orientation towards the Roman Church, brought an alien element into this entity. The conflict of the later ages centred precisely in the irreconcilability of the conceptions of this Romanism and Teutonism.

The bequest of Charlemagne—the *orthodoxus imperator*, as the inscription on his tomb had it—was of a twofold nature. On the one hand, he was, and was taken as, the model of the monarch—not of a mere king or emperor, but of a monarch who autonomously governs the political entity allegedly entrusted to him by God. In his function as a monarch he must be unimpeded by any considerations or regard for any other power: the teachings of the Roman Church are enforceable, not because the Roman Church had given them the force of law, but because the monarch, Charlemagne, in his autonomous function surrounded certain magisterial expressions of the Roman Church with the halo of an enforceable rule. The idea of monarchy was one of the bequests of Charlemagne: and functionally, the monarch was the supreme protector. Just as he alone *qua* monarch considers himself functionally qualified to judge when to issue laws and upon what matters, so also it is he alone who considers himself functionally qualified to know when and how to protect those in need of protection. The monarch's protection is consequently autonomous. The conceptions of monarchy and of protection are complementary and thoroughly Teutonic and royal.

On the other hand, Charlemagne's bequest was the Romanism which was, to him, nothing more nor less than the Christian faith as expounded by the Roman Church: "Romanitas" and "Christianitas" were to Charlemagne tautological expressions. But, as we have seen, the term "Roman" lent itself to a purely religious as well as a purely historical-political interpretation. In the one sense, Romanism meant that the substratum of the empire was the Roman-papal faith; in the other sense, Romanism meant that the substratum of the empire was, not the Roman-papal faith, but the ancient imperial Roman idea of rulership, in which sense the Germanic Rulers were historically to continue the old Roman emperorship. The one kind of Romanism was Christian and spiritual; the other was a historical-political idea and secular.

It may seem paradoxical that the secular brand of Romanism was rejected by Charlemagne, whilst the papacy, on the other hand, interpreted Romanism in the historical-political sense. But this paradox is only apparent. For we should keep in mind the conceptions underlying all papal actions. These conceptions centred in the conception of the Ruler's function within the *corpus Christi*, within the congregation of the faithful. Now the Roman Church was the epitome of this *corpus*: the Roman Church contained in its bosom everything which was dispersed and diffused throughout the Christian world. Hence, if this epitome of a universal entity confers through the pope emperorship, it can be only a universal one, and the only kind of emperorship which was universal was Roman emperorship: it is *conferred* by the pope, therefore it is derivative; it is not autonomous: this papally created universal emperor is conceived entirely on a teleological plane. Genetically and chronologically, the Roman emperor had grown out of the patrician of the Romans; ideologically, the emperor arose out of the Pauline, Gelasian and Isidorian views. Protection and defence of the Roman Church and herewith of the universal Church being the "finis," the "telos," the *raison d'être* of the Roman emperor, the historical-political conception of Romanism was, logically enough, interlocked with papal ideology.

Functionally, then, there was no difference between the patrician and the emperor, according to the papal point of view. But, as we said before, the patrician's was an office. This office was transformed into the dignity of emperorship. The creation of the emperor was the creation of a universal protector—because a universal entity was to be protected—with the title of "emperor of the Romans." The parallelism between Stephen II and Pippin on the one hand, and Stephen IV and Louis I on the other hand, is indeed striking: in the former case the papal unction signified the creation of the king, although he had been king before, for the particular purpose of defence and protection; in the latter case the combination of unction and coronation in one act signified the creation of the Roman emperor, although Louis had been emperor before, for the special purpose of defence and protection. The emperor thus created obtains the dignity of a universal Ruler, though by no means conceived on an autonomous basis by papal doctrine.

That is why Stephen IV brought the crown of Constantine with him to Rheims and that was the view on the emperor's function as classically expressed in this same century by John VIII that the emperor was an *advocatus*, an *adjutor*.

There is therefore no paradox at all in the papacy's interpreting Romanism in the historical-political sense: only in this way the papacy could obtain an effective protector on a conceptually universal scale. The creation of the Roman emperor by the papacy was the visible transplantation of the abstract Pauline, Gelasian and Isidorian ideas into a concrete and tangible framework.

On the other hand, the successors of Charlemagne—and we may well include most of the medieval emperors—embraced the historical-political concept of Romanism, thereby not only deviating from Charlemagne, but also, which is more important, giving that concept of Romanism a meaning that was at variance with the genesis of the idea. The reason for this eager acceptance of the historical-political Romanism by the Rulers was, quite apart from such intangible and elusive considerations as "the glory that was Rome," because this dignity designated the highest available dignity of rulership: it was conceived to be the high-water mark of political power, in its essence universal and incorporating all the characteristic features of true monarchical form of government. Thus far there was no difference between the Frankish conception of monarchy and the ancient historical Roman idea of monarchy. Both were essentially autonomous. In a way one might say that the Frankish conception was refined and sublimated by adopting the Roman conception. The differences, however, emerge at once when due credit is given to the function which the papally created Roman emperor was to play: it was precisely the opposite to what the emperors imagined, for they were made (and sometimes later also unmade) emperors for the protection of the Roman Church. They conceived Roman emperorship on the monarchic and autonomous level, instead of on the functional one: mistakenly they attributed to the papally created Roman emperor autonomous rulership. Seen from another angle, the difference is the same as the one which we witnessed as regards the Roman-papal idea of protection and its Teutonic-royal counterpart. In each case the difference was that between appearance and reality.

## II

Precisely because Charlemagne had written on his banner that the Roman faith was the cementing bond of his empire, the quite unprecedented upsurge of sacerdotal, i.e. hierocratic manifestations in the second decade of the ninth century becomes accessible to understanding. It was through the insistence of Charlemagne that the spiritual element of the faith was the substratum of his empire that the "sacerdotium" in his empire was given a standing, appropriate enough, it is true, and yet ultimately destructive to the monarchic form of imperial government. In the numerous councils of the early ninth century the "sacerdotium" showed, how in a Christian society which Charlemagne's empire was supposed to embody, the régime of the dead emperor was one that could not stand up to a serious examination. It was, in other words, a régime that, according to intellectual and sacerdotal élite of the early ninth century, was inappropriate to the conception of Christian society.

In considering the Frankish ethos in the first decades of the ninth century due prominence must be given to the character of the Carolingian Renascence, so powerfully stimulated by the *orthodoxus imperator* himself. It was a purely Latin Renascence confined to the resuscitation of Latin and patristic works, and one of the effects of this Carolingian Renascence was an accentuated and accelerated impregnation of the Frankish-Western mind with Roman Latinity.[1] Moreover, the diffusion of Roman law principles at that time, again greatly enhanced by Charlemagne himself, contributed its share to the steeping of the contemporary mind with characteristically Roman features. The clergy itself had of course always lived "secundum legem Romanam," and with the concomitant increase of sacerdotal influence this legal feature was of not inconsiderable importance in facilitating the passage from religious Romanism to its secular historical counterpart.

The intellectual and literary background of this Carolingian Renascence could not and did not produce anything like a *Laienethik*. What principles were set forth, broadcast and even partially applied were those of the educated and learned classes, wholly constituted by the sacerdotal members of the Church. And it is not the least symptomatic feature of the effects of this Renascence that its bearers in the ninth century styled Charlemagne "Pharao," the oppressor of his

---

[1] Cf. the pertinent observations by the late P. Koschaker, *Europa und das Römische Recht*, pp. 36, 60.

people (Radbert) or depicted the rider on the equestrian statue of
Charlemagne as a tyrant (Walafrid Strabo).[1] It is, moreover, also
characteristic of the temper of the time that Charlemagne's immediate
successor, Louis I, was wholly under the spell of the great forerunner
of Cluny, Benedict of Aniane. Benedict became the true regent.[2] That
Louis himself had shown a marked predilection for monasticism from
his early youth onwards,[3] only partly explains the overpowering
influence of Benedict of Aniane. The susceptibility of Louis I to
Romanism in both its kinds is, no doubt, partly also the effect of his
father's reign.[4]

Louis I himself bears witness to the prevailing conceptions and at
the same time heralds the tone of later generations. To him the body
of the believers in Christ, Christian mankind, forms one body—the
old Pauline theme—within which he functions as a member but which
membership imposes upon him the duty to eradicate evils within this
*corpus*.[5] This corporate conception of the universal Church which still

---

[1] For details see H. Fichtenau, *Das Karolingische Imperium*, cit., pp. 255–6, 333–4.

[2] Fichtenau, op. cit., 222: "Benedict wurde zum eigentlichen Regenten." Cf. also L. Halphen, op. cit., pp. 228–9.   [3] Fichtenau, op. cit., 212 f.

[4] For our purposes it is not necessary to go into details of Benedict's programme. His influence especially on the Diet of Aix-la-Chapelle in 816, is noticeable, at least as far as the decrees of that Diet relate to the need of purifying the monastic order from alien elements. In effect this meant the emancipation of the monks from contemporary society, the creation of an exclusive organization which was to live under its own laws and rules. This is his *Concordia Regularum*, a fusion of all sorts of monastic rules prevalent in the Frankish kingdom, but based largely on St Benedict's *Rule,* see PL. ciii. 701 ff. Benedict's explanation of the canons, his exposition of patristic literature, his collection of books, his gathering around him of scholars of repute, and so forth, are indeed remarkable achievements, even if they are not as unique as they are sometimes held to be. His symbolism is also characteristic of the scholar as well as of his time: the three parts of the altar correspond to Trinity; the seven chandeliers represent symbolically the sevenfold graces of Holy Spirit, and so on; cf. *Vita s. Benedicti*, PL. ciii. 351–2, and on Benedict himself see H. v. Schubert, *Geschichte der christl. Kirche im Frühmittelalter*, cit., pp. 615 ff.; Fichtenau, op. cit., 214 ff.; Ph. Schmitz, s.v. in DHE. viii. 177–88; D. Knowles, *Monastic Order in England*, pp. 25–7 (here also further literature) ; H. Dörries, "Die geistigen Voraussetzungen und Folgen der karolingischen Reichsteilung" in *Der Vertrag von Verdun*, ed. Th. Mayer, pp. 163 f., and S. Dulcy, *La régle de S. Benoit d'Aniane et la réforme monastique à l'epoque carolingienne*, Nimes, 1935.

[5] See MGH. *Capitularia,* no. 173, p. 356, lines 13 ff.: "Quapropter nos ob amorem et honorem Dei ac Domini nostri Jhesu Christi et ob exaltationem sanctae matris nostrae catholicae ecclesiae, quae est corpus eius in qua et nos membrum ipsius per bona opera effici cupimus, consuetudinem pravam et valde reprehensibilem . . . abolere cupientes . . . statuimus et decrevimus, ut abhinc in futurum . . ." Cf. also the preface to no. 137, pp. 273–5.

has only a mystical head in the person of Christ, is the fundamental theme of papal as well as of imperial standpoints. It is the theme which determines the course of medieval political doctrines.

The impetus which the religious Romanism had given to the awakening of hierocratic thought manifested itself so clearly in the councils. They are indeed a faithful reflexion of the ethos dominating the intellectual and cultural circles. On the whole, the decrees of these numerous councils say extraordinarily little that is new. But this is beside the point. What is to the point, however, is that they put forward the proper hierocratic theme with the help of declarations which were formerly purely theoretical: the synodists cull from all sorts of repositories precisely those statements which assume a particularly great significance in their time. What was formerly said, so to speak, *in vacuo* and what had mere theoretical significance, now becomes a matter of practical politics. Moreover, in that they incorporated, and as often as not copied their sources, the decrees of these councils can be considered as the vehicles which transmit old material to later generations: besides their importance as mirrors of the prevailing contemporary ethos, these councils and decrees function also as the incubators of the hierocratic programme.[1] It is St Augustine, St Jerome, Gregory I, Prosper, Isidore and a number of old councils which form the backbone of the great councils, notably those in the second and third decades.

If we were to give a general heading to all these councils it would perhaps be: the proper ordering of society within the Christian corpus. The synodists stress the role which the sacerdotal members of the Church have to play within this corpus of Christian mankind. They emphasize the functional qualifications of the "sacerdotes" in so far as they alone are qualified to orientate and to direct this corporate society. But because this is their function in the Christian body politic, the second main theme arises, namely the need for a purified sacerdotal order. The first theme prompted the stressing of the fundamental differences between the two ordines which make up the whole Christian corpus; the second theme prompted the reliance on Charlemagne's own legislation concerning the living, education and morality of the clerics.

The accentuation on the "ordo sacerdotalis" by the Council at Aix in 816[2] is perhaps the most significant feature of its decrees. In order to

---

[1] Cf. e.g., the many decrees of these councils which went into Gratian's *Decretum*, see the list in MGH. *Concilia*, ii. 885 ff.

[2] The decrees of this council together with the Rule laid down by Bishop

prove the significance of the sacerdotal order, the synodists rely almost wholly on Isidore of Seville's book on the ecclesiastical offices. On the authority of Isidore they declare that tonsure has a twofold meaning: the tonsured cleric has the "sacerdotium regnumque ecclesiae" and consequently the Petrine statement on the royalty of priesthood is applicable to the tonsured clerics alone.[1] Ordination, moreover, confers upon the cleric the power to bind and to loose and also the power to teach "in toto orbe" and "per totum mundum"[2]—to teach, that is, what is, and what is not, Christian. Christ, according to the synodists of Aix, "est verus dux populorum" since He is the mediator between God and man. The sacerdotal order begins with St Peter by virtue of the Petrine commission, and it is this which constitutes the cleavage between the sacerdotal and the lay orders; it is also the Petrine commission which gives the sacerdotal order its functional qualification in a Christian society. These same synodists of Aix in 816 are, consequently, very much concerned with the purifying of the sacerdotal order since only a purified order can be considered adequate for the functions which its members have to fulfil in a Christian society.[3]

Whilst this council was almost exclusively concerned with the role of the sacerdotal order and the need for purifying the order itself, the Council held at Paris in 825 busied itself with a different theme. The council was prompted by the letter which the Eastern emperors had written to Louis I and in which they had expressed the hope that Louis would side with them in the question of image worship.[4] In a rather

---

\* Chrodegang of Metz (about 760) (PL. lxxxix. 1097 ff.) were to be the model for numerous statutes of medieval cathedral and collegiate chapters. These statutes are only partially edited. For the subject itself see H. E. Feine, *Kirchliche Rechtsgeschichte*, cit., pp. 166–7, 317–21; D. Knowles, *Monastic Order*, cit., p. 26, and above all L. Santifaller's works, see now also his observations in *Oesterreichisches Archiv f. Kirchenrecht*, iv (1953), pp. 86–7, with further literature.

[1] MGH. *Conc.*, ii. 318, lines 36–8: "Utrumque signum exprimitur in capite clericorum, ut impleatur etiam corporis quadam similitudine quod scriptum est, Petro apostolo perdocente 'Vos estis genus electum, regale sacerdotium." The reference is to I *Pet.* ii. 9 and Isidore's *De ecclesiasticis officiis*, ii. 4. The application of the Petrine text to the clerics only is significant and foreshadows later hierocratic thought, cf. e.g., Hugh of St Victor infra p. 440.

[2] MGH. cit., p. 323, cap. 9.

[3] This applies also to the *Capitula canonum*, caps. 38–113 and to the *Regula canonicorum*, caps. 114 ff. The significance of the council's decrees lies also in that the usual canonical norms of the Western Church were now also applicable to the Frankish Church which, by virtue of its peculiar Teutonic development, had sometimes tended to disregard these norms which were valid everywhere in Europe, cf. Fichtenau, op. cit. 223.

[4] MGH. *Concil.* ii. no. 44, pp. 475 ff.

provocative manner the writers of this letter call themselves "Michahel et Theophilus, fideles in ipso Deo, *imperatores Romanorum*," addressing their communication to the king of the Franks and of the Lombards who is "called their emperor."[1] The letter itself is noteworthy for the terminology indicative of the underlying ideas; for instance, the pope is referred to as "papa antiquae Romae";[2] the emperors themselves are "orthodoxi imperatores"; Christ Himself had called them "ad imperii dignitatem," and so forth. And Louis's step is equally significant: he declined to pronounce on the matter of images, but instead asked the pope to permit the holding of a council which was to be composed of Frankish ecclesiastics: this council was to give the verdict on the question of images.[3]

The synodists of Paris, 825, draw a neat line between the "orientalis ecclesia"[4] and the Church centred in Rome which the Easterners so contemptuously called "Old Rome." The insertion of long extracts from the *Legenda s. Silvestri*[5] in these decrees is noteworthy, as also is the strong affirmation of the primatial position of the Roman Church. They address the pope as "the first arbiter amongst men"—"primus in hominibus arbiter"[6]—who had been placed in the apostolic chair by God Himself as the vicar of the apostles.[7] In their address to the pope the synodists declare that he bears a special name "in toto orbe terrarum," namely "universalis papa."[8] Nor do they omit to stress the unique Petrine commission. But a critical appreciation of this council will no doubt take into account that it was primarily concerned with a matter that was of importance to, and provoked by, the East.

The Council held at Rome in 826 under the presidency of the pope viewed the needs of the time from yet another angle. Aix had emphasized the internal, moral purifying needs of the sacerdotal order: Rome laid stress on the proper education of the sacerdotal members of the Church. For they alone are functionally qualified to teach, that is, to permeate the "populus Dei" with Christian tenets, but the presupposi-

---

[1] "Glorioso regi Francorum et Langobardorum, et vocato eorum imperatori."
[2] MGH. *Concil.* ii. no. 44, p. 479, line 36.
[3] *Epistola ad Eugenium directa:* MGH. *Concil.* ii, no. 44, p. 534, lines 15 ff.; see also p. 522, lines 40 ff.
[4] They also speak of the "imperium orientalium Romanorum," p. 521, line 43.
[5] MGH. *Concil.* ii. no. 44, p. 485, cap. 2.
[6] MGH. *Concil.* ii. no. 44, p. 522, lines 9–10.
[7] MGH. *Concil.* ii. no. 44, p. 522, lines 10 ff.: "Quem Deus omnipotens in sede apostolica collocare eorumque vicarium eidem sanctae suae ecclesiae dare dignatus est."
[8] MGH. *Concil.* ii. no. 44, p. 522, lines 12 ff.

tion for this is proper training and education, for without this "quomodo populus Dei doceri possit?"[1] What Charlemagne had so recently decreed for the priests, was now decreed by this Roman synod. Moreover, ordination not only provides the functional qualification for teaching, but also for the administration of the divine mysteries,[2] two aspects of the sacerdotal order which mark it off so clearly from its lay counterpart; two aspects which are also of fundamental importance to the functioning of Christian society. This Roman council not only legislatively laid down the visible gulf between the two orders, as, for instance, was shown in the prohibition that no layman must enter certain parts of the church during mass,[3] but also began to legislate on a number of topics which were of direct concern to lay people: the decrees dealing with matrimonial matters, though not propounding any new point of view—on the contrary, the decree concerned with divorce still adheres to the old doctrine according to which the wife's fornication constituted a valid ground for divorcing her[4]—show clearly the unobtrusive transition from pure doctrine to the legal "non licet."[5] Other decrees containing prohibitions against Sunday work[6] or dealing with the propriety of conduct on feast days[7] are further such indications of the part played by conciliar decrees in regulating social life. Not the least significant of these is that which makes it a duty of the bishop to appoint his own "advocatus" for his diocese: the bishop, in other words, must appoint his own protector, "lest the bishops, whilst attending to human pursuits, lose their eternal salvation."[8]

---

[1] MGH. *Concil.* ii. 556, cap. 6, line 27.

[2] MGH. *Concil.* ii. 557, cap. 7: "Itaque sacerdotes et ministri Christi, qui inter gradus clericorum ordinati existunt, debito officio secundum Deum et doctrinam Patrum in omnibus conversentur, eruditi existentes in divinis libris, valeantque se conspicere et alios emendando docere, ut quibus commissa sunt divina tractare misteria prudenter atque decenter cum Dei timore sua valeant ministeria adimplere, ut Deo, cui assistunt, profecto placere possint. Cavendum quippe est, ut non ineruditi ad ministerium Christi vel inliterati, ut decet, accedant . . ."

[3] MGH. *Concil.* ii. 581, cap. 23: "Nulli laicorum liceat in eo loco, ubi sacerdotes reliquive clerici consistunt, quod presbyterium nuncupatur, quando missa celebratur, consistere."

[4] MGH. *Concil.* ii. 582, cap. 36: "Nulli liceat excepta causa fornicationis adhibitam uxorem relinquere et deinde aliam copulare."

[5] See esp. MGH. *Concil.* ii. 583, cap. 37.

[6] MGH. *Concil.* ii. 580, cap. 30.

[7] MGH. *Concil.* ii. 581–2, cap. 35.

[8] MGH. *Concil.* ii. 575, cap. 19: "Debet ergo unusquisque eorum (scil. episcoporum) tam pro ecclesiasticis quam etiam pro propriis suis actionibus excepto publico videlicet crimine, habere advocatum non malae famae suspectum, sed bonae opinionis et laudabilis artis inventum, ne dum lucra humana adtendunt, aeterna perdant."

The Council held at Paris in 829 must detain us a little longer. Of all the numerous Frankish councils this is the one of greatest importance, since it propounds in decree form a number of highly pregnant doctrines which may, at the time, have been of purely theoretical value, but which nevertheless show us what great strides the hierocratic theme had made as a consequence of Charlemagne's conceptions. Influenced very largely as this council was by no lesser authority than Bishop Jonas of Orleans, it sets forth in its very first chapters the correct view of the nature of contemporary society. The unitary principle, the corporate nature of Christendom, and the distribution of appropriate functions within the Christian *corpus*—these are the main themes dealt with by the Parisian synodists of 829.[1]

The idea of unity dominates the council: the Christians form one body in Christ; the whole universal Church is one body whose mystical head is Christ himself. It is highly significant when these synodists express these fundamental ideas with the help of the Pauline declarations. Their second chapter has this heading:

Quod universalis sancta Dei ecclesia *unum corpus* eiusque caput Christus sit.[2]

The corporate view of the nature of Christian society entails, on the one hand, the close integration and division of functions and, on the other hand, resulting therefrom the different grading of the members composing the *corpus*. In other words, with the help of Pauline statements, the synodists emphasize the teleological principle underlying the working of the Christian body politic. The profound Pauline declaration is here quoted fully: "Since we have many members in one body, not all have the same functions."[3] Immediately afterwards the synodists quote St Paul's further statement in which he had also laid down the teleological principle, namely, that the proper functioning of the corporate body of Christians is guaranteed by all its members being orientated and directed by the head which is Christ.[4] The whole *corpus* receives its purpose and aim through being nourished in all its joints and bands from the head; thus it is a closely knit and integrated entity which will fulfil the purpose given to it by the head, if all the members function in consonance with the office allocated to them.

---

[1] The council like its predecessor of four years earlier, was convoked by Louis: all the four councils of 829 (Paris, Lyons, Toulouse, and Mainz) were summoned specifically by his orders, see MGH. *Concil.* ii. 596–7, where the convocation order is printed.

[2] MGH. *Concil.* ii. 610.      [3] *Rom.* xii. 4.

[4] *Col.* ii. 19; MGH. *Concil.* ii. 610.

The universal Church which is the "corpus Christi"[1] consists, according to the synodists, of the two orders, the sacerdotal and lay. These two orders are represented by two individuals, the sacerdotal and laical persons:

Principaliter igitur totius sanctae Dei ecclesiae corpus in duas eximias personas, in sacerdotalem videlicet et regalem, sicut a sanctis patribus traditum accepimus, divisum esse novimus.[2]

These two individuals symbolically represent the two orders and the synodists quite correctly perceive the significance of Gelasius's statement in this context that in this body politic the sacerdotal person has not only "auctoritas," but also greater weight since he has to render an account for the doings of the regal person on the Day of Judgment.[3]

The invocation of Gelasius's statement necessarily leads the synodists to the Isidorian view of the auxiliary function of the king, or as they style it, of the king's "ministry." The king's "ministerium" consists of ruling the "populus Dei" with equity and justice, so that peace and concord are achieved.[4] Naturally, the nature of equity and that of justice, in a Christian society, can be determined only by a recourse to Christian principles: it is the function of the "sacerdotes" to decide therefore what is equity and justice, because they alone are functionally qualified to pronounce upon these ideas. The *raison d'être* of a regal person, in a Christian society, is, as Isidore had stated, to fortify and to strengthen ecclesiastical discipline; the synodists quote at length the Isidorian passage in which he had declared that what the word of the priests could not achieve, the power of the prince would do "per disciplinae terrorem." The purpose of the king's exercising "terror" is to prevent injustice.[5] The king's function, considered from this point of view, is therefore negative, repressive—in a word auxiliary to the function of the priests. The king is the watch-dog who keeps peace and order within the body of Christians and by virtue of this function he is the defender and protector of the weak and defenceless members of

---

[1] MGH. *Concil.* ii, cap. 2.

[2] MGH. *Concil.* ii, cap. 3, p. 610, lines 33–5.

[3] They continue: "De qua re Gelasius Romanae sedis venerabilis episcopus ad Anastasium imperatorem ita scribit: 'Duo sunt, quippe, . . .' "

[4] MGH. *Concil.* ii. 2, pp. 651–2: "Quid sit proprie ministerium regis. Regale ministerium specialiter est populum Dei gubernare et regere cum equitate et justitia et, ut pacem et concordiam habeant, studere."

[5] MGH. *Concil.* ii. 2, pp. 651–2: "Ipsius enim terror et studium huiuscemodi, in quantum possibile est, esse debet primo, ut nulla injustitia fiat."

this body of Christians, of the clerics, of the individual churches, of the widows and orphans—in short his protective hand is to give security to those who are not in a position to provide security for themselves.

It is, moreover, significant—although of purely theoretical value at the time—that the synodists adduce the Old Testament statement "Per me reges regnant"[1] and that they link this up with another Pauline declaration: "Non est potestas nisi a Deo."[2] These views, when once the pope's vicariate of Christ was fully developed, will become of crucial importance. What the synodists are anxious to emphasize is the moral-religious complexion of the king's ministry. Because he functions as an auxiliary organ, he has not only no autonomous standing in a Christian society—the significance of the biblical "Per me reges regnant" will then become obvious—but he must also orientate his governmental action according to the purpose and nature of his society. The purpose and nature of this *corpus* being Christian, the Ruler's function is to subordinate himself and his government to the task of fulfilling the divine will in this society. This divine will, however, is known only through the sacerdotal order: the "sacerdotes" are the "divinae voluntatis indices" and therefore the "duces fidelis populi";[3] they are the "exemplum aliis et condimentum salutis."[4] The functional qualification of the sacerdotal order for laying down the proper way of living in a Christian society, is the effluence of their unique power to bind and to loose.[5] Views like these, when explicitly addressed to an emperor, had a decidedly significant ring, especially when the power of the keys is joined with Constantine's alleged declaration at the Council of Nicaea to the assembled bishops: "God has established you as priests and has given you power to judge us; rightly therefore we are judged by you, but you cannot be judged by man."[6]

---

[1] *Prov.* viii. 15–16.

[2] *Rom.* xiii. 1; *Concil.*, loc. cit., and cap. 5, p. 655.

[3] The synodists quote from Julianus Pomerius's *De vita contemplativa*, ii. 2, cap. 9, p. 673.

[4] MGH. *Concil.*, i. 38, p. 636, line 29. Cf. also ii. 9, p. 673, again quoting Pomerius: "dispensatores regiae domus, quorum arbitrio in aula regis aeterni dividuntur gradus et officia singulorum."

[5] MGH. *Concil.* ii, cap. 8, p. 673.

[6] MGH. *Concil.* ii, cap. 8, p. 673: " Deus constituit vos sacerdotes et potestatem vobis dedit de nobis quoque judicandi; et ideo nos a vobis recte judicamur, vos autem non potestis ab hominibus judicari." See also i. 19, p. 625. The passage in fact is taken from Rufinus, *Hist. Eccl.*, i. 2 or from Gregory I's *Reg.* v. 36 = MGH. *Epp.* i. 318. The employment of the same quotation by Gregory VII is in his *Reg.* iv. 2; viii. 21; ix. 37. In reviewing the Frankish time the

The function of the Ruler, as the synodists had delineated it—negative, repressive, auxiliary—made them quote the "Render unto Caesar the things which are Caesar's"[1] without thereby detracting from the role which the sacerdotal order alone was qualified to play in a Christian society: in these things which they considered to fall within the purview of the Ruler's function, he could demand obedience. They by no means wish to say that the Ruler has autonomous standing: what he has is "potestas" which is confined to those governmental actions that are related to the purpose of society and to the Ruler's properly auxiliary, repressive function. Since "Caesar" functions in an auxiliary capacity, he does not begin to function thus until the word of the priest has proved inadequate: he does not bear the sword in vain. It is only for particular purposes that he has been given the sword—to ensure the efficacy of the priestly word—and in order to fulfil this purpose he must be rendered obedience by his subjects. So long as he fulfils this supplementary function, he is a legitimate Ruler. Nevertheless we should bear in mind that, according to the synodists, the Ruler had received his supplementary function from Christ, and therefore their invocation of Christ's dictum could have but little practical value at the time—for the proper scope of the "things which are Caesar's" is thereby not determined—but when once the pope's vicariate of Christ was fully developed, Christ's dictum was then readily capable of proper and practical application to the Ruler in a Christian society. For the synodists, the saying of Christ served as the biblical support for the intended reduction of royal power. The expression "things of Caesar" is nothing else but the shell which contains the Pauline and Isidorian substance.

This synod of Paris (829) shows the great stimulus which Charlemagne's ideas had bequeathed to the Frankish intelligentsia. The bishops assembled there set forth a quite advanced hierocratic programme. What we miss in all their decrees is any reference to papal power and authority. It is as if the pope did not exist for them. They

---

late E. Eichmann, *Acht und Bann*, p. 24, said this: "Richtunggebend in dieser ecclesia universalis ist das sacerdotium, welches den göttlichen Willen kennt, interpretiert, verkündet. Nach den von dem sacerdotium verkündeten göttlichen Lehren, "jure ecclesiastico" hat der König das Reich zu lenken; er hat seine Gewalt von Gott zur Freude der Guten, zum Schrecken der Bösen. Da er die Gewalt der kirchlichen Vermittlung dankt, muss er sie im Sinne derjenigen führen, welche sie ihm gegeben haben . . ."

[1] *Matt.* xxii. 21.

still adhere to the point of view that they as bishops are the vicars of the apostles or of St Peter himself as they declare in their address to Louis: "cuius vicem indigni gerimus."[1] What they propound is pure episcopalism—hierocratic thought without its papal ingredient. Or as they say, they aim at episcopal liberty.[2] A good many of the points which they made would have received greater poignancy had they not omitted to take into account the basic element of the papal theme, namely, that the Petrine commission is applicable to the pope alone. Nevertheless, there can be no legitimate doubt that this episcopal-hierocratic set of ideas served as a powerful buttress for the development of the papal theme.[3] And it was barely twenty years later that Rome and Rheims coalesced.

The characteristically episcopal theme without the papal element appears to have been typical of the Frankish ethos in the decades following Charlemagne's death. On the one hand, the very brisk conciliar activity in the 20s and 30s of the ninth century showed the great impulse which the "ecclesiastical" party had been given; indeed, it is hard to imagine anywhere else in contemporary Europe such lively ecclesiastical-political discussions going on as in these councils whose theme was, as we have said, the proper ordering in a Christian society and the role which the sacerdotal order was to play in it. The recourse to Pauline statements is therefore very significant: the universalist conception of the corporate nature of Christian society necessarily leads to the frequent quotation of the "unum corpus sumus in Christo." The aim of all these councils, notably those of Paris and Aix (836)[4] was to demonstrate the unity of the Christian body, and this unitary principle could not, indeed, be better expressed than by this and other Pauline statements. For instance, in his speech at the Council of Kierzy in 838, the deacon of Lyons, Florus, gave a warning against the dangers inherent in dividing the "corpus Christi" by again soliciting support from St Paul's declarations:[5] Christ and His body are one;[6] Christ is the "caput et vertex ecclesiae" from which the universal body of

---

[1] *Concil.* ii. 8, p. 673, lines 7–8. Cf. also their preface, p. 608, lines 4 ff.

[2] See ii. 27, p. 680, line 11: "episcopalis libertas." On this cf. also Fichtenau, op. cit., 261.

[3] The decrees were handed to Louis as the demands of the episcopacy of the whole empire in August 829: MGH. *Capitularia*, ii. no. 196, pp. 26–51 (*Relatio episcoporum*).

[4] MGH. *Concil.* ii. 705–67.

[5] *Concil.* ii. 771, lines 26 ff.

[6] "Rursus caput et corpus Christum et ecclesiam unum Christum esse contestans dicit (scil. Paulus)"; *Concil.* ii. 771, lines 32 f.; I *Cor.* xii. 12.

believers receives nourishment.[1] There is a "mirabilis unitas Domini Iesu et corporis eius . . ."[2] In short, every one of the councils was concerned with the unity of the whole Christian body—universality and unity based upon the corporateness of Christian society are the main tenets of these councils.

But on the other hand, the mystical head of this corporate entity is Christ. The papal claim to headship of this body had not yet apparently made a deep impression on the Frankish intelligentsia, at least as far as its members expressed themselves in conciliar decrees and speeches. It is the hierocratic standpoint of episcopal provenance that is presented to us in these documents. Nor is it different in the literary products of the time, such as the book written by Bishop Jonas of Orleans.[3] This book is merely a re-statement of the decrees of the Paris council of 829 and ideologically adds virtually nothing.[4] It is nevertheless significant of the ethos of the time that these ecclesiastical-political ideas form the subject of a treatise such as Jonas's was. It is in fact one of the first written in Europe on a purely political theme.[5]

The functions which councils and writers attributed to the members of the sacerdotal order in the matter of guiding and shaping contemporary Christian society, of necessity prompted them, as we have seen, to reduce royal power to that of a mere auxiliary organ. The functions of the king in a Christian society are indeed necessary, but they are on a level quite different from those of the priests. The latter alone are functionally qualified to orientate the "corpus Christi," namely universal Christendom. It is, consequently, not surprising that the prevalent system of proprietary churches came under a sharp attack by some Frankish intellectuals. For this system was in fact the precise opposite to what the Frankish intelligentsia considered to be the right ordering

---

[1] *Concil.* ii. 772, lines 7 ff.: "Christus enim Iesus caput et vertex ecclesiae, et idcirco ad vitae aeternae commercium illi conectitur et cohaeret et in illum tota concurrit in ecclesia, ut *fonte capitis totum corpus* irrigetur et vivat . . .", followed by the citation of *Ephes*. iv. 15–16.          [2] *Concil.* ii. 772, lines 26–7.

[3] Jonas of Orleans, *De institutione regia*, ed. J. Reviron, in his *Les idées politico-religieuses d'un évêque du ix siècle*, Paris, 1930.

[4] He was the draftsman of the decrees, see Reviron, op. cit. 33.

[5] Cf. also H. X. Arquillière, *L'augustinisme politique*, p. 98, note 4. In the book itself the episcopal theme, the role of the sacerdotal order and the unitary principle based on the corporate nature of Christian society, are treated in almost literal agreement with the Paris decrees of 829, see esp. pp. 134, 136, 137, ed. cit. Msgr. Arquillière, op. cit., 102, commenting on Jonas, observes: "En somme, le pouvoir séculier n'est qu'un prolonguement necéssaire de l'autorité ecclésiastique. C'est le bras séculier"; and p. 101: "Le roi represente la force, mise au service de l'église."

in a Christian society.[1] We may select Agobard of Lyons as an illustration of this reaction.[2]

To Agobard it is axiomatic that a violation of "canons" constitutes an action against God Himself and against the whole body of Christians;[3] a transgression of "canons" is also an action that endangers the faith itself.[4] For the "canons" were made "Deo auctore" and there can be no excuse whatsoever for their violation. And the "canons" which the archbishop of Lyons has in mind are those concerning church property. By violating these "canons" lay people turn ecclesiastical goods to their own private use.[5] The spread of Christianity, Agobard holds, entailed that emperors, kings, bishops and other potentates began to erect churches and to endow them with goods and treasures,[6] but at the same time Rulers had issued decrees and bishops had promulgated canons intended to protect these goods which were "res

---

[1] For the ideology of the proprietary church system, cf. infra 232,243. One of the first to raise his voice appears to have been Bishop Wala in his memorandum for the Diet to be held in the winter 828-9 at Aix, see *Vita Walae*, MGH. SS. ii. 548-9, and P. Radbert's *Epitaphium Arsenii*, in PL. cxx. 1557–1650, also edited by E. Dümmler, in *Abhandl. der preuss. Akad. d. Wiss.*, 1900, pp. 18 ff., esp. pp. 62 ff., where Wala asks the—for the emperor—awkward question: By what authority does he give away ecclesiastical property and ecclesiastical dignity? It is a weighty question which laical ideology will never answer satisfactorily. It is as if the Investiture Contest had cast its shadows back into the ninth century, cf. also H. Dörries, in *Der Vertrag von Verdun*, ed. Th. Mayer, p. 158. Some of Wala's statements also remind of the situation in the late fifth century. For instance, he says to the emperor (SS. ii. 548): "In divine things you should not hold forth beyond what is needed . . . you know that the whole Church is administered by the two orders;"—"procul dubio his duobus totius ecclesiae status administratur ordinibus." He continues: "Habeat igitur rex rempublicam libere in usibus militiae suae ad dispensandum; habeat et Christus res ecclesiarum quasi alteram rempublicam," ibid., p. 548.

[2] There is a very good study on the background to Agobard's literary products by J. A. Cabaniss, "Agobard of Lyons," in *Speculum*, xxvi (1951), especially pp. 55, 63 ff.

[3] MGH. *Epp.* v. no. 5, p. 167, cap. 4, lines 29 ff.: "Receptum est non aliud esse agere cuiquam adversus canones quam adversus Deum et adversus eius universalem ecclesiam."

[4] MGH. *Epp.* v, no. 5, p. 167, cap. 4, lines 31 f.: "Neque sensum est umquam a quibusque fidelibus ut talia statuta absque periculo religionis violarentur."

[5] MGH. *Epp.* v, no. 5, p. 167, cap. 4, lines 17 ff.: ". . . contra vetitum et contra canones tractant et in usus proprios expendunt homines laici."

[6] MGH. *Epp.* v, no. 5, p. 167, cap. 4, lines 19 ff.: "Postquam enim diffusa est ecclesia Dei toto orbe terrarum et coepit exaltari ac magnificari per omnes regiones et nationes, coeperuntque templa erigi a fidelibus imperatoribus ac regibus atque episcopis vel ceteris potentibus, ditarique rebus et thesauris ornari, fuit enim consequens, ut principum providentia leges promulgarentur et episcoporum canones statuerentur de rebus sanctificatis, id est, sacris locis deputatis, qualiter tuerentur ab improbis, tuerentur a gubernatoribus vel expenderentur."

sanctificatae" because they were assigned to "sacris locis." The gist of
episcopal legislation, according to Agobard, was the prohibition of
alienation of property once assigned to a church or sacred place. The
episcopal decrees fixing the sacrosanct character of this property
"firmati sunt spiritu Dei, consensu totius mundi, obedientia principum,
consonantia scripturarum."[1]

Agobard held that the whole institution of the proprietary churches
was a blatant violation of the principle that these goods should be
removed from the control of the unordained members of the Church.
Once a church had been built, it and the ground upon which it was
erected, could not form the subject of a legal transaction: a transaction
of that kind was nothing less than invasion, usurpation, theft and
sacrilege on the part of the layman who disposed of churches by
appointing his clerics.[2] His point of view, he is anxious to stress, does
not infringe upon the biblical tenet: "Provide neither gold nor silver
nor brass in your purses."[3] For the land and goods assigned to a church
become by virtue of this assignment divine things which are thereby
entirely removed from the disposition by laymen. One must distinguish between theft committed on private, public and divine things.
When even the first two constitute a crime, and the second kind of
theft constitutes a sacrilege even according to imperial laws, how much
more sacrilegious in character must be the third kind of theft. "Apud
nos specialiter sacrilegii nomine censetur."[4] This crime is committed
by giving, accepting or retaining ecclesiastical property.[5] What a
Ruler has a right to is the exaction of taxes and customs duties. Church
property, so far from being the subject of laical transaction, should
not even be administered by lay people; the "sacerdotium" should
itself, through the medium of suitable clerics or monks, administer its
own property.[6] Lay individuals should be the protectors, and not the
administrators, of what they wrongly regard as their privately owned

[1] MGH. *Epp.* v, no. 5, p. 167, cap 4, lines 26 ff. For similar statements during
the Investiture Contest see infra p. 410.
[2] MGH. *Epp.* v, no. 5: see esp. p. 169, cap. 10, lines 43 ff.; p. 170, cap. 12,
lines 40 ff.; p. 172, cap. 15, lines 9 ff.; p. 174, cap. 18, lines 7 ff.
[3] *Matt.* x. 9.
[4] MGH. *Epp.* v, no. 5, p. 174, cap. 18, lines 9–10: "adeo immane scelus esse
manifestum est."
[5] MGH. *Epp.* v, no. 5, p. 174, cap. 18, lines 12–13.
[6] MGH. *Epp.* v, no. 5, p. 174, cap. 19, lines 26 ff.: "Ex laicis denique non solum
possessores sacrarum rerum, sed nec dispensatores fieri permittunt, quin potius
oeconomos de proprio clero eligi precipiunt et agros, vineas atque mancipia ad
usum tribui nonnisi clericis monachis peregrinisque concedunt."

churches.[1] But it took more than 200 years before this demand for a change of the "dominium" into the "patronatus" was realized.

In a letter entitled "De privilegiis et jure sacerdotii" Agobard is equally bitter about the "domestic chaplains" appointed by lay persons.[2] He denounces those clerics who take up clerical positions as a result of laical appointments—such a cleric, Agobard holds, cannot be a "bonus clericus, qui cum talibus hominibus dehonestari nomen et vitam suam ferret."[3] For the lay lord who appoints a cleric does not appoint him "propter religionis honorem," as it is only too clearly seen that the cleric is not held in high esteem by the entourage of the lay lord.[4] In a sarcastic vein Agobard says that a lay lord may well ask somebody to ordain "unum clericionem, quem mihi nutrivi de servis meis propriis" which request of course should be unheeded.[5] Agobard explicitly included in his attacks on the proprietary churches also the episcopal and abbatial owners of churches.[6]

Nevertheless, it would seem that in view of this fundamental opposition to the idea of proprietary churches the ruling of the Roman synod of 826 to which we have already referred, appears particularly odd. In its twenty-first chapter this synod laid down:

A monastery or an oratory, as long as they are erected canonically, must not be removed from the proprietor who is allowed to hand it over to a cleric from his diocese so that divine service may be held there, after the diocesan bishop has been requested to give his consent.[7]

Two observations about this decree must be made. Firstly, there is a great difference between the rulings of a Roman synod presided over by a pope (Eugenius II) and any other synod: the authority attributed to the former was of considerably higher standing than that of the

[1] Cf. also P. Imbart de la Tour, "Les paroisses rurales dans l'ancienne France" in *Revue Historique*, lxvii (1898), pp. 29–30; Fichtenau, op. cit., 233.

[2] MGH. *Epp.* v, no. 11, pp. 203–4.

[3] MGH. *Epp.* v, no. 11, pp. 203–4, lines 32 ff.

[4] MGH. *Epp.* v, no. 11, pp. 203–4, lines 35 ff.

[5] MGH. *Epp.* v, no. 11, p. 204, lines 1 ff. The attitude of the Paris council of 829 was much more moderate, cap. 22, p. 627.

[6] Ep. no. 5, p. 178, cap. 29: "Quicumque . . . noverit omnino non haec nos de solis laicis dicere, sed etiam de episcopis, abbatibus sive quibuslibet clericis, qui aliud faciunt de saepe dictis rebus sacris quam quod faciendum est."

[7] MGH. *Concil.* ii. 576, cap. 21: "De monasterio vel oratorio quod a proprio domino soli edificatum est: monasterium vel oratorium canonice constructum a dominio constructoris invito non auferatur liceatque illi id presbytero cui voluerit, pro sacro officio illius dioceseos et bonae auctoritatis dimissoriae cum consensu episcopi, ne malus existat, commendare, ita ut ad placita et justam reverentiam ipsius episcopi oboedienter sacerdos recurrat."

6

latter. It is assuredly a sign of statesmanship to take into account the realities of the situation, and in view of the widespread system and in view of the facts of the political situation at that time (826), it would have been unwise to proceed to an outright condemnation of the institute. But a littérateur, even though of the standing of Agobard, had greater liberty in denouncing certain features and practices than a provincial council. Secondly, in assessing this decree one should bear in mind that the proprietor's freedom of clerical appointments was restricted, since the decree stipulated that the local bishop's consent must be obtained. Mention therefore must be made in this context of the imperial decree issued three years later, according to which the penalty for appointing a cleric without episcopal consent entailed outlawry for the owner of the church.[1]

As a harbinger of the fusion between the Roman papacy and the Frankish clergy, we may classify Abbot Walafrid Strabo. He wrote his tract between 840 and 842.[2] Whilst, as far as we can see, the councils, speeches and literary products of the time pay no attention to the function and authority of the pope and make the bishops the vicars of all the apostles or of St Peter alone, Walafrid Strabo, on the other hand, perceives the need to base episcopal power upon a firmer foundation than his contemporaries have done. For he squarely bases episcopal authority and, in fact, all the hierarchical offices upon the Petrine commission as the tenet was understood by papal doctrine: he thus makes the pope the apex of the whole sacerdotal hierarchy. It seems, moreover, that he was more interested in this point than in the relationship between the sacerdotal officers and their lay counterparts.

Walafrid's conception of the organic and corporate nature of the Christian body politic is as axiomatic to him as to his contemporaries.[3] This unitary and universal *corpus* has its two orders

ex utriusque ordinis conjunctione et dilectione una domus Dei construitur, unum corpus Christi efficitur,[4]

---

[1] See the Capitulare of Worms, 829, in MGH. *Capitularia*, ii. 12, cap. 1: "De his qui sine consensu episcopi presbyteros in ecclesiis suis constituunt vel de ecclesiis eijiciunt et ab episcopo vel a quolibet misso dominico admoniti obedire noluerint, ut bannum nostrum rewadiare cogantur et per fideijussores ad palatium nostrum venire jubeantur; et tunc nos decernamus utrum nobis placeat, ut aut illum bannum persolvant aut aliam harmiscaram sustineant."

[2] *Libellus de exordiis et incrementis rerum ecclesiasticarum*, ed. in MGH. *Capitularia*, ii. 474 ff.; about the date see p. 473.

[3] See esp. MGH. *Capitularia*, ii. 479, cap. 6.

[4] MGH. *Capitularia*, ii. 516, cap. 32, lines 16 ff.

and his main attention is focused on the hierarchical ordering, that is, the sacerdotal organism, or what he calls the "spiritualis respublica universalis ecclesiae."[1] Nor is it the least interesting feature of Walafrid's argumentation that in demonstrating the hierarchical grading of the sacerdotal order—from the "summus pontifex" downwards—he constructs an entire parallelism between the hierarchical grades of the "sacerdotium" and the "imperium." The pope is paralleled by the Caesars of ancient times who held "totius orbis *monarchiam*": the pope, by virtue of the Petrine commission is raised to the apex of the universal Church.[2]

Comparetur ergo papa Romanus augustis et caesaribus.[3]

The patriarchs correspond to imperial patricians; the archbishops correspond to the kings, metropolitans to dukes, the abbots to military tribunes, the "chorepiscopi" to the "missi" of the counts, and so on down to the lowest ecclesiastical grade.

Walafrid's tract marks an important stage in the development of the hierocratic theory. It bears witness to the realization on the part of some contemporaries that not only a strict hierarchical ordering is necessary, but also that this hierocratic order is instituted from a central agency, the Roman Church. Just as all imperial officers derive their existence from Caesar, in the same way the ecclesiastical officers derive theirs from the supreme pontiff. The consideration underlying this postulate was naturally none other than the function which the sacerdotal order within the universal Church was to play. Being the directive organ of the whole corpus of Christians—and not merely of the Frankish Christians—the sacerdotal order must necessarily be directed by a central organ which is at the same time also the guarantor of unity. The proper working and functioning of the *corpus* of Christians presupposes the execution of the unitary principle by the hierarchical subordination of the sacerdotal order to the guarantor of unity—the Roman Church and herewith the pope.

### III

There can hardly be a better test of the conception of the corporate nature of Christian society in the ninth century than the effects which

---

[1] MGH. *Capitularia*, ii. 514, line 32. On Wala's *Respublica* see supra p. 135 n. 1.

[2] MGH. *Capitularia*, ii. 515, lines 3–5: "Ita summus pontifex in sede Romana vicem beati Petri gerens totius ecclesiae apice sublimatur."

[3] MGH. *Capitularia*, ii. 515, lines 16–17.

excommunication decreed by the ecclesiastical authority produced. The later canonistic and political doctrine of the effects of excommunication are clearly foreshadowed in this century.[1] In this sphere we witness very much the same phenomenon which we noticed in the purely ideological realm: old material is adduced and quoted and thus given a new lease of life, but this old material had, when originally propounded, a purely theoretical value, whilst, by virtue of the changed circumstances, it now begins to display practical effects.[2]

In the early Frankish period excommunication did not seem to have had any effects in the so-called civil sphere. If we take the decrees of the Council of Verneuil of 755 as an example, it becomes clear that the excommunicate is excluded only from participating in certain activities: he must not enter a church; must not eat or drink with any other Christian; must not accept any gifts nor join in prayers with others nor have contact with Christians.[3] Those who are excommunicated by a synod, must be shunned by "all the peoples of the Church."[4] A further effect of such excommunication is that those who have contact with an excommunicate, are themselves excommunicated.[5]

The basic idea of a corporate communion of all Christians could not lead to any other view but to that according to which excommunication was the effective exclusion from membership of this communion: the excommunicate is thus deprived of any standing within the corporate body of Christians. Excommunication displayed effects in every sphere that was considered relevant to the working and functioning of this body. Those individuals who defy episcopal orders for satisfaction "are to be cut out of the body of the universal Church": "tamquam putrida ac desperata membra ab universalis ecclesiae corpore dissecandi."[6] Excommunicate persons are unable to do military service or

---

[1] See esp. E. Eichmann, *Acht und Bann*, pp. 14, 25–6, against Hinschius and others. Cf. now also G. de Vergottini, *Studi sulla legislazione imperiale di Frederico II in Italia*, Milan, 1952, especially pp. 47 ff.

[2] The bases of excommunication were mainly the first and second decrees of the Council of Carthage, 419 (incorporated in Gratian IV. i. 1); cf. also Eichmann, op. cit., loc. cit.

[3] MGH. *Capitularia*, i. 35, cap. 9.

[4] MGH. *Concilia*, ii. 201, cap. 16: ". . . omnino observare debemus, ut qui ab universali synodo pro certis criminibus excommunicatus fuerit, ante emendationem et conversationem non suscipiatur ab aliquo, non episcopus, non presbyter, non diaconus, non laicus et nullus omnino de populis ecclesiae."

[5] MGH. *Concilia*, ii. 201, cap. 16: "Et si quis ante emendationem cum tali communicaverit, juxta canones antiquos excommunicetur cum illo usque ad correctionem et ad emendationem vitae suae."

[6] Council of Pavia, 850, MGH. *Capit.*, ii. 120, cap. 12.

fulfil any public office.[1] In other words, they are excluded from the court of the emperor and from all courtly dignities.[2]

Since the function of the Ruler was auxiliary and since he as a Christian was expected to assist the sacerdotal order in the direction and orientation of the *corpus* of Christians, the bishop was entitled to call upon the civil magistrate if he wished to make a recalcitrant individual conform to ecclesiastical discipline. The bishop, together with the count, could order the individual "ut jussionibus episcopi sui obediens existat";[3] if this should have been of no avail, the individual was to be outlawed by the king and in case of persistency, excommunication followed.[4] But even without preceding episcopal request the Ruler was entitled to outlaw certain individuals who had made themselves guilty of a crime which was such only by virtue of an ecclesiastical decree, as for instance, usury; in this case[5] the emperor made a norm of ecclesiastical laws his own, but without specific mandate or admonition on the part of the bishop.[6] As a last resort excommunication will be decreed.[7] The same observation can be made as regards the refusal to pay tithes.[8]

On the other hand, there is no evidence to support the contention that punishments imposed by the king for the violation of his laws displayed any effects anywhere else but in the strictly limited and confined royal sphere. In other words, outlawry inflicted by the king for transgressions of his decrees, does not entail exclusion from the *corpus* of Christians. This is nothing else but the practical application of the idea that what matters in a Christian society is not the law of the emperor, but the law of those who are functionally qualified to direct this society. Their laws have effects throughout the length and breadth of Christian society, whilst the king's laws and their effects are limited, that is, limited to the scope of his power.

[1] MGH. *Capit.*, ii. 120, cap. 12: "Nullo militiae secularis uti cingulo nullamque reipublicae debent administrare dignitatem."

[2] Cf. also the Convention of Soissons of 853, *Capit.* ii. 266, cap. 10: "excommunicationem ecclesiasticam et *motum indignationis regiae.*"

[3] "Capitulare Olonnense" of 825, *Capit.* i. 327.

[4] *Capit.* i. 327: "Si vero assensum non dederit, bannum nostrum nobis persolvat. Quod si adhuc contumax perstiterit, tunc ab episcopo excommunicetur." A. Nissl, *Der Gerichtsstand des Clerus im Fränkischen Reich,* Innsbruck, 1886, p. 35, note 3, refers to a letter of St Boniface, written to the pope in which he complained of heretical priests who had been condemned to degradation and incarceration in a monastery, but who had refused to go into prison; Boniface asks the pope "ut per litteras vestras mandare curetis duci Carlomanno, ut mittatur (scil. sacerdos) in custodiam, ut semina satani latius non seminet."

[5] See *Capit.* cit., p. 327, cap. 5.      [6] Cf. also Eichmann, op. cit., p. 18.

[7] Cf. the Convention of Lothar and Louis of 851, *Capit.* ii, 73, cap. 5.

[8] Council of Worms of 829, *Capit.* ii. 13, cap. 7.

It is of course true that these views had little practical value in the ninth century. But to them we can justifiably apply what we have said about the purely theoretical value of literary and conciliar expressions. They all serve as powerful incubators of a programme: they are vehicles which not only transmit old material to later times, but which also attempt to apply and to adapt this material to circumstances which had little in common with those which had first given rise to certain fundamental statements. But this, we think, is an observation which does not only apply to this topic.

This survey of the Frankish ethos will have shown that as a result of Charlemagne's own religious conceptions—and despite his own monarchic government—hierocratic forces were released which were from now onwards to give European society its particular "ecclesiastical" complexion. The basic tenet of this hierocratic view was the conception of the community of Christians as one closely knit organic entity—a *corpus* within which the members fulfilled certain functions in consonance with the purpose and character of this society. This being a Christian *corpus*, priestly ordination was the criterion which conferred a functional qualification of rulership, of directing and guiding this *corpus*. Those members of the *corpus* who were not thus distinguished, though still fulfilling important functions, were not functionally qualified to rule, that is, to direct and orientate this *corpus*. The "sacerdotium" alone was thus qualified—the "regnum" alone was qualified to enforce with the help of the sword—"per disciplinae terrorem"— the word of the "sacerdotes." This assistance of the "regnum" to the "sacerdotium" was fundamental to the working of the whole Christian *corpus*. By laying down some general principles obtaining in a Christian society, the Frankish intelligentsia made later European society its debtor. Nevertheless, we ought to be clear about the defect which this episcopalist hierocratic theme showed, namely, its lack of orientation towards the Roman Church and the pope. Even so, this Frankish set of ideas was to prove a very powerful medium for the development of the conception of Christian society. The implementation of the true papalist theme was considerably facilitated by this receptivity and preparation of the soil. The vigorous assertions of the papal-hierocratic theme by contemporary popes, especially Gregory IV and Leo IV, could and did without difficulty lead to the merging of papal and episcopal views—could and did lead to the confluence of Rome and Rheims.

# CHAPTER V

# Symbolism in Coronation Ceremonies of the Ninth Century

## I

THE reception by Charlemagne of Pope Leo III at Paderborn was not apparently distinguished by an elaborate ceremonial: the king's dignitaries gathered around him without any distinction about their clerical or laical status. The reception, seventeen years later, by Louis the Pious of Pope Stephen IV at Rheims, was marked by a careful ceremonial arrangement: the earlier informal manner was dropped; instead, the clerical dignitaries were ranged in a straight line on Louis's right-hand side, whilst on his left-hand side there stood his magnates.[1]

The motive for Stephen's journeying to Rheims was to crown the son of Charlemagne emperor, although he had already become emperor three years earlier, in 813. The significance of the papally performed imperial coronation in 816 was threefold. Firstly, there was the emphasis on the Roman and Petrine origin of the imperial crown; secondly, it was the first papal ceremony which combined unction with actual coronation; thirdly, the Romans themselves were excluded from the creation of an emperor. All this, to be sure, was due to the initiative of the pope himself. For, according to contemporary reports, as soon as Stephen IV became pope, he notified Louis that he desired to meet

---

[1] Ermoldus Nigellus, *In honorem Hludovici Caesaris*, ii. verses 211 ff. (SS. ii. 482 = MGH. *Poetae Lat.* ii. 30); H. Fichtenau, *Das karolingische Imperium*, p. 224. A beginning of the separation of the two estates could be already witnessed three years earlier when, at the council of Mainz, they sat in different groups, as the synodists themselves say: MGH. *Concilia*, ii. no. 36, p. 259: "Convenit in nobis de nostro communi collegio clericorum seu laicorum tres facere turmas, sicut et fecimus." The one estate comprised the episcopal and abbatial participants, the other the dukes, counts and judges, pp. 259–60. Cf. also the council held at Aix-la-Chapelle in 802, *Conc.* ii, no. 29, p. 230, and see also Charlemagne's decree, *Capitularia*, i. 161, c. 1, where he ordered the separation of the clerical and abbatial and ducal elements each of which he was to address separately.

him.[1] Upon the arrival of the pope at Rheims—the day seems to have been a Thursday[2]—Louis dismounted from his horse and prostrated himself three times before the pope. This threefold proskynesis corresponded to the Byzantine ceremonial[3] and the new facet was that it was rendered to the pope alone, and not to a king or emperor.[4] The ceremony of prostration must have been previously arranged, and symbolically foreshadowed the significance of the pope's functions. No less meaningful was the pope's greeting to the king, after the latter had arisen and had himself extended his welcome to the papal visitor:[5] Stephen's greeting formula changed the text of *Kings* slightly:

Benedictus sit Dominus Deus noster, qui tribuit oculis nostris videre *secundum David*.[6]

The significance lies in the allusion to the ceremony of anointing. The coronation itself took place on the following Sunday before mass.[7] After the prayers the pope on receipt of the usual gifts from Louis exclaims:

> Roma tibi, Caesar, transmittit munera Petri
> Digna satis digno, conveniensque decus.[8]

Thereupon the pope orders a most precious crown to be brought which crown turns out to be that formerly worn by Emperor Constantine:

---

[1] Thegan, *Vita Hludowici Imperatoris*, MGH. SS. ii. 594: "Dirigens legatos suos ad supradictum principem, nuncians ei, ut libenter eum videre voluisset in loco ubicumque ei placuisset. Quod audiens, magno tripudio repletus coepit gaudere, et statim jussit missos suos obviam ire sancto pontifici cum salutationibus magnis et servitia praeparare." See furthermore *Annales Regni Fancorum*, ad 816, p. 144: "Duobus post consecrationem suam exactis mensibus quam maximis poterat itineribus ad imperatorem venire contendit, missis interim duobus legatis, qui quasi pro sua consecratione imperatori suggerent." We should also bear in mind that Stephen was the first pope since the political picture in Europe had so radically changed: an arrangement concerning the actual protection to be given to a newly elected pope, was highly desirable. The outcome was the *Ludovicianum*, about which see *Cambridge Hist. Journal*, xi (1953), pp. 114–28.

[2] Cf. *Vita Hludowici*, MGH. SS. ii. 620–21.

[3] See Eichmann, *Kaiserkrönung*, i. 41.

[4] Eichmann, loc. cit., who also draws attention to DP. 9.

[5] With the words of *Ps.* cxviii. 26.

[6] Thegan, loc. cit., p. 594, lines 10–11. I *Kings* i. 48: "Benedictus Dominus Deus Israel, qui dedit hodie sedentem in solio meo, videntibus oculis meis."

[7] So Thegan and Ermoldus; the *Vita Hludowici* says that the coronation took place during mass: "Inter missarum celebrationem."

[8] Ermoldus, verses 423 ff., p. 486. Before he says: "Inchoat, et cunctis monitans dat jussa silendi, ore benigna refert haec pius orsa pio."

> Tum jubet adferri gemmis auroque coronam,
> Quae Constantini Caesaris ante fuit.[1]

The step initiated by Leo III was now concluded by Stephen IV. He brings the crown of Constantine with him from Rome,[2] and this crown is the gift of St Peter to Louis. The pope as vicar of St Peter is merely the bearer of the Petrine gift. The papal blessing of the crown —a ceremony borrowed from the East[3]—is the pope's own personal contribution, as also is his blessing of Louis himself, which is followed by the anointing ceremony—the first such papal ceremony to be performed on an emperor in Europe. The final act is the placing of the crown on Louis's head.[4] The development of papal intervention is straight and clear: first the papal unction of Pippin as "patricius Romanorum," then the liturgically meaningless coronation of Charlemagne as "imperator Romanorum," and lastly the fusion of unction and coronation.

Moreover, whilst during Charlemagne's coronation the Romans were made to play some part in the act, at the ceremony at Rheims they were conspicuously absent: the crown is the gift of St Peter and hence at the disposal of St Peter's vicar; for the Romans there was no more room. Indeed, the pope's wish to exclude the Romans from partaking in the envisaged ceremony constituted an additional and a strong motive for Stephen's undertaking the journey.[5]

The prayer said by Stephen after the blessing of the crown and of Louis himself, makes interesting reading:

O Christ, Ruler of the empire of the world and Master of the ages, you have willed that Rome be the head of the earthly globe, grant our prayers . . .[6]

Rome, therefore, by divine ordinance, is to be the head and the centre of the world—not Constantinople, Aix-la-Chapelle, or Rheims. In

---

[1] Ermoldus, verses 425–6.

[2] Cf. also Thegan, loc. cit., p. 594: "Coronam . . . quam secum adportaverat."

[3] See Eichmann, i. 43.

[4] Thegan, p. 594: "Et in proxima die dominica in ecclesia ante missarum solempnia coram clero et omni populo consecravit eum et unxit eum ad imperatorem et coronam auream mirae pulchritudinis cum pretiosissimis gemmis ornatam, quam secum adportaverat, posuit super caput eius."

[5] The agreement which the pope wished to conclude with Louis was to guarantee imperial protection against the Romans: this was the *Ludovicianum*.

[6] Ermoldus, verses 429 ff.: "Qui regis imperium mundi saeclumque *gubernas* / Qui *Romae censes orbis habere caput* / Exaudi, praecibusque meis, peto, flecte benignam / Christe, aurem; votis rex pie quaeso fave. / Adjuvet Andreas, Petrus, Paulusque, Johannes / Atque Maria Dei mater opima pii; / Induperatorem hunc Hludowicum tempora longa / Servate; abscedant tristia cuncta procul. / Prospera cuncta date, nec non peto noxia longe / Pellite; sit felix, sitque potensque diu."

6 *

this we find expressed the ancient papal idea that the "ecclesia Romana" was the epitome of the whole of Christendom: and here the city of Rome acquires the function of the headship of the whole world: the city of Rome is the epitome of the whole Christian world. The emphasis on the Petrine character of the papal gifts, notably the crown of Constantine, was naturally very apt to endorse the identity between the "imperium Romanum" and the "imperium Christianum." These gifts were despatched by "Roma" which was, so to speak, the custodian of Constantine's donations to St Peter. The iridescent character of "Roma" as the one-time head of a (universal) empire and as the Petrine city is well brought out in the statement:

*Roma, tibi Caesar, transmittit munera Petri.*[1]

And the placing of the Constantinean crown on Louis's head by the pope is accompanied by the following papal declaration:

Hoc tibi Petrus ovans cessit, mitissime, donum.[2]

The circle is closed: the imperial crown because in the possession of St Peter is disposed of by his vicar: it is St Peter who, through the instrumentality of his vicar, confers imperial dignity: it is St Peter who makes the Roman emperor.

The main differences between the act of 800 and that of 816 are obvious. There no liturgical ceremony, merely a simple action devoid of religious meaning although performed in a church; here a fully fledged liturgical ceremony. The former act was largely borrowed from the Byzantine rite; the latter combined Byzantine and Frankish and papal rites. The essential features of the act of 800 were copied from Byzantium (the preliminaries in the form of consultation with senate and army: here with the assembled prelates and the Roman people, followed by acclamation and adoration), but disappeared at the ceremony sixteen years later. If the one chronicle reporting the adoration of Leo III is true,[3] it would have been the first and last adoration ren-

[1] The late Father Eichmann, op. cit., i. 45, drawing attention to the Roman spirit that can be observed at Rheims said: "Beachtenswert ist der römische Geist, der das Gebet durchweht: es ist Gotteswille, dass *Rom* das Haupt des Erdkreises, des Imperiums, sei; nicht Aachen, oder Reims. Der universalistische Zug, der diese Krönung hindurchzieht, ist unverkennbar." See furthermore, C. Erdmann, *Forschungen zur politischen Ideenwelt*, p. 75: "Das Wesentliche an der Feier war danach die Betonung der römischen und petrinischen Herkunft der Krone." [2] Ermoldus, verse 449, p. 486.

[3] *Annales Regni Francorum*, ad 801, p. 112, ed. cit.: "Post laudes ab apostolico more antiquorum principum adoratus est." The *Liber Pontificalis* says nothing about Leo's adoration, which silence in itself would not of course prove that no adoration was rendered by Leo.

dered by a pope to a Western emperor. Moreover, if the one report about the "laudes" at Rheims is true, they had no constitutive character.[1] Neither at Constantinople nor at Rome was the emperor anointed, and this feature constitutes the most essential difference between Rheims and its Roman predecessor.

Even if Stephen had not volunteered the information of the provenance of the crown, the act of 816 presents itself as the perfect translation of papal doctrine centring in the pope's function as a monarch, into visible reality. The conflation of the Cesarean Roma and the Petrine Roma was paralleled by the conflation of sacerdotal and regal powers in the person of the pope. This combination was also expressed in the order of ceremonial procedure: the unction precedes the coronation. In the ceremony of the unction the pope acts as a "sacerdos" and only the pope could do this. In the ceremony of the coronation the pope acts as "rex," and, again, only the pope himself could do so, since to no one else had Constantine entrusted the crown of the Roman empire. If the pope wished, he could have worn it, but he humbly refused it and left its use to Constantine—and he handed it now to Louis.[2] Unction and coronation were combined into one act, of which the former was of Frankish, the latter of Byzantine, origin. This combination of the hitherto quite separate actions[3] was to be of crucial importance for the rest of the Middle Ages. Before disposing of the crown, the pope "consecrated" through unction the king and "unxit eum *ad imperatorem.*"[4] This act, not the coronation, was really the vital religious part of the ceremony and gave it its liturgical meaning. The pope's function as a "sacerdos" was indisputable, and in the ingenious utilization of the purely spiritual unction (hitherto reserved for royalty alone) for *imperial* coronations, lies the true and deep significance of Rheims. Henceforward unction and coronation remained indissolubly linked as the two essential parts of one ceremony.

---

[1] Ermoldus, verses 480 ff.; see also Eichmann, op. cit., i. 29 ff.

[2] Eichmann, i. 46: "Der Papst, der fortlebende Petrus, hat die Krone, die er nach dem Willen des grossen Kaisers 'pro honore beati Petri' tragen sollte, freudig an Ludwig abgetreten."

[3] The Eastern emperors were not anointed. Cf. the report of Theophanes, writing about 810, and ridiculing the (by him) invented unction of Charlemagne in 800: "from head to feet the pope oiled him in," see his *Chronographia*, ed. de Boor, i. 473; see also the translation from the original Greek into Latin by Anastasius Bibliothecarius in his famous letter, MGH. *Epp.* vii. 384: "coronavit . . . perungens oleo a capite usque ad pedes."

[4] See Thegan, p. 594, line 16: "coram clero et omni populo consecravit eum et unxit eum ad imperatorem, et coronam auream . . . posuit super caput eius."

We should not forget, however, that the unction of the emperor demonstrated to the world the superiority which the Western emperors enjoyed when comparing themselves with their Eastern colleagues. For the latter's creation as emperors was not ecclesiastical, but purely mundane—the religious ceremony following it was only declaratory, not constitutive. Here in the West, the emperor was anointed by the supreme "sacerdos." Moreover, we can perhaps still better appraise the significance and imaginative courage of the pope's utilization of unction for imperial coronations, when we bear in mind that not even he as a bishop, nor anyone else in Rome, was anointed: the liturgical act of anointing sacerdotal members of the Church was unknown in ninth-century Rome and was not introduced there until more than a hundred years later.[1]

The symbolic combination of the "Sacerdos" and "Rex" in the person of the pope was also suitably accompanied by the change of name that was now given to the papal residence. This residence had already changed its name once before, from the "episcopium" to the "Patriarchium Lateranense." But now in or about 813 the latter name transformed itself not merely into a "Palatium," but also into a "Sacrum Palatium."[2] Whilst the "sacrum" character of the palace was to designate the sacerdotal function of the pope, the characterization of his residence as a "Palatium" was to convey his imperial-regal function. The basis of this metamorphosis was the Donation of Constantine, according to which the Emperor Constantine had made as a gift to the pope the "palatium imperii nostri Lateranense," so that this "palatium" should excel all other palaces in the whole world.[3] And the further purpose of this gift was that the pope should have his residence "ad imitationem imperii nostri." Indeed, this papal symbolism, so exquisitely shown in the ceremony at Rheims and in the contemporaneous change of title of the papal residence, was to remain a potent factor in the development of the papal idea itself.

---

[1] About 920 from the Gallican liturgy; on this see esp. E. Eichmann, "Königs- und Bischofsweihe" in *SB. Bayr. Ak.*, 1928, pp. 37 ff., also *Kaiserkrönung*, i. 81; Eisenhofer, *Liturgik*, pp. 289 f.; G. Ellard, *Ordination Anointings in the Western Church before 1000 A.D.*, pp. 74 ff. Cf. also supra p. 67.

[2] See especially K. Jordan, "Die Entstehung der römischen Kurie" in *Sav. Z., Kan. Abt.*, 1939, pp. 100–1, notes 2–5; also E. Caspar, *Geschichte des Papsttums*, ii. 629 ff.; idem, "Das Papsttum unter fränkischer Herrschaft" in *Z. f. Kirchenge-schichte*, lii (1935), pp. 139 ff.; R. Elze, "Das Sacrum Palatium Lateranense" in *Studi Gregoriani*, iv. 27 ff.; see also infra p. 326.

[3] "Quod omnibus in toto orbe terrarum praefertur atque praecellit palatiis."

## II

We may pause here and ask ourselves, what was the meaning of imperial unction? Its immediate predecessor was the Frankish royal unction which was modelled on Old Testament prototypes.[1] The conception underlying the anointings in the Old Testament was that the prophet by virtue of his knowledge of the divine will, symbolically appoints a king of his people. The procedure that became the model for the medieval unctions was that laid down in the Old Testament when God ordered Samuel to look amongst the sons of Jesse for a king of Israel as a successor of Saul.[2] David, having been fetched from the pastures, was anointed by Samuel to whom God said: "Anoint him; for this is he."[3] And it was from this day that the spirit of the Lord lived in David.[4]

There are two sides to the unction, both of which are as important in the Old Testament as they are in the Frankish and papal ceremonies. There is the constitutive aspect of unction. The Jews desired a king so that they would be like all the other nations,[5] and it is in this context that royal unctions made their appearance: Saul was anointed,[6] David was twice anointed,[7] Solomon's unction was similar[8] to that of Absalom,[9] Joas,[10] Jehoahaz.[11] The common feature of all these kings was that because they were anointed, they were held to have been divinely appointed, and hence were legitimate rulers of the Jewish people; in this capacity they had the duty of safeguarding their dynasty and of maintaining peace and order amongst the Jews. The ceremony of anointing consists in the prophet's pouring olive oil from the horn of oil over the head of the king.[12] It is this act alone which makes, which creates the king: thereby he becomes "dux populi."[13] He is constituted as the divinely installed and appointed ruler: he is the Lord's anointed,

---

[1] For this see especially E. Müller, "Die Anfänge der Königssalbung im Mittelalter" in *Hist. Jahrb.*, lvi (1938), pp. 317 ff.; Eichmann, SB. cit., passim; M. M. David, *Le Serment du Sacre du XI⁶ au XV siècle*, pp. 24 ff. (offprint from *Revue de moyen âge latin*, vi (1950)), and Eichmann, op. cit., i. 78 f.

[2] I *Kings*, xvi. 1.　　　　　　　　　[3] I *Kings*, xvi. 12.

[4] I *Kings*, xvi. 13: "and the spirit of the Lord came upon David from that day forward."

[5] I *Kings*, viii. 20.　　　　　　　　[6] I *Kings*, ix. 16, etc.

[7] I *Kings*, xvi. 3; and II *Kings*, v. 3 and 17; xii. 7.

[8] III *Kings*, i. 34 and 45.　　　　　　[9] II *Kings*, xix. 10.

[10] II *Paral*, xxiii. 11.　　　　　　　[11] IV *Kings*, xxiii. 30.

[12] I *Kings*, x. 1, and xvi. 13.

[13] II *Kings*, vi. 21: "Dixitque David . . . et praecepit (scil. Dominus) mihi, ut essem dux super populum Domini in Israel."

the *Christus domini*.[1] By virtue of having received unction the external status of the Ruler was raised.

The other aspect of the unction concerns the internal side: whilst externally the anointed becomes king, internally he becomes a prophet: "and the spirit of God came upon him and he prophesied amongst them."[2] Since God's spirit is in him, the king enters into an intimate relationship with God, that of son and father.[3] It is this internal kinship between David and God which transforms his whole being into something fundamentally different from what it was before unction. "God gave him another heart"[4] and consequently, the king's heart is in the hand of the Lord.[5]

This elevated position of the Lord's anointed, the *christus domini*, explains the divine protection which he enjoys: "Nolite tangere christos meos."[6] The unction does not exclude the possibility of the king's being expelled, as the case of Saul proved.[7] The divine appointment includes therefore the possibility of withdrawal of the specific functions conferred on the anointed—and just as the divine appointment was made through the instrumentality of the prophet, so also could the prophet, knowing the divine will, withdraw the previously conferred functions from the anointed.[8]

These essential features of unction had been adopted by the Franks.[9] In obvious dependence on the Old Testament the king was anointed on the head.[10] The papal adoption of this Frankish rite finds its effortless explanation in that, according to the papal view the ruler was to symbolize the "caput orbis"[11] whereby "orbis" signified the "orbis

---

[1] I *Kings*, xxiv. 7, 11 (6, 10); xxvi, 9. 16.
[2] I *Kings*, x. 10; cf. also x. 6.
[3] II *Kings*, vii. 14: "I will be his father and he shall be my son."
[4] I *Kings*, x. 9.       [5] *Prov.*, xxi. 1.
[6] *Ps.* civ (cv), 15; cf. also I *Kings*, xxiv. 6, 7; xxvi. 9, 16; II *Kings*, i. 14, 16.
[7] II *Kings*, i. 21.
[8] For some other details see also Dom Ph. Oppenheim, "Die sakralen Momente in der deutschen Herrscherweihe" in *Ephemerides Liturgicae*, lviii (1944), pp. 46–7.
[9] Frankish bishops were anointed on their hands, see M. Andrieu, "L'onction des mains dans le sacre épiscopal" in RHE. xxvi (1930), pp. 343–7; idem, "La carrière ecclésiastique des papes" in *Revue des sciences religieuses*, xxi (1947), pp. 102–5. The anointing of the bishop's head appears for the first time in the Sacramentary of Gellone which was written (according to the late A. Wilmart, "Le copiste du sacramentaire de Gellone au service du chapitre de Cambrai" in *Revue Bénédictine*, xlii (1930), pp. 210 ff.) between 770 and 780; see on this also G. Ellard, *Ordination Anointings*, cit., pp. 30, 31.
[10] See also L. Duchesne, *Origines du culte chrétien*, Engl. transl. of the 5th ed., p. 375, note 3, with a reference to Amalarius of Metz, *De eccles officiis*, ii. 14.
[11] Cf. also E. Eichmann, op. cit., i. 81.

christianus" and "caput" denoted headship in the specific papal sense, namely the supreme and specially appointed protector. The "Christian world," in other words, had been symbolically given its ruler, its Old Testament king. The king of the Old Testament had now advanced from his position of a king of the Jews to that of a king of the (Roman) Christians. The identification of the "imperium christianum" with the "imperium Romanum" was naturally of great help in this symbolic conferment of supreme ruler dignity. The "imperium Romanum" was the political term for the "imperium christianum." As the successor of the prophet in the Old Testament the pope anoints the supreme king now ruling over the (Roman) Christians; as the successor of Constantine the pope confers the (at least in an ideational sense) universal Roman emperorship upon the anointed. This, we hold, is the symbolic explanation of the combination of the act of unction with that of coronation at Rheims in October 816.

The ideological significance of Louis I's unction can best be understood if the historical antecedents of this unction are taken into account. It will be recalled that the unction of Pippin by Stephen II expressed the idea of the king being made the "patricius Romanorum": the exaltation and protection of the Roman Church was the specific purpose of Pippin's unction.[1] The same idea we meet with Paul I when he declared[2] that God had appointed Pippin as the "defensor" of His Church and the visible means by which this appointment was carried out was by unction.[3] There is therefore no reason to suppose that the unction of October 816 had not the same significance as that of its predecessors. Whilst therefore the function of Charlemagne as "imperator Romanorum" absorbed his function as a "patricius Romanorum," his "imperator" position was derived from an act that was devoid of liturgical meaning. But now, the combination of unction with coronation sanctified the "imperator" himself.

In other words, the missing religious and liturgical link between the "patricius Romanorum" and the "imperator Romanorum" was now supplied by the unction of the emperor. As regards the purpose of unction there was not of course any difference between the "patricius"

---

[1] For this see supra p. 73.　　　　[2] MGH. *Epp.* iii. 513.

[3] The declaration of the synodists assembled at Chelsea, in 787, who designated Offa as *christus Domini* (c. 12), should also be adduced in this context: with specific reference to the king's unction they declare that he owes obedience to the bishops because they have the power of the keys and of binding and loosening, see cap. 11, in Haddan & Stubbs, *Councils and Ecclesiastical Documents*, iii. 452–3. This appears to be the earliest reference to an English unction.

and the "imperator": in each case unction took place so as to make the anointed a protector and defender of the Roman Church. The difference lay in another field: the "patricius" was an officer, no more and no less; the "imperator" was a dignity symbolizing conceptually universal rulership: and linked with unction papally performed, this dignity was considered divinely conferred.[1] But we cannot strongly enough emphasize that as regards the functions which according to papal views, either "patricius" or "imperator" was to fulfil, there was no difference at all.[2] The promotion of the "patricius" to an "imperator" is understandable, we think, if it is set against the Eastern background. The statement of Louis II in 871, writing to the Eastern emperor, entirely bears out our interpretation: Frankish kings, he wrote, were now Roman emperors, because they had been anointed by the Roman pontiff for the specific purpose of protection and defence of the Roman Church.[3]

The papacy by anointing the "imperator" created, not just a mere defender, but an *imperial* defender of the Roman Church: by virtue of his elevation to emperorship, he is functionally the specific protector and defender of the Roman Church, and herewith he is also the protector and defender of all the Romans (= Latin Christians): defence and protection of the Roman Church, the epitome of Latin Christendom, entails necessarily defence and protection of the universal Church. Moreover, unction provides a very special link between the emperor and the pope. As Nicholas I maintained in this same century, unction constituted a "spiritualis proximitas,"[4] or as it was later said there was a "spiritualis conjunctio" between pope and emperor. This is the transference of the Old Testament idea of the fathership and sonship.[5] The emperor becomes the "specialis filius Romanae ecclesiae," or the "unicus filius," and the idea of the pope's fatherhood—thrown against the characteristic Roman background—assumes a still greater significance in its relation to the emperor. A son of the universal Church

---

[1] See infra section III.

[2] In this context the protection sought by the pope and considered to be sufficiently guaranteed in the *Ludovicianum* assumes a particular significance: the emperor has now the duty of protecting the newly elected pope and of defending him even, if necessary, against the Romans. For details see *Cambridge Hist. J.,* cit., pp. 115–7.

[3] MGH. *Epp.* vii. 389, lines 8–10; also infra p. 217.

[4] MGH. *Epp.* vii., in his letter to the Bulgars.

[5] Cf. II *Kings,* vii. 14: "Ego ero ei in patrem, et ipse erit mihi in filium." *Ps.* ii. 7: "Filius meus es tu: ego hodie genui te." *Ps.* lxxxviii. 27: "Ipse invocabit me: Pater meus es tu, Deus meus et susceptor salutis meae."

the emperor had always been, but now through unction he enters into a very specific and most intimate kinship with the pope: he becomes the latter's "special" or "unique" son. Leo IV declared in 852 that the emperor became an "heir of the Roman Church" and as such he was outside the disciplinary powers of any ecclesiastic except the pope. The emperor, Leo IV held, had been "elected" by God and thus was anointed by the pope who for this reason severely took the great Hincmar to task for having excommunicated Lothar.[1] Indeed, because unction makes the emperor the Lord's anointed, he is directly responsible to the pope. The idea underlying these views is that of the mediatory rule of the pope, of his vicariate of the divinely instituted St Peter. For God had anointed the emperor through the instrumentality of the pope.[2] Symbolically, this was to lead directly to the solemn act of the pope's adopting the emperor by suitable and appropriate signs.[3]

The conferment of imperial dignity was consequential upon the unction performed by the pope. A universal dignity such as that contained in Roman emperorship could be conferred only by a universal power. Thus far, as we hope to show later, the medieval (Roman) emperor surpassed all other rulers in excellence and dignity; he was also privileged in that he was not subjected to censure by anyone other than the pope.[4] But on the other hand, the emperor assumed a "servi-

---

[1] See MGH. *Epp.* v. p. 605 to Lothar himself: "In unctum Domini, quem sedes apostolica benedictionis oleo publice consecravit, sibique proprium heredem fecit, anathematis jaculum contra omnem, non solum divinam, imo humanam institutionem inferre praesumpsit . . . mandamus, ut . . . neque contra vos, quem Deus sibi principem et imperatorem elegit, et per manus summi et apostolici pontificis sanctificatum benedictionis oleum super vestrum caput effudit, clam vel publice audeat aliquam quocumque tempore anathematis vel aliam injuriae inferre jacturam." In his letter to the Frankish episcopacy, ibid., p. 604, Leo IV sharply remonstrates against Hincmar's action which violates "divinas pariter et humanas constitutiones."

[2] For Stephen II's identical expressions concerning Pippin's unction as King, see supra p. 84 n. 1.

[3] The enfolding ceremony and so forth, see infra p. 257. The adoption as a "filius" was not without value to the emperors themselves, as Lothar testified in his letter to Adrian II (868): MGH. *Epp.*, vi., p. 240, but it was also of advantage to the popes themselves as regards the episcopal hierarchy. Reference must be made to the exemption of monasteries from episcopal jurisdiction: the papal privileges exempting the monks from diocesan jurisdiction spoke of the latter as the popes' "filii speciales et proprii," cf. e.g., John XIX's privilege of exemption for Cluny, PL. cxli, col. 1136 in 1024; for all details see E. Eichmann, "Das Exkommunicationsprivileg des Kaisers" in *Sav. Z., Kan. Abt.*, i (1911), pp. 186–7. This was an important aspect of the extension of papal control.

[4] Cf. esp. Eichmann, loc. cit., pp. 181–94; idem, "Die Adoption des deutschen Königs durch den Papst," ibid., xvi (1916), pp. 301 ff.

tium," namely the protection of the Roman Church. The privileged position of the emperor was the application of the biblical "Nolite tangere christos meos."[1]

In the ceremony of unction the pope acts as a mere instrument of God's will. This is the gist of the theory of unction as set forth by John VIII in this same ninth century. "Dominus Deus unxit eum," John VIII declares[2] in 877, referring to Charles the Bald: Christ through the pope's instrumentality had made Charles an emperor and constituted him a prince of the people.[3] Furthermore, Charles was anointed "*ad imitationem* scilicet *veri regis Christi* filii sui, Domini nostri."[4] What Christ possessed by nature, the emperor now possessed by grace, John VIII maintained—"quod ipse possidet per naturam, iste consequeretur per gratiam"—and it was he himself who bestowed this grace upon the emperor. The anointed therefore becomes Christ-like, in so far as he obtains the regal powers of Christ through the medium of the pope who is basically "Rex" and "Sacerdos." He becomes "vicar of the King of kings" because the function of Christ as true king is transferred to the anointed emperor. He is a new or second David: "rex et propheta."[5] Hence the anointed becomes "sanctus," "sacratus" or "sacer," because he represents the "typus Christi" or the "figura Christi" in His regal function.

It is, in view of these conceptions, very understandable that contemporaries—and also later generations—regarded the anointed emperor on a level no different from that of a bishop. Berengar's court poet writes that the unction will make the emperor a "sacerdos," and

---

[1] *Ps.* civ (cv). 15. H. Fichtenau, *Das Karolingische Imperium*, p. 305, note 46, refers to the "Capitulare" of Kierzy, 858: MGH. *Capitularia*, ii. 439, which states: "Qui infideliter et contumaciter in unctum qualemcumque domini manum mittit, dominum christorum Christum contemnit." Fichtenau rightly calls this the "social" effect of unction.

[2] Mansi, xvii. App. col. 172. A slight, but inessential amplification of this passage is in Deusdedit's *Coll. canonum*, ed. W. v. Glanvell, p. 439.

[3] Mansi, loc. cit.: "Secundum priscam consuetudinem solemniter ad imperii Romani sceptra proveximus et augustali nomine decoravimus, ungentes eum oleo extrinsecus, ut interioris quoque spiritus sancti unctionis monstraremus virtutem ... Christum hunc oleo laetitiae delibatum extrinsecus faciens, et principem populi sui constituens."

[4] Cf. *Acts*, x. 38: "Jesum a Nazareth, quomodo unxit eum Deus, spiritu sancto et virtute." The phraseology "ad imitationem veri regis Christi" may have been suggested by the Donation of Constantine which had: "ad imitationem imperii nostri."

[5] Cf. Archbishop Odilbert's "Responsum" to Charlemagne: MGH. *Capit.* i., no. 126, p. 247: "David sanctum imitantes qui pro se populi salute *in typo* nostri exhibuit redemptoris."

an Italian bishop writes to Berengar himself that "imperii principem sacerdotem vocari non est dubium,"[1] because "ex uno cornu olei sacerdotes et reges sanctificari manifestum est." The view that by virtue of his being anointed the emperor becomes a priest seemed to be particularly tenacious, as the later conflicts only too clearly showed. This idea of the king's being a "sacerdos" was naturally greatly fostered by the exercise of those functions which were (later) considered exclusively sacerdotal. Charlemagne himself is of course a particularly good example. But this attribution of sacerdotal functions to the emperor rested upon merely external resemblances between him and a bishop.

The imperial unction did not confer what is technically called a "character indelebilis." Neither the Bible nor medieval practice would lend support to this view: Saul was to see David anointed and Louis I himself had to experience the lack of a "character indelebilis" in his papal unction. Furthermore, although in both the imperial and episcopal unctions the oil, namely the chrism, is poured over the head, the most obvious difference between the emperor and the bishop is that the "impositio manuum" is omitted in the imperial ceremony. This, and the further omission of another essential feature of episcopal consecration, namely the placing of the gospel book on the shoulders (the neck), leave no room for doubt that, objectively, the emperor was not to become a "sacerdos." The "impositio manuum" is the intrinsic part of episcopal consecration: and the gospel book opened up and resting on the neck[2] symbolizes the teaching capacity of the bishop: both the "impositio manuum" and the gospel book give the bishop the "cura animarum"—precisely the feature which was absent in the case of an imperial "consecration." Moreover, the anointing of the head of the bishop is accompanied by the appropriate liturgical prayer of the consecrators, whilst there is no corresponding prayer—"unguatur et consecretur caput tuum"—in the case of the emperor's anointing.[3] In both cases, however, it is still the same matter which is used, namely

[1] See P. E. Schramm, "Die Krönung etc." in *Sav. Z., Kan. Abt.*, xxv (1935), p. 257, note 1; Eichmann, op. cit., i. 107.
[2] This goes back to a time long before the eighth century, see *Liber Diurnus*, form. 57, p. 47; also OR. IX. No. 4 (PL. lxxviii. 1006).
[3] The anointing of the bishop's head seems to have come into use (within Frankish domains) in the early ninth century, cf. G. Ellard, op. cit., pp. 74–5. The appropriate liturgical prayer at the episcopal anointing was the "Veni, creator spiritus." For details see also P. Battifol, "La liturgie du sacre des évêques dans l'évolution historique" in RHE. xxiii (1927), pp. 733–63; also E. Eichmann, "Königsund Bischofsweihe" in *SB. Munich*, 1928, fasc. 6; idem, op. cit., i. 82 f.; cf. also H. Fichtenau, op. cit., p. 65 and p. 306, note 58.

chrism. Nevertheless, despite the obvious lack of the proper sacerdotal qualifications—the "cura animarum"—the ascription of sacerdotal functions to the anointed emperor signified in contemporary opinion no less and no more than that the emperor, by virtue of having been anointed, was entitled to perform such acts as were appropriate to a "sacerdos." That is to say, he was credited, not indeed with the specific administration of divine mysteries, but with the rightful performance of those actions which were in fact the effluence of sacerdotal qualifications: conferment of ecclesiastical offices notably of episcopal ones, convocation of councils and the chairmanship in them, the pronouncement of legally binding decrees for the sacerdotal members of the Church, the trial of clerics, and so forth. "Cura animarum" was indeed conceded to the anointed bishop, but this had no practical importance in the life of the social organism. What had practical importance was the action taken, and this action taken by the emperor, was based upon his supposed sacerdotal character. He acted *as if* he had been a "sacerdos."

A further presupposition for the exercise of "sacerdotal" functions was the conception of true monarchy. Ruling over an entity which was substantially Christian makes it imperative that the ruler—the monarch—takes care of precisely those features which are essential for Christian life; in practice this entailed the appointment and control of those who administered to the divine mysteries. As a monarch he alone rules; as a monarch he alone claims the right to turn into a binding and enforceable rule of action, into the law, what the epitome of Christianity, the Roman Church, teaches. The ascription of the "sacerdos" quality to the "Rex" signified the denial of the pope's jurisdictional primacy. The king as the monarch can not tolerate another monarch besides himself: the monarch alone is entitled to endow the teaching with enforceability—a diarchy, for understandable reasons, was rejected. The "sacerdos" function in the "Rex" concerned the exercise of governmental functions in a Christian society: but this function went no further than purely organizational, jurisdictional and administrative matters. Only in this sense may we speak of a *Rex-Sacerdos*.

This monarchic form of government could be exercised effectively so long as the basis of the king's authority was not laid bare: this involved for the monarch the embarrassing question "By what authority?" And when once this question was broached, the monarch ceased to be a monarch and became a mere king charged with the fulfilment of certain specified duties.

## III

It is difficult to over-estimate the powerful precedential character of the coronation of 816.[1] The idea of a co-emperorship (*Mitkaisertum*), it is true, was not at once abolished, for in the following year, 817, Louis I crowned his son, Lothar I, emperor. But on the occasion of the latter's Italian sojourn he was specifically requested by the pope to come to Rome for Easter 823. It is not without interest to note that Lothar had already decided to leave Italy when the papal request reached him.[2] The purpose of the invitation can have been none other than to perform the same ceremony on the son which the father had undergone seven years earlier; and the purpose of the coronation was to be the solemn creation of a specific protector and defender of the Roman Church.[3] The initiative came, for understandable reasons, from the pope—"rogante Paschale papa"—but the place of the coronation was not Rheims, but Rome.[4] What was begun at Rheims, was developed at Rome: the coronation was performed at the main altar of St Peter's. This church was henceforward the right and proper place for imperial coronations. Moreover, whilst in 816 there was no handing over of imperial insignia, at Rome the emperor received a sword from the hands of the pope.[5] The sword is the symbol of physical strength; it furthermore symbolizes the protection of him who has conferred it, the pope—it is for this purpose that the emperor receives this symbol of strength.

[1] No lesser authority than Bonizo of Sutri considered Louis I's coronation as the first imperial coronation of a Frank; see his *Liber ad Amicum*, MGH. *Libelli de Lite*, i. 577: "Quo mortuo (scil. Carolo) Ludoicus ei successit, eius filius, vir mitissimus, qui primus omnium Francorum regum imperiali sublimatus est dignitate." The coronation of Charlemagne is not even mentioned.

[2] *Annales Regni Francorum*, ad 823, pp. 160 f.: "Hlotharius vero, cum secundum patris jussionem in Italia justitias faceret, et jam se ad revertendum de Italia prepararet, rogante Passchale papa, Romam venit." Cf. also *Vita Hludowici*, MGH. SS. ii. c. 36, p. 627: "Cum ... ad patrem de reditu cogitaret, rogatu Paschalis papae Romam imminente sancti paschae solempnitate adiit."

[3] Which was, in view of the Roman situation, advisable. This stands in close proximity to the "pacta" (the *Ludovicianum* and the *Lotharianum* of the following year, 824) which were the documentary basis of imperial protection.

[4] *Ann. Reg. Franc.*, ibid., p. 161: "(Hlotharius) honorifice ab illo susceptus in sancto paschali die apud sanctum Petrum et regni coronam et imperatoris atque augusti nomen accepit." *Vita Hludowici*, p. 627: "Ab eodem papa clarissima ambitione susceptus, ipso sancto die apud b. Petrum diadema imperiale cum nomine suscepit augusti." Cf. also *Vita Walae*, ii. 17, in MGH. SS. ii. 563 f.

[5] See *Vita Walae*, ii. 17, p. 564, lines 6 ff.: "Unde quia coram sancto altare et coram sancto corpore beati Petri, principis apostolorum, a summo pontifice vestro—this is Lothar's report to his father, Louis I—ex consensu et voluntate

This symbolic handing over of the sword—it is for the first time that we read of it in connexion with an imperial coronation—has very deep symbolic significance. The Old Testament makes no mention of a royal sword as a distinguishing sign of kingship, although the very last book of the Old Testament in its very last chapter has a passage which may not have been without influence. Here[1] we read that Jeremiah the prophet had given a sword to the army commander, Judas Machabaeus, designating it as a "holy sword a gift from God," with which the enemies of Israel should be expelled.[2] At the same time we should keep in mind that the sword was also a characteristic Roman symbol; it formed an essential part of the Roman emperor's equipment as he functioned as the supreme commander of the army. Lastly, there is the well-known Pauline statement that the Ruler "beareth not the sword in vain."[3] The very deep significance of the coronation of 823 lay in that this Pauline statement was transformed symbolically, and the manner in which this transformation took place, was by the visible conferment of the sword.[4]

Although utilizing the characteristic Roman symbol of "imperatorial" power, the papacy gave the symbol itself an entirely different meaning. The conferment signified that the emperor received the "physical strength" from the pope, for the specific purpose of defence and protection. What Isidore of Seville expressed in abstract terms, what St Paul had dogmatically asserted, was now moulded into the unmistakable language of visible symbolism. The profound teleological principle underlying St Paul's description of the Ruler as "a revenger *to* execute wrath upon him who doeth evil," is here clothed in a symbolic and visible act. The function of the Ruler is the extermination of evil and for this he receives the sword. The decision of what is, and what is not, evil in a Christian society must necessarily be left to those who are functionally qualified to pronounce upon it, namely the "sacerdotium" or for the sake of convenience the pope.

---

benedictionem honorem et nomen suscepi imperialis officii, insuper diademata capitis et *gladium ad defensionem ipsius ecclesiae et imperii* vestri . . ."

[1] II *Machab.* xv. 16.

[2] "Accipe sanctum gladium, munus a Deo, in quo dejicies adversarios populi mei Israel."

[3] *Rom.* xiii. 4.

[4] Cf. also Cl. Schwerin, "Zur Herkunft des Schwertsymbols" in *Festschrift Paul Koschaker*, Weimar, 1939, iii. 324 ff., especially pp. 346–8: the sword symbol was not of Germanic, but of Roman-ecclesiastical origin. About the "spata sancti Petri" cf. ibid., pp. 332, 335. About Paul I supra p. 68 n. 5.

The auxiliary function of the emperor—clearly suggested in St Paul and Isidore—is brought out in all succinctness and conciseness in the coronation ceremony. The "minister of God" as St Paul characterized the Ruler, will in course of time become the minister of the pope, when once the technical concept of the pope's vicariate of Christ, that is, of his role as mediator, is fully developed. The emperor's function is of a negative kind, the suppression of evil, and this is merely the a-political expression of his function as a protector and defender: in this function lies his whole *raison d'être*, but thereby was also opened up the road to his "demotion" from a monarch to a mere king, who is charged with the specific duty of protection.

The sword thus conferred is not a simple sword, but one that is sacred and hallowed by virtue of the pope's conferring it.[1] And just as the unction was performed by the pope acting as the instrument of God, so was the sword handed to the emperor by the pope as an execution of the divine will. The earlier "patricius Romanorum" had no outward symbol of his function; the emperor from now onwards was given this symbol "ad defensionem ecclesiae et imperii." That the conception of the emperor's function as a protector in the way in which papal doctrine envisaged it, did not tally with the imperial conception of protection, is in no need of further comment: the one conception entailed control by the papacy, the other control of the papacy. Moreover, since the Roman-inspired and Roman-directed faith is the substratum of the empire, the defence of the universal Church is at the same time a defence of the empire: the identity of "imperium christianum" and "imperium Romanum" could not lead to any other view but that expressed in Lothar's report. Yet the term defence does not only apply to the suppression of evil within the "imperium," but applies also outside it. For defence includes also (once again we have recourse to Agobard of Lyons as a witness) the subjugation of "barbarous nations so that they may embrace the faith and widen the frontiers of the kingdom of the faithful."[2]

The next coronation, that of 850 when Louis II was crowned emperor, shows the advance which the papal theme had made: it was now the father, Lothar I, who had sent his son Louis II to Rome in

---

[1] That is, incidentally, the reason of why the emperor or king was later entitled to enter the church "cinctus cum gladio," because his sword was sacred, see for all these details Eichmann, op. cit., ii. 103.

[2] The emperor as "caput orbis" should "adversus barbaras nationes dimicare, ut eas fidei subjugaret, ad dilatandum terminum regni fidelium," Agobard, *Apologeticus pro filiis Ludovici*, in MGH. SS. xv. 275 f.

order to be crowned;[1] no longer was it necessary for the pope to issue an invitation. Moreover, this coronation alone was constitutive, since Louis II had not been made an emperor by his father.[2] At Easter 850 Leo IV anointed and crowned him emperor.[3] That he also received the sword, we know from Nicholas I who also shows us the intimate connexion between St Peter, his vicar, and the symbolic transfer of the sword.[4]

But there is one more aspect of this coronation 850 which demands our attention. We recall that the Donation of Constantine made Constantine explain the reason of his removing the capital. This could now be taken as a prohibition for an emperor to reside in Rome. When the Romans suggested to Louis II that he should take up his imperial residence at Rome, he turned their suggestion down "ob reverentiam beatorum apostolorum." Whether this refusal was papally inspired or whether Louis II himself acted in the spirit of the Donation, cannot be decided.[5] It is nevertheless worthy of remark that the same emperor in other ways implemented the ordinances of Constantine. According to the latter, the emperor should hold the reins of the papal horse as a token of his obsequiousness, that is, he should perform the "officium stratoris" (as distinct from the "officium strepae," the holding of the stirrup). The biography of Nicholas I tells us that Louis II had performed this "officium stratoris"; what is more, he performed this service when the pope was already sitting in his saddle: as soon as Louis saw the pope, he ran towards him and led the papal horse the length of an arrow-shot.[6] Louis II seems to have been a true imitator of Constantine.

---

[1] See *Annales Bertiniani*, ed. G. Waitz, p. 38. "Lotharius filium suum Romam mittit, qui a Leone papa honorifice susceptus et in imperatorem unctus est."

[2] Louis had six years earlier been anointed and crowned as king of the Lombards by Sergius II, see *Liber Pontificalis*, ii. 88; he was also given a sword. See also Halphen, op. cit., 340 ff., 397.

[3] *Chron. Salernitanum*, MGH. SS. iii. 519: "Oleo unctionis est unctus coronaque prorsus suo capite septus et ab omnibus imperator augustus est nimirum vocatus." See also *Ann. Bert.*, loc. cit.                    [4] For this see infra p. 197 f.

[5] See *Libellus de imperatoria potestate in urbe Roma*, MGH. SS. iii. 721 f.

[6] *Liber Pontificalis*, ii. 152, lines 19 ff.: "Augustus obvius in adventum eius (scil. papae) occurrit frenumque Caesar equi pontificis suis manibus apprehendens pedestri more quantum sagittae jactus extenditur, traxit ... imperator equo descendit equmque pontificis iterum ut supra meminimus, traxit." Eichmann, ii. 288, observes: "Der Dienst ist losgelöst von einem wirklichen Bedürfnis: der Papst sitzt ja bereits zu Pferde und bedarf einer Hilfe nicht. Es ist also ein reiner Ehrendienst, der demonstrativ erwiesen wird. Nach dem gemeinsamen Mahl wird die Szene wiederholt. Und nur ein Zügel-, kein Bügeldienst wird erwähnt; auch das Constitutum Constantini kennt letzteren nicht."

Seventy-five years after Charlemagne's coronation, and again on a Christmas Day, the second Charles was solemnly crowned by John VIII. This coronation embodied all the features of the previous coronation ceremonies, and added one more decisive element: papal designation and nomination of the emperor. The death of Louis II provided the opportunity. Since he died without male heirs, his successor according to the law of the time, and also according to the wish of the late Louis, should have been Louis the German.[1] But the pope, John VIII, having consulted his counsellors and the "Roman senate," offered the imperial crown to Charles the Bald: he was called upon because it was hoped that he would provide security for the Christian people and exalt the Roman Church—papal doctrine could hardly have been better summarized than in these few words. The offer to Charles in fact resulted from the solicitude of the pope to provide a successor for Louis II.[2]

The imperial crown which Charles the Bald received on Christmas Day 875, three months after the papal offer had been made, was conferred "through the privilege of the apostolic see."[3] Two years later, the same pope in his great speech at Ravenna gives us a little more insight into papal thought. He had "elected and confirmed" Charles II who "through divine inspiration" had already been designated by Nicholas I: it was this "inspiratio coelestis" which was the basis of John's offer to Charles. The pope appears merely as the mouthpiece of the divine will. In a way one might say that the emperor is "pre-    †

---

[1] For details see P. E. Schramm, *Der König von Frankreich*, Weimar, 1939, pp. 32 ff.; Eichmann, op. cit., i. 51; Halphen, op. cit. 417 ff.

[2] MGH. *Epp.* vii. Ep. 59, p. 311, written in September 875, hence very shortly after the news of Louis's death must have reached Rome; also incorporated in Deusdedit's *Coll. can.* iv. 182, p. 487 ed. cit.: "Igitur, quia, sicut Domino placuit, Hludowicus gloriosus imperator defunctus est (12 August 875) cum nos, qui in loco eius propitia divinitate succedere debuisset, cum fratribus nostris et inclito Romano senatu concorditer tractaremus, devotione et fide tua ad medium deducta, hanc multi dignis preconiis efferre ceperunt. Cuius et nos non solum nostris diebus, sed etiam b. papae Nicholai tempore reminiscentes excellentiam tuam ad honorem et exaltationem sanctae Romanae ecclesiae et ad securitatem populi Christiani eligendam esse speravimus." See also MGH. *Capitularia*, ii. 348: "Dominus Johannes apostolicus et universalis papa primo Romae *elegit* atque sacra unctione *constituit* . . ."

[3] Ep. 7, p. 321, lines 34–5: "Per apostolicae sedis privilegium cunctorum favoribus approbatum sceptris imperialibus sublimavit." Cf. also PL. cxxvi. 658: "Carolus rex, adiens limina apostolorum Petri et Pauli honorifice a nobis exceptus, postquam solemniter vota regia persolvisset ad sepulchrum b. Petri, die nativitatis Domini in ecclesia ipsius b. Petri . . . dignitatem imperialem per impositionem manuum nostrarum adeptus est."

elected" into his emperorship by God[1] and the papal decision transforms the "pre-election" into a final election. The emperor is
"desideratus, optatus, *postulatus* a nobis et *a Deo vocatus* et honorificatus"; the pope promotes the king to the—at the time—highest
accessible dignity.[2] And when once the pope emerges as the constitutionally established "vicar of God" or "of Christ," the Donation
could be dispensed with as a basis of the papal function.[3] Charles the
Bald himself embraces the papal point of view in the most telling
manner when he adopts for his seal the inscription: "Renovatio
imperii Romanorum et Francorum." The Roman and Frankish empires are renovated through the papally performed coronation. This,
indeed, is a resounding victory for the papal theme. Charles's papal
creator leaves us in no doubt about the functions which the Ruler of
the renovated Roman and Frankish empires has to fulfil: not protection
in the old Teutonic-royal sense, but protection and defence in the
Roman-papal sense. The emperor was a *patronus, defensor* and *adjutor*.[4]

John VIII's reference to his consultation with the Roman senate
warrants an observation. One must not read into his statement that he
consulted the Roman senate, the view that the senate had any constitutive function in the creation of the emperor. On the one hand, the
Roman senate was a euphemistic term for the Roman aristocracy, and
on the other hand, John himself tells us in his Ravenna speech that
the whole Roman people, the "gens togata," had assented to his
"election" of Charles.[5] No constitutive role was attributable to the
Romans in 800 nor seventy-five years later. What they did, was to

---

[1] Eichmann, op. cit., i. 53: "Vorwahl."

[2] See Mansi, xvii, App. col. 172 f.: "Et quia pridem apostolicae memoriae
decessori nostro papae Nicolao idipsum (Carolum) jam inspiratione coelesti
revelatum fuisse comperimus, elegimus hunc merito et approbavimus una cum
annisu et voto omnium fratrum et coepiscoporum nostrorum . . . secundum priscam consuetudinem . . . proveximus et augustali nomine decoravimus"; Charles
did not ask for the imperial crown, "sed tamquam desideratus, optatus, postulatus
a nobis et a Deo vocatus et honorificatus, ad defendendam religionem et Christi
utique servos tuendos humiliter et obedientia accessit . . . promptus ad ipsius
promotionem et hoc per sacerdotum Domini manus ministrorum eius officium,
sicut David et Salomon . . ."

[3] Eichmann, op. cit., i. 54, says that John acted as the "Papstkaiser des Constitutum Constantini"; cf. also Biehlmayer-Tüchle, *Kirchengeschichte*, ii. 59: the
pope as the "alleinberechtigte Kaisermacher."

[4] Ep. 48, p. 46, lines 16 ff.: "Nam superna vos majestas sanctae suae ecclesiae
nobis commissae *patronum invictum, defensorem potentem* et *strenuum adjutorem*
concessit . . . quasi vindicem Dei *habeamus ministrum*." This letter was written
to Charles the Bald in 877. The echo of the Pauline statement is obvious. See also
the two letters quoted, infra, p. 224 n. 3.    [5] See Mansi, xvii. App. cols. 172–3.

approve of the "election," namely the decision of the pope.[1] The attribution of a constitutive role to the Romans in the making of an emperor and the assumption of the papal role in the creation of an emperor are incompatible.

The significance of this reference to the Romans lies in a different field. Although the "emperor of the Romans" was the title of the highest available dignity of rulership, its essential ingredient was power and its effective exercise. But this presupposed that the thus "elected" emperor actually exercised some power over the Romans in the geographical sense: the Romans in this sense were merely the epitome of all the Romans. What sort of emperor of the Romans would this be who had no shadow of (royal) power over the (geographical) Romans? It is, we think, this essential ingredient of imperial dignity which accounts for John VIII's reference to his consultation with the Romans; it is this ingredient, too, which explains the later "Rex Romanorum" who in fact had developed out of the "Rex Italicorum," who in his turn had developed out of the "Rex Langobardorum." Seen from the point of view of the emperor title, the actual exercise of power over the Lombards (Italici, Romans) manifested itself in the "Rex Romanorum": the king of Italy (= Romans)[2] was the preliminary to the fully fledged emperor of the Romans.[3]

Considering the function which was attributed to the papally created emperor—the function of a *patronus, adjutor* and *defensor*[4]—John's insistence on the necessity of his approval of the person of the emperor

---

[1] The same feature emerges at Ravenna where the people say to the pope "quem amastis et amamus; quem dilexistis diligimus; quem elegistis eligimus . . . quod in eo . . . gessistis . . . sequimur," Mansi, loc. cit.

[2] The *Regnum Italicum* is referred to by John several times. Cf. Ep. 59, p. 54, lines 6 ff.: "Quapropter tam pro ecclesiasticis quibusdam necessitatibus quam pro statu et pro correctione reipublicae auctoritate apostolica decrevimus reverendorum fratrum et co-episcoporum nostrorum *Italici regni* universale, id est, totius provinciae, advocare concilium"; Ep. 247, p. 217: ". . . Karolomannus gloriosus *rex istius Italici regni*"; Ep. 24, p. 287, lines 14 ff.: ". . . episcopis et comitibus *Italici regni*." For the actual ceremonial at coronations of these kings see E. Eichmann, "Zur Geschichte des lombardischen Krönungsritus" in *Hist. JB.*, xlvi (1926), pp. 522–4; here also, p. 523, the proof of the direct application of the Egbert Pontifical to these Italian coronations.

[3] A precedent was Louis II's coronation as king of the Lombards in 844. See the account in the *Lib. Pont.*, ii. 89, lines 5 ff.: "Tunc almificus pontifex (Sergius II) manibus suis ipsum Hludovicum, imperatoris filium, oleo sancto perungens, regali ac pretiossissima coronavit corona regemque Langobardorum perfecit." Cf. also the account in the *Annales Prudentii*, MGH. SS. i. 440, lines 20 ff.: "Hludovicum pontifex Romanus unctione in regem consecratum cingulo decoravit." It seems that the royal sword was handed over for the first time on this occasion, cf. Eichmann, art. cit., p. 518.　　　[4] See supra p. 162 n. 4

is logical and consistent.[1] The death of Charles the Bald provided him with the opportunity of making his ideas on this point quite clear, ideas which flow from the conception of the emperor as the organ wielding the sword for the sake of the protection of Christianity. Having heard of the attempts of Italian magnates to elect a king—after Karlmann's departure in 879—John writes to the archbishop of Milan to say that the magnates must not accept anyone as their king without papal approval and consent. "Nullum absque nostro consensu regem debetis recipere."[2] For the king whom they wish to elect, must be approved by the pope, since he will become emperor:

Nam ipse, qui a nobis est ordinandus in imperium, a nobis primum atque potissimum debet esse vocatus et electus.[3]

It can readily be seen that the pope as true emperor-maker would not suffer an imperial candidate to be forced upon him. He alone was in a position to judge whom he was going to "ordain" and he alone was to decide who would be an emperor suitable for the fulfilment of the functions as a patron and assistant.[4] Herein we may see the germs of the later papal examination and confirmation of the emperor-elect.[5]

Karlmann incapacitated, and no longer possible as a suitable patron and assistant, the *Papstkaiser* John VIII turned to Count Boso with the intention of creating him emperor. John adopted Boso as his son[6] and his designation fell for the first time upon a ruler who did not belong to the Carolingian dynasty. The adoption of Boso was the outward, formal and ceremonial symbol of his having been found suitable by the pope.[7]

---

[1] E. Eichmann, "Die rechtliche und kirchenpolitische Bedeutung der Kaisersalbung im MA." in *Festschrift f. G. v. Hertling*, Munich, 1913, p. 267, points out that this papal claim to the right of approbation was to expand to the papal right of confirmation of the emperor on the analogy of episcopal procedures.

[2] Ep. 163, p. 133, lines 33–4.

[3] Ep. 163, p. 133, lines 34–5. It is not quite correct when A. Kroener, *Wahl und Krönung der deutschen Kaiser und Könige in Italien*, Freiburg, 1901, p. 19, says that John claimed to decide the royal appointment first, "da der König von Italien zugleich Kaiser sei." Cf. also Eichmann, op. cit., ii. 56.

[4] It may not be quite correct when the late Eichmann said: "Wenn wir alle diese Momente zusammenfassen, so haben wir in Johann VIII den Papstkaiser der Donatio Constantini," see "Die Adoption des deutschen Königs durch den Papst" in *Sav. Z., Kan. Abt.*, vii (1916), p. 309. John's view can be explained also by the ideology underlying the Donation, which, as we have seen, was not an invention of the forger.

[5] The questions put to the emperor-elect are in *Ordo C.*; cf. also Gregory VII infra p. 288 and Innocent III in RNI. 62.

[6] Ep. 110, p. 102, lines 20–1: "Bosonem gloriosum principem per adoptionis gratiam filium meum effeci." Cf. also MGH. *Capit.* ii. 368.

[7] Ep. 94, p. 89, lines 10 ff.: "Bosonem principem . . . permissu Dei ad majores

Boso was dropped, and Charles III was crowned emperor by John VIII in 881.[1] On the occasion of this coronation John VIII produced an imperial crown from the jewel rooms of St Peter's.[2] Although John did not enjoy complete freedom in making Charles III an emperor—he had already been king of Italy for the last two years—the pope never let the initiative slip from his hands.[3] The shadowy Carolingian empire under Charles III received its particular stamp from this imperial coronation.[4]

Stephen V acted entirely within the framework provided by papal ideology and precedent which was so amply supplied by his predecessor, John VIII. The adoption of Wido, Duke of Spoleto, as the "son of the Roman Church" signified his designation as a Roman emperor. The first emperor who was not a Carolingian, was crowned on 21 February 891.[5] And Pope Formosus made Wido's son, Lambert, first a co-emperor and after the death of his father, sole emperor. But at the same time, emperor-maker as Formosus was, he also designated Arnulf and crowned him emperor at St Peter's on 22 February 896, after Lambert had been dropped. Once again constrained by circumstances the papacy under John IX, abandoned Arnulf and confirmed Lambert's emperorship. The vehicle by which this confirmation was carried out was that of a repetition of the unction on Lambert in the Roman synod of 898.[6] Lambert's death in the same year provided the papacy with

---

exclesioresque gradus modis omnibus salvo honore nostro promovere nichilominus desideramus." Cf. again Eichmann, art. cit. (note 4), p. 303: the pope speaks like a "Weltherrscher, der sich einen Mitregenten an die Seite setzt." For further examples of adoption, ibid., pp. 303–5.

[1] For this see Ep. 224, p. 199; Ep. 257, p. 225; Ep. 260, p. 230.

[2] *Erchanberti Breviarium Regum Francorum*, MGH. SS. ii. 330: "Clementissimus Carolus . . . a pontifice Romano de thesauro sancti Petri apostoli corona capiti imposita ad imperium consecratus, et augustus Caesar appellatus, nunc divina clementia favente pacatissimum regit imperium, domina Richarta simul cum eo ad regni consortium ab eodem apostolico sublimata."

[3] The angling for an emperor whose function was that of a "patronus" or "adjutor" of the Roman Church, is understandable only from the point of view of the very real danger presented by the Arabs in Southern Italy. At no other time, perhaps, was this function of the emperor understood in such real terms as at the time of John VIII. For an excellent discussion of this aspect of John's pontificate see F. E. Engreen, "Pope John VIII and the Arabs" in *Speculum*, xxi (1946), pp. 318–30.

[4] Cf. R. Holtzmann, *Geschichte der sächsischen Kaiserzeit*, Munich, 1943, p. 12, and L. Halphen, op. cit., pp. 446–54. The oath of Charles III heralded the oaths taken by later emperors.

[5] Cf. MGH. *Capit*. ii. 194; Flodoardus, *Hist. Ecc. Rem.*, MGH. SS. xiii. 557: Eichmann, op. cit., i. 59.

[6] See Mansi, xviii. 221; for details cf. Halphen, op. cit., pp. 475–81.

yet another opportunity to "make" an emperor in the person of Louis III of Burgundy, and when Berengarius, the effective ruler of Italy, had expelled Louis, John X crowned Berengar emperor in 915. Berengar was the last Roman emperor before the coronation of Otto I on 2 February 962.

# CHAPTER VI

# The Age of Pseudo-Isidore

## I

THE idea of unity embracing all Latin Christians (Romans) in one entity which had all the appearance of a universal union of mankind, was seriously jeopardized by the conflicting aims and aspirations of Charlemagne's successors, the successors of him who had given the idea of (European) unity such pronounced form. The emperor had been the guarantor of the unity of his empire which was virtually identical with the extent of Latin Christendom, virtually co-terminous with the Roman-directed universal Church. The third and fourth decades of the ninth century show that the pope succeeds the emperor as the unifying organ: the Roman Church alone will guarantee the unity of the universal Church, for which the unity of the Roman empire is an indispensable presupposition. Moreover, hierocratic conceptions as expressed in the conciliar manifestations of this period and papal conceptions begin to coalesce in these decades.

The revolt against Louis I which was on the point of breaking out by early in 833[1] gave Gregory IV precisely the handle whereby the authority of the Roman Church could be demonstrated in a most conspicuous manner.[2] It is true that the pope was to be found in the camp of the rebellious Lothar[3] but it would be quite misleading to deduce therefrom that he was merely the tool of the rebels, as Lothar's enemies would have it. The interpretation of the pope's motive for his journey across the Alps, namely, that he wished to be a peacemaker between

---

[1] For factual details see L. Halphen, op. cit., pp. 277 ff.

[2] Gregory IV's order to Louis to take back his wife, Judith, should be considered in this context. As far as we can see this was the first papal order issued to an emperor in a matrimonial affair: the pope uses "jubere" towards Louis. See Thegan, *Vita Hludowici* (MGH. SS. ii. 598), cap. 37, lines 8–9: "Supradicta conjux venit ibi obviam ei (scil. imperatori) quam honorifice suscepit, *jubente Gregorio* Romano pontifice cum aliorum episcoporum justo judicio."

[3] See, for instance, Nithard, *Historia* (MGH. SS. ii. 652–3); *Annales Bertiniani*, ad a. 833; Pascherius Radbertus, *Epitaphium Arsenii*, ed. A. Dümmler, in *Abhandlungen d. Preuss. Akad.*, 1900, p. 81 (ii. 14).

father and sons, is certainly nearer to the truth.[1] For peace within the empire was necessary for achieving unity. In his function as pope Gregory IV considered himself fully justified in attempting to settle a dispute which vitally concerned the empire itself. In other words, the unity of the empire was jeopardized by the filial revolt: the guarantor of this unity was the pope.

Two documents of this Easter time 833 are of especial interest to us; the one is written by Agobard of Lyons, the mentor of the conciliar views which propounded the hierocratic theme so manifestly, and the other was written by the pope himself. Agobard addressed himself to Louis.[2] The emperor's order to Agobard to join him in his court is flatly refused: instead Agobard joins the pope, for "the pope's advent is most reasonable and opportune."[3] Fortified by statements from Pelagius I,[4] Leo I[5] and Anastasius[6] Agobard lifts the whole quarrel between father and sons onto a higher plane altogether. According to him, the quarrel not merely creates disunity within the empire, but, what is much more important to Agobard, affects the unity of the "ecclesia" itself. Empire and Church universal are thus expressions of one and the same entity, according to Agobard: who then should be better qualified to settle a dispute affecting the unity of the universal Church than the pope, hence his appearance is sufficiently reasonable and opportune. He who strives for the unity of the Church, acts as Christ's lieutenant,[7] and Pope Anastasius had reminded the emperor "ut constitutis apostolicae sedis *obtemperet* (scil. imperator)."[8] Knowing the emperor more as an "amator regni coelestis quam terreni," Agobard appeals to him to save the unity of the Church.[9]

The second document is doubly revealing, for on the one hand it shows us the main points made by the "old" imperial party, and on the other hand it contains the salient papal-hierocratic elements in a summarized form. The episcopal adherents of Louis I[10] operated with the old Frankish tenet that the universal Church is headed by the

---

[1] So, for instance, the interpretation by the *Vita Hludowici Imperatoris*, c. 48 (MGH. SS. ii. 635).

[2] MGH. *Epp.* v, no. 16, pp. 226 ff.

[3] "Satis rationabilis et oportunus est eius adventus," MGH. *Epp.* v, no. 16, p. 227, lines 35–6.

[4] J. 939: Mansi, ix. 716.　　　　　　　　[5] J. 407: ep. x, c. 1.

[6] J. 744: Thiel, p. 616.　　　　　　　　[7] Ep. cit., p. 227, lines 29–30.

[8] Ep. cit., p. 227, line 30.　　　　　　　[9] See c. 7, p. 228.

[10] The letter of the pope is addressed to the bishops as a reply to their grievances against the pope's interference; their letter is not preserved, but we can reconstruct it from the papal reply: MGH. *Epp.* v, no. 17, pp. 228 ff.

emperor, and therefore the *sacerdotium*, as part of the universal Church, is subjected to imperial commands. Accordingly, the pope, too, is subjected to imperial authority, since the leadership of the universal Church is not his. He is, logically enough, called the "Brother" of the bishops and as an equal of theirs has no right to issue any orders to them. They would have joyfully joined his company, had there not been an imperial order to the contrary. And it was the imperial command which determined their attitude; a papal command could never override an imperial command. They counsel the pope to subject himself to the emperor, instead of undermining the sacerdotal office by attempting to give orders. If he were to do as they advised him to do, they would then receive him with all the honours due to him, otherwise they would break off relations with him and would depose him.[1]

The only astonishing feature of this episcopal protest is that its draftsmen were so completely oblivious of the radically changed temper of the time. In countering the episcopal arguments the pope has ample opportunity to set forth the papal theme trenchantly. The very first lines of the letter manifest its tenor and trend: he, the pope, was not their brother; on the contrary, homage and respect due to a father had to be shown to him.[2] Papal orders must be obeyed: he had commanded them to join him and they had refused sheltering behind an imperial order.[3] But these are reprehensible words, the pope angrily remarks—"quae verba reprehensibilia sunt"—on two grounds. A pontifical order is no less sacred than an imperial one—"quam illa (jussio) quam dicitis imperialem"—and secondly, the episcopal way of reasoning is utterly opposed to the truth—"quia veritate caret, quod dicitis illam praevenisse," for whenever pontifical and imperial orders clash, the latter must be disregarded: "non enim illa (jussio) praevenit, sed nostra, id est, pontificalis." The pope's orders concern the government of the souls. The contrast between the pontifical "regimen animarum" and the imperial "regimen temporale" unmistakably reveals Gregory's point of view. The idea behind his statement

---

[1] This follows clearly from the wording of the letter, p. 231, lines 30 ff.: "Illud vero quod minari vos cognoscimus periculum gradus, quis explicare poterit . . ." The threat of deposition is also reported by the *Vita Hludowici*, ed. cit., c. 48, p. 635; cf. also *Epitaphium Arsenii*, ed. cit., p. 84.

[2] Ep. cit., p. 228, lines 32 ff.: "Romano pontifici scribentes contrariis eum in praefatione nominibus appellastis, fratrem videlicet et papam, dum congruentius esset solam ei paternam reverentiam exhibere."

[3] Ep cit., p. 228, lines 35 ff.: "Adventu quoque eius comperto, laetari vos dicitis, credentes omnibus principi scilicet subjectis profuturum, et optasse: occursum vestrum nobis non negandum, nisi sacra jussio imperialis praeveniret."

7

Neque ignorare debueratis maius esse regimen animarum, quod est pontificale
quam imperiale, quod est temporale[1]

is that the pontifical government of souls is in itself sufficient to effect
the proper direction of Louis's empire. The "regimen animarum"
when applied to the concrete dispute, emerges here as a definite
"political" measure: it focuses attention on the character and substance
of the empire—papally conferred—as a predominantly spiritual entity.
Differently expressed: the direction of souls will ensure the proper
working of the whole body; the imperial "regimen temporale" is
viewed in the function of an auxiliary organ in the Isidorian sense. In
this theocentrically orientated society the papal reasoning was bound
to penetrate the minds even of his episcopal opponents: the pope could
safely side-step the specific episcopal grievances.

Gregory IV elaborates these points in his letter. He puts into the
mouth of Gregory Naziazenus statements which the latter never made,
but because they illustrate the pope's way of reasoning, they are all the
more interesting on this account.[2] The acceptance of the Christian
faith subjects everyone including emperors to the sacerdotal power—
"lex Christi sacerdotali vos (scil. imperatores) nostrae subicit potestati"
—and to sacerdotal tribunals: "atque istis tribunalibus subdit."[3] For
Christ had given the priests "potestas," that is, a "principatus" so
manifestly more perfect than the imperial power.[4] It would run counter
to the idea of justice if the flesh were to dominate the spirit, if the
terrestrial were to oppress the celestial, if human matters were to be
preferred to divine matters. They, the bishops, as true "sacerdotes,"
that is, as the administrators of the divine cult—and not of a mere
human cult—should heed these words, since the emperor is only one
sheep of the flock of Christ and as such he is committed to the supreme
pastor,[5] to the occupant of Peter's chair, to him who "locum beati
Petri tenet," and reverence, respect and homage must be paid to him
for the sake of the chair itself. "Honoranda est cathedra pontificalis et
propter cathedram sedens in illa."[6]

[1] Ep. cit., p. 228, lines 40–1. One might be inclined to see the hand of Agobard
at work: cf. A. Hauck, *Kirchengeschichte*, ii. 516; Halphen, op. cit., 281.

[2] About the misquotation see Dümmler's note, p. 229, note 1; the quotation is
supposed to come from Gregory's *Oratio* xvii.

[3] Ep. cit., p. 229, lines 2 ff.: "Sic enim ipsis imperatoribus loquitur (Gregorius)
dicens . . ."

[4] "Dedit enim et nobis potestatem, dedit principatum multo perfectiorem
principatibus vestris."

[5] Ep. cit., p. 229, lines 6 ff.

[6] Ep. cit., p. 229, lines 5 ff.

The theme of the episcopalists that the pope *qua* pope had no right to touch matters concerning their own dioceses, unless he did this with their consent—the logical conclusion from their point of view since they regarded the pope as their brother—is met by Gregory IV in a manner that manifests one of the most cherished programmatic points of the hierocratic system. "You say that I have no right to act, or to arrange anything in your dioceses, and that I cannot excommunicate anyone against your will"[1]—but he is impervious to this way of reasoning. His axiom is the unity of the whole body of believers, of the universal Church, and this unity is alone guaranteed by the "cathedra pontificalis," hence the function of the pope as a peacemaker.[2] For it is in the function of a peacemaker—"legatione *fungimur pacis*"—that he crossed the Alps. The body of believers must not be divided, as surely it would be, if the episcopal opponents had their way: but they should bear in mind that this body is Christ's Church, from which neither the Germanic nor the Gallic Church can be separated. The guarantee for the unity of this one "ecclesia Christi" lies in obedience to the Roman Church.[3] The theme underlying this papal remonstration is the insistence on hierarchical subordination of the episcopacy: without this subordination there can neither be a proper functioning of the whole *corpus* of believers nor the necessary exercise of papal authority. Unity of the whole body is guaranteed, according to the Roman Church, by its supreme authority. We should take note, however, that the pope expressly states that the headship of the Church belongs to Christ, and that he ascribes to himself only a Petrine vicariate, not a vicariate of Christ. There is as yet no suggestion of the pope functioning "vice Christi," that is, functioning on behalf of Christ Himself Who heads the *corpus* of believers.

The phraseology chosen by the pope (or by Agobard) to express his contempt for imperial orders—"illa (jussio) quam dicitis imperialem"—is prophetic and defines by implication the emperor's proper function within the body of believers, within the universal Church. These words reflect the papal esteem of the emperor. Nevertheless, the loyal adherence of the Western emperors to the Roman empire concept was, from the papacy's point of view, potentially very useful, as the outgoing ninth century was only too clearly to show.

---

[1] Ep cit., p. 231, lines 4 ff.

[2] Cf. also the rhetorical question: "Quare mihi contrarii cum ecclesiis vestris debetis in legatione pacis et unitatis, quod Christi donum et ministerium est?", Ep. cit., p. 231, lines 8 ff.

[3] Ep. cit., p. 231, lines 16–23.

But this adherence could also, at least theoretically, be usefully exploited against the East: the age of Nicholas I and Adrian II was to demonstrate this usefulness. The potentialities of Gregory's statements, we must repeat, were no less prophetic for the West: they foreshadow the view that the "regimen animarum" is crucial and at the same time a sufficiently great force to orientate society. Transposed onto the plane of government, the maxim of Gregory IV is that those alone who are functionally qualified are entitled to orientate society: hence the "regimen temporale" in this society, is inferior to the "jussio pontificalis." This is the as yet uncouth expression of the regulative or directive principle in Christian society.

## II

It may not be unprofitable to illustrate the permeation of contemporary thought with papal-hierocratic principles by some examples[1] chosen from the imperial, episcopal and papal quarters.

The emperor, Lothar, writes to the pope[2] requesting him to confer the pallium on Hincmar. The Arenga of this letter is extraordinarily revealing: the apostolic see is not merely the head of all the churches, but is the foundation and head of all Christian life and sanctity "in the whole world"—"in universo orbe."[3] Every question, every matter, every cause touching ecclesiastical points, should be referred to the Roman Church, because it is the mother of religion and the fountain head of equity.[4] This imperial communication is a strong endorsement of the jurisdictional primacy of the Roman Church, precisely that primacy which Charlemagne had refused to recognize. Nevertheless, it would be erroneous to say that in Lothar's opinion the jurisdictional

---

[1] In appraising the climate of this time, we should not omit to point out that this was also the period which saw so many able theologians at work. This intellectual *élite* numbered men like Claudius, Hrabanus Maurus, Hincmar, Gottschalk, Walafrid Strabo, Paschasius Radbertus, Christian of Stablo, Heiric of Auxerre, Servatus Lupus of Ferrières, Regino of Prüm, Symphorianus, Amalarius of Metz, Johannes Scotus, Prudentius of Troyes, Ratramnus of Corbie, etc. Due importance should also be given to the "burning zeal for liturgy" resulting in a great number of liturgical refinements and reforms in this ninth century, about which see Th. Klauser, "Die liturgischen Austauschbeziehungen etc." in *Hist. Jb.* liii (1936), pp. 184-5, especially Amalarius.

[2] MGH. *Epp.* v, no. 46, p: 609.

[3] MGH. *Epp.* v, no. 46, p. 609, lines 24 ff.: "Sedem apostolicam, quae per beatissimum apostolorum principem in universo orbe, quaqua versum religio christiana diffunditur, caput et fundamentum est sanctitatis."

[4] MGH. *Epp.* v, no. 46, p. 609, line 27 f.: "Omnes quasi ad matrem religionis, fontemque recurrerent aequitatis."

primacy of the Roman Church comprised also non-ecclesiastical matters: for this view there is no warrant in his letter. This endorsement of the papal jurisdictional power in sacerdotal matters by the emperor, is a sign of the advance which the papal theme had made in the quarter, in which, *prima facie*, most resistance would have been expected.

The other quarter, the Frankish episcopacy, is equally indicative of the trends of the time. Assembled at Paris in 849, the bishops issue a *Synodica* to the Breton duke Nomenojus, upon whom they pour bitter recriminations: by refusing obedience to the pope, the duke had shown his contempt for the whole of Christianity. For the pope had been given by God the primacy in the whole world.[1] Disobedience to the pope entails a "perturbatio populi christiani."[2] The theme underlying this *Synodica* is the conception of Christendom as one body: and the unity of this one body is particularly susceptible to injury if the head of this body is refused obedience. For the whole of Christendom—the universal Church—is affected by everything that affects the pope who has the "primatus in omni orbe terrarum." The "pax christiana"[3] is guaranteed by the pope alone, and he who shows disrespect to the pope disturbs the "pax christiana." These are the opinions of Frankish bishops expressed at the very same time which saw the Pseudo-Isidorian forgers at work. The pope is no mere head of the *sacerdotium*, but head of "omnis orbis terrarum."

Whilst these bishops were concerned with the unity of the *corpus* of Christians, others assembled five years earlier at Diedenhofen (844) pronounce upon the government of this *corpus*, of this universal Church, in a manner which shows the total eclipse suffered by the governmental ideology of Charlemagne. There was no longer, according to these synodists, a unitary combination of regal and sacerdotal powers in a mere king or emperor: this unitary combination was only to be found in Christ Who had decreed that His Church was to be governed by pontifical authority and by regal power.

Bene nostis, ab illo, qui solus merito et rex et sacerdos fieri potuit, ita ecclesiam dispositam esse, ut pontificali auctoritate et regali potestate gubernetur.[4]

---

[1] Mansi, xiv. 923D: "Omnem laesisti christianitatem, dum vicarium b. Petri apostolicum, cui dedit Deus primatum in omni orbe terrarum, sprevisti . . ."

[2] Mansi, xiv. 924B.  [3] Mansi, xiv. 925A.

[4] MGH. *Capit*. ii. 114, no. 227. Cf. also the letter of the synod of Kierzy (anno 858) in MGH. *Capit*. ii. 440, lines 39 ff.: "(Christus) qui solus rex fieri potuit et sacerdos, et in coelum ascendens suum regnum, id est, ecclesiam, inter pontificalem auctoritatem et regiam potestatem gubernandum disposuit" (c. 15). See also the synod held at Fimes in 881, Mansi, xvii. 537.

The different functions are distributed by Christ Himself, and the synodists are careful to repeat the Gelasian contrast between "auctoritas" and "potestas." The mystical head of this one *corpus* was still Christ, and hence the allocation of the different functions—of "auctoritas" and "potestas"—within this *corpus* was Christ's own disposition. Again, there was as yet no suggestion that the same combination of powers was in the hands of a vicar of Christ. Only when this stage was reached, that is to say, when the conception of a mystical headship of Christ gave way to a corporal, vicarious headship, the Gelasian principle became capable of full and practical realization.

Nevertheless, in the same year 844 in which the synodists had gathered at Diedenhofen, there was written a joint letter by the archbishop of Sens and the count of Vienne. This letter[1] deserves some remark, because in it the idea of the functional qualification of the priests—epitomized in the Gelasian "auctoritas"—shows itself in that it is stated that kings should implement or cause to be implemented what the pontiffs teach. The ancient antithesis of "discere-docere" reappears here in the garb of the antithesis "implere-docere," that is, that the (Christian) kings, if they aspire at this dignity, should act as the pontiffs teach.

Rex regum idemque sacerdos sacerdotum, qui solus potuit ecclesiam regere quam redemit . . . potestatem suam ad eandem gubernandam ecclesiam in sacerdotes divisit et *reges*, ut, *quod sancti docerent pontifices, et ipsi implerent et impleri facerent devotissimi reges.*[2]

It seems hardly possible to surpass this concise statement: if the full jurisdictional and legislative power of the Roman Church is brought to bear upon this declaration, the whole hierocratic scheme is here expressed in a nutshell.

The pope himself—Leo IV—fully availed himself of the opportunity of giving and making the last binding decision in matters concerning the ecclesiastical hierarchy—and here the difference between him and his namesake, the third Leo, some fifty years earlier becomes manifest.[3] Moreover, in his letter to Louis II, Leo IV brings out the function of the Roman Church as the epitome of all Christendom and as the organ responsible for everything that affects the universal

[1] MGH. *Epp.* vi. 72 (Servatus Lupus: Ep. 81). The letter was written to the archbishop of Lyons, *ca.* 844.

[2] Ep. cit. p. 73, lines 6–10.

[3] MGH. *Epp.* v, no. 12, p. 591; no. 35, p. 604; nos. 3 and 4, pp. 586–7; no. 10, p. 589; no. 22, p. 599; no. 37, p. 605, etc.

Church. The reason for his accepting supreme pontifical authority was that he be enabled to take care of all that occurs in the world.

Ut nostis, ideo pontificatus culmen suscepimus, ut *de omnibus quae in mundo sunt*, curam et sollicitudinem habeamus.[1]

It is he in fact who is responsible to God for remedying evils: if he were to fail in this papal duty he would have to render an account for it.[2] The whole Christian world is committed to him, and not merely the ecclesiastical hierarchy. The claim to frontierless exercise of papal authority—"quaecumque regio"—heralds the Nicholean pontificate. In short, the Roman Church is the epitome, the crystallization, and the concentrated embodiment of Christendom. It is only as a specific application of this tenet that Leo IV appointed Alfred the Great a "Consul" in 853 and, on the imperial model, adopted him as "quasi spiritalis filius."[3] The successor of the "Consul Dei" appoints a "Consul" on his own authority: not incongruously Leo IV may be likened to an heir of both the "Consul Dei" and the Roman emperors. Hand in hand with this goes Leo's insistence on the universally binding character of the "regulae decretalium" issued by the Roman pontiff. Roman judgments and decrees admit of no other law, and if ecclesiastical tribunals cannot find a solution to a concrete problem, they are ordered to refer the case to the Roman Church[4]

The tenet of the functional qualification of the *sacerdotium* is of particular concern to Leo IV. The "sacerdotes" within the Christian "orbis terrarum" assume specific functions owing to their qualifications as the "sors Domini." Hence they are removed from the jurisdiction of the ordinary tribunals. For the "ecclesiasticus ordo," consisting of the "episcopis et clericis ordinatis"[5] attends to "divinis negotiis"[6] and consequently in this body of believers this "ordo" is raised above the ordinary lay people. We recall that Alcuin had deemed it fitting to quote the (forged) *Constitutum Silvestri* when he referred to the

[1] Ep. 10, p. 589.

[2] Ep. 10, p. 589, lines 23 ff.: "Quod nisi faceremus et malum, quod sive aput vos sive *aput quamcumque regionem* perpetratum valemus agnoscere, auctoritate apostolica emendare dissimulamus, de manibus nostris hoc altissimus requirere non omittet."

[3] Ep. 31, p. 602, to Ethelwulf: "Filium vestrum Erfred, quem hoc in tempore ad sanctorum apostolorum limina destinare curastis, benigne ne suscepimus, et quasi spiritalem filium consulatus cinguli honore vestimentisque, ut mos est Romanis consulibus, decoravimus, eo quod in nostris se tradidit manibus."

[4] Ep. 16, cap. 14, pp. 595–6.

[5] Ep. 16, p. 594, lines 12–13.

[6] Ep. 16, p. 593, line 23.

impending trial of the third Leo before Christmas 800. And we find the same quotation in the letter of the fourth Leo: accusations against bishops can proceed only on the testimony of seventy-two suitable witnesses.[1] But this principle is extended by Leo IV to ecclesiastical goods and possessions: they are the property of the individual church and hence of the universal Church and are therefore removed from lay disposition.[2]

These statements of fundamental principles may not have had all the desired effect at the time, but there can be no gainsaying their precedential character. It was these—and similar—manifestations of the papal point of view which, as a consequence of having been incorporated in collections, assumed the nature of an "auctoritas." It is no wonder that Gratian made nine excerpts from this one letter of Leo IV.

It is very much the same ideology which appears in the confirmation of privileges for Corbie, issued by Leo IV's successor, Pope Benedict III.[3] The Arenga of this privilege points to the function of the Roman Church as the "caput et princeps" of the whole Christian body: to the pontiff as the vice-gerent of St Peter was committed by Christ the *principatus* over the whole body of the Church—"Christus totius ecclesiae committens principatum": the authority of this overlordship lay in the Petrine commission.[4] None of the faithful can doubt that the Roman pontiff is responsible for all the believers in Christ, for the whole body constituting the universal Church.[5] His authority extends "circa universalis ecclesiae corpus per totius orbis latitudinem diffusae."[6] It is not the least interesting feature of this letter that Benedict III

---

[1] Ep. 16, pp. 593–4, quoting canon iii of the *Const. Silv.*: "sicut nobis tradidit b. Silvester et Romana sancta tenere videtur ecclesia."

[2] Ep. 16, p. 595, cap. 10: "Eas possessiones vel praedia, quae justo titulo ad sacrosanctas pertinere videntur ecclesias, vel sub ecclesiastico jure tenentur, indignum est, ut a quibusdam laicis alienentur. Quippe tribuentibus proficit ad mercedem, alienantibus vero scimus exinde provenire delictum." It was precisely this principle which was to play a great role in the eleventh and twelfth centuries, see infra pp. 408 ff.

[3] J. 2663, of 7 October 855: PL. cxxix. 1001 ff.

[4] J. 2663, of 7 October 855: PL. cxxix, col. 1001D: "Cum Romanae sedis pontificem constet omnium ecclesiarum Christi caput atque principatum fatur 'Tu es Petrus . . .'"

[5] "Cunctatio nulli fidelium relinquitur . . . et omnium in Christo credentium saluti, paci atque quieti prospicere nos oporteat, ut et quae prava sunt corrigantur et quae rata roborentur, quae corrupta sunt restaurentur, quae autem integra conserventur."

[6] Cf. also col. 1002: "Igitur cum apostolicae sollicitudinis universalis ecclesiae credita sit dispensatio et pro cunctorum fidelium statu perpetuas nostrae sollicitudinis vigilias pretendere conveniat . . ."

apparently welcomes the opportunity to weave into the texture of the Arenga his ideas about the special place which the emperor occupies in the scheme of things: his care for the Gallican churches is prompted by the fact that they form an integral part of the empire, which itself is constituted by Italy and the Frankish provinces.[1] And it is in the same context and Arenga that Benedict III announces the principle which can have validity only in a Christian society, namely, that the prince's laws should be endorsed by apostolic authority. The implication is clear: the prince, if he wishes to rule legitimately within the universal Church, must subject his laws to pontifical authorization. Then the words of Christ will be fully applicable to that prince "He that receiveth you, receiveth me"[2] as also in the opposite case will other words of Christ be applied: "He that despiseth you, despiseth me."[3] There is no difference between the synodists of Diedenhofen (844) and Benedict III: the former's demand that the prince should implement the teachings of the pontiffs, is stated by the latter's declaration that the prince should submit his laws to pontifical authorization. The echo of the Gelasian axiom seems manifest: "Imperatores Christiani subdere debent exsecutiones suas ecclesiasticis praesulibus."[4]

## III

Perhaps the most characteristic feature of the papal-hierocratic theme had always been its conservatism and reliance on tradition. More often than not, it was a genuine conservatism and a genuine tradition that distinguished the architects of this programme. But there were successful attempts to create a conservatism and a tradition by either antedating documents and ascribing them to earlier authors or by forging documents altogether and dating them in the far distant past in order to be safe enough to escape a check. The most conspicuous example of creating a conservatism and a tradition is provided by that circle to which the three great and not uninfluential forgeries owe their origin.

[1] J. 2663, of 7 October 855: PL. cxxix, col. 1002D: "Quandoquidem utramque provinciam unius imperii sceptrum non dividit et Romanae dignitas ecclesiae una cum terreno principatu utriusque provinciae regnum communi jure disponit."
[2] *Matt.* x. 40.
[3] *Luke*, x. 16: "Aestimantes terrenae reipublicae rectores tunc se feliciter imperare, si suis sanctionibus apostolica confederantur auctoritas, quamdum in nobis suscipiunt ac venerantur, illum se suscipere gratulantur, qui discipulis suis loquitur 'qui vos recipit, me recipit.' Hinc econtrario contemptoribus ait: 'Qui vos spernit, me spernit.'"
[4] Ed. Thiel, p. 293.

7 *

All three—the *Capitula Angilramni, Pseudo-Isidore*, and *Benedictus Levita*—attempt to give the hierocratic point of view the halo of antiquity. Many of the decrees incorporated in them contain absolutely nothing new: what the forgers did was to clothe a particular hierocratic and already virtually accepted tenet in the garb of an ancient decree. Others were of an indubitably genuine provenance, whilst a third group of decrees—and they are the true forgeries—contain certain hierocratic tenets for which no warrant could be found in previous genuine documents. It is this last group which merits a few words.

Collections of this kind, as are the three products under discussion, imply the possibility that their authors had a fair chance of their works being accepted by contemporaries. To undertake all this labour of collecting and inventing documents, if there were little prospect of acceptance, would be hardly more than an exercise in mental gymnastics. To judge by the numerous manuscripts of these forgeries still extant, the assumption is not unwarranted that their authors sensed the climate of the time correctly. By forging documents they clothed the one or the other hierocratic idea in the language of a decree issued by a second- or third-century pope. What the forgers did not invent was ideology; what they did forge was the decree which was to "prove" this ideology. Moreover, the great currency which these products, especially *Pseudo-Isidore* and *Benedictus Levita*, gained, was not only due to the receptiveness of the soil for the views set forth in them, but also to their character as handy reference books. What had been dispersed in all sorts of—for contemporaries—more or less inaccessible repositories, now became easily available: it was all so conveniently gathered into one volume.[1] The atmosphere of the time pervaded as it was with hierocratic ideas, together with the character of these products as useful reference works, account largely for the immediate influence which they exercised. Lastly, these great forgeries symbolize, so to speak, the coalescence of Rome and Rheims. Precisely because they had originated quite independently of the papacy, these products of the Frankish intelligentsia were to become the natural allies of the papacy. Exactly one hundred years after Stephen's journey to the Frankish kingdom, the ecclesiastical intelligentsia of this kingdom repaid the debts it owed to the papacy by presenting it with these collections of materials. Perhaps they were the most welcome gifts the papacy had ever received.

[1] That is what Pseudo-Isidore himself says in the opening paragraph (Hinschius, *Decretales Pseudo-Isidorianae*, p. 17): "Compellor a multis tam episcopis quam reliquis servis Dei canonum sententias colligere et *uno in volumine* redigere et de multis *unum* facere."

## IV

A very short survey of these three great forgeries (made between 845 and 852) may be profitable. We survey them by beginning with the *Capitula Angilramni*. They are alleged to have been sent by Pope Adrian I in 785 to Angilram, bishop of Metz. The aim behind this allegation was to stamp these decrees with pontifical Roman authority. This allegation could be made all the easier as Charlemagne himself had received in 774 a canonical collection from the pope, the *Dionysio-Hadriana*. The main purpose of our collection seems to have been to make accusations against bishops as difficult as possible and to have bishops tried by the ecclesiastical court only. Of course, the claim here set forth in legal form, is nothing new. In the first years of Louis I's reign Theodulf of Orleans had said very much the same[1] when he declared that he was not subject to a royal tribunal, but only to papal jurisdiction;[2] and the decrees of the synod at Aix-la-Chapelle in 836 had laid down that indictments against bishops must be made before a council, and must be tried and proved there.[3] What this forger attempted to do was to pretend that the decrees emanated from the Roman Church which issued them and declared at the same time that the divine ordering prevented a trial of bishops by secular tribunals.[4] Furthermore, the forger transformed earlier conciliar decrees concerning the personality of the accusers of a bishop, into papal decrees: the decree of the Council of Chalcedon laid down personal blamelessness on the part of the accuser of a bishop as a presupposition for a lawful prosecution; this emerges in the forger's *Capitula* too.[5] What is important is that the synod which is to try a bishop must be convoked by the ecclesiastical superior.[6] The forger's insistence on strict hierarchical ordering is

---

[1] MGH. *Poetae Lat.* i. 566, verse 65 f.: "Esto: forem fassus, cuius censura valeret, Dedere judicii congrua frena mihi? Solius illud opus Romani praesulis extat, cuius ego accepi pallia sancta manu."

[2] See preceding note.

[3] MGH. *Concilia*, iii. 718, which decree is literally borrowed from Jonas of Orleans's tract, cap. 2.

[4] Hinschius, ed. cit., p. 757, cap. 1: "Dei ordinationem accusat in qua constituuntur qui episcopos accusat vel condemnat, dum minus spiritualia quam terrena sectatur." But cf. Isidore's *Sententiae*, iii. 39, no. 2.

[5] Hinschius, ed. cit., p. 758, cap. 3, and Concil. Chalced. cc. 17, 21. "Placuit ut semper primo in accusatione clericorum fides et vita blasphemantium perscrutetur. Nam fides omnes actus hominis debet praecedere, quia dubius in fide infidelis est." Cf. also IV Concil. Toletanum, c. 64.

[6] Hinschius, ed. cit., p. 758, cap. 4. The whole is taken from the letter attributed to Felix I: *Pseudo-Isidore*, p. 200 f., cc. viii–xiv. Furthermore, *Cap. Angilramni*,

entirely in line with the dictates of the hierocratic programme.[1] It is in this context that he stresses the primacy of the Roman Church. On the one hand, a provincial synod must be cancelled if papal vicars so demand it,[2] but, on the other hand, any laws contrary to the canons and decrees of the Roman pontiff or to "boni mores" are null and void.[3] The pope himself is immune from any sort of accusation and judgment, the forger declares, by borrowing the forged and identical stipulation of one of the Symmachan products.[4] It will be agreed that the *Capitula* contain extraordinarily little that was not known before: but it will also be agreed that the crispness of these decrees gives them the appearance of true legal enactments.

## V

† *Pseudo-Isidore* is designed to serve as a hand book which contains the literal transcriptions of documents from the earliest Christian times onwards. The basic structure of this collection was that of the old *Hispana*.[5] The first of the three parts of the work consists of "decretals" issued by pre-Constantinean popes and shows most blatantly the labour of the forgers: all the sixty decretals are forged. The second part is only to a small extent the work of the forgers: it contains older forgeries as well as genuine material. Perhaps the most complicated part is the third and last beginning with the (forged) *Constitutum Silvestri*: in this part genuine and spurious material is rather skilfully blended. Altogether there are more than one hundred forged or falsified papal letters in this work. Whilst therefore the *Capitula Angilramni* constituted, so to speak, a legal summary of the hierocratic theme, *Pseudo-Isidore* is supposed to give the full references and the

---

cc. 18–22, p. 762. For the question whether this forger was identical with that of Pseudo-Isidore, see Hinschius, pp. clviii–clxxxii.

[1] Cf. also preceding note.

[2] Hinschius, ed. cit., p. 765, cap. 39: "Ut provincialis synodus retractetur per vicarios urbis Romae episcopi, si ipse decreverit."

[3] Hinschius, ed. cit., p. 764, cap. 36: "Constitutiones contra canones et decreta praesulum Romanorum vel bonos mores nullius sunt momenti."

[4] Hinschius, ed. cit., p. 766, cap. 51: "Neque praesul summus a quoquam judicabitur, quia dicente domino non est discipulus super magistrum." This is in cap. iii of the *Constitutum Silvestri* (also in *Pseudo-Isidore*, p. 449; Mansi, ii. 623).

[5] On the *Hispana* see Fournier-Le Bras, *Histoire des coll. can.*, i. 66 f.; H. E. Feine, *Kirchliche Rechtsgeschichte*, pp. 82, 148; the work was wrongly attributed to Isidore of Seville.

full text of the relevant source material, in short the *pièces justifica-tives*.[1]

At the outset of our brief analysis of *Pseudo-Isidore* we must em-phasize again that the work contains very little new material. It could be passed over in silence, were it not that it exercised great influence on later papal generations as well as on canonists. It was to become the pantheon of all papal prerogatives. What Pseudo-Isidore did was to mould hierocratic tenets—hitherto vaguely floating about—into con-crete papal pronouncements bearing the stamp of apostolic and early Christian antiquity. The work of these forgers was tendentious, de-signed to set forth a programme in the cloak of the "law."

Throughout *Pseudo-Isidore* the paramount theme is that of the functional qualification of the priests in a Christian society. They alone can function, by virtue of their qualifications, as the directing organs of the Christian *corpus*. The priests are the true leaders of the whole body of Christians. They function as the "lieutenants of Christ"—"sacer-dotes vice Christi legatione *funguntur*," Pope Evaristus is made to say.[2] They are the chosen people of Christ—"in sorte Domini electi"[3]— because He Himself had selected them: "ad glorificandum se et divina mandata seminanda . . . eos Dominus elegit."[4] In fact, the priests are the vicars of Christ within the universal body of Christians: "Christi vicarii sunt sacerdotes, qui *vice Christi* legatione *funguntur* in ecclesia."[5] They are divinely pre-ordained.[6] Pope Melchiades is made to refer to the alleged declaration of Constantine in the Council of Nicaea when he exclaimed "Vos a nemine dijudicari potestis, quia solius Dei judicium reservamini: dii etenim vocati estis."[7] By not according to

---

[1] For details of modern literature, see H. Schubert, *Geschichte der Kirche im Frühmittelalter*, p. 537; A van Hove, *Prolegomena*, pp. 305–6; Fournier-Le Bras, *Histoire des collections canoniques*, i. 137; H. E. Feine, *Kirchliche Rechtsgeschichte*, p. 153. Cf. also E. H. Davenport, *The False Decretals*, Oxford, 1916.

[2] Hinschius, ed. cit., ep. 2, c. 4, p. 90; cf. also Clement, ep. 3, c. 57, p. 53; see also idem, p. 52, c. 56 ("qui sacerdotio domini fruimini"); furthermore, Anacletus, ep. 2, c. 22, p. 79; Alexander, ep. 1, c. 3, p. 95, and p. 97, c. 5; Anterus, p. 155, c. 7, etc. Pope Anacletus is made to say, ep. 1, c. 3, p. 68: "Injuria sacer-dotum ad Christum pertinet, cuius vice *funguntur*"; ep. 2, c. 21, p. 77: "Quoniam injuria eorum ad Christum pertinet, cuius legatione *funguntur*." The source of these expressions may have been Gregory I, see supra p. 39 (cf., however, *II Cor.* v. 20).

[3] Pope Urban, p. 143, c. 1.

[4] Clement, p. 43, c. 39.

[5] Eusebius, ep. 3, c. 17, p. 239. Cf. Gregory I supra p. 39.

[6] Fabianus, ep. 2, c. 16, p. 163: "Deus ergo, fratres, ad hoc preordinavit vos et omnes, qui summo sacerdotio *funguntur*."

[7] Melchiades, p. 248, c. 11; for Gregory I's statements see supra p. 39 f.

the priests, the salt of the earth,[1] the place that is due to them in a Christian society, proper reverence is not shown to Christ.[2] For the clerical order alone knows the "divina mandata," whilst the lay members of the universal Church are devoted to carnal things only.

The proper ordering within a Christian society demands, consequently, that clerical persons are exempted from the control and jurisdiction of the inferior lay people; accusations against clerics by lay persons are inadmissible, since inferiors must not accuse superiors. A pupil cannot accuse, still less judge, his master; nor can a lay prince accuse or judge a cleric.[3] How could a lieutenant of Christ be accused or judged by those people who form the "plebs."[4] Having the functional qualifications for directing Christian society the members of the clerical order should not only abstain from "omnes huius vitae occupationes," but also treat lay jurisdiction with contempt.

Of particular interest and importance are Pseudo-Isidore's pronouncements concerning the virtually sacrosanct position of the episcopacy. "Episcopi a Deo sunt judicandi," Pope Pius is made to say.[5] They must be tried by the ecclesiastical tribunal only, but must never be accused by the "vulgus."[6] The proper tribunal is the synod, and yet, this assembly is devoid of any jurisdictional power unless summoned by the pope.[7] These ideas stand in close proximity to the strict hierarchical grading of the sacerdotal order itself, a theme which is so incessantly repeated. This sacerdotal hierarchy has its apex in the Roman Church. The primacy of the Roman Church is, next to ecclesiastical freedom from lay jurisdiction, the most vital principle with which Pseudo-Isidore operates.[8] In a most specific sense the Roman Church

---

[1] Clement, ep. 1, c. 26, p. 38; cf. *Matt.* v. 13, 14, 16; xv. 14.

[2] Anacletus, ep. 2, c. 24, p. 79.

[3] See, for instance, Clement, ep. 1, c. 31, p. 40; c. 42, p. 45, etc.

[4] Evaristus, ep. 2, c. 9, p. 91; Pontianus, ep. 1, c. 3, p. 147; Anacletus, ep. 2, c. 22, p. 78 ("perverted individuals"); Fabianus, ep. 12, c. 13, p. 162; Eusebius, ep. 2, c. 9, p. 234; Julius, ep. 18, p. 473. Lay people on equal footing with "violatores sepulchri, incestuosi, homicidae, perjuri, adulteri, de bellis fugientes," Stephen, ep. 1, c. 2, p. 186.

[5] Ep. 1, c. 4, p. 117.

[6] Evaristus, ep. 2, c. 9, p. 91: "Non est itaque a plebe vel vulgaribus hominibus arguendus vel accusandus episcopus"; Calixtus, ep. 1, c. 3, p. 136.

[7] See preface, p. 19, c. 8, and Marcellinus, decr. i, p. 224, and decr. ii, p. 228, c. 10: "Synodum ergo absque huius sanctae sedis auctoritate episcoporum . . . non potestis regulariter facere, neque ullum episcopum, qui hanc appellaverit apostolicam sedem dampnare antequam hinc sententia finitiva procedat."

[8] But cf. Fournier-Le Bras, op. cit., i. 133: "On a dit, bien à tort, que l'idée dominante d'Isidore était l'exaltation de l'autorité du Saint-Siège. Ce qui est vrai, c'est qu'il poursuit avant tout la restauration de l'indépendance, de l'autorité

epitomizes all that is contained in the sum total of all the other churches. In fact, Christianity as such is epitomized in the Roman Church. All Christian life is derived from its epitome.[1] By Christ's commission St Peter became the "caput totius ecclesiae."[2] Moreover, all the superior status accorded to the clerics, applies to the Roman Church in a concentrated manner: it is the Church of him who was "cephas." The lay parts of the Christian body assume a mere passive role in this scheme of things. For the "ecclesia" being identical with Christendom, must be ruled by the Roman Church and the sacerdotal hierarchy. "Caput enim ecclesiae Christus est; Christi vicarii sacerdotes sunt, qui vice Christi legatione *funguntur* in ecclesia."[3] It is only logical for Pseudo-Isidore to claim that the proper tribunal for all Christians is the ecclesiastical tribunal.[4]

Pseudo-Isidore's other basic view is the organic conception of the Christian body. He knows of Leo I's view[5] but makes Pope Julius propound this theme.[6] This Christian *corpus* includes both the clerical and lay Christians, and "although there are many members in the one body of Christ, not all members have the same functions": but "we all are one body in Christ." It is the organically and closely knit union of this one body—the "connexio totius corporis"—which makes necessary an integration of functions[7] and in a very special sense makes imperative the hierarchical gradation of the sacerdotal members of this body. Priests have all the same *ordo*, but they have not all the same *potestas*. Hence the proper functioning of the *corpus* presupposes dis-

---

et du prestige de l'épiscopat. S'il exalte le Siège Apostolique, c'est sans doute pour rendre hommage à la vieille tradition ecclésiastique et romaine, mais sourtout parce que, ayant compris que l'épiscopat ne peut s'appuyer avec sécurité sur le souverain séculier, il cherche à lui donner un point d'appui très solide dans le domaine purement spirituel."

[1] Cf., for example, Pius I, p. 116, c. 1, quoting *Col.* ii. 19: "Caput, ex quo totum corpus per nexum et conjunctionem ministratum et constructum crescit in augmentum Dei."

[2] Marcellus, p. 223, c. 1.

[3] Eusebius, ep. 2, c. 3, p. 230; and ep. 3, c. 17, p. 239.

[4] The apostolic saying is here applied in a far more general way than it was originally intended: "Quaecumque ergo contentiones in Christianos hortae fuerint, ad ecclesiam deferrantur et ab ecclesiasticis viris terminentur," Marcellinus, ep. 2, c. 3, p. 221; see furthermore Alexander, ep. 1, c. 4, p. 95: "Christianorum causas ad ecclesias deferri et ibidem terminari"; Anacletus, ep. 1, c. 16, p. 74: ". . . sacerdotali judicio terminari."

[5] He incorporates the whole of Leo I's Ep. 14 in his collection, pp. 618–20; the relevant passage is c. 10, p. 620.

[6] J. + 159: Pseudo-Isidore, pp. 456 ff.

[7] Cf. also Pius I, p. 116, c. 1; *Col.* ii. 19.

tribution of offices, so however that the Roman Church obtains "principatum totius ecclesiae," Pseudo-Isidore makes Julius say anticipating Leo I.[1] The organic conception of the Christian body— "ecclesia, quae est corpus eius (scil. Christi)"[2]—together with the necessity for strict monarchical rulership of this one body[3] produces, according to Pseudo-Isidore, the further consequence that the lower placed churches partake in some way in the power of the Roman Church, from which they receive their existence.[4] Here it cannot be denied that Pseudo-Isidore makes a certain advance, for he extends— on the basis of the organic conception—the principle which Leo I had laid down for one particular case, that of his own vicar: Pseudo-Isidore generalizes this principle and makes Pope Vigilius say that the Roman Church "reliquis ecclesiis vices suas credidit largiendas, ut in parte sint vocatae sollicitudinis, non in plenitudine potestatis."[5] This plenitude of power is the pope's alone, for, on the model of the incorporated Donation of Constantine, the pope combines both royal and sacerdotal functions in his own person: he is, as Felix II is made to say, "quasi totius orbis caput."[6]

## VI

Whilst Pseudo-Isidore's aim was to show, by the literal transcription from papal (and conciliar) sources, the right order of living, the canon of life in a Christian society, his contemporary Benedictus Levita pursued the same aim by collecting royal and imperial decrees. Whilst, furthermore, Pseudo-Isidore pretended to work on the basis of Isidore, Benedictus Levita pretended to continue the work of the abbot of St Wandrille, Ansegisus, who had collected (by about 829) the Frankish *capitularia* issued between 789 and 826.[7] This Pseudo-Ansegisus of

[1] Julius, p. 461, and also anticipating Gelasius, Ep. 14, c. 9, Thiel, p. 367.

[2] Euticianus, c. 5, p. 210.

[3] Conflating Leo I's Ep. 14, c. 10, with Rom. xii. 5, he makes Calixtus say, p. 136, c. 1: "Non decet enim membra a capite dissidere, sed juxta sacrae scripturae testimonium omnia membra capud sequantur."

[4] Vigilius, p. 712, c. 7: "a qua omnes ecclesias principium sumpsisse nemo recte credentium ignorat."

[5] Leo I's statement was: "Vices enim nostras ita tuae credimus caritati ut in partem sis vocatus sollicitudinis, non in plenitudinem potestatis," Ep. 14, p. 619, preface. This was written by Leo I to his vicar, Anastasius of Thessalonica, about which see supra p. 8; on Pseudo-Isidore's extension see G. Tellenbach, *Libertas*, p. 166. The letter of Vigilius is genuine, except cap. 7, where the extension is forged, see Hinschius, p. cv.       [6] Felix II, c. 13, p. 489.

[7] They are printed in Mansi, xvii. 698–800; PL. xcvii. 490–590; and MGH. *Leges.* i. 256–325.

Benedictus Levita—the author's name is as much a pseudonym as that of Isidore Mercatus (Pseudo-Isidore)—was to prove that the hiero-cratic theme was set forth by royal and imperial *capitularia*, hence it is the exact opposite number of Pseudo-Isidore. The collection contains 1721 chapters of which only about a quarter is genuine; the oldest genuine law is one of King Childebert of 596, and the most recent a *capitulare* of 829; in this genuine mass there is also a good deal of Roman law.[1] In the preface the author reveals that his collection is destined to serve the interests of the clergy as well as those of the whole Christian people.[2]

Naturally, the role of the papacy also assumes major proportions in this work. The secular laws, the *Capitularia*, are proper norms of conduct, according to Benedictus Levita, because they had been con-firmed by apostolic authority,[3] and for this reason they are binding on the whole Christian people. The function of the pope as the supreme judge in a Christian body was given particular prominence in this collection. Old tenets were here reshaped and expressed in far more decided language than they originally were.[4] The universally binding character of papal decrees is given equal prominence.[5] No synod is legitimate unless approved by the pope.[6] The magisterial primacy of the Roman Church is, for understandable reasons, one more prominent

---

[1] Cf. M. Conrat, in *Neues Archiv*, 1899, pp. 341 ff., and the introduction to MGH. *Leges*, ii. 19–31. For a description and analysis see E. Seckel, "Studien zu Benedictus Levita" in *Neues Archiv*, xxvi–xli, 1900–31, and *Sav. Z., Kan. Abt.*, 1934–5; cf. also Fournier-Le Bras, op. cit. i. 202–9.

[2] Preface, p. 40, lines 14–16: ". . . ea, quae sequuntur, ad sanctae Dei ecclesiae servorumque eius atque totius Christiani populi, utilitatem sunt conscripta capitula."

[3] Preface, p. 40, lines 7–8: "Ut cognoscant omnes haec praedictorum principum (scil. Carolimanni et Pippini) capitula maxima apostolica auctoritate fore firmata."

[4] ii. 64, which is a transformation of c. iii of the Council of Sardica, cf. Seckel, vol. xxxiv. 376 ff. See furthermore, ii. 401 = Sardicum, c. iv = iii. 103; Sard. c. vii = iii. 173. In this process of transformation the original text is often changed beyond recognition. Cf. e.g., iii. 315 (forged): "Placuit, ut si episcopus accusatus appellaverit Romanum pontificem, id statuendum, quod ipse censuerit"; the same in *Additio*, iv. 27, where it is rendered "ex edictis synodalibus sub Theo-dosio imperatore." On the various modifications of texts see Fournier-Le Bras, op. cit., i. 160–2.

[5] ii. 341: "(Rubric) Ut nullus apostolicas sanctiones temerare praesumat. Ita unanimes divinis apostolicis constitutionibus serviatis, ut in nullo patiamini pia canonum decreta violari." Repeated iii. 244. Cf. also i. 85.

[6] ii. 381: "Auctoritas ecclesiastica atque canonica docet non debere absque sententia Romani pontificis concilia celebrare"; iii. 341: "Ut provincialis synodus retractetur per vicarios urbis Romanae episcopi, si ipse decreverit." Cf. also iii. 478.

point.[1] In the emphasis of these cardinal tenets Benedictus Levita pursues the same aim as Pseudo-Isidore and with as little originality as the latter.

Since this collection was one of Frankish secular laws and since these, particularly those of Charlemagne, had dealt so largely with a number of topics which papal legislation had not touched and which were nevertheless important for the shaping of Christian society, we find a very great number of regulations allegedly repeating, modifying or re-enacting decrees concerning the payment of tithes;[2] service on Sundays and holidays;[3] penance;[4] instruction by priests;[5] delivery of sermons;[6] pastoral care;[7] illegality of usury;[8] ordination of clerics;[9] and so forth. These regulations are supplemented by those relating to accusations against clerics and particularly against bishops—the point of vital interest to the contemporary clerical party.[10]

Whilst in all this the forger did not contribute anything new—on the whole his work stands on a far lower level than that of Pseudo-Isidore—he nevertheless makes one point which deserves special mention. This point concerns the inalienability and inviolability of ecclesiastical property. In this Benedictus Levita did not invent anything new, but rounded off, so to speak, a legislative development whose beginning was witnessed in the councils of the second and third decades of his century. The council at Paris, 829, had touched upon this delicate point[11] and seven years later in the council at Aix-la-Chapelle the principle of inviolability and inalienability of ecclesiastical property was made the subject of a decree.[12] Benedictus Levita raises this principle to a higher level when he declares in several forged decrees that whatever has been given for the service of clerics has become divine property, whether it be fields, bridges, books, buildings, rivers, vestments, clothing, parchments, in short all mobile and immobile goods.[13] Any infringement of this so widely conceived ecclesias-

---

[1] i. 35, p. 48, esp. lines 31 ff.    [2] i. 45, 51, 88, 101, 154, etc.    [3] ii. 188 ff.
[4] i. 117 ff.    [5] i. 4; ii. 174.    [6] i. 95; 299.
[7] i. 57, 169; ii. 176; iii. 132.    [8] i. 38.    [9] i. 40.

[10] E.g., i. 36, 187; ii. 307, 357 ff., 381, 403; iii. 84–91, 107–12. Not all of these decrees are spurious, some are in literal agreement with the Council of Carthage, some with that of Toledo IV, and others again with that of Chalcedon, for details see Seckel, vol. xxxv, pp. 474 ff.

[11] MGH. *Concilia.*, i. p. 675, and the *Relatio episcoporum*, cap. 196, see also supra p. 136.

[12] See MGH. *Conc.*, p. 718 f., c. 8, and also the letter of Jonas of Orleans, ibid., pp. 730 ff.

[13] ii. 89; ii. 407: "Quicquid a fidelibus offertur, sive in mancipiis sive in agris, vineis, silvis, pratis, aquis aquarumque decursibus, artificiis, libris, utensilibus,

tical property is consequently a sacrilege, the penalty for which is excommunication,[1] loss of all dignities,[2] and stigmatization and punishment as murderer, thief and church robber[3] by the secular tribunals.[4]

One more observation seems warranted. Episcopal freedom was the battle cry of Pseudo-Isidore, as it was that of Benedictus Levita. But the latter goes a little further than the former when, obviously re-echoing the relevant declarations of the synodists of Paris, 829,[5] he declares that Constantine had given the lead by saying that emperors can be judged by bishops, but not bishops by emperors.[6] This alleged statement by Constantine is the basis of Benedictus Levita's forged declaration of Pippin in which he said:

Praecipimus atque jubemus ne forte, quod absit, aliquis circa episcopos leviter aut graviter agat, quod ad periculum totius imperii nostri pertinet.[7]

The claim to absolute episcopal freedom is based upon the unique function which the bishops fulfil in a Christian society, that is, the binding and loosing committed to them by St Peter.[8] It is this aspect

---

petris, aedificiis, vestimentis, pollibus, lanificiis, pecoribus, pasenis, membranis, mobilibus et immobilibus, vel quaecumque de his rebus, quae ad laudem Dei fiunt vel ad supplementum sanctae Dei ecclesiae eiusque sacerdotibus atque ornatum praestare possunt, domino ecclesiaeque suae a quibuscumque ultro offeruntur, Domino indubitanter consecrantur et ad jus pertinent sacerdotum. Et quia Christum et ecclesiam unam personam esse veraciter agnoscimus, quaecumque ecclesiae sunt, Christi sunt; et quae ecclesiae vel in supradictis vel in quibuscumque speciebus sive pollicitationibus sive pignoribus, sive scriptis, sive corporalibus rebus offeruntur, Christo offeruntur; et quae ab ecclesia eius quocumque commento alienantur vel tolluntur, sive alienando sive vastando sive invadendo sive minorando sive diripiendo, Christo tolluntur." See also ii. 370, 426–8.

[1] ii. 134–6; iii. 265, 409.

[2] ii. 428: ". . . omnes honores, quos habere videbatur, perdat."

[3] iii. 142.

[4] Cap. cit.: " Quod si quis fecerit, tam nostris quam et successorum nostrorum temporibus, poenis sacrilegii subjaceat, et a nobis atque successoribus nostris nostrique judicibus vel comitibus sicut sacrilegus et homicida vel fur sacrilegus legaliter puniatur et ab episcopis nostris anathematizetur, ita ut mortuus etiam sepultura et cunctis Dei ecclesiae precibus et oblationibus careat."

[5] See supra p. 131.

[6] i. 315: "Imperator episcopis ait: 'Deus, inquit, constituit vos sacerdotes, et potestatem vobis dedit de nobis quoque judicandi. Et ideo nos a vobis recte judicamur, vos autem non potestis ab hominibus judicari . . . vos etenim vobis a Deo dati estis dii. Et conveniens non est, ut homo judicet deos.' " See also Gregory I, supra p. 39; the council of Aix-la-Chapelle, p. 179, and Pseudo-Isidore, supra p. 181; also Gregory VII, infra pp. 289 ff.

[7] i. 315.

[8] i. 315: "Et ut omnes cognoscant nomen, potestatem, vigorem et dignitatem sacerdotalem, quod ex verbis Domini facile intelligi potest, quibus beato Petro, cuius vicem episcopi gerunt, ait: 'Quodcumque ligaveris . . .' "

of functional qualification in a Christian world order which makes Benedictus Levita insert another chapter wherein the position of the secular power is made clear:

Nam et episcopos et sacerdotes, quibus omnis terra caput inclinat, per quos et nostrum pollet imperium, admodum honorari et venerari omnes monemus.[1]

And he adds:

Detractio sacerdotum ad Christum pertinet, cuius vice legatione *funguntur* in ecclesia.

The position of the king or emperor within the Christian body is made clear also in the imperial decree in which obedience to the bishops is made the king's or emperor's duty, whilst there is no corresponding duty on the part of the bishops to obey the emperor's decrees.[2] It is therefore perfectly logical when we read that imperial laws in opposition to ecclesiastical canons and papal decrees are null and void.[3]

Lex imperatorum non est supra legem Dei, sed subtus.[4]

As we have said before, these forgeries do not excel in inventing new ideas: what they did was to give certain fundamental theses, already largely accepted, a historical twist and foundation. The chief value of these products, especially *Pseudo-Isidore*, lay in their character as handy reference works, which made time-consuming search and research unnecessary. No doubt, the authors of these products were not unskilful in giving certain ideas a sharper and more accentuated form than they previously might have had. What in particular the author (or authors) of the *Pseudo-Isidoriana* attempted to set forth was the canon of right living in a Christian society: as the preface to the work points out, the term "canon" denotes the "norma recte vivendi,"[5] and to lay down this right way of living was the author's intention, prompted no doubt by existing conditions, namely the visible decay of the once held universal empire. The idea underlying this motive of the author was the conception of society as a Christian body politic—the

---

[1] i. 322.

[2] i. 375.

[3] iii. 346; this is in agreement with *Capitula Angilramni*, cap. 36.

[4] *Additio* iii. 18.

[5] See preface, ed. cit., cap. 3, p. 17: "Canon autem graece, latine regula nuncupatur. Regula autem dicta quod recto ducit, ne quando aliorsum trahit. Alii dixerunt regulam dictam vel quod regat, vel quod normam recte vivendi praebeat, sive quod distortum pravumque quid corrigit." This passage is in fact copied from the genuine *Hispana*.

ideational union of Christian mankind was not the Roman empire, but the universal Church conceived as an empire: the *imperium Romanum* was to be supplanted by the *imperium Christianum* governed by its functionally qualified members. The powerful help which Pseudo-Isidore gave to later papal generations, particularly of the Humbertine-Hildebrandine period, is undeniable. Rheims supplied convenient handbooks to Rome.

# CHAPTER VII

# Three Ninth-century Popes

IT is not the least symptomatic feature of Nicholas's state of mind that the writings of his predecessors in the papal office come so readily to his pen: Leo I, Gelasius I, Gregory I, and a whole host of others whose official communications form the backbone of Nicholas's own products. In accepting the Eastern challenge to the *principatus* of the Roman Church, Nicholas I was given the opportunity of re-stating the papal-hierocratic theme and in so doing he powerfully buttressed papal ideology. But what Gelasius lacked, was now at the disposal of this ninth-century pope, namely all the ideological armoury of his predecessors, fortified by contemporary Western declarations and expressions of a strong hierocratic nature, and ably assisted by Pseudo-Isidore. Nevertheless, whilst the Eastern theatre of war provided, so to speak, only a theoretical battle ground, the transformation of Western society gave Nicholas the opportunity to assert the papal-hierocratic theme most forcefully. Set against the Western background, the papal point of view was forced to accept the Eastern challenge: although there were no reasonable grounds for hoping that the breach between East and West could be healed, Nicholas could not acquiesce in the defiant Eastern denial of the *principatus* of the Roman Church.[1] The assertion of the pope's functions in the West peremptorily demanded a clear re-statement of the papal theme towards the East. The pontificate of Nicholas I shows us the approximation of Western society to the body politic of the *Societas omnium fidelium*.

Standing on the ancient roads as he did, Nicholas had the ability to formulate the hierocratic temper of his time in an articulate manner. His communications are characterized by firmness coupled with the conviction of speaking with authority divinely conferred and sanctioned; by strong-mindedness combined with the knowledge of being superior and unaccountable to any one; by aggressiveness resulting

---

[1] It may be recalled that the argument in favour of Constantinople, because it was the seat of the imperial government and senate (the *urbs regia*) was still employed by Photius, *Nomocanon*, i. 5, ed. Paris, 1615, pp. 7–8.

from impatience at still not seeing ancient and justifiable claims recognized. And he had powerful satellites upon whom to rely. The Frankish
episcopacy had for the most part become one of the firm props of the
papal scheme of things; the "imperium," itself the offspring of papal
aspirations and dreams, had become a reality, though now showing
unmistakable features of decay; the thorough permeation of the Western orbit with Romanism could not but produce the expected results;
and perhaps most important of all, the papacy had effectively emerged
as the empire maker.[1]

## I

Nicholas I had the good fortune of having in Anastasius a great
savant, librarian, chancellor, archivist and church historian.[2] There
can be few parallel cases of such a harmonious association as existed
between Nicholas and Anastasius, when once the earlier differences
between the two men had been ironed out. It is fair to assume that
Anastasius acquainted the pope with Pseudo-Isidore,[3] but too much
weight should not be attached to this facet. On the one hand, a pope,
like Nicholas I, who was able to sense the temper of his time and who
was the personification of an idea, could see in *Pseudo-Isidore* little
more than a useful and handy reference work which made time-consuming search for earlier papal manifestations superfluous; on the
other hand,[4] Anastasius begins his fruitful co-operation with Nicholas

---

[1] The idea is very prevalent that Nicholas I was the builder of the medieval
papacy, e.g., H. Böhmer, in *Realencykl. f. prot. Theol.*, 3rd ed., p. 69: "Nikolaus
hat die mittelalterliche Papstidee geschaffen"; cf. also A. Hauck, *Kirchengeschichte*,
ii. 549, and *Weltherrschaftsgedanke*, p. 14. It seems very difficult to label one pope
as the builder (or according to T. G. Jalland, op. cit., p. 378: as the "creator")
of the medieval papacy: this edifice was built of many stones by many architects.

[2] J. Haller, *Nikolaus I & Pseudo-Isidore*, Stuttgart, 1936, p. 131; E. Perels,
*Papst Nikolaus I und Anastasius Bibliothecarius*, Berlin, 1929, pp. 185 ff., 242 ff.
Cf. also idem, in the Introduction, pp. vi–ix, and G. Lähr, "Briefe und Prologe
des Bibl. Anastasius" in *Neues Archiv*, xlvii (1928), pp. 416 ff.

[3] For this thesis see Haller, op. cit., pp. 187 ff., and Perels, op. cit., pp. 181 ff.
See furthermore H. Schrörs, in *Hist. Jb.*, 1904, pp. 1 ff., 1905, pp. 275 ff.
Jalland's assertion, op. cit., p. 384, that "the belief that Nicholas made use of the
False Decretals to justify his claims, once widely held, has now been generally
abandoned" has little foundation. Cf. P. E. Schramm, "Studien etc." in *Sav. Z.*,
*Germ. Abt.*, 1929, pp. 206–7 about the close association of Anastasius with the
composition of the so-called "Early List of Judges" which was modelled on the
Donation of Constantine, see ibid., pp. 213–14 and 230. That Nicholas avoided a
direct reference to the Donation can be explained: he no doubt perceived the
weakness of the document.

[4] F. Dvornik, *The Photian Schism*, Cambridge, 1948, p. 106, suggests that
Pseudo-Isidore was already known in the papal chancery under Leo IV and
Benedict III.

only after the end of his involuntary exile, that is, after 862. Once the intimate association between the two men was established, they supplemented each other extraordinarily well; the one supplying the *geistige Rüstzeug*, the historical learning and arguments, the other laying down the aim and policy to which the librarian's learning should be harnessed.

It may not be unprofitable to sketch rapidly some of Anastasius's ideas about the role of the papacy, since these ideas form a useful background to the great pope's own. The librarian's expressions are perhaps somewhat flamboyant and rhetorical, but were very efficacious in strengthening the confidence of the pope in the librarian's knowledge and ability.

In Anastasius's letter to the pope[1] the learned author hails the pontiff as the "vicar of God," the "pontiff of universal mankind" without whose authority nothing may be accomplished nor be made known in this world. For he is the "unicus papa," the "peculiar pastor and father" of all men, the judge and arbiter of all and also the doorkeeper of heaven.[2] "In the pope's breast live the tables of the Testament as well as the manna of heavenly savour." What he has bound, nobody can loose, and vice-versa, and what he has opened, nobody can shut again, for

vicem namque in terris possides Dei[3]

he writes to the pope.

Stripped of their exuberance, these expressions manifest the view of the pope's mediatory role, a view which emerges in the pope's own communications. But the language employed by Anastasius was precisely the language which Nicholas wished to hear and read.[4] These and similar adulatory expressions[5] are indicative, on the one hand, of

---

[1] MGH. *Epp.* vii, Ep. 1, pp. 396 ff.

[2] MGH. *Epp.* vii, Ep. 1, p. 397, lines 9–12: "Neque enim fas est, ut absque vicario Dei, absque clavigero coeli, absque curru et auriga spiritualis Israel, absque universitatis pontifice, absque unico papa, absque singulari pastore, absque speciali patre, absque omnium arbitro, aliquid consummetur aut divulgetur."

[3] MGH. *Epp.* vii, Ep. 1, p. 397, lines 12–16. The whole passage runs: "Tu enim tenes claves David, tu accepisti claves scientiae. In arca quippe pectoris tui tabulae testamenti et manna coelestis saporis requiescunt. Tu enim quod ligas, nemo solvit; quod solvis, nemo ligat. Qui aperis et nemo claudit, claudis et nemo aperit; vicem namque . . ."

[4] In order to assess the versatility of the librarian, one should compare his earlier conduct with the language of this letter.

[5] Another example is Bishop Adventius of Metz: he writes that the pope is vice-gerent of God, sitting as he does as a true apostle in the papal chair. See

the general esteem in which Nicholas was held, and, on the other hand, of the susceptibility of the pope himself to these high sounding phrases about the papal office.

## II

The theme dominating the mind of Nicholas I was that of the Roman †
Church's being the epitome of the whole of Christendom: Christians are Christians by virtue of their membership of one of the individual churches: but these in turn receive their life from the Roman Church, which is the head and fountain of all Christian life.

*Universitas credentium* ab hac sancta Romana ecclesia, quae caput est omnium ecclesiarum, doctrinam exquirit, integritatem fidei deposcit.[1]

Consequently, the pope alone has to render an account for all those calling themselves Christians:[2] they on the other hand, submit their request for the forgiveness of their sins to the apostolic chair.[3] In a word, the whole flock of Christians—and this includes the Eastern ones—is committed to his care, because it is solely through the Roman Church that they become Christians.[4]

As far as the earth is Christian, the popes are set above the whole earth: *principes super omnem terram.*[5] Theoretically, the Church in the East is just as much subjected to papal ruling as the body of Christians in the West.[6] The universal Church is epitomized in the Roman Church:

---

MGH. *Epp.* vi, Ep. 8, p. 220, lines 14 ff.: "qui vices Dei tenetis et in reverendissima summi principis cathedra verus apostolus residetis, ut vestris fovear solaminibus . . ." His readiness to obey papal edicts as if they came from God: p. 221, lines 9 ff.: "Ecce paratus sum obsecundare edictis vestrae auctoritatis veluti Deo, in cuius persona cuncta profertis."

[1] MGH. *Epp.* vi, Ep. 86, p. 447, lines 32 ff.

[2] MGH. *Epp.* vi, Ep. 86, p. 447, lines 34 ff.: "Pro quibus tantum consistimus pavidi, quantum consideramus in aeterno examine pro omnibus et prae omnibus, qui Christi censentur nomine, rationem reddituri."

[3] MGH. *Epp.* vi, Ep. 86, p. 447, lines 37 ff.

[4] Ep. 29, p. 296, lines 19 ff., to the Frankish bishops: "Ne forte, quod absit, homini haerentes perverso ab illa petra decidatis, super quam verus architectus totius domus suae voluit fundamentum construere et auctorem pravitatis sequentes amittatis communionem ipsius, a quo et episcopatus et apostolatus sumpsit initium, per quem etiam vos per gratiam Dei non solum episcopi, verum et Christiani estis effecti. Capiti ergo religionis, id est, sanctae apostolicae sedi haerete." Cf. Innocent I supra p. 7 n. 6.

[5] Ep. 29, p. 296, lines 10 ff.: "Cum, licet indigni, pro patribus nati filii vicem eius agentes Dei sumus gratia constituti in domo ipsius principes super omnem terram."

[6] See especially Ep. 88, p.t., and Ep. 31, p. 300, lines 21–2: "Ergo quia totius nos ecclesiae maxima cura praestolatur nostrum praecipue debet ecclesia tota procul dubio judicium promereri."

Universa sancta ecclesia, quae apud nos est.[1]

The conciseness of this statement can hardly be surpassed. The Roman Church is the epitome of all Christendom:

Suscepit ergo ac continet in se Romana ecclesia quod Deus universalem ecclesiam suscipere ac continere praecepit.[2]

Consequently, fullness of power rests solely with the Roman Church: powers are diffused throughout the organism of the universal Church, but the Roman Church contains in epitome all these powers.[3] Whatever the pope does, speaks, and writes, affects the whole body of believers: in a way he represents the universal Church:

Nos ecclesiam Dei, qui ei per abundantiam supernae gratiae praesumus, juxta modum acceptae distributionis exhibere debemus.[4]

All this is the application and elaboration of Pauline expressions.[5] According to Nicholas, Christianity lives solely through the Roman Church—without this Church there is no Christianity. The solicitude for the universal Church is therefore only the other side of the pope's function.[6] The decrees of the Roman Church are therefore binding

[1] Ep. 88, p. 480, line 15; repeated in Ep. 90, p. 491, line 5.

[2] Ep. 88, p. 478, lines 2–3.

[3] Ep. cit., p. 476, lines 4 ff.: "Proinde animadvertendum est, quia non Nicena, non denique ulla synodus quodquam Romanae contulit ecclesiae privilegium, quae in Petro noverat eam *totius jura potestatis pleniter* meruisse et cunctarum ovium regimen accepisse," with a reference to Boniface I, cf. Mansi, viii. 755.

[4] Ep. 77, p. 411, lines 37–8. The soundness of the whole building presupposes firmness of foundations, hence the imperative need for unimpeded authority of the Roman Church:

> Ubi universa fabricae moles innititur,
> ibi firmum validumque habeatur in omnibus fundamentum.

(Ep. 71, p. 394, lines 20–2.) This also means the personal immunity of the pope from any sort of accusation: "Prima sedes non judicabitur a quoquam," Ep. 88, p. 466, lines 22–3, with a reference to the spurious Council of Sinuessa (Mansi, i. 1257). On this apocryphal source see Maassen, *Geschichte*, i. 411 ff. Nicholas also quotes from the *Constitutum Silvestri*, cap. xx: "Neque ab augusto neque ab omni clero neque a regibus neque a populo judex judicabitur," Ep. 88, p. 465, lines 15–16. The text of this forgery in Mansi, ii. 632. Cf. also Ep. 100, p. 606, lines 19 ff.: "Cum enim Christi munere propter primatum ecclesiae Romanae in b. Petro concessum nemini sit de sedis apostolicae judicio judicare aut illius sententiam retractare permissum . . ." since the disciple is not above the master, *Matt.* x. 24, cf. also *Const. Silv.* cap. iii, and Nicholas again in Ep. 88, p. 466, line 28, and p. 467, line 26; see furthermore Pseudo-Isidore, Hinschius, p. 449. See also supra p. 175.

[5] Especially *Col.* ii. 19.

[6] Ep. 71, p. 397, lines 1 ff.: "Totius enim ecclesiae Deo auctore generaliter gerimus sollicitudinem et omnium utique, qui ecclesiae filii sunt, cura constringimur atque omnium . . . nostrum praecipue fidelium statu impigram gerere providentiam." Cf. also Ep. 91, p. 513; this is an application of II *Cor.* xi. 28.

upon the whole Church[1] because the pope has been divinely instituted as the Ruler over the whole (Christian) world:

Nos divinitus . . . constituti principes super omnem terram, id est, super universam ecclesiam.[2]

This whole *corpus* of believers can be compared, according to Nicholas, with a vessel which contains in itself all those species of living beings individually known as men, collectively known as nations.[3] The world, as far as it was Christian, is to him an "ecclesia" —"Terra enim ecclesia est"[4]—which is ruled by its epitome, the Roman Church, through the hierarchically subordinated *sacerdotium*. Consequently, the heads of this epitome are "principes super omnem terram." Reverence shown to the pope is reverence shown to St Peter, whose place Nicholas takes, or rather "reverence is shown to God in his apostle who . . . instituted us as his heirs and successors."[5]

The logical application of this view is that major causes must be submitted to the Roman Church. Hincmar's high-handed dealings with Rothad, the bishop of Soissons, gave the pope the opportunity of proclaiming the supreme jurisdictional powers of the Roman Church in a major cause, such as the deposition of a bishop.[6] From his point of view it was intolerable that a metropolitan should arrogate to himself the rights which were reserved to the pope. In rather sarcastic tones Nicholas reproaches the Frankish bishops for their curious practice of sending lay people to Rome for all sorts of papal decisions, but of refusing to allow an important matter of ecclesiastical discipline and

[1] Ep. 91, p. 523, lines 3–4: "Satis nostis, quae ab ea statuta fuerint, haec universalem ecclesiam semper tenuisse."

[2] Ep. 88, p. 475, lines 32 ff.

[3] Ep. 88, p. 478, lines 1 ff. After the allusion to *Acts* x. 11–12, xi. 5–6, he says: "ipsius vasis instar dignoscatur in se continere universorum animalium, quae homines intelliguntur, spiritualiter nationes." He also refers to *Luke* v. 3. About this allegory and its early history see especially H. Rahner, "Navicula Petri" in *Z. f. kath. Theol.*, lxi (1947), pp. 3–20, 30–1. The Nicholean statement was later utilized by Innocent III, also in a letter to the patriarch, *Reg.* ii. 209.

[4] Ep. 88, p. 475, line 34.

[5] Ep. 78, pp. 412–13 to Charles the Bald. About the notion of the pope being the heir of St Peter, see supra p. 8 n. 4.

[6] In his encyclical, Ep. 71, p. 393, he relies on *Pseudo-Isidore*, p. 393, lines 25 ff.; on this see Hinschius, *Pseudo-Isidore*, pp. ccv ff.; H. Schrörs, *Hinkmar, Erzbischof von Reims*, p. 259, note 82; Fournier-Le Bras, *Hist. d. coll. can.*, i. 228. Cf. also E. H. Davenport, *The False Decretals*, p. 51, note 34. The subject-matter of the dispute could have been dealt with just as effectively without a recourse to *Pseudo-Isidore*, for instance by referring to Leo IV's statement, MGH. *Epp.* v, p. 595; see also Perels, op. cit., p. 172: Nicholas used *Pseudo-Isidore* because the collection assisted the pope's aspirations.

organization to be taken thither. The "sedes apostolica" is the "caput" of all Christianity,[1] including of course the "sacerdotium." Its affairs are more important for the governance of universal Christendom than the "judicia saecularium."[2] The stern hierarchical ordering of the ecclesiastical body and its subordination appear to Nicholas as the pivotal points of government.[3] The "outstanding members of the Church" are the bishops: by virtue of their qualifications they assume a particularly important function within the *societas*, and therefore they must be strictly subordinated to the pope, and through their subordination they partake in the pope's fullness of power.

The insistence of Nicholas on the strict hierarchical ordering is from a governmental point of view consistent: this insistence means in effect centralization of the ecclesiastical government, a claim that was inherent in the idea that "ecclesia universalis (quae) apud nos est." The "sacerdotium" is the vehicle for the transmission of papal decrees which are the "sancta decreta." On the other hand, the episcopal will has to be suppressed if an effective centralization is to be carried out. The reduction of episcopal and metropolitan power was a necessary preliminary to the implementation of the strict monarchic papal rule.

The presupposition for reducing episcopal independence was however the attack on the exuberant proprietary church system: it was this system which presented itself as the most effective bar to the exercise of direct papal control over the higher ecclesiastics. Their installation amounted to an appointment, hence Nicholas's insistence on episcopal elections by the clergy. His protestations and vituperations against the prevalent system are couched in quite unusually strong terms. Clerics, he says, who obtain their "clerical" position through the machinery of the proprietary church system, do not thereby become members of the "sacerdotium": rather they are the property of the layman who appoints them; they are the appointees in the houses of laymen, and by no means can be said to be clerics. It is his duty to see that this poisonous toadstool—"venenatum elleborum"—is uprooted.[4] In the decree sent to the bishop of Besançon, Nicholas lays

---

[1] Ep. 71, p. 393, line 10.

[2] Ep. 71, p. 397, line 15.

[3] Ep. 71, p. 397, lines 20 ff. The significance of a cause being a "major causa" is that the pope acts as a tribunal of first instance, and not as a court of appeal. It was therefore an excellent means of exercising direct control over the episcopacy. Cf. also Perels, op. cit., pp. 171–2.

[4] Ep. 39, pp. 313–14: "Numquid Gerardus comes illum (*scil.* presbyterum) consecravit, numquid de ipsius est diocesi? Ubi hoc legisti—the letter is addressed

down the principle of free episcopal elections; bishops must be elected "non a saecularibus quibusque, sed a clero ecclesiae."[1]

The exercise of papal control over the episcopacy presupposed that the lay power was prevented from intervening in the creation of a bishop. So long as the "sacerdotium" was not extracted from lay control, there was no prospect of its papal control or of a centralized government. That is the underlying meaning of the often misunderstood Nicholean "separation of powers." What he attempts to lay down is the principle that the *societas fidelium*—the term which he himself coined—cannot be ruled by those who are not functionally qualified. The only functionally qualified members of this *societas* are the "sacerdotes" or as he says the "outstanding members of the Church," in effect the bishops. But the presupposition is that they must be free, that is to say, they must be under papal control. For this *societas* is one of the faithful, and consequently, its direction and government—the "regimen" as Nicholas had it—must be in the hands of the "caput religionis"[2] who, however, cannot function properly if the "sacerdotium" is controlled by the lay power, which has no governmental functions within the terms of this *societas*. True monarchic power within this society lies only with the pope: his decrees and laws are binding upon all:

Cui (*scil.* apostolicae sedi) facultas est in tota Christi ecclesia *leges* speciali prerogativa ponere *ac decreta* statuere atque sententias promulgare.[3]

## III

The ideas of Nicholas I on the function and standing of a king within the *societas fidelium* appear as an application of his fundamental view on the epitome character of the Roman Church. At the imperial coronation, the emperor[4] is pontifically conceded the right to use the

---

to the archbishop of Vienne, Ado—ubi hoc didicisti, nisi quia presbyteri non specialiter ecclesiae civitatis aut ecclesiae possessionis aut martirii aut monasterii secundum sacras regulas ordinantur, sed in domibus laicorum constituuntur et cum saecularibus adeo conversantur, ut non jam Dei, non ecclesiae cuiuslibet, sed illius comitis atque illius ducis esse dicantur? Ita ut impletum sit, quod per prophetam dicitur 'et erit populus sic sacerdos' . . . tamquam venenatum elleborum amputari."

[1] Ep. 123, p. 643, cap. iv. Civic authorities have merely the right of consenting to the election.

[2] Ep. 29, p. 296, line 23.

[3] Ep. 29, p. 296, lines 35 ff. With this should also be compared the report of Anastasius, MGH. *Epp.* vii. 409.

[4] It is Louis II whom the pope has in mind.

sword. He is given the right to wield the sword against infidels: the underlying idea is that of protection: by virtue of the coronation papally performed, the emperor is now entitled to draw the sword against the enemies of universal Christianity. He does not bear the sword in vain. Moreover, the emperor receives the empire itself "for the sake of the exaltation and peace of his mother, this holy and apostolic Church."[1] The purpose of creating the emperor was that of obtaining a protector of the Roman Church; since this Church is the epitome of the whole Church, its protection is at the same time the protection of the universal Church; hence the use of the sword pontifically blessed, is the effluence of the emperor's function as a protector. Negatively expressed, without papal intervention, the use of the sword would not be legitimate for a Christian prince.

St Peter had once wielded the physical sword against Malchus, Nicholas declares, whilst he employed spiritual weapons against Ananias and Saphira.[2] This statement leaves no room for doubt that, in terms of later terminology, St Peter possessed both swords, the material as well as the spiritual.[3] If we now bring to bear upon such pregnant expressions Nicholas's idea that the popes had been divinely instituted in the Roman Church as vicars of the two luminaries illuminating the whole world, we shall have no difficulty in appraising the stimulus and direction which his statement was to give to later generations.

Hi ergo (*scil.* apostoli) tamquam duo luminaria magna coeli in ecclesia Romana divinitus constituti totum orbem splendore fulgoris sui mirabiliter illustrarunt.[4]

This declaration expresses metaphorically the doubly apostolic character of the Roman Church, but it lent itself easily to a different interpretation, especially when linked with the metaphor of the "greater

[1] Ep. 34, p. 305, lines 4 ff.: ". . . macherae usum, quem primum a Petri principis apostolorum vicario contra infideles accepit . . . sinatur omnino a Deo protectum imperium suum, quod cum benedictione et sacratissimi olei unctione sedis apostolicae praesule ministrante percepit, ad exaltationem et quietem matris suae, huius sanctae et apostolicae ecclesiae, licenter ac rectissime moderari."

[2] Ep. 123, p. 641, lines 23 ff.: "Beatus scilicet Petrus apostolorum princeps, qui Malchi corporali abscissa gladio aure inobedientiam et in Anania et Saphira spirituali verbi mucrone mendacium et avaritiam perculit."

[3] Cf. also Perels, op. cit., p. 175: it is worthy of remark that Nicholas "dem Petrus ausdrücklich die Verfügung über *beide* Schwerter zuerkannt hat." (Perels's italics.) A passing reference to this important statement of Nicholas in J. Lecler, "La théorie des deux glaives" in *Recherches de science religieuse*, xxi, 1931, p. 306.

[4] Ep. 88, p. 475, lines 12–14.

light"—"majus luminare"—which was St Peter instituted by Christ in heaven:[1] the potentialities of this metaphor were indeed great.

The adaptation of Gelasius's[2] famous views by Nicholas must be set against these statements. The pope's vicariate of St Peter begins to approach his vicariate of Christ. For what Nicholas wishes to show is his role as a mediator, his role as a bridge-builder between Christ and man, his role as the divinely instituted monarch who has the "sollicitudo totius ecclesiae."[3] This adaptation of Gelasius by Nicholas was necessary in order to justify his claim that the popes were "principes super omnem terram": "terra enim ecclesia est." The true significance that lies in this incipient approximation of the pope as a vicar of Christ, is brought out by Nicholas in the changes which he made in Gelasius's well-worn passages: the changes are slight from a purely verbal point of view; they are significant from the point of view of the subject-matter.

In the first place, whilst Gelasius had written: "Quoniam Christus

---

[1] Ep. 103, p. 611, written five years before Ep. 88, from which the words in the text are quoted, see preceding note: "Quem (*scil.* Petrum) Dei filius in sancta ecclesia sua tamquam luminare majus in coelo constituit." The biblical basis may be *Gen.* i. 16. For an eighth-century use of the metaphor cf. Paulinus of Aquileja, MGH. *Poet. Lat.* i. 136, speaking of "praeclara coeli duo luminaria." Cf. also Isidore of Seville, *De ordine creaturarum*, cap. 5 (PL. lxxxiii. 923–4) and esp. his *Quaestiones in Vetus Test.* PL. cit., col. 213, no. 6, which is a very suggestive passage.

[2] The reliance of Nicholas on Gelasius is explicable by the great similarity of the situations. Acacius and Photius are frequently bracketed together by Nicholas. The conclusions of F. Dvornik, op. cit., have no bearing on our enquiry, since what is important, for our purposes, is what Nicholas thought and how his thought was reflected in his writings. That he thought Photius did challenge the Roman primacy, is clear, otherwise Ep. 88 would make little sense, unless one is prepared to attribute to Nicholas the basest motives, as, for instance, E. Dümmler, *Geschichte des ostfränk. Reiches*, i. 657 has done. Nor does it make any difference whether Ep. 88 was actually drafted by Nicholas alone or jointly with Anastasius: it was an official papal communication dispatched in the name of Nicholas I. Cf. N. Ertl in *Arch. f. Urk.*, xv (1938), p. 83; cf. also the cautious appreciation of Dvornik's view by the late E. de Moreau, "La réhabilitation de Photius" in *Nouvelle Revue Théologique* (offprint), January 1950, pp. 180 ff. The Frankish antagonism to the Greek views was, of course, a great help to Nicholas. Cf. e.g., Aeneas of Paris, *Liber adversus Graecos* (in L. D'Achery, *Spicilegium*, Paris, 1723, i. 116–49) who significantly also operates with the Donation of Constantine to prove the *principatus* of the Roman Church; cf. p. 146: there are copies of this document, he says, in the archives of the churches: "Haec et alia quam plurima . . . in eodem releguntur privilegio, cuius exemplaribus ecclesiarum in Gallia consistentium armaria ex integro potiuntur." See also Ratramnus of Corbie, *Liber contra Graecorum opposita* (D'Achery, i. 63–112) also attacking the caesaropapist Eastern regime (p. 64). There is some resemblance with the *Libri Carolini*.

[3] Ep. 31, p. 300; Ep. 90, p. 491.

memor fragilitatis humanae . . . discrevit" Nicholas expands this
slightly and his version of Gelasius is this:

Quoniam idem mediator Dei et hominum homo Christus Jesus . . .
discrevit.[1]

Perhaps no significance should be attributed to Nicholas's omission
of the Gelasian motive[2] but the expansion is important. The qualification of Christ as the "mediator between God and man" in a letter
addressed to the East, is no doubt intended to suggest a very intimate
connexion between Christ and the pope; to suggest, in other words,
the pope's own role as a mediator. The point to bear in mind is that
Christ's distribution of the functions, sacerdotal and regal, is now
suggested to be vicariously in papal hands.[3]

   This is an important statement, subtle, no doubt, but at least it
enables us to understand the *prima facie* cryptic and usually misinterpreted passage which he addresses to the Eastern emperor as well as to
the Eastern bishops and metropolitans.

Ingrati filii circa matrem vestram, ex qua imperandi fastigium vos et patres
vestri ordine coelitus disposito percepistis, nullatenus appareatis.[4]

This again is Gelasius in slightly modified form. Gelasius had written
to the Eastern bishops that the emperor had the privileges of his power
divinely conferred upon him and "for these benefices he should not
show himself ungrateful and should not usurp anything in contradiction to the divine ordering of things."

Et eius *beneficiis* non *ingratus* contra *dispositionem coelestis* ordinis nil usurpet.[5]

The idea behind Nicholas's statement is again that of the mediatory
role of the pope. What Gelasius had declared to be a divine benefice
and privilege, is now suggested to be the effect of the function of the
Roman Church, the "mother of the Eastern emperors." Differently

---

[1] Ep. 88, p. 486, lines 6 ff. The passage went into Gratian in its Nicholean form
and was correctly attributed to Nicholas (*Dist.* xcvi, c. 6). This Ep. 88 was later
"exploited to the utmost by the canonists of the Gregorian and post-Gregorian
periods," F. Dvornik, op. cit., p. 106. Gratian has no less than twenty-four
excerpts from this one letter of Nicholas. The biblical basis for the expansion is
I *Tim.* ii. 5.

[2] "Memor fragilitatis humanae" is omitted by Nicholas.

[3] Cf. also Ep. 60, p. 371: "Privilegia namque Romanae ecclesiae totius sunt
Christi." In Ep. 71, p. 398, he says that Christ's ordinances are alive in the Roman
Church.

[4] Ep. 90, p. 508, lines 30–2; the same words in Ep. 91, p. 530, lines 10–12.

[5] Ep. 1, p. 293, ed. Thiel. Immediately before Gelasius says: "Habet privilegia
potestatis suae, quae administrandis publicis rebus divinitus consecutus est; et
eius beneficiis . . ."

expressed, nothing, including the obtaining of rulership and of power —"fastigium imperandi"—occurs in a Christian world without divine disposition: but the Roman Church is divinely instituted; it has the "*principatus* divinae potestatis"[1] and therefore whatever occurs, occurs through the intervention of the Roman Church. By this somewhat circuitous route Nicholas could indeed claim that the Eastern emperors had achieved the height of their power by means of their mother, the Roman Church. In all the long development of papal doctrine, this is perhaps the most far-reaching claim ever made on a practical plane. Divine will is transmitted through the Roman Church: the Eastern emperor—in whose making the pope played not the slightest role—has his power divinely willed, hence the divine will intervenes through the medium of the Roman Church.[2]

The mother-function of the Roman Church is, by virtue of the approximation of the pope's vicariate of St Peter to a vicariate of Christ, greatly, though logically, extended to those who even refused to acknowledge the primacy of the "mother church." Nevertheless, the mother-function of the Roman Church is paralleled by the father-function of the pope himself. Again, in the Western world, where the primatial position of the pope was fully acknowledged, this was rather

---

[1] Ep. 82, p. 433.

[2] This passage, as is well known, has caused a good deal of misunderstanding. Cf. e.g., A. Hauck, *Weltherrschaftsgedanke*, p. 21, who overlooked the rather obvious fact that the Roman Church had no share whatsoever in the creation of the Eastern emperor. J. Haller, op. cit., p. 142–3, maintained that this passage refers to the emperor's standing in the ecclesiastical hierarchy. But Haller was right in rebuking Hauck for reading "a qua" instead of "ex qua." John VIII has "a qua" instead of the Nicholean "ex qua." See infra p. 222 n. 5. All difficulties concerning the interpretation of this passage would be cleared away, if the Donation of Constantine could be shown to have been in Nicholas's mind. But he explicitly states that the Eastern emperor is not an emperor of the Romans (see infra 202 n. 5) and he addresses the Eastern emperor personally ("vos") and in the present tense. The Donation could have been the basis, if the passage had referred to the predecessors of the present emperor only, and if Nicholas had not used "ex qua" which when juxtaposed to John VIII's "a qua" shows a difference of meaning. Cf. also Louis's "a qua" in the passage quoted infra 217 n. 2. Statements similar to that of Nicholas were made by Pope Agatho in 680 on the occasion of the Easter synod at Rome, but it is doubtful whether Nicholas knew of them. Agatho wrote to the emperor, Constantine IV Pogonatus (Mansi, xi. 239): "Apostolica et evangelica traditio quam tenet spiritualis vestri felicissimi imperii mater apostolica Christi ecclesia"; cf. also ibid., col. 242: "Haec spiritualis mater vestri tranquillissimi imperii, apostolica Christi ecclesia, quae per Dei omnipotentis gratiam a tramite apostolicae traditionis numquam errasse probabitur." Cf. also col. 243: "Apostolica Christi ecclesia, spiritualis mater a Deo fundati imperii." However, things had radically changed between the pontificate of Agatho and that of Nicholas I.

8

commonplace: but Nicholas extended his father-function to the Eastern emperors as well. And the father-function of the pope is based upon the same mediatory principle as the mother-function of the Roman Church.

Patres etenim vestri per gratiam Christi sumus et vos tamquam karissimos diligimus filios nec possumus vobis nisi viam veritatis ostendere; terrenam gloriam vestram augeri divinitus exoptamus; sed quid peccamus, si coelestem ac aeternam vos capessere nihilominus exoramus?[1]

Once this step was taken the following suggested itself. Obedience to a carnal father is self-evident—and the *argumentem a fortiori* at once comes to the fore—how much more justifiable is the demand of obedience to the spiritual father.[2] And another argument is also at once at hand, namely, that of the spirit excelling the flesh, with the inescapable consequence that matters pertaining to the spirit must be placed before carnal things.[3]

The other slight change of a Gelasian passage effected by Nicholas was the insertion of the single "tantummodo" into a sentence of his predecessor. Whilst the Christian emperors needed the priests for eternal salvation, the priests on the other hand, should make use of the imperial laws *merely* for the management of their material affairs. The insertion of the "merely" strikingly brings out the essence of the Gelasian passage.[4]

It is nevertheless worthy of remark that Nicholas denies that the Eastern emperor is the (universal) Roman emperor. The Roman empire is where the pope wishes it to be—the contents of the Donation of Constantine—and it certainly is not in the East, but in the West. What sort of Roman emperor are you, he writes to Michael III, who know no Latin? It is just ridiculous for you to call yourself emperor of the Romans: you say that Latin is a barbarous language, because you do not understand the language of the Romans.[5] The empire in the

---

[1] Ep. 88, p. 484, lines 34 ff.

[2] Ep. 88, p. 463, lines 22–4: "Si ergo carnales quanto potius spirituales digna penitus a filiis debent veneratione potiri."

[3] Ep. 88, p. 463, lines 24–5: "Quanto enim spiritus carnem praecellit tanto magis ea quae sunt spiritualia carnalibus oportet omnibus anteponi." The same in Ep. 92, p. 535 to Photius himself, whom the pope calls in this same letter a "viper": "porro si te viperam appellamus non fallimur."

[4] Ep. 88, p. 486, lines 11 ff.: ". . . et pontifices pro cursu temporalium *tantummodo* rerum imperialibus legibus uterentur."

[5] Ep. 88, p. 459, lines 18 ff.: "Si ideo linguam Latinam barbaram dicitis, quoniam illam non intelligitis, vos considerate, quia ridiculum est vos appellare Romanorum imperatores et tamen linguam non nosse Romanam . . . quiescite igitur

East is but a kingdom, not the universal Roman empire which is in the West, for it is the pope who "ex inspiratione coelesti" decides upon the emperor's person.[1]

## IV

In pursuance of this theme Nicholas's language towards secular rulers is that of the master who issues orders.[2] A ruler who does not obey the mandates and decrees of the Roman Church must be considered "quasi minus Christianus" and should be anathematized.[3] No ruler must give a mandate which is "contra ecclesiasticas regulas."[4] It is in his function as the interpreter of the divine and human law that Nicholas issues his lengthy catalogue of injunctions and prohibitions to the Bulgars,[5] in which his detailed regulations concerning the social life are of particular interest.[6] As Christians, rulers have the duty of extirpating heresy within their boundaries, and a heretic should be treated as an "extraneus." The function of the king is the establishment of peace for the sake of the universal Church: in this way kings serve their mother "unde spiritualiter nati sunt."[7] Naturally, in a Christian society the determination of what is and what is not heresy, belongs to those who are qualified to pronounce on the issue, the members of the "sacerdotium." Moreover, in this Christian society kings are not entitled to sit in judgment over the priests: they are exempt from the formers' jurisdiction, since judgment is the effluence of authority which the kings have not:

---

vos nuncupare Romanorum imperatores, quoniam secundum vestram sententiam barbari sunt quorum vos imperatores esse asseritis."

[1] John VIII's reference to Nicholas's choice of the future emperor, see supra 161 and Eichmann, *Kaiserkrönung*, i. 53, with special reference to John's report: it is the "Entschluss des Papstes, der zum Imperium beruft."

[2] E.g., Ep. 15 to Lothar II; Ep. 23, p. 288, lines 12–13; Ep. 26, p. 291, lines 24–5; Ep. 60, p. 370, lines 36 ff.

[3] Ep. 90, p. 504, lines 15 ff.

[4] Ep. 88, p. 465, lines 29–30, referring to Pelagius's letter to Childebert, MGH. *Epp.* iii. 76.

[5] Ep. 99, pp. 569–600.

[6] Ep. 99, cc. 26–32, pp. 580–1.

[7] Ep. 99, c. 17, p. 578, lines 12 ff.: "per hoc jam merito per potestates exteras tamquam extraneus opprimatur ... nam nisi moverentur potestates Christianae adversus huiusmodi, quomodo rationem redderent de imperio suo Deo? Quippe cum pertineat ad hoc reges saeculi Christianos, ut temporibus suis pacatam et sine diminutione velint servari matrem suam ecclesiam, unde spiritualiter nati sunt."

Non autem vobis licet clericos judicare, cum vos magis ab ipsis conveniat judicari.[1]

The functions which the clerics have to fulfil in the Christian society exclude their subjection to lay tribunals: the functionalist principle made the principle of the *privilegium fori* a necessity.[2]

There are also other ideas within the jurisdictional sphere which germinate in the important pontificate of Nicholas I. The one concerns widows—one of the categories constituting the "personae miserabiles" in later times—because widows are worthy of special protection. Their judge was Christ—"quarum judex Christus est"[3]—and when the pope emerged as the vicar of Christ in the full technical and constitutional sense, it was not difficult to claim the ecclesiastical tribunal as the proper *forum* for widows.[4] Christ is "pax nostra"[5] and because the universal Church is the manifestation of Christ's peace, the pope—who presides over this body[6]—has to watch that peace is kept within its boundaries. In practical terms this vigilance of the pope extends in particular to treaties made between Rulers, for treaties promote peace and concord, and a breach of a treaty is therefore of fundamental concern to the pope. Here[7] we find another germ for later medieval theories of ecclesiastical jurisdiction and arbitration concerning "international" treaties. Lastly, Nicholas's step in the marriage affair of Lothar II heralds the later doctrine of the exclusive jurisdiction of the ecclesiastical tribunal in matrimonial matters.[8] No doubt Gregory IV's handling of the affairs of Judith and Louis[9] influenced Nicholas. But whilst

---

[1] Ep. 99, cap. 83, p. 595, lines 12–13; cf. also ibid., cap. 70, p. 592, lines 8 ff.: "Verum de presbyteris qualescumque sint, vobis, qui laici estis nec judicandum est nec de vita ipsorum quippiam investigandum." The echo of Gelasius is again unmistakable, cf. supra p. 27 n. 4.

[2] In another context he quotes with full approval Leo IV's citation from the *Const. Silvestri*: Ep. 107, p. 621, lines 1 ff.; on Leo IV, see supra 175. Cf. also A. Nissl, *Gerichtsstand des Clerus im fränk. Reich*, pp. 182 ff., and pp. 240 ff.

[3] Ep. 44, p. 319, line 15.

[4] The biblical source may have been *Ps.* lxvi. 6.

[5] Ep. 33, p. 302, line 7; *Eph.* ii. 14.

[6] Ep. 33, line 12: "sancta mater ecclesia, cui mea humilitas per habundantiam divinae miserationis praeest."

[7] Ep. 33, pp. 302–3.

[8] On the subject itself see J. Calmette, *La diplomatie Carolingienne*, pp. 66 ff.; J. Haller, op. cit., pp. 5–15; 35–74; and L. Halphen, *Charlemagne & l'empire Carolingien*, pp. 375 ff.

[9] See supra 167. Cf. also Leo IV's statement made in 847: MGH. *Epp.* v. Ep. 16, p. 595, cap. 9: "Scriptum est, 'Quod Deus conjunxit, homo non separet' (*Matt.* xix. 6). Tamen nuptiae, ut multi maximi et religiosi viri sanxerunt, suo ordine peragendae."

the former pope did not supply any theoretical justification for his step, Nicholas supplied it when he declared that it was his "pastoralis cura" which prompted him to have the matter decided by his "legati a latere, apostolica auctoritate fulti."[1]

According to Nicholas I matrimonial matters belong to that wider sphere of matters which directly affect the salvation and faith of the Christian people: the interests of the "populus Dei" and of the "grex dominicus" make ecclesiastical, that is, papal jurisdiction in matrimonial matters imperative.[2] The pope as the pastor of the "dominicus grex" must see that the people devoted to the divine cult do not live in a reprehensible manner.[3] Matrimony as a divine institution appertains to the spiritual sphere of a Christian's life, and as such is of direct concern to the pope. It is a spiritual issue and therefore touches the very foundation of the whole society. For this society is the *societas omnium fidelium*[4] which is an organic and closely knit body, whose sole substratum is the spiritual element of faith as expounded by the Roman Church. The corporate character and the bond that creates this *corpus*, namely the spiritual-moral element of Roman-papal provenance, is exquisitely brought out by Nicholas's designation: *societas omnium fidelium*. Hence on the assumption that marriage affairs are matters falling within the precincts of faith which is the cementing bond of this *societas*, the pope is bound to take the view that a setting aside of a matter of faith by one member affects the whole society. From this point of view the pope is not only entitled, but in duty bound to decide matrimonial matters.[5] And it is also from the same point of view that an effortless explanation can be given for the threat of excommunication in the case of disobedience.[6] On this basis the pope can approach the king—Charles II—and admonish him not to tolerate in his kingdom any longer a woman who has fled from her

[1] Ep. 3, p. 269.
[2] Ep. 3, p. 269, lines 5 ff. (Theutberga and Waldrada).
[3] Ep. 1, p. 267, lines 14 ff.: "Canonica auctoritas hoc omni in loco praedicare non cessat, ut populus divino cultui mancipatus inreprehensibilis existat. Quo enim mediante fieri melius poterit quam illorum sollicitudine, qui pastorum loco curam dominici gregis susceperunt? Quapropter vestram admonemus fraternitatem . . . ut vestram diocesim non sinatis pollui fornicariis."
[4] Ep. 1, p. 267, line 23.
[5] J. Haller, op. cit., p. 13, remarks that nobody could seriously say that the marriage of a king affected the whole Church. A grosser misunderstanding of the premises upon which Nicholas worked, and of the papal theme in general, is hardly possible.
[6] So in the case of Engeltruda and Count Boso: Epp. 1 and 2, pp. 267–8 and in the case of Lothar himself: Ep. 44, p. 319, line 1; also Ep. 32, p. 301, line 1.

husband.[1] No doubt the papal measures were something new at that time; no doubt also that contemporaries were somewhat apprehensive,[2] but a good deal of the supposedly revolutionary attitude of Nicholas I disappears when it is set against the previous ideological development. What Nicholas did, was to draw the obvious conclusions from this.

The same observation may be made as regards Nicholas's views on the relationship between ecclesiastical and secular laws. It is axiomatic for him that in the *societas fidelium* the ecclesiastical laws must take precedence over those laws issued by princes. "Terra enim ecclesia est" he had once said. Hence, civil laws can in no way override ecclesiastical laws—"ecce quemadmodum imperiali judicio non possint ecclesiastica jura dissolvi"—for the latter stand on a par with divine laws: "ecce qualiter, quod lex humana concessit, lex divina prohibeat."[3] This is not to say that Nicholas has no use for the civil laws: he accords to them subsidiary character in so far as that they may be applied if no ecclesiastical laws exist for the particular case and if they do not contradict the underlying principles of the canons.[4] Civil laws can on no account diminish canonical authority.[5]

These are indeed very important declarations of principles. They are ideologically firmly based upon the nature of the *societas fidelium* in which the individual king fulfils a function in relation to the whole *societas*. This *societas* being a Christian society must necessarily be guided by those who are functionally qualified and through the machinery provided for government, namely through the laws issued by the functionally qualified members of this *societas*. That means that the king's laws must be in accordance with this regulative principle; that means that the king must issue only such laws which contribute

---

[1] Ep. 2, p. 268.

[2] It is, of course, true that these papal steps in a matrimonial matter had not been taken before, and Hincmar's reaction is characteristic of a contemporary; cf. his opinion in PL. cxxv. 623–772; K. Sdralek, *Hinkmar's Gutachten*, pp. 93 ff.; Cf. also A. Esmein, *Le mariage en droit canonique*, 2nd ed., i. 70 ff., and G. Tellenbach in *Hist. Z.*, 1939, pp. 341–2, referring to Loening's *Geschichte des deutschen Kirchenrechts*, ii. 630, note 2.

[3] Ep. 57, p. 357, lines 31–3.

[4] Ep. 57, p. 357, lines 21–3: "Cum constet enim jus mundanum legum et imperatorum non omnibus ecclesiasticis controversiis utendum esse, praesertim cum conveniatur evangelicae ac canonicae sanctioni aliquotiens obviare." Gratian (*Dist.* x, c. 1) has a different and possibly better reading: "Lege imperatorum non in omnibus . . ."

[5] Ep. 57, p. 357, lines 35–6: "Eas (*scil.* leges) evangelicis apostolicis atque canonicis decretis quibus postponendae sunt, nullum posse inferre praejudicium asseramus." It will be recalled that this was the principle throughout the medieval period: it assumed particular importance as regards the Roman law.

to the wellbeing and proper functioning of his kingdom, which in itself forms part of the wider *societas fidelium*. Royal laws, in other words, must fit in with the purpose for which the whole *societas* exists. It is the teleological principle which Nicholas expresses with the new term of the *ordinabilitas legum*: for it is the function of the civil laws to adjust themselves to the underlying purposes of society—to help to bring about the realization of the aim of society and thus to contribute to its proper working:

Nemo ita justius operari debet quam cui commissa videtur legum ordina-bilitas.[1]

Seen from a different angle: that prince will fulfil his role as a Christian prince whose laws fall in line with the character and purpose of the whole *societas fidelium*.[2]

These views stand in close proximity to Nicholas's ideas about the duties of clerics as subjects of a king. The bishop of Metz, Adventius, justified his conduct at a recent synod by declaring that he was a subject of his king and hence owed loyalty to him. Although Nicholas cannot impugn the validity of the biblical passage invoked by the bishop,[3] he nevertheless counsels him to examine whether or not a particular king or prince deserves to be treated as such, and the first criterion upon which a decision can be based is whether he governs himself well, and secondly whether he governs his people well.[4] In other words, sacer-dotal loyalty to a king depends upon the qualification of the king and on the manner in which he fits into the framework of the *societas fidelium*. It is the lawful exercise of government which is the criterion: "videte, si jure principantur."[5] Or expressed on the moral-religious plane: is the king the personification of virtue? What, however, is "jus," what constitutes "virtue," cannot be decided in the *societas fidelium* but by Christian principles. And it is the *sacerdotium* alone which by virtue of its qualifications has the knowledge and capability of judging whether or not the individual king lives according to the principles of Chris-

---

[1] Ep. 2, p. 268, line 10.

[2] This is the same principle which the synodists at Diedenhofen had expressed in 844, see supra 174. Cf. also Benedict III concerning the authorization by the Roman Church of civil laws, supra 177. This too was a principle which was at work throughout the medieval period.

[3] The bishop probably referred to I *Pet.* ii. 13. Ep. 31, p. 299, lines 34 ff.: "Illud vero quod dicitis regibus et principibus vos esse subjectos eo quod dicat apostolus 'sive regi tamquam praecellenti' placet."

[4] This may be an Isidorian echo of the "bene regere," cf. the passage cited supra p. 30.

[5] Ibid., line 37.

tianity.[1] If the king does not conform to what the *sacerdotium* lays down as the "jus," if the king's government as part of the *societas fidelium* is opposed to "canonicis decretis," disobedience is counselled. For that king is a tyrant and as such is to be resisted.[2] What is "vitium" and what constitutes virtue must be left to the judgment of those who are the "sors Domini." A tyrant is consequently put on the same footing as a heretic.[3] Disregard of papal mandates naturally comes under the heading of "vitia," and disregard of the divine law—as expounded by the Roman Church—is another item in the same category.[4] For every decision or decree issued by the Roman Church is final.[5] The visible effect of a deliberate disregard of papal decrees is exclusion from Christian society with the attendant consequence of social isolation.[6]

We have singled out only some of the leading ideas of Nicholas I. It will have become sufficiently clear that there are few original themes

[1] Ibid.: "Verumtamen videte, utrum reges isti et principes, quibus vos subjectos esse dicitis, veraciter reges et principes sint. Videte, si primum se bene regunt, deinde subditum populum; nam qui sibi nequam est, cui alii bonus erit? Videte, si jure principantur: alioquin potius tyranni credendi sunt quam reges habendi. Quibus magis resistere et ex adverso ascendere quam subdi debemus. Alioquin si talibus subditi et non praelati fuerimus nos, necesse est eorum vitiis faveamus. Ergo 'regi praecellenti,' virtutibus scilicet et non vitiis, subditi estote . . ."

[2] See preceding note and Ep. 24, p. 288, lines 21 ff. addressed to all the bishops in France, Burgundy and Germany telling them: "Si unanimes fueritis, quis est, qui vobis resistat? Patres nostri etiam regibus restiterunt."

[3] Cf. Ep. 88, p. 469, line 13; Ep. 90, p. 500, line 21; and Ep. 92, p. 535, line 38.

[4] Ep. 31, per totam.

[5] Ep. 52, p. 339, lines 21 ff.: "Nam sedis apostolicae sententia tanta semper consilii moderatione concipitur, tanta patientiae maturitate decoquitur tantaque deliberationis gravitate profertur, ut retractatione non egeat nec immutari necessarium ducat . . ." Cf. also Ep. 53, p. 348, lines 13 ff., and Ep. 71, p. 398.

[6] Ep. 68, p. 384, lines 15 ff.: ". . . omnibus alienus et tamquam violentus invasor atque tyrannus sit Christianorum communione privatus, ita, ut qui huiusmodi in communione susceperit, simili poena teneatur adstrictus."

It may not be unprofitable to record a few testimonies of contemporaries concerning their reaction to Nicholas's pontificate. Gunther of Cologne, for instance, held that Nicholas had raised himself to the level of an emperor of the whole world: *Ann. Bertiniani* (SS. RR. GG.) ad 864, p. 68 (ed. G. Waitz): "Nicolaus, qui dicitur papa et qui se apostolum inter apostolos adnumerat, totiusque mundi imperatorem se fecit." Regino of Prüm said that Nicholas had ordered kings and tyrants "with such authority as if he had been the master of the world" (*Reginonis Chron.*, in SS. RR. GG. ed. F. Kurze, ad 868, p. 94). Cf. also Walafrid Strabo in MGH. *Capit.*, ii. 575. Amongst recent judgments on Nicholas cf. Halphen, op. cit., p. 393 and p. 395: "La volonté du pape tromphait. Elle triomphait pareillement dans tous les domains de la vie politique ou religieuse de l' Europe carolingienne." Bihlmeyer-Tüchle, *Kirchengeschichte*, 12th ed., 1948, ii. 56: "Der Anspruch auf eine 'directive' Gewalt der Kirche bezw. des Papstes über die Herrscher in bezug auf religiös-sittliche Fragen ist bei ihm bereits deutlich ausgeprägt."

in his views. Yet, it was precisely by a skilful adaptation and combination of old papal expressions that Nicholas I greatly added to their poignancy and bequeathed to them a stimulating flexibility. It is the vigorous assertion of the Roman *principatus* which, when logically pursued, was to lead to the conception of the *societas fidelium* as the supra-regal, autonomous, corpus of Christendom.

## V

If the test of political ability is to sense the temper of the time and to act accordingly, Adrian II emerges as an equal of his great predecessor, Nicholas I. The hallmark of his five years' rule was the exercise of pontifical authority within the *societas fidelium*.

The very first lines of his first pontifical letter set the tone. These lines peremptorily order Lothar II to take back Theutberga. The justification for this order lies in Adrian II's function: he functions as the vicar of St Peter to whom Christ had committed "oves suas, *totam* videlicet ecclesiam."[1] The *ecclesia* is the whole corporate union of all Christians, that entity which Nicholas had termed the *societas fidelium* and which Adrian himself calls also the *populus Dei*.[2] The emphasis on papal functions within this *ecclesia* or *societas* is therefore very marked in Adrian II—"nos qui per supernam gratiam apostolorum principis *fungimur* vice"[3]—because the exercise of his authority within this body is based upon his function as the vicar of St Peter: thereby also the fullness of the Petrine commission is demonstrated. For Christ's commission to St Peter—"Whatsoever thou shalt bind . . ."—does not suffer any exception. The power to bind and to loose is all-embracing and comprehensive: whatever means whatever.

In quibuscumque omnia sunt, quantacumque et qualiacumque sint.[4]

By virtue of this power the pope is entitled to exclude individuals, including kings, from this Christian society.[5] As the supreme monarch

---

[1] MGH. *Epp.* vi, Ep. 1, p. 695, lines 10 ff.: "Quia b. Petro apostolorum principi Dominus noster oves suas, totam videlicet ecclesiam precioso jam sanguine suo redemptam . . . nos *vice* utique *apostolatus* illius Domino in omnibus cooperante *fungentes* . . ."

[2] Ep. 21, p. 725.          [3] Ep. 19, p. 721, lines 39–40.

[4] Ep. 4, p. 701, lines 4–5. In the immediately preceding lines he wrote this: "Nemo plane dubitet nullum facinus esse quod ecclesia data sibi potestate ab eo desistentibus non possit absolvere vel poenitentibus relaxare, cui dicitur 'Quaecumque dimiseritis super terram, dimissa erunt et in coelis . . .' In quibuscumque . . ." as text. This seems a literal borrowing from Gelasius, see supra p. 20 n. 1.

[5] Ep. 4, p. 701, lines 10 ff. See also Ep. 1, p. 697, lines 3 ff.: "Si vero quilibet . . . nocere, sciat se a nobis perpetui anathematis vinculo esse procul dubio

8 *

within the *societas fidelium*, the pope has to care as much for the spiritual well-being of his subjects as for the stability of the kingdoms themselves.[1] For the stability of a kingdom rests upon the security of its foundations which are of a spiritual nature. The kingdom is but a part of the wider *societas* which in itself is based on the spiritual element of faith. Hence the pope's *jus apostolicum* to concern himself with a kingdom's stability: the king, if necessary, must accept papal "correctionem."[2]

The reason for Adrian's invectives against Charles the Bald is not, as he points out, an earthly or mundane desire: he does not inveigh against the king "ambitione regni, sed justitia commovemur."[3] It is not territorial ambition that prompts him—"et non terrarum spatia quaerimus"—but his function as head of the *societas fidelium*, that is, of the universal Church. It is this function which lays upon him the duty of rendering an account on the Day of Judgment for the doings of the kings under his care: "An non pro te, rex, rationem coram Domino ponere compellemur si . . . factum tuum non reprehendimus"?[4] Gelasius's theory was being applied to such an extent that even the omission of the king (Charles the Bald) to receive papal legates "more regali" would be made an item in the pope's eventual rendering his account for the king.[5] The king's doings did not harmonize with *justitia*; and *justitia* is manifested in papal decrees, because through them St Peter speaks:

> Praecepta . . . beati Petri per os nostrum prolata.

Papal decrees are Petrine decrees: papal judgments are St Peter's judgments.[6] But since St Peter was instituted by Christ Himself, his decrees are therefore God's voice made known through the Roman Church.[7] And since, furthermore, the external ferment of the *societas*

---

innodandum, et ab omni Christianorum consortio separandum, te (rex) autem, si talibus consensum praebueris, *omnimodis excommunicandum.*"

[1] Ep. 1, p. 695, lines 16 ff.: "Os nostri apostolatus . . . pro regni stabilitate felicitateque perpetua . . . vicibus indefessis aperientes excellentiam tuam . . . *jure apostolico* exhortemur." See also Ep. 19, p. 722, line 8: "Coelesti magisterio exoramus, ut pro regni stabilitate vos nunc . . . satagatis."

[2] Ep. 1, p. 695, lines 24–5.　　　　　　　　[3] Ep. 21, p. 726, line 1.

[4] Ep. 21, p. 724, lines 21–2.

[5] This is inserted in parentheses between "si" and "factum" in the quotation in the text: "si—ut illud interim sileamus, quod missos apostolicae sedis more regali recipere contempsisti—factum . . ."

[6] Ep. 36, p. 745, lines 33 ff.: "Quod praefati canones et decreta decernunt . . . decernimus, et quod statuunt statuimus; et quod judicant, judicamus."

[7] Ep. 37, p. 747, lines 12 ff.: "Quoniam, tranquillissime imperator, audisti vocem Dei per apostolicae sedis officium tibi delatam . . ."

*fidelium* is justice, it is the *jus apostolicum* to decree that nobody's rights are violated: "ad unicuique jus proprium reservandum."[1] Having assumed the authority of the supreme arbiter as to what is and what is not just in the *societas fidelium*, the pope has the *jus apostolicum* to issue binding instructions to the members of this *societas*, in all matters in which justice is involved. Hence his order to the barons of Charles the Bald's kingdom not to take up arms or to make any military preparations under pain of excommunication.[2] The outlines of Hildebrand's conceptual framework begin to become discernible.

Hand in hand with this function as the supreme arbiter, or as the supreme repository of *justitia*, goes the other function of the pope, namely that of a peace maker and peace preserver. Peace is a virtue, and Christians have to cultivate virtues, of which none is of greater moment than this one, peace. "Omnes quidem virtutes Christi cultoribus sectandae sunt, sed nulla utilius quam pax."[3] Moreover, the duty incumbent upon the pope as the organ of preserving peace is also based, Adrian II argues, on the angelic message at the time of Christ's birth: "Gloria in excelsis Deo et *in terra pax* hominibus bonae voluntatis."[4] The intimate relationship between him and Christ—a line so clearly indicated by Nicholas I—that emerges from this argumentation, should not pass without notice: just as the coming of Christ signified "peace on earth," so it is the pope's office now to keep that peace as the head of the whole Christian commonwealth.[5] Peace amongst the component parts of the *societas fidelium* is a necessary presupposition for the fulfilment of the purpose and aim of this society.[6] These are

[1] Ep. 18, p. 720, lines 25 ff.: "Praeterea noveris misisse nos epistolas quasdam in Gallicanarum partium regiones, tam reges quam praesules et omnes omnino regnorum primates ad comprimendum ambitum et unicuique jus proprium reservandum." The invasion by Charles the Bald's of Lothar's kingdom is to Adrian II a flagrant violation of the law because this kingdom belongs by right to Louis II: "regnum quondam regis Hlotharii quod carissimo filio nostro domino imperatori *jure* debetur" (Ep. 18, p. 720, lines 32 ff.); cf. also on the same topic Ep. 19, p. 722, lines 15–16.

[2] Ep. 32, p. 736, lines 34 ff.: "Alioquin quisquis vestrum contra Karolomannum castra moverit, arma sustulerit vel laesionis exercitia praeparaverit ac per id, ut effundatur fidelium sanguis, construxerit, non solum excommunicationis nexibus innodabitur, verum etiam vinculis anathematis obligatus in gehenna cum diabolo deputabitur."

[3] Ep. 16, p. 717, line 15.     [4] *Luke* ii. 14: Ep. 6, p. 703, lines 31 ff.
[5] Ep. 6, p. 703, lines 5–6.

[6] That despite his authoritative language Adrian did not meet with conspicuous success, is beside the point. What is to the point, however, is that his pontificate stands out as a reign which crystallizes the Nicholean welter of ideas. It may well be that Anastasius drafted most of Adrian's letters, cf. Perels, op. cit., pp. 231 ff.

indeed powerful ideological agencies by which the minds of contemporaries and of later generations became saturated. And this saturation in its turn was the presupposition for erecting a legal edifice upon this set of ideas.

This programme has all the characteristic Roman imprints: Adrian II was perhaps the most Roman of all the ninth-century Roman popes.[1] His letters reveal the typical Roman stamp: authority and command; demand for subordination and obedience, for order and for consequent gradation of organized authority. Christian elements and Roman elements are blended into one consistent whole in his letters. In a way, the Christian idea of "pax" is complementary to the Roman idea of "justitia."[2] It is in the function as a "pater familias" that Adrian II attempts to preserve peace and to guard justice. Hence also the authoritative, commanding language; hence also the stress he lays upon the qualifications of the "sacerdotium": the limited "jus episcopale" corresponds to the universal "jus apostolicum"; in support of this "jus episcopale" Adrian II invokes Gregory I[3] as well as Leo's counsel: "unusquisque suis terminis contentus."[4] All this is of course nothing else but the principle of functional order, expressed in legal terminology. Hence also Adrian's insistence on the episcopal control of monastic institutions—"omne monasterium in potestate episcopi consistere debet juxta canonum auctoritatem."[5] Hence also Adrian's addiction to the conception of the Roman empire: to him the "regnum Romanum," merely a preliminary to the "imperium Romanum," was of quite an especial concern. The emperor is "imperator noster."[6]

## VI

It is from the point of view of the Roman empire ideology that one can understand the significance of Adrian II's letter to Charles the Bald in 872. This letter[7] is certainly somewhat puzzling when set against other letters written by the same pope to the same king. In these latter communications Charles is taken to task for all sorts of

---

[1] But cf. L. Halphen, op. cit., p. 401: "Hadrien II . . . se trouve un prêtre romain assez efface. Borgne et boiteux, c'est un homme sans grand préstige."

[2] Cf., for instance, Adrian's bracketing of the "paterfamilias" with the conception of the "domus Domini" and the "civitas Dei": p. 714, lines 8 ff. The biblical reference is *Ps.* lxviii. 10, and *John* ii. 17.

[3] Ep. 6, p. 714; Ep. 34, p. 740, etc. The "jus episcopale" in Ep. 20, p. 723, line 9.

[4] Ep. 18, p. 720, line 31; cf. also Ep. 30, p. 735 p.t., and Ep. 35, p. 742.

[5] Ep. 35, p. 742, lines 29–30.　　[6] Ep. 36, p. 745, line 17.　　[7] Ep. 36.

wicked action—"Inter cetera excessuum tuorum . . . illud quoque nihilominus objicitur, quod etiam bestiarum feritatem excedens . . ." —is the cheerful beginning of a letter sent barely a year earlier.[1] Now in 872 that same king is held up as a model of piety, justice, and zeal.[2]

The background of this enigmatic letter is the communication sent by Charles the Bald and written by Hincmar to Adrian II in which they severely and provocatively criticize the pope, because by his earlier remonstrations he had so bitterly insulted the king. Although assuring Adrian of their veneration for the vicar of St Peter, Charles and Hincmar nevertheless find it apposite to remind Adrian of the fate which had once befallen Vigilius. It was hardly possible to utter a graver threat.[3] In order to make the picture complete, we should bear in mind that in 871 Charles the Bald was on his way to Italy[4] and had taken up stations at Besançon. The combination of the threat expressed in the letter of Charles with his actual movement was no doubt intended to create the worst forebodings in the papal mind.

But the pope had not yet played his trump card. The problem of imperial succession had become acute—the choice lay between Louis the German and Charles the Bald—and in order to ward off the menacing attitude of Charles, Adrian II wrote to him this enigmatic letter. He, the pope, would never acquiesce in anyone else but Charles being the future emperor.[5] The letter shows traces of hurried composition and indicates that the pope thought that only the employment of superlatives and unequivocal statements would achieve his end and ward off the execution of the threat. The most confidential tone adopted by the pope—"ut sermo sit secretior et litterae clandestinae nullique nisi fidelissimis publicandae"[6]—was to add a personal and intimate note to this letter. It may, however, be open to doubt whether Adrian's explanation of his earlier letters to which Charles had taken such strong exception, was accepted by the king.[7]

The acquisition of the Roman imperial crown was the offer which

---

[1] Ep. 31 p. 735, lines 26 ff.    [2] Ep. 36, p. 743.    [3] PL. cxxiv. 881–2.
[4] *Ann. Bertiniani*, ed. cit., ad 871, p. 118; cf. also Halphen, op. cit., p. 414; in the same year Emperor Louis II was made a prisoner at Bari and rumour had it that he was already dead.
[5] Ep. 36, p. 745.    [6] Ep. 36, p. 745, lines 16–17.
[7] Ep. 36, p. 744, lines 15 ff.: "Et si quaedam litterae delatae vobis sunt, aliter se habentes in superficie vel subreptae vel a nostris infirmantibus extortae vel a qualibet persona confictae, durius aut acrius mordaciter sonantes: id tamen nobis fixum semper mansit in mente, quod vobis significavimus devote, nec alienum judicavimus, judicamus et judicabimus a nostra communione mentis devotione, quam diligimus tota animi intentione."

the pope made to Charles. The offer was sure to fall on fertile soil: in a few words Adrian II manages to summarize the function of the papally created Roman emperor:

Si contigerit te imperatorem nostrum vivendo supergredi, te optamus omnis clerus et plebs et nobilitas *totius orbis et urbis* non solum ducem et regem, patricium et imperatorem, sed *in praesenti ecclesia defensorem* et in aeterna cum omnibus sanctis participem fore.[1]

The role which the pope plays in the making of the Roman emperor is here unambiguously stated;[2] no less unambiguously is stated the role of the emperor within the *societas fidelium* or, as Adrian II expresses it, within the *ecclesia*. The imperial crown was the allurement to Charles.

. The full appreciation of the papal point of view presupposes some observations on the larger background which produced this communication of the pope. It will be recalled that the eighth ecumenical Council of Constantinople had come to an abrupt end in March 870. Anastasius was the joint papal and imperial legate at that Council. His report on the Council's proceedings throws some interesting light on papal and Western-imperial points of view. Moreover, in the late summer of 871 Adrian performed a festive coronation on Emperor Louis II after his recent release from captivity.[3] And in the same year Louis II despatched his famous letter—drafted by Anastasius—to the Eastern emperor, in which the papal Roman empire conception is set forth in classic manner. Set against such manifestations of the imperial theme, this letter of Adrian II sent to Charles only a few months afterwards, contained not only the bait of the imperial crown for Charles, but it was also prompted—like Louis's festive coronation—by the turn which the eighth ecumenical Council had taken. Let us first briefly review Anastasius's report, and then Louis's letter to the Emperor Basilius.

[1] Ep. 36, p. 745, lines 22 ff. The whole passage runs: "Igitur ergo integra fide et sincera mente devotaque voluntate—ut sermo sit secretior etc. (as text)—vobis confitemur devovendo et notescimus affirmando, salva fidelitate imperatoris nostri, quia, si superstes ei fuerit vestra nobilitas, vita nobis comite, si dederit nobis quislibet multorum modiorum auri cumulum, numquam adquiescemus, exposcemus aut sponte suscipiemus alium *in regnum et imperium Romanum*, nisi te ipsum. Quem, quia praedicaris sapientia, et justitia, religione et virtute, nobilitate et forma, videlicet prudentia, temperantia, fortitudine atque pietate refertus, si contigerit . . ." as text.

[2] "exposcemus aut sponte suscipiemus."

[3] Eichmann, op. cit., i. 49–50. A "festive coronation" (*Festkrönung*) is not an original coronation: it is merely the repetition of a coronation on certain occasions, such as on feast days, or as here on release from captivity. A "festive coronation" may also be called a crown-wearing ceremony.

(1) The report of the learned librarian allows us a welcome insight into the mentality of the official imperial and papal legate.[1] He reports that Basilius, the emperor, had in the course of the conciliar debates arrogantly and aggressively designated himself "emperor of the Romans" and had thereby touched upon a very sore point. In refuting the Eastern theme the versatile librarian re-states the papal theme that the Eastern emperors, as a consequence of divine judgment, had lost their empire in the West. They may legitimately call themselves "emperors of the Greeks," but not "emperors of the Romans." They had sought to sow dissension into the universal Church; and not satisfied with this, they had continued to prevail upon the Roman pontiffs with crooked methods and even now attempted to infringe the privileges of the Roman Church.[2] The genuine irritation that appears from these few lines in the report, can well be explained by the Eastern disregard for vital papal principles, principles in fact on which the history and herewith the development of the papal theme had hinged for so long. In a way Anastasius's irritation is understandable when one considers that apart from arranging the planned marriage between Ermengard, the daughter of Louis, and the son of the Eastern emperor, the purpose of this council was the establishment of unity in the Roman empire. And according to the librarian's opinion, this unity of the empire was the presupposition for the liberty of the universal Church, for the spheres of empire and universal Church were identical.[3]

The two empires, the Greek and the Roman ones, will be united only when the primatial function of the Roman Church is acknowledged and this unity of the whole empire will consequently lead "ad totius Christi ecclesiae libertatem." The function of the Roman Church as the epitome "totius Christi ecclesiae" necessarily guarantees the unity of the empire: imperial unity depends upon the recognition of the Roman Church as the one unitary principle. Behind all these statements there lurks the latent claim to the specific role which the Roman Church plays in the making of the only one universal Ruler, the "imperator Romanorum." The emperor of the Greeks is *an* emperor, but not the specific universal ruler which can only be he who is "emperor of the Romans," that is, who is thus created by the pope. The

---

[1] MGH. *Epp.* vii. no. 5, pp. 403–15. The joint papal and imperial commission is at p. 410, lines 15 ff. The report is addressed to Adrian II.

[2] Ep. cit., p. 411, lines 35 ff.

[3] Ep. cit., p. 410: "In tam enim pio negotio et quod ad utriusque imperii unitatem, imo totius Christi ecclesiae libertatem pertinere procul dubio credebatur, praecipue summi pontificii vestri quaerebatur assensus."

"ecclesia Romana" and the "imperator Romanorum" are indissolubly linked together.

(2) The letter of Emperor Louis II[1] presents the papal Roman empire theme in classic form. Its main theme is the emphasis on the correct meaning of the term "Roman" which, according to the letter, denotes the Latin Christian. Roman emperorship is the supreme dignity that can be acquired only within the Roman orbit. The "Roman" idea is the Latin-Christian idea: Romanism thus understood is a convenient term to denote all Christians who derive their spiritual life blood from the Roman Church. In so far, then, the *imperium Romanum* and the *ecclesia Romana* are expressions of one and the same idea, looked at from different angles.

The tone and theme of the letter[2] are set by the inscription: Louis, "imperator augustus Romanorum" writing to his brother, Basilius, "imperatori novae Romae" in order to remonstrate against the latter's use of the title arrogated to himself. If Basilius had taken the trouble to delve into books and other records, he would have found out that the term "basileus" could be applied to all sorts of rulers who were merely kings, and not emperors. The Old Testament offers examples of this use of the word, and so does history: for not only the Greeks had their "basilei," but also the Persians, Indians, Armenians, Saracens, Goths, and so forth.[3] The Eastern emperor should therefore realize that the term "basileus" is in itself indifferent and its use can be detected in all nations at all times.[4] When Basilius points out that, ever since apostolic times, the prayers referred to "unum imperium," Louis (and Anastasius) retort that this means the "imperium patris et filii et spiritus sancti." It is simply not true as Basilius had written that he, Louis, had

---

[1] That Anastasius was the author of this letter is certain. Cf. A. Kleinclausz, "La lettre de Louis II a Basile V" in *Moyen Age*, viii (1904), pp. 48 ff.; W. Henze, "Ueber den Brief K. Ludwigs II" in *Neues Archiv*, xxxv (1910), pp. 663 ff., esp. 670 ff.; N. Ertl, "Dictatoren frühmittelalterlicher Papstbriefe" in *Arch. f. Urkundenforsch.*, xv (1938), pp. 128 ff. Anastasius was the dictator of most of (Nicholas's) Adrian II's and John VIII's letters, see Ertl, art. cit., pp. 83 ff.

[2] MGH. *Epp.* vii, pp. 385 ff. The letter is a reply to a letter sent by the Eastern emperor Basilius which Louis answers point by point. Cf. also W. Henze, art. cit.

[3] MGH. *Epp.* vii, pp. 386–7.

[4] MGH. *Epp.* vii, p. 387: "Et certe, ut de Latinis codicibus interim tacemus, si Graecos etiam noviter editos revolvas codices, invenies procul dubio plurimos tali nomine (scil. basilei) vocitatos et non solum Graecorum, set et Persarum, Hepierotarum Indorum Bithiniensium, Parthorum, Armeniorum, Sarracenorum, Aethiopum Guandalorum et Gothorum atque aliarum gentium praelatos "basileon" appellatione veneratos. Intuere, igitur, frater, et considera, quod multi fuerint qui basilei diversis temporibus et in diversis locis et nationibus nuncupati sunt vel hactenus nuncupentur."

assumed a new title; nor that his grandfather had usurped the title "imperator Romanorum." The truth is—as can be read in the records —that divine wish and judgment of the Church and of the supreme pontiff made his family the bearers of Roman imperial dignity.[1]

Roman imperial dignity, however, can be conferred only by and upon Romans, and not by and upon Greeks. Hence, when Basilius suggests that Louis should call himself "emperor of the Franks," he should bear in mind that there can not be an emperor of the Franks unless he is first an emperor of the Romans. The greater includes the smaller. This dignity is conferred by the Roman Church upon the Franks, so that they may defend and exalt the Roman Church. They alone are anointed by the Roman pontiff with holy oil for this purpose. The function of the Roman emperor as the defensive and protective organ of the Roman Church is here stated by the emperor himself: his creation entails the function and duty of a protector and defender.[2]

It is a pardonable mistake for the Eastern emperor to state that a Frank cannot be a Roman, although this statement reveals a profound lack of understanding of the point of view which he wishes to attack. For he overlooks that the biological or racial or national element plays no role in this ideology: he is a Roman who acknowledges the primatial function of the Roman Church. A Roman is a Latin Christian. It is not the person that matters—"quoniam non est personarum acceptator Deus"—but, as the apostle had said, it was the spiritual element, the idea as such, which determines whether or not an individual was a Christian.[3] But the Greeks adhere to "kacodosiam," that is, they follow the wrong views and that is why they cannot be "emperors of the Romans": they cannot be emperors over those who hold the right views, "bonam opinionem, id est, orthodosiam." Christianity and

---

[1] MGH. *Epp.* vii, p. 387: ". . . quantum ad lineam generis pertinet, non sit novum vel recens, quod jam ab avo nostro non usurpatum est, ut perhibes, set Dei nutu et ecclesiae judicio summique praesulis inpositionem et unctionem manus obtinuit, sicut in codicibus tuis invenire facile poteris."

[2] MGH. *Epp.* vii, p. 389: "Praeterea mirari se dilecta fraternitas tua significat, quod non Francorum, set Romanorum imperatores appellemus, set scire te convenit, quia nisi Romanorum imperatores essemus, utique nec Francorum. A Romanis enim hoc nomen et dignitatem assumpsimus, apud quos profecto primum tantae culmen sublimitatis et appellationis effulsit, quorumque gentem et urbem divinitus gubernandam et matrem omnium ecclesiarum Dei defenden-dam atque sublimandam suscepimus, *a qua* et regnandi prius et postmodum imperandi auctoritatem prosapiae nostrae seminarium sumpsit. Nam Francorum principes primo reges, deinde vero imperatores dicti sunt, hii dumtaxat, qui a Romano pontifice ad hoc oleo sancto perfusi sunt."

[3] Reference is made to *Acts* x. 35.

Latinity and Romanism are interchangeable terms: hence the pope alone is entitled to confer Roman imperial dignity, for the Roman Church is the epitome of Christendom which follows "orthodosia"; the term "Roman" has nothing to do with nationality. If this papal right were denied, one might just as well deny the legality of Samuel's anointing David after the lapse of Saul; nobody had ever said that Arcadius and Honorius and others were not Roman emperors, because they were originally Spaniards. Moreover, the Frankish line has rightly achieved the apex of power, because of their services to that Church which holds the right views. Christ's dictum, therefore, had a prophetic application to the Eastern emperor—"The kingdom of God shall be taken from you and given to the nation bringing forth the fruits thereof."[1] And St John's the Baptist's promise was also fulfilled.[2]

Ideologically the other points made by Louis-Anastasius yield little new material. There is the natural retort that the Easterners had even deserted Rome, which was the seat of the empire, as well as the Roman nation and language.[3] There is the linguistic argument, this time accentuated by Basilius's use of the term "riga" and "rix" which gives Anastasius welcome opportunity of making fun of the emperor's inadequate mastery of the language. There are the elegant allusions and alliterations which convey an air of superiority in a subtle, but nevertheless unmistakable manner.

This letter of Louis-Anastasius is a document of first class importance. The historical development of the ninth century was skilfully woven into the texture of pure ideas. The transaction based upon the Donation of Constantine had lost its earthly connexion and was transposed onto a higher plane: the removal of the empire from the East to the West was an act of God. But the "emperor of the Romans" was charged with definite duties: his *raison d'être* was the defence and protection of his mother, the Roman Church, "a qua imperandi auctoritatem sumpsit." This is an idea which is to leave its imprint upon the next centuries. And in the course of time the Nicholean *societas*

---

[1] *Matt.* xxi. 43.

[2] *Matt.* iii. 9. "Sicut ergo potuit Deus de lapidibus suscitare filios Abrahae, ita potuit de Francorum duritia Romani suscitare successores imperii."

[3] Ibid., p. 390, lines 12 ff. In many ways this letter is complementary to the denunciations of the Greek errors by the synod of Worms (Mansi, xv. 866 ff.) held in 868. Cf. *Annales Fuldenses* (SS. RR. GG.) ad 868: "Synodus apud Wormatiam mense Maio habita est praesente Hludowico rege ubi episcopi nonnulla capitula de utilitate ecclesiastica conscribentes *Graecorum ineptiis* congrua ediderunt responsa."

*fidelium* will emerge in the shape of the Gregorian *societas christiana* as the one body corporate and politic, which will reduce the Roman empire to an integral and vital part of this whole, autonomous *societas*.

Three years after this letter was written, and seventy-five years after the Great Charles's coronation, another Charles—the Bald—was crowned by Adrian II's successor, John VIII, on Christmas Day 875.

## VII

The conceptions of John VIII, Adrian II's immediate successor, show a very considerable deepening of the papal-hierocratic theme. With ever-increasing clarity the notion of the corporate unity of all Christians emerges: this body, called by Nicholas I the *societas fidelium*, by Adrian II the *populus Dei*, and by John VIII the *respublica christiana*,[1] is a definite and concrete society: it is the visible Church made manifest and tangible—a body politic, for want of a better term, which in its underlying premises is universal, comprising all Christians who derive their spiritual life blood from the Roman Church. And within this body the functionalist principle is at work: functions are distributed according to the qualifications of the members of this society. Those who are functionally qualified to rule and to direct, have rights and duties different from those who are not so qualified, but who still have to play an important part within the framework of the *respublica christiana*.

The Roman Church, according to John VIII, has the *principatus* over all nations of the world: the Roman Church is the unifying principle of the many nations which acknowledge it as their mother and head.[2] The character of the Roman Church as the epitome of Christendom is expressed in a manner which suggests John's close acquaintance with Nicholas's declaration. For according to John "the whole Church of God is with us"—"ecclesia Dei, quae penes nos est."[3] Consequently, the *respublica christiana* is entrusted to the care of the pope.[4]

[1] MGH. *Epp.* vii. Ep. 150, p. 126, lines 30 f.: "status christianae religionis ac reipublicae."

[2] Ep. 198, p. 159, lines 18 f.: "Quae (scil. Romana ecclesia) omnium gentium retinet principatum et ad quam totius mundi quasi ad unam matrem et unum caput conveniunt nationes." This may be an elaboration of a Gelasian passage, cf. supra p. 15.

[3] Ep. 9, p. 326, line 19 (an almost literal borrowing from Nicholas I, see supra 194); cf. also Ep. 7, p. 277, lines 25 ff.

[4] Ep. 8, p. 323, lines 26 ff.: "ministerii nostri est universalis ecclesiae Dei sollicitudinem beati Petri apostoli sententiam circumferre." Cf. also Ep. 103,

The closely knit organic nature of this society entails that whatever affects one of its particles, affects the whole society, and in a particular sense the Roman Church.¹ Nevertheless, there are some faint vibrations of the later theory that the *imperium Romanum* and the *respublica christiana* are by no means identical conceptions.²

John issues binding decrees to the whole society: they are binding because they are issued "judicio Dei omnipotentis."³ Disobedience to them is equal to disobedience to divine commands.⁴ The sanction for disobedience is exclusion from Christian society "auctoritate omnipotentis Dei"⁵ with the further consequence that no member of society may have contact with the excluded member.⁶ It is only an application of this point of view that kings are bound to enforce ecclesiastical laws within their domains.⁷ Moreover, the preservation of peace within the "tota Christianitas" is a major obligation imposed upon the holder of the papal office. "Nolite socialia bella committere" John VIII writes to the barons in Louis the German's kingdom.⁸ And it is in this function as a peacemaker that in 878 he announces his intention to go to Troyes and to preside over the meeting of the four kings.⁹ As the supreme head of the *respublica christiana* he declares that treaties are not to be made with pagans, especially not with the Saracens, since such transactions turn out to be detrimental to the whole of Christendom: the underlying idea being that these treaties need papal approval.¹⁰

---

p. 97: "nobis pro totius sanctae ecclesiae statu laborantibus." We note the conflation of *Matt.* xvi. 18 with II *Cor.* xi. 28, about which see also supra p. 5 n. 4.

¹ Ep. 8, p. 323, lines 28 ff.: "Quid in qualibet mundi parte congruat sive non congruat, censoria gravitate depromere, quatinus oves dominicae, quae vocem pastoralis nostrae sollicitudinis cognoscentes pastorum principem humiliter audiunt . . ." See also Ep. 257, p. 225, lines 16 ff.

² Evildoers, he writes to Charles the Bald, will not only defile his empire, but will inflict harm on the whole of Christianity. Ep. 24, p. 23, lines 1 ff.: "Totum idem imperium coinquinabunt, et omni Christianitati dispendium generabunt, quia, cum sint ipsi oves morbide, totum gregem contaminant." Cf. also Ep. 31, pp. 29 f.: "vestrum vilescat imperium et totae Christianitati nascatur dispendium."

³ Ep. 54, p. 308, lines 3–4.

⁴ Ep. 8, p. 235, lines 22 ff. with a reference to *Rom.* xiii. 1–2 and to *Prov.* viii. 15: "Per me reges regnant."

⁵ Ep. 303, p. 263, line 13. Cf. also Ep. 56, p. 309, lines 29 ff., and Ep. 54, p. 308, line 4; etc.

⁶ Ep. 57, p. 310.

⁷ Ep. 35, p. 293, to the king of Mercia, Burgrad, to see that Gregory I's matrimonial statute is kept.

⁸ Ep. 8, p. 325, line 27.

⁹ Ep. 107, pp. 99–100; cf. also Ep. 136, 137, pp. 119, 120. For factual details see L. Hartmann, *Geschichte Italiens im MA.*, iii/2, pp. 56 ff.

¹⁰ Ep. 279, p. 246, lines 10 ff. (concerning the bishop of Naples who had made

John's reason for insisting on the functionalist theme within the *respublica christiana* is evident. The "sacerdotes" on the model of Gregory I, are the "dei," or "angeli," to whom the Old Testament pronouncement applies: "He who toucheth you toucheth the apple of His eye."[1] The *privilegium fori* is only the reverse side of the functional qualification of the priests: laymen have no right to sit in judgment over those whose function is a "ministerium sacerdotale"; judgment on them is reserved to God alone.[2] For the priests are the properly qualified organs of the whole *Christianitas* who thereby assume functions which raise them above the level of laymen: it would be a reversal of the proper ordering of society if laymen were to pass judgment on the "sacerdotes." John VIII is perfectly aware of the duplicity of meaning attributable to *ecclesia*:

Ecclesia nihil aliud est nisi populus fidelis, sed praecipue clerus censetur hoc nomine.[3]

This society being an *ecclesia* must needs be ruled by the "clerus" who at times may also be designated as "the Church." It is they, the priests, whose task it is, to lay down the faith, the foundation of the whole building, and in this way they direct the society, whose cementing bond is the spiritual element of the faith.[4] This society—it may be termed *respublica christiana* or *Christianitas*[5]—forms one body corporate and politic. "La Chrétienté est donc une patrie—mais une patrie tout à

---

a treaty with the Saracens; on this see also F. E. Engreen, in *Speculum*, xxi, 1946, p. 319); Ep. 217, p. 194 to the Prefect Pulcaris. The bishop of Naples was then excommunicated, p. 247, lines 6 ff., where the sentence of excommunication will be found.

[1] *Zach.* ii. 8, Ep. 303, p. 263.

[2] Ep. 155, p. 129, line 26. The archbishop of Bourges had been seized by the men of Count Bernard who himself was excommunicated in September 878: Ep. 142, p. 122. "Episcoporum judicium, fili karissime, suo tantummodo Dominus servavit arbitrio, nec de episcopis vult Deus laicos judicare. Unde monemus dilectionem tuae caritatis (Bernard), ut, quicquid in hac causa praedicti episcopi deliquistis, sub celeritate et legaliter officio ac ministerio sacerdotali emendare studete, quia nos illud . . . inultum remanere nullo modo patimur."

[3] Ep. 5, p. 332, line 30.

[4] Ep. 113, pp. 104–5: "Canonica instituta servantes oportet nos, quotiescumque inierunt passiones, sacerdotum collegia aggregare, ut simul venientibus salubre universae ecclesiae consilium et totius Christianitatis fidem eidem imponant." See furthermore Ep. 210, p. 187, lines 27 ff.: "Divina potestate, quam accepit ecclesia Christi, cuncta solvuntur vincula, quando per pastoralem auctoritatem quae fuerant ligata, solvuntur."

[5] See preceding note, and Ep. 208, p. 177, line 45: "universus in orbe terrarum christianus populus." Ep. 78, p. 74, lines 23 and 28: "tota christianitas."

la fois temporelle et spirituelle."¹ Being a Christian society, it can be directed only by the functionally qualified members, that is, the "clerus."

John VIII's views on the derivation of Roman imperial power are worth mentioning. The Roman Church is not only the "caput nationum"² and the "caput orbis et mater omnium fidelium"³ but, by virtue of the see of St Peter, the city of Rome itself is also raised to a "civitas sacerdotalis et regalis *per* sacram sedem."⁴ That this designation of Rome is directed against the East, seems clear; it seems equally clear that this designation also has specific reference to the imperial question in the West; and in the last resort it is the transposition of the "regale sacerdotium" onto a different plane. Charles the Bald had received his power to rule as well as his faith from the Roman Church.⁵ The discretionary but decisive role played by the Roman Church is brought out by John's statement that the Roman Church could have selected Louis the German instead of Charles the Bald as Roman emperor: nevertheless, Charles was chosen by the Roman Church "in the manner of God"—"more Dei"—as another David.⁶

The mediatory role of the Roman Church and the pope, to which we have drawn attention in our survey of Nicholas I's ideology, is here delineated in very concrete terms. Charles should not think that he had received the empire as a mere human *beneficium*, but rather as a *divinum beneficium*, handed to him by the instrumentality of the pope.⁷ The empire is a divine institution, or as John VIII has it: "Dei omnipotentis ordinatio"⁸ and rebellion against it is not rebellion against the person of the emperor, but against God Himself Whose kingdom the

---

¹ J. Rupp, *L'idée de Chrétienté*, Paris, 1938, p. 38.
² See supra p. 219.                     ³ Ep. 78, p. 74, line 25.
⁴ Ep. 78, p. 74, lines 36–7. About Leo I's expression see his *Sermo* 82, c. 1, supra p. 77.
⁵ Ep. 22, p. 20, line 32: "a qua (scil. Romana ecclesia) non solum regnandi sed et in unum Deum et verum credendi exordium percepistis." With this cf. Nicholas I's statement, supra 200 and Adrian II's, supra 217. Cf. also John's Ep. 87, p. 82, lines 27 ff. to Louis the Stammerer: ".... matri vestrae, *a qua* et potum praedicationis in proavis et infulam imperii accepistis."
⁶ Ep. 22, p. 20, lines 20 ff.: "Spreto magno et bono fratre, vos more Dei gratuita voluntate tamquam alterum regem David elegit et praeelegit atque ad imperialia sceptra provexit."
⁷ Ep. 7, p. 321, lines 20 ff. Repeated in Ep. 8, p. 324, lines 44 ff.: "Quando ad imperium, quod ei constat non humano collatum beneficio, licet per nostrae mediocritatis ministerium, sed divino pertingere potuisset." About Gelasius see supra p. 22. Eichmann in *Festschrift f. Hertling* rightly stresses John's view on the mediatory role of the pope, p. 267.
⁸ Ep. cit., p. 325, line 23.

empire is.[1] There is no need to comment upon the Gelasian origin of the idea of *beneficium*; suffice it to say that, as a consequence of the mediatory role of the pope, the Gelasian *beneficium* was divinely conferred by the pope. What was implicit in Gelasius, is now explicit.[2] "Vos auctore Deo in imperium coronaverimus," says John.[3]

In pursuance of this theme John writes to Charles that he had obtained the empire as a divine benefice because he had been "divinitus praescitus et praedestinatus."[4] This divine pre-selection was revealed through John's predecessor, Adrian II:

Divina ergo majestas excellentiam vestram prae ceteris elegit Romani imperii altitudine sublimare augustalique voluit diademate coronare.[5]

This statement is all the more interesting as John combines it with the duty which the divine selection of the emperor throws upon him: protection and defence of the Roman Church and thereby of the universal Church, that is, of the whole of Christendom.[6] The emperor is the sworded organ of the Roman Church against internal and external enemies, because he is the "filius specialis" of the Roman Church.[7]

The responsibility of the pope for the rulers, and especially for the Roman emperor follows as a natural corollary of this theme. For he as the head of "tota Christianitas" appoints its temporal protector and the account which the pope will render on the Day of Judgment about the Ruler, will depend on how the protector has discharged his duty. If therefore despite papal admonition, protection of the Roman Church is not forthcoming, the pope's account on the Day of Judgment

[1] Ep. cit., lines 24 ff., reminding the barons in Louis the German's kingdom of their duty not to invade the empire: "neque enim contra Karolum est murmur vestrum, sed contra Dominum, cuius est regnum et cui voluerit ipse dat illud."
[2] Cf. also supra 199 on Nicholas I, and infra 341 on Adrian IV.
[3] Ep. 32, p. 31, line 27.        [4] Ep. 32, p. 325, line 7.
[5] Ep. 56, p. 51, lines 8–9.
[6] Ep. 56, p. 51, lines 9–12: ". . . coronare, ut Deo nostro clementer auxiliante potentiae vestrae brachio triumphali ecclesiam Christi voce suave petram verae fidei fundatam tueremini semper et ab immani crudelique paganorum infestatione . . . defenderitis." As soon as John had crowned Louis the Stammerer king at Troyes (for details see P. E. Schramm, *Der König von Frankreich*, Weimar, 1939, pp. 62 ff.) he pointed out the new king's duty, namely "defensionem, liberationem atque exaltationem sanctae Romanae ecclesiae," Ep. 115, *Allocutio*, p. 106, lines 7–8. Here also the application of *Rom.* xiii. 4 that the prince does not bear the sword in vain. That Louis the Stammerer was also "selected" by divine majesty through the instrumentality of John VIII to become Roman emperor—after Charles the Bald's death—is certain, even though the candidate was eventually dropped, see supra 164, and Eichmann, op. cit., i. 55, Schramm, op. cit., loc. cit., and L. Hartmann, op. cit., iii/2, pp. 58–9, who draws attention to John's imitating Stephen II at Troyes.        [7] See supra p. 152.

will be adverse.[1] On the other hand, defence of the Roman Church is a guarantee of reward on the Day of Judgment.[2] This duty of protection and defence and exaltation of the Roman Church is in fact the price which the emperor has to pay for receiving the Roman imperial crown. The emperor is not a protector *ex se* and *per se*, but is made one: he is a patron, an adjutant, an advocate.[3]

Murdered by his own entourage,[4] John VIII stands out as one of the very great medieval popes who had advanced the theme of papal-hierocratic views quite considerably. John's pivotal idea was that contemporary society formed one body corporate and politic: it was an organic whole which was headed by him and which was to be ruled through the instrumentality of the *sacerdotium*. The emperor is created for the sake of protection and defence of the Roman Church, and he receives his empire, through the medium of the pope, as a *divinum beneficium*. And since the Roman Church can confer only universal power, the emperor created by the pope becomes the master of all

---

[1] Ep. 193, p. 155, lines 17 ff.: "Nam si, quod absit, per vos forte remanserit, ut ecclesia Dei in praesenti defensionem non habeat et taliter turbata consistat, videte, ne ante tribunal Christi et coram apostolorum principum praesentia vestrae animae patiamini detrimentum, quia nos paterna vos ammonitione hortantes secundum ministerium nostri officii ea, quae Dei sunt, et saluti vestrae proficua, agere incunctanter convenimus." Cf. also Ep. 78, p. 74, line 32: ". . . ne . . . districtam Domino cogamur reddere rationem."

[2] Ep. 180, p. 145, lines 3–5: "Nam si per vos sancta Romana ecclesia fuerit exaltata atque defensa, vester honor et gloria hic et in futuro sine dubio coram Domino multiplicata manebit." This was written to Charles III (the Fat) in 879, before he was made an emperor and when John was still angling for an emperor.

[3] This is made quite clear by John VIII in two letters both dealing with his making Charles II Roman emperor. In the one (Ep. 36, p. 36, lines 1 ff.) he combines this idea with his responsibility to God for the emperor and the empire (which is a divine benefice) and writes to the hierarchy in Charles's territory: "Unde et eum adversus omnes hostes ecclesiae non solum *defensorem*, sed etiam *patronum et advocatum nostrum* existere proposuimus, ut, quod ei nos apud Deum esse satagimus, ipse inter homines pro nobis fieri non detrectet." The other letter is written to Charles himself (Ep. 32, p. 31, lines 25 ff.). After depicting the tribulations besetting Rome, John writes: "Haec sunt, karissime, de innumerabilibus pauca, quae mater vestra Romana, pro dolor! diebus vestris perfert ecclesia, quasi nos non *vos auctore Deo in imperium coronaverimus* . . ." and hence his appeal for help: "unde iterum iterumque totis singultibus totisque imploramus praecordiis et per Christum Dei filium suppliciter adjuramus, qui vos ad tantum provexit fastigium et imperium: vel nunc citatum extendite clementiae brachium et periclitanti patriae quin potius mundo, auxilii jamjamque porrigite dexteram." See also Ep. 48, p. 46, quoted supra p. 162 and Ep. 4, p. 318: the emperor as "Christi patronus."

[4] First he was poisoned, and when the poison did not work quickly enough, his head was battered with a hammer. The epitaph of John is printed by Duchesne, *Lib. Pont.*, ii. 223, note 4.

kingdoms: Roman emperorship is universal lordship. The theme of the letter of Louis II emerges in unsurpassable succinctness in John's letter to a possible future emperor in the year 879:

Si Deo favente Romanum sumpseritis imperium, omnia vobis regna subjecta existent.[1]

## VIII

The advance made in these three pontificates is also mirrored in the new coronation *ordo* (B) which was composed then. The visible changes effected in it are significant enough to warrant a few observations, because the coronation *ordines* are an excellent means of fathoming contemporary ideas.[2]

There is, considering on the one hand the pronounced manifestations of papal-hierocratic conceptions during the pontificate of John VIII and on the other hand the period of ideological stagnation in the succeeding decades, some justification for subscribing to the view that *Ordo B*[3] was composed relatively soon afterwards.[4] No change was effected in the emperor's standing as a *persona sacra*.[5] He was not

---

[1] Ep. 205, p. 165, written to Louis the Stammerer: "Scitote pro certo, quia nullus parentum vestrorum tantam gloriam et exaltationem a decessoribus nostris percepit, quantam nos vobis, si veneritis, totis multipliciter viribus desideramus impendere . . . sedes apostolica, quae caput est omnium ecclesiarum Dei, vos magno desiderio quasi *unicum et carissimum filium* praestolatur, vestra speciali visione celeriter perfruatur, quoniam, si Deo favente Romanum sumpseritis imperium, omnia vobis regna subjecta existent." Reviewing John's activity, Schramm observes that "the papal court had always been the unsurpassable master in the art of justifying each of its steps by reference to divine order, morals, law or tradition," *König von Frankreich*, p. 35.

[2] Cf. the pertinent observations of P. E. Schramm, "Die Ordines der Kaiserkrönung" in *Archiv f. Urkundenforschung*, xi (1930), p. 285: "So eng war diese Beziehung zwischen Zeremonie und Politik, dass man geradezu sagen darf, eine Ideengeschichte der beiden Gewalten beruhe so lange auf unsicherem Boden als es nicht gelungen ist, die verschiedenen Entwicklungsphasen der römischen Kaiserkrönung mit Sicherheit festzulegen."

[3] We adopt Eichmann's nomenclature. This *Ordo B* (ed. E. Eichmann, *Kaiserkrönung*, i. 135–8) was previously called *Cencius I*, because it was the first *Ordo* entered by Cencius in his *Liber Censuum*. *Cencius II* is the *Ordo C*, about which see infra 253. Cf. also E. Eichmann, "Das Verhältnis von Cencius I und Cencius II" in *Grabmann Festschrift*, Munich, 1935, i. 204–45.

[4] Schramm, loc. cit., p. 354, between 880 and 890. On the other hand, Eichmann, op. cit., i. 149, and C. Erdmann, *Forschungen*, p. 70, would date *Ordo B* somewhere in the 20s or early 30s of the tenth century. But there is unanimous agreement that this *Ordo B* was used for the Ottonian coronations, cf. Erdmann, op. cit., p. 71. Cf. also the attractive suggestion by M. Uhlirz, art. cit., pp. 269–70, about the possibility of reconciling the controversy concerning the Salian *Ordo* (Schramm) and the purely liturgical coronation *ordines*.

[5] Cf. also Ph. Oppenheim in *Ephemerides Liturgicae*, lviii (1944), p. 47.

a "sacerdos" in any meaning of the term, because the "cura animarum" was not entrusted to him, this being the effluence of ordination. The promise which the emperor made on the occasion of his coronation in front of St Peter's was one of a protector defending the Roman Church.[1] The external setting of the emperor's consecration and unction is parallel to the consecration of the pope himself: the same three bishops who take part in the consecration of the pope—those of Albano, Porto and Ostia—also take part in the anointing of the emperor.[2]

This brings us to the first change in *Ordo B.* The ceremonies of unction and coronation are separated: the former is carried out by the three bishops, whilst the latter is solely the pope's prerogative. The symbolic significance of this division of functions and ceremonies lies in that the pope's function is thereby brought into clearest possible relief: until the climax of all the coronation ceremonies is reached, namely the imposition of the crown, the pope remains inactive; he stands erect in front of the main altar of St Peter's:

> Pontifex vero stet sursum ante altare et imponat ei diadema.

The pope becomes active when the final act begins.

The second change is this. We have already had an opportunity of pointing out that the coronation of 816 signified the fusion of Byzantine and Frankish elements. Now in *Ordo B* we find another Byzantine

---

[1] The promise of *Ordo B*: "In nomine Christi promitto, spondeo atque polliceor ego N. imperator coram Deo et beato Petro apostolo me protectorem ac defensorem esse huius sanctae Romanae ecclesiae in omnibus utilitatibus, in quantum divino fultus fuero adjutorio, secundum scire meum ac posse." About the possible derivation of the formula from Pippin's promise cf. P. E. Schramm, in *Sav. Z., Kan. Abt.*, xxvii (1938), pp. 186–91.

[2] This is modelled on *Liber Diurnus*, form. 57, pp. 46–7; cf. also OR. IX cap. 5 (PL. lxxviii. 1006). The pope was consecrated by the bishop of Ostia (already testified for 336) who ranked first amongst the seven Lateran bishops; he anointed the emperor, after the bishop of Albano (the third in rank) had said the first *Oratio* over the emperor, followed by second *Oratio* spoken by Porto (second in rank). All this is closely modelled on OR IX, cap. 5 and *Lib. Diurn.* form. cit.; see also F. Wasner, "De consecratione . . . pontificis" in *Apollinaris*, viii (1935), pp. 108–9, *Ordo B* and Eichmann, op. cit., ii. 218–19. According to the privilege of John XIX of 17 December 1026 (PL. cit., appendix to OR XI, col. 1055) the bishop of Silva-Candida was to say the first *Oratio* over the emperor: "Ad unguendum consecrandumque imperatorem primum vestram et vestrorum successorum episcoporum fraternitatem convocamus." In 1037 Benedict IX confirmed this privilege (PL. cxli. 1356) adding that the bishop of Silva-Candida was to be the "bibliothecarius" of the Roman Church and one of the two bishops who were to enthrone the pope "in apostolica sede." Since the bishopric of Silva-Candida was not filled by the end of this century, the privilege became a dead letter. The three Rhenish bishops (Cologne, Mainz, Trier) at the royal coronation, corresponded to these three Roman bishops.

influence. The pope whilst imposing the crown no longer says the old prayer "Accipe coronam," but prays

Accipe signum gloriae in nomine patris et filii et spiritus sancti.

The reason for this change is, on the one hand, that the old formula denoted the principle of hereditary kingship,[1] whilst the function of the pope was thought to have been brought out more clearly when the emperor received the "sign of glory in the name of the Father, the Son and the Holy Ghost." He was then indeed "a Deo coronatus" as his official title had it. On the other hand, the Byzantine emperor, too, claimed this distinction, though he was crowned only by the patriarch: the new title and the accompanying prayer was adopted in the West in order to demonstrate the mediatory role of the pope between Christ and the emperor.[2]

The third and most important change concerned the anointing. Whilst previously the emperor had been anointed on the vertex, he is now anointed on the right arm and between the shoulders—"brachium dexterum et inter scapulas"—no longer with chrism, but with an inferior kind of oil.[3] In both these changes the papal-hierocratic point of view is exquisitely manifested. And both were in fact dictated by the Gallic liturgy relating to the unction of the head of the bishop and by the introduction of this liturgy in Rome, as a consequence of which the pope too was anointed on the head.[4]

[1] See Eichmann, op. cit., i. 142: the new formula betrays its Byzantine model; cf. also ii. 61 f.

[2] The whole prayer runs: "Accipe . . . sancti, ut spreto antiquo hoste spretisque contagiis omnium viciorum sic judicium et justitiam diligas et misericorditer vivas, ut ab ipso Domino nostro Jesu Christo in consortio sanctorum aeterni regni coronam percipias, qui cum patre et spiritu sancto vivit et regnat Deus per infinita saecula saeculorum. Amen." Biblical models: *Eccl.* xlvii. 7; *Is.* xxviii. 5; *Jer.* xiii. 18. The "antiquus hostis" may be the dragon of *Rev.* xii. 9 and xx. 2. For further interpretative details see Eichmann, op. cit., ii. 62 f.

[3] Liturgically three kinds of oil must be distinguished, cf. H. A. Wilson, *The Gelasian Sacramentary*, no. XL, pp. 69–74; no. LXX, p. 113, and no. LXXII, pp. 114–15; Eisenhofer, *Liturgik*, pp. 130–1, 270–1; E. Eichmann, "Königs und Bischofsweihe" in *SB. Munich*, 1928, fasc. 6, pp. 21 ff.; idem, in *Hist. Jb.*, lxix (1949), pp. 611–12. They are: (1) the "oleum infirmorum"; (2) the "oleum catechumenorum" or "exorcitatum" which is the one used for imperial coronations since *Ordo B* and which has the function of driving out evil spirits (exorcism): it is purifying and re-invigorating; and (3) the "chrisma" or olive oil mixed with balsam, embodying the Holy Spirit: a "compound oil," see L. W. Legg, *English Coronation Records*, pp. xxxiv f.

[4] Cf. M. Andrieu, *Le Pontifical Romain*, ii. 264; Eichmann, *SB.* cit., pp. 37–8, and G. Ellard, *Ordination Anointings in the Western Church*, pp. 75 ff., 88 ff., 98: there was no liturgical anointing in Rome before John X. Ellard bases his conclusions on MS. BM. Add. 15222. Cf. also supra p. 67 n. 3.

Unction with chrism on the head is what came to be called sacramental in character, whilst unction with oil bestows no such specific distinction. *Ordo B* constitutes therefore an explicit "demotion" of the emperor.[1] The underlying assumption is that the function of those parts of the (imperial) body which are anointed, is thus sanctified. Anointing of the head would symbolize headship, whilst anointing of the right arm and between the shoulder blades—the seat of physical strength—symbolizes the sanctification of the physical support and protection of the head. The idea of protection (in the Roman-papal sense) is thus most exquisitely symbolized in the ceremony of anointing.[2]

---

[1] Cf. Eichmann, *SB.* cit., p. 37 and the quotation from Amalarius of Metz, ibid. The late Erdmann, op. cit., p. 71, does not accept the distinction between ordinary oil and chrism for the tenth century. But the texts in Ellard to which Erdmann refers (p. 71, note 3) are partly in pontificals of Southern France (Ellard, p. 83) showing Dunstan's influence (p. 82), and in part they make the distinction between oil and chrism: for episcopal consecration anointing with chrism on the vertex appears quite distinct from the anointing of priests' hands with oil, see p. 87 (Troyes) and pp. 95, 98. The exception is Verona, p. 93.

[2] We should take note of Pseudo-Isidore's view which was attributed to Pope Clement, according to which the anointing of the head of the bishop made him "quasi Christi locum tenens," see Hinschius, op. cit., p. 53, cap. 59. We should also refer to the declaration of the council of 881: "Tanta est dignitas pontificum major quam regum, quia reges in culmen regium sacrantur a pontificibus, pontifices autem a regibus consecrari non possunt," Mansi, xvii. 538. This is Gelasian theory expressed in liturgical terms (cf. Gelasius, *Tract IV*, cap. 13, p. 569, quoted supra p. 26). It is well known that Innocent III later expressed the classic theory of the significance of unction (*Extra:* I. xv. un.): "Refert autem inter pontificis et principis unctionem: quia caput pontificis chrismate consecratur, brachium vero principis oleo delinitur, ut ostendatur quanta sit differentia inter auctoritatem pontificis et principis potestatem." This too is Gelasianism. Imperial or royal unction is not a sacrament, but a sacramentale. That English kings were anointed with chrism on the head is well known, cf. the *Liber Regalis*, ed. Legg, op. cit., at p. 93; cf. also P. E. Schramm, *History of the English Coronation*, Oxford, 1937, pp. 120, 128–9, 132, and the interpretation of Becket adduced by Schramm, p. 122, note 2. In a pontifical of the twelfth century (MS. Trinity College, Cambridge: B. 11. 10, fol. 106r) we read a rubric which is almost identical to that of the fourteenth-century *Liber Regalis* (i.e. unction with chrism on the king's head), but on which a marginal gloss in a thirteenth-century hand comments: "Dicit tamen Innocentius III in tit. de sacra unctione, quod rex non debet inungi in capite, sed in brachio, humero vel armis." For another six MSS. of this so-called *Anselm Ordo* see Schramm, "Ordines Studien III" in *Archiv f. Urkundenforsch.*, xv (1938), p. 320, who considers the possibility of St Osmund being the author of this *ordo*. The evidence, however, would go to show that the medieval kings were always anointed with chrism on the head. Whether Peter of Blois used terms in a technical sense is not quite clear when he wrote to the pope on behalf of Eleanor to secure her son's release from captivity; Henry VI committed a sacrilege: "O impie, crudelis et dire tyranne, qui non es veritus manus sacrilegas immittere in *christum Domini*, nec te regalis unctio nec sanctae viae reverentia nec timor Dei a tanta inhumanitate cohibuit," PL. ccvi. 1270.

# CHAPTER VIII

# Imperial Hegemony

## I

THE end of the ninth and the first half of the tenth centuries demonstrate the truism that the Roman emperor was indeed of vital importance for the functioning of the papacy. The *raison d'être* of the Roman emperor was the protection and defence of the Roman Church, but these decades would also show that the Roman Church depended for its very existence on its protector. With the disappearance of the powerful Frankish monarchy, there disappeared also the special protector of the Roman Church which rapidly began to degenerate in these decades; the popes climbed down to depths which must be classed unparalleled. There is every justification for saying that the Roman Church was tossed about like chaff in the wind at the time when its "brachium" was in abeyance.

Ideological advance under these circumstances can hardly be expected: the popes' personalities; the overpowering domination of the Roman nobility; the frequent changes in the papal chair itself; the strong influence exercised by women of a shady past with no less shady ambitions; the depravity of the papal personnel—these indeed are not factors conducive to the development of ideas. Nevertheless, the idea that Roman emperorship could only be received from the hands of the Roman pontiff, had not suffered any eclipse. This idea was as important to the new dynasty in Germany as to the papacy itself. The early Saxons bear witness to the enduring attraction and fascination of the empire conception. The foremost of European Rulers, the first Otto, after his successful Italian campaign, had to return home in 951 as a mere king: his request submitted to Pope Agapetus II for the imperial crown was refused.[1] It is an illustrative sidelight that before his Italian campaign, Otto I had already ordered the striking of the characteristic imperial *bulla*—a somewhat premature governmental action.[2]

The appeal of John XII to Otto I ten years later naturally fell on †

[1] Cf. also R. Folz, op. cit., p. 59.
[2] For this see W. Ohnsorge, *Das Zweikaiserproblem*, pp. 51, 59, with specific reference to DO. I. 135.

fertile soil: it was the old appeal of the papacy for protection and defence, couched in terms reminiscent of some two hundred years earlier. Otto's help was invoked against the advancing armies of Berengar and his son Adalbert. Otto eagerly followed the call: he undertook the second Italian campaign in the function of a protector and defender of the Roman Church having been thus designated by John XII. Otto went in the capacity of the "brachium Romanae ecclesiae." On 31 January 962 at the gates of Rome, through his legates, Otto took the characteristic oath of protection and defence, particularly as regards the papal territories: and in the function of a protector (in the Roman-papal sense) he was crowned by the pope on 2 February 962. Eleven days later he made the compact with John in which he confirmed the Carolingian donations. In his function as a protector he set out to subject the hostile forces in Italy, on 14 February 962.

It was in the following months that Otto's role as a protector in the papal sense changed into one in the royal sense. In the districts which he conquered and which he had recently confirmed as papal territory he made the inhabitants take an oath to himself instead of, as the pope expected, to the Roman Church. To John XII therefore Otto I appeared no longer as the protector whom he had wished to see, but as the oppressor, in no way different from an Aistulph, Desiderius or Berengar. Thus the pope called upon new protectors, against Otto, namely the Hungarians, the Byzantines—and Berengar. To Otto I the pope appeared as a traitor, no better than any other Roman. The insurrection instigated by John made it imperative for Otto that the root of the trouble should be eradicated: hence Otto's return to Rome in November 963, the summoning of Pope John XII before the synod held at St Peter's under Otto's chairmanship, and the eventual deposition of the pope by this synod on 6 December 963.

† 

On this occasion the compact issued in February 962 was falsified by the insertion of clauses, of which the most important was that which dealt with the promise by the Romans, given on oath, that they would insist on an oath to be taken by the pope to the imperial legates before his consecration. The significance of this lies less in the actual falsification than in the changes made in another document which then served as the model for the *Ottonianum* which has been preserved until this day.[1] That other document was the so-called *Sacramentum Romanorum* of 824[2] which, we hold, did not contain an oath to be taken by the

*

[1] For details see *Cambridge Historical Journal*, xi (1953), pp. 114–28.
[2] MGH. *Capitularia*, i. 235.

pope, but the stipulation that, for the sake of being effectively protected, the pope should notify the emperor of his election, so that the pope's consecration should proceed in the presence of the imperial legates. This notification was changed into an oath in December 963 and the falsified *Sacramentum Romanorum* served as the basis of the falsification of the original *Ottonianum*. In other words, what was previously laid down in the interests of the papacy, was now modified in the interests of the empire: the idea of protection in the papal sense, expressed in the no longer extant original *Sacramentum Romanorum*, changed into one in the royal sense and was expressed in the falsified, transmitted *Sacramentum Romanorum*.

Whilst originally, therefore, the papacy notified the emperor so as to be protected, mainly against the unruly Romans, the emperor now appeared as the protector in the royal sense of the Roman Church, and the latter became a protectorate of the empire. The root of the papal notification to the emperor was, ideologically, the conception of the emperor as the "brachium" of the Roman Church; in documentary form this root could be found in the old *Liber Diurnus* regulation according to which papal elections had to be announced to the emperor (or to the exarch at Ravenna) so as to be confirmed: the papacy made use of this *Liber Diurnus* regulation, after the creation of the (Roman) empire in the West, but changed its meaning: the emperor should be notified, not in order to obtain confirmation from him, but protection. This papal notification was therefore the signal given to the emperor to act as the "brachium" of the Roman Church: it was the invocation of the service which was the emperor's *raison d'être*, according to the papal point of view. And it was this (papal) idea of protection which was changed into its royal counterpart: the way in which this was done was by falsifying the document which originally contained a stipulation concerning a mere announcement of the papal election to the emperor: this was transformed into an oath to be taken by the pope to the imperial legates. The emperor, according to the *Ottonianum* in its transmitted form, is the supreme protector in the Teutonic-royal sense.

That change in the role of the protector on the part of Otto could be effected all the more easily as this was precisely the role which he had played towards the imperial churches. The ninth and tenth centuries had not only witnessed the exuberant growth of the proprietary church system, which, from an ideological point of view, is characterized by the application of the Teutonic idea of protection to the individual churches, but also the application of the true monarchic principle to all the important bishoprics. That is to say, the *imperium* as a Christian entity and monarchically ruled, was to be given its appropriate ecclesiastical officers in the shape of suitable bishops and abbots. Hence, fundamentally and as regards royal control, there was no difference between a royal proprietary church and any bishopric or abbacy. Both were essential organs of the imperial government—both kinds of churches were subjected to the monarch, and by the mid-tenth century this distinction had been obliterated. Every important church was now an imperial church. To leave the creation of a bishop to an electing body would have been a serious infringement of a correctly understood monarchic principle. And the *Ottonianum* in its falsified form is a clumsy attempt to adapt the Roman Church to imperial conditions: and there was no safer way of so doing than of basing this document on "previous" documents. This arrangement in the *Ottonianum* is the nearest approach to a full transformation of the Roman see into an imperial see.[1]

## II

The coronation of Otto I in 962 is perhaps the most eloquent testimony of the enduring efficacy of that part of the papal theme by virtue of which only the pope of Rome can confer Roman imperial dignity.

* [1] About the requirement of suitability, cf. also infra 244. This requirement of a suitable incumbent in the case of a proprietary church is clear: the church was the owner's property, hence the need to protect it by installing a suitable cleric.

† In the case of imperial churches, which were not originally proprietary churches, the king—and especially the Ottonians—supplied the bishop with rich lands and so forth, and hence here too the necessity arose of appointing a suitable and loyal bishop. Cf. also H. Schmidinger, "Die Besetzung des Patriarchenstuhls von Aquileja" in MIOG., lx. 1952, p. 344: "Für die ottonische Kirchenpolitik, die ihren Grundsätzen entsprechend die Bischofssitze reich mit Ländereien und Regalien ausstattete, um sie auf diese Weise zu den mächtigsten Lehensträgern des Reiches zu machen, war es von entscheidender Bedeutung, die wichtigsten Bischofssitze in die Obhut treuer Anhänger zu bringen." It seems that in the case of a proprietary church, property was the basis upon which the system could grow: the erection of the church was the effluence of ownership. In the case of the imperial churches (the *Reichskirchen*) property was handed to the imperially appointed bishop so that the episcopal church was the cause of providing the bishop and his see with property. The protection of property was therefore intimately and intrinsically bound up with this system which was clothed in feudal garb: the bishop (or abbot) did homage and took the oath of fealty to the lord. And just as the idea of protection was vital to the feudal system, so it was the ideological ferment of the proprietary church and the imperial churches. And when we allow ourselves a glance ahead into the twelfth century, it will become clear that the *temporalia*, or as they were appropriately called, the *Regalia*, played a crucial role in the relations between the episcopacy and the crown.

And five years later—it was another Christmas Day—Otto had his son crowned emperor at St Peter's. Although Charlemagne served as the model for all three Ottos,[1] his main theme of an unpolitical and religious Romanism had unobtrusively, but steadily, transformed itself into a fully fledged political Romanism: it was this avowed political Romanism which became a permanent feature of the medieval European landscape.[2] This political Roman empire ideology was so firmly entrenched in men's minds that no other imperial conception could hope to be a serious competitor.[3]

To this Romanism, however, the dispensatory role of the pope was axiomatic and fundamental. Only he is a Roman emperor upon whom the pope had conferred the title and dignity.[4] And yet, neither title nor dignity added anything of tangible value to the power of the first Otto. Before his imperial coronation he had been hailed as "caput totius mundi," as "dominus pene totius Europae"; his power before coronation was said to stretch into Asia and Africa;[5] he occasionally called himself in several Diplomata before his coronation "imperator augustus";[6] he was the most powerful European Ruler who could count not only Denmark and Burgundy as virtual satellites, but who also was invoked as an arbiter in France, who interfered in Spain on behalf of the Christians, whose influence was effectively felt in Norway and Sweden, who had strong ties to Anglo-Saxon England—but in spite of all this, he was a mere "Rex." What he did not have was power over Italy. But in order to be a Roman emperor, he had to have control of the geographical Romans. In order therefore to be Roman emperor he

[1] See the already quoted excellent work of R. Folz, *Le souvenir et la légende de Charlemagne*, pp. 45 ff. The coronation of Otto II may have been inspired by this "imitatio Caroli"—and yet what difference between 813 and 967.

[2] Cf. the observations of F. Schneider, *Rom und Romgedanke*, p. 191, which, though exaggerated, deserve quotation: "Die umbarmherzige Logik des Geschehens forderte, dass die besonders naturwidrige Pseudomorphose des abendländischen Imperiums sich in Phantasmen und Illusionen verzehren sollte."

[3] For the Frankish or Western imperial idea, see C. Erdmann, *Forschungen*, pp. 44 ff.: "Die nichtrömische Kaiseridee," especially Widukind of Corvey.

[4] Cf. now also W. Holtzmann, *Das mittelalterliche Imperium und die werdenden Nationen*, Cologne, 1953, p. 8: "Otto I hat an der Tradition festgehalten, das nur der Papst die Kaiserkrone vergeben kann."

[5] So Widukind of Corvey, see the passage quoted by Erdmann, op. cit., p. 46, note 2; cf. also R. Folz, op. cit., pp. 56 f.

[6] In the protocol of DO. I. 132, p. 212, of 951; DO. I. 195, p. 276, of 13 June 958; DO. I. 209, p. 288, of 960; cf. also DO. I. 31, p. 117, line 35: "Defendatur imperiali sceptro"; DO. I. 46, p. 131, line 16: "hoc imperiali regiae auctoritatis praecepto"; DO. I. 177, p. 257, line 15: "imperiali nostra auctoritate constituimus."

9

had to exercise some control over the "Romans" who, so to speak, physically epitomized the Romans (= Latin Christians) everywhere. Hence Otto's eagerness to deal with Italian affairs and his emergence as king of Italy—"rex Francorum *et Italicorum*"—on 23 September 951 at Pavia.[1] The king of Italy was the king of the geographical "Romans" epitomized—the later "Rex Romanorum"—and this status was an indispensable preliminary to the dignity of the emperor of the Romans.[2]

The other reason for the Italian campaign of Otto stands in closest proximity to the advance of the Byzantine troops in Southern Italy: they were the armies of him who had never given up the claim to be the true "imperator Romanorum."[3] The Eastern emperor, in Western conceptions, was a mere Greek emperor,[4] and the Ottonian acknowledgment of the Donation of Constantine was the implicit confirmation of the papal point of view that the Roman empire was at the disposal of the pope, by virtue of Constantine's action.[5]

And, so it was held, this Roman empire could never perish: that empire which is, according to tenth-century conceptions, the idolized political manifestation of Christianity, must be defended against him who arrogates to himself the title "emperor of the Romans." This, so it was held, was the proper interpretation of the prophecy of Daniel:[6] the four empires of this prophecy were the Assyrian-Babylonian, the Persian, the Greek and the Roman empires. This fourth kingdom "shall be diverse from all kingdoms and shall devour the whole earth and shall tread it down and break it to pieces."[7] Already widely current in the middle of the ninth century, this eschatological interpretation of the biblical prophecy furnished a strong ideological ferment in the tenth century as also in later times.[8] In a way, this eschatology was a spiritualized teleology of history.

---

[1] For details see R. Holtzmann, *Geschichte der sächsischen Kaiserzeit*, Munich, 1943, pp. 143–9.

[2] Cf. also supra p. 163.

[3] The aim of the Byzantine armies was Rome, as we know from Liutprand's *Legatio*, cap. xviii (ed. SS. RR. GG., by F. Becker), pp. 184–5.

[4] Liutprand, *Legatio*, cap. lxvii, p. 200.

[5] Liutprand, *Legatio*, cap. xvii, p. 184.

[6] *Dan.* vii. 14.

[7] *Dan.* vii. 23.

[8] R. Folz, op. cit., p. 41, note 13, and R. Holtzmann, op. cit., p. 193. About the patristic interpretation in the same sense see C. Trieber, "Die vier Weltreiche" in *Hermes*, xxvii (1892), pp. 321 ff., especially pp. 340–2 (St Jerome), and W. Kamlah, *Christentum und Geschichtlichkeit*, Cologne, 1951, pp. 302 ff. (St Augustine). Cf. also H. Löwe, "Von Theoderich d. Gr. zu Karl d. Gr." in *Deutsches*

At this stage of the development it is perhaps advisable to state the one point on which both imperial and papal conceptions were in agreement, namely on the exclusive and universal character of Roman emperorship. Because he was the Roman emperor, the medieval emperor surpassed all other Rulers in dignity and excellence.

But as regards the substance of this Roman emperorship the two points of view differed fundamentally. According to the papal standpoint, this dignity is universal, because it is conferred by the Roman Church. The universality of the Church is reflected in the ideational universality of Roman emperorship. The emperor's universality is a reflexion, not indeed in degree, but in kind of that universality which is epitomized in the Roman Church which confers the dignity of emperorship through the medium of the pope. This may be a subtle, though we hold, a necessary distinction.[1] And the emperor is created for the specific purpose of protecting the Roman Church—hence the protector of the Roman Church, itself the epitome of the universal Church, must needs be conceived on the plane of an ideational universality.

On the other hand, the imperial standpoint did not view the substance of Roman emperorship from this functionalist angle. Accordingly, emperorship is universal, because it is Roman emperorship. The Ottonians (and later imperial generations) put upon Charlemagne's empire the complexion of the Roman empire; they interpreted his Romanism in the historical-political sense. To them Charlemagne appeared as the model monarch, *because* he was held to have been a Roman emperor. This imperial view of Roman emperorship was based, in the last resort, upon the ancient Teutonic idea of royal monarchy. Being the strongest monarchs in Europe, the German kings deemed it their right to be the Roman emperors.[2] The conferment of the Roman

---

*Archiv*, ix (1952), pp. 363 ff., and note 124. It is interesting to observe that the prophecy still played some part in the capture of Constantinople: according to Salimbene's report (MGH. SS. xxxii. 23–4) the Greeks fought fiercely against the Latin invaders and the inspiration of the Greeks was the Daniel prophecy (I owe this to Dr C. H. Talbot). Later at the end of the thirteenth century to the four empires was added a fifth, the empire of Christ "qui fuit verus Rex et verus *Monarcha*," Ptolomy of Lucca in his continuation of Thomas Aquinas's *De regimine principum*, about which see C. N. S. Woolf, *Bartolus of Sassoferrato*, pp. 318–20.

[1] This reflexion of the universality of the Roman Church in the empire is, we think, the ideological germ out of which later grew the allegory of sun (pope) and moon (emperor).

[2] And consequently universal rulers. And in periods of crisis and tension attempts will be made to restore the waning confidence by asserting the ideational

imperial crown by the pope was a necessary formality of a declaratory character. The substance of this emperorship was monarchic and autonomous, according to the imperial standpoint. There is no need for us to comment upon the ideological metamorphosis which Charlemagne had undergone, nor upon the inconsistencies of this point of view which tacitly brushed aside the genesis of medieval Roman emperorship. Genetically and ideologically he had grown out of the patrician of the Romans, and was always considered by his creator an *ad-vocatus*, an *adjutor*, a *brachium* of the Roman Church.

As we have said before, the identification of the *imperium christianum* with the *imperium Romanum* was one of the bequests of Charlemagne. This identification was of considerable weight with later imperial generations, and the temptation to identify both "empires" had by no means spent all its impetus by the time of the Staufens. But, however much, in a rough sense, Charles's identification corresponded to reality, from the mid-tenth century onwards these two terms began to express different ideas: this was one more feature which the imperial point of view disregarded. According to it, the *imperium christianum* was still the same as the *imperium Romanum*. This identification appears as a salient feature of the century between the first Otto's coronation and the third Henry's death. Hand in hand with this goes—again quite in accordance with the historical-political conception of Romanism—the quickening insistence on the Roman features of the empire, reaching its apogee in Otto III; and with this goes, again for evident reasons, the rivalry with the Eastern emperor and the concomitant borrowing of

---

universality of the emperor in concrete terms. For instance, in the stormy days of Frederick I, so full of stress and tension, Staufen ideology will operate with the ideologically significant term of "kinglings" (*reguli*) to denote kings as mere provincial governors within the empire; and the Eastern empire will sink to a mere "regnum Graeciae." Cf. on this now W. Holtzmann, op. cit., pp. 20, 22–3, with a special reference to Frederick's threat to the independence of France. Under his son, Henry VI, this threat to France was no less real, cf. Roger of Hoveden, iii. 301 (Rolls Series) ad 1195: "Notum erat regi Angliae, quod praedictus imperator (Henry) super omnia desiderabat, ut regnum Franciae Romanorum imperio subjaceret." The term *reguli* seems to have been coined by Benzo of Alba who wrote his poem for the imperial cause also in a period of crisis and stress; cf. P. E. Schramm, *Kaiser*, i. 256, note 5, and for details infra 387. In obvious allusion to the papalist sun-moon allegory, the Cistercian Caesar of Heisterbach, Henry VI's contemporary, says: "Just as the sun excels in size and splendour all the stars, in the same way the Roman empire shines forth more magnificently than all the kingdoms of the world. Here is the *monarchia*: as the stars receive their light from the sun, so have the kings their power from the emperor," *Dialogus miraculorum*, quoted from Th. Toeche, *Kaiser Heinrich VI*, Leipzig, 1867, p. 270.

Byzantine imperial features, and finally the utilization of the proprietary church system for governing the "imperium." These appear to be the salient features of that century. We can but briefly touch on these features and we do this merely in an attempt to bring the contrast between this system and its successor into clearer relief.

The title of Otto I for some years after his coronation was the simple "imperator" or "imperator augustus" without the epithet "Romanorum." This may or may not have deeper significance, although the assumption cannot be dismissed out of hand that this title without "Romanorum" was considered sufficient indication of the Roman character of this empire. But that this self-same (Roman) empire was also the Christian empire *par excellence*, cannot be legitimately doubted, considering the actual policy of Otto: he appeared as, and was, the foremost protector of Christianity in contemporary Europe. To all intents and purposes Otto considered his empire identical with the Christian empire, that entity which is made up of the Latin Christians.[1]

The intelligentsia of the Ottonian period bears witness to this Carolingian bequest of the identification of the empire with the Christian empire. At first Otto's empire was the "imperium Romanum" pure and simple, so, for instance, in the poems of the nun, Hrotsvita of Gandersheim. To her the empire could bear no other complexion than a Roman one: it was the "imperium Romanum" or "Caesarianum" or "Octavianum."[2] Almost simultaneously another school of thought appears which programmatically identifies the Roman empire with the Christian empire. Its chief representative was Adso of Montier-en-Der.[3] On the basis of his eschatological interpretation of the prophecy of Daniel he entirely identifies the Roman and Christian empires: "Roman" and "Christian" were interchangeable terms and ideas to

---

[1] Governmentally, of course, Otto I was *Rex-Sacerdos* (in the sense in which    †
we use the term, see supra 156) and this explains his strong hand in the liturgical reforms carried out during his long stays in Italy: it was he who transported into Italy and enforced in the Italian churches the rich liturgy so highly developed as it had been during the preceding decades (Pontifical of Mainz). On all this see Th. Klauser, "Die liturgischen Austauschbeziehungen etc." in *Hist. Jb.*, liii (1936), pp. 186–9. The pope installed after John's deposition, Leo VIII, was a layman and the first pope consecrated according to the new liturgy, see Klauser, p. 187, and M. Andrieu, "La carrière ecclésiastique des papes" in *Revue des sciences religieuses*, xxi (1947), pp. 109–10.
[2] See the fine study of C. Erdmann, "Das ottonische Reich als imperium Romanum" in *Deutsches Archiv*, vi (1943), pp. 421–6, where the hitherto overlooked and very significant expressions of the nun are given *in toto*.
[3] See Erdmann, art. cit., pp. 426–33.

him.[1] This empire was the last of the four and its idea is therefore imperishable although its material form was nearly ruined.[2] Hence under the presupposition that both empires were ideologically identical, the collapse of the Roman empire would mean the ruin of the Christian empire: the germs of the "Renovatio Romani imperii," the task of the Latin Christian, were contained in this point of view.[3] But when we now look at Odilo of Cluny, a representative of yet another school, though still French, writing in the first decade of the eleventh century, we shall see that, although to him too the idea of the "imperium Romanum" is of crucial importance, it is no longer identifiable with the "imperium christianum."[4] This is all the more important since Odilo of Cluny is one of the foremost Cluniacs: with them certainly the idea of a Christian empire begins visibly to detach itself from the idea of the Roman empire. As regards the functions of the Roman empire, there seems no divergence between Odilo and Adso: to both the Roman empire is indispensable for Christianity at large; to both the Christian empire needs the Roman empire as its protector.[5]

## III

Seen against the political and ideological background of his time, the "Wonder of the World," Otto III, may become accessible to understanding. His motto was Charlemagne:[6] his seal was Charlemagne's, upon which was engraved the head of an old man so as to leave no possible room for doubt; and ROMA on the other side of his seal was surrounded by the inscription: RENOVATIO IMPERII ROMANORUM.[7] But

[1] Erdmann, art. cit., p. 429: "einfache Gleichsetzung von Römer- und Christenreich."

[2] Erdmann, art. cit., p. 427.

[3] Erdmann, art. cit., p. 429: "Die Erneuerung des römischen Reiches wurde zu einer christlichen Aufgabe."

[4] See the passages cited by Erdmann, pp. 433–40.

[5] The deeper reason for the Cluniac attitude is to be sought in their ideas of "reform": they hoped to "reform" contemporary society, including of course the "sacerdotium," through the medium of the Roman empire. Hence the close connexion they had with the emperor in the early eleventh century, and hence also why the emperors appeared to them the providential saviours of Christendom. But cf. now G. Ladner's views on the Ottonian Renascence in "Die mittelalterliche Reformidee und ihr Verhältnis zur Renaissance" in *Festschrift f. A. Löhr* (MIOG. lx, 1952), pp. 54–5.

† [6] See especially R. Folz, op. cit., pp. 78 ff.

* [7] The sources concerning the coronation of Otto III are now well assembled by M. Uhlirz, "Zur Kaiserkrönung Ottos III" in *Festschrift f. E. E. Stengel*, Münster, 1952, pp. 263–7.

the fundamental difference between him and his great model is too obvious to need any comment: for Charlemagne the *Renovatio* was exclusively religious and orientated by Christian Rome; for Otto III it was exclusively political and orientated by ancient Rome. Otto's idea behind his *Renovatio* was that of Adso: in order to save Christianity, the fourth empire must be resurrected: the empire of the Romans is the vehicle, the only vehicle, which can raise Latin Christendom from the quagmire into which it had sunk. Undertaken in the interests of Christendom, this "renovation" was to be carried out by the wholesale adoption of old Roman official titles no less than by the wholesale borrowing of Byzantine models. Naturally, as "imperator Romanorum" Otto III could not tolerate that even in a detail the self-styled "Imperator Romanorum" in the East could surpass him.[1] Even the lance as an imperial standard carried before Otto III is reminiscent of the Byzantine model of the emperor's standard.[2] The former purely religious "renovatio" had now turned into a thoroughly political "renovatio": the former's unpolitical Romanism was replaced by a political Romanism.[3]

This "renovatio" however was only a transitory step in the ideological development of Otto III. For after the Gnesen campaign when he adopted the title "servus Jesu Christi," he advanced in 1001 to the height of "servus apostolorum."[4] There is in fact a consistent line of development on the part of the young emperor within the space of three years. First he introduces the "Renovatio" in April 998 on his seal;

[1] For details see Schramm, *Kaiser*, i. 105 ff.

[2] See Arnold, *De sancto Emmerano*: "(Otto) ex more precedente sancta et crucifera imperiali lancea exivit de civitate (Ratisbon) petiturus Italiam," quoted by Eichmann, op. cit., i. 186, who held that the lance was "das abendländische Gegenstück zu der byzantinischen Kaiserstandarte, die, von einem Kreuz überhöht, dem Kaiser vorangetragen wurde." On the history and the problem as to whether the lance had political significance or was merely a relic (which guaranteed victory in battle) see W. Holtzmann, *König Heinrich und die heilige Lanze*, Bonn, 1947, pp. 15 ff., 58 ff. (here also a review of the relevant literature). The older view that the *Libellus de ceremoniis* was composed in Otto III's time, must be rejected, see Schramm, op. cit., i. 193 ff., 202 ff.; against this is A. Michel, *Papstwahl & Königsrecht*, Stuttgart, 1936, p. 172, note 161, and p. 195, note 230.

[3] About the probable time and the source which directly inspired his *Renovatio* (Gerbert with his triumphant exclamation: "Nostrum, nostrum est imperium Romanum") see Erdmann, *Forschungen*, pp. 107–9, supporting an earlier view of Schramm (*Hist. Z.*, cxxix, 1924, pp. 462–3.)

[4] One is inevitably reminded of the Eastern ἰσαπόστολος, the emperor being the thirteenth apostle; cf. also Ohnsorge, op. cit., p. 70. We think that this title of Otto III was not only an attempt to combine papal and Byzantine conceptions, but also a (daring) attempt to repudiate the Leonine theory of the jurisdictional primacy of the Roman Church.

then, on 17 January 1000, he adds to the title "imperator Romanorum" the designation "servus Jesu Christi";[1] this is replaced in the following year by the designation "sacrarum ecclesiarum fidelissimus et devotissimus dilatator";[2] and lastly there emerges in his title the "servus apostolorum":

Otto servus apostolorum et secundum voluntatem Dei salvatoris Romanorum imperator augustus.[3]

The "imperium christianum" is identified with the "imperium Romanum" and hence its leadership must be in the hands of the one "imperator Romanorum." The identity of the two empires entailed that there must be identity of rulership; as head of the Roman empire Otto III was "imperator Romanorum"; as head of the Christian empire he was "servus apostolorum."[4] The government of this one body was concentrated in the one who, by his title, expressed his most intimate relationship with the apostles, especially with St Peter. Otto III was emperor and "pope."[5] Or in the more familiar terminology of bygone days, Otto III was *rex* and *sacerdos*.[6] The Renovatio of the Roman empire entailed the Renovatio of the Christian empire.

This new double function of the emperor appears first in the famous Diploma which is of particular concern to us. Issued between 18 and

[1] DO. III. 344 ff.

[2] DO. III. 388, issued in Rome under this title: "Otto tercius secundum voluntatem Jesu Christi Romanorum imperator augustus sanctarum ecclesiarum . . . dilatator."

[3] DO. III. 389, and its contents (see infra 241) leave no doubt about the significance of the title emerging in precisely this Diploma.

[4] If the year 1001—the last of his life—is any indication of the trend of his ideology, it seems that the title "servus apostolorum" was going to oust the "imperator Romanorum" altogether. In the following DD. after 389/90, the intitulatio is simply: "Otto tercius servus apostolorum"; DO. III. 407, 409, 412, 414–16, 419, 422.

[5] The court proceedings of DO. III. 396, of 4 April 1001, were first signed by "Otto servus apostolorum subscripsi" to which the pope adds his signature: "Ego Silvester s. catholicae et apostolicae ecclesiae Romanae praesul huic refutationi et sponsioni ut supra legitur, praefui et subscripsi." Cf. also Schramm, op. cit., i. 158, note 5.

[6] As early as November 998, Otto III presided together with Gregory V in a synod at St Peter's, Rome, in which a Spanish bishop was deposed and another put in his place. This is, we think, a clear instance in which the emperor acting on his claim as an ideational universal *Rex-Sacerdos* intervened in a purely ecclesiastical and organizational matter. On the affair itself see R. Holtzmann, op. cit., p. 352; here also the facsimile of the document (J. 3888) with Otto's signature; cf. now also W. Holtzmann, op. cit., p. 15: "Otto III hat aus seiner Kaiserwürde Folgerungen gezogen, welche über den gewohnten geographischen Bereich des Imperiums hinausgingen. *Sie sind aber beschränkt auf das Kirchenregiment.*" (Italics mine.)

23 January 1001[1] this document also expresses the double function of Rome itself: Rome is no longer the apostolic city, but the *urbs regia*, hence the capital of the world, and *therefore* the Church of Rome is the mother church of all other churches. It is as a consequence of his double function, the imperial and apostolic, that Otto III has the authority to testify to this:

Romam caput mundi profitemur, Romanam ecclesiam matrem omnium ecclesiarum testamur.

And because he testifies to this position of Rome,[2] he finds it particularly exasperating that the pontiffs have so much blackened the record of the city.

(Testamur), sed incuria et inscientia pontificum longe suae claritatis titulos obfuscasse.

Not only have they claimed what is not theirs, but what they had, had sold, spoilt or embezzled. And when all had gone, they came to the emperor asking for more. Asking for more, he exclaims, basing their claims on those false tales which they fabricated under the name of the Great Constantine and which they made the deacon John write in golden letters. The popes base their claims on those other figments by which they say that a certain Charles (II) had given to St Peter "our public goods." "To which we reply that Charles could not give anything away by right. He had given away what he did not possess. Brushing aside these imaginary scraps of paper and fairy tales, *we*, out of our munificence, make a present to St Peter from those territories which are ours. Just as *we* have elected for the love St Peter the Lord Silvester, our teacher, and as *we* have by God's will ordered and *created him pope*, so do we now confer on St Peter through Silvester gifts from our public imperial property." This gift consisted of the eight counties of the Pentapolis.[3] The pope was not, however, the owner of these eight counties, but merely their administrator.

[1] According to Th. Sickel, ad DO. III. 389, p. 819.

[2] As a "novus Constantinus" Otto III built new churches at Rome, about which see E. Mâle, *Rome et ses vieilles églises*, Paris, 1944, pp. 133–59.

[3] DO. III. 389. About editions, literature and authorship (Bishop Leo of Vercelli) see Sickel, loc. cit., and Schramm, op. cit., i. 166, ii. 65. We quote from Schramm's edition, pp. 66–7: "In nomine sanctae et individuae Trinitatis Otto servus apostolorum et secundum voluntatem Dei salvatoris Romanorum imperator augustus. Romam caput mundi profitemur, Romanam ecclesiam matrem omnium ecclesiarum esse testamur, sed incuria et inscientia pontificum longe suae claritatis titulos obfuscasse. Nam non solum, quae extra Urbem esse videbantur, vendiderunt et quibusdam colluviis a lare s. Petri alienaverunt, sed—quod absque

9 *

It is plain that according to Otto III the papacy had no right to the territories hitherto claimed as their own. The title-deed of their claim is declared null and void—the Donation of Constantine is a fabrication from which no rights can flow. This fictitious basis of papal possessions must be supplanted by an act of the emperor himself. On account of his imperial and apostolic capacity he could not allow any other title-deed to possessions than his own. The Ottonian Donation is therefore the effluence of imperial omnipotence. It is moreover a Donation which is prompted by the recognition of the services which he had received from his former master, Gerbert, now created pope by the imperial will.[1] Perhaps no particular significance should be attached to the omission of the usual designation of the pope as "spiritualis

---

\*   dolore non dicimus—si quid in hac nostra Urbe regia habuerunt, a maiori licentia evagarentur, omnibus judicante pecunia in commune dederunt et s. Petrum, s. Paulum, ipsa quoque altaria spoliaverunt et pro reparatione semper confusionem induxerunt. Confusis vero papaticis legibus et jam abjecta ecclesia Romana, in tantum quidam pontificum irruerunt, ut maximam partem imperii nostri apostolatui suo conjungerent, jam non quaerentes, quae et quanta suis culpis perdiderunt, non curantes, quanta ex voluntaria vanitate effuderunt, sed sua propria, utpote ab illis ipsis dilapidata, dimittentes, quasi culpam suam in imperium nostrum retorquentes, ad aliena, id est ad nostra et nostri imperii, maxime migraverunt. Haec sunt commenta ab illis ipsis inventa, quibus Johannes diaconus cognomento digitorum mutilus, praeceptum aureis litteris scripsit, sub titulo magni Constantini longa mendacii tempora finxit. Haec sunt alia commenta, quibus dicunt, quendam Karolum s. Petro nostra publica tribuisse. Sed ad haec respondemus ipsum Karolum nichil dare jure potuisse, utpote jam a Karolo meliore fugatum, jam imperio privatum, jam destitutum et adnullatum. Ergo: quod non habuit, dedit; sic dedit, sicut nimirum dare potuit, utpote qui male adquisivit, et diu se possessurum non speravit. Spretis ergo commenticiis preceptis et imaginariis scriptis, ex nostra liberalitate s. Petro donamus, quae nostra sunt, non sibi, quae sua sunt, veluti nostra conferimus. Sicut enim pro amore s. Petri domnum Silvestrum magistrum nostrum papam elegimus et Deo volente ipsum serenissimum ordinavimus et creavimus, ita pro amore ipsius domni Silvestri papae s. Petro de publico nostro dona conferimus, ut habeat magister, quid principi nostro Petro a parte sui discipuli offerat." Then follows the enumeration of the eight counties.

The deacon mentioned here, Johannes, had to make an ornamental copy of the Donation of Constantine by order of John XII, on the occasion of Otto I's Roman sojourn in 962. Later, but before 964, John XII had the deacon's fingers chopped off, hence his nickname. He fled to Otto's court revealing the secret of the Donation, hence Otto III's knowledge; on all this see Schramm, op. cit., i. 70–1, 163, and I. M. Watterich, *Romanorum pontificum vitae*, i. 42. The text of the Donation may have been supplied by that contained in *Pseudo-Isidore*, see G. Tellenbach, *Libertas*, p. 221.

[1] It seems fairly certain that the choice of the name Silvester by Gerbert aroused some suspicions in his "creator," especially as Otto was familiar with the secrets contained in the bosom of the Roman Church which were revealed to his grandfather by John the deacon.

pater noster": but there can be little doubt about the functions allotted to Silvester by Otto: he was no more than the chief metropolitan within the ambit of the "orbis Romanus."

On the other hand, the Ottonian Donation is also directed against the Eastern aspirations. Not only is Rome—and not Constantinople—the *urbs regia*, but also the Byzantine Church stands in a filial relationship to the Roman Church. Indeed, it is the whole "orbis Romanus" that is seen by Otto in his twofold capacity.[1] According to him, the "orbis Romanus" was nothing else than the political conception of Christianity. Hence, *Roma caput mundi*, and the unity of this universal body politic presupposes unity in its government: Otto appears as the supreme monarch.

But this Ottonian Donation signifies more than the mere assertion of the emperor's imperial and apostolic capacity. It brings into clearest possible relief Otto's function as the supreme monarch and protector. We think that here is the link with the prevalent institution of the proprietary church system, whose ideological strength lay in the king's affording protection to a weak and defenceless body, the sacerdotal hierarchy. In the exercise of his monarchical rule, the king had the right to install the bishop in his ecclesiastical functions: the bishop thereby came under the special protection of his "creator." It is this idea of protection (in the royal sense) which cemented the proprietary church system ideologically. The protection afforded by the owner of the church—and in the widest sense the king was "owner" of every bishopric—was the inner ferment of the system, fortified as this was by the oath of fealty taken by the bishop. The bond thus created was a very personal one. As a protector the king had a very natural interest in the maintenance of his property. He could, if he considered it expedient, concede to certain collegiate bodies, the right to elect their superior,[2] but in the case of the important episcopal sees and as the one

---

[1] Cf. DO. III. 390, of 23 January 1001.

[2] The examples of these *Wahlprivilegia* are too numerous to be quoted. Cf. e.g., DO. III. 269: "Insuper etiam statuimus et confirmamus per hanc nostri praecepti paginam atque inviolabilem auctoritatem ut quandoquidem abbas de ipso monasterio ex hac luce migraverit . . . tunc qualem digniorem et meliorem de ipsa congregatione fratres invenerint, licentiam habeant eligendi et ipse qui electus est a nostra imperiali potestate . . . sine ulla contradictione inimicorum investiatur"; or DO. III. 319: "Insuper etiam privilegium dedimus monachis praesentibus et cunctis qui post eos futuri sunt in eodem loco, abbatem inter se eligere secundum regulam sancti Benedicti"; for Otto II cf. DO. II. 142: "Concessimus etiam praedictis sanctimonialibus ex imperiali majestate per privilegii huius munitionem licentiam eligendi inter se abbatissam Dei servitio aptam . . ."

most directly interested in the administration and organization of his churches, he himself exercised the right to see that a suitable incumbent was appointed: in these cases the king proceeded by simple nomination; and of Silvester II Otto says: "elegimus . . . ordinavimus et creavimus."

There is therefore a noteworthy parallel between the protective function of the Teutonic king and the protective function of the prototype of every *Rex-Sacerdos*, Justinian. Although in their origins independent, the two conceptions of rulership had so many elements in common that for all practical purposes they were identical. Teutonic and Byzantine ideas[1] in this respect were so similar to each other that the wholesale borrowing of Byzantine ideas and forms by essentially Teutonic rulers may have a simple explanation. Both governmental systems relied heavily on the *sacerdotium*, and the Teutonic manner of harnessing the *sacerdotium* to the governmental machinery by way of the proprietary church system was, in our opinion, merely a practical modification of the same principle, perhaps furthered by the prevalent feudal conceptions.[2] To both systems, the Eastern and the Western, it was essential that a *suitable* candidate was appointed for the see. Here we find the principle of idoneity or suitability which was of such crucial importance to the hierocratic system too. But whereas in the latter system the suitability concerned the Ruler himself, in the former it concerned the ecclesiastics, above all, the bishops, and of course the pope. To all three systems, the *sacerdotium* was an indispensable vehicle by which the respective policies were to be carried out. And in a way one might say that the later Investiture Contest was essentially a fight over the control of the *sacerdotium*.[3]

---

[1] See, for instance, the prefaces to Justinian's *Novellae*, vi; lxxxv; and lxxxvi.

[2] That the proprietary church was not unknown in the East has been proved, cf. P. Thomas, *Le droit de propriété des laiques sur les églises*, Paris, 1906, especially pp. 3–11.

[3] The Ottonian (and Salian) governmental systems stand and fall with the *sacerdotium* as the agency of the government. The benefits accruing to imperial power can hardly be exaggerated; by virtue of the proprietary church system the king was free to install the ablest cleric wherever he found it necessary; for good examples under Otto I see R. Holtzmann, *Kaiser Otto d. Gr.*, Leipzig, 1936, pp. 96–7; the king had no need to take into consideration territorial or regional motives; the system was also immune to the cancer of hereditary succession with all its inherent dangers of decomposition; the members of the *sacerdotium* were —one has only to look at the DD and the immediate entourage of the kings— highly cultured men, versed in literature, history and politics: the *cancellaria* of the kings was staffed with precisely these men. Indeed the chancery was the nursery of influential bishops and archbishops, since the vacant sees were filled from

What seems important was that the idea of royal protection was carried by Otto III to its logical conclusion. Indeed, the *Ottonianum* made an attempt at this when it initiated the somewhat clumsy machinery of an oath to be enforced by the Romans from the pope. The *Ottonianum* was a patched-up document which did not make any fundamental pronouncement, and because of this shortcoming the third Otto may have refused to confirm it; he also recognized that the donations contained in the document were based upon slender foundations. But in the Ottonian Donation we have in fact a programmatic declaration of him who was supreme monarch and therefore supreme protector of everyone in his "orbis Romanus," including the papacy. And the angry outburst of Otto about the squandering of papal possessions by the pontiffs is the outburst of one who believes that his own property has been the subject of wanton spoliation. Hence a clean sweep has to be made. And he programmatically declares that the pope —in no way different from any other bishop—owes his position to him: he also declares that the pope *qua* pope has no right to territories. The donation to St Peter through the hands of the pope who is to be the trustee of the territories, is the effluence of Otto's imperial and apostolic omnipotence.

Monarchy means supreme rulership carried out by means of the law and the appropriate agencies. For the Ottonian system this entailed a function of the pope which was not unlike that accorded to him by Otto's great model, Charlemagne. Whether or not Otto acknowledged the magisterial primacy of the Roman Church is of no concern to us, but what is of concern is that the jurisdictional primacy of the Roman Church was denied. The pope was not, and could not be, given the right to surround his pronouncements with the halo of a legal sanction. The conception of true monarchy militated against this. The pope is, in Otto's conceptions, the chief priest in the "orbis Romanus," appointed by the "servus apostolorum." The former Justinianean prescription of an imperial confirmation of the elected pope had now degenerated into a straight imperial appointment. This manner of making a pope was, naturally enough, based upon the principle

---

the ranks of the royal chancery personnel. Cf. now also W. Holtzmann, *Das mittelalterliche Imperium*, cit., p. 7, who speaks of the great advantage which the Ottonian empire had through the "Hereinnahme der Kirche in den Staat"; the Capetians at the same time lost all influence on the *sacerdotium*, ibid. For the composition of the German royal chancery and its tasks in the tenth and eleventh centuries, see H. W. Klewitz, "Königtum, Hofkapelle und Domkapitel" in *Arch. f. Urkundenforsch.*, xvi (1939), pp. 102-34.

of suitability, and Otto had every reason for finding Gerbert suitable. The spirituality of the papal—as indeed of every sacerdotal—office made it imperative that in this Christian "orbis Romanus" only the best and most suitable should be raised to this dignity. It is at this point that the "reforming" Cluniacs come into the picture, and Otto III himself was very much influenced by Odilo of Cluny. As the supreme protector Otto III, not unlike Justinian, had to see that his empire, Roman and Christian as it was, was given the best men. This astonishing parallelism between East and West led to a still more intensified copying of Eastern features and the adoption of ancient Roman elements, particularly by contemporary littérateurs, of which none is perhaps more significant than the *Graphia* circle. And the renascence of Roman legal studies was an inescapable consequence.

To sum up, Otto III's standpoint was focused upon the implementation of the monarchic principle. The monarch rules over that body politic which, by virtue of its universal character, is Roman and Christian. The basis of this view is the idea that this political entity is entrusted to him by God: he as the divinely appointed monarch must therefore rule, that is, guide and direct that body politic, of which the cementing idea was that of the Christian faith. In this sense his empire was indeed Roman—in the other, political, sense the empire could call itself Roman only as a result of accepting papal ideology, according to which the Roman empire was dispensed by the pope. In either sense the ideological weakness of Otto's position is apparent. It was a governmental theory which bore all the germs of its own destruction within itself. Was he functionally qualified to lead a body politic whose substratum was a spiritual element, the Christian faith? Was not his own Romanism the tacit acceptance of the papal theme?

## IV

The implementation of the monarchic principle by Otto III's successors is still more pronounced. They considered themselves as monarchs in the most literal sense of the term. They bore themselves as the divinely appointed Rulers over the entity which they called the empire of the Romans. In this capacity they had at heart all the interests affecting that body. And since this body over which they ruled was substantially Christian, they had a particular predilection for the regeneration of the *sacerdotium*.

Henry II's title

Heinricus servus servorum Christi et Romanorum imperator augustus secundum voluntatem Dei et salvatoris nostrique liberatoris[1]

neatly expresses the monarchic function in its twofold aspects: he is "servus servorum Christi," an obvious borrowing of the papal title, and he also is emperor of the Romans. As the monarch of this Christian body politic calling itself Roman empire, his foremost function as a protector is to see that the spiritual life is regenerated. The protecting hand of the emperor can be witnessed in every vital sphere of contemporary life.

Henry II is an effective reformer of monastic institutions: on his behalf and by his order monastic reforms are carried out at Prüm, Hersfeld, Berge near Magdeburg, Reichenau, Fulda, Corvey, Stablo-Malmedy, St Maximine near Trier, Gandersheim, and so forth.[2] Certain organizational matters also fall into the competency of the emperor: a number of smaller monastic institutions were incorporated by his order into the framework of great episcopal churches, a measure which greatly increased their economic efficiency.[3] It is probably true that Henry II's zeal was to a great extent inspired by the Cluniacs.[4] Vacant episcopal sees were filled by simple nominations—"dono regis episcopus fiebat" as a chronicler reported[5]—having had due regard to the principle of suitability. He it was who erected Bamberg,[6] and who

[1] DH. II. 284, issued at Rome, on the occasion of his imperial coronation in 1014. In this context attention should be drawn to the picture of Henry II which depicts him crowned by Christ Himself, see P. E. Schramm, *Die deutschen Könige & Kaiser in Bildern ihrer Zeit*, Table 85a; cf. also Table 85b which shows Henry crowned by a hand reaching down from heaven (with this should be compared the Roman picture reproduced by Alföldi, supra p. 17), whilst yet a third shows him crowned by the Holy Ghost, Table 86. The crown is the characteristically Byzantine crown showing the *pendilia* on both sides, see Schramm, Text, p. 110. Cf. also Table 81 showing Christ Who crowns Henry being sponsored by St Peter, whilst his wife, Cunigunde, is sponsored by St Paul, Text pp. 107–8, 197. The difference between Henry II and Otto III emerges clearly—and hence also the difference in their titles—when one looks at Table 78 showing Otto III crowned by SS. Peter and Paul; cf. also Text, pp. 101–2. In this context attention should also be drawn to the intitulation of the Spanish king, Ordonius III in 954: "Servus servorum Domini," see E. E. Stengel, in *Deutsches Archiv*, iii (1939), p. 9, note 1, who also noted the parallel to the papal title.
[2] One should beware of exaggerating the decadence of monastic life in imperial monasteries, cf. now K. Hallinger, *Gorze-Kluny*, in *Studia Anselmiana philosophica-theologica*, xxii–xxv, 1950–1.
[3] For details of Henry's "church policy" see the lucid account in H. Mikoletzky, *Kaiser Heinrich II und die Kirche*, Vienna, 1946.
[4] Cf. Mikoletzky, op. cit., pp. 11 ff., who observes that the Cluny movement could never have succeeded without Henry II.
[5] *Chron. s. Laurentii Leodiensis*, MGH. SS. viii. 267.
[6] For details see now Th. Mayer, "Die Anfänge des Bistums Bamberg" in *Festschrift Stengel*, 1952, pp. 272–88.

revived the suppressed bishopric of Merseburg, who transformed the abbey of Bobbio—Columban's foundation—into a bishopric. Numerous ecclesiastical synods were held under his presidency, the convocation having been in his hands. It is in his function as monarch that he confirms papal privileges[1] or that he confers on abbots and monks the privilege of having the imperial tribunal as their proper court.[2] Externally, too, Henry II appeared as the personification of the monarchic idea: he used to wear a gown which was said to denote universal dominion, the so-called *Weltenmantel*.[3] It was a garment ornamented with apocalyptic and zodiacal figures, and had been worn by the biblical high-priests:[4] it manifested his regal-sacerdotal position.[5] In short, Henry's empire was a priest-state: the "populus Christianus" as he understood the term, was entrusted to him, and being a Christian people they had to be given suitable ecclesiastical officers. The *sacerdotium* was to be regenerated because it was vital to the governmental machinery of Henry II.

From the point of view of protection the confirmation of the *Ottonianum* by Henry II[6] becomes understandable. The natural assumption is that this so-called *Privilegium* would have been confirmed at Henry's imperial coronation in 1014,[7] provided always that it really was a privilege conferred on the Roman Church. What was not done in 1014, was done six years later, at Bamberg, on the occasion of Pope Benedict VIII's memorable visit to the emperor. The pope obviously considered the Ottonian Donation unsatisfactory from every point of view: above all, there was no undertaking of protecting the territories ceded. The pope's visit to Bamberg was prompted by the advance of the Byzantine armies in Southern Italy which clearly threatened the city of Rome. And in order to obtain a firm undertaking of protection of the patrimony of St Peter from Henry II, Benedict undertook the

---

[1] Cf. DH. II. 494, of 2 September 1023, to the monastery of Fruttuaria.

[2] DH. II. 475, to the monastery of S. Salvator near Isola.

[3] See Schramm, in *Studi Gregoriani*, ii. 429; Eichmann, *Kaiserkrönung*, i. 149. About Otto III's dalmatic see M. Uhlirz, "Zur Kaiserkrönung Ottos III" in *Festschrift Stengel*, pp. 263–4.

[4] Cf. *Ex.* xxviii. 4; *Lev.* viii. 7.

[5] Schramm, *König von Frankreich*, p. 160, note 2.

[6] DH. II. 427 = MGH. *Const.* i. no. 33, pp. 65–70.

[7] This was indeed assumed by no less an authority than Baronius, *Ann. Ecclesiastici*, ad 1014, ed. Lucca, 1744, xvi. 487. Although he does not know when the privilege was conferred, Baronius says, "nihilominus tamen ex consuetudine praedecessorum imperatorum, qui similia privilegia statim post imperialem a pontifice susceptam coronam eidem tradiderunt, facile possumus colligere" that it was given at Henry's coronation in 1014.

journey across the Alps. Naturally, as the supreme protector Henry did not refuse Benedict's request. The price which the pope paid for the promise of protection was high: for we recall that the *Ottonianum* also contained in its second part severe restrictions imposed upon the papacy. Henry, from his monarchic point of view, had of course no scruples in confirming what the first Otto had enacted. The reason why there was no re-issue of the document on the occasion of Henry's coronation seems rather obvious: the pope considered it incongruous and incompatible with his function as the dispenser of imperial dignity to ask for confirmation of the *Ottonianum*. For it was at Henry's coronation that *Ordo C*, the herald of a new age, was first applied, and the ideas underlying this *Ordo* militated against submitting a request for the confirmation of the *Ottonianum* with its severe restrictions on the papacy.

The ruthless exploitation for governmental purposes of the *sacerdotium* by Conrad II, the first Salian emperor, is perhaps the most characteristic feature of his reign. Consequently, the criterion he applied to episcopal appointments and depositions was not so much that of suitability for the spiritual office, but rather that of usefulness to the crown. Against useless ecclesiastics Conrad proceeded severely and adamantly. Archbishop Burchard of Lyons was kept in chains for years; Archbishop Aribert of Milan was arrested and deposed by imperial decree; the bishops of Piacenza, Cremona and Vercelli were exiled. In Conrad II one meets an upright and stern, though coldly calculating monarch, to whom the *sacerdotium* was a mere machine. That the Roman Church was perhaps not even credited with magisterial primacy, may well be true. The public burning by the bishop of Constance of a bull of John XIX on Maundy Thursday 1033 throws significant light on the frame of mind of a part of the episcopacy; nor is it less significant that the archbishop of Mainz addressed Conrad as "vicarius Christi."[1] There can have been few medieval monarchs who

---

[1] See Wipo, *Gesta Chuonradi imperatoris*, MGH. SS. xi. 260, ad 8 September 1024, the day on which Conrad was anointed and crowned at Mainz. About the jubilations on this occasion Wipo says that "si Carolus magnus cum sceptro vivus adesset, non alacrior populus fuisset nec plus gaudere valeret de tanti viri reditu." In his speech the archbishop of Mainz said, amongst other things, this: "Omnis potestas fluitantis saeculi de uno fonte purissimo derivatur . . . is omnipotens rex regum, totius honoris auctor et principium, quando in principes terrae alicuius dignitatis gratiam transfundit . . . tecum et propter te nobis est sermo, domne rex. Dominus, qui te elegit ut esses rex super populum suum, ipse te prius voluit probare et postmodum regnare . . . passus es injurias, ut nunc scias misereri sustinentibus injurias; pietas divina voluit te esse sine disciplina, ut post coeleste

acted so faithfully in the spirit of the Roman Caesars as Conrad did, the first to adopt the title which was the preliminary to full imperial dignity, that of "Rex Romanorum." And on his seal the inscription embodied his ideological programme:

Roma caput mundi tenet orbis frena rotundi.[1]

Logically enough, the Roman laws were bolstered up, at least as far as Rome was concerned:[2] as we indicated before, the "Renovatio" of the Roman empire entailed a "renovatio legum Romanarum." Nevertheless, despite the accentuation of the Roman character of his empire, Conrad was not Roman emperor until he had received the imperial crown from John XIX's hands.[3]

The appellation of Henry III as the apotheosis of the medieval ideal of a monarch, would not seem inadequate: in fact, he was the personification of the monarch who, appointed by God to rule his people, had, in his function as supreme protector, to take care of all their interests. And since his empire was Christian, Christian interests came before every other consideration.[4]

---

magisterium christianum caperes imperium. Ad summam dignitatem pervenisti, *vicarius es Christi*." Cf. also Thietmar of Merseburg, quoted infra 264. Because he considered himself *christus Domini*, Frederick I, some 130 years later applied to himself the vicariate of Christ: "Imperatoria majestas, quae regis regum et domini dominantium vicem gerit in terris, in gubernatione universitatis . . .", MGH. *Const*. i. no. 240, p. 335.

[1] On this and the literary source see Schramm, *Kaiser*, i. 212, 227, 284 f. It was in Conrad's time that the *Graphia* came to be written in its original form which was made up of all sorts of sources, mainly Byzantine, because its author held that in Constantinople the unadulterated "Romanism" could be found, see Schramm, i. 203–4, 216; ed. of the text, ibid., ii. 73 ff. Of particular interest is the *Libellus de ceremoniis aule imperatoris*, ed. ibid., ii. 90 ff., modelled on the *Liber de cerimoniis* of Constantine Porphyrogenitos and adapting the latter's ideological symbolism for Roman-Western conditions. Significantly enough the emperor is correctly styled: *Monokrator* (cap. 4).        [2] MGH. *Const*. i. no. 37, p. 82.

[3] Raoul Glaber living in this time, reflects the temper of the period when he says that nobody can be called emperor who is not crowned by the pope. See his *Historia*, MGH. SS. vii. 59, lines 11 ff.: "Illud nihilominus nimium concedens ac perhonestum videtur atque ad pacis tutelam optimum decretum, scil. ut ne quisquam audacter Romani imperii sceptrum praeporerus gestare princeps appetat, seu imperator dici aut esse valeat, nisi quem papa sedis Romanae morum probitate aptum delegerit reipublicae eique commiserit insigne imperiale." About a general review of this writer cf. P. Rousset, "Raoul Glaber interprète de la pensée commune au xi siècle" in *Revue d'histoire de l'église de France*, xxxvi (1951), pp. 5–24; and about the plan of dividing the world and the churches into East and West reported by him, see A. Michel, "Die Weltreichs- und Kirchenteilung des R. Glaber" in *Hist. Jb.*, lxx (1951), pp. 62–4.

[4] About the deep religiosity of Henry III see G. Ladner, *Theologie und Politik vor dem Investiturstreit*, Vienna, 1936, pp. 70–1.

It is only from this point of view that one can understand his episcopal and papal appointments. In each case he, as the monarch of the Christian empire, had to see that the candidate was suitable for his office, and also that he was useful to the monarch. Since the episcopacy was a governmental organ as well as the body administering to the spiritual, Henry's predilection and zeal for reform is understandable. Again, the frequent councils in his reign furnish abundant evidence of his deep religious concerns. Naturally the "reform" of the episcopacy was without practical avail, so long as the "caput sacerdotum" was not reformed—and the papacy at the time of Henry's accession presented a spectacle peremptorily demanding reform. As supreme protector of Christendom—as far as this was realized in his empire—he could not but be resolved to take matters into his own hands. The papacy being the chief protectorate of the empire—in fact an episcopal see on a magnified scale—had to be purged of the unsuitable and useless individuals. Constitutionally inclined as he was, Henry III would not act and depose the two popes without a synod, at which he presided himself.[1] Sutri signifies the consummation of the monarch's supreme protective functions: Christendom had to be protected against these unworthy individuals.

It is nevertheless worthy of remark that Henry III, insisting on strict constitutional principles, had conferred upon himself the office of a patrician by the Romans. This office was to give him the handle by which he proceeded to the direct appointment of the popes. By this step he pursued the aim, on the one hand, of depriving the Roman nobility of their hold over the papacy[2] and, on the other hand, of being in a position to appoint the popes directly—in a no wise different manner from that of the appointment of a bishop in the empire. We may observe in parenthesis that although this constitutional device enabled Henry to treat the papacy as just another bishopric, the office of the patriciate additional to the imperial dignity was something of an historic anomaly. For no emperor had ever been a patrician—the latter was appointed by the former.[3] In Frankish times we recall, the emperor absorbed the office of the patrician.

[1] For the whole question see the detailed study of G. B. Borino, "L'elezione e deposizione di Gregorio VI" in *Archivio della R. societa Romana*, xxxix (1916), pp. 141–252; 295–410, especially pp. 208 ff.; R. L. Poole, "Benedict IX and Gregory VI" in *Proc. Brit. Acad.*, viii (1917), pp. 199 ff., at pp. 212 ff., and also G. Tellenbach, *Libertas*, pp. 212–17.

[2] The Crescentii had the title conferred on themselves by the Roman nobility, but the title seems to have disappeared since 1012, see G. B. Borino, art. cit., pp. 361 ff., and Schramm, op. cit., i. 189, 230; also Tellenbach, op. cit., p. 216 note.

[3] This was emphasized by the author of the *Libellus*, cap. 20. ed. cit., ii. 103:

Henry III utilized his authority of appointing popes to the full; and those whom he appointed were throughout men of the highest calibre —Clement II, Damasus II, Leo IX, and Victor II—whose suitability for the office could never be called into question. If ever a monarch acted in consonance with the functions and principles that animated his policy, it was Henry III. As a Christian monarch in the most literal meaning of the term, Henry, by exercising his protective functions, demonstrated how a true monarchic form of government could be practised. He gave his Christian empire an episcopacy and a papacy, in short ministers who were commensurate to their calling. His papal appointments were the effluence of his duty as the supreme monarch ruling a Christian empire. In an inverted sense he may be spoken of as the "brachium sanctae Romanae ecclesiae," whose help proved of inestimable and historic value for the implementation of the hierocratic system.

To say that Henry's fatal mistake lay in the—to him and to others —attractive and persuasive equation of Christian empire with his Roman empire, is to state a truism. The idea of universality inherent in Roman emperorship was understood in a factual manner, instead of in a functional sense. By its very nature Roman emperorship gave the papacy a strong preponderance; and, considering the previous development of hierocratic ideology, it was incongruous to admit the magisterial primacy of the Roman Church and at the same time deny its jurisdictional primacy, epitomized as this was in the Petrine commission. But this is precisely what Henry III—and his predecessors— failed to grasp. All were insistent on the essential Christian-theocentric nature of their own body politic—which was, from any objective point of view, merely a part, albeit an important one, of a greater and wider society—and this insistence on the character of their society so largely explains their policy and governmental systems. But was the monarchic rule of a king—even if he was also called "imperator Romanorum"— compatible with the essence of the society over which he ruled and which in any case was only a part of a larger body? If this society was Christian, by what authority do kings and emperors preside as monarchs over it? Are they functionally qualified to govern monarchically a society that is Christian, which in other words receives its life blood from the Roman Church? Could the king or emperor be a

---

the patrician appointed by the emperor "sit enim valde notus imperatori, sit fidelis et prudens, non elatus . . ." About Otto III's appointment of patricians and its significance see Erdmann, *Forschungen*, pp. 105–6.

monarch in a completely Christo-centric world that acknowledged the primatial function of the Roman Church, the epitome of the whole Christian world? Was not the function of the king or emperor in this kind of society on quite a different level?

To these questions the lay point of view could not find a satisfactory answer. What the hierocratic point of view had hitherto lacked was the kind of men whom Henry III was to provide by violating one of the most cherished hierocratic tenets, that is, by direct imperial appointment. Hierocratic tenets were ready to be implemented—Henry III, the supreme protector, furnished the men who were to make his son a protector in a different sense, because he was "filius, non praesul, ecclesiae" which latter term denoted the corporate union of all Christians, the *societas christiana*.

## V

A brief consideration of the new coronation *Ordo C* may provide a suitable transition to the succeeding age. The—to all seeming—imposing edifice of royal monarchy had already been gravely undermined: the very act that made the king an "imperator Romanorum," symbolized the strength of the papal theme, and at the same time also exposed the inconsistency of the laical-monarchic standpoint.

Despite some controversy about the date of this *Ordo C*,[1] there is overwhelming evidence that it was composed in the early eleventh century, and that this *Ordo C* formed in fact the coronation rite for the imperial coronations in this century, beginning with the coronation of Henry II in 1014.[2] Still based on the *Liber Diurnus*[3] as well as on

---

[1] Formerly known as *Ordo Cencius II*, see supra p. 225.

[2] We accept Eichmann's reasons for the dating of *Ordo C*, see his "Der Krönungsordo Cencius II" in *Misc. F. Ehrle*, 1926, ii. 322 ff.; "Zur Datierung des sog. Cencius II" in *Hist. Jb.*, lii, 1932, pp. 265–312; "Das Verhältnis von Cencius I und II" in *Festschrift f. Grabmann*, 1935, i. 204 ff., at pp. 238–45; *Kaiserkrönung*, i. 151 ff., 234 ff., ii. 303; and in *Hist. Jb.*, lxix (1949), pp. 613–5 (a reply to his critics). Against Eichmann's dating and for a later date (end of twelfth century) and for the view that *Ordo C* was a mere programme that was not put into practice, see Schramm, "Die Ordines etc." in *Arch. f. Urkundenforschung*, xi (1930), pp. 285 ff.; idem, "Der Salische Kaiserordo & Benzo von Alba" in *Deutsches Archiv*, i (1937), pp. 390 ff.; M. Andrieu, *Le Pontifical romain au MA.*, ii. 291 ff., 292 n. 1 ("nature theorétique"); M. David, *Le Serment du sacre*, 1950, p. 229, n. 24; H. W. Klewitz, "Das Papsttum & Kaiserkrönung" in *Deutsches Archiv*, iv (1941), pp. 421 ff. (for late eleventh century); idem, "Die Krönung des Papstes" in *Sav. Z., Kan. Abt.*, xxxi (1941), pp. 96 ff. Cf. now also M. Uhlirz in *Festschrift f. E. E. Stengel*, 1952, p. 270, tentatively suggesting that *Ordo C* (or an early redaction) was used for Otto III's coronation.

[3] *Liber Diurnus*, from. 57, pp. 46–7.

\* †
\*

OR. IX, our *Ordo C* takes the "demotion" of the emperor several stages further than did its immediate predecessor.[1] Structurally, symbolically and ideologically *Ordo C* appears as an elaboration of *Ordo B*.

A comparison of the rubrics in *Ordo B* and *Ordo C* reveals a not inconsiderable change. The heading of *Ordo B*—"Incipit ordo Romanus ad benedicendum imperatorem quando coronam accipit"—is continued in its successor: "a domno papa in basilica beati Petri apostoli ad altare sancti Mauritii."[2] The important point of this *Ordo C* is that the function of the pope as the sole crowning agency is considerably stressed. Whilst the actual coronation and conferment of the imperial insignia was no longer performed by the pope on the main altar of St Peter's, but on a side altar, that of St Maurice, the liturgical-religious act of the unction was still performed at the main altar in the same manner and by the same high ecclesiastics and with the same kind of oil as prescribed in *Ordo B*. What appertained to the actual coronation including the specific coronation prayers, was performed by the pope personally—at a side altar. The insignia were the ring, the sword, the crown and the sceptre.[3] Perhaps nothing illustrates the ideas underlying

---

[1] It should be remembered that just as *Ordo IX* (the *ordo* for papal consecrations) knew nothing of the *Credo* as part of the (Roman) mass, so there is no *Credo* in *Ordo C*. The *Credo* was introduced into the Roman mass in the eleventh century, after Henry II had expressed his astonishment at its absence, cf. Th. Klauser, "Die liturgischen Austauschbeziehungen" in *Hist. Jb.*, liii (1933), p. 188; Eisenhofer, *Liturgik*, ed. cit., p. 200 f.; Eichmann, op. cit., i. 133, 214, n. 88. There is no mention of the curia in *Ordo C* nor of the college of cardinals, which would indeed exclude the late date suggested.

[2] Text ed. by Eichmann, op. cit., i. 169 ff., and Schramm, *Arch. f. Urk. forsch.*, cit., p. 375 (*Cencius II*) and p. 371 (*Cencius I*). We print the full text in the appendix.

[3] The orb is not yet part of the imperial insignia, but according to Glaber's report (*Historia, MGH. SS.* vii. 59) Benedict VIII handed to Henry II a globe surmounted by a cross. This sign was produced on papal orders: "Praecepit (scil. papa) fabricari quasi aureum pomum atque circumdari per quadrum pretiosissimis quibusque gemmis ac desuper auream crucem inseri. Erat autem instar speciei huius mundanae molis, quae videlicet in quadam rotunditate consistere perhibetur . . ." The symbolism was unmistakable, even though the orb was handed to the emperor outside the actual coronation ceremony. The orb became part of the insignia at Henry VI's coronation by Celestine III. Cf. now J. Deér, *Der Kaiserornat Friedrichs II*, Bern, 1952, Table XXI (3) and XXV (10) depicting Henry VI holding the orb in the left hand; earlier emperors held the orb, but not as part of the insignia: it signified subjection of all nations "in cuncto orbe" to the emperor, cf. *Lib. de ceremoniis*, ed. cit., c. 13, p. 99 (about 1030). The *lorum* too seemed to have been worn first by Henry VI, see Schramm, *Hist. of the English coronation*, pp. 135–6 and Eichmann, op. cit., ii. 152: only in the fourteenth century the stole became "via facti" an imperial sign, Eichmann, ibid., p. 151. For the *lorum* (the stole royal) in Constantine's Donation, see supra p. 79, and

*Ordo C* better than the consistent appellation of the future emperor as "electus." The opening sentence sets the tone: "At the break of Sunday dawn the 'electus' with his wife descends . . ." and this designation is kept up throughout the *Ordo* until the future emperor has received the last imperial sign, the sceptre.[1] Although of biblical origin,[2] this appellation has nevertheless ideological significance when it is brought into connexion with the *scrutinium* of the emperor by the pope: this too was an innovation of *Ordo C*.[3]

The procession of the imperial train from Monte Mario across the Via Triumphalis to St Peter's is of little symbolic significance, except that upon reaching the city boundary at the foot of Monte Mario the

---

*Lib. de cerem.*, cap. 6, p. 97. At the opening of Edward I's grave in the eighteenth century, it was found that he too had worn the stole in priestly fashion, see Schramm, *Arch. f. Urkundenforsch.*, xv (1938), p. 355.

[1] There is some parallel as regards the coronation of Richard I who was termed "Duke" in all stages of his coronation prior to unction, see L. W. Legg, *English coronation records*, p. 46. About the symbolic meaning of the sceptre—originally the most outstanding sign of rulership and gradually degraded to a mere ornamental piece (Gregory IX)—and the rod, see Eichmann, op. cit., ii. 83–92; cf. also the complaint of Charlemagne about the bishops carrying the signs of rulership, ibid., ii. 85. The ring was first worn by the Frankish bishops in the ninth century as "signum pontificalis honoris" and as "signaculum fidei" and the Frankish royal coronation *ordines* have a ring as a royal insigne. Henry IV appeared with the "anulus pontificalis" in Rome, see Eichmann, ii. 95: invested with the "virga" and the "anulus," the signs of "sacri regiminis," the emperor was "in der Tat bischofsgleich." It disappeared in Innocent III's *Ordo D*. Cf. also his *Reg.* i. 519: the ring as a "sacramentalis ornatus."

[2] I *Kgs.* ix. 2: "Saul electus et bonus"; *Ps.* cv (cvi). 23: "Moyses electus eius"; *Is.* xlii. 1: "Ecce servus meus . . . electus meus"; cf. also I *Pet.* ii. 4. It is true that Gregory VIII uses the term "electus" in MGH. *Const.* i. no. 411, pp. 586–7 but we think it would be too hasty to conclude therefrom that *Ordo C* was composed in the late twelfth century. Quite in conformity with hierocratic-papal ideology Gregory VII lays stress on the election of the candidate, see his *Reg.* iv. 3, p. 299, iv. 7, p. 305, and vii. 14a, p. 484, also iv. 25, p. 340. With special reference to Rudolf of Swabia—*Reg.* vii. 14a—see H. Mitteis, *Die deutsche Königswahl*, pp. 22, 61.

[3] The omission of a formal enthronement of the emperor in this *Ordo* and its successor (*Ordo D* of 1209, the last medieval coronation *Ordo*) is very significant; and this all the more so as the ORi (beginning with OR. IX) lay great stress on the formal enthronement of the pope. Enthronement symbolizes the taking of physical possession of a dominion. This omission indicates the essential function which the emperor, according to papal ideology, is to perform: he was created an *advocatus*, a *defensor*, a *patronus*, and for this there was no need for an enthronement. As far as it is known, no emperor was ever enthroned in his capacity as an emperor. The late Eichmann, op. cit., i. 103, thought that the absence of an enthronement could be explained by a recourse to the Donation of Constantine (cap. 18), but it may be suggested that the papal view on the emperor's function affords an equally plausible explanation.

future emperor is solemnly and in great state received by the Roman
authorities, the judges, military leaders, guilds, and so forth; and upon
reaching the Leonine city, near the Church of Maria Transpadina, the
future emperor is received by the local Roman clergy—the "clerici
minores," the sub-deacons in their tunics, the deacons in their dal-
matics, and the presbyters in their own liturgical vestments, the monks,
and so forth, who all extend their welcome to the future emperor with
incense, crosses, flags, and other appropriate symbols.[1] Here at the
Church of Maria Transpadina the two chief authorities of Rome are
also present, the city prefect of Rome and the Count Palatine of the
Lateran. The ceremonial bears a strong resemblance to Byzantine
customs. The solemn—and by now—lengthy procession moves along
the "porticus" of the Via Cornelia[2] and comes to a halt in front of
St Peter's. Here on the top of the flight of steps leading into St Peter's,
the pope seated—so as to indicate his authority and to bring into clear
symbolic relief the position of the emperor as the one who submits a
request[3]—waits for the emperor to approach him: bishops and the
other ecclesiastical dignitaries are grouped around him. The emperor
(and the empress) ascend the flight of steps followed in strict hierarchical order by the ecclesiastical and lay dignitaries, by the bishops,
abbots, knights, barons, ladies-in-waiting, and so forth. And here in
the view of "all the world"—"urbis et orbis"—some important
symbolic acts take place.

[1] For all details see Eichmann, op. cit., i. 184 ff.

[2] It is here on the Via Cornelia before the train reaches St Peter's that the
emperor receives gifts and homage from the strangers, from Greeks and Jews in
their native tongues, the reception symbolizing the universality of imperial rule;
cf. also the (Graphia) *Libellus de ceremoniis aule imperatoris*, cap. 19 (ed. Schramm,
*Kaiser*, ii. 102). This also seems to be the place about which Thietmar of Merseburg, an eye witness of Henry II's coronation, says that twelve senators—six
shaved and six unshaved—surround the emperor with their staffs; see his *Chronicon*, viii (vii). 1, p. 193 (ed. R. Holtzmann): "Heinricus Dei gratia rex inclitus a
senatoribus duodecim vallatus, quorum VI rasi barba, alii prolixa mistice incede-
bant cum baculis, cum dilecta suimet conjuge Cunigunda ad ecclesiam s. Petri
papa expectante venit." Eichmann, op. cit., i. 187, considers it possible that the
twelve senators represented the old lictors; Schramm, in *Studi Gregoriani*, ii. 428,
considers that the twelve senators represented the twelve apostles who accompanied Christ: this, according to Schramm, is the mystagogy in the imperial
ceremonial.

[3] This is of ancient Roman origin, cf. Th. Mommsen, *Römisches Staatsrecht*,
i. 397–8. The magistrate sat, whilst the citizen submitting a request, had to stand.
This prerogative was then adopted by the emperors, who then alone had the right
to sit, whilst everybody else had to stand, see A. Alföldi, "Die Ausgestaltung des
monarchischen Zeremoniells am römischen Kaiserhof" in *Mitt. d. deutschen
archaeologischen Instituts*, Rom. Abt., xlix, 1934, pp. 42–4.

The ceremony begins with the kissing of the pope's feet, the emperor's oath, his solemn assurances that he had come in peaceful intentions, and his adoption as a "filius" of the Roman Church. All these are new items in *Ordo C*. Upon reaching the pope the future emperor —and empress—kiss the pope's feet as a token of their humility, submission and veneration.[1] Immediately after this ceremony the emperor takes the oath to the pope and his successors who enter into their office canonically: he swears fidelity to, and protection and defence of, the Roman Church and the pope personally.[2] It is at this point that lay and papal points of view were so far apart: what the one meant by protection did not exactly harmonize with the meaning attached to it by the other. The kiss of peace given by the pope to the emperor in the form of a cross on forehead, chin and cheeks, seals the oath and the emperor's threefold assurance of his peaceful intentions.[3] Thereupon, as a sign that some important step is to be taken, the pope rises from his seat and thrice asks the future emperor if he wishes to be "a son of the Church." "Et ego te recipio ut filium ecclesiae" is the pope's answer: the emperor thus becomes the "filius-defensor," he is the "unicus" or "specialis filius" of the Roman Church and thereby of the universal Church: as such he has the special duty of protection and defence. This is followed by the symbolic act of the pope's adopting the emperor as the special protector. In the view of the whole large congregation the pope enfolds the "filius" under his mantle ("mantum") whilst the latter kisses the pope's breast.[4] Bearing in mind what we said when analysing John VIII's ideology, namely that the pope elects, designates and postulates the (future) emperor, we shall have no difficulty in appreciating not only the continuity of the papal-

---

[1] This is the Western transformation of the Eastern proskynesis, the actual prostration on the ground before the emperor as the earthly representative of divinity. Cf. also OR. VIII, cap. 7 (PL. lxxviii. 1002).

[2] The changes of *Ordo C* are typographically indicated by Schramm, *Archiv* cit., pp. 371, 375. The emperor's is not a feudal oath, but an oath that he will keep faith, cf. also infra 339. The reference to the "popes canonically entering" will not escape attention: the validity of the oath depended upon the fulfilment of this criterion. It was no doubt a veiled attack on the practice of papal installation by the emperor. Cf. also Leo IX's reference to the term: PL. cxliii. 631, 684, 690, and Gregory VII in his *Dict. Papae*, cap. 23.

[3] Here *Ordo C* has the admonition that the emperor must come cleanshaven— "rasus enim debet esse"—because the Saxons had adopted the un-Roman beard: as a "novus Constantinus" the emperor had at least to look like a Roman.

[4] For the origin of this see H. Planitz, *Deutsche Rechtsgeschichte*, Graz, 1950, p. 21: "Einhüllung in den Mantel," and E. Eichmann, "Die Adoption des deutschen Königs" in *Sav. Z., Kan. Abt.*, vi. 1916, pp. 237 ff.

hierocratic theme, but also the deep symbolism which manifested itself in the enfolding ceremony: the "filius" is now solemnly adopted by the pope: no other European king was ever adopted by the pope. Hierocratic ideas could not be expressed more suitably than in this symbolic act designating the fatherhood of the pope,[1] and the sonship of the emperor.

The ceremony of adoption is immediately followed by the pope's taking the right hand of the "electus." This act symbolizes again the fatherhood of the pope and also his function as a helper to the (future) emperor.[2] It is as the father of the emperor that the pope presents himself to the view of the crowd: and the crowd now acclaims the emperor—the last remnant of the popular acclamation: indeed this is the natural consummation of the scene enacted on Christmas Day 800.[3]

The acclamation by the Romans finished, the pope's archdeacon takes the emperor's right hand and leads him into the interior of St Peter's, where the bishop of Albano says the first *Oratio* "Deus in cuius manu" over the emperor. The pope himself accompanied by the chanting of "Petre amas me?"[4] leaves the emperor behind with the bishop of Albano, and enters the basilica proper. This chant also has symbolic significance in so far as the pope is praised as the living Peter to whom the words of the gospel apply.[5] The end of the chant signals the beginning of a new important act, the *scrutinium*. The pope taking his seat on a "Rota" in the central aisle is faced by the "elected." The *scrutinium* is the formal examination of the future emperor. His assistants are the archpresbyter and the archdeacon, sitting left and right of him. On the pope's side sit the other Lateran bishops. The rest stand

[1] Cf. I *Paral.* xxviii. 6–7: "Dixitque mihi: Salomon, filius tuus, aedificabit domum meam et atria mea; ipsum enim elegi mihi in filium et ego ero ei in patrem et firmabo regnum eius."

[2] Cf. *Ps.* lxxii (lxxiii), 23–4: "Jumentum factus sum apud te; et ego semper tecum. Tenuisti dexteram meam et in voluntate tua deduxisti me et cum gloria suscepisti me." Cf. also *Ps.* cxvii (cxviii), 16, *Is.* xli. 10, and esp. 13: "Quia ego Dominus Deus tuus, apprehendens manum tuam dicensque tibi, Ne timeas, ego adjuvo te." For the Babylonian and Byzantine usage of the same ceremony see Eichmann, op. cit., i. 195, and note 48.

[3] This acclamation by the Romans is attested at all the Salian coronations in the eleventh century. F. Schneider, *Rom & Romgedanke*, p. 207, seems to think that the Romans exercised a constitutive right of election. Against this view rightly E. Kantorowicz, *Laudes regiae*, pp. 79–80: the acclamation was a mere "collaudatio"—an acclamation "in stunted form"—without any constitutive meaning.

[4] *John* xxi. 15–17.

[5] As Eichmann, loc. cit., observes, the chant must be taken as a whole, and the "Pasce oves meas" assumes in this context very great significance.

in a half circle around. The pope himself opens the examination which is modelled on that of a bishop: it is of course true that the examination is a pure formality, but this should not deceive us into thinking that it was devoid of deeper significance.[1] This, in fact, is the adoption of another Byzantine usage, namely, the confession of faith which the Byzantine emperor had to make before his coronation.[2] In the *scrutinium* of *Ordo C* lies the root of the later formal approbation by the pope of the emperor.[3]

The pope then betakes himself into the sacristy, where he puts on his vestments, that is, amice, alb and cingulum, tunic and dalmatic, but not the pallium and the mitre. Thus dressed he awaits the "electus" who after having been clothed by the two high ecclesiastics in the chapel of St George, is now taken before the pope in the sacristy, always assisted by his two papal clerics. It is then that the pope makes him a cleric by conceding to him the wearing of specific clerical, though not sacerdotal, vestments.[4] This is the so-called "immantatio" amplified in this case by the characteristic imperial garments, such as the tunic, dalmatic, pluviale and mitre.[5] What are not conceded to the emperor are the proper sacerdotal regalia, stole, maniple, planeta, nor of course the pallium.[6] There is no need to underline the significance of all this, and its intimate connexion with the Donation of Constantine. The

---

[1] For the actual questions see Text of *Ordo C*.

[2] See Eichmann, i. 201.

[3] The fact is undeniable that later papal approbation of the candidate could without any efforts be based upon the *scrutinium*; cf. also Schramm, art. cit., pp. 326 f., and Eichmann, i. 271; Gregory VII, infra 288, and Innocent III in RNI. 62.

[4] Eichmann's transcription has "faciat clericum," whilst Schramm has "fatiit" (p. 379). In his "Krönungs und Bischofsweihe" in *SB. Munich*, 1928, p. 53, Eichmann reads "facit."

[5] About the grant of the mitre to other potentates see also infra 313. If the description of the imperial mitre in the (Graphia) *Libellus* is applicable to this time, the mitre of the emperor was worn from front to back (and not as the later episcopal mitre from left to right): the mitre looked the same from the front as from the back and was called by the author of the *Libellus* a crown. It was meant to symbolize the emperor's Janus-like face and his knowledge of what is going on behind and in front of him; see *Libellus de ceremoniis aule imperatoris*, cap. 4 (ed. Schramm, *Kaiser*, ii. 94): "Sexta corona est mitra, qua Ianus et reges Troianorum usi sunt, per quam innuitur, quod *monocrator* que ante et que retro sunt, sollicita mente advertere debet."

[6] We may perhaps be allowed to refer to a later medieval jurist, Baldus, who says that the consecration of the emperor constitutes an "ordo ecclesiasticus, sed non sacer": *Super Decretalibus*, I. vi. 34, no. 3. According to Schramm, *König von Frankreich*, p. 161, the garments of the French king were not clerical: "Die Dynastie bleibt bei der laikalen Kaisertracht."

stage is now set for the next great event—the solemn procession to the main altar of St Peter's. The pope now wears his mass vestments, his pallium and mitre. The train is headed by the ecclesiastics in strict hierarchical order followed by the pope, then the "electus" still assisted by the two high ecclesiastics, and lastly the empress with her ladies-in-waiting. The act of ordination—consisting of unction and the conferment of the imperial insignia, the latter act being performed at the side altar of St Maurice—is built into the coronation mass between the *Kyrie* and the *Gloria*.[1]

A few observations appear warranted about the prayers which the pope says when conferring the sword. It is he himself who fastens the sword on the emperor—"cingit eum cum gladio"—and the accompanying prayer makes it clear that the sword is conferred on him "cum Dei benedictione."[2] Acceptance as a "filius-defensor" of the Roman Church, his adoption through the enfolding ceremony, and lastly the conferment of the sword as the concrete means of protection—these are the acts which translate an abstract idea into symbolic language: it is a rich symbolism whose underlying ideas stand in glaring contrast to the idea which the emperors themselves had of their function as monarchs and protectors of the Roman Church. If we recall that Charlemagne had prided himself on being a "filius et defensor sanctae Dei ecclesiae"[3] and when we find this phrase in *Ordo C*, we shall have no difficulty in appraising the fundamentally divergent standpoints that inspired the two literally agreeing statements.

*Ordo C* forms the bridge which spans the age between Henry II and

---

[1] For the reason of this see Ph. Oppenheim, in *Ephemerides Liturgicae*, lviii (1944), p. 47, and for all other details Eichmann, i. 205–17; about the feast which the pope gives in honour of the emperor, ibid., 217–22. It is during the coronation mass that the *laudes* are chanted by two groups—the one headed by the archdeacon and consisting of the six other palatine deacons and subdeacons; the other consisting of the "scola cum notariis," the latter representing the officials who had to issue papal documents and who actually acclaimed the emperor in this official capacity at the end of the antiphon, see E. Kantorowicz, *Laudes regiae*, p. 84. Innocent III's *Ordo D* was to change the arrangement: higher orders could be received only during mass, but since the emperor did not receive any higher orders, the whole anointing ceremony was performed before mass, no longer at the main altar, but also at the side altar of St Maurice; the coronation was still performed between epistle and gospel, see *Ordo D*, ed. Eichmann, op. cit., i. 259 f., and 279 f. The ring—the episcopal sign—also did not appear in *Ordo D* as an imperial sign, but the orb did which was handed over without any prayers.

[2] Cf. also *Mach.* xv. 16: the sword, like the pallium, was taken from St Peter's altar.

[3] MGH. *Concilia*, ii. 158, No. 19F. Cf. also MGH. *Cap.* i. 44, p. 19: "devotus sanctae ecclesiae defensor atque adjutor in omnibus."

Otto IV. Ideologically there is therefore an uninterrupted development. The original idea, first aired by Stephen II, of the role of the
Frankish king, through the intermediate stages of a patrician of the
Romans and of the emperor of the Romans, remained basic to the
conceptual framework of papal-hierocratic ideas. It subsequently
formed the foundation of the coronation *ordines* upon which was
erected a detailed and elaborate liturgical and symbolic edifice.

# CHAPTER IX

# Gregory VII

THE designation of the papacy as Reform papacy from Leo IX onwards expresses the fallacious view that with the accession of this pope the era of "reform" begins. If indeed "reform" was what distinguished the Hildebrandine papacy, one may be forgiven for asking why this epitheton ornans is not bestowed upon the emperors immediately preceding this period. For, as we hoped to show, the Saxon and quite especially the early Salian emperors were indeed imbued with the spirit of reform and were successful to a not negligible extent. In a way one might say that whatever "reform" the post-Leonine popes carried out or tried to carry out, was largely conditioned by the previous imperial reform measures. This point of view which sees in the papacy a mere "Reform" papacy, would restrict its objectives to the removal of certain evils and abuses: did the papacy in the second half of the eleventh century really aim at nothing higher than this barren and negative end?

What the papacy attempted was the implementation of the hierocratic tenets, that is, the translation of abstract principles into concrete governmental actions. It is no doubt true and understandable that the first concrete application of these principles is apt to give a contemporary a somewhat severe jolt,[1] but this sensation is a reaction, however natural, to the application of the idea, not to the idea itself. The unparalleled advantage which the papacy had over any other institution was its own storehouse of ideological memory, the papal archives. On the other hand, it would have been impossible for any power, including the papacy, to achieve so much within so short a time, had there not been a potent permeation of the contemporary mind with the very same ideas which were now applied in practice. Moreover, there were unobtrusive channels which preserved the hierocratic theme, such as the symbolism expressed in *Ordo C*, which was a faithful mirror of the

---

[1] Cf. e.g., Bonizo of Sutri, *Liber ad Amicum*, viii (MGH. *Libelli de lite* (henceforward quoted: LdL.), ii. 609): "Postquam de banno regis ad aures personuit, universus noster Romanus orbis contremuit."

advance which hierocratic ideas had made. To this must be added a number of institutionalized manifestations: these are effective carriers of ideas and are, so to speak, its conservators. It was in these incubators of its own theme that the papacy had always found great support.[1]

## I

(*a*) It would be wholly erroneous to assume that the Roman papacy was the only guardian of hierocratic principles. At the time which witnessed the exercise of sacerdotal functions by the prototype of a *Rex-Sacerdos*, Henry III, there came from across the Alps the (fragmentary) tract *De Ordinando Pontifice*. Written in the year following Sutri[2] the tract demonstrates the ideological preparedness in regions far away from Rome. With unusual alacrity and alertness the author[3] pursues the hierocratic theme. To him Henry's action at Sutri was nothing more nor less than illegitimate: it was pure usurpation on his part, and compulsion on the part of the popes concerned. Henry is a "coactor" who perpetrated an offence.[4]

The title of this tract might well be: "By what authority did Henry III act?" Was Henry functionally qualified to sit in judgment over the popes at Sutri? As a Christian he no doubt belongs to the Church, but is this sufficient qualification for the exercise of judicial functions over

[1] The usual denunciations of the early eleventh-century papacy should no longer be repeated. Cf. e.g., W. Kölmel, *Rom und der Kirchenstaat im 10. und 11. Jarhrhundert bis in die Anfänge der Reform*, Leipzig, 1935, who shows how much the Tusculan popes had contributed to purely organizational matters. See also K. Jordan, in *Studi Gregoriani*, i. 119 f. This recent and only partial re-orientation towards the eleventh-century papacy makes a thorough study of these popes very necessary; cf. now also R. Elze, in *Studi Gregoriani*, iv. 33 ff. With special reference to papal insignia the late Eichmann, *Weihe & Krönung des Papstes im Mittelalter*, 1951, pp. 30–1, points out that the "Reform" papacy did not emerge as suddenly as is usually maintained. It is also in the early eleventh century that papal documents came to be written on parchment (instead of on papyrus), for which see now L. Santifaller, *Beschreibstoffe im Mittelalter* (MIOG., suppl. vol. xvi/1, 1953), pp. 87–9: the oldest parchment document of 967 by John XIII (cf. also infra p. 328) but this was an isolated case, and from 1007 onwards parchment begins to oust papyrus in the papal chancery, see Santifaller's list, p. 88, and pp. 89–90.

[2] Between 1047 and 1048, see G. B. Borino, "Invitus ultra montes cum domno papa Gregorio abii" in *Studi Gregoriani*, i. 30, note 63.

[3] About the authorship see F. Pelster, "Der Traktat 'De ordinando pontifice' und sein Verfasser Humbert von Moyenmoutier" in *Hist. Jb.*, lxi (1941), pp. 88 ff.: Humbert's authorship is denied by A. Michel, "Die folgenschweren Ideen des Kardinals Humbert" in *Studi Gregoriani*, i. 87, but accepted by J. de Ghellinck, *Le Mouvement théologique du XIIe siècle*, 2nd ed., Paris, 1949, p. 438.

[4] *De Ordinando Pontifice*, in MGH. LdL. i. 13.

priests and popes? For Henry's decision was a judgment which concerned in particular the alleged sinful (because simoniacal) conduct of Gregory VI. But where is the scriptural or other unimpeachable evidence of the emperor's qualification to judge priests and popes? For he who sits in judgment over a pope, must take the place of Christ:

> Ubi enim inveniuntur imperatores locum Christi obtinere?

Our author puts the finger on the vital spot: this was precisely the function which Henry as supreme monarch had assumed:[1] it was precisely in the function as a vicar of Christ that he and his predecessors had acted basing themselves on the view that they had received their power and authority directly from God.[2] And it was precisely on this question that the whole regal-sacerdotal scheme floundered, because the lay point of view had no answer to this question of the legitimate origin of the emperor's power to judge priests and popes. It is this question which was of crucial importance at a time which was thoroughly soaked with Christo-centric principles. Emperors might have all history and tradition in their favour, but this says nothing about the legitimacy of the functions exercised, however much based upon history and tradition. Could emperors apply to themselves the Petrine words? This was the basic query, and the lay standpoint had no answer to it.

It is from this premiss, and this premiss alone, that the fundamental principle of functional qualification can be understood. The power to bind and to loose, the power to forgive sins, is a specific sacerdotal qualification; hence our author very pertinently asks:

> Cui erat confessionem reddere, cuius erat exigere? Quo loco, quo ordine?

And the answer which he gives leaves nothing to be desired as regards lucidity and pungency:

> In ecclesia populus sacerdoti, sacerdos episcopo potest confiteri, episcopus summo et universali pontifici, ille autem soli Deo, qui eum juditio reservavit. Quod autem jure non debet converti.

---

[1] About him see supra 251 and cf. also his characterization as "vicarius Dei" by G. Ladner, *Theologie und Politik vor dem Investiturstreit*, Vienna, 1936, pp. 60 f. and 154 f. Cf. also following note.

[2] Cf. the pictorial presentation of the idea, supra p. 247 and see also as a characteristic contemporary example Thietmar of Merseburg, *Chronicon*, i. 26, p. 16, ed. cit.: "Quin potius reges nostri et imperatores summi Rectoris vice in hac peregrinatione praepositi . . . hii quos Christus sui memores huius terrae principes constituit"; bishops therefore must be subjected to the emperors, because the latter act "vice Christi." Cf. also Wipo's report supra p. 249.

What the author does here is to combine the Gelasian principle[1] with the principle laid down in the *Constitutum Silvestri*,[2] one of the Symmachan forgeries, namely, that the supreme pontiff may not be judged by anyone.[3] This sacerdotal qualification is the presupposition for exercising jurisdictional functions over the members of the sacerdotal hierarchy, and we are not therefore surprised to find here the old statement allegedly made by Constantine in the Council of Nicaea, in which he called the bishops "gods" who are not subject to any earthly tribunal.[4] Not only is Constantine held up as the example to be followed by all rulers, because he had shown himself obedient to Pope Silvester, but the authority of Charlemagne is also invoked for the following statement which he was supposed to have made: "Praesul summus a quoquam non judicabitur."[5] In a word, laymen are not qualified to exercise any functions for which they have not been given authority.[6]

(*b*) Whilst the principle of functional qualification is applied to a specific question by the anonymous author, in the case of Cardinal Humbert it is the basis of what may well be called a system. In his literary products[7] he gives the hierocratic theme its permanent com-

[1] See *Tract. IV*, cap. 13, p. 569: "Sed dicatur forsitan: non imperator absolvit, sed a pontificibus poposcit absolvi . . . inferior quippe potiorem absolvere non potest: solo ergo potior inferiorem convenienter absolvit."

[2] *Const. Silv.*, cap. iii, Mansi, ii. 623: "Neque praesul summus judicabitur a quoquam, quoniam scriptum est 'Non est discipulus super magistrum'" (*Matt.* x. 24). Cf. also supra p. 117 n. 4.

[3] The bishop of Liège, Wazo, who wrote his *Sententia de Gregorio VI pontifice* at the same time as the tract under discussion was written, also operated with the *Const. Silv.*: "Inter haec ad mentem redit, quod cum papa Clemens ex episcopo Bavembergensi in apostolica sede sublimatus de hac vita discessit, imperator de subrogando in locum illius alio consilium eius quaerere animum induxit. Ille autem ut erat in omnibus et in talibus maxime scrutator studiosissimus, vigilanter cum aliis, quibus laboris huius partes expenderat, hinc gesta pontificum Romanorum, hinc eorundem decreta, hinc autenticos canones, capitulare recensere sollicitus fuit. In quibus diligenter revolutis nichil aliud quam summum pontificem, cuiuscumque vitae fuerit, summo honore haberi, eum a nemine unquam judicari oportere, immo nullius inferioris gradus accusationem adversus superiorem recepi debere, invenire potuit," I. M. Watterich, *Pontificum Romanorum Vitae*, i. 79–80. It will be seen that, not unlike Humbert a few years later, Wazo combined the *Const. Silv.* with an Isidorian statement; cf. *Studi Gregoriani*, iv. 113 ff.

[4] "Vos a nemine judicari potestis, quia Dei solius juditio reservamini; dii etenim vocati estis, idcirco non potestis ab hominibus judicari," ibid, p. 12.

[5] Charlemagne of course never said this. Our author takes it from Benedictus Levita, i. 302, or the *Capitula Angilramni*, cap. 51, Hinschius, p. 766.

[6] In support of this the author cites Pseudo-Isidorian statements of Popes Pius I, Telesphorus, Pontianus and Xistus; the relevant passages are in Hinschius, pp. 120, 147; see also pp. 108, 111.

[7] We can but briefly survey them here: an exhaustive monographic treatment of the cardinal's ideas is long overdue.

10

plexion. His work is a summary of old tenets and maxims, but a summary which everywhere shows a master mind at work: in a way his work looks back, and yet in another it looks forward, precisely because of the masterly moulding of old material. And the actual personal influence exercised by Humbert on the papacy in the fifties of the eleventh century, gives his work the stamp of added significance.

The pivotal point in the programme of Humbert is the closely reasoned, sharp hitting and high spirited attack on the prevailing *Rex-Sacerdos* ideas and practices. The proprietary church system and the concomitant lay investiture are but manifestations of one and the same principle, namely, disregard of the principle of order: in this disorder, as he witnessed it, the government of the Church lies in the hands of its unordained members with the result that the priesthood, the ordained members of the Church, are dominated by laymen. Lay ideology as such is made the chief target of Humbert's constructive criticism.

What he wishes to see established is the *ordo rationis*, so as to prevent *confusio*.[1] That in its argumentation Humbert's work shows itself a veritable storehouse of ancient material and that this argumentation necessitated an exhaustive utilization of the pantheon of all papal prerogatives, namely Pseudo-Isidore, cannot by any means diminish the value of the cardinal's ideas. To him the implementation of the primacy of the Roman Church was the cardinal point: the Roman Church is the hinge and head—"cardo et caput"—of all the other churches.[2] The Roman Church is the fountain head of all Christian life and order and principles. It is the epitome of all Christendom embracing as it does "universam terram."[3] In practical terms these

---

[1] *Adversus simoniacos*, in MGH., LdL. i. 205: "Ad totius . . . religionis conculcationem praepostero ordine omnia fiunt." See also Humbert's *Sententiae* (the former *Diversorum patrum sententiae* or *collectio minor*) in Anselm's *Collectio canonum*, ed. F. Thaner, iv. 8, p. 195. The "Sentences" of Humbert have rightly been called by A. Michel "Das erste Rechtsbuch der Reform"; its influence cannot be exaggerated. Cf. also the characterization by the late de Ghellinck, *Mouvement théologique*, p. 436: "C'est le premier véhicule des principes de la réforme qu'elle fait pénétrer dans tout l'occident." An edition is very much wanted.

[2] *Sententiae*, cc. 2, 12 (Thaner's Anselm, i. 20, p. 7; i. 9, p. 10); cf. also Leo IX's letter in Corn. Will, *Acta et Scripta*, cap. xxxii, pp. 81–2; also A. Michel, *Die Sentenzen des Kardinals Humbert*, Leipzig, 1944, p. 18. A comparison between the headings of the *Sententiae* and the DP. of Gregory VII (infra 292) is very instructive, cf. the conspectus of W. Peitz, "Das Originalregister Gregors VII" in *SB. Vienna*, clxv (1911), pp. 282–3.

[3] Cf. the similar expression of Nicholas I, supra 195, and see Humbert's *Fragmentum B*, printed by P. E. Schramm, *Kaiser*, ii. 133. Cf. also ibid.: "Romana ecclesia . . . afficit totius Christianitatis membra," p. 131. See furthermore his *Sententiae*, cc. 2, 10, 12, 17 = Gelasius I, ep. 42, c. 1, Thiel, p. 455, and cf. also

axioms of Humbert denote the jurisdictional and legislative primacy of the Roman Church.[1]

Before the formal break of 1054 the Cardinal's standpoint is universalist in the best meaning of the term. The primacy of the Roman Church, according to him, must be the principle working wherever the Christian faith is the norm of conduct, and this comprises also the Eastern half of Christendom.[2] The Christian world was to him indeed an "ecclesia," the "corpus Christi" become manifest, concrete and tangible. "Our emperor" is Christ.[3] Consequently, the Gelasian "mundus" is exchanged by Humbert for the *ecclesia*, and the lay ruler is merely a part of this *ecclesia*, by virtue of his being a Christian. The cardinal employs a terminology that is as significant as it is lucid. In comparing royal and sacerdotal dignities one should say that

*sacerdotium in* praesenti *ecclesia* assimilari animae, regnum autem (scil. in praesenti ecclesia) corpori, quia invicem se diligunt et vicissim sese indigent ... sicut praeeminet anima et praecipit, sic sacerdotalis dignitas regali, utputa coelestis terrestri.[4]

The Christian world was the *ecclesia*, the body corporate and politic of all Christians, which derives its sustenance from the epitome of all Christendom, the Roman Church.[5]

But pre-eminence of the soul over the body is not merely a religious, or moral or philosophic pre-eminence: it is a nomological pre-eminence: it is a function which the soul exercises over the body by prescribing to it what is and what is not to be done in the interests of the whole human organism. The soul decrees, orders, directs and orientates the body. The body is a mere instrument of the soul, necessary indeed, but on no account autonomous: in fact, the cardinal's point of view is of course nothing but a truism in Christian cosmology which, when transplanted onto the governmental plane, emerges in the axiom

just as the soul commands the body, so does sacerdotal dignity command royal dignity.

---

Anacletus in Pseudo-Isidore, Hinschius, p. 83, c. 30: "Haec vero sancta Romana apostolica ecclesia non ab apostolis, sed ipse beato Petro dixit 'Tu es Petrus . . .' "

[1] See especially *Sententiae*, cap. 3.

[2] We hold that the cardinal's mission to Constantinople in 1054 was prompted by this aim.

[3] *Adv. sim.*, ii. 27, p. 174.      [4] *Adv. sim.*, iii. 29, p. 225.

[5] For the more correct appellation of the Roman Church as the "corporate epitome" of Christendom, see infra p. 319, and our paper in *Studi Gregoriani*, iv. 111 ff.

The *sacerdotium* within the Christian body corporate has the same function as the *anima* within the individual human body. The priesthood commands, because it alone is functionally qualified to issue orders. The *clericalis ordo* is the soul of the Christian body politic:

> Est enim *clericalis ordo in ecclesia* praecipuus tamquam in capite oculi, de quo ait Dominus "Qui tetigerit vos, tangit pupillam oculi mei."[1]

The consequence is that the unordained members, including kings and emperors, of the Church are subjected to the priesthood, which after all is the hallmark of the hierocratic theme. The "laicalis potestas," Humbert says, is the organ which executes the commands of the priesthood: the lay order, if the principle of *ordo rationis* is to be established, must be obedient to the clerical order:

> Est et laicalis potestas (scil. in ecclesia) tamquam pectus et brachia ad obediendum et defendendum ecclesiam valida et exerta.[2]

Hence, the priesthood and the secular arm of the Church stand to each other like soul and body, sun and moon, head and limbs. The Western and Eastern emperors are the arms of the pope.[3]

In consequential pursuit of the hierocratic theme Humbert considers the function of the kings and emperors as protectors and defenders in the sense of being advocates. In fact, the only meaning which the cardinal is able to attribute to royal (and imperial) anointing is that by

---

[1] *Adv. sim.*, p. 235; *Zach.* ii. 8.

[2] Ibid., p. 235.

[3] See Leo IX's letter written by Humbert, in C. Will, *Acta et Scripta*, p. 87; cf. also A. Michel, *Sentenẕen*, p. 67, and in *Studi Gregoriani*, i. 85, and Humbert himself in *Adv. sim.*, iii. 29. Leo IX made lavish use of the Donation of Constantine in his letter to the patriarch, Michael Kerullarios, where the pope says that the patriarch, after having been shown the testimonies, should now be satisfied "*de regali sacerdotio* sanctae Romanae et apostolicae sedis"; this should be acknowledged by all those who wish to be, or be spoken of as, Christians. PL. cxliii. 753 (= Will, op. cit., p. 68): "His et quamplurimis testimoniis jam vobis satisfactum esse debuit de terreno et coelesti imperio de regali sacerdotio sanctae Romanae sedis precipue super speciali eius dispositione in coelis, si quoquo modo Christiani esse vel dici optatis, et si ipsam evangelii veritatem aperte, quod absit, non impugnatis." The testimonies referred to are, on the one hand, the Petrine commission, and, on the other hand, the Donation of Constantine which is here copied *in extenso*. Cf. also ibid.: "Tantum apicem (i.e. summi sacerdotii privilegium) coelestis dignitatis in beato Petro et eius vicariis prudentissimus terrenae *monarchiae* princeps Constantinus intima consideratione reveritus, cunctos usque in finem saeculi successores eidem apostolo in Romana sede pontifices, per b. Silvestrum non solum imperiali potestate et dignitate, verum etiam infulis et ministris adornavit imperialibus, valde indignum fore arbitratus terreno imperio subdi quos divina majestas praefecit coelesti." The text of the Donation as incorporated in this letter agrees with the text in Pseudo-Isidore.

this visible liturgical act kings and emperors are thereby stamped as specially selected protectors of the Church. Kings, according to him, are not self-styled or self-appointed protectors: they do not receive their sword from God: it is the "priests of Christ" who confer upon kings the sword for the specific purpose of protection and defence. By accepting the symbol of the sword from priestly hands the king assumes the solemn duty—solemn because fortified by unction—of defending the Church universal and herewith also the individual churches.

Ad hoc enim gladium a Christi sacerdotibus accipiunt (scil. reges), ad hoc inunguntur, ut pro ecclesiarum Dei defensione militent et, ubicumque opus est, pugnent.[1]

Far from being entitled to erect churches, kings have only the duty of defending existing ones. But erection of churches is only one of those actions which are based upon the assumption of "sacerdotalis officii"[2] entailing "duplicem confusionem." The worst offenders in this respect were the "Ottones, prae omnibus ante se regibus sacerdotalis officii praesumptores."[3] But the "ordo rationis" demands that the temporal rulers should be especially assigned—"assignati" is the cardinal's succinct term—as "tutors and defenders" by the priests. Kingship is *tutela*.

Inde est, quod reges saeculi et principes ecclesiis Dei tutores et defensores *assignati*,

otherwise they would bear the "sword in vain."[4] From this follows conclusively that, in order to establish the principle of *ordo* within the Christian body politic, clerics must have precedence over kings, just as kings have precedence over the lay people whom they rule:

Sicut enim regum est ecclesiasticos sequi, sic laicorum quoque reges suos.[5]

The adherence to this principle will be "ad utilitatem ecclesiae et patriae."

Two observations are here warranted. Firstly, the *ecclesia* is one body corporate and politic, one indivisible and undivided *corpus*.[6] Its

---

[1] *Adv. sim.*, iii. 15, p. 217.     [2] *Adv. sim.*, iii. 15, p. 216.
[3] *Adv. sim.*, iii. 15, p. 217.
[4] *Adv. sim.*, iii. 5, p. 204; *Rom.* xiii. 4; cf. Isidore supra p. 29.
[5] *Adv. sim.*, iii. 21, p. 225.
[6] The unitary principle also works in purely theological problems: God hates duality ("dias . . . scismatica") and loves the oneness: "monas," see *Adv. sim.*, iii. 24, p. 229, line 27 ff.; on this see Ladner, op. cit., pp. 34; 58, note 132; 289, who considers that Humbert borrowed the term "monas" from Johannes Scotus's *De divisione naturae*; cf. also Thaner in the edition of Humbert's *Adv. Sim.*, p. 97.

direction lies in the hands of the *sacerdotium*: it is the latter which assigns to everyone within this body his function. This assignment constitutes then the *ordo*, and the well-being of this body politic will be furthered if each keeps to the sphere of action allotted to him. Consequently, the right order will be disturbed if priesthood or lay people intervene in—or rather interfere with—matters which do not belong to their legitimate sphere of action: the basis of legitimacy is the allocation by the *sacerdotium*. This applies within each section[1] as well as to the relations between the two sections.[2] In other words, the principle of order demands that there be a horizontal and a vertical limitation of spheres of action, otherwise there will be confusion and disorder. But the presupposition is that the allocation of functions in this Christian body politic is the task of its *anima*, the *sacerdotium* and eventually of the "caput sacerdotum" who epitomizes all the powers and functions widely diffused as they are throughout the length and breadth of the Christian body.

Secondly, the king's function is purely auxiliary and supplementary: his function is negative: he functions for the sake of the Church universal and is instituted and sanctified by the *sacerdotium* for the purpose of defence and protection in the widest meaning of the term. Protection and defence however are not exclusively focused on the individual churches, but are also concerned with the suppression of evil by force. Of course, this constitutes proper defence of the Christian body politic, particularly defence from enemies within the body itself. This forcible suppression of what the *sacerdotium* alone is in a position to judge evil and wicked—always presupposing a Christian body politic —is the foremost function of the king in the Christian society. Hence, if there were no evil doers, no criminals—and we may add, looking ahead: no heretics—there would be no need for a secular power within the Church. Humbert relies on, and quotes from, Isidore's famous passage.[3] Evil actions, however, are sins and, according to contemporary and accepted beliefs, promoted by the devil: they are the devil's doings. Consequently, the secular prince exists in order to suppress these actions instigated by the devil: if there were no sinful conduct in a community, there would be no need for a power whose sole *raison d'être* is the physical suppression of this kind of conduct, for by ful-

---

[1] For instance, no metropolitan should interfere in those spheres which are assigned to the bishops, or archdeacons, etc., and *vice-versa*.

[2] *Adv. sim.*, iii. 9, p. 208.

[3] *Adv. sim.*, iii. 21, p. 226. Isidore, *Sententiae*, iii. 51, no. 4, quoted supra p. 29.

filling this function allotted or assigned to him, the prince protects the whole corporate body of Christians. All this is in the tradition of the hierocratic theme; it was soon to be given its permanent and perhaps most famous clothing by Gregory VII.[1]

As we said before, the period from the fifties of the eleventh century onwards, is not a period which witnessed the evolution of a new doctrine, but a period which saw the application and implementation of a—by now—old ideology. This hierocratic doctrine by virtue of being applied became the governmental basis of the papacy. What pure doctrine declared ought to be done, is now being done. Hierocratic doctrine emerges in the shape of the hierocratic system, the essence of which is the conception of the universal Church as a body corporate and politic, comprising all Christians. This is the *societas christiana*, to use Gregory VII's distinctive terminology,[2] in which the authority of the Roman pontiff holds sway; in which the pope's function as legislator and judge of appeal is effective; in which the mandate of the pope creates binding effects. For practical purposes this *societas christiana* is Western Europe, whose paternity can be traced back to Charlemagne and to the first Gregory's prophetic vision. This *societas christiana* is an entity which is to be governed on the monarchic principle: it is the *corpus* of the Christians over which the Roman Church exercises its monarchic *principatus* through the medium of the pope as the vicar of St Peter. This European society is technically a body politic, and despite its cementing bond, the spiritual element of the Christian faith, it is also earthy and has all the appurtenances and paraphernalia attendant upon civil society: its legislative, consultative, administrative, executive offices. Indeed, the *societas christiana* or what Cardinal Humbert called the *ecclesia*, is a *societas perfecta*.

[1] For the application of this tenet by Gregory VII, see his *Reg.* viii. 21, p. 552 and *Reg.* iv. 2, p. 295 (ed. E. Caspar). Perhaps no other doctrine of Gregory VII has caused so much misunderstanding as this alleged "devilish or sinful origin of the State." But when looked at from the point of view of functionalism and hierocratic ideology, the statement of Gregory is rather commonplace and says absolutely nothing new: Isidore's statement contained all the ingredients. Incidentally, this is a good example of how misleading it is to speak of the "devilish" or "sinful" origin of the *State*, as if this makes any sense at all. Cf. St Augustine, *Civ. Dei*, xi. 1; xiv. 28; xv. 5 and 7; xvi. 3 and 4; xvii. 6; xviii. 2; etc.

[2] Originally the term *societas* (and its related notions *sociatus, societas coetus, multitudinis*, and the like) is Ciceronian ("Quid enim est *civitas* nisi juris societas?") and denotes *respublica*, State or commonwealth (cf. *De Republica*, i. 32; 49; iii. 31; iv. 3) and was transmitted to the Middle Ages through the medium of St Augustine's *Civ. Dei*.

We turn to Gregory VII and omit the hierocratic manifestations of the pontificates of Nicholas II and Alexander II, because not only did he give the whole period its stamp and complexion, but also because he appears as the personification of the hierocratic idea. Indeed, he is hierocratic doctrine brought down to earth and made eminently concrete. None sensed the temper of his time better than he—his warlike phrases, speeches and appeals, are not a reflexion on the man, but rather on contemporary society. None had that passionate vision and that impelling conviction which he embodied—his dramatic performances are a mirror of the man and of contemporary society. None possessed the same inflexibility and stubbornness as he—and this is a reflexion of the man, and not of contemporary society. Rarely had an idea found such a protagonist who was at once its personal manifestation, effective expounder and fearless executor.[1]

## II

Some preliminary remarks on Gregory VII's premisses may profitably precede the survey of his thought.

Firstly, it is axiomatic for him that the *ecclesia* is a body corporate and politic the constituent element of which is the spiritual element of the Christian faith. As such this society knows no territorial frontiers: it is literally universal. As a body politic it is territorially confined to Latin Christendom. But this society despite its constituent spiritual substance, is not by any means a pneumatic body, but has all the appurtenances of real earthiness. As such it must be governed and the substratum of this society necessitates its government by those who are uniquely qualified to function as the directing and governing organs, namely by the ordained members of the Church. The principle of functional qualification must be translated into a workable governmental machinery. The *sacerdotium* alone is qualified and entitled and bound to function as the governmental organ of the *societas christiana*. The correct application of this principle rests, on the one hand, on the delineation of the *ordo laicalis* and the *ordo sacerdotalis* and, on the other hand, entails strict hierarchical ordering within the functionally qualified part of the *ecclesia*.

Secondly, it is axiomatic for Gregory that order, that is, the neat demarcation between the two *ordines* must be preserved: order within

---

[1] In the words of the *Breviarium Romanum*, ad 25 May, he was "acerrimus ecclesiae defensor."

the *societas christiana* is the second vital principle of Gregory VII. It means that each and every member must fulfil the functions allotted to him, functions, that is to say, which are determined by the nature of the body of the Christian society. The function of each member of this *societas* is orientated by the purposes of this society. When therefore everyone acts according to the function allotted to him, there will come about what Gregory VII calls *concordia* entailing *pax* within the *ecclesia*.[1] Its opposite is *discordia*, which emerges when the individual members do not adhere to the functions which they are called upon to fulfil.

Thirdly, it is fundamental to Gregory VII that the basis of the allocation of the functions is *justitia*. *Justitia* is not a purely religious-ethical idea, nor is it a purely nomological idea: it partakes of both. It contains the totality of all those ideological principles which flow from the substratum of the *societas christiana*, namely the Christian faith. The substance of *justitia* is the right *norm of living*, and *justitia* answers the question: what is the appropriate norm of conduct in a Christian society? *Justitia* is the crystallized and most abstract expression of hierocratic doctrine.[2] It is according to Gregory the Christian norm of conduct, a regulative principle which yields an applicable criterion for measurement.[3] Just conduct is unquestioned acknowledgment and acceptance of the ideological principles constituting *justitia*. He who thus acts, shows *humilitas*; he who refuses to acknowledge and to accept these principles shows *superbia*. *Superbia* is the deliberate setting aside of the norm of conduct as prescribed in and by *justitia*. *Justitia* is the canon of Christian world order, according to which the functions are allotted in Christian society and its life consequently regulated. *Justitia* shows what is right conduct, and what, therefore, ought to be the law—in a Christian society.

Fourthly, and lastly, *justitia* is unshaped *jus*: it stands in the ante-chamber of *jus*. It is "quasi juris status" as Bishop Atto of Vercelli

---

[1] See especially infra p. 289 f. for the texts quoted from Gregory VII and St Augustine.

[2] The verdict of E. Emerton, *The correspondence of Pope Gregory VII*, New York, 1932, p. xxiv, partakes somewhat of crudity: "Whatever was favourable to the Roman Church system, came within the definition of *justitia*." Emerton seems at least to have felt however that the term "righteousness"—the usual interpretation (Bernheim, Whitney, Tellenbach)—is quite inadequate to render the sense of the profound idea appropriately.

[3] Considered by itself, *justitia* is an indifferent term: Emperor Henry III could have invoked it, so could and did Luther: *justitia* becomes meaningful only by the means of the ideology which is infused into it.

10 *

and Abbot Thietland of Einsiedeln exquisitely expressed it.[1] The conduct prescribed by *justitia* need not be one that can be found in the mould of the *jus*, as, for instance, in a papal letter or a conciliar decree, and the like. It is, as we have said, the pure idea of right conduct, but nevertheless this idea is also a norm and as such demands conformity which is nothing else but *obedientia*, the direct effluence of *justitia* being "quasi juris status." Deliberately setting aside the principles of *justitia* not only shows *superbia*, but also *inobedientia*. The pair "humilitas-superbia" refers to the religious-ethical side, whilst the pair "obedientia-inobedientia" refers to the nomological side, of *justitia*. Or differently expressed: "humilitas-superbia" concerns the internal, psychic-emotional state; "obedientia-inobedientia" relates to external conduct.[2]

It will be seen that these premises of Gregory's thought contain nothing new, except the terminology. But this terminology reflects the maturity of the hierocratic view: it is assuredly a symptom of a matured view when its many aspects can be neatly expressed in a few pregnant terms. And, apart from the actual application of hierocratic principles, the most important consequence of this maturity of thought was Hildebrand's clear perception of the need to have a law with which to govern the *societas christiana*. That law for which he repeatedly expressed his wish, was to show the distillation of *justitia* into *jus*, into generally binding rules of conduct.[3] Hierocratic principles as evolved in times gone by in papal statements and in historical events[4] constitute in their

---

[1] See Denifle, *Die abendländische Schriftauslegung bis Luther*, Freiburg, 1906, pp. 25, 27. It should be noted that the "justitia Dei" in *Rom.* i. 17 (cf. also iii. 21–2; x. 3–4) was thus defined only by these two authors: "Justitia dicitur quasi juris status. Justitia ergo est, cum unicuique proprium jus tribuitur; unde et justus dicitur, eo quod jus custodiat"; all the other interpreters adopted the purely theological or moral explanation, e.g. of St Augustine or of Walafrid Strabo.

[2] It may be that the idea of *justitia*, as a consequence of legal studies, reappeared later in the "jus naturale" which has exactly the same amphibious character as *justitia*, and, just as *justitia*, its substance is determined by the prevailing ideology. The conception of natural law is not of Roman law origin, but is an excrescence of Greek legal philosophy: in the *Institutes* of Ulpian which contain the "Roman" law definition of natural law, this definition was "probably a post-classical insertion," see F. Schulz, *History of Roman legal science*, Oxford, 1946, p. 137; cf. also pp. 71–2, 136, 337, note O. But cf. for Roman law itself C. A. Maschi, *La concezione naturalistica del diritto e degli istituti giuridici Romani*, Milan, 1936, pp. 162 ff., and on "naturalis ratio" in Roman law, ibid., pp. 236 ff.

[3] See Peter Damian's *Opusculum* no. 5: *De priv. Romanae ecclesiae ad Hildebrandum* (PL. cxlv. 89). The actual biblical basis of this view on the need for a law in a Christian society may possibly have been *Rom.* i. 17 (*Hebr.* x. 38). The living as such, the human actions, must be regulated in a society.

[4] This is what the reference to "Gesta" means, i.e. the history as recorded in the *Liber Pontificalis*. In contemporary terminology the expression "Gesta"

totality *justitia*, and these detailed principles should be made available for the actual government of the *societas christiana*. And of these principles none was more important than the function of the Roman Church as the epitome of all Christendom—that see, because it had been St Peter's, which has the *principatus*.

One might well say that, according to Gregory VII, the Roman Church is the embodiment of *justitia*:[1] the Roman Church headed by the pope knows the canon of the Christian world order—the *norma justitiae*—and hence the pope alone, by virtue of this self-same point of view, is entitled to issue on the basis of *justitia* concrete and detailed laws which bind everyone, without exception, in the *societas christiana*.[2] In a way, therefore, the concrete chapter headings of the *Dictatus papae* may be said to embody *justitia* in the mould of *jus*. The compilation of the *Dictatus Papae* is the conspicuous answer to Hildebrand's request, a request which showed his realistic appreciation of the situation, namely, that pure doctrine without the *jus* is little more than an illusion. The other and equally important symptom of this maturity of hierocratic doctrine is the concomitant canonistic activity assiduously assembling those previous utterances which in their totality contain *justitia*. The beginning was made with Humbert's *Sentences*, closely followed by the great collections of the late eleventh century, all of which show the execution of the one fundamental principle with its

---

always was understood in this sense. Cf. the advice given by the "Magister" to his "Discipulus" in the anonymous contemporary tract discovered by H. Weisweiler, "Un MS inconnu de Munich sur la querelle des investitures" in RHE. xxxiv (1938), pp. 245 ff.; see p. 268: "Lege libellum, qui gesta pontificum dicitur." It seems that in the ninth century the term "Gesta pontificum" referred to the ORi, as is shown by the use of the term by Gottschalk's *Opusc. II*, ed. D. C. Lambot, *Oeuvres theologiques et grammaticales de Godescalc d'Orbais*, Louvain, 1945, p. 494, no. 137.

[1] According to Innocent II the Roman Church was the "sedes justitiae," see e.g., his *Epp.* 347 and 380, PL. clxxix. 397 and 436. Cf. also Alexander III, *Ep.* 43 (PL. cc. 115): the Roman Church is divinely instituted "ut ad similitudinem aeterni et justi judicis unicuique pro meritorum qualitatibus responderet"; cf. also *Ep.* 766, PL. cit., col. 706. Innocent III called the Roman Church the "fundamentum legis totius Christianitatis" in *Reg.* ii. 217; cf. also *Reg.* ii. 105, 197, etc.

[2] This, we consider, is the germ out of which the later theory grew that the pope "omnia jura in suo pectore habet." The idea inherent in this axiom was later also expressed thus: "Summus pontifex non humanae adinventionis studio, sed divinae potius aspirationis instinctu leges statuens," Innocent IV in MGH. *Epp. sel. XIII s.*, ii. 55, p. 41. The view that the Roman Church alone knows the *norma justitiae* is, we think, also the germ of the later principle that the pope is "judex ordinarius omnium," as, for instance, expressed by Huguccio, the master of Innocent III.

many ramifications and derivations and applications, namely, the function of the Roman Church in the *societas christiana*, exercising the
monarchically conceived *principatus*. All this Rome-orientated legal
activity was to present the *jus* as it appeared when derived from
*iustitia*.[1]

# III

In consonance with traditional views Gregory VII conceives the
Church as the *corpus Christi*.[2] This *corpus* is composed of the ordained
and unordained members of the Church: it is the christian society—
"corpus Christi, quod est fidelium congregatio"[3]—and as such is an
autonomous body of all Christians who thus form the *orbis Romanus*.[4]
This body has all the concreteness and tangibility of an organically
integrated and earthy society. Those who live by the maxims of
Christianity as expounded by the Roman Church are Romans, the
others are Greeks.[5] In this we recognize the remnants of the old
imperial ideology: the *societas christiana* embodies the Roman empire
—"quibus imperavit Augustus, imperavit Christus"[6]—although this
Christian society stands on a level different from that of the Roman
empire: "Plus enim terrarum lex Romanorum pontificum quam imperatorum obtinuit."[7]

---

[1] For details see infra, ch. XI.

[2] See *Reg.* vi. 10, p. 412 (ed. E. Caspar): "Eos velut putrida membra a toto
corpore Christi quod est ecclesia catholica, anathematis gladio resecamus." The
Registers of Gregory VII (preserved in the Vatican Library: Reg. Vat. no. 2)
were the original registers of the papal chancery, according to W. Peitz, "Das
Originalregister Gregors VII" in *SB. Vienna*, 1911, fasc. 5. Peitz's opinion has
held virtually undisputed sway, despite some hesitations expressed here and there,
e.g., by R. L. Poole, *Lectures on the history of the papal chancery*, Cambridge,
1917, p. 127, note 2. But Peitz's views are now severely impugned by L. Santifaller,
*Beschreibstoffe im Mittelalter* (MIOG. suppl. vol. xvi/1, 1953), pp. 94–113.
Santifaller holds that Gregory's Register as preserved, is an *aide-memoire*, and
not the original Register: "Sammlung des politisch und administrativ wichtigen
Schriftenmaterials der Regierung Gregors VII, bestimmt zur Orientierung und
Verwertung für die Nachfolger ... eine Art Verbindung von Gedenkbuch für
den inneren Gebrauch und von Farbbuch für äussere Zwecke" (p. 112). In this
respect there is then no difference between Gregory's Register and Innocent
III's Registers, especially the RNI, about which see F. Kempf, *Die Register
Innocenz III* (Misc. Hist. Pont., ix. 1945), pp. 102 ff., esp. pp. 105–7, 117–19.

[3] *Reg.* ii. 73, p. 234. Cf. also *Reg.* vi. 16, p. 422. See also R. Morghen, "Questioni Gregoriane" in *Archivio della R. Deputazione di storia patria*, lxv (1942),
p. 61; idem, ibid., lxix (1946), pp. 97–116.

[4] *Reg.* viii. 5, p. 522.

[5] *Reg.* viii. 1; and for the "Romans" viii. 5 and 12, pp. 522, 532.

[6] *Reg.* ii. 75, p. 237.

[7] *Reg.* ii. 75, p. 237.

Over this *societas christiana* comprising as it did Latin Christendom, the pope rules by virtue of the Petrine commission. The *orbis Romanus* is directed by its epitome, the Church of Rome. For the whole Christian people had been entrusted to St Peter's care by Christ, the "summus imperator."[1] Hence this people is in the charge of the pope and he alone is entitled to demand unqualified obedience to his decrees.[2] Through the instrumentality of St Peter God had given to the pope the unique power to bind and to loose on earth as well as in heaven.[3] This power is indeed a concession of universal validity.[4] It is all embracing and comprehensive. And it is this power contained in the Petrine commission which confers the *universale regimen* upon the pope, excepting no Christian and no Christian's affairs.[5] The universality of government cannot, logically enough, be confined to particular aspects or to particular persons. The "universalitas suscepti regiminis"[6] knows in theory no frontiers. For as the *Dictatus* of Avranches had it, on the authority of Gelasius, "to the pope every power of the world must be subjected."[7] Should one really assume, Gregory asks very pertinently, that this universal government stops short of the power "judicare de terra? Absit."[8] The pope is the common father and master of all Christians—"communis pater et dominus"[9]—and therefore his authority cannot be subjected to any restrictions. God Himself had given St Peter the "regimen totius ecclesiae"[10] and consequently to him as St Peter's vicar is entrusted "universalis ecclesiae regimen,"[11] that is, the government over the whole *corpus* of Christians.

---

[1] *Reg.* viii. 21, p. 557. On the Gelasian origin of the term see supra p. 26.

[2] *Reg.* iii. 6*, p. 253: "Placet, ut populus christianus specialiter tibi (scil. beato Petro) commissus mihi obediat pro vice tua mihi commissa."

[3] *Reg.* iii. 6*, p.253: "Mihi tua gratia est potestas a Deo data ligandi et solvendi in terra et in coelo."

[4] See *Reg.* viii. 21, p. 548, and iv. 2, p. 295: "Nullum excipit, nichil ab eius potestate subtraxit." Cf. also *Reg.* vi. 4, p. 396, and vii. 6, p. 465. On the Gelasian model of this see supra p. 20.

[5] *Reg.* ii. 51, p. 193: "Nos equidem jam nunc non solummodo regum et principum, sed omnium christianorum tanto propensior sollicitudo coartat, quanto ex universali regimine quod nobis commissum est, omnium ad nos causa vicinius et magis proprie spectat."

[6] *Reg.* ii. 44, p. 180: "Ex universalitate suscepti regiminis, omnibus qui in Christo sunt . . ."

[7] See the quotation from the *Dictatus* of Avranches (DA) infra p. 283 n. 2.

[8] *Reg.* viii. 21, p. 550: "Cui ergo aperiendi claudendique coeli data est potestas, de terra judicare non licet? Absit."

[9] *Reg.* ii. 25, p. 157; ii. 67, p. 223, and in many other places.

[10] *Reg.* i. 15, p. 24.

[11] *Reg.* i. 9, p. 14.

From the hierocratic point of view one can but sympathize with the exasperation of Gregory VII which underlies the following question:

If the holy and apostolic see, through the principal power divinely conferred upon it, has the right to judge spiritual things, why then not secular things?[1]

The purely physical and material aspects of a Christian's life must of necessity be subjected to the direction of the spirit, indeed a commonplace enough statement, but one that seemed to have the peculiar fate of escaping the attention of contemporaries.[2] It is this commonplace idea that is contained in the other purely rhetorical question of Gregory VII:

For if the see of St Peter decides and judges celestial things, how much more does it decide and judge the earthly and secular.[3]

It is the same point of view, only seen from a different angle, which prompted Gregory to this statement:

Since the apostle has ordained obedience to mundane powers, how much more has he enjoined obedience to the spiritual powers and those who are the vice-gerents of Christ amongst Christians.[4]

He, as the vicar of St Peter, whom Christ had made the prince over all earthly kingdoms[5] has the power "universo orbi imperare."[6] But governing this whole societas christiana is indeed a heavy load on papal shoulders and places so much responsibility upon him. Thus he writes to Hugh of Cluny:

---

[1] Emerton's translation, which in one or two places we have slightly changed. Reg. iv. 2, p. 295: "Quodsi sancta sedes apostolica divinitus sibi collata principali potestate spiritualia decernens dijudicat, cur non et saecularia?" Cf. I Cor. vi. 3.

[2] Of Gregory VII and of some later writers, too. Cf. e.g., E. Voosen, Papauté et pouvoir civil, Louvain, 1927, pp. 247 ff., and A. Fliche, Le reforme Grégorienne, Paris, 1932, ii. passim; Gregory did not claim "temporal" powers. This is an oblique point and prevents an adequate appraisal of the profundity of hierocratic ideology.

[3] Reg. iv. 24, p. 338: "Si enim coelestia et spiritualia sedes beati Petri solvit et judicat, quanto magis terrena et saecularia." This statement sets the tone for all the hierocratic manifestations down to the fourteenth century, e.g. Aegidius Romanus, De eccles. potestate (ed. R. Scholz, Weimar, 1929), iii. 4, p. 163.

[4] Reg. i. 22, p. 38: "(Apostolus) ait 'omnis anima sublimioribus potestatibus subdita sit.' Cum ergo mundanis potestatibus oboedire praedicavit, quanto magis spiritualibus et vicem Christi inter Christianos habentibus."

[5] Reg. i. 63, p. 92: "Petrus apostolus, quem Dominus Jhesus Christus rex gloriae principem super regna mundi constituit." Cf. also Reg. iii. 15, p. 267, where the Normans are said to desire to have St Peter as the only "dominus et imperator post Deum."

[6] Reg. iii. 31, p. 166; and Reg. ii. 45, p. 183: "Nos . . . qui ad regendum populum praelati . . . vocati et constituti sumus."

Portamus in hoc gravissimo tempore non solum spiritualium, sed et saecularium ingens pondus negotiorum.[1]

This Gregorian point of view, as we shall presently see, is little more than a truism when the import of hierocratic doctrine is properly appraised. Moreover, this society over which the pope rules, is so closely knit and so much an organism that an injustice or damage inflicted upon a single part of it, redounds to the detriment of the whole *corpus*.[2]

From these premises which can have validity only in a wholly Christian society, the claim follows conclusively that papal commands are divine commands and that therefore those who deliberately set aside papal orders expose themselves to the charge of having committed idolatry.[3] For papal commands are issued "ex parte omnipotentis Dei"[4] or "auctoritate Dei";[5] being the "deputy of St Peter" the pope has inherited the apostle's fullness of power.[6] Governing the Christian people not only entails issuing binding decrees by divine authority, but also supervision of those who in actual fact rule the people, namely the kings and emperors. For they too had been entrusted by St Peter with rulership over their peoples,[7] and St Peter's function has now been taken over by the pope. This is what Gregory tells the king of France, Philip I: his kingdom as well as his soul are in the power of St Peter.[8] And to the king of Ireland, Terdelvach, Gregory writes that Christ Himself had instituted St Peter over all the kingdoms of the world—"super omnia mundi regna constituit"—and to St Peter and his successors He wished all the powers "in saeculo" to be subjected.

---

[1] *Reg.* i. 62, p. 91.

[2] *Reg.* v. 7, p. 358 to Archbishop Udo of Trier and his suffragans: "Agite ergo, dilectissimi fratres . . . quoniam, si causa neglecta fuerit et ad graviorem, quod absit, exacerbationem venerit, non solum genti vestrae et regno Teutonicorum, sed quoad fines Christianitatis sunt, dampna pericula confusionem et inaestimabiles miserarum causas pariet." *Reg.* iv. 23, p. 335: "Hoc autem, quod inter eos agitur, negotium tantae gravitatis est tantique periculi ut, si a nobis fuerit aliqua occasione neglectum, non solum illis et nobis, sed etiam universali ecclesiae magnum et lamentabile pariat detrimentum." This view was of course intimately associated with the corporate nature of Christendom, cf. supra p. 6 f.

[3] *Reg.* iv. 24, p. 338: "Qui apostolicae sedi oboedire contempserit, scelus idolatriae incurrit"; see also *Reg.* iv. 23, p. 336; vi. 10, p. 411; viii. 15, p. 536; ix. 20, p. 601, and in many other places.

[4] *Reg.* v. 15, p. 375, etc.

[5] *Reg.* ix. 35, p. 624.

[6] See *Reg.* i. 63, p. 92.

[7] *Reg.* ii. 50, p. 192, to King Sancho II of Aragon: "A beato Petro apostolorum principe ad regendum tibi commissum populum."

[8] *Reg.* viii. 20, p. 543: "Beatus Petrus, in cuius potestate est tuum regnum et anima tua."

"The whole universe must obey and revere the Roman Church."[1] In a word, because Christian society means a society that is directed by the conceptions of Roman-papal-Petrine ideas, the pope as vicar of St Peter exercises supreme rulership over the *societas christiana*.

Although not claiming the vicariate of Christ for himself, Gregory nevertheless in his function as vicar of St Peter applies to himself the same fullness of power with which St Peter was credited. Gregory entirely operates with the Petrine commission; he does not say or imply that he was Christ-like or that he was Christ's vicar. Because St Peter had been set over the kingdoms, so he too as Peter's vicar has the same authority. In other words, the pope continues Petrine powers. The important point here is that the Petrine commission was not yet conceived to constitute a vicariate of Christ: the pope merely inherited the fullness of power which Christ had given to St Peter. But by virtue of this fullness of powers the—later—claim could be raised that this fullness constitutes a vicariate of Christ in the person of St Peter and consequently of the pope as his successor. Although, as we have said, Gregory VII himself did not claim the vicariate of Christ for himself *qua* pope, there can be no legitimate doubt that his pontificate and his

---

[1] See J. Usserius (Ussher), *Veterum epistolarum Hibernicarum sylloge*, Dublin, 1632, p. 76: "Cui (scil. Petro) principatus et potestates et quicquid in saeculo sublime videtur esse, subjecit . . . beato Petro eiusque vicariis (inter quos dispensatio divina nostram quoque sortem annumerari disposuit) orbis universus obedientiam similiter et reverentiam exhibere debet, quam mente devota sanctae Romanae ecclesiae exhibere reminiscimini." This letter of Gregory is now newly edited on the basis of MS. Claud. A. i, fol. 38, by A. Gwynn, in *Studi Gregoriani*, iii. 115. On the letter itself and its date see the excellent discussion ibid., pp. 113–22. Cf. also Gregory's similar statement: "Cui (scil. papae) omnes principatus et potestates orbis terrarum subjiciens, jus ligandi et solvendi in coelo et in terra contradidit," Ph. Jaffé, *Mon. Greg.*, p. 386. This Gregorian phraseology shows a kinship with Peter Damian's statement in *Disceptatio synodalis*, in LdL., i. 78, lines 7–8. The conception of Peter being the head of the kingdoms, could without undue difficulty lead to the thesis which adduced, and applied to the pope, the passage in *Jer.* i. 10. Cf. in this context also Innocent III writing to Philip Augustus, *Reg.* ii. 251: "*Christus*, rex regum et dominus dominantium . . . et corpus et animam tibi contulit . . . *regnum tibi concessit*, qui et vivere tibi contulit et moveri, et universa quae habes bona donavit"; also *Reg.* iii. 18: Christ, "qui tibi praeter excellentiam regiae dignitatis et vitam contulit . . ." Of non-papal sources we may quote Peter of Blois's letter to Celestine III on behalf of Queen Eleanor (1193), entreating the pope for his effective intervention with Henry VI to secure Richard I's release: "Nonne Petro apostolo et *in eo vobis*, a Domino *omne regnum* omnisque potestas regenda committitur? . . . Non rex, non imperator, aut dux a jugo vestrae jurisdictionis eximitur. Ubi est ergo zelus Phinees? Ubi est auctoritas Petri? . . . non degeneret in *haerede Petri* dignitatis apostolicae reverenda successio" (PL. ccvi. 1267). In the third letter (PL. cit., col. 1270) there is then the reference to *Jer.* i. 10.

vigorous assertion of the Petrine fullness of powers materially contributed to the crystallization of the conception that St Peter was given
vicarious powers by Christ.[1]

On the presupposition that St Peter exercises supreme rulership over
the *societas christiana*, the deposition of kings by St Peter's vicar was
a logical consequence of this premiss. From this also followed that in
the case of a prince's unwillingness to implement instructions issued
to him by the episcopacy, the latter was entitled to proceed against the
recalcitrant prince "spiritualibus et saecularibus armis."[2] Bishops are
ordered to attack a count alleged to be a tyrant "with weapons, both
carnal and spiritual."[3] By the same token the pope is entitled to invoke
the help of a duke against a disobedient bishop who is to be ejected
from his see forcefully by the duke.[4] And again by the same token the
pope authorizes a count to reproach his king for deeds which in
Gregory's eyes are wicked, and to threaten the king on the pope's
behalf with excommunication.[5]

It is an axiom of a correctly understood hierocratic doctrine that the

[1] For some of the reasons why the pope was not "vicarius Christi" at that time
see G. Tellenbach, *Libertas*, app. xvi, pp. 228–30, against Harnack's well-known
thesis. G. Ladner, op. cit., p. 155, note 412, points out that none of the "Reform"
popes claimed the title "vicarius Christi." The pope could not appear as vicar of
Christ until the Petrine commission was considered to constitute a vicariate of
Christ in St Peter, and hence also in his successors. When this concept was
evolved, the Donation of Constantine could be dispensed with, as in fact was
done by Innocent III. The development of the constitutional position of the pope
as vicar of Christ was necessitated by the very concept of the congregation of
the faithful forming the *corpus Christi*, that is, an autonomous, juristic entity
whose head was Christ. But this entity had to be governed, hence the pope
acted on behalf of Christ on earth, as Innocent III was to make abundantly clear;
hence also the notion of Christ's visible vicar (cf. infra 444) became indispensable
for purposes of government. The notion was also used to uphold the papal view
of episcopal power being derived from the pope.

[2] *Reg.* ii. 5, p. 133: "Quod si facere contempserit (i.e. Lancelin of Beauvais)
spiritualibus et saecularibus armis eum insequi et urgere non prius desistatis . . ."

[3] *Epp. coll.*, no. 34, p. 562 (ed. Ph. Jaffé). The bishops were those of Liege and
Verdun, and the count was Arnulf of Chiny; cf. also *Reg.* vii. 13, pp. 477–8. On
this letter see also A. M. Stickler in *Studi Gregoriani*, iii. 101. The immediate
model of this letter may have been Nicholas II's letter to the bishops of France
in 1059, telling them to proceed against the archbishop of Trier (Eberhard)
"spirituali simul et materiali gladio" (PL. cxix. 783; partly incorporated in
Gratian, XV. vi. 2 and ascribed to Nicholas I).

[4] *Reg.* ii. 8, p. 137: "Ducem (Wratislaw of Bohemia) vero rogavimus, ut si
episcopus nobis non oboediret, ut eum de castro expelleret." The same idea in
*Reg.* viii. 18, p. 540: a papal order to Count Ebulus of Roucy to resist Archbishop
Manasses of Rheims.

[5] See *Reg.* ii. 18, pp. 150–1 to Count William of Poitou ordering him to make
strong representations with Philip I of France.

principle of superiority and inferiority shows itself in all spheres of the *societas christiana*. It is on the basis of this axiom that royal power must be directed by the instructions of the apostolic see.

Qua tamen majoritatis et minoritatis distantia religio sic se movet Christiana, ut cura et dispositione apostolica dignitas post Deum gubernetur regia.[1]

Again, considering the nature and substance of the body corporate over which the pope presides, this principle is self-evident. In logical pursuit of this theme and by raising the famous Gelasian words to the level of a scriptural testimony—"divina testatur scriptura"—Gregory tells the Conqueror that the apostolic and pontifical authority has to represent Christian kings and all others before the divine tribunal in order to render an account of their doings.[2] Quite in consonance with Gelasius I Gregory VII speaks of all Christians as his "subditi," precisely because he as head of the *societas christiana* is responsible for the doings of its members before the divine tribunal.[3] In classic form Gregory expresses one of the principal hierocratic tenets by declaring that apostolic and royal powers are to be likened to the two luminaries, sun and moon.[4] The ingenious bracketing of the sun and moon

---

[1] *Reg.* vii. 25, p. 506, to the Conqueror.

[2] *Reg.* vii. 25, p. 506, continuing: "Licet fili karissime, tua non ignoret vigilantia, tamen, ut pro salute tua indissolubiliter menti tuae sit allegatum, divina testatur scriptura, apostolicam et pontificalem dignitatem reges Christianos ceterosque omnes ante divinum tribunal representaturam et pro eorum delictis rationem Deo reddituram." It is not easy to see what new idea Gregory VII was supposed to have expressed here, as A. Fliche, op. cit., ii. 319, maintains. Cf. also E. Voosen, op. cit., p. 247, where the Gelasian background is overlooked. It is sometimes alleged that the supposed Two-Power theory of Gelasius I does not fit into Gregory's scheme: of course not, if Gelasius had propounded a "dualism." But on that reading of Gelasius this dualistic theory would also constitute an alien element in Pseudo-Isidore as well as in every papal communication that uses Gelasius. The reference to "divina scriptura" was no doubt chosen by Gregory to impress the Conqueror. This Gelasian background was also overlooked by the late Z. N. Brooke, "Pope Gregory's demand for fealty from William the Conqueror" in EHR. xxvi (1911), p. 235, where the passage was given a feudal meaning. In *Reg.* viii. 21, p. 553, Gregory quotes Gelasius directly from the source.

[3] *Reg.* ii. 51, p. 193 to Sven of Denmark: "Nosti, quod reges . . . et quodom nes ad districtum judicium futuri examinis venturi sumus, quod nunc non solum nobis, qui sacerdotes sumus, sed et regibus ceterisque principibus tanto concussius timendum et expavendum est, quanto pro nobis et *subditis nostris* rationem posituri sumus."

[4] *Reg.* vii. 25, to the Conqueror, p. 505 f.: "Sicut enim ad mundi pulchritudinem oculis carneis diversis temporibus representandam solem et lunam omnibus aliis eminentiora disposuit luminaria, sic, ne creatura, quam sui benignitas ad imaginem suam in hoc mundo creaverat, in erronea et mortifera traheretur pericula, providit, ut apostolica et regia dignitate per diversa regeretur officia." The

allegory with the Gelasian principle of the priestly rendering an account for the crimes of the kings, shows the maturity which hierocratic thought had reached. Indeed, "Christi sacerdotes" are the "patres et magistri" of all the faithful, including kings and princes—what a pitiable madness, he exclaims, if the son were to subjugate the father or the pupil his master: and has not Pope Gelasius said exactly the same to his contemporary emperor, and fortified by such declarations some pontiffs have excommunicated kings, whilst others excommunicated emperors. Henry IV's second excommunication and final deposition are thus expressly based upon Gelasian authority.[1] And the *Dictatus* of Avranches in the chapter corresponding to the *Dictatus* of Gregory, dealing with the deposition of kings, supports this by invoking the testimony of Gelasius I.[2] In other words, Christian royal power can be exercised so long as the king accepts the ruling of the pope. Or looked at from a different angle, the deposition of a Christian king is the rightful exercise of the supreme power contained in the pope's *universale regimen*.[3]

Closely allied to this conception of Gregory VII is his view of the duty of the king in a Christian society, and of the function of the priesthood. He sees the foremost duty of the king in the implementation and execution of *justitia*, in carrying out the sum total of all the precepts contained in "pura religio." This, as we know, is nothing else but Christian cosmology brought down to earth.[4] The "justitia Chris-

---

biblical reference is *Gen.* i. 17. Sacerdotal dignity and royal power stand to each other like gold and lead: *Reg.* viii. 21, p. 553, quoting from "Ambrosius" that is, *De dignitate sacerdotali*, c. 2 (PL. xvii. 569–70). This tract though ascribed to Ambrose, was written in the second half of the fifth century, cf. H. Rahner, *Abendl. Kirchenfreiheit*, p. 175, note 5; cf. also supra p. 78. This comparison was later also used by Thomas Becket, see D. Knowles, *Episcopal colleagues of Archbishop Thomas Becket*, Cambridge, 1951, p. 147; it seems that Becket quoted from Gregory's letter, cf. the report of Grim, quoted by Knowles, note 3. Gilbert Crispin, too, quoted from this pseudo-Ambrosian tract, cf. J. Armitage Robinson, *Gilbert Crispin*, Cambridge, 1911, pp. 68, 113.

[1] *Reg.* viii. 21, p. 553.

[2] See DA. cap. 10: "Papae omnis potestas mundi subdi debet Clemente Gelasio teste. Regna mutare potest ut Gregorius Stephanus Adrianus fecerunt."

[3] See *Reg.* vii. 14a, p. 487: "Si potestis in coelo ligare et solvere, potestis in terra imperia, regna, principatus, ducatus, marchias, comitatus, et omnium hominum possessiones pro meritis tollere unicuique et concedere."

[4] *Reg.* iv. 28, p. 344, to the kings and princes of Spain: "Exhibentes vos fideles ministros faciendam justitiam"; *Reg.* vi. 20, p. 432, to Count Centullus: he deserves to be called "christianus princeps, quia sis videlicet *amator justitiae*, defensor pauperum et propagator pacis"; *Reg.* viii. 20, p. 542, to Philip I, admonishing him to be "*amator justitiae*"; in the same sense already *Reg.* i. 75,

tianae legis"[1] made known through the mouth of the Roman Church, is to be executed by the Christian kings. Hence no one may call himself a Catholic who disregards the norms of living as expounded by the epitome of the universal Church, that is to say, ignores the "norma justitiae":[2] "Quod catholicus non habeatur qui non concordat Romanae ecclesiae."[3]

Obedience is thus the hallmark of the Christian and particularly of the Christian prince: obedience to the decrees of the Roman Church must be unqualified: he who contradicts the decrees shows unheard-of "superbia" and has consequently no right to exercise governmental power.[4] This claim to unquestioned obedience flows from what may be called the legalization of the faith and, in the last resort, from the true monarchic position of the pope who exercises the *universale regimen*. In the case of a prince disobedience entails deposition.[5] This penalty itself is, logically enough, *justitia*.[6] The *societas christiana* can live, can exist, can develop, can come to its full fruition only if the (papally decreed) "*justitia* christianae legis" is made the norm and standard of living. Obedient kings are members of the "corpus veri regis Christi"; disobedient kings are members of the "corpus diaboli."[7] It is not the pope, but St Peter who excommunicates and deposes kings through the instrumentality of the pope.[8] On the other hand, kings rule by the

---

p. 107; *Reg.* vi. 29, p. 442, to Ladislaw of Hungary: "De cetero prudentiam tuam monemus, ut *viam justitiae* semper studeas . . ."; *Reg.* i. 70, p. 101, to the Conqueror: "Justitiae per omnia, cum oportunum est, inmodo insudare, ne desistas"; cf. furthermore the protocol of the Lenten synod in Rome, 1078, *Reg.* v. 14a, p. 370, no. 6, where Gregory announces his intention to send legates "a latere apostolicae sedis" to Germany who will convoke "omnes religiosos et *justitiae amatores* in Teutonici regni partibus . . ."; see also *Reg.* viii. 21, p. 559: Constantine, Theodosius, Honorius, Charlemagne, and Louis the Pious were "*justitiae amatores*, Christianae religionis propagatores, ecclesiam defensores . . ."; *Reg.* ix. 34, p. 622 to Count Robert I of Flanders: it behoves a Christian prince to have "in hoc negotio *justitiae amorem*."

[1] *Reg.* ii. 9. p. 140.　　　　[2] *Reg.* vi. 29, p. 441, to the king of Hungary.
[3] DP. 26.
[4] See Gregory's letter to Henry IV: *Reg.* iii. 10, p. 267.
[5] *Reg.* iii. 6*, p. 253: "Per auctoritatem Heinrico regi, filio Heinrici imperatoris, qui contra tuam ecclesiam inaudita superbia insurrexit, totius regni gubernacula Teutonicorum et Italiae contradico, et omnes Christianos a vinculo juramenti . . . absolvo." See also *Reg.* iii. 10a, p. 270, and *Reg.* iv. 23, p. 336: threat of deposition and excommunication in the case of not affording safe conduct to papal legates: "Resistite et totius regni gubernacula contradicendo . . ." Cf. also infra p. 301.
[6] Cf. the remarks of Gregory concerning the affection of a mother towards a deposed son whose deposition was the execution of justice, in *Reg.* iv. 3, p. 299.
[7] *Reg.* viii. 21, p. 557.　　　　[8] *Reg.* iii. 6, p. 255.

consent of the Roman Church or, as Gregory puts it, those whom the (Roman) Church after mature deliberation has called to government, should humbly obey:

Quos sancta ecclesia sponte sua ad regimen vel imperium deliberato consilio *advocat*, non pro transitoria gloria, sed pro multorum salute, *humiliter obediant*.[1]

All these views, we repeat, can only be propounded and accepted in a Christian society, that is, a society which is not held together by a mere biological or linguistic element or by sheer force, but one whose substratum is the spiritual element of the Christian faith. Only under this presupposition can the function of a king be understood, and under this presupposition royal power is not and cannot be monarchic or absolute, referring as it does to the mere exercise of physical-material power. Royal power receives its meaning and purposeful function only in relation to the substratum of the society or part of the society over which this physical-material force is to be executed. Royal power is not autonomous: it must be considered in relation to the character of contemporary society, that is in relation to the purpose and aim of the *societas christiana*. As we said before, the constitutive element of contemporary society was not force, nor a racial or national or biological element, but the spiritual element of the Christian faith: or what Gregory himself called "pura religio." This alone is the directive principle; this alone is the orientating factor, and this alone is the criterion which enables us to understand the function of the king as well as of the "temporal" or "secular."

For the king is a Christian and as such is subjected to the decrees of the Roman Church: in fact it is his specific duty to show himself an *amator justitiae*. True royal power can be had in a Christian society "by bowing before Christ, king of kings" and hence by accepting the decrees of the Roman Church.[2] Had there not been sin, instigated by the devil, there would have been no need to have a physical-material power to repress sinful conduct: from the teleological point of view kingship owes its origin to the devil, because he made man deviate from the path of *justitia*;[3] consequently, the king's function, as an

---

[1] *Reg.* viii. 21, p. 561.    [2] *Reg.* ii. 30, p. 164, to Henry IV.

[3] This is of course Isidorian doctrine. Cf. also Humbert supra 270, and Innocent III in RNI. 18, speaking of the "causa institutionis" of priesthood and secular rulership: the "sacerdotium" was instituted "per ordinationem divinam, regnum autem *per extorsionem humanam*." That is why metaphorically expressed, "regalis potestas praeest noctibus" (*Solitae*, Rainer, ii. 2 (PL. ccxvi. 1184); also *Reg.* i. 409; vii. 79 and RNI. 2). Cf. infra p. 423 n. 4.

*amator justitiae*, is the suppression of evil, but what is, and what is not evil, must necessarily be left to those who in a Christian society are qualified to pronounce upon it, that is, the ordained members of the Church: for they alone are qualified to function as the directing organs of this society; they alone are functionally qualified to direct society according to its underlying purpose; they alone, therefore, are functionally qualified to lay down the *norma justitiae*. The king, through being an *amator justitiae*, functions as a means to an end. The suitability of the king for his office is consequently of vital concern to the directing organs of the *societas christiana*; so is the king's usefulness. But these are criteria which can be established only by a recourse to the substance and essence of the *societas christiana*.[1]

The function of any member of the *societas christiana* can be determined only through relating it to the constituent element of this society, namely, the Christian faith as expounded by the Roman Church. Hence in this society, because he fulfils a higher function, the lowest exorcist stands higher than an emperor: in fact he is a "spiritualis imperator." And if this can be said of exorcists, "quanto amplius sacerdotes!" Another Gregory had said that the priests alone have the "sensum Christi." Which, transplanted to the sphere of government, means that they alone are qualified to direct Christian society: they alone have *auctoritas*; they alone are functionally qualified to rule. On the other hand, the "temporal" or "carnal" has a no doubt valuable function, according to Gregory, namely the function of a means to an end: considered from the teleological point of view, the "temporalia" are indeed indispensable to the proper working and functioning of the whole *societas*. Precisely because this society is endowed with real earthiness, the "temporal" is useful, but it becomes useful only by its being related to the aim and purpose, the "finis" or "telos" of society. It must be harnessed to the purpose of this *societas*, whose constitutive element is the spiritual element of the faith; the temporal must, in other words, serve the purpose of a substantially spiritual society. Then it will become purposeful, useful and meaningful. Then it will lose its inert character and become useful in the promotion of the health of the whole organism. By itself the "temporal" has no

---

[1] We think that this is the substance of the letter to Hermann of Metz, *Reg.* viii. 21, especially pp. 555 ff. What Gregory is anxious to impress is the teleological principle underlying the working of the Christian body politic. Considered from his point of view his exclamations show a justifiable note of irritation: "Quis igitur vel tenuiter sciolus sacerdotes dubitet regibus anterferri?" and so do many other statements in this letter.

indigenous function: if related to the spiritual substance of society, it will then be auxiliary and instrumental to the realization of the purpose underlying society. Matter, in hierocratic doctrine, is logically the servant of the spirit.[1]

Kings dealing as they do with matter, are, for governmental considerations, on the same level as matter, or the "temporal." The king is matter personified. The Christian king who acts on the basis of unqualified obedience to the Roman Church, is a king who deserves the epithet "useful"; he who does not, is "useless." The king functions —just as much as the "temporal" does—as a means to an end. Each is useful, provided each is harnessed to the purpose and substance of the society in which each exists. Usefulness to the *societas christiana* is the hallmark of the Christian king, and he proves himself useful by accepting the principles of *justitia*. This idea of usefulness underlies a number of statements made by Gregory VII which have not always been appreciated properly. For according to him, the function of a king is the defence and protection of the universal Church in general and of the Roman Church in particular: he who thus fulfils this function is useful to the whole *corpus*; he who does not is useless and loses his standing as a king.[2] It is far better, he counsels, to wait for a suitable

---

[1] This view on the "temporal" is in fact the germ out of which later grew the theory that the pope was entitled to dispose of the world's temporal goods (cf. Aegidius Romanus, Cardinal Bertrandi, etc., *Medieval Papalism*, pp. 133 ff.). This theory is extraordinarily consistent and the only one that seemed compatible with the notion of the *societas christiana*. Considering the purpose of this society it was logical that the pope (and with him the *sacerdotium*) alone knew to what use—from the point of view of this society—the temporal goods were to be put. It may be that the further penetration into the texture of Roman law (cf. e.g., *Cod. Just.*, VII. xxxvii. 3) facilitated the emergence of this theory. Cf., for example, Innocent III in RNI. 18: "Principibus datur potestas in terris, sacerdotibus autem tribuitur *et* in coelis. Illis solummodo super corpora, istis *etiam* super animas." Gregory IX writing to Frederick II (23 October 1236) says that the pope had not only "animarum imperium," but also "in universo mundo *rerum et corporum principatum*" (MGH. *Epp. sel. XIII s.*, i. 604, no. 703). Or as Innocent IV expressed it, the universal Church itself possesses the temporal goods: "Christus dominium et possessionem rerum ecclesiae habet . . . vel ecclesia habet possessionem . . . id est aggregatio fidelium quod est corpus Christi capitis" (ad X: II. xii. 4; I owe this passage to my former pupil, Dr B. Tierney). On the basis of the directive principle the pope as the monarch governing the *corpus* was considered to be in the best position to direct the actual use of temporal goods. The problem of papal taxation, especially in the fourteenth century, stands in closest proximity to this theory.

[2] *Reg.* ix. 3, p. 575, instructing Altmann of Passau and Abbot William of Hirsau, about the procedure to be adopted in the election of the new king (March, 1081): ". . . defensorem et rectorem, sicut eam (scil. ecclesiam) decet, clementer tribuat. Nisi enim ita obediens et sanctae ecclesiae humiliter devotus ac *utilis*,

king than to hurry matters and perhaps elect an unworthy man.[1] And in the fateful autumn days of 1076 he writes to all the faithful in Germany that if Henry should not repent, a new king should be elected who "shall bind himself unquestionably to carry out the measures" which the pope decrees: at the same time Gregory demands, so as to be in a position to confirm the election, prior notification of the elected candidate—"inform us at the earliest possible moment of the matter itself, the person and the character of the candidate."[2] The principle upon which this demand is based, is that of suitability—the pope alone is in a position to judge whether the king elected is a suitable king within the *societas christiana*.[3] But behind this there stands as a logical corollary the papal right of examining the election itself.[4] From here it is only a short step to the programmatic declaration of Innocent III.[5] Naturally, the principle of suitability assumes major importance in the case of him who is eventually to be the special defender of the Roman Church.[6] Within the realm of government the principle of

---

quemadmodum Christianum regem oportet, et sicut de R(udolpho) speravimus’ fuerit procul dubio ei non modo sancta ecclesia non favebit, sed etiam contradicet." Cf. also *Reg.* viii. 21, p. 554, where he declares that Childeric was deposed, not because of his iniquities, but because "non erat *utilis*." This conception was one of the germs from which the later theory grew (particularly after the intensified study of Roman law) of "public *utilitas*": the pope as the monarch of the Christian body politic knows what is required by *publica utilitas*. Cf. also infra p. 425 n. 2.

[1] *Reg.* ix. 3, p. 575: "Melius quippe fore arbitramur, ut aliqua mora secundum Deum ad honorem sanctae ecclesiae *rex* provideatur *idoneus* quam nimium festinando in regem aliquis ordinetur indignus."

[2] *Reg.* iv. 3, p. 299 f.: "negotium, personam et mores eius quamtotius potestis nobis indicare."

[3] In a way one might see in this demand, logical as it is, a reversal of the former imperial demand for notification of the elected pope to the exarch of Ravenna for confirmation.

[4] *Reg.* cit.: "Ut autem *electionem* . . . apostolica auctoritate firmemus."

[5] In RNI. 62.

[6] For the historical background of Gregory's letter and its significance see the important contribution of W. Berges, "Gregor VII und das deutsche Designationsrecht" in *Studi Gregoriani*, ii. 189–209, especially pp. 198–200. Berges points (note 24) to the development of Gregory's views as regards Pope Zacharias's participation in the affair of Childeric: in *Reg.* iv. 2, p. 294, the pope merely deposed Childeric; in *Reg.* viii. 21, p. 554, Childeric was deposed by the pope who himself "set in his (Childeric's) place Pippin, the father of Charlemagne." This latter statement comes nearer to historical truth (see supra p. 53) than that concerning the deposition. The passage in *Reg.* iv. 3—"ut . . . *novam ordinationem* nostris temporibus corroboremus, sicut a nostris patribus factum esse cognoscimus"— might possibly refer to the *scrutinium* of the coronation procedure. Cf. also *Reg.* i. 20, to which Berges himself draws attention (p. 199)—"Rex et Romae Deo

suitability manifests itself in the king's being useful to the *societas christiana*; and he is useful when he executes with his sword what the Roman Church decrees. The abstract Isidorian thesis comes near to its practical realization.[1]

## IV

These considerations of Gregory VII are the effluence of his basic view of the hierarchical ordering of society itself. Diversity of offices, that is, of functions and orders, is, according to him, necessary for the integration of any organism.[2] In a most memorable passage—indeed lacking neither in profundity nor in beauty—the first Gregory had declared and the seventh was to repeat it:

Neque enim universitas alia poterat ratione subsistere, nisi huiusmodi magnus eam differentiae ordo servaret.[3]

The proper working of society is the result of what the two Gregories call the *ordo differentiae*. By this they mean the differential grading of the members of society: by fulfilling the functions attached to each individual grade, to each individual order, there will come about what the seventh Gregory styled "una concordia ex diversitate."[4] This was "divinae dispensationis provisio"[5] which instituted "gradus diversos ordines distinctos," so, however, that the lower orders show due reverence to the higher orders. Therefrom *pax* will emerge and society

---

annuente *futurus imperator*"—pointing out the connexion between idoneity and the making of the emperor.

[1] From Gregory's point of view it is consistent that the king should become a "miles beati Petri," cf. *Reg.* ii. 49, p. 190; ix. 3 and 4, pp. 576, 578; or that he should become a "fighter in the service of the apostolic court," as he makes plain to King Sven II of Denmark, *Reg.* ii. 51, p. 194: "If our holy mother, the Roman Church, should have need of your aid in fighting men against God's enemies, we would like to know how much hope we can place in you. Not far from here there is a very wealthy province near the sea which is now in the hands of vile and miserable heretics, where we desire to put one of your sons as duke and prince and defender of Christianity, that is, if you are willing, as one of your bishops has told us of your intention to give him as a fighter in the service of the apostolic court ('apostolicae aulae militandum') together with a good following of faithful troops." The province mentioned may be Dalmatia.

[2] This point of view stands in closest proximity to the organic conception of the *societas christiana*; for the fully developed organic conception see infra ch. xiii on John of Salisbury and Hugh of St Victor.

[3] *Reg.* vi. 35, p. 450. Gregory I: *Reg.* v. 59, p. 371, lines 15–16. The biblical basis of this principle is I *Cor.* xii. 6: "diversity of operations."

[4] Ep. cit., p. 450.

[5] We shall not miss the allusion to the Gelasian "dispensatio."

as a whole will fulfil the purpose for which it exists. The purpose of this society will be achieved if there is concord, itself the result of the integration of diverse orders—unity of the whole organism, not in spite of, but because of the diversity of functions.[1] Unity results from accepting the principles contained in *justitia* which allots specific directive functions to the sacerdotal order, functions, that is to say, which are explicable only by the character of society as a *societas christiana*. It is also *justitia* which allots the auxiliary function and servile role to the "temporal" and its human personification, the temporal ruler. This functionalist approach based upon the teleological principle, is of the greatest importance to the conceptual framework of Gregory VII.

His sharp distinction between the two *ordines* composing the *societas christiana*, the sacerdotal and laical orders, is not merely a matter of principle, but a matter of government. For the sacerdotal order is, by virtue of its members having received ordination, alone functionally qualified to lead and to direct the whole Christian people. Through ordination the members of the sacerdotal order alone are given the power to bind and to loose—and this power alone creates, on the one hand, the deep cleavage between them and their unordained lay counterparts, and, on the other hand, gives them the functional qualification for their governing the *societas christiana*, which is genetically and substantially a spiritual society. The role which, in this society, the lay order, headed by king or emperor, has to play, will have become sufficiently clear.

It is consequently in keeping with the basic and traditional tenets of the hierocratic theme, when the sacerdotal order is raised to the level of divine agents: to them alone is applicable the biblical "He who toucheth you, toucheth the apple of my eye"[2] and "Touch not mine anointed."[3] The sacrament of ordination lifts its recipient out of the ordinary mass of individuals. He obtains thereby the qualification of guiding the unordained members of society. The transition from mere guidance into leadership is carried out by transforming "pura religio" into an enforceable, binding rule, into the law.[4] The *sacerdotium* is the

---

[1] Cf. St Paul, loc. cit., and also St Augustine, *Civ. Dei*, xix (13): "Pax omnium rerum tranquillitas ordinis. Ordo est parium dispariumque rerum sua cuique loca tribuens dispositio."

[2] *Reg.* ix. 37, p. 631; *Zach.* ii. 8.          [3] I *Chron.* xvi. 22.

[4] Evidenced, for instance, in the transformation of the "claves regni coelorum" into "claves juris" by the twelfth-century canonists; cf. also infra ch. xi. As far as can be seen, the author of the *Summa Coloniensis* (written in the late sixties of the twelfth century) was the first to do so.

vehicle which makes *justitia* articulate. The functional qualification is conferred upon them by the "caput sacerdotum."[1] Since the whole "christianitas" was handed to St Peter by Christ Himself, it is consequently St Peter's vicar upon whom falls the duty to judge and to legislate upon all matters affecting this *societas*. Judgment and legislation being the two vital channels through which any form of government can be carried out, must therefore be the preserve of those functionally qualified to govern the Christian body. Hence, the priests alone are the "sors Domini" and hence they alone are qualified to function as the directing organs of the "corpus Christi, quod est ecclesia catholica."[2] This idea of functionalism stands and falls with hierocratic doctrine or more correctly, with the idea of the Roman Church being the epitome of the *ecclesia universalis*, the corporate body of all Christians.

Several consequences could be, and were, drawn from this functionalist approach.

Firstly, having obtained their specific function from the pontiff, the lower churches logically partake in the authority of the Roman Church, though never in the fullness of its authority. Gregory brings the earlier doctrine to its fruition.[3]

Sancta Romana ecclesia vices suas ita aliis impertivit ecclesiis, ut in partem vocatae sunt sollicitudinis, non in plenitudinem potestatis.[4]

Supreme sacerdotal power is concentrated in the pontiff alone as the head of the Roman Church which diffuses its power throughout the ecclesiastical hierarchy.

Secondly, centralization of government is a further consequence of the functionalist principle correctly understood and applied. Centralization is not, however, confined to sacerdotal matters, but concerns, by virtue of the epitome character of the Roman Church, all matters affecting the *societas christiana*.[5]

---

[1] *Reg.* viii. 21, p. 552.    [2] *Reg.* vi. 10, p. 412.

[3] The original phrase came from Leo I, see supra p. 8, who had used it for a special occasion only (Ep. 14, c. 1). The phrase also appeared in Pseudo-Vigilius, see Hinschius, *Pseudo-Isidore*, p. 712; it was appended to a genuine Vigilius letter as the seventh chapter, cf. Hinschius, p. cv., and p. 712 notes ad cap. 7.

[4] PL. cxlviii. 783. Cf. also Gratian, II. vi. 11 (and 12). It was not so very difficult to construct a corporation theory on this basis. On this see the unpublished (Cambridge) thesis of B. Tierney.

[5] This is the theme of the twenty-seven sentences of the *Dictatus Papae* (DP) which in their totality are a concise re-statement of the Roman primacy. What they contain is hierocratic ideology in the garb of the law. The riddle which the DP has hitherto presented, is most satisfactorily solved by G. B. Borino, "Un

This applies specifically to the following items.

(*a*) The legalization of the headship of the whole universal Church: the pope is by law—"de jure"—the universal pontiff, since the Roman Church is divinely founded.[1] The name of this head is now legally monopolized, and the pope alone applies to himself the epithet "sanctus."[2]

(*b*) The institution of papal legates who are the prolonged arms of the pope and invested with papal powers. They carry out direct papal government through the length and breadth of the *societas*. From this follows that they have precedence over all other ecclesiastical orders.[3] The papal legates being "a latere papae" are "pars corporis papae" and consequently function on behalf of the pope[4] who applies to himself Christ's dictum "He who despiseth you, despiseth me"[5] when he issues instructions to his legates who are, in a sense, papal apostles.[6] To disregard their instructions which are papal instructions, is to disregard "ipsam Veritatis sententiam."[7]

(*c*) The supreme jurisdictional powers of the pope himself. In his capacity as pope he is outside the bounds of any tribunal,[8] whilst as an appellate tribunal the verdicts given by the pope are incapable of revision.[9] Every member of the Christian society is entitled to appeal

---

ipotesi sul DP di Gregorio" in *Archivio della R. deputazione di storia patria*, n.s. x (1944), pp. 240 ff.: these twenty-seven sentences are the chapter headings of a lost canonical collection. Borino's solution is now generally accepted, cf. St. Kutner, in *Studi Gregoriani*, ii. 400; K. Hofmann, ibid., i. 531 ff.; P. E. Schramm, in *Göttinger Gelehrte Anzeigen*, 1953, p. 131. Cf. already W. Peitz, op. cit., pp. 280 ff.

[1] DP. 2 and 1.

[2] DP. 11, and 23. For details concerning the DP. see K. Hofmann, *Der Dictatus Papae Gregors VII*, Munich, 1933; cf. also R. Koebner in *Festschrift f. Robert Holtzmann*, Leipzig, 1933, pp. 64–92.

[3] DP. 4.

[4] Cf. also the observations of P. E. Schramm, in *Studi Gregoriani*, ii. 440: "Auf sie bezog das Dekretalenrecht, was das römische Recht auf die Consuln und die kaiserlichen Legaten aussagte"; also G. Tellenbach, ibid., ii. 138; and J. B. Sägmüller, in *Theologische Quartalschrift*, lxxx (1898), p. 71: "rein delegatäres Beamtentum." See also H. E. Feine, *Kirchliche Rechtsgeschichte*, Weimar, 1950, p. 270.

[5] *Luke*, x. 16.

[6] See the many passages in which Luke is quoted in this sense: *Reg.* i. 17, p. 27; ii. 40, p. 177; ii. 73, p. 234; in iii. 10, p. 265 writing to Henry IV he says: "Non nobis, sed Deo omnipotenti debitam non denegaris reverentiam, quamquam apostolis eorumque successoribus Dominus dicere dignatus sit 'qui vos audit . . .'"

[7] *Reg.* i. 17, p. 27: "Non eos (scil. legatos), sed ipsam Veritatis sententiam spernunt."

[8] DP. 19. On the genesis of this see *Studi Gregoriani*, iv. 111 ff.

[9] DP. 18.

to the head of the Roman Church.[1] Supreme jurisdiction is in effect *justitia* made concrete. For the Roman Church is the repository of *justitia*, of the sum total of the principles of hierocratic theory.[2]

It was only a specific application of this tenet that the papal chancery from Gregory VII onwards abandoned in the solemn *privilegia* the usual clause binding the pope's successors[3] and adopted phrases[4] which denoted the freedom of the issuing pope himself and of his successors to effect changes prompted by *justitia*. This chancery peculiarity is not an adoption of a mere phraseology because the clause which was adopted, expressed in documentary form the papal plenitude of power and signified the pope's legal and jurisdictional freedom from any cramping restrictions imposed by a predecessor. Privileges, conferred by the Roman Church, can always be altered, Gregory declared, or abolished, "si necessitas vel utilitas major exegerit."[5] The pope as a monarch stands above the law.[6]

(*d*) The supreme legislative functions of the pope,[7] which include the papal right to set aside conciliar decrees.[8] Legislation the basis of which can only be *justitia* must necessarily be concerned with any

---

[1] DP. 20.

[2] In the widest sense this applies also to DP. 17, the authorization of dogmatic-canonical books, about which see St. Kuttner in *Studi Gregoriani*, ii. 387 ff.

[3] Cf. *Liber Diurnus*, form. 95, p. 125: "Statuentes auctoritate b. Petri principis apostolorum, sub divini judicii obtestatione et anathematis interdictum, ut nulli umquam nostrorum successorum pontificum . . . liceat ipsum praenominatum fundum quoquo modo aufferre vel alienare . . ."; almost the same phrase in form. 91, p. 120; cf. also form. 88, p. 117: ". . . omnino interdicentes nostris posteris ac successoribus . . ."

[4] Such as "Salva per omnia justitia sanctae Romanae ecclesiae."

[5] *Reg.* vi. 2, p. 393.

[6] There were isolated instances of this chancery peculiarity before Gregory's pontificate, cf. Sergius II in 844 (J. 2586: Mansi, xiv. 807) conferring the apostolic vicariate on Archbishop Drogo of Metz "salvo in omnibus huius universalis Romanae sedis primatu nostrique praesulatus honore vigoreque"; Benedict III in 855 (J. 2664, Mansi, xv. 110) spoke of "salvo in omnibus jure apostolicae sedis." On the whole question see F. Thaner, "Ueber die Entstehung und Bedeutung der Formel 'Salva sedis apostolicae auctoritate'" in *SB. Vienna*, lxxi (1872), pp. 807–51; J. B. Sägmüller, "Zur Entstehung etc." in *Theologische Quartalschrift*, lxxxix (1907), pp. 93–117; idem, *Zur Geschichte der Entwicklung des päpstlichen Gesetzgebungsrechts*, Rottenburg, 1937, pp. 9 ff.; cf. also idem, "Die Idee Gregors VII vom Primat der römischen Kirche" in *Theol. Quartalschrift*, lxxviii (1896), pp. 571–613.

[7] DP. 7. The claim to supreme legislative power is the application of the Roman law principle "What pleases the prince has the force of law," about which see G. Le Bras "Le droit romain au service de la domination pontificale" in *Revue hist. de droit français et étranger*, xxvii (1949), pp. 390–1.

[8] DP. 16 and 25.

topic or aspect which affects the working of the *societas*. Legislation, next to jurisdiction, is, as we have said, the vital channel through which any government, if it deserves this name, must function. And this legislation cannot, and does not, stop short of either persons or things: it is comprehensive, because it emanates from the epitome of all Christendom, which alone knows how matters existing, and persons living, in this *societas*, should be directed, if the purpose of this society is to be realized and its substratum come to its full fruition.[1] The deceptively sudden onrush of the numerous canonical collections in the Gregorian period is perhaps the best symptom of the state of preparedness of hierocratic doctrine: from now onwards these canonical collections stand in sharp contrast to the older models, since the former have universal and centralized character, orientated as they were by Rome. The episcopal bias of the earlier collections is swept aside in favour of the Roman bias.[2]

Thirdly, only from the functionalist point of view the full meaning of Gregory's battle cry "libertas ecclesiae" becomes understandable. That "ecclesia" does not mean the universal Church is plain and needs no further comment. What this slogan means is "libertas sacerdotii." We have here in fact one of the instances in which the meaning of the term "ecclesia" is restricted to the sacerdotal order of the universal *ecclesia*. That this terminology could and did cause a good deal of confusion is clear. For nobody could assert that the Church, that is the universal body of believers, the *societas christiana*, was oppressed; in actual fact, the eleventh-century emperors considered their actions and government exercised in the interests of the universal Church. The numberless benefactions, grants, immunities and so forth, bestowed upon the sacerdotal order, indeed do not indicate any oppression. But what these benefactions and so forth represented was the idea of protection in the royal sense. The emperor, and kings, acted as Christian overlords, and by virtue of their being divinely appointed "protectors" of the whole body of believers, including the sacerdotal order, they necessarily defended this body and one of the aspects of defence and

---

[1] Shortly afterwards St Anselm was to express this principle thus: "Certum quippe est quoniam qui non obedit Romani pontificis ordinationibus, quae fiunt *propter religionis Christianae custodiam*, inobediens est apostolo Petro, cuius vicarius est, nec de grege illo qui ei a Domino commissus est, *Ep.* xiii (PL. clix. 208). Cf. also *Ep.* lxv (PL. cit. col. 103): apostolic decrees are issued "ad robur Christianae religionis" because they emanate from "Petro utique apostolo, cuius vice *fungitur* (scil. papa)."

[2] Cf. A. Michel, "Die folgenschweren Ideen des Kardinals Humbert" in *Studi Gregoriani*, ii. 65 ff.

protection was the conferment of *beneficia* on the *sacerdotium* as a token of "exaltation." Defence and protection are only one aspect of "exaltation." But this function of the emperors and kings necessarily entailed control of the sacerdotal order. The way in which control was exercised was by the utilization of the proprietary church system for governmental purposes.[1] And the form in which this was symbolically carried out was that of investiture. The ceremony of investing the "elected" bishop[2] was the visible sign of the conferring of protection upon him by his royal lord.[3]

That this point of view was incompatible with the idea of functionalism and that it was diametrically opposed to the "pura religio," since the sacerdotal status was conferred by the lay lord, is understandable; so also is the fierceness of the battle against the whole lay standpoint which underlay the proprietary church system now thoroughly ossified. The deeper meaning of the battle cry "libertas ecclesiae" lies in the opposition to the royal idea of protection: not control of the *sacerdotium* by the protector, but control by the *sacerdotium* of the protector.[4] Control of the sacerdotal order by the emperor or king was

---

[1] The so-called lower churches (*Niederkirchen*) do not come within the purview of this essay, but the principles are the same. On the lower churches see especially the important investigations of H. E. Feine, "Studien zum langobardisch-italienischen Eigenkirchenrecht" in *Sav. Z., Kan. Abt.*, xxxi–xxxiii (1941–3); idem, "Ursprung, Wesen und Bedeutung des Eigenkirchentums" in *Festschrift f. L. Santifaller* (MIOG. lviii, 1950), pp. 195–208; idem, "Kirchenreform und Niederkirchenwesen" in *Studi Gregoriani*, ii. 505 ff. The financial and general economic benefits of this proprietary church system, including the lower churches, to the lay lords was of considerable importance to the latter. As Feine, in the last mentioned contribution has shown, in the neighbourhood of Lucca one church went through six generations of priests in the tenth century, whilst the more regular arrangement was inheritance to the priest's son and grandson only. For valuable comparisons and historical developments see now again, H. E. Feine, "Kirchleihe und kirchliches Beneficium" in *Hist. Jb.*, lxxii (1953), pp. 101 ff. For Cluniac priories or cells many of which were originally lay churches, their absorption into the Cluniac circle, the serious breaches thereby caused to the proprietary church system, and the resultant economic and social consequences, see the fine study by G. Schreiber, "Cluny und die Eigenkirche" in *Archiv f. Urkundenforsch.*, xvii (1942), pp. 359–418. For some post-Conquest examples see also D. Knowles, *Monastic Order in England*, pp. 596–7.

[2] See the lucid account by Z. N. Brooke, "Lay investiture" in *Proc. Brit. Acad.*, xxv (1939), pp. 223 f.

[3] According to Brooke (p. 224), lay investiture "was not the means by which the king maintained his control, but rather the outward sign of that control and of its character."

[4] The statutory beginning was made in the synod of April 1059, MGH. *Const.* i. 547, no. 384, cap. 6: "Ut per laicos nullo modo quilibet clericus aut presbyter obtineat ecclesiam nec gratis nec pretio."

irreconcilable with the control of the same body by the "caput sacerdotum." In a Christian society the control of the sacerdotal order was essential for both emperor and pope. The effective government of each depended upon the effectiveness of the control exercised over the priests. Hence the ferocious nature of the Investiture Contest. "Libertas ecclesiae" therefore meant freedom of the *sacerdotium* from the control of the protector and its subjection to papal control. In order to execute the *universale regimen* the pope was forced to subject the *sacerdotium* to his control, for its members were the transmitters of *justitia* made articulate by the Roman Church. And participating in the plenitude of power of the Roman Church they were alone qualified to function as the governing and directing organ of the *societas christiana*, in consonance with its underlying purpose. In fact and in theory the royal-laical control of the sacerdotal order turns into a sacerdotal control of the lay order. The protector becomes a "patronus" or "advocatus."

This subjection of the sacerdotal order to papal control was implemented by the insistence on strict hierarchical ordering within the ranks of the order, that is, by unqualified obedience to superior authority. This duty of obedience is reinforced by the specific episcopal oath.

Ego N. episcopus ab hac hora et inantea fidelis ero et obediens beato Petro et papae Gregorio suisque successoribus, qui per meliores cardinales intraverint.[1]

Disobedience was consequently a violation of this oath. The *sacerdotium* was the civil service of the pope—the role once intended for its members by the emperors and kings—through which the *societas*

---

[1] *Reg.* vi. 17a, p. 428. About the nature of this oath see infra 337. It should be noted that the words "et obediens" were omitted in the episcopal oath as incorporated in the *Compilatio Prima* and in the *Liber Extra* (II. xxiv. 4). On the other hand, these words occur in the oath prescribed for archbishops and bishops and abbots in the thirteenth-century formularies of the papal chancery, see M. Tangl, *Päpstliche Kanzleiordinungen*, Innsbruck, 1896, "Juramenta" nos. xviii (archbishops) and xix (bishops and abbots), pp. 50, 51. They are also in the modern episcopal oath, see *Pontificale Romanum*, ed. 1891, pp. 38–9. Gregory's episcopal oath also contained this: "Romanam ecclesiam per saecularem militiam fideliter adjuvabo, cum invitatus fuero." In this addition the late C. Erdmann, *Entstehung des Kreuzzugsgedankens*, Stuttgart, 1935, p. 196, saw the whole *Kriegsmann* Gregory, "den ganzen Gregor." But the passage may merely mean that the bishop, when ordered, would assist the Roman Church with a secular militia, and in so doing he would only execute a papal order. This passage was omitted in canon law, in the formularies, and in the *Pont. Rom.* However, Gregory IX in 1229 ordered under pain of ecclesiastical censures bishops to hasten to Rome personally

*christiana* was to be governed and directed. Consistently enough, the *sacerdotium* controlled by the pope and freed from lay control, was the *domina* of kingdoms.[1] It was precisely the crime of Henry IV in Gregory's opinion, that by exercising control over it he had acted "contra libertatem sanctae ecclesiae": subjection of the sacerdotal order to lay control redounds eventually to the detriment of the whole Christian *corpus*, hence "libertas ecclesiae" according to Gregory, for the sacerdotal order is then not in a position to direct and govern according to the principles underlying the *societas christiana*; it is then not in a position to act in accordance with the principles of *justitia* as enunciated by the Roman Church. Centralization of the ecclesiastical government and the enforcement of strict obedience on the part of the bishops, was the answer to the problem of effective papal control of the *sacerdotium*. Hence also the repeated attempts in this same century to secure the "purification" of the priesthood.[2]

---

with an armed force to defend the Roman Church against a possible attack by Frederick II; to Robert, archbishop of Lyons: "sub debito juramenti districte mandantes ac in remissionem peccaminum . . . inungentes, quatenus sine more dispendio cum congruo exfortio bellatorum ad nos personaliter venire festines" (MGH. *Epp. sel.* XIII *saec.*, i. no. 403, p. 323); the same to William, bishop of Paris (no. 404, pp. 323–4); cf. also no. 405, p. 324 to Henry, archbishop of Milan.

[1] *Reg.* iv. 3, p. 298: "Non ultra putet (scil. Heinricus) sanctam ecclesiam sibi subjectam ut ancillam, sed praelatam ut dominam." Of the many echoes which this statement of Gregory produced, we may single out that of St Anselm, writing to Baldwin I in Jerusalem: "*Ne putetis* vobis, sicut multi mali reges faciunt, ecclesiam Dei quasi *domino* ad serviendum esse datam, sed sicut *advocato et defensori* esse commendatam . . . *liberam* vult esse Deus sponsam suam, non *ancillam*," *Ep.* ix (PL. clix. 206).

[2] "Libertas ecclesiae" thus understood naturally contained the strongest condemnation of simony and concubinage. In each case sacerdotal liberty was endangered and sacerdotal subjection to the "caput sacerdotum" made problematic. As regards concubinage Gregory said this: "Non liberari potest ecclesia a servitute laicorum, nisi liberantur clerici ab uxoribus." Moreover, simony and concubinage are fundamentally opposed to the spiritual function of the cleric. Their designation as "haeresis" and the fierce fight against these two evils are thus explicable. Nor should the danger be overlooked which lay in the diversion of revenues from their proper purpose and the other danger of hereditary priestly offices. On the principle to which we have drawn attention (see supra 281) lay princes were ordered to suppress simony and concubinage, see *Reg.* ii. 45, 62, etc. It was only a corollary that lay people were ordered to resist simoniacal and married priests who thus could not enjoin obedience. The proclamation of a lay strike against married clerks was one means of enforcing liberty of the sacerdotal order, cf. e.g., the decree of the synod of 1059, cc. 3 and 8. On the whole question of the battle against simony in particular, see the fine study by I. Parisella, "Ecclesiae Romanae dimicatio contra simoniam" in *Apollinaris*, xv (1942), pp. 95–140; here also a full bibliography, pp. 96–8. That the underlying reason for

11

The function of the emperor or king is reduced to that of a protector in the Roman-papal sense, a defender who acts in the interests of, and when called upon by, the sacerdotal order. The transmutation of the royal protector into a papal protector, of the owner of the individual church into the patron of the church, was a necessary consequence of these premisses. We have had an opportunity to point to the attempt made by a ninth-century council[1] to effect this change, but the attempt could not succeed because it was premature. The successful transmutation of the owner into a patron by Gratian[2] was conditioned by the firm hold which hierocratic principles had gained upon the contemporary mind. On numerous occasions Gregory VII wrote to kings commanding them to do their duty and to defend "ecclesias," because this defence was the proper function of the Christian king: the transmutation of the king into the patron was inevitable.[3]

The means by which lay control or even influence was to be excluded was the implementation of the old principle of the "juste et canonice" electing of the pope and the bishops. The mechanism of the one was provided by the decree of Nicholas II (1059) which will engage our attention later, and which began the development culminating in the decree of Alexander III. The mechanism of the other was the "canonical election" of the bishops. Although the compromise of Worms (1122) still provided for the bishop's election by diocesan clergy and people, seventeen years later, in 1139, the second

---

the battle was not always understood, is testified, inter alia, by the *Annales Augustani* (MGH. SS. iii, ad 1076): "Papae (Gregorii) enorme decretum de continentia clericorum per laicos divulgatur. Sacerdotes a laicis pro connubiis et ecclesiarum emptione miserabiliter ejiciuntur." Considered from this point of view, the magnitude of the vexatious problem of the validity of simoniacal ordinations is understandable, see the classic work of L. Saltet, *Les Réordinations*, Paris, 1907, especially pp. 182 ff.; A. Michel, "Die antisimonistischen Reordinationen" in *Römische Quartalschrift*, xlvi (1938), pp. 29 ff.; F. Pelster, "Die römische Synode von 1060" in *Gregorianum*, xxiii (1942), pp. 66 ff. The first literary product concerning the condemnation of simony, is alleged to come from the musician Wido of Arezzo (*ca.* 1030, cf. F. Thaner in his introduction to LdL. i. 2–3) printed in LdL. i. 5–7, but according to Michel, art. cit., this was written by Humbert, *ca.* 1054–5.
    [1] See supra pp. 134 ff.
    [2] Cf. especially U. Stutz, "Gratian und die Eigenkirchen" in *Sav. Z., Kan. Abt.*, i (1911), pp. 15 ff.
    [3] Cf. *Reg.* i. 75, p. 107 (to Philip I); i. 70, p. 101 (to the Conqueror); vi. 20, p. 432 (to Count Centullus of Béarn); vi. 29, p. 442 (to Ladislaw of Hungary); viii. 20, p. 542 (to Philip I); the protection asked for, also concerned the property of the individual church: *Reg.* ii. 8 (to Wratislaw of Bohemia); vi. 37, p. 454 (to Count Jordan of Capua), etc.

Lateran Council under Innocent II excluded the lay element altogether, restricting the election to the "religiosi viri"[1] which in actual fact meant election by the chapter until finally in 1171, Alexander III established the exclusive right of the cathedral chapter to elect the bishop.[2]

## V

An attempt has been made to set forth the main ideological principles of Gregory VII. It will have become sufficiently clear that Gregory's thought-pattern is hewn in one mould: he stands firmly on the old tenets and pursues their logical implications to the very utmost. To him, as we have repeatedly pointed out, the multitude of Christians forms one corporate entity, constituting the *societas christiana*, whose essence is the spiritual element of faith, but which has nevertheless all the appurtenances of real earthiness. There are several features which are characteristic of this society showing us more clearly than any theoretical disquisition its basic spiritual structure and at the same time its very real earthy character.

Firstly, *excommunication* is the effective exclusion of individuals from membership of the *societas christiana*. The character of this society and its underlying idea made it self-evident that the authority which was to pronounce sentence of exclusion from the Christian *corpus* was the sacerdotal order; and the essence of this society also rendered obvious the grounds upon which this exclusion was to be based. Primarily a sanction laid down for setting aside the "justitia legis christianae," itself the crystallization of "pura religio," the effects of excommunication were by no means confined to the purely religious spheres of life. Intercourse with the excommunicate individual was prohibited: he was

---

[1] Mansi, xxi. 533, cap. 28; Gratian, *Dist.* lxiii. 35.
[2] In his letter to the chapter of Bremen, PL. cc. 1270. The great importance which the sacerdotal members of the Church assumed in the hierocratic scheme, necessitated their special penal protection. The second Lateran Council (1139) decreed the *Privilegium canonis* (cap. xv = Gratian, XVII. iv. 29) according to which any corporal injury inflicted on a cleric entailed automatic excommunication from which only the pope could absolve upon the personal request and appearance of the excommunicate individual. On the other hand, proceedings by laymen against clerics (except in the case of heresy) were denied, obviously an application of the principle of (hierarchical) functional ordering, according to which only an equal or a superior could charge an equal or inferior individual. According to the later canon law, moreover, no cleric was to stand his trial in civil or criminal matters before the secular tribunal, no matter whether he was plaintiff or defendant.

to all intents and purposes socially isolated. He was to be shunned because outside the norm of living prescribed for the members of the *societas*. Having been declared an outcast, he was considered to be infected with a contagious disease,[1] hence contact with him was prohibited, with the further consequence that those who disregarded this prohibition became themselves, so to speak, infected and therefore shared the fate of him with whom they communicated. And one of the grievances of Gregory against Henry was that the latter had not given up intercourse with the five excommunicate counsellors, and consequently he found himself excommunicated.[2] Excommunication is the juristic and concrete social exclusion from the corporate body of Christians. Only wives were allowed to be in direct contact with their excommunicate husbands, children with their parents and the low manual workers with their masters.[3] To those unaware of the excommunication the prohibition did not apply.[4] A further consequence was that those, for instance vassals, who were tied to the excommunicate individual by an oath of fealty, were for obvious reasons released from the obligations into which they had entered.[5]

These measures were applicable to private individuals as well as to kings. The latters' standing in Christian society was thereby clearly brought out. What amounted to a mere social isolation on the part of private individuals,[6] amounted in the case of a king to a virtual deprivation of government. For if nobody except his nearest relatives were

---

[1] Cf., for instance, in the twelfth century Alexander III, *Ep.* 768, PL. cc. 707: "Excommunicatio enim ad modum leprae quae totum corpus corrumpit, totum hominem contaminat et deturpat."

[2] Gregory VII, *Reg.* iv. 2, pp. 293–4, and *Reg.* ii. 52a, p. 196.

[3] See *Reg.* v. 14a, cap. 16, p. 373.

[4] Ibid.; cf. also *Reg.* iii. 10a, p. 269; iii. 16, and 17; ix. 24, pp. 605–6.

[5] *Reg.* v. 14a, cap. 15, p. 372; also iv. 6, p. 304.

[6] In later canonistic doctrine and conciliar and papal legislation this social isolation of the excommunicate individual will lead to the concept of "civil death" ("civiliter mortuus"): all acts of the excommunicate are invalid. He is incapable of performing "actus legitimi" (this term originated in Roman law: *Dig.* 50. 17. 77, cf. E. Eichmann, *Acht & Bann im Reichsrecht*, Paderborn, 1909, p. 67). This means that the excommunicate is incapable of making a last will, of testifying before a court, of accepting donations, of disposing his property or of acquiring new property—in short he is outlawed. He is declared infamous: he cannot occupy public offices; if he is a judge, his verdicts are null and void; he is excluded from the bar; his acts as a notary public are invalid, and so forth; see especially Innocent III's *Vergentis*. It goes without saying that he is excluded from the sacraments, that he cannot have a christian burial, that he cannot enter a church, and so forth. In order to prevent contamination, incarceration was decreed, cf. Innocent III, *Reg.* ii. 99 (imprisonment of an abbot "ne contaminet gregem intactum").

allowed to communicate with him, he was obviously in no position to govern, that is, to issue binding decrees, in the sphere conceded to him, to his Christian subjects.[1] The prohibition of social contact was made plain in the case of Philip I of France. In his letter to William of Poitou, Gregory threatened Philip's excommunication as well as the excommunication of everyone "who showed Philip royal honours and obedience."[2]

Secondly, formal *deposition* of a reigning king must, in theory, be distinguished from his excommunication. Whilst the latter was the consequence of a purely religious or moral disobedience and could be inflicted upon any member of Christian society, deposition was the consequence of the king's uselessness. He was no longer useful, because as a consequence of his disobedience to papal orders, he did not execute *justitia* laid down by the pope. Hence he was to be deprived of his title-deed to rule. And we may recall that, according to Gregory, Childeric was deposed by Zacharias, not because he was iniquitous, but because he was useless. Incapacity to govern was the effect of excommunication. Deposition, on the other hand, concerned the title-deed, the basis, of the king's position: it was this which was taken away and he therefore had no longer any right to rule. In his action against Henry IV, Gregory distinguishes between excommunication and deposition by declaring "totius *regni* Teutonicorum et Italiae *gubernacula contradico*." Excommunication concerned Henry the Christian, deposition Henry the king. Exercise of rulership was, according to hierocratic ideology, an honour or a privilege, and this must be lost if the ruler tries to follow his own views of government to the detriment of the whole body.[3]

Deposition is, therefore, strictly speaking independent of excommunication: the latter is focused on the internal sphere, the former on the external sphere, of a ruler. In each case the criteria are different.

---

[1] These considerations applied later also to a prince who turned out to be an apostate: he is to be deprived of his governmental power, according to St Thomas Aquinas, because this prince intends "homines separare a fide. Et ideo quam cito aliquis per sententiam denuntiatur excommunicatus propter apostasiam a fide, ipso facto eius subditi sunt absoluti a dominio eius et juramento fidelitatis, quo ei tenebantur," *S. Theol.*, II. ii. qu. xiii. a. 2.

[2] Gregory VII, *Reg.* ii. 18, p. 151.

[3] *Reg.* ii. 18, p. 151: "Dignum est enim, ut qui studet honorem ecclesiae tuae imminuere, ipse honorem amittat, quem videtur habere." The numerous papal documents decreeing excommunication of kings, princes, etc., and the release of their subjects from the obligation of obedience are assembled (down to Boniface VIII) by G. B. Pallieri and G. Vismara, *Acta pontificia juris gentium*, Milan, 1946, pp. 52 ff., documents nos. 207–324.

Inability to govern is the indirect consequence of excommunication; it is the direct consequence of deposition. Seen from the hierocratic point of view, excommunication was the effluence of the pope's supreme sacerdotal powers, whilst deposition was the effluence of his function as the supreme monarch of the Christian body politic. Empires, kingdoms, princedoms, and so forth, form parts of this body politic: but it is the pope's duty to see that *justitia* is carried out through the instrumentality of the secular prince. Hence it is the pope's right to take the basis of kingship away, if an individual king should prove himself useless, and to transfer kingship to some other suitable, and therefore useful, individual.[1] This distinction between deposition and excommunication makes it clear why the latter is not even mentioned in the *Dictatus* of Gregory, whilst the former is given due prominence.[2]

In the case of Henry IV the sentence of deposition was never revoked by Gregory. Canossa concerned Henry's re-admission to Christian society, and had nothing to do with his exercise of governorship. Had he not also been deposed, this re-admission at Canossa would have been sufficient to re-instate him in his kingship. This is clear from Gregory's speech at the synod of 7 March 1080:

(Henry) came to me in Lombardy begging me to release him from excommunication. And when I had witnessed his humility and when he had promised me reforms of his life, I restored him to communion only, but *I did not re-instate him in his kingship* from which I had deposed him in the Roman synod.[3]

The deposition of 1076 was only what may be called a preliminary deposition amounting to a suspension from kingly power, but this sentence was never revoked by Gregory: the preliminary deposition was made final in 1080.[4] Hence, in the intervening years between 1076

---

[1] *Reg.* vii. 14a, p. 487: "Omnis mundus intelligat et cognoscat, quia, si potestis in coelo ligare et solvere, in *terra imperia, regna, principatus* . . . et *omnium hominum possessiones* pro meritis *tollere* unicuique *et concedere.*" The same idea emerges in the communication concerning Philip I of France which Gregory writes to the French clergy: "Commanded and bound by apostolic authority . . . separate ourselves from all service and communion with him (Philip) and forbid throughout France the celebration of divine worship in public. But if this measure should not bring him to his knees, we wish to leave no doubt in anyone's mind that, with the help of God, we will make every effort to take away from him the kingdom of France by all possible manner of means," *Reg.* ii. 5, p. 132 (". . . quin modis omnibus regnum Franciae de eius occupatione adjuvante Deo temptemus eripere").     [2] DP. 12.     [3] *Reg.* vii. 14a, p. 484.

* † [4] Against A. Fliche who held that at Canossa Henry was re-instated, see now H. X. Arquillière, in *Studi Gregoriani*, iv. 1 ff. Cf. also W. Berges, ibid., ii. 201–2, and Schramm, *Göttinger Gelehrte Anz.*, 1953, p. 92.

and 1080 the royal office in Germany was in suspense, until in 1080 Gregory transferred royal power to Rudolf of Swabia: "Rudolf for his humility, his obedience and his truthfulness, is granted the power and dignity of kingship."[1]

Closely allied to formal deposition is the release of the subjects from their oath of allegiance to the ruler. This release is only a specific application of the view that the pope is entitled to release anyone from the obligation to fulfil an oath, in itself a faculty that is directly based upon the power to bind and to loose.[2] The formal release from the oath was not superfluous in the case of deposition, for, theoretically, the deposition of the king does not affect the oaths taken to him. Hence, immediately after the (preliminary) deposition of Henry IV Gregory declares solemnly:

Et omnes christianos a vinculo juramenti, quod sibi fecerunt vel facient, absolvo et, ut nullus ei sicut regi serviat, interdico.[3]

Thirdly, the *repression* of actions and movements which threaten the continued existence of society or attack its foundations, is the duty of any responsible ruler. If need arises, this repression takes the form of employing force.

One kind of repression may be called police action, that is, forceful repression of internal activities considered hostile to the fabric of society: the activities to be repressed constitute the denial of *justitia*. There is the case of Robert Guiscard and the Normans who were declared rebels because they threatened the liberty of the Roman Church. The proper function of a prince was to be a protector (in the Roman-papal sense) of the Church by specifically protecting the Roman Church. But since the Normans threatened the Roman Church, repressive measures were called for: Gregory issued a summons to Count William of Burgundy who, moreover, had taken an oath to the effect that he would lend his hand for the defence of the goods of St Peter.[4] "If necessary, you should come with your army in the service of St Peter."[5] Gregory's hope was that the mere show of military

---

[1] *Reg.* cit., p. 487. The sentence of Henry's final deposition, ibid., p. 486: "Omnem potestatem et dignitatem illi regiam tollo."

[2] Cf. the tone of irritation on this point in Gregory's letter to Hermann of Metz, *Reg.* viii. 21, pp. 547–8. Could any legitimate doubt exist in Hermann's mind about the right of Gregory to release subjects from this oath?

[3] Reg. iii. 10a, p. 270.

[4] *Reg.* i. 46, p. 70: ". . . ut quacumque hora necesse fuisset vestra manus ad dimicandum pro defensione rerum sancti Petri non deesset, si quidem requisita fuisset."

[5] *Reg.* i. 46, p. 70 ". . . quatinus praeparetis vestrae militiae fortitudinem ad

force would teach the Normans a lesson so that bloodshed amongst Christians might be avoided and the Normans "facilius subdantur justitiae."[1]

It was by the same token that—ironically enough—Robert Guiscard and the Normans were summoned in 1080 for a police action against Ravenna, where Wibert was in residence. But this time the leadership of this expedition was to be in the hands of the pope himself. After referring to the oath of protection and defence of the Roman Church taken by Guiscard and others, Gregory continues his summons by saying:

We propose by the beginning of September, after the cooler weather has set in, to enter the district of Ravenna with an armed force, in order to restore the church (Ravenna) to its father, the blessed Peter.[2]

The same idea is contained in Gregory's communication of the same year (27 June 1080) which voices the threat that if the Castilian king, Alphonso VI, who had allegedly supported the simoniacal activity of the monk Robert and who had meted out some rough treatment to a papal legate, were not to give satisfaction, and if the papal demand for the people's insurrection against their king went unheeded, he himself would not find it too grave a labour to cross over to Spain, so as to take drastic measures against the king.[3] But a police action, such as envisaged by Gregory, if successful, would entail that the pope himself would temporarily have to assume the function of the king deprived of his kingdom. This possibility was reckoned with by Gregory: the violation of the principles of *justitia* by Philip I would impose upon the pope the duty to use both hands "when there is no prince to care for such matters, to watch over the lives of the religious."[4] In this we witness the—logically consistent—theory that in the case of negligence or disobedience on the part of the temporal ruler or secular justice,

---

succurendum Romanae ecclesiae libertati, scilicet, si necesse fuerit, veniatis huc cum exercitu vestro in servitio sancti Petri."

[1] *Reg.* i. 46, p. 70, lines 28–9.

[2] *Reg.* viii. 7, p. 525.

[3] *Reg.* viii. 2, p. 518: "Qui si minus praeceptioni nostrae obedirent, non gravem existimaremus laborem nos ad Hispaniam proficisci et adversum eum, quemadmodum Christianae religionis inimicum, dura et aspera moliri." Erdmann, op. cit., p. 160, remarks: "Diese Worte können vernünftigerweise keinen anderen Sinn haben als den einer Drohung mit einem eigenen Kriegszuge des Papstes nach Spanien." In Gregory's letter to Alphonso himself we read: *Reg.* viii. 3, p. 520: "Beati Petri gladium super te evaginare cogamur."

[4] *Reg.* ii. 49, p. 190.

the pope must supply what is wanting.[1] Moreover, this "taking over" by the pope was in perfect harmony with the function allotted to a king within the *societas christiana* and the function of the pope himself in ruling it.

Into this category of repression by a police action will soon come also the persecution of heretics. The treatment meted out to the unorthodox or erring members of the *societas christiana* or those defiantly challenging the authority of the Roman Church in doctrinal matters can be understood by a proper appraisal of the nature of the *societas* as a corporate entity held together solely by the spiritual bond of the faith. Hence deviations from faith, heresy, attacked the foundations of this society and made drastic measures necessary.[2] Heresy, in hierocratic doctrine, is the very negation of the foundation upon which society rests: it is the open denial of—not merely disobedience to—the papally expounded *justitia* as a norm of living; the function of the Roman Church as the epitome of universal Christianity is implicitly denied. Hence, heresy, as canonistic doctrine will evolve the theory, is high treason; it is a *crimen publicum* because it strikes at the very foundations of contemporary society, and if not checked, will eventually destroy the unity of the whole *corpus*, so that its former constituent parts will emerge as autonomous units.[3] As the monarch

[1] Cf. also Erdmann, op. cit., p. 148, referring to Peter Damian's interpretation of the two hands: PL. cxliv. 463, 368. Obviously, the "gladius b. Petri" had only one meaning at that time, when used by the pope, as the hierocratic two-swords theory had not yet been developed: A. M. Stickler, "Il gladius nel Registro di Gregorio VII" in *Studi Gregoriani*, iii. 89–103, is therefore quite right in his explanation of Gregory's "gladius beati Petri." About Henry IV's view see infra pp. 345 f.

[2] At times, however, the notion of heresy was capable of liberal application. For instance, Henry IV was considered a heretic in 1102 by Paschal II; and it is against him, the "chief heretic," that Count Robert of Flanders is ordered to marshal his forces. The pope's letter is not only an early instance of a "crusade" against a heretic, but also of the employment of the ambiguous phrase "for the remission of sins" (other examples supra 297): "Justum enim est ut qui semetipsos a catholica ecclesia segregarunt, per catholicos ab ecclesiae beneficiis segregentur. Nec in hac parte tantum, sed ubique, cum poteris, Henricum haereticorum caput, et eius fautores pro viribus persequaris. Nullum profecto gratius Deo sacrificium offerre poteris quam si eum impugnes qui se contra Deum erexit, qui *ecclesiae regnum auferre* conatur, qui in loco sancto Simonis idolum statuit, qui a principibus Dei sanctis apostolis eorumque vicariis de ecclesiae domo s. spiritus judicio expulsus est. Hoc tibi ac militibus tuis in peccatorum remissionem et apostolicae sedis familiaritatem praecipimus," *Ep.* lxxxviii, PL. clxiii. 108.

[3] For imperial legislation on heresy, particularly under Frederick II, see now G. de Vergottini, *Studi sulla legislazione imperiale di Frederico II in Italia*, Milan, 1952, pp. 97 ff., and its influence on French legislation, pp. 265 ff. For the canonistic background see ibid., pp. 179 ff. (*De Brabantionibus, Ad abolendam, Vergentis*).

11*

ruling this corporate entity the pope has to ensure the safety of the fabric of the society through various agencies.[1]

There is one more kind of action which is prompted however by other considerations. There are, on the one hand, the massacres of Christians in the East—"unheard-of slaughter, daily slain like so many sheep by the pagans" as Gregory put it[2]—and, on the other hand, the attempt at liberation of the Holy Sepulchre from the hands of the Turks.[3] Although both considerations are of a defensive nature, they nevertheless stand in closest proximity to the division of Christianity into an Eastern and Western half. And it was this division—caused by the Eastern refusal to acknowledge the primacy of the Roman Church —which provided the special motive for Gregory to issue his summons for a military campaign against the East:

Illud etiam me ad hoc *premaxime* instigat, quod Constantinopolitana ecclesia de sancto spiritu a nobis dissidens concordiam apostolicae sedis expectat.[4]

Again, considering the nature of the *societas christiana* as a corporate entity monarchically ruled, it is only logical and consistent for Gregory VII himself to lead the expedition as its "dux et pontifex."[5]

---

[1] Cf., in this period, Bonizo of Sutri's defence of a "war against error," *Liber ad Amicum*, MGH. LdL. i. 568 ff.; cf. also Anselm of Lucca, "Quod ecclesia persecutionem possit facere," see on this A. M. Stickler, *Studi Gregoriani*, ii. 259.

[2] *Reg.* ii. 31, p. 166.

[3] *Reg.* ii. 31, p. 166, lines 31–2.

[4] *Reg.* ii. 31, pp. 166–7. Cf. C. Erdmann, op. cit., p. 152: "Wir dürfen es ihm aufs Wort glauben, dass dieser Plan, eine Union . . . und den römischen Primat dort zur Anerkennung zu bringen, sein Hauptmotiv gewesen ist." About the story of Emperor Michael III's request to Gregory see W. Holtzmann, "Studien . . . zur Entstehung des ersten Kreuzzuges" in *Hist. Vierteljahrschrift*, xxii (1925), p. 173 f., and C. Erdmann, op. cit., p. 149, note 66. Cf. also the cautious formulation by S. Runciman, *History of the First Crusade*, Cambridge, 1951, p. 98. Innocent III was later to express the effect of the crusade when he wrote to the patriarch of Constantinople: "Nos ergo, qui per gratiam Redemptoris ipsam Constantino-politanam ecclesiam nuper ad obedientiam apostolicae sedis, tamquam ad sinum reduximus matris suae . . ." *Reg.* viii. 153 (PL. ccxv. 728).

[5] This, he says, was the condition under which the 50,000 men had accepted his call: "Quam ammonitionem Italici et ultramontani Deo inspirante, ut reor, immo etiam omnino affirmo, libenter acceperunt et jam ultra quinquaginta milia ad hoc se preparent, ut, si me possunt in expeditione pro duce et pontifice habere, armata manu contra inimicos Dei volunt insurgere et usque ad sepulchrum Domini ipso ducente pervenire." According to Gregory's programme, the protection and defence of the Roman Church was to be in the hands of Henry IV, whilst the pope's companions were to be the old empress Agnes and Countess Mathilda. C. Erdmann, op. cit., p. 151, remarks: "Wüssten wir das nicht alles aus Gregor's eigenen Briefen, so würden wir es vielleicht für den schlechten Witz eines boshaften Gegners halten." S. Runciman, op. cit., p. 99, holds Gregory's plan "a stroke of imaginative statesmanship." Later papal ideology expressed the view of

In the same year, 1074, Gregory had issued a general summons to all those willing to defend the Christian faith,[1] and in this summons the theme of liberating the Christians in the East from the danger of the pagans is made the object of the campaign to be undertaken. The magic word "liberation"—"pro liberatione fratrum"—gives the proposed military undertaking its defensive complexion: but liberation of the Christians would result in the union between East and West, and thereby the acknowledgment of the Roman primacy in the East would be brought about.

That Gregory's intended military campaigns were not "wars" in the accepted modern sense, seems clear. His idea about these envisaged measures was that of the later crusades: Gregory VII must be credited with giving the crusading idea its first concrete formulation; and none recognized this more freely than Urban II himself explicitly adopting Gregory's aim and idea.[2] But it seems equally clear that this crusading

---

the pope being "dux et pontifex" of the expeditionary force in terms such as contained in the arenga of a letter of Gregory IX to Frederick II: "Post vicarium Iesu Christi Romanum pontificem, qui disponene Domino Christiani dux est et magister exercitus, fidem catholicam defendere ac tueri consuevit augustus, qui non inaniter accepisse nec sine causa portare gladium cernitur," *Epp. sel. XIII saec.*, i. 553, p. 447.

[1] *Reg.* i. 49, p. 75.

[2] See *Liber Pontificalis*, ed. cit., ii. 293: "Audierat iste praeclarus et devotus pontifex predecessorem suum Gregorium papam praedicasse ultramontanis Iherosolimam pro defensione Christianae fidei pergere et Domini sepulcrum manibus inimicorum liberare, quod facere minime potuit, quia persecutio Heinrici regis nimium eum undique urguebat." The evidence would indicate that the appeal of Sergius IV (J. 3972, of 1011) is a forgery of the early twelfth century, cf. J. Haller, *Papsttum*, ii/2, p. 531, against Erdmann, op. cit., p. 102 f. The savants of the crusades do not mention this appeal of Sergius, cf. Runciman, op. cit. The words which Hildebrand spoke in the Council of Tours some twenty years earlier in 1054, have a prophetic ring: "Romam fide atque armis semper fuisse invictam," see B. Sudendorff, *Berengarius von Tours*, Gotha, 1850, p. 217. In examining Gregory's crusading idea one should not leave out of account its eschatological aspect. There was, we believe, a strong eschatological element in it. A perusal of his letters impresses the reader with the author's being tormented by an overpowering anxiety to rescue Christianity from the clutches of anti-Christ. In some mystical prophecies current in his time, the theme of anti-Christ is central, so especially in Adso's *Epistola ad Gerberdam Reginam de ortu et tempore anti-christi*; this work (ed. E. Sackur, *Sibyllinische Texte und Forschungen*, pp. 104–113) may have been some source of inspiration of Gregory, but the place of the Roman emperor who is to lead his army into Jerusalem, is taken by the pope as "dux et pontifex." According to Adso, the expedition to Jerusalem by him who "Romanum imperium ex integro tenebit" will bring about the "finis et consummatio Romanorum christianorumque imperii." The Triburtine Sibylla (Text in Sackur, pp. 177–97; now newly edited and translated into German by A. Kurfess, *Sibyllinische Weissagungen*, Cologne, 1951, pp. 262–79) would be

idea implicitly contains the germs of the later theory of the "just war":
again, the qualification of a war as just or unjust is the result of measur-
ing its aims by the standard of *justitia*. Defence and liberation were to
become the criteria of the just war, and defence and liberation can be
correctly measured only by the prevailing ideas, epitomized as they
were in *justitia*.[1]

Whatever shape the employment of force took, the presupposition
was that the action was undertaken in conformity with *justitia*: therefrom resulted the duty of individuals and rulers to participate in these
actions. In characteristically medieval fashion the justness of the undertaking was symbolically expressed: the symbol showing to all the world
that the action was just, was the papal banner. The "vexillum sancti
Petri" symbolized the blessing of the undertaking by the seat of
*justitia*, hence this symbol was also called the "vexillum sedis apostolicae." This symbol is despatched or handed over by the pope and
thus publicly signifies action undertaken on behalf, or with the approval,
of the Roman Church.[2] Its bearer was called the "signifer papae."[3] In
all its profundity of meaning this symbol emerges in Gregory's predecessor, Alexander II, and stands in closest proximity to the character
of the *societas christiana* as an autonomous body politic embracing all
the "Romans." As such this body must have an outward symbol—like
its constituent, but smaller royal and imperial parts—which at the

nearer to Gregory's time (about 1047, see Sackur, p. 217), though its influence
appears negligible, cf. E. Bernheim, *Mittelalterliche Zeitanschauungen*, p. 224.
About eschatological influences on the crusading idea in the late eleventh century
see C. Erdmann, "Endkaiserglaube & Kreuzzugsgedanke" in *Z. f. Kirchengeschichte*, li (1932), pp. 386–414.

[1] The dynamic element of the crusading idea reflects also in its theoretical
development the idea of a military campaign undertaken, not for the sake of
liberation and defence, but for the sake of implanting the Christian faith in non-
Christian territories, in order to expand the scope and size of the *societas christiana*.
Here again the previous campaigns under the leadership of emperors, beginning
with Charlemagne, should be appraised from the ideological point of view. For
the roots of the *Missionskrieg*, see Erdmann, op. cit., pp. 6–9, also G. Combès,
*La doctrine politique de s. Augustine*, pp. 255 ff., 417 ff. About the whole question
of Christianity and war, cf. Erdmann, op. cit., p. 8 ff.; cf. also R. H. Bainton,
"The early church and war" in *Harvard Theological Rev.*, xxxix (1946), pp.
189–212 (dealing with the second century) and now also H. v. Campenhausen,
"Der Kriegsdienst der Christen" in *Festschrift f. C. Jaspers*, 1953, pp. 257–64.
For the views of medieval theologians on war see H. Finke in *Festschrift Grab-
mann*, ii. 1426–34.

[2] It was therefore also called "signum Romanum," see Erdmann, op. cit.,
p. 175, note 37.

[3] So Ordericus Vitalis, *Hist. Eccl.* iii. 3 and 5, quoted by Erdmann, op. cit.,
p. 119, note 52.

same time also signified that those to whom it was given, acted in conformity with *justitia*. In a way, this symbol reflects the spiritual and
earthy nature of the *societas christiana*.[1] But this topic of external
symbols belongs to the next chapter in which we propose to survey
some other signs by which the government of the *societas christiana*
is revealed.

---

[1] For details of the papal banner see Erdmann, op. cit., pp. 166–84; idem,
"Kaiserfahne und Blutfahne" in *SB. Berlin*, 1932; idem, "Kaiserliche und päst-
liche Fahnen" in *Quellen & Forschungen aus ital. Archiven*, xxv (1934), pp. 8–18,
and also P. E. Schramm, in *Studi Gregoriani*, ii. 441 f. In our period the following
cases in which a papal banner was despatched or handed over, are worth mentioning: to Count Roger of Sicily who was to fight the Moslems (1063); to Count
Erlembald of Milan (1064); to Duke William of Normandy (1066); to William
of Montreuil as the general in the Campagna (1064); to the leader of men (William
of Aquitaine?) fighting for Barbastro (1064?); to the inhabitants of the maritime
Italian towns for their campaign against North Africa (1087); for the further cases
see Erdmann, op. cit., especially from the time of Urban II onwards. The new
mosaics ordered by Innocent III (*Gesta*, cap. cxlv; PL. ccxiv. cciv) are characteristic: they depict Christ flanked on the left by St Paul and on the right by St Peter,
and Innocent III himself standing in the foreground with a female: he is clad in
full pontifical vestments with the tiara, whereas the female described as "ecclesia
Romana" wears a crown holding in the left hand a book and in the right hand a
banner, in whose flag the keys of St Peter are woven. For further details and a
full description see K. Burdach, "Walther von der Vogelweide's Kampf gegen
Innocenz III" in *Z. f. Kirchengeschichte*, lv (1936), pp. 499–502, here also further
literature, note 74. Innocent appointed Byzantine artists for these mosaics, ibid.,
pp. 512–13. About the picture depicting Leo III see supra p. 95.

# CHAPTER X

# The Court of the Pope

THIS brief analysis of Gregory VII's thought will have shown the basic conception underlying hierocratic doctrine, namely, the conception that the *societas christiana* was an autonomous, juristic entity: conceptually, it was an organic unit, and as such embraced the whole of Latin Christendom of which the individual kingdoms and the empire formed constituent parts. This unit transcends all biological or linguistic or racial frontiers, and for this reason is stronger and more resilient than the incidental bonds of birth, language, race or geography. This *societas* is the corporate body of all the "Romans."

## I

This autonomous, corporate entity made adequate government necessary, necessitated, in other words, the establishment of certain institutions and governmental organs, in short necessitated a machinery of government. Government means orientating and directing this corporate unit according to the principles of *justitia*. On the basis of the Petrine commission this government was monarchic in form. The transmitters of *justitia* were the members of the sacerdotal hierarchy. And by the decrees, orders, and instructions emanating from the seat of *justitia* social life within this body corporate became effectively permeated with the idea of papal monarchy and the idea of central authority.

The form of government was monarchical. But it was not sufficient to state this monarchic form of government in ideological terms: it was necessary that the monarch also appears as a monarch to the world. The way in which this was achieved was by making the pope a monarch in form as well as in idea: he was the sole Ruler of the *societas christiana*. The crisp expression of Gregory VII merits its quotation:

He alone may use the imperial insignia.[1]

[1] DP. 8: "Quod solus uti possit imperialibus insigniis." About the source of this statement see supra p. 81.

And of these imperial insignia none was more important or more symbolic than the crown. It is entirely in line with the development of the hierocratic theme for the monarch of the *societas christiana* to personify in a symbolic manner the unique concentration of power. In order to show this in the most concrete and visible manner, he alone was entitled to wear imperial insignia. That he was thus entitled did not mean that he could not allow the imperial crown to be used by a king: the entitlement meant that the pope alone might use the imperial insignia, if he so wished. According to hierocratic tenets the use of the imperial insignia was a concession, symbolically expressed in the ceremony of the imperial coronation.

The crown—the *corona* or the *regnum*[1]—worn by the pope was of no liturgical significance: liturgical significance was reserved to the mitre alone. This was in fact the stage of development in the second half of the eleventh century. We read that Gregory VII in 1075 went in procession "*coronatus* et cum omni laude episcoporum atque cardinalium" to the Lateran palace.[2] By the end of the same century we are informed by Bishop Bruno of Segni that in solemn processions the pope wears the *regnum* as well as the *purpura*, and that in his external appearance there was no difference between him and the former emperors.

Unde in magnis processionibus omnis ille apparatus pontifici exhibetur, qui quondam imperatoribus fieri solebat.[3]

In order to understand this development we must recall that, according to the Donation of Constantine, the emperor had wished to put the

---

[1] The name *tiara* was adopted at the very end of the eleventh century, see "Vita Paschalis" in *Lib. Pont.*, ii. 296, lines 21–22: immediately after his election (1099) Paschal II "clamide coccinea (on this see the passage from the Donation infra 318) induitur a patribus et *thyara* capite eius imposita . . ." Cf. also p. 297: "Domnus Paschalis II *coronatus* in urbem rediit convaluitque ecclesia." See also Duchesne's note 6, p. 307. Later the tiara was adorned with the orb on its top and a cross. The papal tiara is still the extraliturgical head gear of the pope when he is carried through the Vatican. We should note, however, that the tiara was also worn by Sicilian kings, especially Roger II and Tancred, in imitation of Byzantine practices, see J. Deér, *Der Kaiserornat Friedrichs II*, Bern, 1952, p. 22, note 82.
[2] See *Lib. Pont.*, ii. 282, lines 20–21.
[3] PL. clxv. 1108. The whole passage runs: "Summus autem pontifex propter haec et regnum portat (sic enim vocatur) et purpura utitur non pro significatione, ut puto, sed quia Constantinus imperator olim beato Silvestro omnia Romani imperii insignia tradidit. Unde et . . ." as text. Cardinal Deusdedit echoes the same view when he says "quod Constantinus imperialem coronam eidem contulerit et definierit terrenum imperium Romae potestatem non habere," Deusdedit, *Collectio canonum*, iv. 1 (ed. Wolf von Glanvell, Paderborn, 1905, pp. 24 f.)

imperial crown on Silvester's head, but that the latter refused to wear it over his clerical tonsure: the Emperor Constantine in the place of the imperial crown had then put the *phrygium* upon Silvester's head. This head gear was "candido nitore" and designated, according to the forger, "splendidam resurrectionem dominicam."

Now, we know that the forger gave certain existing practices some political twist and historicity. This becomes quite clear in the case of the *phrygium*. We know that Pope Constantine when entering Constantinople had worn the *camelaucum*[1] which was a white silk cap of high conical shape and identical with the forger's *phrygium*.[2] Moreover, in view of the terminology adopted by the eighth-century Roman *Ordo*,[3] the entry in the *Liber Pontificalis* which informs us about the pope's *camelaucum* deserves particular mention: the emperor meets the pope and performs the proskynesis "cum regno in capite."[4]

From the account in the Donation of Constantine it is evident firstly that Silvester did not use the imperial crown, and secondly that the pope did wear the *camelaucum* = *phrygium*. We must therefore distinguish between a latently papal head gear—the imperial crown—and the patently worn papal head gear, the *phrygium*. This head cover was in liturgical and extraliturgical use down to the mid-eleventh century. It seems that there was only this one head cover, in this period, and that the only change which occurred was that of name: the *phrygium* came to be called the mitre.[5]

---

[1] See *Lib. Pont.*, i. 390, line 15.

[2] See especially E. Sachsse, "Tiara und Mitra der Päpste" in *Z. f. Kirchengeschichte*, xxxv (1914), p. 489, and F. Wasner, "De consecratione . . . pontificis" in *Apollinaris*, viii (1935), pp. 430–1.

[3] See the quotation from OR. IX infra p. 314 n. 2.

[4] *Lib. Pont.*, i. 391: "Augustus christianissimus cum regno in capite sese prostravit." Cf. E. Kantorowicz, *Laudes regiae*, p. 136: the *camelaucum* was the insigne of the Byzantine emperor and other Eastern rulers. According to J. Deér, op. cit., p. 21, the *camelaucum* ranked as an imperial crown immediately below the diadem since the end of the sixth century.

[5] For all this see E. Wüscher-Becchi, "Ursprung der päpstlichen Tiara und der bischöflichen Mitra" in *Römische Quartalschrift*, xiii (1899), pp. 96 ff., and Table VII, nos. 3, 4, 6, 9; the classic work of J. Braun, *Die liturgische Gewandung*, Freiburg, 1914, pp. 458 f., 499, where the changes in the forms of the mitre from a bonnet to the characteristic mitral shape are depicted, p. 459. H. W. Klewitz, "Die Krönung des Papstes" in *Sav. Z., kan. Abt.*, xxxi (1941), pp. 108–9; Sachsse, art. cit., pp. 487–9. According to Braun (pp. 455–6) the *camelaucum* was not taken off by the pope whilst functioning liturgically and this *camelaucum* was also worn by cardinals, i.e., the priests of the titular Roman churches, cf. also Klewitz, art. cit., p. 113. In his post-humously published work, *Die Weihe & Krönung des Papstes im Mittelalter*, 1951, pp. 29–30, Eichmann does not accept the view of Klewitz (which we have adopted) that there was only one head gear

Leo IX in a number of privileges gave permission to individual bishops to wear the *mitra Romana* on certain feast days.[1] That these permissions pursued definite aims is clear, the foremost being to establish stronger hierarchical ties.[2] But there was no visible difference between the episcopal and papal mitre, and this lack of differentiation made it imperative that the head gear of the pope and a bishop should be distinguished. The distinguishing feature was found in the papal tiara, or as it came to be called the *regnum* or the *corona*. The liturgical head gear of the pope remained the mitre: the extraliturgical head cover appropriate to him alone, was the *regnum* or *corona*.[3]

About the "coronation" of Nicholas II we are informed by Benzo of Alba. Despite his tendentious report, the concrete details which he gives about the head cover of the pope cannot have been the fruit of his rather fertile imagination. Gregory as Hildebrand, Benzo says, in the Lenten synod of 1059 "regali corona suum coronavit hydolum (Nicholas II)"[4] and Nicholas II "quasi rex in synodo

---

of the pope before the mid-eleventh century. Eichmann maintained that, as a direct result of the Donation of Constantine, two kinds of papal head gear became necessary and that the pope certainly before 1000 wore "eine liturgische, pro sacerdotio, und eine weltliche, pro regno." But the evidence which the late savant on medieval coronations adduces, seems too tenuous to support his view.

[1] To the archbishop of Trier in 1049: "Romana mitra caput vestrum insignivimus, qua et vos et successores vestri in ecclesiis officiis Romano more utamini," PL. cxliii. 595; for further examples see Braun, op. cit., pp. 452 ff. The mitre was also conferred on abbots, the first abbot being Aethelsig of Canterbury in 1063, see D. Knowles, *Monastic Order in England*, p. 579. There is some resemblance between the grant of the pallium and that of the mitre, see Sachsse, art. cit., p. 490. The mitre was later also granted to secular princes, so, for instance, by Nicholas II to Duke Spitignew of Bohemia (*ca.* 1060), see Deusdedit, *Coll. can.* iii. 150, p. 385; by Alexander II to Duke Wratislaw of Bohemia (1072) and confirmed by Gregory VII (*Reg.* i. 38, p. 60: "Ad signum intimae dilectionis, quod laicae personae tribui non consuevit"); by Lucius III to Roger II of Sicily (Otto of Freising, *Gesta*, MGH. SS. RR. GG., ed. G. Waitz, cap. 29, p. 46: "Papa concessit Siculo virgam, et anulum, dalmaticam et mitram atque sandalia"; see also Deér, op. cit., p. 12, and cf. his Table XXXIII); by Innocent III to King Peter of Aragon (*Reg.* vii. 229: "papa . . . largiens ei (scil. Petro) regalia insignia universa, mantum videlicet, et colobium, sceptrum et pomum, coronam et mitram"). Cf. about this also Eichmann, *Kaiserkrönung*, ii. 145; and about the emperor's mitra see supra p. 259.

[2] See especially Klewitz, art. cit., p. 113, and Eichmann, *Weihe des Papstes*, p. 27.

[3] Cf. E. Kantorowicz, op. cit., p. 137, who says that the adoption of the tiara was "to provide the pope with a badge which he did not share with any bishop and which clearly distinguished him amongst the members of the hierarchy."

[4] Benzo of Alba, *Ad Heinricum IV*, MGH. SS. xi. 672: "Corrumpens igitur Prandellus (Hildebrand) Romanos multisque perjuriis induxit synodum, ubi regali corona suum coronavit hydolum. Quod cernentes episcopi facti sunt velut

coronatur."¹ From the description of Benzo it is clear that the head cover of Nicholas II had undergone some change: it was no longer the simple mitre which covered his head, since the mitre was enlarged by two *circuli*, that is, two rings. In order to understand this, we recall that an early Roman *Ordo*² had termed the *phrygium* of the pope *regnum*.³ At the time of the composition of this *ordo*, *phrygium* and *regnum* were the same and symbolized the kingship of the pope.⁴ But in the succeeding period this symbolic meaning seems to have been forgotten. When however the papal mitre became the *mitra Romana* and when this mitre was also worn by other prelates and princes, the necessity of devising a distinguishing feature for the papal mitre led—as a result of the general raking up of pertinent sources in precisely this decade— to a recollection of the Donation of Constantine, and its *phrygium*⁵ was now considered to be the appropriate and distinguishing head gear of the pope. What in actual fact was done was to surround the gold lace at the bottom of the mitre with a circle, above and below. The *regnum*, according to the description of Benzo of Alba, was a modified mitre, modified by the addition of the two rings which in fact were no more than the upper and lower trimmings of the gold lace. The mitre thus modified was the *corona* or *regnum* (*phrygium*).⁶ It was an extraliturgical head cover.⁷ When we now juxtapose the relevant passages in the

---

mortui. Legebatur autem in inferiori circulo eiusdem serti ita: corona regni de manu Dei; in altero vero sic: diadema imperii de manu Petri."

¹ Almost the same words he uses for Alexander II: "Talis super christianum populum exaltatur et quod auditu nedum visu horribile est, quasi rex in synodo coronatur," p. 692.

² See OR. IX, PL. lxxviii, cap. 6, col. 1007: "Accedit prior stabuli et imponit ei (scil. papae) in capite regnum quod ad similitudinem cassidis ex albo fit indumento." F. Wasner, art. cit., p. 431, is of the same opinion, namely, that the *phrygium, camelaucum* and *regnum* are one and the same thing; cf. also G. Ladner, "Die Statue Bonifaz's VIII und die Entstehung der dreifach gekrönten Tiara" in *Römische Quartalschrift*, xlii (1934), p. 52, note 66, p. 56, and Schramm, in *Hist. Z.*, clii (1935), pp. 308 and 309. Against this identification was Eichmann, *Weihe des Papstes*, p. 30, although he did not seem to have read Wasner's important articles.

³ Cf. also supra p. 312.

⁴ In consonance with the Donation of Constantine and with the head gear of the Eastern emperor.

⁵ Which had already been identified with the *regnum* in OR. IX.

⁶ We should not omit to mention that Isidore of Seville defined the mitre thus: "Mitra est pilleum *phrygium*, caput protegens, quale est ornamentum capitis devotarum. Sed pilleum virorum est, mitrae autem feminarum," *Etymologies*, XIX. xxxi. 4, ed. W. M. Lindsay in *Scriptorum classicorum Bibl. Oxoniensis*, 1911. This definition is under the rubric: "De ornamentis capitis feminarum."

⁷ See H. W. Klewitz, art. cit., pp. 114–15, who also observes that the mitre began to change its form from the end of the eleventh century, for which change

Donation, in the *Dictatus* of Avranches, and the *Dictatus* of Gregory VII, the development seems to have been thus:

| Donation | DA.10 | DP.8 |
|---|---|---|
| Statuentes eundem phrygium omnes eius successores pontifices singulariter uti in processionibus. | Soli papae licet in processionibus insigne quod vocatur regnum portare cum reliquo apparatu imperiali.[1] | Solus (papa) uti possit imperialibus insigniis. |

The confirmation of all this is in the statement of Bruno of Segni that the pope wears the *regnum*, "quia Constantinus imperator olim beato Silvestro omnia Romani imperii insignia tradidit." Indeed, the pope is a *sacerdos regalis* as well as an *imperialis episcopus*: he was the *apostolicus* on earth.[2] The pope is *sacerdos* and *rex*.[3]

The monarch of the *societas christiana* therefore appears as a true emperor clad with all the imperial garments. One more such symbolic manifestation of his supreme Rulership was the kissing of the feet[4] which was the Western counterpart of the Eastern proskynesis, the actual (and humiliating) prostration before the emperor as divinity on earth.[5] Into this category of public demonstrations signifying the

---

there would have been no occasion, had not the phrygium been revived. For the different shapes of the mitre see Braun, op. cit., p. 459. About the mitre of the emperor in the *Libellus de ceremoniis aule imperatoriae*, see supra p. 259.

[1] Cf. also DA. 11: "Solus utitur rubra cappa in signum imperii vel martirii." We think that the DA. should be dated earlier than the beginning of Gregory's pontificate, cf. *Studi Gregoriani*, iv. 118.

[2] See the eleventh-century description of the Lateran services, where the pope is characterized thus: "Qui sacerdos est regalis et imperialis episcopus, immo patriarcha et apostolicus" quoted by Klewitz, "Die Entstehung des Kardinalkollegiums" in *Sav. Z., kan. Abt.*, xxvi (1936), p. 123, note 1.

[3] Cf. E. Kantorowicz, op. cit., p. 138, speaking of an "imperialization of the Church as one of the outstanding features of the Reform papacy." Biblical models might have been Eccl.us, xliv. 14: "*Corona aurea super mitram* eius expressa signo sanctitatis, et gloria honoris; opus virtutis et desideria oculorum ornata."

[4] DP. 9: "Solius pedes omnes principes deosculentur." The OR. IX mentioned kissing of the feet in cap. 4 (PL. lxxviii. 1006). The *Lib. Pont.* (ii. 107) also knew of the kissing of the feet of the pope in the ninth century. About the adoration of the Norman kings in Sicily and the kissing of their feet (heels) see J. Deér, op. cit., p. 14, note 20.

[5] E. Eichmann, *Kaiserkrönung*, i. 189; here also further literature. Cf. also Eisenhofer, *Liturgik*, p. 57: indubitably adoption of the Roman-Byzantine imperial ceremonial. On the origins of the proskynesis in the ancient empire, cf. M. P. Charlesworth, "Some observations on Ruler Cult" in *Harvard Theol. Rev.*, xxviii (1935), pp. 16 ff., and especially A. Alföldi in *Mitt. d. deutschen archaeolog. Instituts*, Rom. Abt., xlix (1934), pp. 59 ff. (directly derived from the divine position attributed to the emperor, but strenuously opposed by the Christians, pp. 74–9). Kissing of the feet was not, however, unknown in ancient Rome, see

unique monarchic position of the pope belong also the *laudes* which were sung to the pope on the model of the imperial *laudes*.[1] Papal coronations and papal festive coronations ("crown-wearings")—on certain feast days[2]—were also to bring into clear relief the monarchic appearance of the pope: kings and emperors since the tenth century had attached great significance to these festive coronations.[3] And the Byzantine festive coronations were the direct model of the papal festive coronations.[4]

The papal coronation and its ideological significance make a few observations necessary. It is proved that the ceremony of papal coronations—as distinct from the consecrations—was performed in the case of most twelfth-century popes.[5] Nevertheless, papal coronation, consisting of the imposition of the *corona* and the enthronement accom-

---

Alföldi, pp. 54–5, nor kissing of the emperor's cheeks and hands, pp. 40–2. Sometimes the proskynesis was combined with the kissing of the hem of the emperor's garment, ibid., pp. 62–3 (Persian origin). Kissing of the pope's hands is mentioned in OR. I, cap. 8, PL. cit. col. 941 (late eighth century). Washing of the feet by the pope is mentioned in OR. X, c. 12; OR. XI, c. 41 and OR. XII, c.25.

[1] See especially E. Kantorowicz, op. cit., pp. 129–32; Schramm in *Studi Gregoriani*, ii. 443; and R. Elze, "Das Sacrum Palatium Lateranense," ibid., iv. 49–50.

[2] See H. W. Klewitz, "Krönung des Papstes" *Sav. Z.* cit., pp. 99–100, quoting from Albinus's entry in the *Liber censuum*. On the eighteen specifically mentioned feast days the pope "debet coronari": 8 November, 11 November and 23 November; the first three Sundays of Advent; Christmas Day; St Stephen's day, Epiphany; Sunday Laetare; Easter Sunday and Monday; second Sunday after Easter; Ascension; Whitsun; 29 June; 31 December, and finally the anniversary of the pope's election. Cf. also OR. XI, *Additio*, PL. cit. col. 1053. The officers who assisted the pope in this ceremony were the "addrextatores."

[3] See E. Eichmann, op. cit., i. 189. How much during Gregory's pontificate the pope was considered as holding the Roman empire may be gleaned from the dating of some Burgundian documents: "Domno nostro papa Gregorio Romanum imperium tenente," quoted by E. Kantorowicz, op. cit., p. 140, note 93, from the *Cartulaire de l'abbaye de S. Bernard de Romans*.

[4] E. Eichmann, *Weihe des Papstes*, p. 40. At the same time the liturgical *ordines*, beginning with OR. I, inherited a good deal of ancient Roman emperor ceremonial, e.g. thuribles, torches, etc. Cf. also P. Batiffol, *Études de liturgie et d'archéologie chrétienne*, Paris, 1919, pp. 193 ff.; also Alföldi, op. cit. (supra, 315 n. 5), pp. 114 f. About the imperial *sella* (the chair) see idem, ibid., pp. 104–6, 110; the papal *sella* figures prominently in the ORi. On the genuflexion before the Roman emperor see Alföldi, ibid., pp. 46 ff., and Batiffol, op. cit., pp. 137 ff.

[5] For detailed evidence see H. W. Klewitz, art. cit., p. 98, note 7. Whether Gregory VII himself was crowned, is not certain, except that he appeared at the Christmas procession of 1075 "coronatus" (see supra p. 311), but this can have been only a festive coronation, and not an original one.

panied by the *laudes*, never displayed the same effects as their counter-part, the imperial coronations. For the latter was constitutive: before the imperial coronation the king was a mere candidate for emperor-ship. It was different with the pope: his coronation was merely declara-tory, not constitutive. For the *regnum* was the symbol of imperial-royal power. As we have tried to show, royal power in hierocratic thought was merely the "temporal" personified: it was the personal expression of the lifeless "temporal" or "secular." And pontifical authority by virtue of the character of this authority and the society over which it was exercised, entitled the pope to dispose of the "temporal" or royal power. Hence the solemn imposition of the *corona* could not and did not add anything as regards authority which the pope had not already possessed.[1] Just as it was necessary at times to remind contemporaries of the full meaning of papal authority, so it was necessary to emphasize this authority by the solemn act of papal coronation. Papal coronation was a mere symbolic act demonstrating the pope's supreme monarchical position by contemporary and ack-nowledged means.[2] The wearing of the papal crown at festive corona-tions had solely symbolic meaning.[3]

Although the crown was a monarch's most pronounced outward

---

[1] We do not think it is right to say that the "immantation" of the pope after his election with the *cappa rubea*, the imperial purple, had constitutive effects: in this sense H. W. Klewitz, art. cit., p. 120, and E. Kantorowicz, op. cit., pp. 138–9. It too had merely declaratory effects: this seems also the opinion of Eich-mann, *Weihe des Papstes*, p. 34 (a sign of the "rechtmässige Antritt"); cf. also infra 318. n. 2. F. Wasner, art. cit., pp. 118–21, also seems to be of this opinion. The same may be said of the pope's solemn induction into the palace: this too had no constitutive effects, see Wasner, ibid. The constitutive act was the election, see the decree of Nicholas II (MGH. *Const.* i. 538, cap. 8) and later Innocent III, *Sermo in consecratione*, iii (PL. ccxvii. 663). About the inthronization of the pope, i.e. his elevation into the "sedes beati Petri" by the two cardinal bishops, see Wasner, art. cit., pp. 255–6, 258, esp. pp. 269, 271; Eichmann, op. cit., pp. 13–17; the juristic nature and the consequences of this elevation are dealt with by Wasner, loc. cit. Cf. also A. Menzer, "Die Jahresmerkmale etc." in *Römische Quartal-schrift*, xl (1932), pp. 68–70.

[2] Little more than a century afterwards Innocent III exquisitely expressed these ideas thus: *Sermo* cit. (preceding note): "Solus autem Petrus assumptus est in plenitudinem potestatis. In signum spiritualium contulit mihi mitram, in signum temporalium dedit mihi coronam; mitram pro sacerdotio, coronam pro regno, illius me constituens, vicarium, qui habet in vestimento et in femore suo scriptum 'Rex regum et dominus dominantium, sacerdos in aeternum secundum ordinem Melchisedech" (col. 665). Cf. also *Sermo VII in festo beati Silvestri*: "Romanus itaque pontifex in signum imperii utitur regno et in signum pontificii utitur mitra: sed mitra semper utitur et ubique, regno vero nec ubique nec semper" (PL. cit., col. 481). Cf. also G. Ladner, art. cit., p. 57.

[3] See especially H. W. Klewitz, art. cit., pp. 118 ff.

symbol of his position, it was only one of several symbols. The author of the Donation of Constantine had taken great care to say that the pope was to be given all imperial garments, so as to leave no doubt about the papal function as an emperor-monarch.[1] Imperial garments were scarlet red, so had those of the pope to be: the *cappa rubea* which is the "chlamys purpurea" of the Donation, is a scarlet mantle, which the pope puts on immediately after his election.[2] Of the other pieces of papal attire we mention the *rubia calciamenta papalia*, the papal scarlet shoes, the *caligae de rubeo panno*, the stockings, and the *infula rubea*.[3] The *Dictatus* of Avranches merely echoes the Donation when its author declares: "Solus utitur rubea cappa in signum imperii vel

---

[1] "De praesenti contradimus . . . diadema . . . phrygium, necnon et super-humerale, videlicet lorum, qui imperiale circumdare adsolet collum, verum etiam et chlamydem purpuream atque tunicam coccineam et omnia imperialia indumenta . . . etiam et imperialia sceptra simulque et cuncta signa atque banta etiam et diversa ornamenta imperialia et omnem processionum imperialis culminis at gloriam potestatis nostrae." The *Libellus de ceremoniis aule imperatoris* (ca. 1030) gives the monokrator (the emperor) most of these garments, including the "tunica coccinea," the "chlamys" and the "phrygium" as well as the dalmatic, cap. 5 and 6 (ed. P. E. Schramm, *Kaiser*, ii. 95–7). It seems that the author of the *Libellus* wished to recover from the Constantinean grant as much as possible for the emperor.

[2] By the mid-twelfth century this mantle was considered as symbolizing the "investiture" of the pope. Cf. the vivid description of the scene in which the anti-pope Victor IV took the "mantum" away from Alexander III in the view of all ("a collo nostro propriis manibus violenter excussit et secum . . . asportavit") in Alexander III's *Ep.* i, PL. cc. 70–1; see also Klewitz, art. cit., p. 120, referring to Victor's decision to renounce the papacy by laying down the *cappa rubea*. The terms used for this mantle were not always consistent: it was also called "pluviale," "mantum," or "clamis," see Eichmann, *Weihe*, p. 34. Eichmann thought that the scarlet mantle originated at about the time of the fabrication of the Donation of Constantine, "weil das Bedürfnis, es dem Kaiser gleich zu tun, in Rome lebhaft gewesen ist, und gerade dieses Kleidungstück durch seine Farbe und Bezeichnung den kaisergleichen erkennen liess." The OR. XIII (Gregory X) in the thirteenth century and OR. XIV gave, however, great prominence to the "immantation" which was to symbolize the "investiture" of the pope with the papacy. See OR. XIII, cap. 2 (PL. lxxviii. 1105): immediately after the election the prior of the deacons puts the purple mantle on the pope and says: "Investio te de papatu Romano, ut praesis urbi et orbi." The same procedure was followed in OR. XIV, cap. 10 (PL. cit., col. 1126). According to the *Caeremoniale Romanum* of 1486 the essential features of this investiture were still kept, but the words were not spoken, "so as not to provoke the secular rulers," Eichmann, *Weihe*, p. 56. Nevertheless, in 1090, the Irish Bishop Gilbert knew of a "chlamys coccinea" as part of the episcopal attire, see J. Usserius (Ussher), *Vet. Epist. Hib. Syll.*, Dublin, 1632, p. 87. For the alleged gift of a "cappa valde pretiosa aurifrigio ex omni parte ornata" by Aegelnoth, cf. Eadmer, *Hist. nov.*, PL. clix. 416–18.

[3] Cf. Eichmann, *Kaiserkrönung*, ii. 49 ff., 131 f. P. E. Schramm in *Studi Gregoriani*, ii. 444, considers that the red sandals of the Eastern patriarch may possibly have been the model for Roman adoption.

martirii,"[1] whilst the *Dictatus* of Gregory VII has indubitably the better and more concise diction:

Solus uti possit imperialibus insigniis.[2]

## II

The form of the government of this *societas christiana* was monarchic. But the scope and manifold nature of this government exercised over that vast society made a consultative body necessary: the universality of this government necessitated the establishment of a permanent council around the monarch. In the terminology of contemporary kings this body surrounding them was called the *curia regis*, but the papal curia was infinitely better organized and had more ramifications than its royal counterparts. The most important section of this papal curia was the permanent senate around the pope, which by the end of the eleventh century had become a constitutionally defined body—the college of cardinals or the sacred college. This corporate body, consisting by the end of this century, of the three orders, the cardinal bishops, the cardinal priests, and the cardinal deacons, and headed by the pope, had become the corporate epitome of the universal Church. This body was in fact the Roman Church which was no longer the epitome of Christendom plain and simple, but its corporate epitome. The corporate nature of the Roman Church corresponded to the corporate nature of the *societas christiana*.

The formation of this corporate body proceeded by utilizing the existing organization of the Roman clergy. Although their original functions—liturgical, pastoral, parochial, alternating in weekly turns, hence called hebdomadal functions—were not at first abolished, they were bound to take second place when once a constitutional corporate entity was created for the specific purpose of functioning as the senate of the pope. The nucleus of this organized body was formed by the

---

[1] See DA. 11, and Klewitz, art. cit., p. 120, note 77.

[2] The sceptre was one more of the papal insignia derived from the Donation of Constantine, see the quotation supra 318. It was used as early as Leo VIII's pontificate, see Liutprand, *Historia Ottonis*, ed. cit., cap. 22, p. 175: Benedict V "pallium sibi abstulit, quod simul cum pontificali ferula, quam manu gestabat, domno Leoni papae reddidit." The sceptre was the sign of the pope's "weltlichen, nicht der geistlichen oberhirtlichen Gewalt, die beim Papst schon durch das Pallium symbolisiert war," Eichmann, ii. 82–5; *Weihe*, p. 33. The monarchic position of the pope (in conjunction with his imperial insignia) is well brought out by the late twelfth-century author of the *Summa Reginensis*: "Omnes autem reges christiani subsunt domino apostolico, qui etiam imperialia signa habet," ed. by A. M. Stickler in *Salesianum*, xiv, 1952, p. 491.

cardinal bishops, those seven "episcopi cardinales ebdomadarii" of whom first mention is made during the pontificate of Stephen III: the cardinal bishops were to be joined by the cardinal priests and then by the cardinal deacons.[1] Very significantly Leo IX called ecclesiastics from beyond the Alps to Rome[2] where they joined the ranks of the cardinal bishops and cardinal priests after the dismissal of a number of simoniacal cardinals.[3] The cardinals began to function as the pope's counsellors and senators. The avocation of non-Roman elements to the cardinalate sufficiently demonstrated the epitomizing character of this body.[4] This marked not only the beginning of the corporate establishment of the senate, but also the essential change in the functions of this body: the previous liturgical functions of an unorganized body became the senatorial functions of the corporate epitome.

It is to the need of a senatorial body that St Peter Damian refers in a well-known passage: the Roman Church must imitate the ancient curia of the Romans—"Romana ecclesia, quae sedes est apostolorum, antiquam debet imitari curiam Romanorum"[5]—for just as at that time the senate directed the multitude of the nations, so that they should be subjected to the Roman empire, in the same way St Peter Damian holds that the senators of the universal Church should subject mankind to the laws of the true emperor Christ.[6] In programmatic assertions of

†　[1] For all this see J. B. Sägmüller, *Die Tätigkeit und Stellung der Kardinäle*, Freiburg, 1896; idem, in *Theol. Quartalschrift*, lxxx (1898), pp. 596–614, and lxxxiii (1901), pp. 45–93; J. Lestocquoy, "Administration de Rome et des diaconies du VII au IX siècle" in *Rivista d'archaeologia cristiana*, vii (1930), pp. 261 ff.; M. Andrieu, "L'origine du titre de cardinal dans l'église romaine" in *Miscellanea G. Mercati*, 1945, v. 113 ff.; H. W. Klewitz, "Die Entstehung des Kardinalkollegiums" in *Sav. Z., kan. Abt.*, xxv (1936) pp. 115–221 (cardinal bishops: pp. 127–47; priests: pp. 147–76; and deacons: pp. 176–92); St. Kuttner, "Cardinalis" in *Traditio*, iii (1945), pp. 129 ff., at pp. 146–52, 172–98. For the early history of the "diaconiae" and their contribution to the making of "un organismo romano" see the important work of O. Bertolini, "Per la storia delle diaconiae romane" in *Archivio della Societa Romana di storia patria*, lxx (1947), pp. 1–145.

[2] For instance, the abbots of Monte Cassino, Vendôme, St Victor-Marseilles, see Kuttner, art. cit., p. 175, note 102.

[3] See Sägmüller, op. cit., pp. 25, 38; H. W. Klewitz, art. cit., p. 117; Kuttner, art. cit., pp. 173, 175, note 103.

[4] It is from Leo IX onwards that the college of cardinals begins to take concrete shape, Klewitz, p. 118, who has worked out this most intricate process. Cf. also A. Dumas in E. Amann and A. Dumas, *L'église au pouvoir des laiques*, Paris, 1951, pp. 155–9.

[5] Peter Damian, *Opusc.*, no. 31: *Contra phylargyriam*, cap. 7 (PL. cxlv. 540).

[6] Peter Damian, *Opusc.*, no. 31: *Contra phylargyriam*, cap. 7 (PL. cxlv. 540): "Sicut enim tunc terrenus ille senatus ad hoc communicabant omne consilium, in hoc dirigebant et subtiliter exercebant communis industriae studium, ut cunctarum gentium multitudo Romano subderetur imperio, ita nunc apostolicae sedis

this kind we recognize the concrete realization of the *societas christiana* as an autonomous body politic which is in need of a proper governmental machinery. The same ideas underlie the statement of Cardinal Deusdedit who declares that the place of the old patricians is now taken by the Roman clergy: "Inde Romani clerici locum antiquorum habent patriciorum."[1] What the term cardinal came to mean was a very intimate connexion with the pope and papal government, so intimate in fact that Cardinal Humbert could speak of the cardinals as participants in the papal plenitude of power, that is, as co-bearers of the primacy of the Roman Church. The term "Romana ecclesia" as a result of the initiation of this corporate body, acquired a corporate complexion: it became, as we have said, the corporate epitome of the *societas christiana*. When formerly the senators were called the "pars corporis imperatoris," the new senators, the cardinals, became the "pars corporis papae."[2] Consequently, the Roman Church was the "caput et cardo" of contemporary Christian society: it was its corporate head. Cardinal Humbert as the draftsman of Leo IX's letters, writes to the patriarch of Constantinople:

Like the immovable hinge that sends the door forth and back thus Peter and his successors have the free judgment over the entire Church . . . therefore his clerics are named cardinals, for they belong more closely to the hinge by which everything else is moved.[3]

---

aeditui, qui spirituales sunt universalis ecclesiae senatores, huic soli studio debent solerter insistere, ut humanum genus veri imperatoris Christi valeant legibus subjugare. Et sicut tunc Romanorum consules ex diversis mundi partibus reportabant . . . sic isti nunc animas hominum de manu diaboli, debent liberare captivas . . . et regi suo Christo signa gaudeant victricia reportare." Cf. also Peter Damian's *Disceptatio synodalis* (MGH. LdL. i. 83, lines 17–18) where he says that SS Peter and Paul had possessed the principate of the apostolic senate; the "defensor Romanae ecclesiae" declares: "Non ignoras, quod inter omnes sanctos martyros Petrus et Paulus in apostolici senatus culmine possident principatum."

[1] Deusdedit, *Collectio canonum*, iv. 1 (ed. Wolf von Glanvell, p. 17). According to Peter of Blois the cardinals are the *Patres conscripti*, PL. ccvii. 377, *Ep.* 126.

[2] On this see Sägmüller, op. cit., pp. 225–6.

[3] Cornelius Will, *Acta et Scripta*, cap. xxxii, pp. 81–2. It is the same idea that emerges from the statement of Cardinal Deusdedit when he declares that the cardinals are the bases and hinges by which the "plebs Dei" is ruled: etymologically the *basilei* are derived from *basis*: "Sicut a basibus, quae sunt fulturae columnarum a fundamento surgentes basilei, id est reges dicuntur, quia populum regunt, ita et cardinales derivative dicuntur a cardinibus januae, qui tam regunt et movent, quod plebem Dei . . . ad amorem Dei moveant," op. cit., ii. 160, p. 268. For the difference between Peter Damian and Deusdedit, see Kuttner, art. cit., p. 176, note 109. In his *Carmen*, no. LXXII, Peter Damian makes St Peter "basim aedificii" (PL. cxlv. 941).

Nevertheless, the initiation of this corporate body brought about what we have called the problem of the cardinalate, that is, of the precise constitutional standing of the cardinals. Can they exercise authority over the pope, participating as they do in his primacy? Is the pope bound by the cardinals' advice or can he legitimately disregard it? We can only mention this problem in passing, since it is outside the scope of this essay, and we confine ourselves to the statement that when once the theory of corporations was fully worked out, it was sure to be applied to this body too, with the inevitable consequence of restricting the pope's functions.[1]

But the function of the cardinals was not merely senatorial. The manner in which popes were made and unmade in the fourth and fifth decades of the eleventh century, extraordinarily resembled the Eastern spectacle of the creation of the imperial domestic prelate, the patriarch. The regime of Henry III had shown the unadulterated application of the idea of protection in the purest royal sense. This interpretation of the idea meant control by the emperor of the papacy; the papal conception of protection meant control by the papacy of the emperor. But the Henrician government had plainly manifested the exercise of imperial control over the papacy, thus cutting right across the fundamental axioms of hierocratic doctrine: this making and unmaking of popes was the most palpable negation of the pope as the supreme monarch in the *societas christiana*. It was the concrete denial of the pope's being the *sacerdos regalis*.

The pattern for "canonical and just elections" was provided by the old Roman decree of 769 passed in the synod under Stephen III.[2] Although the synodists excluded the laity, they could do little more than say that the election of the pontiff lay in the hands of the (Roman) clergy. It was nevertheless significant that the account of this decree of 769 referred to cardinal presbyters and deacons.[3] In the intervening years between 769 and 1059 the local Roman clergy had crystallized into distinct and very prominent offices, the seven cardinal bishops, the twenty-five cardinal priests, and the cardinal deacons. They alone had performed the hebdomadal services in the Lateran: the conferment upon these prominent ecclesiastical officers of the exclusive right of electing the pope was therefore understandable. The utilization of these

---

[1] Cf. *Studi Gregoriani*, iv. 111 ff.

[2] See supra p. 87. On the importance of this decree see F. Wasner in *Apollinaris*, viii (1935), pp. 251 ff.; cf. also M. Andrieu, "La carrière ecclésiastique des papes" in *Revue des sciences religieuses*, xxi (1947), pp. 90 ff.

[3] Cf. *Lib. Pont.*, i. 478; 484.

(Roman) cardinals for non-liturgical functions was a measure that suggested itself.[1] In short, the "cunctus clerus" of 769 had shrunk to the "cardinales clerici" and in a specific sense to the cardinal bishops who functioned as metropolitans in designating and raising the elected candidate to the pontifical office.[2] In a way, the cardinals took the place of the cathedral chapter.

The acclamation laid down in the decree of 769 re-appeared in 1059 in a somewhat different shape. The remaining clergy and the people "should accede to consent to the new election."[3] Considering the tenor and the ideas underlying the decree there can be no doubt that the passage did not have in mind a ratifying, legal consent by clergy and people, but merely the acclamation in the form of the popular *laudes*.[4] Lastly, Henry IV was given in this decree the personal right of "consenting," that is, of acclaiming; his successors also should have this right, provided that they submitted a specific request to the Roman Church and that this request was granted.[5] The old *Liber Diurnus* regulation had indeed undergone some drastic changes. From a notification to the emperor (or exarch) requesting him to confirm the papal election through the intermediate stages of the Carolingian and post-Carolingian period, when the *Liber Diurnus* was utilized, not in order to obtain confirmation, but protection by the emperor, to the decree of

[1] See the decree of 13 April 1059, MGH. *Const.* i, no. 382, pp. 539–40, cap. 3: † "Ut, obeunte huius Romanae universalis ecclesiae pontifice, in primis cardinales episcopi diligentissima simul consideratione tractantes, mox sibi clericos cardinales adhibeant: sicque reliquus clerus et populus ad consensum novae electionis accedant." The procedure, therefore, was that the cardinal bishops designated the candidate to the other cardinals, and all cardinals then elected the candidate formally. About the theological importance of this synod see A. J. Macdonald, *Berengar and the reform of sacramental doctrine*, London, 1930, pp. 108 ff.; also G. Schreiber, "Studien über Anselm von Havelberg" in *Analecta Praemonstratensia*, xviii (1942), pp. 68–70. About the probable author of the decree concerning the election, i.e. Humbert, see now also A. Michel, "Humbert und Hildebrand bei Nikolaus II" in *Festschrift f. G. Schreiber* (*Hist. Jb.*, lxxii, 1953), pp. 143–50 (offprint).

[2] Cap. 4, p. 539: ". . . cardinales episcopi procul dubio metropolitani vice funguntur, qui videlicet electum antistitem ad apostolici culminis apicem provehunt."

[3] See the passage quoted supra, note 1.

[4] Of which we read in subsequent election accounts. If ratification had been intended, the diction would have been different, but the employment of the term "accedere" militates against interpreting the passage in the sense of legal ratification.

[5] Cap. 6, p. 540: "Salvo debito honore et reverentia dilecti filii nostri Henrici, qui in praesentiarum rex habetur et futurus imperator Deo concedente speratur, sicut jam sibi concessimus, et successores illius, qui ab hac apostolica sede personaliter hoc jus impetraverint."

1059, when the "right of acclaiming" the new pope was made the issue of a specific papal concession, was a long and tortuous way; and a way, as we have seen, which was not without grave dangers to the papacy. The sixth chapter of this decree of 1059 was the last remnant of the old *Liber Diurnus* rule: it was hardly recognizable any more. The reason is clear. The preceding ninety-seven years had all too clearly shown to what excesses the erstwhile invocation of protection had led: it was this invocation in fact which enabled the emperors to exercise their control over the papacy. On the other hand, this decree in its eighth chapter excludes any intervention by the emperor between election and inthronization of the newly elected pope. The pope once elected assumes full pontifical powers. Moreover, the act which made the future emperor a special protector of the Roman Church was the imperial coronation. And since in 1059 there was little prospect of Henry IV becoming emperor in the near future, the "protector of the Roman Church" was to be found in the Normans who became in the summer of this year the vassals of the Roman Church.[1] In this function they were to safeguard papal elections as laid down in the decree.[2]

The senatorial and electoral functions of the cardinals led to the fixation of a number of specific privileges to be enjoyed by them.[3] We can but indicate some of these privileges here. The development of these privileges began at the time at which the cardinals became the senators and electors of the pope, although it was not concluded until well into the following century. The importance of the cardinals is perhaps best seen in the strenuousness of the efforts which Wibert (the anti-pope Clement III) made in order to win their adherence to his cause: in so doing he considerably hastened the development of the specific privileges appertaining to the cardinals[4] who, even after the schism had ended, would not renounce any of the rights won in

---

[1] The oath of vassalage is in the *Liber Censum*, ed. P. Fabre and L. Duchesne, i. 421, no. clxii, and clxiii: "Adjutor ero ad tenendum et ad acquirendum regalia sancti Petri contra omnes homines . . ."

[2] "Etsi tu vel tui successores ante me ex hac vita migraveritis, secundum quod monitus fuero a melioribus cardinalibus clericis Romanis et laicis, adjuvabo ut papa eligatur et ordinetur ad honorem sancti Petri." It is indeed a long way from the *Ludovicianum* and the *Lotharianum* to this oath taken by the Normans.

[3] Membership of the college of cardinals was not a presupposition for papal candidature, see cap. 5: "Eligant autem de ipsius gremio, si reperitur idoneus, vel si de ipsa non invenitur, ex alia assumatur." A great number of popes in the twelfth and thirteenth centuries were not cardinals.

[4] St. Kuttner, art. cit., p. 174; cf. also Sägmüller, op. cit., pp. 235–6; and H. W. Klewitz, art. cit., p. 173.

"schismatic" times.[1] Not only did the cardinals claim precedence over any bishop; not only were the requirements of the Symmachan forgeries—the testimony of three dozen witnesses—applied to the trial of a cardinal; but also the cardinals obtained the right which in fact was the logical application of the hierarchic principle, to judge any bishop in the Roman empire[2] as well as the right to subscribe to papal acts.[3] Lastly, the meetings of this senatorial body supplanted the former synod: the meeting of the cardinals became the consistory,[4] the cabinet of the pope.[5]

## III

The pope was not only a *sacerdos regalis*, but he also appeared as such. And this made it advisable for him to live in a place which suitably brought into relief his monarchic function. We recall that the residence of the popes had changed its name during the ninth century: from a mere *episcopium* the residence became the *sacrum palatium Lateranense*. This nomenclature symbolically projected on to the residence of the popes their sacerdotal (*sacrum*) and their regal-imperial functions (*palatium*). It was in this *palatium* that the pope resided with his entourage and his officials. The papal residence was also the seat of the curia of the pope—the *curia Romana*—which shows such great affinities with a royal or imperial curia. In both curiae the monarch is surrounded by his dignitaries, officers, title bearers; in each case all the administrative appurtenances appertaining to a court will be found.[6]

[1] Klewitz, art. cit., pp. 166, 175; and K. Jordan, "Die päpstliche Verwaltung im Zeitalter Gregors VII" in *Studi Gregoriani*, i. 127.

[2] *Descriptio sanctuarii Lateranensis ecclesiae:* "qui potestatem obtinent judicium faciendi super omnes episcopos totius Romani imperii in omnibus conciliis vel synodis quibuscumque accersiti vel praesentes fuerint," quoted by Klewitz, art. cit., p. 123, note 1.

[3] J. B. Sägmüller, op. cit., pp. 62, 184, 216, 246; Klewitz, art. cit., p. 201; St. Kuttner, art. cit., p. 177. For cardinals' signatures see J. B. Sägmüller, op. cit., p. 74, notes 6 and 8; and Bresslau, *Handbuch der Urkundenlehre*, 2nd ed., ii. 52, note 2, and the further development, ibid., pp. 55–61 (Gregory IX: Potthast 9368; Nicholas IV: Potthast 23010). Since the pope is merely the mouthpiece of the Roman Church, Cardinal Hugh asserts that without the cardinals' signatures, the pope's declarations are invalid: *Ad Mathildam*, MGH. LdL. ii. 419.

[4] See H. W. Klewitz, art. cit., pp. 133, 203; and J. B. Sägmüller, op. cit., pp. 48–58, 97–8. "Le consistoire est une transposition du synode romano-byzantin," J. Rousset de Pina in *Hist. de l'église*, Paris, 1953, ix. 236. Constantine's council was the "sacrum consistorium," see G. Ostrogorsky, *Gesch. d. byz. Staates*, p. 20.

[5] The conferment of specific garments on the cardinals began in the time of Innocent IV, see P. Hinschius, *Kirchenrecht*, i. 357.

[6] See K. Jordan, art. cit., p. 134; E. Eichmann, *Kaiserkrönung*, ii. 212; P. E.

In the case of the *sacrum palatium* the basis was the Donation of Constantine, in which the emperor had handed over to Silvester "palatium nostrum" which the emperor himself had built. Consequently, in the ninth century the term *palatium Lateranense* was adopted and the former *episcopium* (or *patriarchium*) disappears from papal documents altogether.[1] It was not only the official residence of the pope; it became also in the course of time the place in which regular payments have had to be made—in a way corresponding to a royal exchequer—as John XIII in 970 had laid down.[2] It also housed the papal chancery, the archives, and was the seat of the highest tribunal in the *societas christiana*. In a word, the *sacrum palatium* was the physical centre of the government exercised by the pope over the *societas christiana*: here converged all the multifarious and diverse channels from the whole of Christendom.[3]

A few observations on the organization of the *palatium* appear pertinent. It must not be supposed that the old organization was suddenly thrown overboard in the second half of the eleventh century. Within the purview of papal organization we find in fact the same gradual growth over a long period as we witnessed in other fields. New offices come slowly into their own, whilst old offices either merge with new ones, or vanish altogether. This latter was the case with the old palatine judges—the Seven Palatine Judges ("septem judices palatini") —who were not removed, but their importance was so diminished that in the second half of the eleventh century they vanished from sight altogether. The reason for this evanescence was clearly because these seven judges were not only not necessary members of the higher

---

Schramm, in *Studi Gregoriani*, ii. 438; K. Jordan, "Die Entstehung der römischen Kurie" in *Sav. Z., Kan. Abt.*, xxviii (1939), pp. 97 ff.

[1] Only during the time of Otto III's Roman sojourn the title *sacrum palatium* vanishes for a little while, see R. Elze, "Das Sacrum Palatium Lateranense" in *Studi Gregoriani*, iv. 40, who considers it possible that this suppression was due to Otto's view on the Donation.

[2] See K. Jordan, "Entstehung," p. 101 and "Verwaltung," p. 112; R. Elze, art. cit., p. 36. Cf. J. 3742. The payment concerned annual dues to be made "in palatio nostro" by the senatrix Stephania of ten gold solidi for the town of Preneste.

[3] Later under Innocent III it was found necessary to erect a number of new buildings at St Peter's, see *Gesta*, c. cxlvi (PL. ccxiv. ccxi): "Quia vero non tantum honorabile, sed utile censuit, ut summus pontifex apud s. Petrum palatium dignum haberet, fecit ibi fieri domos istas de novo: capellaniam (the residence of the "capellani"), cameram et capellam, pannatariam (baking house?), buccellariam, coquinam et marescalciam; domos cancellarii, camerarii et eleemosynarii . . . totumque palatium claudi muris et super portas erigi turres."

ecclesiastical hierarchy, but also, since Ottonian times, had been styled and had functioned as "judices Romani imperii." This fusion of functions prevented an important office from being developed or from being merged into new offices; the consequence was that it petered out and the judges for a time became purely local justices.[1] The development of the palace organization freely adopted features provided by Western patterns,[2] but it should be pointed out that these Western models were by no means slavishly copied.

For obvious reasons the papal chancery was a department that was most directly concerned with the actual administration of the *societas christiana*. This department provided the means transmitting *justitia*. As a consequence of the adoption of the name *palatium* new styles were created which had so far only appeared in an imperial *palatium*. The style and office of a chancellor—*cancellarius*—is found for the first time under John XVIII.[3] In the early eleventh century we find papal documents written as well as dated by "Petrus abbas et cancellarius sacri Lateranensis palatii."[4] For a while the office of librarian—the old head of the papal chancery—and that of chancellor were united, but by the mid-eleventh century the chancellor became the head of this department. Next to the chancellor's office there was the office of the "notarii et scriniarii sacri Lateranensis palatii."[5] It was the chancellor together with the notaries who formed, so to speak, the personal secretariat of the pope and who wrote the important correspondence.[6] The influence of this department became particularly marked when Clement II introduced non-Roman notaries and joined them to his personal "secretariat."[7] A further consequence of this organization

[1] P. E. Schramm, art. cit., p. 213 ff. But see also A. Dumas in E. Amann and A. Dumas, *L'église au pouvoir des laiques*, pp. 159–60.
[2] R. Elze, art. cit., attractively draws attention to the imperial palace at Pavia as the prototype of the papal palace and its organization from the tenth century onwards.
[3] See J. 3947, of December 1005, and R. L. Poole, *Lectures on the papal chancery*, Cambridge, 1917, p. 59; idem, "Imperial influences on papal documents" in *Proc. Brit. Acad.*, viii (1917), pp. 244, 248; K. Jordan, "Verwaltung," p. 112.
[4] Cf. R. L. Poole, op. cit. and loc. cit. See also A. Dumas, op. cit., p. 164: "Brusquement en 1005, pour mieux assurer l'unité de direction, le pape Jean XVIII inaugura un nouveau système. Il mit ses scribes sous l'autorité d'un chef specialisé, qui reçut le titre de chancelier."
[5] R. L. Poole, op. cit., p. 62; K. Jordan, "Verwaltung," p. 112. Under Benedict VIII the new title is "scriniarius et notarius sacri nostri palatii sanctaeque nostrae Romanae ecclesiae," Jordan, loc. cit., note 9.
[6] See K. Jordan, art. cit., p. 113; Poole, op. cit., p. 63.
[7] The separation of the *scrinium* from the *palatium* (the residence of the popes) is not directly concerned with the papal chancery, as P. Kehr once thought, see

was that the connexions between papal administration and city administration became more and more tenuous.[1] Moreover, the old curial script[2] which was a corruption of the old Roman cursive and somewhat akin to the Beneventan script, was replaced by the non-Roman minuscule "which acquired in the papal chancery a delicacy and refinement unmatched elsewhere."[3] This replacement was in fact a necessity since the old curial script—the *Littera Romana*—was illegible to those outside Rome; the effective exercise of governmental functions made a change imperative.[4]

his "Scrinium und Palatium: ein Beitrag zur Geschichte des päpstlichen Kanzleiwesens" in MIOG., suppl. vol. vi, pp. 70 ff., especially pp. 73–4; cf. also R. L. Poole, op. cit., p. 14 and 64–5, but see now R. Elze, art. cit., p. 39; idem, "Die päpstliche Kapelle" in *Sav. Z., kan. Abt.*, xxxvii (1950), p. 157, note 72, and P. E. Schramm in *Göttinger Gel. Anz.*, 1953, p. 117. It should be pointed out that the chancery as an independent organ—the *cancellaria*—probably did not come into being before Innocent III, see H. W. Klewitz, "Cancellaria" in *Deutsches Archiv*, i (1937), p. 78, and the references to "cancellaria" in the *Epp. Cantuarienses* and in the *Liber censuum*, quoted by R. Elze, in the last mentioned article, p. 175, note 173. The term "cancellaria nostra" is used by Lucius III, see *Lib. Extra*, I. iii. 10.     [1] See Kehr, loc. cit.

[2] It was called the "scripta notaria," Wattenbach, *Anleitung zur lateinischen Paleographie*, Leipzig, 4th ed., 1886, p. 20.

[3] R. L. Poole, op. cit., p. 58. This became the curial minuscule, see H. Bresslau, op. cit., ii/2, p. 533, or half-curial: C. Paoli, *Grundriss zu Vorlesungen über lateinische Paleographie*, transl. K. Lohmeyer, Innsbruck, 1902, p. 297 (this section is omitted in the new edition of C. Paoli's *Diplomatica*, by G. C. Bascapè, Florence, 1942). Cf. also H. Foerster, *Abriss der lateinischen Paleographie*, Bern, 1949, pp. 146–7.

[4] Cf. the example of Archbishop Ralph of Tours, quoted by A. Lowe, "Handwriting" in *The Legacy of the Middle Ages*, Oxford, repr. 1948, p. 220. The first occasion on which the minuscule appears on a papal document, though in the dating line only, was in a privilege of John XIII, of 15 April 967 (J. 3714): R. L. Poole, art. cit., p. 245, note 2. This is also the first document of the papal chancery written on parchment (instead of on papyrus), see H. Schmidinger, "Die Palliumverleihung Benedict VIII für Ragusa" in *Festschrift f. Leo Santifaller*, 1950, p. 32, and supra 263. It was from the late tenth century onwards that the un-Roman minuscule at first juxtaposed to the *Littera Romana*, gradually ousted the latter altogether, see R. L. Poole, art. cit., p. 245, H. Schmidinger, art. cit., pp. 32–3, with many examples of the co-existence of the two scripts. Two other effects of imperial influences should be noted: under Leo IX the *Rota* appears: the cross is separated from the *Bene Valete*, placed in the left hand corner under the scriptum line and surrounded by two circles with an appropriate motto written between them; under the same pope the monogramme appears as a derivative of the *Bene Valete*: it is placed in the right hand corner and shaped in rectangular form. "The monogramme is unquestionably derived from that which reproduced the emperor's name in his diplomas . . . (Leo) took the whole idea from the imperial diploma," Poole, art. cit., p. 247. See furthermore, C. Paoli, *Diplomatica*, ed. cit., 1942, p. 148. For the history of the *Rota* and its possible prototypes (coins), see H. Hartmann, *Arch. f. Urkundforsch.*, xvi (1939), pp. 388–410. For the *gratia* formula see infra p. 332 n. 1.

As a department and office of the *palatium* from which emanated the laws governing the *societas christiana*, the papal chancery had to issue documents which reflected the great care which was taken in their composition; hence the great value attached to the *cursus* or prose rhythm of papal documents. To have drawn attention to this important point was the merit of John of Gaeta, the chancellor under Urban II, the later Gelasius II.[1] It is however more than doubtful whether the *Liber Diurnus* came to be "replaced" as a consequence of John's chancellorship.[2] But no doubt is permissible about the dating of papal documents. Whilst previously the chancery conservatively followed the traditional pattern of dating papal documents according to imperial years, this practice ceases altogether under Leo IX. Henceforward papal documents are dated exclusively according to the pontifical years. Papal documents can no longer take imperial years as the measure of time and date: in the *societas christiana* the regnal years of the papal monarch alone count.[3]

For understandable reasons the financial side of the curia begins to assume an importance proportionate to the exercise of the *universale regimen* over the Christian world.[4] The chamberlain, or *camerarius*,

---

[1] See the entry in the *Lib. Pont.*, ii. 311, lines 26 ff.: "Tunc papa (Urbanus) ... fratrem Johannem ... ordinavit, admovit suumque cancellarium, ex intima deliberatione constituit, ut per eloquentiam sibi a Domino traditam antiqui leporis et elegantiae stilum, in sede apostolica jam pene omnem deperditam ... ac leoninum cursum lucida velocitate reduceret." Cf. also R. L. Poole, op. cit., pp. 74–5, 84–4, and the *cursus* itself, ibid., ch. iv, with numerous examples of various kinds of a *cursus* ("velox," "tardus," "planus").

[2] So the general opinion, cf. Poole, op. cit., p. 84. But L. Santifaller has cast serious doubt on the validity of this view, cf. his "Die Verwendung des LD in den Pivilegien der Päpste" in MIOG., xlix (1936), pp. 225–366; idem, "Neue Forschungen zur älteren Papstdiplomatik" in *Hist. Z.*, clxi (1940), pp. 532–8; idem, in Th. Sickel, *Römische Erinnerungen*, Vienna, 1947, pp. 174–80 (here also an outline of the problems which still need examination); idem, *Beschreibstoffe im Mittelalter* (MIOG., suppl. vol. xvi/1), 1953, pp. 93–4 ("niemals im praktischen Gebrauch der Papstkanzlei gestanden"). See furthermore C. L. Mohlberg, "Neue Erörterungen zum LD" in *Theolog. Revue*, xxxviii (1939), pp. 297 ff.; R. Ritzler, "Intorno al LD" in *Misc. Franciscana*, xlii (1942), pp. 77–82. But see especially W. Peitz against Santifaller, *Liber Diurnus: Methodisches zur Diurnusforschung* (Misc. Hist. Pont., ii. 1940).

[3] R. L. Poole, art. cit., p. 242, and A. Menzer in *Römische Quartalschrift*, xl (1932), pp. 75 ff.

[4] It is well known that Gregory VII attached great value to an orderly financial administration, but it seems an exaggeration to say that money alone played a decisive part in his "policy," cf. J. Haller, *Papsttum*, ii/1, p. 346; cf. also C. Erdmann, op. cit., pp. 142–4: church money used for military purposes. About the alleged Jewish origin of Gregory see G. Picotti, "Della supposta parentela ebraica di Gregorio VII" in *Archivio storico Italiano*, c (1942), pp. 3 ff. (denying

appears to have developed partly from the earlier papal chamberlains, and partly from the *cubicularii* and *vestararii*.[1] By the time of Urban II the "camerarius domini papae" becomes the curial officer responsible for the administration of papal finances, whilst under Urban's successor, Paschal II, a new financial official in the person of the "camerarius curiae Romanae" makes his appearance.[2] The "camera apostolica" as the financial department of the *palatium* comes into being[3] and seems to take the place of the ancient "vicedominium."[4]

Of the other officials constituting the curia in the widest sense we can but mention in passing the "vice-dominus" whose office seems to have been absorbed by that of the archdeacon[5] who in the case of a papal vacancy, functioned as the "vicarius" together with the arch-presbyter and the "primicerius," before the college of cardinals assumed this role.[6] Urban II, probably on the model of the French court, introduced the "dapifer" or lord high steward, and later in the twelfth century we witness the papal cup bearer—"pincerna domini papae"—as well as the marshals of the papal court, as palatine officers.[7]

Lastly, mention must be made of a "department" which, though

---

it); and R. Morghen, "Questioni Gregoriani" in *Archivio della R. societa di storia patria*, lxv (1942), pp. 1 ff., and ibid., lxix (1946), pp. 119–30. See also G. Marchetti-Longhi, "Richerche sulla famiglia di Gregorio VII" in *Studi Gregoriani*, ii. 287 ff., 312 ff., who refers (p. 313) to William of Malmesbury's characterization of Gregory as coming from "despicabilis parentela." The argument centres in the problem whether there was only one family of the Pierleone or two. But cf. also O. Lehmann-Brockhaus, *Schriftquellen zur Kunstgeschichte des 11 und 12. Jahrhunderts*, Berlin, 1938, i. 720, no. 3035, who refers to the report of the Saxon Annalist according to which Gregory's father was a carpenter. Cf. also *Annales Palidenses*, MGH. SS. xvi. 69, lines 9–10.

[1] See E. Eichmann, "Die Krönungsservitien etc." in *Sav. Z., kan. Abt.*, xxix (1939), pp. 10 ff.; *Kaiserkrönung*, ii. 249 f., 259 ff.; but cf. K. Jordan, "Zur päpstlichen Finanzverwaltung" in *Quellen und Forschungen aus italien. Archiven*, xxv (1934), pp. 91 ff.; idem, in *Studi Gregoriani*, i. 128 (origins in Cluny?), and R. Elze, art. cit., p. 194, at note 314.

[2] See K. Jordan, loc. cit.

[3] Schramm, *Studi Gregoriani*, ii. 439.

[4] E. Eichmann, op. cit., ii. 249–50. The development of the system of papal taxation does not belong to this period. But as every body politic must have properly organized revenues, so also were taxes prescribed by the government of the *societas christiana*: "church taxes" fell on both clerics and laymen, but, for understandable reasons, the former were exempted from provincial laical taxes.

[5] See K. Jordan, in *Studi Gregoriani*, i. 120.

[6] About this see G. B. Borino, "L'arcidiaconato di Ildebrando" in *Studi Gregoriani*, iii. 463–516; see also R. Elze, ibid., iv. 41.

[7] Schramm, loc. cit., p. 440. Cf. also Boso's "Vita Hadriani IV" where he also speaks of the "pincerna domni papae" in Watterich, *Pontificum Romanorum Vitae*, ii. 336.

borrowed from the royal courts, came in time to assume great importance. This is the papal *capella*, whose members were the *capellani* or chaplains. The beginnings of this curial department can again be found in the second half of the eleventh century. But the papal chaplains assumed functions different from their models in the royal courts, for they were subdeacons and "scriptores." First mentioned in their plurality by Urban II,[1] it seems however that a "capellanus" was found as early as 1026 in the papal administration.[2] By the end of this century the importance of the *capellani* showed itself in the promotion of nine of them to the cardinalate.[3] Throughout the following century the administrative and constitutional importance of the *capellani* increased, so that by the time of Innocent III the *capella* of the pope formed, so to speak, a reservoir on which the pope could and did draw for specific tasks.[4]

## IV

Every royal or imperial court had its feudal vassals—and so had the papal curia.[5] It is no doubt true that as time went on, the papal curia counted the greatest number of feudal vassals in medieval Europe. Nevertheless the harnessing of feudal principles to the hierocratic

[1] For all this see the study of R. Elze, "Die päpstliche Kapelle" in *Sav. Z.*, *kan. Abt.*, xxxviii (1950), pp. 145–204; idem, in *Studi Gregoriani*, iv. 46–7. It is the great merit of Elze to have drawn attention to the importance and development of the papal *capella*.

[2] K. Jordan, *Studi Gregoriani*, i. 114, drew attention to this. For the threefold meaning of *capella* see H. W. Klewitz in *Arch. f. Urkundenforsch.*, xvi (1939), p. 119, note 1.

[3] See the entry in *Lib. Pont.*, ii. 311–12.

[4] Particularly connected with legations, liturgical reforms, chancery organization; judicial business in the curia came more and more into the hands of the *capellani*, so that when the *Rota* was established, it was entirely staffed by the *capellani*. Under Innocent III there were about fifty of them, who also belonged to the pope's *familia*, see his *Gesta*, cap. cxlvi, and they were fed from the papal kitchens. Most of these *capellani* seem to have come from Bologna. For all details concerning them see R. Elze, art. cit. For the *Rota Romana* and its further development, see N. del Re, *La Curia Romana*, Rome, 1952, pp. 217–19. And for the development of all curial officers in the thirteenth century including the papal tribunals and welfare offices (papal alms house, hospital, etc.) see the excellent work of B. Rusch, *Die Behörden und Hofbeamten der päpstlichen Kurie des 13. Jahrhunderts*, Königsberg, 1936. Reviewing the process of imitation by the curia, G. Le Bras, "Le droit romain au service de la domination pontificale" in *Rev. hist. de droit français et étranger*, xxvii (1949), pp. 377–98, says (p. 393): "Pouvoirs, services, offices: le Saint-Siège imite toute la structure de l'empire (romain). Au terme de cette longue accomodation, la papauté domine non seulement l'église mais le siècle. Elle a soumis tous les fidèles, tous les princes et finalement tous les hommes." [5] P. E. Schramm, in *Studi Gregoriani*, ii. 404.

theme, it seems to us, was merely one more symptom of its implementation, a feature that has caused considerable misunderstanding and many oblique judgments on the working and the government of the medieval papacy. This feature which becomes very pronounced from the mid-eleventh century onwards, can be explained, however, only by contemporary criteria, principles and views. It is admitted on all sides, firstly, that a most personal relationship exists between lord and vassal; secondly, that the feudal lord affords a protection to the vassal which forms the essence of the feudal contract; and thirdly that a feudal nexus provided the contemporary means in public law to obtain specific services.

If we keep these principles in mind, it will be easier to understand the entry of feudal principles into the Roman curia. To begin with, the very idea of the pope—or, if we wish to be painstakingly correct, St Peter—becoming a feudal lord, strikingly illustrates his function as a monarch: for it was precisely the feature of a powerful monarch to give protection to the weaker. Hence, by assuming this very same character the pope, through admitting a ruler into the "patrocinium beati Petri," as plainly and palpably as it was possible by contemporary means, demonstrates himself as a protector in the same sense in which the king or emperor had previously understood the term.[1] The assumption of feudal lordship therefore means that the pope is in a position to give effective protection: the feudal lordship of the pope must not, however, be thought of in terms identical to those relating to a king or emperor whose protection lay in a field different from that which could be provided by the pope. The protection offered, accepted and given, by the pope was that which flowed from his function as the supreme *sacerdos regalis*. The vicariate of St Peter manifested itself in a feudal lordship of the pope which, by contemporary standards, meant the personal protection of St Peter through the medium of the pope. By accepting a ruler into the "patrocinium beati Petri" the authority of the pope was by no means increased: what was achieved was that St Peter through the pope afforded special protection to a king who had become a feudal vassal of the Roman Church.

---

[1] It is also from Gregory's time onwards that the royal grace formula—hitherto exclusively employed by kings and emperors in their documents ("si *gratiam* nostram habere vultis")—makes its appearance in papal letters. Cf. his *Reg.* i. 66, p. 96: "Sicut *gratiam* sancti Petri et nostram habere vultis"; *Reg.* iv. 4, p. 301: "Sicut beati Petri apostoli nostrique . . . *gratiam* obtatis." For this see C. Erdmann, "Untersuchungen zu den Briefen Heinrichs IV" in *Arch. f. Urkundenf.*, xvi (1939), pp. 196 ff., 198, note 5.

On the other hand, the entry of a king or prince into this feudal nexus presupposes that the pope was in fact held to be an effective protector, for otherwise not a single enfeoffment carried out by the papacy would be accessible to understanding. In order to enjoy St Peter's protection, the king or prince had to surrender his land into full papal ownership—"jus et proprietatem beati Petri"—and received it back as a fief, so that he became legally an usufructuary. In recognition of his usufruct and of the Petrine protection the king or prince undertook to render certain services, be they in the form of an annual money payment—*census* or tribute[1]—or in the form of military duties. We hold therefore that the feudalism as practised by the papacy brings into clearest possible relief the function of the *sacerdos regalis* who is now held to be strong enough to protect. The wheel has come full circle.

The motives for seeking the papal monarch's protection were varied. In general, it was the weak rulers who sought protection from a stronger one, in this case from the pope. The legitimization of an illegitimate rulership was one such motive, as is evidenced in the case of the Normans.[2] A disputed succession to the throne prompted the occupant of the throne to seek papal protection, as is evidenced in the cases of Croatia and Dalmatia[3] and Russia,[4] to mention only the obvious instances of our period. In other cases the pope himself could suggest to the king to enter into the "patrocinium beati Petri"; this suggestion was made when the country itself was considered to belong by right

[1] On the terminology, whether *census* or tribute, cf. W. E. Lunt, *Papal revenues*, New York, 1934, i. 63, and idem, *Financial relations of the papacy with England*, New York, 1939, i. 130.

[2] This is also admitted by A. Fliche, *La réforme Grégorienne et la reconquête chrétienne*, Paris, 1947, p. 115; cf. also Lunt, *Financial relations*, i. 131. The obvious example of the following century is Portugal, see K. Jordan, "*Das Eindringen des Lehenswesen in das Rechtsleben der römischen Kurie*" in *Archiv f. Urkundenforschung*, xii (1932), pp. 72, 89. Innocent III in accepting the Portuguese king as a feudal vassal writes to him: "Personam tuam et regnum Portugalense . . . sub b. Petri et nostra protectione suscipimus et praesentis scripti pagina communimus," *Reg.* i. 441.

[3] In 1076. The oath of King Zvonimir is printed in Deusdedit's *Coll. can.*, iii. 278, ed. cit., p. 383, and in *Liber Censuum*, ed. P. Fabre and L. Duchesne, i. 356, no. lxxii. The king was invested with his kingdom by the papal legate "per ensem, vexillum, sceptrum et coronam."

[4] Gregory VII, *Reg.* ii. 74, p. 236, to the Russian king, Isjaslaw: ". . . asseverans (filius vester: Iaropolk) illam suam petitionem vestro consensu ratam fore ac stabilem, si apostolicae auctoritatis gratia ac munimine donaretur." This feudal passage is now quoted at length by Pius XII in his letter to the Russian peoples of 7 July 1952, see *Acta Ap. Sedis*, xliv (1952), pp. 506–7.

to the Roman Church, such as the islands on the basis of the Donation of Constantine.[1] This approach is made by Gregory to Spain,[2] Besalù,[3] Provence,[4] Poland,[5] Brittany,[6] and probably also England. In close proximity stand the intimations of the pope in those cases in which certain promises had been made by a king and which the pope interpreted in the sense in which he wished them to be interpreted, as, for instance, in the case of Denmark.[7] As regards Hungary, Gregory based himself, rightly or wrongly, on the fact that the country had been "olim beato Petro cum omni jure et potestate sua oblatum et devote traditum."[8]

The important point in all these cases is that the protection of the pope was an effluence of the strength of his position: the feudal lordship of the pope was nothing less than the transmutation of his vicariate into a contemporary mould and frame, into that of a feudal lord protector. Considering the multitude of feudal vassals which the papacy counted, it is clear that the pope was in theory at least the strongest European feudal monarch. This arrangement gave the pope the possibility of obtaining troops[9] or regular money payments: the *feodum censuale* must be clearly distinguished from Peterspence.[10] The afford-

[1] On this thesis see L. Weckmann, *Las Bullas Alexandrinas*, Mexico, 1949, pp. 25 ff., 69 ff., 156 ff. See also supra p. 80. The oath of Robert Guiscard should also be considered in this context. Sicily had not yet been conquered in 1059, but Robert's oath included the island. Sardinia and Corsica were the other two islands of immediate concern whose property was deduced from the Donation of Constantine.

[2] Gregory's *Reg.* iv. 28, pp. 345–6 to the Spanish princes: "Notum vobis fieri volumus, quod nobis quidem tacere non est liberum . . . videlicet regnum Hyspaniae, ex antiquis constitutionibus beato Petro et sanctae Romanae ecclesiae in jus et propietatem esse traditum." Cf. also *Reg.* i. 7. The obvious basis (the Donation of Constantine) is denied by L. de la Calzado, "La proyeccion del pensimiento del Gregorio VII" in *Studi Gregoriani*, iii. 41–2, who would prefer to take the general hierarchical tendencies of Gregory as a firmer basis.

[3] K. Jordan, art. cit., p. 78.　　　　[4] Idem, ibid., p. 78.

[5] On the basis of the donation of Miseko (Meiscko I), the first Christian ruler of Poland, see E. Maschke, *Der Peterspfennig in Polen und dem deutschen Osten*, Koenigsberg, 1933, pp. 20 ff. and 304 ff. About this see also Weckmann, op. cit., pp. 148–50.

[6] Cf. B. A. Pocquet du Hout-Jusse, "La Bretagne a-t-elle été vassalle du saint-siège?" in *Studi Gregoriani*, i. 189–96.

[7] *Reg.* ii. 75.　　　　　　　　　　[8] *Reg.* ii. 13.

[9] Cf. the observation of C. Erdmann, *Kreuzzugsgedanke*, p. 206: "Die Lehenshoheit über weltliche Fürsten sollte unter anderem dazu dienen, ein *päpstliches Heer* zustande zu bringen. Es ist keine Uebertreibung: Gregor VII strebte darnach, das Papsttum zu einer Militärmacht zu machen . . . alle denkbaren Wege zur Erreichung dieses Zieles hat er versucht."

[10] Nevertheless we should note that later the *Liber Censuum* maintained that those

ing of St Peter's protection by the pope was naturally a highly welcome means of increasing his power. Yet, the exercise of papal authority did by no means depend upon any sort of feudalism. The cases of Henry IV and of Philip I, to mention only two clear instances, need no comment: neither was a feudal vassal.[1] The rulership of the *societas christiana* was not of course conditioned by the creation of a feudal nexus, whilst the authority and exercise of this rulership was the basis upon which papal feudalism could proceed, proceed to such an extent that by the end of the twelfth century the Roman curia was the most powerful feudal curia in Europe.[2]

The effect of becoming a feudal vassal of the pope was that the king and his country enjoyed the special protection of the pope: king and country came into the "patrocinium beati Petri";[3] that the country

---

countries which paid the *census*, could be rightly considered "in jus et proprietatem b. Petri et sanctae Romanae ecclesiae persistentes," see *Lib. cens.*, ed. cit., i. p. 2, and editorial note 3. Cf. also P. Fabre, *Étude sur le Liber censuum*, Paris, 1892, pp. 129 ff., especially 146–7. The important countries paying the "denarius b. Petri" were: England, Denmark, Sweden, Norway, Orkney Islands, Hungary, Croatia and Dalmatia, Poland, and probably also some parts of Russia. On the origins and development of Peterspence in England see Fabre, op. cit., pp. 129 ff.; E. Maschke, op. cit., pp. 33–5, and the exhaustive treatment by W. E. Lunt, *Financial relations*, i. 3–129. Peterspence could also be conceived of as a ground rent. For details of sums, etc., see *Liber censuum*, i. 223 ff. (England); 226 (Wales); 230 (Scotland); 232 (Ireland). Cf. also the entry for Sweden, p. 229: "Notandum quod singulae domus Suetiae singulos dant denarios monetae ipsius terrae." For further details, see the translated documents in Lunt, *Papal revenues*, ii. nos. 238–65.

[1] Innocent III's exercise of jurisdiction over Philip Augustus in *Novit ille* was based entirely on the "ratio peccati."

[2] In a far too sweeping manner St Thomas Aquinas states: "Reges sunt ergo vassales ecclesiae," *Quodlib.* XII, qu. xiii, a. 19, ad sec. Only when the term "vassal" is used in an untechnical sense, Thomas's statement is correct.

[3] *Reg.* ii. 75, p. 238, to the Danish king, Sven II: ". . . nobile *patrocinium* eius (Petri) acquireres." *Reg.* ix. 17, p. 597, to Robert Guiscard: "Quapropter b. Petrum, cuius tibi adesse *patrocinium* grandia facta testantur, prae oculis habere semper memineris." Innocent III's enfeoffment of Peter of Aragon offers a good example: "Ego Petrus . . . cupiens principaliter, post Deum, b. Petri et apostolicae sedis *protectione muniri* . . . spero et confido, quod tu et successores tui, me ac successores meos et regnum praedictum auctoritate apostolica *defendetis*," *Reg.* vii. 229 (= *Gesta*, cap. cxxi). Of course, papal protection without a feudal nexus was still possible. A simple priest could be taken into protection, e.g. Alexander III, *Ep.* 549; or a dean of a chapter, Innocent III (*Reg.* ii. 67, dean of Toledo; *Reg.* iii. 21, dean of Magdeburg); or a count (idem, *Reg.* ii. 297, Count of Montpellier); or a queen, by Gregory IX (Queen of Bohemia, Constance, MGH. *Epp. sel. XIII s.*, i. 351, no. 436: "Personam tuam cum omnibus bonis . . . sub protectione suscipimus apostolicae sedis et nostra specialiter") or a landgrave (idem, ibid., no. 557, p. 451). The protection enjoyed by the crusaders was merely a specific application of affording papal protection without feudal nexus;

could not be legitimately offered to some other ruler;[1] that any injury inflicted upon the king or the country was considered to be an injury inflicted upon the Roman Church itself;[2] that this feudal arrangement was to redound to the "glory and honour 'utriusque vitae' of the vassal" himself.[3]

It would be quite misleading to think that all this was the result of a sudden inspiration. On the contrary, this process was in some ways only a specific extension of the principles which had been followed in the monastic sphere, namely the institution of the so-called papal proprietary monasteries.[4] They had come under papal protection and tutelage—"tuitio," "protectio," "libertas," "tutela" are the technical terms in the papal privileges which take monasteries into the "patrocinium beati Petri."[5] By virtue of having been given "in proprium beati Petri" these monasteries were papal monasteries; on the other hand, they came "sub patrocinio et defensione sanctae Romanae ecclesiae."[6] "La donation est le moyen, la protection le but."[7] It was St Peter who protected the monastery. And this privileged position of the monastery was epitomized in the pregnant formula of Hildebrandine coinage that the monastery enjoyed the *Libertas Romana*.[8]

---

having taken the cross, they enjoyed the *Libertas Romana*. The main privileges which a crusader enjoyed were: automatic excommunication of those who attacked person or property of the crusader; plenary indulgence; exemption from ordinary tribunals and from paying certain taxes; immunity from prosecutions arising out of debts contracted before the crusade, and so forth. The crusader became, so to speak, a member of the pope's *familia*.

[1] This becomes clear in the case of Hungary, *Reg.* ii. 63, p. 218. In France a vassal could be a vassal of several lords from the late ninth century onwards, see F. L. Ganshof, "Depuis quand a-t-on pu, en France, être vassal de plusieurs seigneurs?" in *Mélanges Fournier*, Paris, 1929, pp. 261 ff.

[2] Cf. e.g., Gregory's letter to the knight Wezelin, *Reg.* vii. 4, p. 363: "Quicquid in illum (regem) ausus fueris, procul dubio te in apostolicam sedem facturum."

[3] E.g., *Reg.* ii. 63, p. 219, line 3; *Reg.* ii. 75, p. 238, line 19; etc.

[4] For this institution see P. Fabre, op. cit., pp. 27 ff.; G. Schreiber, *Kurie und Kloster*, Stuttgart, 1910, ii. 6 ff.; H. Leclercq, in DAC. vii. 338 ff.; D. Knowles, *Monastic Order*, pp. 570 ff.; H. Hirsch, "Untersuchungen zur Geschichten des päpstlichen Schutzes" in MIOG. liv (1942), pp. 392 ff.; A. Amann in Amann and A. Dumas, op. cit., pp. 343 ff.

[5] See now especially W. Szaivert, "Die Entstehung und Entwicklung der Klosterimmunität" in MIOG. lix (1951), pp. 286 ff.; and the numerous examples cited by P. Fabre, op. cit., pp. 37–68; also Amann and Dumas, op. cit., pp. 347 ff.

[6] So in J. 3777 of Benedict VII, April 974; cf. W. Szaivert, art. cit., p. 288, note 148; also the foundation charter (979) of St Peter Besalù: "Tradimus . . . ut sub eius (beati Petri) defensione atque munimine consistat ad perpetuum," Fabre, op. cit., p. 63; cf. also Leo IX taking a monastery upon request "sub nostri regiminis tuitione" and "sub nostra defensione," *Ep.* xcix, PL. cxliii. 744.

[7] Fabre, op. cit., p. 44.     [8] See Fabre, op. cit., pp. 71 ff., 76 ff.

The enfeoffments carried out by the papacy, in a modified form expand this principle appertaining to the monasteries. Instead of the monastery entering the "patrocinium beati Petri," it is now the king or prince and his country that assume this relationship. The ruler personally enters into this close relationship with the pope and as a consequence he and his country are protected by St Peter.[1] The form in which protection of St Peter was promised to a monastery, namely the solemn *privilegium* was kept: the pope issued to the feudal vassal personally also a *privilegium* of protection (*Schutzprivileg*). The actual manner of making the king or the prince a feudal vassal of the Roman Church naturally followed the established pattern of investing him "per vexillum" and so forth, whilst on the other hand, he had to swear fealty to the pope, in return for which he enjoys St Peter's protection.[2]

These considerations will enable us to understand why the oath of the bishops[3] can on no account be taken as a feudal oath, although this has in fact been maintained. But the bishop never became a vassal of the pope; he never entered into the "patrocinium beati Petri"; he was never invested with anything.[4] His oath was nothing but an oath of obedience, stringent indeed, but by no means a feudal oath. For one of the constituent elements of the two-sided feudal contract was absent: the special protection by the pope. Indeed the bishop swore to defend the Roman papacy and St Peter's *regalia*—"papatum Romanum et regalia sancti Petri adjutor ero ad tenendum et defendendum salvo meo ordine"[5]—but this reflects his function as a direct subordinate of the pope.

These considerations will also enable us to understand the difference

---

[1] What has been said about the effects of papal protection in the sphere of monasteries, can *mut. mut.* be applied to the effects of protection in the sphere of feudal vassals: P. Fabre, op. cit., p. 73: "Le but de la protection apostolique est d'assurer l'integrité de l'objet sur lequel elle s'exerce. Aussi tous les privilèges donnés aux censiers de l'apôtre garantissent contre les convoitises l'objet protégé. Deux sortes de dangers sont à craindre pour l'être organisé les atteintes du monde extérieur et la diminution de l'énergie vitale. Les monastères protégés par l'apôtre sont assurés contre ce double péril."

[2] Robert Guiscard's oath is in *Liber censuum*, i. 422, no. clxiii, which formed the model for later feudal oaths, including that of John.

[3] Cf. Gregory's *Reg.* vi. 17a, p. 428–9.

[4] The same applies to the oath of the Roman senator, see OR. XII (PL. lxxviii. 1100), cap. 86. This oath is directly modelled on the episcopal oath, as also is that taken by the later vice-chancellor, notaries, correctors, auditors, secretaries, etc., see Tangl, *Kanzleiordnungen*, "Juramenta" nos. I, III, IV, X, XIII, pp. 33, 35, 36, 45, 47.

[5] Cf. again the senator's oath and that of the chancery personnel; cf. also the modern episcopal oath, in *Pont. Roman.*, ed. 1891, pp. 38–9.

12*

between the position of the emperor and that of the king who had become a papal vassal. Again, the same constitutive element is missing: the emperor does not enter into the "patrocinium beati Petri."[1] The emperor never sought the special protection of the pope; what he did seek was the imperial crown from the hands of the pope. What distinguished the emperor from any other king, be he feudal vassal of the pope or no, was that he was created a "specialis" or "unicus filius" of the Roman Church, whose duty it was to obey the orders of his father, the pope.[2] Episcopal oath and imperial oath show much more kinship with each other than does either with the feudal oath.[3] The emperor, in other words, is the king specially selected—"designated" we recall John VIII and may now add Paschal II[4]—for the protection of the Roman Church and hence of the whole of Christendom. The emperor alone stands in a unique relationship to the pope, for he is made—and sometimes also unmade—by the pope.

Nos igitur imperatoriae dignitatis plenitudinem tibi concedimus.[5]

There is no imperial crown without the emperor's special sonship of, and filial nexus to, the pope.[6] The difference between the emperor and the king who is a vassal of the Roman curia, is obvious.

[1] The oath suggested by Gregory VII for Hermann of Salm (*Reg.* ix. 3, p. 576) cannot be adduced, since this text appears to be suspect. Book ix of the Register does not seem to be free from doubt, cf. A. Fliche, *La réforme Grégorienne*, ii. 12, esp. 23: the texts "ressemblent singulièrement à des interpolations." It may be that the whole ninth book was inserted afterwards (between 1081 and 1083), see E. Caspar, "Studien zum Register Gregors VII" in *Neues Archiv*, xxxviii, 1913, pp. 190, 202; cf. also W. Peitz, in *SB. Vienna*, 1911, fasc. 5, p. 48, who does not maintain that there were the usual signs of original registration in the ninth book. See now also L. Santifaller, *Beschreibstoffe im Mittelalter*, 1953, p. 100.

[2] See also supra p. 257 f.

[3] Cf. in the late twelfth century Huguccio: "Nam et qui accipiunt pallium a domino papa, juramentum praestant. Dicimus etiam episcopi et archiepiscopi et imperator jurant fidelitatem papae," ad *Dist.* xxiii, c. 6, MS. Pembroke College, Cambridge, No. 72, fol. 133 va.

[4] In the *Relatio Registri Paschalis II* we read that Henry V "a pontifice imperator *designatus* est," MGH. *Const.* i. 147, no. 99, lines 40–1. Concerning the (abortive) coronation of Henry V on 12 February 1111, the "Vita Paschalis II" by Cardinal Peter of Pisa relates: "Proceres, judices, advocati . . . venerunt . . . atque dicentes: 'Henricum regem sanctus Petrus elegit,' " Watterich, *Vitae*, ii. 8. It is all in the fashion of John VIII. In the following century there is the example of nominating the king of the Romans, Rudolf of Habsburg: "Te regem Romanorum nominamus": MGH. *Const.* iii, no. 66, p. 55 (Gregory X). About Innocent III see infra p. 343 n. 2.

[5] Innocent II to Lothar: MGH. *Const.* i. 168, no. 116.

[6] See Innocent II again., ibid, no. 117, p. 169 (Lothar as the "specialissimus ecclesiae defensor") and no. 116, p. 168: "Te christianissimum principem et

The emperor takes a "juramentum subditi," an oath which characterizes the subordinate position of the subject to his superior: he takes an *Untertaneneid* which creates a "vinculum subjectionis."[1] The king who has become a vassal of the pope, takes a "juramentum fidelitatis," an oath of fealty.[2] On the basis of the emperor's oath the claim can be raised that he is the "officialis papae" and that he has to draw his sword "ad nutum pontificis Romani."[3]

---

inter speciales beati Petri filios unicum ac praecipuum defensorem ad imperii fastigium . . . sublimavimus."

[1] We cannot agree with M. David, *Le serment du sacre*, Strasbourg, 1950, p. 232, who repeats the old theme in cautious terms when he says: "L'empereur jure fidelitatem au pape. Par là ce dernier cherche probablement à accréditer l'idée d'une dépendance féodale de l'empereur à son égard et une telle prétention provoquera bien des remous un peu plus tard."

The origin of the "oath of allegiance" (as it may somewhat incorrectly be called) was Roman-imperial, see Th. Mommsen, *Römisches Staatsrecht*, ii/2, pp. 792–3; it was developed from the oath taken to the princeps as the supreme military commander, and in imperial times "senatus milesque et populus" swear this oath, see the passage of Tacitus, quoted by Mommsen: all officials, all citizens, and all subjects take it. Cf. also A. Alföldi in *Mitt. d. deutschen archaeolog. Inst.*, Rom. Abt., 1935, p. 78. For the development in Frankish and post-Frankish times see R. Schröder, *Lehrbuch der deutschen Rechtsgeschichte*, pp. 109, 481. About the differences between this oath and the oath of fidelity see H. Brunner, *Deutsche Rechtsgeschichte*, ii. 58 f.; cf. also H. Planitz, *Deutsche Rechtsgeschichte*, pp. 44 f., and P. E. Schramm, *Hist. of the Engl. Coronation*, pp. 183–4. The "crimen laesae majestatis" was the violation of this oath, see Schröder, op. cit., p. 117, note 65 and G. Waitz, *Deutsche Verfassungsgeschichte*, iii. 307 f.

[2] The distinction between the two kinds of oaths is in the *Libri Feudorum*, ii. 5, and the gloss on this chapter; cf. also cap. 7 with the details of the feudal oath. For the need to distinguish between these two kinds of oaths, see especially the late F. Lot, "Le serment de fidélité a l'époque franque" in *Revue belge de philogie et d'histoire*, xii (1933), pp. 569–82 ("serment de fidélité du vassal" and "serment d'allégeance du sujet"); F. L. Ganshof, "Benefice and vassalage" in *Cambridge Historical Journal*, vi. (1939), p. 171, note 113; also C. E. Odegaard, "Carolingian oaths of fidelity" in *Speculum*, xvi (1941), pp. 284 ff., especially pp. 292–6.

[3] Cf. St Bernard infra 431; Hostiensis, *Summa aurea*, ad I. vi. 34; Eichmann, *Kaiserkrönung*, ii. 178–9; *Medieval Papalism*, p. 140. None saw the need to eliminate a possible ambiguity clearer than Innocent III. In his coronation *Ordo D* (ed. Eichmann, i. 259) he excised the formula of the oath as used in *Ordo C* ("Juro . . . fidelitatem tuisque successoribus . . .") and substituted this: "Ego enim N., Rex Romanorum, annuente domino futurus imperator, promitto, spondeo polliceor atque juro Deo et b. Petro, me de cetero protectorem et defensorem fore summi pontificis et S.R.E. in omnibus necessitatibus et utilitatibus suis . . . secundum scire et posse meum, recta et pura fide." But the oath of Peter of Aragon, a real feudal oath taken to Innocent III, runs: "Ego, Petrus rex Aragonum, profiteor et polliceor, quod semper *ero fidelis et obediens* domino meo papae Innocentio. . . ." *Reg.* vii. 229, PL. ccxv. 550 (= *Gesta*, c. cxx). John's oath as a vassal omits "obediens," see *Reg.* xvi. 77 (PL. ccxvi. 880). Only once Innocent III used the term "investire" in connexion with imperial affairs: RNI. 29. But here the term has not the technical feudal meaning. And in RNI. 62

It is indubitably true that feudal language and Roman-papal language are exasperatingly identical. This linguistic phenomenon has been the cause of a good deal of confusion and exacerbation in medieval and modern times. The terms "fidelis," "fides," "fidelitas" and so forth may have a thorough feudal meaning, but they may also bear a Roman-papal meaning. The bishop, the emperor, the anti-pope,[1] the Romans[2] and the feudal vassal of the pope—they all swear and make promises in terms hardly distinguishable from each other. And popes and emperors address their encyclicals "omnibus Christi fidelibus." In the one sense "fidelitas" means faithfulness,[3] in the other it denotes fealty. Other such terms are "defensor," "miles," "servitium," "beneficium." The latter term particularly is susceptible to most contradictory interpretations. *Beneficium* may be a Roman term, in which sense Gelasius I had used it; but it may also be a feudal term. This identity of language and divergence of meaning of daily occurring and important terms accounts for much misunderstanding and resultant ill-feeling. The alleged "demand" of Gregory VII for fealty to the Conqueror appears to have had all the makings of such misunderstanding on the part of the latter, who may well have misinterpreted Gregory's (Roman) terminology. But no definite conclusion can be advanced in this case, because the actual words used by the pope are of crucial importance, and Gregory's letter is lost.[4] But we have the classic example in the following century when the misreading and misunderstanding had serious repercussions. Even at the risk of a digression a few observations are called for.

---

which is so largely based on RNI. 29, the term is dropped altogether. He refers the "juramentum fidelitatis" to vassals only, *Reg.* iii. 29. A comparison between the two kinds of oaths will be found in his *Reg.* i. 577 and 578 (the oath of the city prefect and the oath of Count Hildebrand). The same clear distinction is to be found in Innocent IV's deposition of Frederick II. In the manifesto after the deposition Innocent declares that Frederick "nobis *fidelitatis* et *subjectionis* vinculo sese astringit" (E. Winkelmann, *Acta imperii inedita*, ii. 699, no. 1035). In the bull itself the pope refers Frederick's "juramentum fidelitatis" explicitly to Sicily only (MGH. *Const.* ii. 510, no. 400 = *Epp. sel. XIII s.*, ii. 124, p. 90) whilst as an emperor "juravit honores, jura et possessiones Romanae ecclesiae pro posse suo servare ac protegere bona fide."

[1] Cf. Silvester IV's renunciation, MGH. *Const.* i. 147, no. 98: "Promitto *fidem* et obedientiam Deo digno et catholico papae Paschali."

[2] See *Sacramentum Romanorum*, MGH. *Capit.*, i. 324: "Promitto ego . . . in futurum *fidelis* ero dominis nostris . . ."

[3] In this sense the modern canon law speaks of the oath which the bishops have to take: "jusjurandum *fidelitatis*," see CIC. can. 332 §2.

[4] Only the Conqueror's reply is extant, see Lanfranc's *Opera*, ed. Giles, Ep. x, p. 32.

We refer to the incident at Besançon. Adrian IV used the term *beneficium* in its original Roman sense, and not in the feudal sense in which Frederick I had understood it.[1] Adrian's explanatory letter retracts not one syllable from the first letter: he had conferred—"contulimus"—the distinction of imperial dignity[2] as a "bonum factum."[3] It is a *beneficium* which the pope confers when making the † king an emperor. There is no duty upon the pope to confer imperial dignity—and the emperor has no right to it.[4] That is the meaning of *bonum factum* (= *beneficium*): nobody has a right to expect a good deed. "We have placed the crown upon your head, so that it may be judged a good deed by everyone." This "good deed" is a *beneficium*

---

[1] The situation was aggravated by the imperial curia recollecting the picture in the Lateran palace which showed Lothar doing liege homage to Innocent II and which had this caption: "Rex venit ante fores, jurans prius Urbis honores, *post homo fit papae* sumit quo dante coronam," Rahewin, *Gesta Friderici*, ed. G. Waitz, p. 177, and also Gerhoh of Reichersberg, *De quarta vigilia noctis*, LdL. iii. 512. There can be no doubt about the mischievous ambiguity of picture and caption, but neither is proof that Lothar became a papal vassal in his function as an emperor: he was a papal vassal as regards the Mathildine estates with which he was enfeoffed by the pope, MGH. *Const.* i. 169, no. 117. Cf. also Frederick's complaint in *Const.* i. 234, no. 167: "It began with a picture, from a picture it went on to a letter, from a letter it tries to go on to authority." The picture was destroyed some time in the fourteenth century, cf. the "reconstituted" engraving (sixteenth century) in P. E. Schramm, *Kaiserbilder*, Table 129, text pp. 148–9 and 219–20.

[2] MGH. *Const.* i. 235, no. 168 = Rahewin, *Gesta*, iii. 23, p. 196: ". . . nos . . . honorifice imperialis dignitatis insigne tuo capiti imposuimus ut bonum factum valeat ab omnibus judicari." It is not quite correct to head this letter "Litterae excusatoriae."

[3] There is absolutely no warrant for saying that Roland, at Besançon, suggested "that in all probability 'fief' was the meaning intended by the pope in using the term *beneficium*," as Abbot Hicks maintains, "Adrian IV" in *Downside Review*, lxiv (1946), p. 149 (here also other questionable statements). Rahewin, op. cit., p. 177, reporting the scene at Besançon says this: "His omnibus in unum collatis, cum strepitus et turba inter optimates regni de tam insolita legatione magis ac magis invalesceret, quasi gladium igni adderet, dixisse ferunt unum de legatis: '*A quo ergo habet, si a domino papa non habet imperium?*' Ob hoc dictum eo processit iracundia, ut unus eorum . . . exerto gladio cervici illius mortem intentaret." From the traditional hierocratic point of view the legate's question was perfectly justifiable; the question itself reveals a certain naïve astonishment which, in the circumstances, is understandable.

[4] "Per hoc enim vocabulum 'contulimus' nil aliud intelligimus nisi quod superius dictum est 'imposuimus.'" Cf. the first letter, *Const.* i. 230, no. 164: Consider, Adrian says, "quam gratanter et quam jocunde alio anno mater tua, sancta Romana ecclesia, te *susceperit*, quantam tibi *dignitatis plenitudinem contulerit* et honoris, et qualiter imperialis insigne coronae libentissime conferens . . . si majora beneficia excellentia tua de manu nostra suscepisset . . . non immerito † gauderemus." Cf. with this Innocent II's declaration, supra, p. 338.

divinely conferred,[1] conferred by God through the pope. Adrian, far from sending a letter of appeasement in which an enraged emperor was to be pacified and in which terms were to be explained away, moves entirely within the framework of traditional ideology.[2] Gelasius had provided the pattern. He had said that the emperor had the "privilegia potestatis suae" as a divine *beneficium*[3] and, we recall furthermore, Gelasius had seen the imperial Christian power as a *beneficium* divinely conferred by Christ.[4] In Adrian's communication the claim is implicit that he acts as "vicarius Christi" and that in this function he confers the *beneficium* of imperial power. What he pronounces here—though still in somewhat veiled terms—is his vicariate of Christ, his vicariate of the "mediator between God and man": imperial power, dignity and crown are conferred by Christ through him. And did not his predecessor and the pupil of St Bernard, Pope Eugenius III, designate himself as "vicarius Christi"?[5] As the vicar of Christ, the "true king and priest," the pope consequently combines both royal and sacerdotal powers vicariously and in this function he confers imperial dignity as a *beneficium* in the Gelasian sense.[6]

[1] See the explanation of Adrian: "Hoc enim nomen ex 'bono' et 'facto' est editum et *dicitur beneficium apud nos*, non feudum, sed bonum factum. In qua significatione in universo sacrae scripturae corpore invenitur, ubi ex beneficio Dei, non tamquam ex feudo, sed velut ex benedictione et bono facto gubernari dicimur et nutriri. Et tua quidem magnificentia liquido recognoscit, quod nos ita bene et honorifice imperialis dignitatis insigne tuo capiti imposuimus, ut bonum factum valeat ab hominibus judicari." Cf. also ibid.: "Licet enim hoc nomen, quod est beneficium, apud quosdam in alia significatione, quam ex inpositione habeat, assumatur, tunc tamen in ea significatione accipiendum fuerat, *quam nos ipsi posuimus*, et quam ex institutione sua noscitur retinere." Cf. already John VIII, supra, p. 222.

[2] We would be inclined to think that the very similar conflict between Henry VII and Clement V about the emperor's "juramentum fidelitatis" arose out of the same duplicity of meaning attributable to "fidelitas"; cf. *Clem*. II. xix. un.

[3] Ep. 1, cap. 10, Thiel, p. 293: "Habet *privilegia potestatis* suae quae administrandis publicis rebus divinitus consecutus est et eius *beneficiis* non ingratus . . . nil usurpet . . . ne contra illius *beneficia* pugnare videatur, *a quo* propriam consecutus est potestatem."

[4] Cf. also Ep. 12, cap. 4, p. 353: "Itane verum est, princeps egregie, qui non solum praesentia *Christi beneficia*, sed desideras et futura . . ."

[5] See the curial officer's report in MGH. SS. xx. 543, and especially the realistic re-enactment of the Last Supper at Easter in which the pope played the part of Christ, the cardinals that of the apostles and a curial official that of Judas, in OR. XI, cap. 48 (composed 1140–1) and repeated in OR. XII, cap. 35 (late twelfth century). For details see my contribution to *Misc. Hist. Pont.*, 1954.

[6] On Innocent III's vicariate of Christ see infra 443 n. 5. Our interpretation is entirely born out by Gervase of Tilbury. In his *Otia imperialia* (MGH. SS. xxvii), a work which he sent to Otto IV in about 1209–10, he says that it was by the "gratia" of Innocent that Otto obtained his imperial title (p. 379) and he

On the other hand, Frederick no doubt also had Gelasius in mind when, in obvious opposition to the famous Gelasian passage, he declares:

Duo sunt, quibus nostrum regi oportet imperium, leges sanctae imperatorum et usus bonus predecessorum et patrum nostrorum. Istos limites excedere nec volumus nec possumus.[1]

The significance of this passage is that pontifical authority as a means of government is excised, and its place is taken by the sacred laws of the emperor. The role of the pope as a "mediator Dei et hominis" is denied—"*liberam* imperii nostri *coronam divino* TANTUM *beneficio* ascribimus"—and in disregard of history, ideology and fact, Frederick depicts himself as the *christus* to whom the empire has come directly from God. This is the classic expression of the lay standpoint concerning the government of the empire, a pronouncement, however, that blatantly disregards the genesis of the medieval empire as well as the function of the emperor himself.[2] And from here it is only a short step to the *imperatura* later in the same century.[3]

---

goes on to say (p. 382): "Imperium tuum non est, sed Christi, non tuum, sed Petri. Non a te tibi obvenit, sed a vicario Christi et successore Petri . . . Petro Constantinus imperium occidentis dedit, cui servierat regnum Francorum, regnum Teutonum, regnum Brittonum, quin imo totus occidens et totus circumfusus orbis. Hic Petro voluit sub Christo totum servire occidentem. *Beneficio* pape, non suo, Roma tempore Karoli nomen recepit imperii; *beneficio* pape Francorum regi confertur imperium; *beneficio* pape regi nunc Teutonum et non Francorum debetur imperium. Nec dedit imperium cui vult Teutonia, sed cui cedendum decrevit papa."                            [1] MGH. *Const.* i. 233, no. 167.

[2] As is well known, Innocent III shortly afterwards expressed in unsurpassable conciseness genesis and function of the emperor by the two terms *principaliter* and *finaliter* (RNI. 18, 29, 31, 33, 47). Therefrom arose his right to nominate the imperial candidate (RNI. 62: "Ottonem reputamus et *nominamus* regem justitia exigente" and ibid.: "(Ottonem) nos ad coronam imperii disponimus *evocare*"; also RNI. 65 and 32: "Regiam magnificentiam ad suscipiendam imperii Romani coronam *vocabimus*."). This nomination is based upon the principle of suitability ("persona idonea"), cf. RNI. 29, p.t., and RNI. 21: the princes should consider him who "ad regendum imperium est *idoneus*," for the Roman Church "nec debet idoneo defensore carere" (RNI. 48, also RNI. 62, 98). From this functionalist point of view Innocent's repeated complaints (e.g. RNI. 15, 33, 85, 92) that malicious people impute to him the desire to destroy the empire are, of course, justified.

[3] For this see RNI. 14, and especially H. Mitteis, *Die deutsche Königswahl*, pp. 99–110. Consequently, according to Staufen ideology, the imperial coronation is a mere formality, whilst papal-hierocratic ideology held it to be constitutive: the emperor received his "plenitudo potestatis" from the pope, see Innocent II supra, 338, and Innocent III in RNI. 33: "*A nobis* imperator imperii recipit diadema in plenitudinem potestatis." With this should be compared Frederick I's manifesto, *Const.* i. 231, no. 165, which also exemplifies the royal idea of protection: the papal-hierocratic view is "inaudita novitas." A little later he claimed the vicariate of Christ for himself, *Const.* i. 335, no. 240: "Imperatoria majestas

# Royal Reaction and Episcopal Resistance

## I

IT might not appear unprofitable to give a very brief survey of the reaction which the first application of the hierocratic theme entailed. A study of the official documents on the royal side, particularly those of Henry IV, justifies the statements, firstly, that the royal party had nothing at its disposal with which effectively to counteract hierocratic tenets, let alone their translation into practice; secondly, that the reaction itself showed all the features of a rearguard action; and thirdly, that the underlying ideas of the hierocratic programme were insufficiently understood. No wonder, therefore, that the reaction lacked consistency, fibre and, so necessary in these matters, the enthusiasm based upon the force of conviction. The reaction was, on the whole, ill-tempered, vulgar and not free from contradiction.

The adequate understanding of this reaction presupposed a clear perception of the hierocratic theme, above all the nature of the society, of that autonomous unit which Gregory VII had called the *societas christiana*. Substantially a spiritual body, it was nevertheless also earthy. As such this society was to be governed by those functionally qualified. The functional qualification depended upon the nature of this society and its constitutive element, the Christian faith as expounded by the Church of Rome. Under the presupposition of the primatial function of the Roman Church, its *principatus*, the pope is the *sacerdos regalis*, the monarch: monarchy in this context is the political term for the concrete exercise of primatial jurisdictional and legislative authority. The consideration of the nature of this *societas* as a spiritual and yet earthy society, the consideration, in other words, of the idea upon which

---

* quae regis regum et domini dominantium vicem gerit in terris." A dualism must necessarily lead to a dual vicariate of Christ, one in the pope (so Frederick in his letter to King Henry II: *Const.*, i. 254, no. 183) and one in the emperor: the kingship of Christ is vicariously in the emperor; the priesthood of Christ vicariously in the pope.

this society is erected, and of the purpose for which it exists, naturally militates against ascribing autonomous character to what is called the temporal and its human personification: it can, consistently enough, have a mere auxiliary function. Whatever exists and whatever activity is displayed in this *societas*, must be judged according to its underlying ideas and purpose. This means that the government and the working of this society can be understood only from the teleological angle. This means, furthermore, that those not so functionally qualified—the lay individuals—and with them inert matter, must be directed by the functionally qualified members of this corporate *societas christiana*. In brief, then, this society was a body politic and corporate, in which the monarchic principle was realized to its fullest possible extent: monarchical rule of persons and things existing within the *societas christiana*. The pope alone is qualified to function as the monarch and consequently to direct and govern the *societas christiana*, the universal Church become corporate.

Henry IV had no adequate answer to these tenets of hierocratic doctrine. One may well wonder whether in fact this would have been possible at all in the existing circumstances. What he held to be an answer was a partial withdrawal from his father's ideological position as *Rex-Sacerdos*, and the concession he made was—a dualism of government. A dualism which he argued existed by reason of God's ordinance in appointing him as a king; a dualism which was to signify a separation of powers in the spiritual and temporal spheres; a dualism which is allegorically represented by two swords. But this dualism propagated by an excommunicate and deposed king is, as can readily be seen, the result of a misconception of the nature, idea and purpose of the *societas christiana* as a corporate body. This dualism—and we note that Henry IV was not only the first to use the two-swords doctrine in a purely allegorical-political sense, but also to use the very term *dualitas*[1]—denies the fullness of power contained in the Petrine

---

[1] The deep significance of this Henrician statement seems not sufficiently stressed by J. Lecler, "L'argument des deux glaives" in *Recherches de science religieuse*, xxi (1931), pp. 307–8; about Edgar's address to St Dunstan, in 969, see ibid., p. 306, and also St Peter Damian's quite unpolitical reference, ibid. In their profound investigation, C. Erdmann and D. v. Gladiss, "Gottschalk von Aachen im Dienste Heinrichs IV" in *Deutsches Archiv*, iii (1939), pp. 135 ff., have proved that Gottschalk was the author of these important letters and manifestos of early 1076, including the letter under discussion and the famous one ending "Come down, come down, to be damned throughout the ages" addressed to the "false monk," see pp. 149, 154, 159, 169–70. The dualism propagated here was the conceptual offspring of Gottschalk, "an eccentric theologian, who was no prac-

commission, denies, therefore, the mediatory role of the pope which is the (already incipient) idea of the pope's vicariate of Christ, and consequently charges the pope with "usurping both kingship and priesthood." According to Henry IV, the universal Church has one head, that is Christ, Who (according to Henry's view) had appointed him king, but not Gregory pope. It is clear that Henry denies the *societas christiana* its corporate character and the true monarchic function of the pope as a *sacerdos regalis*, who because he is priest, is also king.[1] This denial is indeed indispensable to a *dualitas* of government.

He (i.e. Gregory) usurped for himself the kingdom and the priesthood without God's sanction, despising God's holy ordinance which willed essentially that they—namely the kingdom and the priesthood—should remain not in the hands of one, but, as two, in the hands of two. For the Saviour Himself, during His passion, intimated that this was the meaning of the typical sufficiency of the two swords. For when it was said to Him "Behold, Lord, here are two swords" He answered "It is enough" meaning thereby that a duality is sufficient, that a spiritual and a carnal sword were to be wielded in the Church, and by them every evil will be cut off.[2]

The significance of this passage is that Henry IV refuses to accept the conception of a *societas christiana* as a corporate universal body that transcends linguistic and biological frontiers and that is governable by the papal monarch. It is true that the "temporal sword" is to be wielded within the "ecclesia," but this "ecclesia" can be no more than a vaguely conceived spiritual-mystical brotherhood of Christian believers: it certainly can be no corporate, juristic and organic entity. The tenor of this passage—and of the whole letter—is the assertion of Henry's kingship: he is a king and as such he considers himself autonomous: his power came to him directly from God without any inter-

---

tical politician" (p. 157: "Es versteht sich, dass dieser verstiegene Theologe kein praktischer Politiker war"). Gottschalk later retired into more suitable surroundings, into a monastery, after he had risen to the position under Henry IV of chief royal chaplain and provost at Aachen. The tract *De unitate ecclesiae conservanda*, written in the nineties of the eleventh century and ascribed to a monk at Hersfeld, shows some remarkable affinity with Gottschalk's views and expressions.

[1] Henry's opposition was directed against the incipient idea that the pope was vicar of Christ, that is vicar of the "Rex et sacerdos secundum ordinem Melchisedek."

[2] MGH. *Const.* i, no. 63, pp. 112–13 = C. Erdmann, *Die Briefe Heinrichs IV*, Berlin, 1939, no. 13, p. 19. Cf. also ibid.: "Me also whom God called to the kingdom—not, however, having called him to the priesthood—he strove to deprive of my royal power, threatening to take away my kingdom and my soul, neither of which he had granted, because he saw me wishing to hold my rule from God and not from him."

mediary. The *dualitas* of government means that, as a king in his sphere of action, he stands next to the pope, that he is on an equal footing with the pope, in those matters which he as king considers exclusively appertaining to him. Now, the logical pursuit of this Henrician dualist theme—and we must always keep in mind that this dualist theme was propounded by an excommunicate and deposed king—must lead to an ascription to other European kings of the same function which he claimed for himself: in other words, the pope is not only no universal monarch, but he is also confronted by as many European kings as there are who are all the pope's equals: what the pope is supposed to be in spiritual matters, these kings would then be in all those matters which they regard as their exclusive scope of rulership. This tenet, logically pursued, leads back to the conception of royal monarchy in which the king functioning as monarch autonomously determines the scope of his rulership.

But whilst Henry IV misconceived the nature of the society he was living in, his axiom nevertheless merits due attention, because it bears very great significance as regards the future. His *dualitas* is based on the conception that the temporal ruler, the king, who on his own showing deals only with, and confines himself to, temporal inert matter, is autonomous. Because he deals with the temporal, he demands his independence from the pope in temporal matters. And this temporal, according to Henry's ways of reasoning, is so important that God Himself had instituted him directly to deal with it. We do not wish to argue on the soundness or unsoundness of this axiom, but confine ourselves to the statement that, in pursuit of this dualist theory, the necessity became paramount to distinguish between the temporal and the spiritual: where was the line of demarcation? And who laid this line of demarcation down? What, in a Christo-centric world, are the criteria by which the temporal can be marked off from the spiritual? If the temporal and hence the king enjoys autonomy, then it and he must have closely defined autonomous and independent spheres. Hence, from the time when the dualist programme became official policy of the emperors, we witness the strenuous and hapless attempts to find that sphere of autonomous action allegedly reserved to the king. But more important than these futile efforts is that once the king, on account of his function as an independent ruler over the "temporalia," claimed autonomy, there was, logically enough, only a short step to the theoretical creation of the modern entity, the State, which can very well exist without the addition of a spiritual element. Henry IV's manifesto of April 1076, by virtue of a *dualitas* of papal and regal power, marks the faint beginnings of the autonomous modern State. It was, moreover, as a result of the opposition to the hierocratic thesis that the very significant conception of the *Regalia* came to be worked out: as *Regalia* were considered those temporalities which were "regal," that is, the king's property over which he alone exercised jurisdiction; and here a concrete basis of the temporal entity, the State, could be detected. We will return to this topic.

It must not be supposed that Henry IV faithfully adhered to his own axioms. In March 1076 he, "Heinricus Dei gratia rex"—"licet indignus inter christos ad regnum sum unctus"[1]—proclaimed that only for aberrations from the faith he could be deposed. Ten months later we find him supplicating the pope at Canossa for release from excommunication which by no manner of reasoning could be construed as having been inflicted for Henry's aberration from faith. Moreover, Henry who had so defiantly proclaimed a dual form of government now takes an oath to the effect that he would, within a term prescribed by the pope, either implement *justitia* according to papal judgment— and about the meaning of this there should be no doubt—or make peace, *concordia*, according to the pope's council, with his opponents.

Infra terminum, quem domnus papa Gregorius constituerit aut justitiam secundum judicium eius, aut concordiam secundum consilium eius faciam.[2]

Nor would Henry put any obstacles into the path of the pope who was to come into Henry's kingdom to decide the dispute between him and the princes, to end, in other words, the vacancy on the royal throne.[3] The oath taken at Canossa is the execution of the surrender which Henry made at Oppenheim in the preceding October.[4] The king who

---

[1] MGH. *Const.* i. 111 = ed. Erdmann, p. 16.

\*　[2] *Reg.* iv. 12a, p. 315.

[3] On this see Lambert of Hersfeld, *Annales*, MGH. SS. v. 254 f.

†　[4] MGH. *Const.* i, no. 64, p. 114 = ed. Erdmann, appendix B, p. 69. The change of front effected by the German episcopacy and above all by the princes at Tribur, is outside the scope of this enquiry. It would seem, however, that one cannot refute Haller's argument out of hand, namely, that it was Humbert's *Sententiae* which effected the change: "Pseudo-Isidor's erstes Auftreten im Investiturstreit" in *Studi Gregoriani*, ii. 91 ff.; idem, "Der Weg nach Canossa" in *Abhandlungen zur Geschichte des Mittelalters*, Stuttgart, 1944, pp. 130 f., 143 ff., 157 ff., 162–8; against Haller's thesis C. Erdmann, "Tribur etc." in *Deutsches Archiv*, iv (1940), pp. 486–95; A. Michel, "Pseudo-Isidor etc." in *Studi Gregoriani*, iii. 154 ff.; cf. also idem, *Die Sentenzen des Kardinal Humbert*, pp. 139 ff. That Henry was a cunning diplomat and that especially the *promissio* at Oppenheim was a clever diplomatic trick, was the theme of A. Brackmann, "Heinrich IV als Politiker beim Ausbruch des Investiturstreits" in *SB. Berlin*, 1927, pp. 410 ff. We do not think

in April had held himself autonomous and independent of papal power, promises in October "to observe *in all things* the *obedience* due to the apostolic see and to you, Pope Gregory." The kingdom which, so he alleged, was conferred on him by God directly, was now to be the subject of a papal verdict. Henry's kingdom had become the *negotium* of the pope.[1]

Constructive criticism was not the strength of the episcopal resistance. The bishops' resistance was entirely focused on the practical exercise of Roman jurisdictional and legislative primacy. They revolted because their freedom, as they understood it, was threatened by the recent papal measures. But we will look in vain for constructive ideas in their vehement denunciations of Gregory VII, characterized as they were by an appeal to the lowest vulgar emotions: their references to Gregory's "cohabitation with a strange woman," their statement that "all the decrees of the apostolic see have been set in motion by women," their allegation that "this new senate of women administers the church"[2] are singularly devoid of reasoning. The material point in their manifesto was that the hierarchical ordering within the *sacerdotium* was not based upon divine law, and hence Gregory's actions presented themselves as usurpations. They were particularly aggrieved by Gregory's insistence that all ecclesiastical matters and appointments were to be eventually decided by him himself. The subjection to papal commands, the unquestioned obedience postulated by Gregory in the interests of a centralized government, were the demands which aroused the episcopal wrath. Gregory's battle-cry of the "libertas ecclesiae" had not apparently been understood by those who were to benefit from this freedom: what they understood was the liberty which they enjoyed as firm adherents of episcopalism. "We renounce the obedience which we never promised to you, nor shall we in future observe it at

---

that Henry was privy to the last sentence of the *Promissio* (where it is said that the pope would disavow all the ugly assertions which were current about him) because this amounts to a virtual nullification of the preceding clauses. We think that despite the Swabian Annalist's explicit statement (MGH. SS. v. 284 ff.) Henry himself had perpetrated the forgery (p. 286: "litteras . . . sigillatas, quas tamen deinceps ipse clam alteravit et ad libitum suum mutavit"), it was the royal chancery which added the sentence: possibly it was one of the five councillors who had been excommunicated; on this see B. Schmeidler, *Heinrich IV und seine Helfer*, Leipzig, 1927, pp. 304–10.

[1] Thus Gregory VII in his report about Canossa, *Reg.* iv. 12, p. 312. On the term itself, see H. X. Arquillière, "Gregoire VII à Canossa a-t-il réintegré Henri IV" in *Studi Gregoriani*, iv. 12, note 31.

[2] MGH. *Const.* i, no. 58, p. 108 = ed. Erdmann, appendix A, p. 68.

all." The purely constitutional question as to whether this council at Worms—of which the episcopal manifesto was the product—was entitled to proceed to such an important decision as the deposition of the pope, need not be investigated: the council was only a provincial council—two Italian bishops were present: Bruno of Verona and Eppo of Naples—and it was against all tradition that an accused should not be heard, that in his absence he should be condemned, and that he should not even be informed of the charges brought against him.

Whilst episcopal resistance and royal reaction could not, from the autumn months of 1076 onwards, present a united front, the two opposition camps, from the spring months of 1080 onwards, co-operated and showed a considerable vigour in pressing home their attack on the hierocratic theme. What is important to notice here is that the leadership of this united front was in the hands of the episcopacy, greatly assisted by the two enemies of Gregory, Archbishop Wibert of Ravenna and Cardinal Hugh the White. Moreover, Henry IV himself seems to have dropped all his former dualist mollifications and to have returned to the more virile and certainly more promising monistic *Rex-Sacerdos* conception of his father. But the stimulus, we must keep in mind, came from the episcopacy.

It was the Lenten synod of 1080 which brought matters to a head: apart from the second excommunication of Henry the synod once again prohibited lay investiture, but went considerably further than the respective condemnations of the synod of 1078,[1] by decreeing that no one who had received a bishopric from a layman was a bishop and by extending this to the lower churches; excommunication was also decreed for those laymen who conferred ecclesiastical benefices upon clerics who in turn were forbidden to enter the churches thus conferred. And the fifth chapter is directed to the lay population: they should dissociate themselves from those "false pastors" who are not sufficiently equipped and who have not the "via religiosa nec consulendi scientia." This chapter was a formidable challenge to the pastoral office of those clerics who had received their churches from laymen. It is clear therefore that these synodal decrees were directed against the bishops particularly who were to be cut off from the masses of the people: it was the legalization and sanctioning of the lay strike.

The first outspoken reaction against the synod came quite naturally from the bishops: it was they who provided, again for understandable reasons, the leadership, and not the excommunicate and deposed Henry.

---

[1] *Reg.* v. 14a, pp. 370 ff., and *Reg.* vii. 14a, pp. 480–1.

It was at Bamberg, where at Easter 1080 a number of bishops assembled, that the first condemnation of the Lenten synod was made public. Henry IV was far away, at Liège, where he was spending Easter.[1] It was from Bamberg that the bishops attempted to inflame public opinion against Gregory.[2] That they also began to show a lively interest in the position and function of the king, is understandable, for it was only by a recourse to the old and familiar *Rex-Sacerdos* that they could hope to keep their "liberty." The forces which brought forth the Roman synodal decrees—the recalcitrant episcopacy and the recalcitrantly disobedient king—coalesced and were welded together.

At Whitsun 1080 we witness Henry IV joining the nineteen bishops at Mainz. There fortified and stimulated by the episcopal rebels Henry seems to have reverted to his father's functions. It was here at Mainz that the bishops showed their concern primarily "super regni perturbatione regiaeque potestatis derogatione" and only secondarily "super vacillante statu ecclesiae," as we read in Bishop Huzmann's letter to the Lombard archbishops, bishops, dukes and counts.[3] Henry's kingdom was thus made the chief episcopal concern: and Henry himself was put up as a protective wall behind which the bishops could safely shelter. He and the bishops were agreed upon the cause of all the evils— Hildebrand, "that head of a serpent which spread poison," and through whose "venomous breath all the evil sores had burst." The remedy proposed was to disown Hildebrand[4] and to proceed to the election of a worthier man, a "good pastor" who would bring peace. Again, peace would redound to the advantage of royal power and the kingdom itself.[5] The means of achieving this was the synod at Brixen—presided over by King Henry and held on 25 June 1080. Outwardly Henry no doubt appeared as the pivotal point,[6] but considering the genesis of this synod appearances should not deceive anyone into thinking that

---

[1] This is proved by the *Annales s. Jacobi Leodiensis*, MGH. SS. xvi. 639; and *Ruperti Chronicon s. Laurentii Leodiensis*, MGH. SS. viii. 277; cf. also Meyer v. Knonau, *Jahrbücher*, iii. 275.

[2] Evidenced by Archbishop Gebhard of Salzburg in his *Epistola ad Herimannum* (MGH. LdL. i. 270, c. 15): ". . . inhonesta in domnum papam convicia jaculantes, qui congregati sunt, denuntiaverunt extunc in reliquum nequaquam pro apostolico habendum esse. *Ibique incipientes* pertransierunt per universum regnum eadem praedicando, adjunctis sibi et aliis eiusdem verbi ministris . . ."

[3] MGH. *Const.* i, no. 69, p. 118.

[4] "Ille sedis apostolicae subdolus invasor, divinarum humanarumque legum execrabilis perturbator."

[5] "Ut regni perturbatio sedetur regiaque potestas redintegretur."

[6] As the decree of the synod proclaimed it: "Mediante serenissimo rege Heinrico quarto."

the initiative and leadership really lay with Henry: the initiative belonged to the episcopacy, to Wibert and Hugh. The revolt was conducted within the traditional pattern and framework of the *Rex-Sacerdos* presiding over a council which elects a new pope in the person of the archbishop of Ravenna: the schism had begun which eventually led to Henry's imperial coronation at the hands of Clement III.

Whilst the decree of the Brixen synod[1] makes, like its Worms predecessor of four years ealier, no constructive proposals and is a document without substance,[2] the result was nevertheless important. On the earlier models a new pope was made: but the initiative still lay with the episcopal participants and not with Henry. The forms of the old proceedings were kept, though the contents were not the same. The important point to notice is that the *Rex-Sacerdos* could not act—however little his action would amount to—without the episcopacy: but the episcopacy was there at Brixen, not at the behest and by command of Henry,[3] but on account of their own opposition and resistance to Gregory. Henry IV was but a feeble and emaciated reflection of his great father.

## II

The abandonment of the dualist conception and its substitution by the old *Rex-Sacerdos* conception seemed indeed the only way by which the hierocatic thesis could effectively be assailed. But the weakness of Henry's position was too glaring to be overlooked even by his most enthusiastic supporters. Hence the attempt to support his function as a *Rex-Sacerdos* by an appeal to documentary history. Documentary history was to provide what Henry could not supply himself. That in the attempt to provide these documentary tools, anti-hierocratic

[1] MGH. *Const.* i, no. 70, pp. 118 ff.

[2] It is very largely a conglomeration of vituperative charges against Gregory: he was a wicked money-maker who had poisoned four popes before him, who had preached arson and condoned perjury, etc.

[3] That much lamented medievalist, C. Erdmann, has pointed out the change in the epistolary style of Henry's letters. Whilst before him, royal and imperial letters are characterized by the employment of phrases giving orders (*mandamus; praecipimus; jubemus*; etc.), with Henry IV there is a remarkable change: instead of giving orders he requests (*petimus; rogamus*; etc.); he adopts a confidential tone; threats of deprivation of royal grace disappear. "The whole character of his letters shows a fundamental change." See Erdmann, "Untersuchungen zu den Briefen Heinrichs IV" in *Archiv f. Urkundenforschung*, xvi (1939), pp. 195–9. About the personal part which Henry took in the drafting of his letters (which incidentally destroys the legend of Henry's lack of education) see Erdmann, ibid., pp. 247 ff.; here also contemporary testimonies about Henry's education.

thoughts turned to Charlemagne and the first Otto is understandable. Their reigns were to show that the hierocratic scheme was wrong and at variance with history. Certain documents were extant which demonstrated that the pope was in fact made by the emperor and not vice-versa; that the popes themselves had given the right of supervision and control over the Roman Church to these two models of monarchs.

It is weakness which leads to forging documents. The falsification of the *Ottonianum* little more than a century earlier, was a promising beginning. Now in the early eighties the royal party took refuge in a wholesale fabrication of documents, but in so doing showed none of the versatility and skill which distinguished its great antagonist in this same field. These documents were supposed to show the ancient and right order of things. They are: (1) the *Hadrianum*;[1] (2) the *Privilegium Minus* of Leo VIII;[2] (3) the *Privilegium Majus*;[3] and the *Cessatio donationum* concerning the restitution of a number of territories in the patrimony of St Peter to Otto I and his wife Adelaide, but this is of no interest to us.[4]

The purport of these forged documents is to show the singular rights which the king or emperor possesses as regards the pope. Let us be clear about one point, namely that the pivotal point in both the hierocratic and anti-hierocratic camps was the monarchical position of pope and emperor. What was at stake in either doctrine was the unfettered exercise of monarchic rule: the pope by virtue of the Petrine commission claimed the *principatus* of the whole *societas christiana*, of which the empire (and every Christian kingdom) formed an integral part, but no more than a part. The emperor, by virtue of his conception

---

[1] Also called the "Hystoria Karoli Magni Regis Francorum et decreta beati Stephani Adrianique papae" in MGH. *Const.* i, no. 446, pp. 659–60.

[2] MGH. *Const.* i, no. 448, pp. 665 ff.

[3] Also by Leo VIII, ibid., no. 449, pp. 667 ff.

[4] Its author was also supposed to be Leo VIII, ibid., no. 450, pp. 674 ff. The first to suspect the genuineness of these documents was Baronius. Cf. now Weiland in MGH. edition, loc. cit.; Meyer von Knonau, op. cit., iii. 298 ff.; P. E. Schramm, *Kaiser, Rom & Renovatio*, i. 235, 282; K. Jordan, "Der Kaisergedanke in Ravenna zur Zeit Heinrichs IV" in *Deutsches Archiv*, ii (1938), pp. 88 ff.; idem, "Ravennater Fälschungen aus den Anfängen des Investiturstreites" in *Archiv f. Urkundenforschung*, xv (1938), pp. 426–48; R. Folz, op. cit., pp. 126 ff. Most likely the imperial version of the papal election decree of 1059 was also fabricated at the same time, but is in this context of no interest to us. It is printed in MGH. *Const.* i, no. 383, pp. 541–6; Meyer von Knonau, op. cit., iii. excursus IV, pp. 653 ff. Cf. also A. Michel, *Papstwahl und Königsrecht*, 1936, pp. 33 ff. Against the general opinion that Peter Crassus was the forger of these documents, see the observations of Schramm, op. cit., loc. cit., and Jordan, *Deutsches Arch.*, ii. 119 f. For a diplomatic discussion of these forgeries, cf. idem, *Archiv*, pp. 432 ff.

of his office as directly divinely conferred, considered himself the monarch of the empire as regards all spheres affecting its working. Hence neither could concede any point to the other: each tried to be a monarch to the fullest possible extent. How do now these three forged documents argue the point? In examining them one is but struck by the similarity as regards the vulnerable points between these documents and the Donation of Constantine. The latter derived the unique regal position of the pope from a constitutional grant of the emperor: it was an imperial "privilegium" of Constantine that formed the pope's basis. Here we meet with exactly the same vulnerable point, only of course in the reversed order. The emperor's unique position and function as regards the pope was derived from a *privilegium* of the popes. Two of these documents are in fact called "Privilegia."

According to them, the emperor has the right to "elect," that is, to nominate the pope, because this right was conceded to the emperor by the pope,[1] the one by Pope Adrian I, the other by Pope Leo VIII.[2] The documents also speak of the imperial right, papally conceded, of investing archbishops and bishops.[3] It is not difficult to see how much the forger laid himself open to a hierocratic counter-attack. For these "rights" of the emperor were based upon a papal concession contained in a *privilegium*. Was not the whole Gregorian idea focused on the

---

[1] *Hadrianum*, ed. cit., p. 660: "Adrianus papa . . . *tradidit* Karolo augusto *omne suum jus et potestatem eligendi pontificem* et ordinandi apostolicam sedem . . . soli regi huiusmodi reverenda tribuatur facultas . . . Adrianus papa haec omnia *concessit*, laudavit et affirmando constituit." This is followed by the sanctio. In somewhat modified form the passage was incorporated by Gratian in his *Dist.* lxiii, c. 22.

[2] *Privilegium Minus*, ed. cit., p. 666: "Nos quoque Leo servus servorum Dei episcopus constituimus, corroboramus, et confirmamus et per nostram apostolicam auctoritatem *concedimus* atque largimur domno Ottoni primo (!) Teutonico regi . . . eiusque successoribus huius regni Italiae in perpetuum tam sibi facultatem successorem eligendi quam summae sedis apostolicae pontificem ordinandi . . . soli regi Romani imperii hanc reverentiae tribuimus facultatem." This reappears in Gratian, *Dist. cit.*, c. 23. See also *Priv. Majus*, ed. cit., p. 673, cap. 38: "Solus rex Romani imperii summae sedis apostolicae pontificem eligendi ac ordinandi facultatem habere sanctimus et per nostram apostolicam statuimus auctoritatem." We would believe that the expression "rex Romani imperii" in two documents was not inadvertently chosen: it might have been used to circumvent the ideology inherent in the imperial coronation. The author of the *Priv. Majus* avoids discussing imperial coronation and its import: we do not think that this was a mere omission on his part.

[3] *Hadrianum*, p. 660; *Priv. Minus*, pp. 666–7; also *Priv. Majus*, cap. 39, p. 673: "Insuper episcopos in provinciis eligendi et ordinandi habeat (scil. rex) potestatem, ut si quis episcopatum desiderat, ab eo reverenter anulum ac pastoralem suscipiat virgam."

supreme legislative power of the pope, a power which included the right to cancel any privilege that a predecessor might have granted?[1] Later papal opposition and theory took precisely this line in their counter-attack.

Whilst the *Privilegium Minus* purports to be a proper official document, the *Privilegium Majus* is an exposition of the ideas underlying the official act.[2] Its author tries to prove by Old Testament passages that the king has the right to nominate the pope. In introducing his argument he uses an expression which is not insignificant. "We all know, because it is old law, that the *rex Romanum gubernans imperium* should elect the pontiff of the apostolic see."[3] The subtlety and profundity of the Caroline formula had escaped the author who took it as a mere political expression, because it was of ancient Roman origin:[4] as we shall presently see, he was quite well versed in Roman law. The "renovation of the empire of the Romans" led, as we have said, to a "renovatio legum Romanarum" and as a result of this, certain ideas and formulae, such as "the king governing the Roman empire" were culled from usage in the ancient Roman empire. After a somewhat confused account of the installation of Boniface I by the emperor, the author proceeds to explain that the Old Testament king had the right to appoint the ecclesiastical-priestly officers. He singles out King Solomon's dismissal of Abiathar[5] and his appointment of Zadok.[6] David, too, proceeded in the same manner as Solomon: he appointed Asaph as the "princeps tabernaculi"[7] as well as a number of lower officers, such as porters and those engaged in burning offerings.[8] Lastly, Moses also invested Aaron with pontifical garments by conferring on him the mitre:[9] Moses, instituted by God "princeps et dux

---

[1] Cf. Gregory VII's *Reg.* vi. 2, p. 393: "Si necessitas vel *utilitas* major exegerit, licenter valent commutari (scil. privilegia)"; cf. also *Reg.* vii. 24 and ix. 19.

[2] Cf. K. Jordan, art. cit., p. 107, who says that the *Priv. Majus* should rank amongst the *Streitschriften* of the Investiture contest, because it is not a document in the strict meaning of the term.

[3] *Priv. Majus*, p. 669: "Cuncti enim novimus, quod non est novi juris, ut rex Romanum gubernans imperium sanctae sedis apostolicae pontificem eligere et ordinare debeat."

[4] See especially cap. 19, in which the old Roman emperors are thus designated (Valentinianus etc.).

[5] *Priv. Majus*, p. 669: "Ejecit ergo Salomon Abiathar, ut non esset sacerdos Domini." (I *Kgs*. ii. 28.)

[6] *Priv. Majus*, p. 669, and cap. 35: "And Zadok the priest did the king put in the room of Abiathar."

[7] I *Chron*. xvi. 37.          [8] Cf. I *Chron*. xvi. 38 ff.

[9] "Constituit Aaron unumquemque sacerdotem et filios eius sacerdotes." See *Lev*. viii. 7, 10, 13.

super filios Israel," acts as a true *Rex-Sacerdos* and functions in this dual capacity.

The recourse to Roman law in the *Privilegium Majus* is one more of its distinguishing features, and this recourse concerns the utilization of the *Lex Regia*. Once, the author tells us, it was possible for the Romans to make laws, but it became difficult to summon all the Romans for each and every law-making act into one place, whence they considered it expedient and advisable to transfer all their power and rights to the emperor: "Unde suum jus et potestatem imperatori concesserunt."[1] But whilst, according to the old Roman constitution, there was at least theoretically the possibility of an "abrogatio" of this grant, that is, a revocation,[2] our author made this transfer irrevocable. The construction he chooses to put upon the matter is that the originally voluntary act of the people was seen to have become an act dictated by Reason of State:

Voluntas populi postea in necessitatem convertitur,[3]

and therefore there no longer exists a possibility "de regno eum expellere." Again, he believes that he finds support for this in the Old Testament, when the Jews as a people asked for a king[4] and when Samuel anointed Saul as a king.[5] The choice of the Jews was final and irrevocable. The making of a king is a matter for the people: nobody can make himself a king.

Nemo enim seipsum potest regem facere, sed populus primum se creavit regem, quem voluerat.[6]

Once made a king, he cannot be deposed.

No doubt, this is a remarkable interpretation of the *Lex Regia*; no doubt also, this is a considerable advance in political thought: but was it the most appropriate choice of means by which to combat the hierocratic scheme effectively? Quite apart from all difficulties of reconciling the idea of kingship based upon popular will (*Lex Regia*) with the prevalent idea of the divine origin of royal power, the author's point of view reveals an astonishing misjudgment of the whole situation. By declaring the king's power to be derived from the people's will, in this respect he naturally puts his king in a very disadvantageous position compared with the pope's. For it was precisely the contention of the

---

[1] *Priv. Majus*, p. 667, quoting *Inst.* I. ii. De jure nat.; *Hadrianum*, p. 660.
[2] Cf. K. Jordan, art. cit., p. 111.　　　[3] *Priv. Majus*, p. 673.
[4] I *Kgs.* viii. 5–6.　　　[5] I *Kgs.* x. 1.
[6] *Priv. Majus*, p. 673, cap. 37.

hierocrats that the Petrine commission constituted a divine conferment of powers. In a theocentrically orientated society the hierocrats
could reap every advantage, and the idea of the popular origin of the
king's powers only accentuated the gulf that existed between pope and
emperor. Instead therefore of promoting the cause of the emperor, the
author generously and gratuitously handed a good deal of ideological
ammunition to his opponents. Not only did the contemporary literary
product of Manegold of Lautenbach explain the *Lex Regia* in a totally
different manner by making it out to be a revocable grant[1] on the
basis of which the people had the right to depose the king, but the
hierocrats were also soon to make the popular and divine origin of
royal and papal powers a major point in their discussion, a point that
could without undue difficulty be pressed to its fullest advantage.[2]

Whilst thus the "historical documents" of the royal party, produced
as they were at the time when documentary evidence for the resuscitated monarch was wanted, cannot be reckoned as serious attacks on
the hierocratic theme, they nevertheless assume importance, in so far
as in them, especially the *Privilegium Majus*, we witness one of the
earliest attempts to harness the Roman law as well as the Old and New
Testaments to the cause of the monarch's functions. True, cumulatively
the two lines may present some difficulties of reconciliation, but they
at least face the problem squarely: the flabbiness of an unworkable
dualism of government was rightly discarded in favour of a theoretically at least workable monarchism: this line of attack had at least the
merit of forcefulness and virility. It might even have been thought that
this line offered a promising breach into the fortifications of hierocratic
doctrine, but the presupposition for this was the destruction of the
Petrine theory with its consequent tenet of primacy and the resultant
transformation of this tenet into the law. Hence, these documents do
not meet hierocratic doctrine on its own ground: in fact, none of these
approaches this problem: to do away with the primatial function of the
pope—jurisdictionally and legislatively—would have been the only
means to set up the king as a monarch in his own right. Only one
writer of this period saw this vital point: the Anglo-Norman Anonymous vigorously and originally assailed the Petrine basis.[3] Nevertheless, the Petrine theory with all its attendant consequences was so firm
and apparently unshakable that within the realm of ideas it could not

[1] See his *Liber ad Gebehardum*, MGH. LdL. i. 365, 391, cc. xxx and xlvii.
[2] Cf. *Medieval Papalism*, pp. 165 ff.
[3] Cf. infra pp. 394 ff.

be dislodged from its habitation. When ideas prove insufficient to combat an opposing set of ideas, force must step into the breach: and that indeed is the meaning of the act perpetrated by Henry III's grandson, the fifth Henry, in 1111. Can there be a more convincing proof of the strength of an idea than when force has to be employed in combating it?

# CHAPTER XI

# Juristic Theology

## I

In a previous chapter we have referred to the importance which Gregory VII as pope and already as archdeacon Hildebrand attached to the value of having assembled in one "volumen parvum" ancient texts of papal prerogatives.[1] The result was a spate of canonical collections, beginning with Humbert's *Sententiae* which, by virtue of their incisive and mature hierocratic theme, set the tone for all subsequent collections.[2] These collections were in scope, orientation, subject-matter and the amount of material assembled, quite different from any of the previous collections. With these eleventh-century works the medieval canon law begins to take shape as a universal law governing the *societas christiana*, to which law all other legal systems became subsidiary.[3] With Gratian in the following century the science of canon law emerges as a universal science. But in order to understand this development some observations seem justified.

Not the least significant feature of the medieval period is the great reliance placed upon authority: authority—*auctoritas*—either in the

---

[1] P. Damian in PL. cxlv. 89.

[2] See J. de Ghellinck, *Le Mouvement théologique du XII siècle*, Paris, 2nd ed., 1949, p. 442.

[3] The main collections of the second half of the eleventh century are these (for details reference is made once and for all to P. Fournier-G. Le Bras, *Histoire des collections canoniques*, Paris, 1932, vol. ii).

(a) The previously known *Sententiae diversorum patrum* or *collectio minor* (as Anselm's source), but now, thanks to A. Michel's researches, known to be the work of Cardinal Humbert. For a brilliant summary see J. de Ghellinck, op. cit., pp. 435–7.

(b) Cardinal Atto's *Capitulare*.

(c) Anselm of Lucca's collection.

(d) Deusdedit's collection.

(e) Bonizo of Sutri's *Liber de Vita christiana*.

(f) Lanfranc's collection.

(g) The *Britannica*.

(h) Ivo's *Decretum* and his *Panormia*.

Besides those there are many other smaller collections.

shape of custom or tradition, or preferably in that of documentary evidence. The value of an *auctoritas* increased proportionately with its age: the older the *auctoritas* the more weight and greater standing it had. The aversion to innovations—and this characterizes in fact all governments, whether royal, imperial or papal—explains the otherwise inexplicable readiness to forge documents which in themselves as often as not said absolutely nothing new, but gave a practice or an institution the halo of moss-green antiquity. This aversion also explains the incessant insistence of the papacy, especially Gregory VII's, on the ancientness of the ideas put forward and applied. At no other period of its long history has the papacy so loudly and in so shrill a manner proclaimed the old, the traditional, the conservative elements of its theme as in the second half of the eleventh century. Having ourselves attempted partially to retrace some of the ground of the development of papal-hierocratic doctrine, we can but endorse the correctness of this assertion. The correspondence of the popes, and this applies to a particularly high degree to the popes of the second half of the eleventh century, teems with references to the "statuta," the "decreta," the "dicta," the "regulas," the "sanctiones," the "canones," the "constitutiones predecessorum nostrorum" and so forth.

The denominator common to all these manifold expressions or rather the idea behind them all is that that which the "decreta" etc. contain is what is right: what councils, popes, fathers, doctors said was reducible to a norm, the norm being that of the right conduct: this norm is the *canon* of living within the *societas christiana*, the "norma recte vivendi."[1] Hence it is not right conduct in the absolute sense which the texts set forth and which is applicable to any society, but the right conduct, the norm, or the canon which is applicable to the *societas christiana* only. Now the collectors of the "decreta" or the "constitutiones" and so forth provided an assemblage of texts which in their totality showed what is, and what is not, right in the *societas christiana*: what is right however becomes a question of what is and what is not lawful, if set against the background of the pope's jurisdictional and legislative primacy. The nature of a "norm" or a "canon" can be attributed only to statements made by an authority: the attribution of a canonical character to a papal statement presupposed the authoritative character with which the pope was credited. Transferred to society at large, the pronouncement of the pope loses its mere

---

[1] As Pseudo-Isidore had it copying from the genuine *Hispana*, see the quotation supra p. 188 n. 5.

literary character or its expression of opinion, and emerges as an expression of his judicial or legislative capacity: the papal letter in short becomes a canonical statement. Incorporating right conduct in a Christian society, a canonical statement becomes the law of God:

Constat et indubitanter verum est canonicam auctoritatem Dei esse legem. Qui ergo contra canones facit, contra legem Dei facit . . . ac per hoc impius est.[1]

For obvious reasons as a corporate entity, the *societas christiana*, with its basic Roman-legal inheritance, was in need of a law, that is of rules which universally bound and regulated the life of its members. But law in the meaning of "lex," as an individual injunction or prohibition endowed with a sanction, was provided only to a very small extent. The bulk of what was considered the law of the universal Church was contained in individual letters of popes, in passages of the fathers and so on—and these were not strictly speaking sources of the law, but sources which set forth the right conduct, which declared what should be the norm. In their totality these norms or canons constitute the *jus, Recht, Droit, Law*. The individual text provides a canon: the totality of the canons supplies Law (*jus*) and in the course of time this whole body of rules will be called *jus canonicum*. Behind each and every canon declaring what is right and therefore lawful, there must be *justitia*, otherwise the totality of the canons cannot be *jus*. Accordingly, since the Roman Church in hierocratic doctrine was, within the *societas christiana*, the only and exclusive repository of *justitia*, explicit or implicit approval by the Roman Church of a norm raised it to the level of a canon: the jurisdictional and legislative authority of the pope could not produce any other effects.[2]

The material source of a canon was *justitia*; the formal source of a canon was the pope himself. Naturally, therefore, the collections of the eleventh century strove to assemble as many papal letters or extracts from them as could be had, because they were most obvious sources of the canons both in their material and formal respects.[3] And the whole-

---

[1] Siegfried of Gorze to Poppo of Stablo in 1043, quoted by G. Ladner, *Theologie und Politik vor dem Investiturstreit*, p. 43.

[2] In the following century Gratian expresses this thought classically: "Sacrosancta Romana ecclesia *jus* et auctoritatem sacris canonibus impertitur," D.p.c. 16, C. XXV., q. i. For modern pronouncements which are substantially the same as their medieval predecessors, cf. G. Del Vecchio, "Jus et Juristae in sermonibus Pii Papae XII" in *Apollinaris*, xvi (1943), pp. 82–7.

[3] The collection known as *Britannica* is a particularly good example of assembling pontifical letters; the collection is of Italian origin; for details Fournier-

13

sale reliance on the pantheon of papal prerogatives, Pseudo-Isidore, cannot cause any surprise. But this orientation towards the Roman Church provided not only a highly welcome means, therefore, of discarding the numerous provincial or local "canons"—not having been approved by the Roman Church they did not constitute a binding norm, hence could not constitute a canon—but also an opportunity to separate allegedly spurious or apocryphal texts from genuine ones: recourse to explicit or implicit approval of a text by the Roman Church supplied the means to establish the canonical character of a text as well as the authenticity of texts if their genuineness was disputed.[1] It is well known that contemporaries knew of the apocryphal character of a number of texts,[2] but the means by which they could be distinguished from the genuine material presented difficulties. Hence approval by the Roman Church, in whatever guarded or implicit form the approval may have been given, was the criterion by which the authenticity of a text could be established.[3] Consequently, what contradicted the "Roman" tradition was excised from the collections; what was doubtful was accepted, if approved by the Roman Church. What was favourable to the Roman Church was received. Into this last category there belong the conciliar decrees, patristic expressions as well as the legislation of Eastern and Western emperors: this source was accepted without further examination.[4] In brief, the principle of Roman approval enunciated by the collectors is the application of the old hierocratic principle which we have met before, namely that the decrees of councils

---

Le Bras, op. cit., ii. 155 ff., especially p. 157. There are also some significant fragments from the Digest of Justinian, about which see M. Conrat, *Geschichte der Quellen des römischen Rechts im Mittelalter*, Leipzig, 1906, pp. 345–7, 351–4, 370–2; and C. G. Mor, "Il Digesto nell'età pre-irneriana a la formazione della Vulgata" in *Per il XIV Centenario della Codificazione Giustinianea*, Pavia, 1934, pp. 631–47, 679–92. About the *Britannica* cf. now my observations in *Ephemerides Juris Canonici*, xi (1953), no. 4.

[1] It should be pointed out in this context that the "liber canonicus" in DP. 17 has nothing to do with our topic; on this see S. Kuttner in *Studi Gregoriani*, ii. 387 ff.

[2] Cf. the statements made by Peter Damian and Cardinal Atto and referred to by Fournier-Le Bras, op. cit., ii. 6. Cf. also Bonizo of Sutri, *Liber de vita christiana*, ed. E. Perels, ix. 25: "Haec duo capitula [matrimonial impediments] nominibus Romanorum pontificum, Innocentii scil. et Gregorii, titulata apocrifa sunt, tumque in decretalibus eorum epistolis non inveniuntur inscripta tumque sanctorum patrum regulis videntur sentire contraria."

[3] See Fournier-Le Bras, ii. 7.

[4] This applies especially to the *Epitome Juliani*, cf. Fournier-Le Bras, ii. 13. It is nevertheless noteworthy that Humbert's *Sententiae* have only six fragments from secular legislation, see Fournier-Le Bras, ii. 17–18.

do not become universally binding canons, until and unless the Roman Church has approved of them. In itself this is an application of the axiom that every council, in order to have universal effects, must have been summoned by the pope or with the pope's approval.

The collections of the eleventh century are not so much collections of "canon law" in the strict meaning of the term as guide-books or handbooks of sources which contain in their totality the *jus*, the presupposition being that each individual text was based on *justitia*. Hence, these collections excised all the texts of Celtic, Frankish or Germanic provenance, precisely those texts which figured so largely and prominently in, say, Burchard's *Decretum* of the beginning of the eleventh century. Furthermore, they all have a tendency to give documentary and justificatory evidence in favour of the hierocratic theme: they are selective in the sources. They are therefore guide-books in the literal meaning of the term. They pursue a theme: in order to support the theme, they give long extracts from the sources to show what is the canon of lawful activity in the *societas christiana*.[1] Their concentration on the primacy of the Church of Rome and on its consequences as regards episcopacy, kings, and so forth, is therefore self-evident. The other main items in the collections are texts profusedly adduced to demonstrate the uncanonical character of simony, concubinage, lay investing of bishops, alienation of ecclesiastical property and related topics.

The character of these collections will become clearer if we glance at the actual sources which the collectors used in order to provide the canon of right living. There are extracts from purely historical accounts, such as the *Liber Pontificalis*, or fragments taken from the ecclesiastical histories of Eusebius and Rufinus, or from the work of Paulus Diaconus, of Anastasius's *Chronographia*, or Cassiodorus's *Chronica*, and other historical writers. One cannot very well maintain that these works are "sources of law"; but they contain texts and records which show what is right and lawful, what in other words is the canon for a particular action.

---

[1] The work of Bonizo of Sutri, *Liber de vita christiana* (1089–95) is a characteristic example: as the title sufficiently indicates, this work in its ten books sets forth the canonical maxims by which life in the Christian society is regulated for all its orders, classes and strata. It is a very methodical composition assembling on a somewhat selective basis many texts showing the canon of right living. For a characterization see E. Perels in his Introduction to his edition; Fournier-Le Bras, op. cit., ii. 142–4, 147–50; and Ursula Lewald, *An der Schwelle der Scholastik: Boniẓo von Sutri und das Kirchenrecht seiner Tage*, Weimar, 1939.

†

If we wish to appraise the import of these Gregorian collections, we should also bear in mind, not only the diversity of sources utilized, but also the diversity of topics for which the canon was found. The *jus* by which the *societas christiana* is to be ruled must necessarily be intimately associated with the character of this society, unique as it was in its double aspect, a spiritual as well as a civil-earthy society. This consideration applies not merely to the issues which in other kinds of society are accessible to juristic treatment, concerning mainly the relations between individuals or between individuals and a collective entity, but also to those issues which the basic spiritual character of this society called forth, that is, sacramental and liturgical issues. Since this *societas christiana* is an organized entity and since its basic substratum is a spiritual element, the administration of sacraments as well as the qualification of those who administer them, are naturally susceptible to juristic formulation. The problem of the validity of sacraments —baptism, confirmation, matrimony, penitence, eucharist, ordination, extreme unction—is one the solution of which must rest on a binding rule, a canon. Validity means lawful administration and reception of the sacraments. Consequently, sacramental jurisprudence forms a large topic in the collections of the eleventh century, and quite particularly the issue of valid ordinations. Sacramental jurisprudence is a necessary consequence of functionalism properly understood. Moreover, membership of the *societas* entitles the individual to receive sacraments, but this right is denied to those who have severed their membership: excommunication is the exclusion from the *corpus* of Christians, and this entails not only the deprivation of the excommunicate members' right to partake in the sacraments, but also has equally severe civic consequences. The proper juristic fixation of these sacramental topics is therefore conditioned by the character of the *societas*. Lastly, orthodoxy of faith and its counterpart, heresy, are further items which are in need of juristic formulation, again only from the point of view of the organized entity. The great reliance of these collections on the penitentials can therefore be explained without undue difficulty.

Whilst the sacraments are the visible means by which the individual member of the *societas christiana* achieves salvation,[1] the external forms of the cult, especially those performed in public, are comprised in liturgy. Next to sacramental jurisprudence there is liturgical juris-

---

[1] Later Innocent III was to explain the sacraments thus: "Ad hoc in ecclesia Dei visibilis est sacramentorum species instituta, ut per exteriora, quae cernimus, ad interiora, quae intelligimus, transmittamus," *Reg.* i. 519.

prudence which we find in the Gregorian collections: like its counter-part, so liturgical jurisprudence too is treated from an exclusively Roman point of view. Unification of liturgical actions throughout the *societas christiana* corresponds to the unification and centralization of the government itself. Just as the latter was necessary, so was the former: government and liturgy, both concerned with the external, must within the realm of the *societas* be Roman-directed. The numer-ous extracts from the *Ordines Romani* in the collections serve there-fore the same purpose as the extracts from, say, the *Liber Pontificalis* or, for that matter, from the *Liber Diurnus*: namely to demonstrate what is, and what is not, the canon, what is and what is not lawful, in the sphere of liturgy.

What all these collections present to us is what for want of a better name might be called juristic theology. Speculation was conspicuously absent from these works: there is as yet no attempt to develop on scientific lines certain notions; there is no attempt to interpret, to argue, to harmonize or to make the—considering the diversity of the material—so necessary distinctions.[1] These features were reserved to speculative theology which as a direct result of the great Gregorian stimulus, that is, of the implementation of hierocratic doctrine, de-veloped more freely and easily than its juristic counterpart. Indeed, this is not surprising at all: the juristic theologians, by the very nature of their occupation, were conservative. It was, as we were at pains to show, precisely the justifiable axiom of the hierocratic government that what was applied and done, was in strict concord with the ancient ideas and that accordingly the idea of innovation was abhorred. Before the juristic theologians could proceed to develop juristic notions, they were forced to dig up the material in support of their theme: and it was this search in the libraries, so characteristic of the juristic theolo-gians, which produced so many hitherto unknown texts and fragments that had been buried in various repositories.[2] *Jus* by its very nature is conservative, and the juristic theologians therefore looked backwards rather than forward.

[1] To judge by the preliminary account of the late J. de Ghellinck, "Magister Vacarius: Un juriste théologien peu aimable pour les canonistes" in RHE., xliv (1949), pp. 173 ff., it seems that the observation made in the text was still appli-cable to Vacarius in the following century; cf. here also the bitter remarks about the canonists, especially Gratian, pp. 176–8.

[2] On this search see especially P. Fournier, "Un tournant de l'histoire du droit" in *Nouvelle Revue historique de droit français et étranger*, xli (1917), pp. 132, 138, 154 f., 168; Fournier-Le Bras, op. cit., ii. 7–14; and de Ghellinck, op. cit., p. 433.

At the same time there can be no doubt about the nature of this juristic theology: the accent still lies on theology. The theocentric nature of thought and of society itself makes this rather self-evident. Moreover, a differentiation between the various departments comprised in the collective name theology, could not take place until the scientific tools were provided. It is misleading to speak of canonists or of liturgical scholars, and so forth at that time: liturgy, canonistics, theology in the narrow meaning, philosophy and so on, as different aspects of one and the same theocentric science, were the results of specialization, itself the consequence of the deepening of departmental knowledge. The flowering of these branches of learning after the Gregorian period symptomatically demonstrates the comprehensiveness of the *societas christiana* in the world of pure learning. We venture to say that the implementation of hierocratic doctrine was an indispensable condition for the unprecedented cosmopolitan ascendancy of scholarship in all spheres.[1] The spheres most directly affected were those which originally were mere departments of theology in the widest sense: these departments—such as canonistics, liturgy—became henceforward branches of learning in their own rights, whilst theology proper could concentrate with all the greater vigour on its own peculiar problems. The former branches of theology became virtually autonomous although, for obvious reasons, never quite losing their original theological nexus.[2]

---

\*
†    [1] Including what is usually called the humanistic and classical sphere as represented by Marbod of Rennes, Baudry of Bourgeuil, Hildebert of Lavardin and many others. About Godfrey of Rheims see J. R. Williams, "Godfrey of Rheims: A Humanist of the Eleventh Century" in *Speculum*, xxii (1947), pp. 29–45; cf. also the impressive list of French writers of this period provided by the late F. Lot in *Bulletin du Cange*, xvi (1942), pp. 5–59, and G. Stegew, "Les lectures classiques etc.," ibid., ix (1935), pp. 88 ff. About Benzo of Alba see infra pp. 387 ff.

†    [2] This intimate connexion between theology and law exists for a little time after Gratian: on the "communité des matières" see the classic observations by J. de Ghellinck, *Mouvement*, cit., pp. 422–65. The early decretists consider Gratian's book a theological treatise, cf. e.g. Rufinus: "Unde palam est summam quandam totius theologiae paginae contineri in hoc libro" (*Summa*, ed. H. Singer, p. 1). Another early decretist begins his glosses thus: "Inter ceteras teologiae disciplinas sacrorum patrum decreta et consiliorum non postremum obtinent locum," quoted by St. Kuttner, *Repertorium der Kanonistik*, Città del Vaticano, 1938, p. 14, note 1; for a similar gloss see de Ghellinck, op. cit., p. 463. In its early days French canonistics was strongly influenced by theological trends, see St. Kuttner, "Les débuts de l'école canonique française" in *Studia et documenta historiae et juris*, iv (1939), pp. 186 ff. Some of the earlier decretists, such as Sicard of Cremona and Gandulph, were notable theologians and canonists, cf. de Ghellinck, op. cit., pp. 297 ff., 460. Parts of the *Gemma ecclesiastica* of Gerald of Wales with their numerous theological, canonistic and Romanistic illustrations,

## II

Every system of law is the product of those forces that created the society to which the law is to apply. Law reflects the ideology of any organized community of men. This is as true of the *societas christiana* as it is of the society that was ruled by Justinian. Although his statement "nec multum differant ab alterutro sacerdotium et imperium"[1] is not quite correct, his own legislation on ecclesiastical matters showed that to him there was no really substantial difference. The privileges which by virtue of his monarchic position he conferred upon the *sacerdotium*, could be and were embodied in the canonical collections of the eleventh century.[2] But this could not conceal from contemporaries that the ideas manifested in Justinian's codification were diametrically opposed to hierocratic ideas. For his work was the classic legal expression of the imperial-laical standpoint. As such it had all the glamour and the glory that was Rome; it had all the "authority" of documentary evidence; it had above all every advantage in the realm of jurisprudence: it was a law which had omitted hardly any item necessary for the regulation of its contemporary social life.[3]

That this Justinianean codification, for brevity's sake called the. Roman law, had always been a living law at least in certain parts of Europe, has been proved beyond any doubt.[4] It has also been proved that this Roman law was studied at Ravenna[5] where it reached a very

are probably not his own work, but that of Peter the Chanter, cf. A. Boutemy, "Giraud de Barri et Pierre le Chantre" in *Revue du Moyen Age Latin*, ii (1945), pp. 45 f., also de Ghellinck, *L'éssor de la littérature Latine au XII siècle*, Paris, 1947, pp. 142 ff. On Geoffrey of Monmouth's probable use of the collection of Anselm of Lucca, see Schafer Williams, "Geoffrey of Monmouth and canon law" in *Speculum*, xxvii (1952), pp. 186–7.    [1] *Nov.* vii, cap. 2.

[2] And indeed in some earlier collections, cf. C. G. Mor, "Le droit romain dans les collections canoniques des X et XI siècles" in *Revue historique de droit français et étranger*, vi (1927), pp. 512 ff.; idem, "La rezezione del diritto romano nelle collezione canoniche die secoli IX–XI in Italia a oltr' Alpe" in *Acta Congressus juridici internationalis*, ii. 287 ff.; idem, "Un manoscritto canonistico francese del secolo IX" in *Rendiconti del R. Istituto Lombardo di scienze e lettere*, lxxvi (1943), especially pp. 6 ff. (of the offprint). See also Fournier-Le Bras, op. cit., i. 238 (*Anselmo dedicata*); 250 (Regino of Prum); 327 (Abbo of Fleury), 421 and ii. 12 f.

[3] Cf. the fine observations of Paul Koschaker, *Europa und das Römische Recht*, Munich, 1947, pp. 80 ff.

[4] It suffices to mention the names and works of Maassen, Solmi, Calisse, Besta, Leicht, Calasso, Mor. About the Digest see especially the latter's important work in *Per il XIV Centenario della Codificazione Giustinianea*, pp. 559–697.

[5] Cf. K. Jordan, "Der Kaisergedanke etc." in *Deutsches Archiv*, ii (1938), pp. 85 ff., and P. S. Leicht, "Ravenna e Bologna" in *Atti del congresso internazionale*

high standard.[1] But what is of particular importance to us is that the familiarity gained through the scientific study of Roman law, suggested its utilization for ideological purposes. It is not always appreciated that the contemporary application of hierocratic doctrine provided a powerful incentive to make use of Roman law as a means to combat hierocratic tenets. It was, we hold, as a result of this ideological stimulus that Roman law studies came so much to the fore, precisely from the Gregorian period onwards. The "rediscovery" of Roman law concerned not the law, which was being studied in any case, but its underlying ideas.[2] Without the familiarity with Roman law its ideological wealth would not have been grasped: and the realization of ideological opulence exhibited in Roman law, led to the unparalleled intensification of Roman law scholarship from now onwards.[3] What is of further interest to us is that the Justinianean codification was considered a guidebook for the imperial-laical government. The study of Roman law, therefore, provided the supply of technical and jurisprudential con-

---

*di diritto romano*, Pavia, 1934, i. 279–90; and about Pavia, see P. Vaccari, "Pavia e Bologna," ibid., i. 293–312, who holds that Roman law was studied at Pavia earlier than at Bologna. For the "antiqua schola Papiensis" of the eleventh century, see L. Moriani, "Influenza della università di Pavia negli studii della giurisprudenza civile" in *Per il XIV Centenario della codificazione Giustinianea*, pp. 153–8. For a contemporary product of the Pavia school see the *Expositio ad librum papiensem*, ed. MGH. *Leges*, iv. 290–585. About the influence of Pavia on Normandy and hence on the Conqueror, cf. N. Tamassia, "Lanfranco arcivescovo di Canterbury e la scuola pavese" in *Mélanges Fitting*, Paris, 1908, ii. 189 ff., and now especially R. Foreville, "Aux origines de la renaissance juridique" in *Moyen Age*, lviii (1952), pp. 43 ff., at pp. 78–82.

[1] As regards Ravenna, cf., for instance, Peter Damian's discussion in about 1062 with the Ravenna jurists on the computation of the degrees of consanguinity "De parentelae gradibus" in PL. cxlv. 191–208; cf. also Alexander II himself in his bull of April 1063, J. 4500 (Gratian: XXV. v. 2) where the Ravenna view is styled "novus et inauditus error."

[2] This applies to a special degree to the Ravenna school of Roman law: we must bear in mind that Ravenna was the historic rival of Rome (cf. H. J. Schmidt, "Die Kirche von Ravenna im frühen Mittelalter" in *Hist. Jb.*, xxxiv (1914), pp. 729 ff.; and K. Brandi, "Ravenna und Rom" in *Arch. f. Urkundenforschung*, ix (1924), pp. 1 ff.; also K. Jordan, art. cit.) and that Gregory VII's anti-pope, Clement III, was archbishop of Ravenna (Wibert). We alluded before to the possibility that the Wibertist-Henrician forgeries were fabricated at Ravenna. Cf. also Leicht, art. cit., pp. 284 ff.

[3] As the late P. Koschaker, op. cit., remarked, p. 70: even if the Roman law had been a hundred times more perfect than it is said to have been, "so wäre doch kein einziger Student zu den Glossatoren nach Bologna gezogen, wäre es nicht das Recht des *Imperium Romanum* gewesen." On the influence of Roman law on "legal culture" see W. Engelmann, *Die Wiedergeburt der Rechtskultur in Italien durch die wissenschaftliche Lehre*, Leipzig, 1938, pp. 15 ff., especially pp. 31–41; cf. also pp. 62 ff. and pp. 305 ff.

cepts; it was also used as a means to be directed against the application of hierocratic doctrine: in this respect Roman law studies were a defensive measure.

The differences between Roman law and its later rival are obvious. In the one case there was a guide-book ready made at the disposal of its users; in the other case this guide-book had yet to be made. Likewise the advantages and disadvantages are obvious. The advantage inherent in Roman law was that it was a law book with minute regulations concerning all sorts of conditions of men and things: it was a law in any sense of the term. Its disadvantage was—leaving its underlying ideas apart—that it was not readily applicable to contemporary society, there being so many items in Roman law which had no meaning at all in the eleventh century, and there being equally many items of which the old Romans knew nothing, but which were very important in the eleventh century. The disadvantage thus presented by Roman law proved to become the advantage of the "canon" law, for this was a law continually being shaped, modified and, if need be, drastically altered. Roman law could never avail itself of this natural advantage possessed by canon law: being a fixed body of law, fixed that is to say by the Romans, it would have been the height of frivolity to change it in any detail or particular.[1] On the other hand, the well-defined, lucid and sharp jurisprudential and legal concepts which accrued from a study of Roman law[2] could not but turn out to be an advantage for the law to be created for the *societas christiana*.

The intensified study of Roman law at Ravenna, and shortly afterwards at the European legal citadel, Bologna, though so largely conditioned by the application of hierocratic doctrine, was to exercise lasting influence upon the "jus canonicum," precisely because of the specifically Roman juristic technique and concepts. Differently expressed, there could not be a canon law worthy of the name without Roman law technique and schooling. The proper juristic equipment, the technical legal tools, were provided by the Roman law.[3] In this

---

[1] The question of whether it was admissible and "rational" for the present emperor to change the Roman law was treated by the author of the *Quaestiones de juris subtilitatibus*, and denied, see H. U. Kantorowicz, *Studies in the glossators of the Roman law*, Cambridge, 1938, p. 185.

[2] We refer to such concepts as "dominium," "bona fides," "traditio," "praescriptio," "usucapio," "contractus," "dolus," "culpa," and so forth.

[3] Cf. P. Koschaker, op. cit., p. 81: "Was wir aber am römischen Recht bewundern ist der hohe Grad seiner juristischen Durchbildung." For some interesting aspects of rhetorical (Ciceronian) and consequently Roman law influence on canonistics, especially on Sicard of Cremona, see E. Lange, "Rhetorische Einflüsse

13*

respect, then, Roman law was an indispensable auxiliary science to canonistics, that is, Roman law minus its ideology.[1] Canonistics, the proper science of canon law, could not emerge until the juristic theologians had been trained in systematic jurisprudence, which could be provided only by an intensive study of Roman law. Gratian utilizes Roman legal jurisprudence and the Roman law pattern. His book shows the influence of Roman law thought upon a juristic theologian. Precisely because he disposed of Roman law knowledge and training, his work is so markedly different from anything else produced before his time. He rests securely on the results of the intensive Roman law studies in the first decades of the twelfth century at Bologna.

But in this alone does not lie the whole importance of Gratian's work. The title he gave to it, *Concordia discordantium canonum*, indicates his intention, namely to present a reconciliation of contradictory texts. This could not have been done until proper juristic hermeneutics had been made available. For it was due to the combination of legal and interpretative technique that Gratian initiated a new branch of learning, canonistics; rightly has Gratian been called the Father of the science of canon law.[2] Although the immediate source acquainting him with the

---

auf die Behandlung des Prozesses in der Kanonistik des 12. Jahrhunderts" in *Festschrift f. E. Eichmann*, Paderborn, 1940, pp. 69 ff.

[1] In the course of time this will lead to the theory that Roman law was a "lex suppletoria" provided that there is no canonical regulation and that the Roman law does not violate some underlying canonical principle. Cf. Lucius III in *Extra*: V. xxxii. 1, and Innocent III, ibid., I. ii. 10. The auxiliary function of the Roman law is the parallel to the auxiliary function of the emperor himself. For a succinct canonistic view see the *Summa Reginensis* (late twelfth century): "Quomodo potuerunt imperatores aliquid statuere de rebus ecclesiae? Respondeo, non quia imperatores aliquid statuerunt, sed quia ecclesia approbavit," ed. A. M. Stickler, "Vergessene Bologneser Dekretisten" in *Salesianum*, xiv (1952), p. 491. Indeed, this is a long way from Justinian's view on his own ecclesiastical legislation.

[2] See Sarti-Fattorini, *De Claris archigymnasii Bononiensis professoribus*, i. 344: "Quasi parens et auctor juris canonici deinceps habitus est." Our observations on Gratian are not affected by the vexatious problem of whether he was the sole author of the *Decretum* or whether he had collaborators. Some modern experts are inclined to the latter alternative. Cf., e.g,. A. Vetulani, "Gratian et le droit romain" in *Rev. hist. de droit français et étranger*, xxiv (1947), p. 47: "Le Décret, tel qu'il a été reçu par l'école et que nous connaissons d'après les manuscrits parvenus jusqu'à nous, n'était pas l'œuvre d'un seul auteur, mais résultait d'une collaboration. Gratien n'a pas été l'auteur unique du Décret." In the forthcoming *Studia Gratiana* (Bologna) we tentatively suggest that the *Decretum* went through three main phases of which only the first was Gratian's work. Through the research of W. Peitz, the relationship between Gratian, his sources and the papacy has become a major problem. Peitz holds that Gratian composed his *Decretum*, not in Bologna, but in Rome, with the knowledge and support of the pope; that he utilized the

new technique may have been Abelard,[1] the attempts at a reconciliation of the *contrarietates* go back to the period immediately after the end of Gregory VII's pontificate. Collectors of "canons" as well as the Roman jurists were faced with the same difficulty: in the latter case the difficulty concerned the reconciliation of legal texts as embodied in Justinian's codification; and in the former case the difficulty concerned the reconciliation of texts which, though not all of them had the force of a binding canon, had nevertheless at one time or another been considered as "norms." Hence in both cases a satisfactory method had to be devised to do away with textual and substantial *contrarietates*. That theology in the narrow meaning of the term was also faced with exactly the same difficulty goes without saying. None saw the need for a reconciliation, at least in the field of juristic theology, better than Pope Urban II who, in a seemingly insignificant routine letter, pointed the way by advising the recipient that distinctions should be drawn between texts which contain norms of an immutable character and texts which were prompted "pro temporum necessitate et pro personarum qualitate" and which therefore could be considered changeable. This is a most important hermeneutic principle resting as it does on the thesis of cosmological unity: contradictions are merely apparent, not real. The means to solve these apparent *contrarietates* is the basic mental operation of a *distinctio*.

Post-Urban canonical collections, especially that of Ivo of Chartres[2] and Alger of Liège,[3] were to adopt and partly to develop this principle suggested by Urban II.[4] It is an extraordinarily fruitful principle,

---

papal archives and used the manuscript of Dionysius (still preserved at that time) for his work. See Peitz's contribution to the *Studia Gratiana*, "Gratian und Dionysius Exiguus," of which the illustrious author has kindly sent me the typescript.

[1] In this sense St. Kuttner, "Zur Frage der theologischen Vorlagen Gratians" in *Sav. Z., kan. Abt.*, xxiii, 1934, pp. 243 ff. About the whole question of non-juristic influences on Gratian see J. de Ghellinck, op. cit., pp. 494 ff.; Fournier-Le Bras, op. cit., ii. 334 ff.; cf. also Denifle-Chatelain, *Chartul. Univ. Parisiensis*, i. p. xxvii.

[2] Cf. Ivo's Prologue, 'De consonantia canonum" in PL. clxi. 74 ff.; also Fournier-Le Bras, op. cit., ii. 110 ff.

[3] On this see P. Fournier, "Un tournant etc." in *Nouv. Rev. hist. de droit franç. et étranger*, xli (1917), pp. 165–9; also G. Le Bras, "Le Liber de misericordia et justitia d'Alger de Liège," ibid., xlv (1921), pp. 80–118; cf. also de Ghellinck, op. cit., pp. 62 ff.

[4] J. 5383 of December 1088; see S. Loewenfeld, *Epp. pontificum Romanorum*, p. 61. Parts of this letter in Gratian: I. vii. 24. The significance of this letter is stressed by Fournier-Le Bras, op. cit., ii. 357–8; in Fournier's art. cit., pp. 157 f.; by de Ghellinck, op. cit., pp. 432–3; and G. Ladner, *Theologie & Politik vor dem Investiturstreit*, pp. 48 f.

applicable by canonists, Romanists[1] and theologians who developed it to the point of perfection. And from the hands of the pure theologian Abelard, the juristic theologian Gratian accepted it[2] and applied it with consummate skill to his own work: the *concordia discordantium canonum* created thereby a new discipline of learning, canonistics, in so far as juristic theology ceases to be a branch of theology and becomes a science in its own right—the result of specialization.[3] The employment of proper hermeneutic principles in itself is scientific and scholarly treatment of the sources: it is scholarship. The accent now lies on the juristic, and no longer on theology. This could not have been achieved without the juristic and interpretative technique with which Gratian had so perfectly equipped himself,[4] in order to create what had not been done and could not have been done before, namely

---

[1] About them see E. Genzmer, "Vorbilder für die Distinctionen der Glossatoren" in *Acta Congressus Juridici Internationalis*, 1935, ii. 343 ff.; P. Koschaker, op. cit., pp. 62–3, 91; cf. also H. Fitting, *Die Anfänge der Rechtsschule in Bologna*, Berlin, 1888; also E. Seckel, "Die Anfänge der europaeischen Jurisprudenz im 11. und 12. Jahrhundert" in *Sav. Z., Rom. Abt.*, xlv (1925), pp. 391 ff., and P. Torelli, "Glosse preaccursiane alle Instituzione" in *Studi in Onore Enrico Besta*, Milan, 1939, iv. 231 ff.

[2] Abelard also strongly influenced the Romanists, cf. E. Genzmer, "Die justinianische Codification und die Glossatoren" in *Atti del Congresso internazionale di diritto romano*, cit., ii. 383.

[3] Gratian's work was not, however, a book to be used by the untrained, as a Cistercian enactment makes clear: "Liber qui dicitur corpus canonum et Decreta Gratiani, apud eos qui habuerint secretius custodiantur, ut cum opus fuerit proferantur; in communi armario non resideant, propter varios qui inde possunt provenire errores," *Statuta capitulorum generalium ordinis cisterciensis*, ed. J. M. Canivez, Louvain, 1933, i. 108, sub anno 1188, no. 7 (I owe the reference to this edition to Dr C. H. Talbot). As is well known, Sohm attached great value to this Cistercian enactment—he had to rely on its defective edition in Martène-Durand —but Sohm's theory on this point was demolished by U. Stutz, "Die Cistercienser wider Gratians Decret" in *Sav. Z., kan. Abt.*, ix (1919), pp. 63–96, who put the enactment into its Cistercian framework. Nevertheless, the passage does not say that Gratian's *Decretum* itself contained errors: all it says is that errors may arise from the perusal of the *Decretum*. This seems also the opinion of B. Jacqueline, "Bernard et le Droit Romain" in *Bernard de Clairvaux*, Paris, 1953, p. 430, note 9.

[4] It is well known that a modern *lumen juris canonici* has called Gratian a mediocre compiler, but this does little justice to the man's intentions which assuredly were not to compile what previously was scattered, but to compose on the basis of the available material something like a system, a text-book of canonistics. His *Decretum* was a technical handbook, and it is as a result of his perfecting legal and interpretative technique that at the right time and in the right place Gratian bequeathed his work to posterity. As regards the texts compiled by Gratian, see van Hove, in *Apollinaris*, xxi (1948), p. 18: "Speciales laudes Gratiano non sunt tribuendae in colligendis textibus. Paucissima monumenta compilationi suae addidit, quae non reperiantur in anterioribus collectionibus, quibus usus est."

a theory or doctrine of the canons binding upon all members of the *societas christiana*.[1]

It is hardly possible to exaggerate the full implications which this new specialized branch of learning was to have for the working of the *societas christiana*. Barely a generation after Gregory VII's pontificate the *societas christiana* was given its fully equipped army of field workers or technicians, the canonists. The rapidity with which canonistics became, in a quite unprecedented manner, the most important intellectual activity, at once combining pure and applied science, invading all existing seats of learning and potently contributing to the creation of new ones, symptomatically demonstrates the necessity and usefulness of this new science. Hierocratic theory having become a practical governmental scheme, was to be worked by those trained in the science of government which was at that time the science of law. The—again unprecedented—spate of papal legislation of post-Gratian times is at once cause and effect: a cause in so far as it provided a further incentive to the systematic and scientific penetration of canonical jurisprudence; an effect in so far as the popes themselves were fully fledged canonists brought up in the schools of Bologna. The canonist became the technician who in actual fact worked the mechanism of the *societas christiana*.[2] No wonder that an early decretist, still a contemporary of Gratian himself, refers to the standing of a canonist with not unjustifiable pride: "Cuius est magna in ecclesia Dei auctoritas."[3]

---

[1] Cf. the remarks of St. Kuttner, art. cit., p. 244. In this respect an immediate  †
predecessor of Gratian was Alger of Liège, see supra 371, and G. Le Bras, "Alger de Liège et Gratien" in *Revue des sciences philosophiques et theologiques*, xx (1931), pp. 5 ff. Cf. also *Dict. Droit Can.*, s.v. Alger. The specialization to which we have referred later affected canonistics itself, as is evidenced by the monographic literature on certain topics, such as the numerous tracts *De matrimonio, De usuris, De decimis, De electionibus*, the many *ordines judiciarii*, and so forth.

[2] Medieval canon law was not a mere ecclesiastical law: it was a law that pro-  †
vided a canon of right living ("recte vivendi") in the *societas christiana*. To this system all other legal systems, including the Roman law, were subsidiary, a tenet which transferred hierocratic ideology to the sphere of law. Canon law was the law emanating from the *sedes justitiae* of the Christian body politic, hence it was the law of its monarch.

[3] Quoted by de Ghellinck, op. cit., p. 298. Modern critics of medieval papalism cast aspersion on the obvious fact that the popes from the mid-twelfth century onwards were canonists: they ought to have been theologians. This criticism is quite unjustified, because it fails to take cognizance of the function of the pope as a monarch who was primarily concerned with the translation of the *principatus* of the Roman Church into practice. A theologian is assuredly not qualified to govern: government must lie in the hands of someone who is trained, and that training could be had only by canonistics. This explains the uninterrupted sequence of canonist popes; it also explains the utility of studying canonistics:

## III

The evolution of canon law and of canonistics was in fact the evolution of *theologia practica externa*.[1] Law by its very nature can have reference only to the *forum externum*. But complementary to this forum is the *forum internum*, an aspect that stands in closest proximity to the conception of the *societas christiana* as a basically spiritual body corporate which at the same time is also civil-earthy. In order to be effective, the hierocratic scheme must be made to work in the *forum externum* as well as in the *forum internum*. The means by which this was to be effected was that of compulsory sacerdotal confession of crimes and sins. This, however, was merely the application of the power to bind and to loose to individual Christians. It is the power which is hierarchically transmitted downwards to the lowest priest. From this consideration alone it follows that membership of the sacerdotal order is the indispensable presupposition for the exercise of the judicial function contained in this power.[2] Whilst this function was constitutive, basic and vital, there were other functions with which the priest was credited, namely that of a "Corrector" and "Medicus."[3] It seems, moreover, that the medicinal function of the priest, to whom faults, sins and crimes were revealed, was more emphasized in the early eleventh century than his judicial function: priests were spiritual doctors according to Burchard;[4] according to Bonizo of Sutri, however, they were

---

. without it, it was quite impossible to rise in the sacerdotal hierarchy. The part played by the medieval papacy in pure theology was not overwhelming.

[1] Cf. van Hove, *Prolegomena ad Codicem Juris Canonici*, 2nd ed., Louvain, 1945, p. 345; cf. also p. 455.

[2] The well-known biblical passages (*Matt.* xvi. 19; *John* xx. 23) had always been invoked to justify the thesis that the priests alone can legitimately bind and loose. Cf. Burchard of Worms, *Decretum*, xix. 153 (PL. cxl. 1013), borrowing from the *Poenitentiale Romanum*, a spuriously Roman penitential, about which see Fournier-Le Bras, op. cit., i. 351 f., and van Hove, op. cit., p. 300. St Peter Damian speaks of the "sacramentum confessionis," *Sermo* xix (PL. cxliv. 901). About some comparative aspects cf. also R. Pettazzoni, "La confession des péchés dans l'histoire des religions" in *Annuaire de l'institut de philologie et d'histoire orientale*, iv (1936), pp. 899–901.

[3] Cf. Burchard's book xix, preface, col. 940, PL. cit. : "Liber hic corrector vocatur et medicus, quia correctiones corporum et animarum medicinas plene continet."

[4] *Decretum*, xix. 29, PL. cit., col. 985: "Nam et corporum medici diversa medicamenta componunt, ut aliter vulnera, aliter morbum, aliter tumores, aliter putredines, aliter caligines, aliter contractiones, aliter combustiones curent. Ita et spirituales medici diversis curationum generibus animarum vulnera sanare debent."

comparable to experienced doctors who with "judiciali magisterio" discerned the faults of the penitents.[1]

What is clear is that doctrine down to the second half of the eleventh century maintained the advisability of the individual Christian's revealing his faults to a priest,[2] but not the necessity of doing so. All there was were "recommendations" which were rarely followed.[3] Confession to laymen was widespread and universal, and was considered sufficient to obtain remission of sins.[4]

---

[1] *Liber de vita christiana,* ix. 1 (ed. cit., p. 277): "Liber iste medicinalis inscribitur, eo quod aegrotantium continet varia medicamenta animarum. Et sicut peritorum medicorum est ad tactus venarum et adspectum urine morbos cognoscere singulorum, sic prudentum est sacerdotum considerata penitudine penitentis, quid quibusque conveniat, judiciali magisterio dispertire."

[2] Of earlier statements on the value and importance of confessing sins, cf. the Council of Chalons (813), cap. 33, Mansi, xiv. 100, and the almost universally current *Penitentiale* attributed to Theodore of Canterbury as well as the numerous other penitentials: they are little more than lists of possible (and sometimes also impossible) crimes committed and the penance to be imposed as well as the tariffs for commutation. The tariffs were given in order to facilitate the task of the priests; this can be found mainly in the Teutonic penitentials, see B. Poschmann, *Die abendländische Kirchenbusse im frühen Mittelalter,* Breslau, 1930, pp. 8–11, and P. Anciaux, *Le Théologie du sacrement de pénitence au XII siècle,* Louvain, 1949, p. 27, notes 4 and 5. For the penitentials see J. MacNeill and H. Gamer, *Medieval Handbooks of Penance,* New York, 1938 (with many extracts in English translation), and R. Mortimer, *The Origin of private penance in the Western Church,* Oxford, 1939. Since a good deal of later penitential enactments was based upon Visigothic Spanish practices and councils, reference should be made to the very useful survey of J. Ferd. Alonso, "La disciplina penitencial en la España Romano visigoda" in *Hispania sacra,* iv (1951), pp. 243–311. For Irish penitentials cf. Poschmann, op. cit., pp. 3–37, 58–72; and T. Oakley, "Celtic penance" in *Irish Ecclesiastical Record,* 1938, pp. 147–64, 181–201. Cf. furthermore the survey by Le Bras in *Dict. Théologie Catholique,* s.v. Pénitentiels: they were "des catalogues des péchés et de peines expiatiores destinés principalement à guider les confesseurs," col. 1160. About the great civilizing influence of the penitentials see T. Oakley, *English penitential discipline and Anglo-Saxon Law,* London, 1923, the same author's "The co-operation of medieval penance and secular law" in *Speculum,* vii (1932), pp. 515–24, and "The penitentials as sources for medieval history," ibid., xv (1940), pp. 210–23; cf. also Le Bras, loc. cit., cols. 1178–9.

[3] So one of the best informed writers on the subject, P. Anciaux, op. cit., p. 36: "Malgrè ces recommendations multiples et l'existence de rites déterminés, les chrétiens ne se confessaient que très rarement à cette époque (eleventh century)"; also p. 164: "Au XI siècle les auteurs s'efforcent de mettre en relief la valeur de l'aveu des fautes au prêtre"; cf. also p. 609: in the eleventh century "les canonistes considèrent les aspects pratiques et se contentent en général de fournir les listes de tarifs et des règles générales pour l'administration de la pénitence. Les théologians ne s'interessent guère à la doctrine pénitentielle."

[4] See especially the late A. Teetaert, *La confession aux laiques dans l'église Latine,* Louvain, 1926.

Now we may recall that in two synods, that of autumn 1078 and that of Lent 1080, Gregory VII makes "vera" and "falsa penitentia" the subject of one of the synodal decrees.[1] The decrees give warning against "false penitence" and insist on "vera penitentia" which Gregory considers is necessary if remission of sins is to be validly obtained.[2] "Vera penitentia," however, can be obtained only through the medium of properly qualified priests, that is those who are "religione et scripturarum doctrina instructi" so that they may show "viam veritatis." The two points which emerge from this decree are firstly the necessity of sacerdotal confession, and secondly the harnessing of the functionalist principle to confession, that is to "vera penitentia." Because sacerdotal confession is necessary, only those properly qualified can validly bind and loose. The thesis of functional qualification is intimately linked up with the thesis of the necessity of sacerdotal confession.

It is certainly no coincidence that the contemporary tract which was to prove so influential in the sphere of confessional-sacramental jurisprudence and theology bears as its heading the cue words of these synodal decrees: *De vera et falsa penitentia*.[3] That the tract sailed under the name of St Augustine was symptomatic of the authority which it was to have and in fact did have.[4] This tract was one of the bases upon which the exuberant theologians of the twelfth century were to hammer out the purely theological problems connected with priestly confession. For our purposes it will be sufficient if we concentrate on the two main tenets of the tract which are, firstly, the necessity of confession, and, secondly, the necessity of confessing to a priest. Lay confession as distinct from sacerdotal confession is the exact parallel of lay ideology in the wider political field: just as the laical-imperial standpoint had not found, and could not find, an answer to the embarrassing question, "By what authority does the emperor judge

---

[1] *Reg.* vi. 5b, cap. 6, p. 404; *Reg.* vi. 14a, p. 481, cap. 5.

[2] *Reg.* vii. 14a, p. 481, cap. 5: "Valde necessarium est, ut, qui se aliquod grave crimen commissum cognoscit, animam suam prudentibus et religiosis viris committat, ut per veram penitentiam certam peccatorum suorum consequatur veniam."

[3] PL. xl. 1113–30.

[4] Nothing is known about the author. About dates suggested see E. Amann in *Dict. Théol. Cath.*, s.v. Pénitence (towards the end of the eleventh century or even beginning of the twelfth); Fournier-Le Bras, op. cit., ii. 321 ("Vers le milieu du XI siècle); P. Anciaux, op. cit., p. 15, note 2: "vers le milieu du XI siècle." In view of Gregory's wording we would be inclined to place the tract somewhere in the eighties of the eleventh century.

popes?",[1] in the same way no satisfactory answer could be had for the justification of lay confession. Nor is it quite without significance that the author who so pointedly asked the vital question "By what authority" links this up with the power to bind and to loose in the case of mere lay Christians.[2] Sacerdotal confession is a necessary effluence of the tenet of functional qualification. Just as the emperor failed to justify his function in judging popes, so did the layman fail to justify his function in remitting crimes, sins and faults: in neither case had there been given the power to bind and to loose.[3]

It is precisely on this principle that the author of *De vera et falsa penitentia* constructs his theme. He concentrates on the old theme of the priestly power to bind and to loose: indeed this power is a *potestas judiciaria*: it is judicial power in every sense of the term.[4] And as a judge the priest can legitimately demand unquestioned obedience from the penitent: this obedience[5] to be exhibited to the judge is a necessary presupposition for salvation. Punishment is to be imposed in a judicial manner;[6] the criminal is God's enemy.[7] Should the priest misuse his judicial power, he will lose it and may be reinstated only by pontifical decree.[8] Through the priest's exercising judgment on the penitent, God Himself has made a judgment:

Quibus enim remittunt (scil. sacerdotes), remittit Deus.[9]

The judicial power of the priest is not a mere arbitrary or discretionary power, but a power that is strictly based upon *justitia*.[10] Hence the

[1] See supra on the *De ordinando pontifice*, p. 264.

[2] Cf. supra p. 264.

[3] The widespread lay confession may possibly have some roots in Cyprianic theses.

[4] See cap. 20. It was probably the juristic complexion of this tract which appealed to Gratian through whom it gained wide currency, cf. Anciaux, op. cit., p. 302.

[5] Cap. 15: "Ponat (scil. penitens) se omnino in potestate judicis, in judicio sacerdotis, nihil sibi reservans sui ut omnia eo jubente paratus sit facere pro recipienda vita animae, quae faceret pro vitanda corporis morte."

[6] Cf. cap. 8: "Penitentia enim est quaedam dolentis vindicta, puniens in se, quod dolet commisisse." Cf. also Isidore's *Etymologies*, ed. cit., VI. xix. 71: "A punitione poenitentia nomen accepit, quasi punitentia."

[7] Cap. 9: "Scio Deum inimicum omni criminoso."

[8] Cap. 20: "Caveat (scil. sacerdos) ne corruat, ne juste perdat potestatem judiciariam. Licet enim penitentia ei possit acquirere gratiam, non tamen mox restituit in primam potestatem . . . nisi statutum fuerit a Romano pontifice."

[9] Cap. 10.

[10] Cap. 10: "Dixit (scil. Dominus) enim, 'Quodcumque solveritis super terram, erit solutum et in coelis,' hoc est Ego Deus et omnes ordines coelestis militiae, et

priestly judge requires adequate knowledge, the requirement stipulated by Gregory VII in the Lenten synod of 1080.[1]

Although sacerdotal confession is necessary, the author of the tract realizes that a priest may not be at hand. In this case lay confession may be made which does not, however, display the same effects as sacerdotal confession. There is no remission of sins, because the layman lacks judicial powers. What is effected by a lay confession in these circumstances is that the penitent is considered worthy of pardon—"fit tamen dignus venia."[2] But this lay confession cannot be considered a sacrament.[3] The chief point in the tract is the necessity of sacerdotal confession which alone provides full remission of sins, by virtue of the judicial capacity which the priests alone have.[4]

In so far as penitence is a juristic matter,[5] it will engage the attention of the juristic theologians, and quite especially that of the canonists who will transform the "keys of the kingdom of heaven" ("claves regni coelorum") possessed by the priests, into "keys of the law" ("claves juris"). The necessity of annual compulsory confession to

---

omnes sancti in mea gloria laudant vobiscum et confirmant quos ligastis et solvitis. Non dixit, quos putatis ligare et solvere, sed in quos exercetis *opus justitiae* aut misericordiae."

[1] Cap. 20: "Caveat spiritualis judex, ut sicut non commisit crimen nequitiae, ita non careat munere scientiae." It should be noted that according to the old penitentials the priest had no judicial power. All he was expected to do was to impose, according to the catalogue provided, punishment. Cf. also F. Russo, "Pénitence et excommunication: étude historique sur les rapports entre la théologie et le droit canonique dans le domaine pénitentiel du IX au XIII siècle" in *Recherches des sciences religieuses*, xxxviii (1947), pp. 257–79; also 431 ff.

[2] Cap. 10: "Tanta itaque est vis confessionis, ut si deest sacerdos, confiteatur proximo. Saepe enim contingit quod poenitens non potest verecundari coram sacerdote, quem desideranti nec locus nec tempus offert. Et si ille cui confitetur potestatem solvendi non habet, fit tamen dignus venia, ex desiderio sacerdotis."

[3] The late Teetaert, op. cit., pp. 50–4, 243–5, over-emphasizes the part of the tract dealing with laical confession. He himself recognizes (p. 54) that the author does not attribute sacramental character to laical confession. But by concentrating on this part of the work, Teetaert gives a somewhat incorrect impression of the tenor of the book. Although he is correct in pointing out the great influence which this work had, owing to ascription to St Augustine, its influence, we think, lies precisely in the opposite direction envisaged by Teetaert, namely in the direction of the thesis of necessary sacerdotal confession. The work of Anciaux provides a wholesome corrective, at least as far as theory is concerned.

[4] Cf. also Lanfranc, *Libellus de celanda confessione*, PL. cl. 629; and Bonizo of Sutri, *Liber de vita christiana*, ix. 3.

[5] The priest's function resembled that of a civil judge, cf. A. Teetaert, "Quelques Summae de penitentia anonymes de la Bibl. Nat. de Paris" in *Misc. G. Mercati*, ii. 315: "Le ministère du prêtre au confessionel présentait des multiples ressemblances avec l'activité du juge civil."

parish priests is made the subject of Innocent III's decree in the Lateran Council.[1] But this necessity posed many problems with which the juristic theologians and still less the canonists could concern themselves, namely the purely theological aspects of penitence, such as the substance of the sacrament, the problems of repentance and expiation, the elements constituting contrition and its distinction from attrition, the theological position of the priest himself acting as a confessor—a problem that had to be faced ruthlessly when once theology had established the unique efficacy of contrition: but if God alone remits sins, what precise theological significance was to be attributed to the intervention of the priest?[2] These and numerous other extremely difficult theological questions were to be thrashed out in the twelfth century in such a manner which brought into clear relief the differences between speculative and juristic theology. What we would maintain is that the emergence of these problems was conditioned by the tenet of necessary sacerdotal confession.

Penitence is a classic example of the intimate connexion between speculative theology and its juristic counterpart: it is an amphibious institute equally partaking in both departments of theology.[3] But the

---

[1] For details see P. Browe, "Die Pflichtbeichte im Mittelalter" in *Z. f. kath. Theologie*, lvii (1933), pp. 335–83. The view of K. Burdach, "Walther's Kampf gegen Innocenz III" in *Z. f. Kirchengeschichte*, lv (1936), pp. 463–5, 475–8, overlooks the juristic element in confession. In this context attention should be drawn to the thirteenth-century introduction of a second laying on of hands at a priestly ordination, specifically signifying the ordinand's power to forgive and retain sins. The juristic temper of the time also accounts for the emergence of the intitute of indulgences, i.e. the remission of the *temporal* punishments for sins, according to a certain scale. One of the earliest indulgences was granted by Urban II in 1096 (PL. cli. 447–9; translated by W. E. Lunt, *Papal revenues*, cit., ii. no. 510). The excrescences of this institute, too well known, belong to the late medieval period. Cf. the classic work of N. Paulus, *Geschichte des Ablasses*, vols. i and ii, Paderborn, 1922.

[2] Cf., e.g., the interesting distinction which Roland (Alexander III) made between the two aspects of sin: this distinction reflects Roland's juristic temper: "Licet in cordis contritione sit peccatum remissum, non tamen superfluit oris confessio seu operis satisfactio. Peccando enim Deum et ecclesiam offendimus, Deum offendimus male *cogitando*, ecclesiam scandalizamus perverse *agendo*, et sicut duos offendimus, et duobus satisfacere debemus, Deo per cordis contritionem, ecclesiae per oris confessionem et operis satisfactionem," quoted from Anciaux, op. cit., p. 211, note 3. Roland was a faithful adherent of Abelard (Anciaux, p. 208) as was also Gratian himself (supra 372), see Anciaux, pp. 196–208 and pp. 302–12, for an exhaustive treatment of Gratian's doctrine. For the importance of Robert Pulleyn and his influence, see ibid., pp. 231 ff. and 335 ff., 609.

[3] Cf. also A. Teetaert, art. cit., p. 316: "Une fusion intime entre les domaines de ces deux sciences."

energizing of both theological branches and the subsequent acquisition of an autonomous status by canonistics as the twelfth century proceeds, brought about the necessity of providing the "simplex sacerdos" with appropriate manuals of instruction. The old penitentials would no longer do, since they were far too crude and generalizing to be of any use now that both speculative and juristic theology had made such great strides in the penetration of the sacrament.[1] Moreover, by their very nature the penitentials left no scope to the priestly judge for the exercise of any judicial functions as they were understood as a result of the deepening of legal studies: the priest's function consisted of imposing the punishment.[2] On the other hand, there were the learned theological[3] and juristic works which dealt with the subject, but they were far too intricate and difficult to be understood by the ordinary priest who after all was to administer the sacrament.[4] The way out of this impasse created by the increased specialization was the literary species of the *Summa Confessorum*[5] which conveyed in a diluted and easily understandable manner—not unlike that of a modern textbook— the theological and canonistic doctrines appertaining to penitence. They were destined for the ordinary priests who were to apply academic doctrines in their daily work. They might be called manuals of confessional instruction,[6] hence they were severely utilitarian and practical, and were shorn of all literary apparatus, but they fulfilled a great need which arose out of the increase in sacerdotal confession. To judge by the number of still surviving manuscripts these *Summae Confessorum* appear to have successfully answered the need of the time. They were the practical transmitters of hierocratic tenets in its day-to-day

---

[1] On this cf. also Oakley in *Speculum*, xv (1940), p. 212.

[2] See supra p. 375 n. 1.

[3] The feature of specialization to which we have referred before, applies to speculative theology also: here the number of *libelli* or *opuscula* dealing with penitence alone is extraordinarily high.

[4] A. Teetaert, art. cit., p. 314: these works were "trop érudites et trop coutaux ... destinés aux professeurs et aux hommes verses dans le droit canon et les études théologiques."

[5] Also called *Summa de penitentia*, or *Liber penitentiarius* or *Summa de casibus conscientiae*, or *Speculum manuale sacerdotum* or *Confessionale* or *Formulae confessionis quotidianae* or *Flores penitentiae*.

[6] Cf., e.g., the tract of Peter of Poitiers which stands somewhat between the old penitentials and the new confessional literature; it was written before 1215, but during Innocent III's pontificate, see A. Teetaert, "Le Liber Poenitentiarius de Pierre de Poitiers" in *Festschrift f. Martin Grabmann*, Munster, 1935, i. 310–31; parts of the tract are here edited, pp. 318 ff.

application; they were potent agencies in the service of the *societas christiana.*[1]

[1] The whole subject of the *Summae Confessorum* is far too little studied. Cf., apart from Teetaert's article, J. Dieterle, "Die Summae confessionum" in *Z. f. Kirchengschichte*, xxiv (1903), pp. 353–74, 520–48; xv (1904), pp. 248–72; xxvi (1905), pp. 59–81, 349–62; xxvi (1906), pp. 70–9, 166–88, 296–310, 431–42; xxviii (1907), pp. 401–31. The English contribution seems to have been very great. Apart from Guy of Southwick (Cf. A. Wilmart, "Un opuscule sur la confession, composé par Guy de Southwick" in *Recherches de théologie médievale et ancienne*, vii (1935), pp. 337–52) and Bartholomew of Exeter's *Penitentiale* (ed. A. Morey, *Bartholomew of Exeter*, Cambridge, 1937, pp. 175–300) there are the little known, but influential works of Robert of Flamesbury, Thomas of Chabham, whose *Summa* seems to have been a best seller, William Rovying, John Walleys, Edmund Rich, Richard Wethershet, and so forth, none of whom is edited.

# CHAPTER XII

# The Defence of the Lay Thesis

A STUDY of the growth of hierocratic doctrine requires that some account be given of the opponents, that is, of the literary exponents of what in default of a better term we may call the lay thesis. Since no exhaustive account of the diversified literary products can be given in this essay, we must confine ourselves to the presentation of a few outstanding literary adherents of the lay thesis. We should bear in mind, however, that the paucity of manuscripts containing these anti-hierocratic works would suggest that there was no great public demand for them; hence the assumption is justified that their influence was limited.

## I

Peter Crassus, the Ravenna jurist, entitles his tract significantly enough *In Defence of King Henry*.[1] The tenor of the work is on the whole defensive, but, as is so often the case, from the clear statement of a defensive position, some constructive ideas emerge. Most of the tract concerns itself with the problem of whether the monk Hildebrand —Gregory VII is never referred to in any other way—was entitled to excommunicate King Henry: Peter Crassus denies the pope that right. His work assumes especial significance in that it utilizes Roman law ideology in order to buttress the monarchic function of Henry.[2] And from this point of view, the *Defence* is a remarkable piece of writing and symptomatically demonstrates how energizing and vitalizing the implementation of hierocratic doctrine must have been.

To Peter Crassus the king's position is that of a "tutor of the peace," appointed for this particular purpose by divine dispensation: and in the exercise of this function he is and must be unimpeded by anyone, including the "pastor" of the Patarini, Gregory VII.[3] The

[1] Ed. in MGH. LdL., i. 434 ff.

[2] Cf. C. N. S. Woolf, *Bartolus of Sassoferrato*, Cambridge, 1913, p. 70: "The treatise announces the entry of Roman law into medieval political thought."

[3] Cap. 3, p. 437: "Ad haec rex Henricus dispensatione divina in regno successit, ut eisdem pacis tutor existeret, sine controversia vestri pastoris regnum gubernaret."

Lord Himself had given to Henry his kingdom and nobody else.[1] Henry's kingdom is not the "kingdom of your pope," he addresses the Milanese party leaders, but is a "regnum Dei," of which the pope has no right whatsoever to dispose. The kingdom is entirely in the king's hands. Peter's idea of the function of the king is the old idea of a royal protector: as such he is responsible not only for law and order, but also for the true orthodox faith, as it is evidenced by the invocation of *Cunctos populos*.[2] The faith propounded by the "Romans" and thus prescribed is orthodox, not by virtue of any authority of the Roman Church, but by virtue of the authority which had deemed it advisable to endorse that faith and make it the issue of the law. In his function as a protector in the royal sense, the secular ruler issues his laws, not only the one to which reference has just been made, but all his laws, for it is he who supplies the laws for the sake of the whole of Christianity. The *leges* are indeed "sacratissimae."[3] Hence, the king's laws, because they emanate from him who was divinely appointed, must be obeyed by everyone, including popes: for these laws had been issued "pro sua et suorum *utilitate*."[4] The interference—and it is nothing less —of monk Hildebrand has therefore done untold harm to all and everyone.[5] What the hierocratic opponents forget, according to Peter, is that St Ambrose himself had declared the prince to be the image of God and that, consequently, the prince "*vicem Dei* agit."[6] The appeal to St Paul's exhortation suggested itself.[7] Considering this derivation of power, the king's laws are not merely "sacratissimae," but in fact

[1] Cap. 3, p. 437: "Illud enim et divinutus datum testatur liquido Daniel propheta 'Domini est regnum et cui vult, dabit illud' " (*Dan.* iv. 14).

[2] *Cod. Just.* I. i. 1: "Cunctos populos quos clementiae nostrae regit imperium, in tali volumus religione versari, quam divinum Petrum apostolum tradidisse Romanis religio usque adhuc ab ipso insinuata declarat . . ."

[3] Cap. 6, p. 443: "Attendite, quaeso, quod leges, quas piissimi imperatores pro vestra vestrorumque filiorum ac totius christianitatis salvatione condiderunt, unius monachi pertinacia solvere ac delere laborat."

[4] Cap. 6, p. 443: In support Peter quotes *Cod. Just.* I. xiv. 9: "Leges sacratissimae, quae *constringunt vitas omnium*, *ab omnibus* intelligi debent."

[5] Cap. 3, p. 437: "In Henrici itaque regis laesione pacis auctorem, pacis praedicatores pacisque tutores insolentia vestri papae pariter omnes laesos esse, cunctorum sententia absoluta est."

[6] Cap. 7, p. 450: "Ambrosius: 'Principes hos dicunt reges, qui propter corrigendam vitam et prohibenda adversa creantur; Dei enim habent imaginem, ut sub uno sint caeteri.' Idcirco ideo dicit apostolus praestare subjectionem regibus, per quam sciant non esse liberos, sed sub potestate agere, quae ex Deo est, id est, sub principe suo, qui *vicem Dei agit*." The passage ascribed to Ambrose comes from the Ambrosiaster, not from Ambrose himself. Cf. Ambrosiaster, in CSEL. l, pp. 63, 147, cc. 35, 91 (*Quaestiones veteris et novi testamenti*).

[7] *Rom.* xiii. 1–2; cf. also I *Pet.* ii. 13–14.

"divinae," and disobedience to them exposes the offender to the charge of sacrilege.[1]

These views of Peter Crassus are the effluence of his thesis that human society is divided into two distinct classes, the "clerus" and the "populus." Not, we take note, Christian society, but human society as such, shows this division into separate parts; consequently the two systems of law, the secular and ecclesiastical laws, apply to two different sets of people. The consequence is that "clerus" and "ecclesia" become identical, that, in other words, the hierocratically conceived Christian body politic as an autonomous, juristic and universal entity is denied: this hierocratic concept begins to evaporate into a mere fellowship of Christian brotherhood devoid of organic and juristic elements.

The Creator of all things, Petrus argues, had given mankind two sets of laws—"*duplices* ei contulit *leges*"—of which the one set He assigned through the instrumentality of the apostles and their successors to ecclesiastical men,[2] the other through emperors and kings to secular men.[3] There can be little doubt that Peter Crassus's tract presents to us an early revolt against the canon law as understood by the hierocrats, namely, a universally binding set of rules: Peter restricts the applicability of canon law to the ecclesiastics and wishes to see in canon law merely an ecclesiastical law. There must be no interference by this ecclesiastical law of the *leges*.[4] These civil laws were given by God and it was through them, and through no other set of laws, that the Romans governed their empire: for once having conquered a people, the Romans set about to rule them by law—"Romanis deinceps *legibus regere* curabant"—and the vital necessity of these Roman laws for rulership is also proved by the Preface of Justinian to the

---

[1] Cap. 4, p. 439: with a quotation from *Cod. Just.* IX. xix. 1: "Qui divinae legis sanctitatem aut nesciendo omittunt aut negligendo violant et offendunt, sacrilegium committunt."

[2] Cap. 4, p. 438: "Harum unam per apostolos successoresque eorum *ecclesiasticis* assignavit *viris.*"

[3] Cap. 4, p. 438: "Alteram vero per imperatores et reges saecularibus distribuit hominibus." He believes to find support in St Augustine's dictum: "Ipsa jura humana per imperatores et reges saeculi distribuit humano generi," *Expositio Johannis Evangelii*, c. i, tract. 6, no. 25. It is not without interest that Peter Crassus knew the significance of Gelasius's famous *Duo quippe* letter too well to adduce it in his support, although he was perfectly familiar with Pseudo-Isidore, which must have acquainted him with Gelasius's letter. Nor does Peter operate with the *Lex Regia* as the forged documents did and thus he does not lay himself open to the easy hierocratic counter-attack. His king is God's representative on earth.

[4] Loc. cit., with a reference to *Cod. Just.* IX. xix. 1.

*Institutes*.[1] Just how necessary these laws were at his time, Peter says, could be seen when they were not enforced: then there will reign *injustitia*. Abolish the civil laws, he declares, and the result is that that monk Hildebrand, that despiser of the sacred canons, takes a delight in the royal command of an army.[2] The excommunication of Henry, the sowing of all sorts of treacheries in his kingdom by monk Hildebrand, are indeed actions not sanctioned by the *leges*: they are in fact actions "contra leges."[3] All this is against divine ordinance; it creates instability and insecurity within the kingdom, which to prevent is precisely the task of the *leges*. More than that: Hildebrand, having prepared the murder of Henry, was a common criminal who had violated the *leges* and must thus stand his trial as a criminal before the monarch's tribunal.[4] Monk Hildebrand is an enemy of the laws, an enemy of peace, an enemy of the whole of Christianity: "Monachus Hildebrandus, hostis legum, hostis pacis, totius christianitatis hostis."[5]

[1] "Imperatoriam majestatem non solum armis decoratam, sed etiam legibus oportet esse armatam."

[2] "Sed quia leges, per quas imperatores et reges iniquitatem malorum hominum compescere debent, abolitae sunt et nusquam apparent, vexat regnum injustitia, gaudet habere regiam in militia potestatem Ildebrandus monachus, sanctorum canonum contemptor." Cf. also cap. 6, p. 445: "Abolitis legibus nonne parum vivere a brutis animalibus redarguimur?"

[3] Cap. 6, p. 441.

[4] Cap. 4, p. 441: "Quis igitur huic legum inimico hanc poenam merito, qui filio (!) necem paravit, legibus addictam esse non censeat?", and cap. 6, p. 452: "Sed cum ecclesiasticis privilegiis destitutus penitus hoc maleficus cognoscatur, quae mora est removere eum ab ecclesia?" Cf. also p. 435: Hildebrand violated the "lex Julia et lex Plautia." What obstacle is there to putting him on trial as an outcast of the Church: "Quid ergo restat, nisi ut submotus ab ecclesia a competenti judice saeculari sententiam accipiat?" The kind of procedure envisaged by Peter is that laid down in Justinian's *Nov.* cxxiii, cap. 21, § 1 = *Epitome Juliani*, cxv, cap. 34, namely that the criminal clerk or monk should be deprived of his clerical status by the bishop and then handed over to the secular justice for punishment according to human civil law. Cf. Constitutions of Clarendon, cap. iii.

[5] Cap. 6, p. 445. It is no doubt interesting to note that in the early fourteenth century John of Paris posed the problem of a pope fomenting a rebellion against the king (of France) and, anti-hierocrat as the Dominican was, stated that the king could proceed against the pope. *De potestate regia et papali*, cap. xx (ed. J. Leclercq, Paris, 1942, p. 239): the king concludes by "probabilibus vel evidentibus argumentis quod papa vellet inimicari vel . . . aliquid machinari intenderet contra se vel regnum suum. Est enim licitum principi *abusum* gladii spiritualis repellere eo modo quo potest, etiam per gladium materialem, precipue ubi abusus gladii spiritualis vergit in malum rei publicae cuius cura regi incumbit: aliter enim sine causa gladium portaret." Cf. also ibid., p. 148, 150. This is the germ of the Gallican *Recursus ab abusu*, about which see R. Génestal, *Les origines de l'appel comme d'abus*, Paris, 1950, pp. ix ff. Later still the question was discussed whether the "most Christian king of the French" could legitimately render

Some observations seem warranted. Firstly, he restricts the civil and ecclesiastical laws to the two sets of men who are not conceived of as forming one unit, but are distinctly divided. From this follows, according to Peter, secondly that the ecclesiastical law can have no binding effects upon the "populus," whilst, on the other hand, the *leges* are applicable to the clerics: the king being the divinely appointed protector of peace within his kingdom is entitled to punish those who violate the *leges*. Thirdly and lastly, the pope's jurisdictional powers are denied. Canon law is a mere disciplinary code of law for the ecclesiastics. The pope should act in a fatherly manner—"more paterno"—but cannot exercise "patria potestas." In other words, it is religion as such with which the pope should busy himself: he should be its guardian.[1] Religion alone cannot, of course, be a governmental basis: it is the transformation of what Gregory VII had called "pura religio" into an enforceable rule, which Peter contests. What is in his mind is the conception that a kingdom can be governed only by the *leges*: the supremacy of the civil law and its exclusiveness is what Peter wishes to establish. The criterion of lawful conduct is not contained in a canon, but solely in the *lex* which is "sacratissima" and "divina."

None the less, the defence of kingship must necessarily lead to the abandonment of all universalist ideas. Peter Crassus, despite all his predilection for the universalist cause of the Roman empire, must of necessity concede to every territorial king the same basic standing as regards the civil laws as he claims for King Henry's *leges*. There must therefore be as many civil law systems as there are kingdoms. Although the Christian religion may be the same for all of them, its custodian may give paternal admonition only, but no binding rule or canon for those who are not ecclesiastics. This thesis of Peter Crassus contains the germs of the later "Rex in regno suo est imperator." Or seen from yet a different angle, his thesis will in course of time lead to the separation of law from morals: what the king has at his disposal, is the coercive law; what the priesthood and herewith the pope have at their disposal, is morals unenforceable.

No doubt these are remarkable features in a tract written in the eighties of the eleventh century. As a Roman jurist he clearly realizes

---

assistance to his allies if they were attacked by the pope "caco demone suadente" and answered in the affirmative. Cf. the *Repetitio* of Pierre d'Angleberme discovered by M. Boulet-Sautel: *Rev. hist. de droit français et étranger*, xxvi (1948), pp. 323 ff., at pp. 329 ff.

[1] Cap. 6, p. 449: "Et idcirco tota christiana religio est confusa, ex quo illum habuit custodem."

the threat which the "canons" present to the Roman law. Only in a strict adherence to, and enforcement of, the *leges sacratissimae* can peace be achieved. The character of canon law as a universally binding law is denied. But this is nothing else but the presentation of the monarchic thesis in the garb of Roman law. And yet, despite these features, the weakness of the tract lay in disregarding the character of contemporary society. Was it, at that time, sufficient to operate with the colourless "humanum genus"? Since the tract contented itself with stating that the king's function was the preservation of peace through the laws—assuredly a negative aim—what positive goal did the king pursue? These are questions which should have been answered at that time: later generations would not be perturbed by the lack of an answer to this embarrassing question. Peter Crassus's tract was not a serious threat to hierocratic doctrine since it failed to deal with the teleological problem so powerfully and attractively posed by the hierocrats.

## II

We now turn to Bishop Benzo of Alba. His attack on hierocratic tenets breathes an atmosphere entirely different from that of Peter Crassus. Here was the vision of the idealist, the exuberant enthusiast, a writer soaked in the ancient hellenistic and Roman world, an eleventh-century humanist of the purest kind, whose poetic and fluent pen indeed knew no bounds of imagination when praising the ideal of empire and the idol of emperor, whose sonorous phrases and rhymes raise his poetry above the ordinary publicistic literature of the time. The *Renovatio Romani imperii* was to him the panacea for the world's evils; steeped as he was in Romanism, his contemporary emperors, Henry III and Henry IV, were to him the successors of the Caesars. This resuscitation of the Roman empire and the resurrection of the Caesars make him dispense altogether with an attack on the primacy of the Roman Church: the Roman Church as the primatial Church of Christendom —the sheet anchor of hierocratic ideology—simply did not exist for him. In a way, Benzo's *Liber*[1] is the perfect antithesis of Cardinal Humbert's works.

Benzo's long poem is not an arid exposition of abstract theories. There is no system at all in it; it is an ingenious *tour de force*, although

---

[1] *Liber ad Heinricum IV*, ed. MGH. SS. xi. 591 ff. For a biographical sketch of the bishop see A. Fliche in DHE. viii. 298–9.

its material contribution to ecclesiastical-political thought should not be overrated. What makes it worth studying, is the very deep culture that pervades it. He is as well versed in Roman statesmen and writers and poets—Scipio, Cicero, Fabricius, Cato, Horace, Virgil, Lucan, Quintilian, Terence, and so forth—as he is familiar with Greek language and writers: Homer, Socrates, Demosthenes, Diogenes, and so forth.[1] Nor was he any less acquainted with ancient mythology—references and allusions to Hercules, Hector, Rhadamantes, are frequent. The fiery enthusiasm which he has for the emperor turns into a fiery contempt when he comes to write of contemporary popes: Alexander II is the "Asinandrellus" or "Alexandrellus," "Asinander," "papa noctulanus contra totam christianitatem." Gregory VII is invariably spoken of as "Folleprandus," "Prandellus," "Merdiprandus." All his poetical zest is directed against Hildebrand who is to him nothing more or less than "anti-christellus" or "falsissimus atque diabolicus monachellus" or "diabolus cucullatus," "stercorentius" and so forth.[2] The emphasis upon the part which he himself played in imperial affairs, through his personal contacts and his appearance at crucial moments, is another feature that characterizes the work and its

---

[1] Cf., for instance, his Latinization of Greek terms: e.g. ephemerida, p. 653, line 44; Baburrus (βαβύρρας), p. 632, line 41; hembada, p. 629, line 18; hoestum (οἶστρον), p. 619, line 2; bravium (βραβεῖον), p. 605, line 14; rampnos (ῥάμνος) = rhamnos, p. 605, line 8; prohelempsis (προέλευσις) = processus publicus, p. 602, line 23; hempyrium, p. 641, line 22; psiaticus (ψίαθος), p. 641, line 24; rexcleonus = conflation of κλέος and νέος, p. 649, line 22; tegnas (τέχνας), p. 676, line 40, and so on. On the general aspects of Greek culture cf. B. Bischoff, "Das griechische Element in der abendländischen Bildung des Mittelalters" in *Festschrift f. Dölger*, 1951, pp. 49 ff. Another of the eleventh-century humanists and the personal friend of Manasses of Rheims, Godfrey of Rheims, also seems to have taken up his pen in the cause of "Caesar," cf. J. R. Williams in *Speculum*, xxii (1947), p. 37.

[2] That Benzo particularly strongly objected to Gregory's monetary dealings and his connexions with Jewish bankers, is clear, cf. pp. 614, 616. The following verses give some indication of the author's contempt for Gregory VII (p. 659, lines 42 ff.):

> Saonensis Buzianus est quidam humuntio,
> Ventre latro, crure curto, par podicis nuntio,
> Tale monstrum non creavit sexuum conjunctio.
> Falsus monachus Prandellus, habet mille vitia,
> Quem cognoscimus deformem, carne leprositia,
> Ab ecclesia tollendus hac sola malicia.

> Protheus est monstruosus in diversis vultibus,
> Modo ridet, modo plangit in amixtis singultibus,
> Nocte carnibus abutens, die tantum pultibus. (p. 666, lines 15 ff.)

author.[1] This self-importance is also revealed in the opening verses of the poem.[2]

Romanism, universalism and imperialism are tautological expressions for Bishop Benzo. When the hierocratic watchword was that the pope exercised the *universale regimen*, Benzo contrasted this claim which to him was sheer usurpation, with the emperor's power. The emperor, being the true successor and heir of the Caesars,[3] represents "majestas Julii et Tyberii."[4] Rome it was that subjected the whole world to its rule; Europe was made by Rome, the "caput mundi."[5] Rightly is the emperor extolled, ruling as he does over all the kings of the world: "magnificatur super omnes reges universae terrae,"[6] for he is the *imperator orbis terrarum*.[7] What difference there is between him and the mere kinglings, the "reguli provinciarum" or the "regulelli"! The grandiose idea embodied in Roman emperorship is best seen when imperial and royal coronations are compared. The latter is performed by two "episcopelli" who raise the princeling of the one region to the status of a "regulellus" and the "solemn procession" at a royal coronation consists of an iron cross bearer followed by an illiterate, rustic rabble. What splendour, what ceremonial, what profound meaning there is in an imperial coronation.[8]

The universal rulership of the emperor, his monarchic rule, is the

[1] Cf. his lively and graphic description of the events after the death of Nicholas II and the stress on his personal part, pp. 612–13.

[2] Cf. the prologue, p. 597. In another place Benzo contrasts his approach with that of the lukewarm imperial bishops whom he treated "ferreis increpationibus durisque exortationibus," whilst different methods of dealing were indicated in the case of Adelaide: "Sed alia manu erat agendum cum domna Adeleida, cuius parem non assignat ephymerida. Ipsa igitur, quasi regina piscium, ammirabilis balena, non poterat capi neque hamo neque catena. Quapropter adgressus est eam frater Benzo mellifluis verbis porrigens ei escas ex floribus, necnon aromaticis herbis. Et quia noverat eam dilectari planetarum cantilenis, cottidie infundebat auribus eius Ambrosianas melodias, maritimis associatis Syrenis, et ita lyrizando, organizando, deduxit eam in sagenam fidei, traxitque ad litus ante pedes imperatoris Heinrici . . ." pp. 653–4.

[3] See p. 611; cf. also p. 603, line 35: "imperatorum succesor factus."

[4] p. 656, line 22.

[5] p. 598: "Heuropam his jungentes fecerunt *monarchiam*, Roma dehinc exaltatur eiusque imperium . . . subjugavit totum mundum Romana potentia."

[6] p. 600, line 2.

[7] p. 602, line 13. In parenthesis we may note that Benzo's archiepiscopal brother, Alfanus of Salerno, had showered on the future pope almost the same epithets in the poem dedicated to Archdeacon Hildebrand. Hildebrand was the successor of Marius and Caesar: St Peter was "Consul Caesarque," cf. on this N. Lenkeith, *Dante and the Legend of Rome*, London, 1952, pp. 9–10. On Alfanus see P. E. Schramm, *Kaiser*, i. 248–50.

[8] p. 602, lines 25 ff.:

direct effluence of his being the successor of the Caesars. Imperial
power, in an ideational sense at least, is universal monarchic rule:

Tantus es, Caesar, quantus et orbis.[1]

Not only are the various kinglings of the provinces subjected to the
Roman empire in its medieval shape, but they have also to render
services, as a sign of their subjection.[2] Man's language is incapable of
expressing the glory and honour of Rome adequately—"nulla humana
lingua potest explicare talem gloriam tantumque honorem"—unless
indeed one sees in the Roman empire, in Rome herself, the manifestation of God's will. For it was through the merits of the apostles that
Rome's empire was sanctified.[3]

O Roma, Romani, ideo super gentes omnes preposuit vos Creator generis
humani.[4]

According to the poet, the whole world awaits the emperor as if
he were a redeemer: "Omnis terra expectat eum quasi redemptorem."[5]

---

> Portatur ante eum sancta crux gravida ligni dominici
> et lancea sancti Mauricii.
> Deinde sequitur venerabilis ordo episcoporum.
> Tunc rex indutus bysino podere
> auro et gemmis insertis, mirabili opere
> terribilis calcaribus aureis, accinctus ense,
> adopertus Frisia clamide, imperiali veste,
> habens manus involutas cyrotecis lineis (!)
> cum anulo pontificali
> glorificatus insuper diademate imperiali
> portans in sinistra aureum *pomum*,
> quod significat *monarchiam regnorum*,
> in dextera vero sceptrum imperii,
> de more Julii, Octaviani et Tyberii;
> quem sustentant ex una parte papa Romanus,
> ex altera parte archipontifex Ambrosianus.
> Hinc et inde duces, marchiones et comites,
> et diversorum procerum ordines.

Contrasted with a royal coronation, ibid.:

> Duo igitur episcopelli
> sustentant manus unius provinciae regulelli,
> antecedit eum ferrea crucicula,
> retro prosequitur agrestis plebicula.

[1] p. 668, line 36; cf. also p. 644.
[2] p. 647: "Decet utique quatenus omnes ordines ex provinciis regnorum,
quae sub se continet Romanum imperium, ut afferant *suo imperatori* munera,
unusquisque juxta suae professionis ministerium."
[3] p. 603, lines 7–8: "Per quorum (scil. apostolorum) sanctum meritum Roma
tenet imperium."          [4] p. 631, line 8.
[5] p. 605, line 4. About the ancient idea of a saviour and redeemer see supra,
p. 16 n. 3.

Directly descending from the heavens, the emperor is no man of mere flesh—"De coelo missus, non homo carnis"[1]—but the "vicar of the Creator";[2] he is the true image of God.[3] He is divinity become flesh, he is the "christus Domini"[4] and God walks, so to speak, of front of him.[5] What therefore Christ has said of Himself, is directly applicable to His vicar: "He who despiseth you, despiseth me."[6] The government of the world exercised monarchically by the emperor, is the divine way of governing. The whole Christian world should rise in praise of the Creator Who had chosen His vice-gerent.[7]

It is consistent with Benzo's point of view that the emperor regulates all sacerdotal life. Whatever the priests have, whatever they are, whatever status they occupy, it is through the medium of the "vicar of the Creator." They are set in the house of God by the will of the emperor, not by that of a "Folleprandus."[8] Accordingly, they owe subjection to their "plantator" and not to a "supplantor."[9] They should rise in praise of their lord, who had given them all they have.[10] The bishops in particular should show their gratitude to the emperor by some form of military service on his behalf: military service is the outward acknowledgment of the emperor's instrumentality in raising them to the height of their position. The pope himself, according to Benzo, must be created by the emperor: the creation of Clement III appears to him the ideal way of making a pope: "Caesare praecipiente, papa benedicitur." This was so in the time of the Ottos and Henry's father, and so it should be. This imperial right of appointing a pope flows also from the emperor's duty to protect the apostolic see and to govern it.[11] It is therefore against all historical evidence when the "Sarabaita" (Gre-

---

[1] p. 669, line 1.

[2] "Vicarius Conditoris" (p. 609, line 37).

[3] p. 606, line 4; cf. also p. 655, line 30: "Vult enim Deus, quo geras reipublicae sarcinam cum eo, qui regnorum regit monarchiam."

[4] p. 656, line 12.

[5] p. 605, line 2: "Ipse Deus vadit ante Heinricum christum suum, praeparans ei victoriae cumulum."

[6] p. 655, line 25 (*Luke* x. 16).

[7] p. 601, lines 35–6: "Tota igitur christianitas assurgat in laudem Creatoris, qui contra hostiles impetus reddit terribiles aquilas christianissimi imperatoris."

[8] p. 634, line 17: "In domo etenim Domini estis plantati manibus regis, non manibus Folleprandi."

[9] p. 634, line 18: "Oportet itaque ut sitis subjecti plantatori, minime autem supplantori."

[10] p. 599, lines 16 ff.: "Omnes surgant ad scribendum victorias Caesaris." The "omnes" are "praesules et sacerdotes, abbates et clerici, quicumque sunt de sorte Dei ordines angelici."

[11] p. 671, lines 4 ff.

gory VII) asserts that he can promote to imperial dignity whomsoever he pleases.[1]

It is something unheard of, Benzo holds, for the election of the most important official of the *sacerdotium* to be in the hands of monks. Papal elections are not the business of monks. They are fugitives of St Benedict if they try to meddle in papal elections.[2] And what monks! Perjurors and ravishers![3] Nothing better can be said about the Normans who should be called "Nomans" ("Nullimanni") interfering as they do in papal elections: this really amounts to a degradation of the papal office, for they do nothing but roam about in the streets and squares "utpote frenetici."[4]

The apotheosis of imperial power was reached at the time of Otto III:

> O vir virorum, o imperator imperatorum,
> cuius liberalitas erit memorialis per saecula saeculorum,

whilst Henry is gently taken to task for earlier dualist mollifications:

> Duobus servire qui nititur,
> Stultissimus omnium dicitur.[5]

Man cannot serve two masters[6] and man's salvation depends upon his obedience to the divine word revealed as it is in the person and the laws of His vicar, the emperor. By rendering to Caesar what is his, God is thereby rendered what is His.[7]

> Regis enim victoria
> Salus est populorum
> Et ecclesiarum gloria.

There is no need for us to stress that the Italian bishop's vivacious poem represents the exact parallel to the hierocratic thesis. According to him, autonomous and universal character can be attributed only to the *Imperium Romanum*, and not to the corporate Christian body politic. What the hierocrats applied to the latter, Benzo applies to the

---

[1] p. 670: "Dixerat enim ille Sarabaita, quod in sua potestate esset, quem vellet ad imperium promovere, et quem nollet removere."

[2] p. 671, lines 27 ff.: "Fugitivi estis sancti Benedicti, sub nulla regula vultis esse districti."

[3] p. 672, lines 40 ff.: "Monachos dico, et quales monachos! Perjuriis infamatos, stupris monialium sordidatos Et isti sunt creatores paparum."

Cf. also p. 614, lines 29 ff.: "Non est auditum a saeculis saeculorum, Quod ordinatio papae est in manibus monachorum."

[4] p. 622, line 22.　　　　　　　　　[5] p. 645, line 51.
[6] *Matt.* vi. 24.　　　　　　　　　　[7] p. 602, lines 4–5.

former. "Christianitas" is to him no more than a religious concept: it is not what the hierocrats conceived it to be, namely the notion designating a corporate juristic organic entity. The Christian faith is not the constitutive element of the universal Roman empire. Hence the pope cannot appear as the monarch: the emperor alone is monarch because he alone is the vicar of the Creator. This is the true monarchic conception in a universal framework within which the kings become mere provincial governors ("reguli"). And the utilization of the apostolic sojourn in Rome heralds later and very similar interpretations.[1] The pope's function is that of a head of the priesthood, and no more. But the priests are members of the universal empire, and so is the pope, and accordingly he and they owe subjection to the emperor.

Benzo avoids one great difficulty, namely that afforded by the proprietary church system. To him, it appears, all clerical appointments are direct imperial nominations; the appointed clerics constitute merely a kind of imperial civil service. But whilst he bypasses this difficulty, his theory has nevertheless serious flaws. Firstly, he does not even attempt to answer the Gregorian argument of the binding and loosing: is his idol, the emperor, not a Christian and as such subjected to the papal "potestas ligandi et solvendi"? And if he is, what are the limits of this papal "potestas" when applied to the emperor? And if he is not, where is the evidence for exempting the emperor? Secondly, by what unimpeachable documentary authority does the emperor function in the way in which Benzo wishes him to function? And thirdly, how did this universal Roman empire come about? These are vital questions for the answers of which we will look in vain in Benzo's poem. One feels that the author was somewhat uneasy when in the midst of all the din of eulogy and poetry, he writes about the Franks and Teutons having reached the apex of imperial dignity and in the same context speaks of the Greek emperor who is a mere "Rex Bizanzenus." How did this degradation of the Eastern emperor come about? How in other words does Benzo's emperor become a truly universal "Imperator Romanorum" if not through papal volition? To these questions Benzo could not give an answer without jeopardizing all that his venerated idol, the emperor, stood for.

---

[1] Cf. E. Jordan, "Dante et la théorie romaine de l'empire" in *Nouvelle Revue historique de droit français et étranger*, xlvi (1922), pp. 203 f. Miss Nancy Lenkeith, op. cit., takes no account of Benzo's poem.

## III

From yet another angle the hierocratic thesis and its application are vigorously assailed by the Anglo-Norman Anonymous, the author of the *York Tracts*.[1] There is none of the lively imagination and enthusiasm so characteristic of the Italian bishop: here writes a scholarly theologian in a detached, severe and cool manner. He fixes upon the strongest point of hierocratic thought, that namely because all the believers in Christ form one concrete, coherent, organized body, because they constitute a corporate entity, the papal monarch alone is functionally qualified to govern that body. The author of the tracts rightly perceives that the primatial claim of the Roman Church must be assailed, if hierocratic doctrine is to be effectively attacked. He rightly saw that a mere restriction of the papal primacy to certain issues only, would not do: if hierocratic doctrine was to be uprooted, it must be assailed at its most vital point, the Petrine commission. This attempt to demolish the papacy's primatial claim is the negative side of the author's thesis. Its positive and constructive side is focused upon the establishment of a link between Christ and the king. For the hierocrats the link between Christ and the pope was established by Scripture: for their anonymous opponent that link between Christ and the monarchical king was established by theological speculation.

He too operates with the conception of the corporate entity of the "populus Dei" or the "congregatio fidelium Christi" which form the "house of God."[2] He argues that the hierocratic claim rests upon the tenet of the primacy of the Roman Church, through which the pope appears as the "apostolus Christi."[3] If this claim is correct, then the pope "suscipiendus est a nobis quasi apostolus Christi in omni reverentia et honore propter mittentis auctoritatem."[4] Nevertheless, if one looks at the mandates issuing forth from the pontiff in Rome, one

---

* 
†    [1] That these thirty-five tracts were not written by the same author was the theme of Ph. Funk, "Der fragliche Anonymus von York" in *Hist. Jb.*, lv (1935), pp. 251–76. The ideological and linguistic unity of all these tracts cannot be disputed. Cf., apart from Böhmer's works, P. de Lapparent, "Un précurseur de la réforme anglaise: l'anonyme d'York" in *Archives d'histoire doctrinale et littéraire du Moyen Age*, xxi (1946), pp. 149–68; this author is inclined to accept Böhmer's earlier ascription of these tracts to Archbishop Gerard of York (p. 165). About a new and not unattractive ascription to Archbishop William Bona Anima of Rouen see G. H. Williams, *The Norman Anonymous of 1100 A.D.*, 1951 (Harvard Theological Studies, vol. xviii), especially pp. 102–27.

[2] Ed. MGH. LdL. iii, tract iv, p. 663, lines 14–19.

[3] Ed. MGH. LdL. iii, tract v, p. 680, line 17.

[4] Ed. MGH. LdL. iii, tract v, p. 680, lines 23–35.

cannot very well say that they contain the "voluntas Christi," that in other words, what is prescribed by the pope, harmonizes with evangelical or apostolic doctrine.[1] For these are either openly against established Christian doctrine or they circumvent apostolic teachings, with the result that the corporate body of the Christians, is divided between those who follow the pope and those who do not.

But this corporate union of all the Christians, the universal Church, does not and can not suffer division, for it is "unum corpus," that is, the "populus fidelium." Just as one part of the human body is not the human body itself, so no part of the universal Church constitutes the whole Church.[2]

The head of the one and undivided body is Christ Himself.[3] The bond that unites all the members of this one universal body is "una fides, unum baptisma,"[4] but certainly not obedience to the pope in Rome. And when the hierocratic doctrinaires base themselves upon the Petrine commission, they are very much mistaken in their interpretation of Christ's words to St Peter. In the first place, St Peter was not constituted as a judge over the other apostles, or as their head or prince who could command obedience from them.[5] And in the second place, the crucial words—"Tu es Petrus . . ."—did not specifically apply to St Peter alone, but to all the apostles: "Ego dico tibi, *quia* tu es Petrus . . ." St Peter only received these words from Christ on behalf of the others: "pro omnibus ab ipso responsum accepit."[6] Consequently, each apostle was equal to St Peter, each individual church represents

[1] There follows a list of gravamina against the papal government, for instance, the command to bishops to visit Rome annually, p. 680 (often leading to the bishops divesting themselves of their clerical habits "ne agnoscentur, ut episcopi sint," p. 681); the resulting absenteeism, p. 681; the exaction of obedience from bishops and abbots, pp. 681–2; excommunication and deposition in cases of disobedience; unwarranted translation of bishops, p. 684; prohibition of concubinage; and so forth.

[2] "Nulla igitur pars unius ecclesiae per se ecclesia est, nulla pars corporis per se corpus Christi est, sicut nulla pars corporis humani per se hominis corpus est," tract no. 2 in H. Böhmer, ed. in his *Kirche und Staat in England*, Leipzig, 1899, p. 439.

[3] *Kirche und Staat in England*, p. 439: "Omnes insimul partes una sunt ecclesia, unum corpus Christi . . . quorum omnium caput est unum, Christus" with a reference to *Col.* i. 18: "And he is the head of the body, of the church."

[4] *Kirche und Staat in England*, p. 440.

[5] *Kirche und Staat in England*, p. 443: "Licet enim b. Petrus apostolorum princeps dictus sit, non tamen apostolorum judex constitutus esse vel de illis judicasse vel subjectionem ab eis expetiisse legitur."

[6] *Kirche und Staat in England*, p. 443. It may be that the author here relies on the Cyprianic exposition in *De catholicae ecclesiae unitate*, cap. 4 (ed. CSEL. iii. 209 f.). Cf. also Cyprian's *Ep.* lxxxi, cap. 3.

St Peter in so far as Christ is acknowledged as "the Son of the living God."[1] Moreover, "petra" (rock) means not St Peter at all, but Christ Himself[2] who alone is the "petra": "qui est petra," and from Christ all those who believe in Him, have received the power to bind and to loose.[3] Hence, none of the other apostles had received this power from St Peter, but from Christ Himself: "sed ab ipso Christo, Deo et homine."[4] It is an unwarranted assertion to say that Christ had made St Peter a prince of the apostles who thereby had become his satellites.[5] All apostles were equal.[6]

There is, then, no biblical foundation at all for the primatial claim of the Roman Church. For if St Peter was not superior to the other apostles, the pope cannot be superior to the other bishops. Being without any scriptural basis, the primatial claim can rest only on human grounds, of which the most conspicuous is the purely historical fact that the city of Rome was once the capital of the Roman empire (as well as, he adds, the head of many errors) and so it became through the physical presence of Peter and Paul the capital of religion: but let there be no mistake about it that the two apostles could not be what they were without—Jerusalem.[7] The alleged divine origin of the Roman Church's primacy gives way to a human explanation.[8] If any church can claim primacy, it is Jerusalem alone, which is the mother of all. For here in Jerusalem, Michael, the "princeps coelestis exercitus," had his "principatus," and Gabriel had his "municipatus";[9] in Jerusalem also there were the patriarchs and prophets to whom God Himself had spoken in person and had shown His secrets.[10] And from this

---

[1] *Matt.* xvi. 16: "Thou art the christ, the son of the living God."

[2] See I *Cor.* x. 4: "Petra autem erat Christus."

[3] ". . . petra, et ab ipso accepit claves regni coelorum et potest ligare et solvere."

[4] Also according to St John's gospel, St Peter received his power together with the others (*John* xx. 22): "Qui (scil. Christus) resurgens a mortuis et veniens ad eos sufflavit et dixit eis . . . hoc itaque Petrus non fecit eis nec hanc gratiam contulit, sed pariter cum eis accepit," p. 443.

[5] Ibid., "Neque legitur quod a Christo vel ab eius apostolis Petrus apostolorum princeps sit nuncupatus; neque legitur, ut huius principis ceteri apostoli satellites vel ministri sint appellati vel a Petro judicati."

[6] Tract 23a, p. 475, ed. cit.: "Divina institutione nullus inter apostolos major fuit, nullus magisterium vel principatum in alios habuit . . . fecerat eos equales." Cf. also ibid., p. 476: "In his omnibus apostolorum equalitas intelligitur, quia haec omnia equaliter acceperunt."

[7] Tract iii, LdL., p. 660, lines 22–5: "Romana ecclesia praefertur, hoc fit propter potentiam imperii et dignitatem urbis, ut quae videlicet erat caput orbis et princeps erroris, caput quoque fieret religionis."

[8] Tract iii, LdL., p. 660: "Verumtamen hoc ab hominibus institutum est, non a Christo Deo vel ab apostolis."　　[9] Tract no. 12, ed. Böhmer, op. cit., p. 458.

[10] Tract no. 12, op. cit., p. 458: "Ipsa sanctos habuit patriachas et prophetas, quibus Deus locutus est et ostendit eis secreta sua et regni coelestis misteria."

seed came Christ and the redemption of the whole world originated.[1]
Here in Jerusalem it was that Christ was made priest in the order of
Melchisedek:[2] and here was the throne of David and the kingdom
"super quod Christus sedet in aeternum." It was also in Jerusalem that
all the apostles had received the powers of the keys: in short, in
Jerusalem Christ was made the head of the Church universal, of the
corporate body of Christians. What claim has Rome to counterbalance
these obvious facts? Apart from the imperial position nothing but the
apostolic sojourn, but the two apostles did not cease to be members of
the Church of Jerusalem because they happened to stay in Rome.[3]
Whatever the Roman Church may have, it has through its connexion
with Jerusalem which is the "ecclesia primitiva." It is this see which
"jure primatum obtinet, et propter primatum obtinere debet principatum."[4]

Perhaps the most formidable difficulty confronting the anti-
hierocratic writers was how to establish the monarchic principle in a
Christo-centric world. The difficulty concerned nothing more nor less
than the king's direct derivation of powers from Christ, so that it could
be demonstrated in a plausible manner that the king's link with Christ
was direct. Often enough before, as we have seen, has it been maintained that the king (or emperor) was vicar of Christ, but never has
there been an attempt to prove this link. In order to show it, and at the
same time to disprove the hierocratic theme, the scriptural basis of the
pope's monarchic function—the result of the Petrine commission—
had to be supplanted by a rather involved theological and christological
speculation. Our author is one of the very few medieval writers who,
seeing the virtually inexhaustible strength of the pope's primatial
position, attempts on a purely doctrinal basis to reason out the
monarchical position of the king by virtue of his continuing Christ's
powers and functions in his kingdom. How, in other words, can it be
established that not the pope, because there was no such a thing as a
primacy of the Roman Church, but the king is the legitimate, sole,

---

[1] Tract no. 12, op. cit., p. 458: "De quorum semine Christus natus et salus
et redemptio totius mundi orta est."

[2] "In ea quoque sacerdos factus est in aeternum secundum ordinem Melchisedek." On the transmission of Melchisedek in liturgical poetry, see B.
Bischoff in *Festschrift Dölger*, p. 50, note 1.

[3] "Non tamen Hierosolimitanae membra esse desierunt atque discipuli nec
principatum eius vel primatum abstulerunt nec eius auctoritatem vel dignitatem
vel meritum imminuerunt," ibid., p. 459, ed. cit. This argument was later dealt
with by Innocent III in *Reg.* ii. 209.

[4] Ibid. 461, cap. 2.

hence truly monarchic authority that rules the corporate body of Christians? Where, in short, is the link between the king and Christ, since there is no link between the pope and Christ?

The anonymous author and his hierocratic opponents share the thesis that Christ is "Rex et sacerdos secundum ordinem Melchisedek." But whilst hierocratic doctrine stressed, for obvious reasons, the sacerdotal part in Christ, the anonymous author stresses the regal part in Christ. Although it is true, he says, that Christ is "verus rex et sacerdos," the universal Church, His spouse, is not His spouse by virtue of His sacerdotal functions, but by virtue of His regal functions. The Church is called "regina," queen, and not "sacerdotissa," priestess.[1] Apart from this, Christ was heralded in the Old Testament in several places and no prophet can be shown who had announced Christ's coming in His function as a priest: all prophets heralded Christ as king.[2] We must realize, he says, that the priestly nature of Christ was of inferior rank in Him. The construction he chooses in order to prove his thesis—a construction which is admittedly somewhat artificial, though no doubt original—namely that there is a direct link between king and Christ, is this: Christ was not created or made or constituted a king, for He had been king from all eternity, and therefore He was equal to the Father. This equality to the Father accounts for His royal nature's being the really divine part of His being. On the other hand, He was made a priest because He allowed Himself to become Man. Christ's human nature is represented in His sacerdotal part.

Christus enim Deus et Homo, verus et summus rex et sacerdos. *Rex* est, sed *ex eternitate* divinitatis, non factus, non creatus, non inferior vel diversus a patre, sed equalis et *unus cum patre*. *Sacerdos* vero est ex assumptione humanitatis, factus secundum ordinem Melchisedek, et creatus et ideo *minor patre*.[3]

The two natures in Christ, God and Man, are symbolized by His royal and priestly functions. As king He is one with the Father, hence divine; as priest He is merely man and thus inferior to the Father.[4] It is quite in consonance with this speculation when our author holds

---

[1] He appeals to St Augustine who had called the Church "regina" of Christ, but I was unable to verify the quotation.

[2] He refers, by way of exemplification, to *Jer.* xxiii. 5–6 and to *Zach.* ix. 9: Tract iv, LdL., p. 662.

[3] Tract iv, LdL., p. 667.

[4] Tract iv, LdL., p. 667, lines 10–11: "Sacerdos inferioris officii et naturae, id est humanitatis, rex superioris, id est divinitatis."

that Christ had given promise of the kingdom of heaven, but never of the "priesthood" of heaven.[1] The important point to bear in mind, according to the author, is that when Christ created and changed things, He could do this only in the exercise of His royal functions, and not in the exercise of His sacerdotal functions: as a king He ruled, that is governed, men and angels, whilst as a priest He never performed governmental actions, but only redeemed man. The redemption of man by Christ—the effluence of His sacerdotal part—is the means by which Christians may in fact partake of His royal-divine government. As king alone He would not have been able to make His followers, all Christians, partake in the divine ordering of things: their redemption was necessary for this.[2] On the other hand, Christ could not have become priest, that is Man, without first being a king, that is, God. Christ's royalty was prior and superior to His priesthood, because in His royalty He was equal to the Father.[3] He died as a priest, not as a king.

The same relationship can be observed in the case of the king. Christ was the prototype of any king: a Christian king represents Christ on earth, in so far as not only His royalty, but also His priesthood is typified in him. The king is in every respect a *rex* and a *sacerdos*.[4] The king is "figura et imago Christi et Dei"[5] and just like his prototype he rules and governs the Christian people, by virtue of his kingship: "regnat et regit populum suum." Because Christ as king was one and equal to the Father, so the king as king too was one and equal to Christ and God: "Unde et rex Deus et Christus est"; and in so far as he governs, he exercises divine powers. If on the other hand the priests were to govern, this would mean that a certain governmental act, as for instance, the appointment and installation of the king himself, would be based upon the human side of Christ: and as a priest Christ never exercised governmental actions, being unable to do so, because

---

[1] Tract iv, LdL., p. 667, lines 17–18: "Regnum enim coelorum ubique scripturarum promittit fidelibus, nusquam autem sacerdotium."

[2] Tract iv, LdL., p. 667: "Secundum vero quod sacerdos est, homines tantum redemit, ut secum regnare faciat. Haec enim est tota intentio, qua sacerdos factus est, et se ipsum obtulit, in sacrificium, ut homines regni sui et potestatis regiae faceret esse participes."

[3] Tract iv, LdL., p. 667: "Hinc igitur apparet majorem esse in Christo regiam quam sacerdotalem potestatem et praestantiorem, tanto scilicet, quanto divinitas eius major est humanitate atque praestantior."

[4] p. 665, lines 21 ff.

[5] p. 667, line 8. On this cf. E. Kantorowicz in *Harvard Theol. Rev.*, xlv (1952), pp. 253 ff.

only in His royal functions could He create and make things, but not in His purely sacerdotal-human function. But when the king institutes the priests, this indeed is the effluence of the divine functions in Christ: it is a governmental act which a priest can not perform.[1] The consequence is that the government of the *corpus fidelium* must be in the hands of the monarchic king because he alone is the "figura et imago Christi" and hence alone functionally qualified to govern.

In pursuance of this idea the author logically claims that the *ecclesiasticum regimen* must be in the hands of the king as Christ's vicar. The unity of royal and sacerdotal powers in Christ, the unity therefore of these powers in his "figura," the king, is a necessary guarantee for the achievement of unity in the *unum corpus*. Unity of government, that is the monarchic form of government, is the necessary presupposition for unity of the body politic itself. Hence the two powers must, so to speak, be glued together—"in glutino Dei unita conventio"[2]—to ensure unity of the whole body. Monarchy alone will guarantee this. And just as royal power in Christ is superior and original, so also it is with the king.[3] Only under this presupposition can the terrestrial kingdom become a faithful and true reflexion of the celestial one when the former is presided over by the king functioning as a true monarch, that is, by the "figura Christi" who continues Christ's function as head.[4] The "terrena civitas" is the copy of the "civitas Dei" but only if it is ruled by the monarchic king[5] who is "summus typus" and "summa figura" of Christ.[6] Christendom is a corporate body politic; it is the *respublica Dei omnipotentis*.[7]

It is therefore the basic contention of our author that the (royal)

[1] "Verum si sacerdos per regem instituitur, non per potestatem hominis instituitur, sed per potestatem Dei; potestas enim regis potestas Dei est."

[2] p. 669, line 7.

[3] "Quare et a quibusdam estimatur, ut in hominibus similiter major sit et praestantior regia potestas quam sacerdotalis, et rex major et praestantior quam sacerdos, utpote melioris et praestantioris Christi naturae imitatio sive potestatis aemulatio," p. 667.

[4] Tract v, p. 685, lines 33 ff.: "Haec quidem sublimis et gloriosa investitura est, qua Deus imperatorem sive regem investit, ut habeat potestatem coelitus datam super omnes homines ad hoc, ut qui bona appetunt, adjuventur, ut coelorum via largius pateat, et terrestre regnum coelesti regno famuletur, et ut manui suae sacerdotes suos Christus committat et eisdem dominari concedat."

[5] p. 673: "Regnum enim eorum (scil. regum) figura est coelestis regni."

[6] For ideological support he draws on St Augustine again, Ep. 185, c. 5, nos. 19 and 20, quoted in full on p. 673, lines 22–41.

[7] p. 674, line 19. Cf. also p. 676: "Unde manifestum est, reges habere sacrosanctam potestatem ecclesiastici regiminis super ipsos etiam pontifices Domini et imperium super eos, ut et ipsi pie fideliterque regnant sanctam ecclesiam."

vicar of Christ has the task of providing the priesthood with adequate ministers, so that, in his words, the priests may serve the Church "pie fideliterque." Hence the king appoints and creates ecclesiastical officers. All this, he declares, is foreshadowed in the Old Testament where we read of priestly appointments by kings. Moses, who was not even a king, but a mere "dux populi," had power over the priests[1] and made Aaron and his sons priests: he also consecrated the tabernacle and the altars and the liturgical objects.[2] But Moses could not have done all this if he had not been given power to do so by God Himself.[3] The same holds true as regards Joshua and the five kings of Israel. King Solomon in particular was such a shining light that he has rightly been called "ecclesiastes."[4] He enlarged the number of priests, laid down a new liturgy, himself caused a temple to be constructed and consecrated it himself:[5] "In his igitur omnibus per figuram Christus Domini fuit et Christi futuri vices exercuit."

The visible act of anointing during the coronation of the king creates an intimate union between him and the *corpus* of all believers and hence he becomes *sanctus*. "The king is felt to be almost physically transformed into a sanctus by the holy chrism in which flows the cleansing potency of the Holy Spirit."[6] Oblivious or unaware of the change effected in the kind of oil used for imperial unctions, our author holds that this unction contains a higher degree of sanctity than a mere episcopal unction, for the king's unction is performed after the example of Christ Who was anointed by God Himself "ante saecula," whilst that of the bishops is modelled on that of Aaron and the apostles.[7]

---

[1] Tract iv, p. 666, lines 24 ff.: "Sed de Moysi quid dicemus, qui non fuit rex unctione sacratus, non fuit sacerdos, sed dux tantum populi? Nonne et ipse super sacerdotes potestatem habuit et imperium?"

[2] ". . . et tabernaculum et altaria et omnia vasa eius sanctificavit et totum dedicavit sanctuarium."

[3] Tract iv, p. 666, lines 24 ff.

[4] p. 666, lines 34–5.

[5] p. 666, lines 39–40.

[6] Williams, op. cit., p. 159.

[7] p. 669, lines 23 ff.: "Major regis quam sacerdotis et unctio et sanctificatio et potestas . . . secundum interiorem gratiam et veritatem invisibilis et spiritualis unguenti et maxime secundum exemplum filii Dei, ad quod instituta est, major sanctior videtur unctio et sanctificatio et potestas regis quam sacerdotis. Nam unctio et sanctificatio sacerdotum ad exemplum Aaron instituta est, quem Moyses unxit et sanctificavit, et quod majus est, ad exemplum apostolorum quos unxit Deus pater . . . regis vero unctio instituta est ad exemplum illius quem Deus pater unxit ante saecula . . . Jesu Christi Domini nostri." Reference is made to *Ps*. xlv. 7, and *Hebr*. i. 9. As regards royal coronations in England, the author merely states the practice.

14*

This sanctification confers the highest kind of priesthood upon the king. He is alone *Deus-Homo*.[1]

As the "figura Christi" the king represents Christ on earth: he is *Deus-Homo*. It is not consequently surprising that the famous Gelasian passage is adduced by the author in support of his monarchic scheme.[2] What Gelasius had related to Christ, is now related to the "figura Christi." Whereas, on the authority of Gelasius, Christ had distributed the two powers, so also does the king, the "figura Christi" do now. Because the author has set aside the primacy of the Roman Church and the pope's mediatory role, he is theoretically entitled to call upon Gelasius as his supporting witness. This view is indeed hierocratic doctrine turned upside down. Moreover, because the king is also a priest, he may function as a priest: he may remit sins;[3] the power of the keys is conferred upon him through the act of anointing, and is based upon his theory of the priesthood of all Christians: St Peter had received this power on behalf of all the others. The king's priesthood also entitles him to sacrifice bread and wine.[4] No wonder, then, that the author's king may also proclaim doctrine and faith, because he is "summus pontifex."[5] He convokes councils,[6] issues ecclesiastical laws and is the supreme ecclesiastical tribunal—the *solium justitiae*.[7]

We recall that the hierocratic thesis stressed the function of the soul as the directing agency of the body; hence the priests alone were considered functionally qualified to issue binding instructions for the proper use of the corporeal or material. It is the same teleological and directive principle which we meet in the anonymous author of our tracts, only in an inverted sense. There are some, he says, who declare that kings should have power over the bodies, priests power over the souls—as if, he exclaims with a note of irritation, souls could be ruled without the bodies, and bodies governed without the souls,[8] which to maintain "is manifestly without reason." The unitary view on human personality militates against the theory of a diarchy. For if the bodies are to be well ruled, the souls too must be well ruled, and vice-

---

[1] p. 664, lines 26 ff.: "In uno quippe erat naturaliter individuus homo, in altera per gratiam christus, id est, Deus Homo."

[2] Quoted in three places: tract iv, p. 663, line 26; p. 668, line 32; tract v, p. 684, line 45.

[3] p. 672, lines 15 ff.; 677, lines 10 ff.

[4] p. 678, lines 18 ff.: "Quare et peccata remittere et panem et vinum in sacrificium potest offere quod utique facit in die quo coronatur." For this cf. also Williams, op. cit., p. 169.

[5] p. 677, line 33.

[6] p. 675, line 25; p. 676, line 7.

[7] p. 674, line 21.

[8] p. 663, lines 29 ff.

versa.[1] The human body is the temple of the Holy Ghost, that is, of the soul.[2] The soul must necessarily follow the direction of the body which houses it. If we transfer these ideas to the larger question of government it becomes clear to our author "quod rex habet principatum regendi eos, qui sacerdotali dignitate potiuntur."[3]

There is no gainsaying the originality of this author, his trenchant utilization of sources and materials, and his theological acumen. Concentrating as he does on the essential point, namely the link between Christ and the king, he establishes in his king a *Deus-Homo*, the "figura et imago Christi." This author saw the necessity of making the king a true monarch in a Christo-centric world, hence his christological argument. In consequential pursuit of his theme the teleological conceptions fall into line with his principles of government. It would be quite misleading to dub our author a materialist, because he adheres to the view that the body alone gives direction to the soul: for, quite unlike the conceptions of kingship which the dualist opponents of the hierocratic scheme embraced, his king is not a mere personification of inert matter, and for this reason alleged to be autonomous: quite on the contrary, his king is "Deus et Christus," not because he deals with matter, but because Christ's royal nature was directly continued in him, and Christ's royal nature was the true divine part of His being. The reason, we suggest, why our author arrives at this view is that the priestly office cannot concern itself with government. Government is *dominium* in the literal meaning of the term manifesting itself in the promulgation of binding decrees, the laws, and in their enforcement: government, according to the view of our author, means to take effective measures, to shape and to alter, to direct and to command: this is what he comprises under the term "creation." Because Christ had created, He was king, that is, He governed. Although perhaps somewhat tortuous, this is indubitably an original theory. But there looms many a large question in the background. Could this highly speculative theory conquer the hierocratic theme? Could this purest kind of speculative theology do away with the scriptural argument, so easily accessible? Where was the documentary evidence for the author's ingenious assertions of the divinity of Christ's kingship, and the humanity of His priesthood?[4]

[1] p. 663, lines 32 ff.: "Necesse est enim, si bene regantur corpora, bene regantur et animae et econverso, quoniam utraque ideo reguntur, ut in resurrectione simul utraque salventur." [2] He refers to I *Cor.* vi. 19, and to II *Cor.* vi. 16.
[3] Loc. cit., lines 41–2.
[4] In view of his christological arguments it is erroneous to say that he almost

## IV

We must now turn to another representative of anti-hierocratic thought, the author of the *Liber de unitate ecclesiae conservanda*.[1] It should not be assumed that because we survey him his work had exercised any influence.[2] The reason for giving this tract any prominence at all is that it contained ideas which were not only extraordinarily similar to those expressed by Henry IV in the early months of 1076,[3] but which also in the following century gained great currency. The tract is merely symptomatic of a certain kind of anti-hierocratic opposition.

So far we have surveyed three authors who firmly adhered to the monarchic conception of rulership. This author, however, is one of the early specimens who wished to propound an anti-hierocratic doctrine in the shape of a diarchy of government. He maintained that the Petrine power to bind and to loose was not comprehensive: the binding and loosening concerns only those things which should be bound and

---

anticipated the fourteenth-century attacks on the papacy or that he was unique. He was one of the few, if not the only one, and one of the last, if not the last one, who attempted to rescue the monarchic king by establishing a link between him and Christ. Nor is it quite correct to say that the York Tracts were the only "English" contribution to contemporary controversial literature. Even if Williams's thesis is accepted, there are indubitably English contributions from Theobald of Étampes writing from Oxford to Roscellinus at Compiègne (LdL. iii. 603 ff.), Bishop Herbert Losinga of Norwich (ibid., iii. 615 ff.) and others whose writings have disappeared; cf. Böhmer, op. cit., pp. 168 ff., Wattenbach-Holtzmann, *Geschichtsquellen im Mittelalter*, Tübingen, 1948, i. 772 ff. The politically important tract of Gilbert Crispin (a pupil of St Anselm, see R. W. Southern, "St Anselm & his English pupils" in *Medieval & Renaissance Studies*, i (1943), pp. 19–22) is edited by J. Armitage Robinson, *Gilbert Crispin*, Cambridge, 1911, pp. 111–24, and also by W. Holtzmann, "Zur Geschichte des Investiturstreits" in *Neues Archiv*, l (1933), pp. 255–70. Of a little later date is the Oxonian and later Cardinal Robert Pulleyn writing in the thirties of the twelfth century.

[1] Ed. MGH. LdL., ii. 173 ff.

[2] In actual fact this work was completely unknown in the medieval period: only in 1519 Ulrich van Hutten discovered it in the library of Fulda and published it the year after; and since then, even this one manuscript has vanished. For details see R. Holtzmann in Wattenbach-Holtzmann, *Geschichtsquellen im Mittelalter*, cit., i. 406–7, here also modern literature.

[3] The tract was written in the early nineties of the eleventh century. The usual designation of the author today is "the monk of Hersfeld" because it is believed that a monk of the monastery of Hersfeld wrote it. The possibility, however, that Gottschalk, the provost of Aachen and Henry's chief chaplain, was the author, cannot be entirely dismissed, cf. supra 345, and see also the remark of C. Erdmann in his examination of Gottschalk, *Deutsches Archiv*, iii (1939), p. 172, sub no. 17 and in *Archiv f. Urkundenf.*, xvi (1939), p. 203, note 1.

loosed.[1] In vain, however, we shall look for a definition of matters which should not be bound and loosed. Nevertheless, the author contends that by disregarding the essentially limited power given to St Peter, Hildebrand had disturbed the peace and unity of the one Church. But when there is no unity, one cannot speak of a catholic Church, that is, a universal Church, because then it is not the Church of Christ, but the Church of the wicked.[2] By this treacherous conduct towards Henry IV Hildebrand had transgressed the divinely set frontiers: he not only caused disunity and untold harm, but he also took it upon himself to wield the sword which alone belonged to King Henry: the pope had thereby doubled and trebled the sword and sown dissension.[3] Moreover, Hildebrand had violated the apostolic command "Fear God, honour the king" for the king has his power directly from God—"cui potestas a Deo concessa est"[4]—that is, the power to coerce and punish evildoers. It is for this purpose that he wields the sword—"cui gladius est permissus ad vindictam noxiorum"[5]—which the recently deceased Hildebrand had arrogated to himself. In this way, he had usurped the height of royal power.[6] The remedy proposed by the author was the separation of the two swords, their distribution to pope *and* king, in short a dual form of government.

[1] i. 4, p. 190: "Ecce, qualem s. Petrus a Domino potestatem accepit ligandi atque solvendi, talem et ipse tradidit eius successori, scilicet in his, quae oportet ligari et quae expedit solvi."

[2] i. 5, p. 191: "Ideoque, ubi non est totum quod dicitur catholica, hoc est universalis ecclesia, ibi non est Christi, sed malignantium ecclesia, quae divisa est in aliqua parte."

[3] i. 5, p. 198: "Non solum duplicavit gladium, juxta quod in Ezekiele legitur (Ez. xxi. 14), vel triplicavit, sed et multiplicavit, et non solum divisit populum Christianum, sed et sacerdotia, ut multi sunt episcopi in parte ista, plurimi autem in parte altera." Cf. also ii. 11, p. 222: "Sed jam facta divisione imperii simul et sacerdotii, surrexit rex adversus regem, gens adversus gentem, episcopus contra episcopum, populus contra populum." And ii. 3, p. 214: "Scandalorum orta sunt genera; exinde crevit grave et diuturnum bellum et non solum civile bellum . . . vastatationes ecclesiarum et caedes hominum; exinde etiam corruptae sunt divinae et pariter humanae leges, sine quibus non subsistit *ecclesia Dei* vel *imperii respublica*; exinde violata est fides et publica et catholica."

[4] i. 10, p. 198; cf. also ii. 13, p. 224.

[5] i. 10, p. 198.

[6] ii. 15, p. 230: "Hildebrant et episcopi eius vendicaverunt sibi absque dubio *fastigium regiae regulae*, immo usurpaverunt sibi officia potestatis utriusque." Cf. also ibid.: "Hanc Dei dispositionem quisquis diligenter considerat juxta divinam utriusque potestatis ordinationem, perspiciet sane in hoc quoque per Hildebrantum et episcopos eius magnam operatam esse iniquitatem, qui, cum pro pontificali dignitate non deberent vel negotiis saecularibus sese implicare, usurpaverunt sibi ordinationem regiae dignitatis contra Dei ordinationem et contra usum et disciplinam ecclesiae."

This point of view can be propounded only when firstly, the corporate, juristic and organic character of the universal Church is denied: when in other words, the universal Church, the *congregatio fidelium*, is considered to constitute merely a spiritual fellowship held together by the bonds of charity, peace and love. In this way the author would look forward to a period radically different from his own, to a time, that is, when Christianity had become a "moral force" having no organic, corporate and juristic character. Secondly, *ecclesia* and *imperium* are two distinct entities which are autonomous, or rather whose rulers are autonomous, having been both directly instituted by God. *Ecclesia* therefore means to him no more than the *sacerdotium*.[1] Thirdly, and arising out of these two points, is his contention that Christ is the true head of Christendom. In other words, the monarchic principle is assailed by him, but he can do this only by denying the—hierocratically conceived—mediatory role of the pope, that is, the fullness of the Petrine commission, the plenitude of power.[2] Christ has instituted both powers: He had given only specific power to St Peter, whilst others He had given to the king; or if we were to employ the terminology of the twelfth century, He had not created St Peter His sole vicar:[3] and for this the author believes that he finds support in no lesser authority than Gelasius I.[4]

The consequence is that the author must deny the decrees of the Roman Church binding, that is, juristic character: the pope's weapon is not the law or anything else but the "verbum Dei."[5] What the pope

---

[1] Cf. ii. 3, p. 214: "*Ecclesia* Dei" and "*imperii respublica*." Furthermore ibid.: "Certe Deus Romanorum praeparavit regnum, ut ibi et *ecclesia* et *imperium* haberet principatum; huic divinae ordinationi qui resistit, Deo resistit." Also i. 12: "Haec potestas (scil. regia) quae a Deo ordinata est et quae jubetur honorificari, ubi tandem debet judicari? Utrum in *ecclesia* an in *curia*? Si in ecclesia, fortasse ecclesia fit curia, quae a cruore dicitur . . . et cum ecclesiastica prohibeant decreta . . . ut inferior quilibet gradus non praesumat superiorem accusare, quis accusabit regem quasi praecellentem?"

[2] In substance this attack on the pope's plenitude of power—an attack essential to every dualist—foreshadows the (more effective) fourteenth-century opposition to the hierocratic ideology; cf. Dante, *Monarchia*, iii. 8 (ed. A. C. Volpe, Modena, 1946), pp. 162–4; Marsiglio of Padua, *Defensor Pacis*, II. xxiii. 5 (ed. R. Scholz, Hannover, 1933), pp. 445 ff.; Ockham, *Breviloquium de potestate papae*, caps. xiv–xix (ed. L. Baudry, Paris, 1937), pp. 43–59; idem, *Octo quaestiones*, III. iv; etc.

[3] As indeed Staufen ideology was to conceive of a double vicariate of Christ, cf. supra p. 343 n. 3.

[4] See i. 3, where he quotes the relevant passage from *Tractatus IV* of Gelasius.

[5] i. 3: "Sacerdotale judicium non habet nisi gladium spiritus, quod est verbum Dei." Cf. *Ephes.* vi. 17.

can do is to submit a humble petition to the prince, but on no account may the latter be deposed[1] or even excommunicated, because he is "minister Dei" and as such may not be judged by anyone,[2] the underlying reason being that he—just as much as the pope—is directly instituted by God. There is a *regia auctoritas* and next to it a *sacerdotalis auctoritas*. The papal insistence on the binding and juristic character of the canons issuing forth from the Roman Church is in reality the main grievance of our author: it is this which he means by the charge that the Gregorian party would like that "totus mundus vadat post eos, non post Christum";[3] it is this which he means by the multiplication of swords in the hands of Hildebrand. His ideal pope— and he considered Clement III ideal enough to eulogize him—was one who admonishes by using the "verbum Dei," but who does not issue binding laws. Government, or what he calls the coercion of evildoers, is the task of the autonomous secular ruler. The pope is given no more than *magisterium*, but no *jurisdictio*. The *respublica imperii* and the *ecclesia* are two independent societies, the aims of which are never stated.[4] The negation of the pope's jurisdictional powers, the narrowing down of the concept of *ecclesia* and the concomitant emergence of the *respublica imperii* are heralds of an—as yet distant—time when the problem was no longer pope *versus* king-emperor, but the very real separation of Church and State.

There is a great ideological kinship between the school of thought represented by this author and a group of writers who, though insistent on a diarchy of government, nevertheless introduced a topic which at the time was of mere practical importance but which later was to assume an equally great theoretical importance. These writers were of a more practical bent. In order to combat the hierocratic thesis effectively, this school of thought was forced to look for some concrete basis of royal power; they directed attention less towards the origins of royal power than towards the actual and concrete objects with which royal power was concerned. And these objects were found in property and material possessions. What was the position of the bishop (or abbot) as holder of estates and goods connected with the bishopric

---

[1] i. 3: "Sic solebant Deo digni pontifices Romani *suppliciter deprecari* pro ecclesiastica pace, non quaerentes, immo numquam concipientes animo, aliquos de regibus sive imperatoribus deponere . . ."

[2] Cf. the passage quoted supra, p. 406, note 1.

[3] See ii. 14, p. 225.

[4] Unless one takes the punishment of evildoers by the king's sword as the aim of the *respublica imperii*.

(or abbacy)? Although these writers cannot be said to have contributed materially to questions of principle, they nevertheless deserve attention because of the possibilities inherent in their theory of a separation of ecclesiastical office and ecclesiastical possessions.

The theorists of the *Regalia* assert the exclusive rights of the king as regards the "temporalia" of the invested bishop (or abbot) and consequently deny ecclesiastical jurisdiction over these "temporalities." It was undeniable that the bishops by way of investiture had received, not only their pastoral office, but also substantial property, such as houses, estates, manors, granges, and so forth. In order to ward off the comprehensive hierocratic claims some anti-hierocratic littérateurs with a practical sense withdrew the *rex-sacerdos* from his exposed position, and maintained the king's inalienable and untransferable rights over the material possessions with which the bishop was invested. These royal rights associated with the temporal goods, houses, estates, and so on, received the significant name of *Regalia*.[1] The first to draw attention to this distinction between the (spiritual) office and the (temporal) possessions was Wido of Ferrara.[2] According to him, royal investiture is divided into two quite separate spheres, into the bishop's *spiritualia*, his episcopal and pastoral office, and the bishop's *saecularia*, consisting of manors, fields, and the like. The office is spiritual, the possessions are secular.[3] But the term *secularia* comprises also, according to Wido, "omnia placita saecularia et juditia et regalia et *publica jura* et *vectigalia*."[4] All these items were withdrawn from the bishop's jurisdiction, Wido declared, and the king alone was entitled to dispose of them. What the bishop had during his tenure, was legally a mere usufruct of the "possessions," which therefore remained the king's property. Hence every newly installed bishop must be invested anew

---

[1] The best recent account of the theory of the *Regalia* will be found in Irene Ott, "Der Regalienbegriff im 12. Jahrhundert" in *Sav. Z.*, *Kan. Abt.*, xxxv (1948), pp. 234–304.

[2] See A. Scharnagl, *Der Begriff der Investitur*, Stuttgart, 1909, pp. 47–50, and Ott, art. cit., p. 238. Wido's tract was written in the spring of 1086 and entitled *De schismate Hildebrandi*, ed. MGH. LdL., i. 532 ff.

[3] Wido, *De schismate Hildebrandi*, lib. ii, p. 564, lines 32 ff.: "Duo siquidem jura conceduntur episcopis omnibus, spirituale vel divinum, aliud saeculare; et aliud quidem coeli, aliud quidem fori. Nam omnia, quae sunt episcopalis officii spiritualia sunt, divina sunt, quia, licet per ministerium episcopi, tamen a sancto spiritu conceduntur. At vero judicia saecularia et omnia, quae a mundi principibus et saecularibus hominibus ecclesiis conceduntur, sicut sunt curtes et praedia omniaque regalia, licet in jus divinum transeant, dicuntur tamen saecularia, quasi a saecularibus concessa. Itaque divina illa a sancto spiritu tradita imperatoriae potestati constat non esse subjecta."      [4] p. 565, line 42.

with these temporalities, otherwise "revertuntur ad imperialia jura."[1]

It is an important distinction which the bishop of Ferrara draws, although its flaws are obvious; it is a distinction which has all the appearance of eminent practicability, even though theoretically open to all manner of opposition; it is a distinction which has all the makings of a compromise and as such will eventually be utilized for the truce signed at Worms (1122). What is important, however, is that in the stormy February days of 1111 Paschal II and Henry V drew up a document in which certain rights were declared to be the king's rights, and were termed as such: *Regalia*. By virtue of their nature, the *Regalia* are withdrawn from the jurisdiction of anyone else but the king. The bishops and abbots were to be satisfied with the tithes, offerings and voluntary gifts. The *Regalia* according to this document are:

Cities, duchies, markgravates, countships, mints, tolls and customs, markets, hundredcourts, manors, soldiery and fortifications.[2]

Even though all this remained a dead letter, the careful enumeration of these royal rights, the *Regalia*, and their embodiment in an official document, would indicate that as regards these material goods kingly rights were acknowledged, that is to say, rights which the king had independent of any other authority, and solely emanating from the fact of his materially possessing them. Royal ownership alone was the criterion. It is however plain that the proposal that the bishops should divest themselves of all temporal possessions, was unacceptable to the logical and consistent papal-hierocratic mind: this is made manifest by Placidus of Nonantula writing in the same year 1111 and obviously attacking the proposal.[3]

Not the least interesting facet of this tract of Placidus is that although it deals largely with this question, the author studiously avoids the

---

[1] p. 564, lines 41 ff.: "Quae vero sunt ab imperatoribus tradita, quia non sunt ecclesiis perpetuo jure manentia, nisi succedentium imperatorum et regum fuerint iteratione concessa, dicuntur profecto quoddammodo regibus et imperatoribus subdita, quia nisi per succedentes imperatores et reges fuerint ecclesiis confirmata, revertuntur ad imperialia jura."

[2] MGH. *Const.*, i, no. 90, p. 141: "Interdicimus etiam et sub districtione anathematis prohibemus, ne quis episcoporum seu abbatum, presentium vel futurorum, eadem *regalia* invadant, id est, civitates, ducatus, marchias, comitatus, monetas, teloneum, mercatum, advocatias regni, jura centuriorum et curtes, *quae manifeste regni erant*, cum pertinentiis suis, militiam et castra regni, nec se deinceps nisi *per gratiam regis* de ipsis regalibus intromittant."

[3] See Ott, art. cit., p. 246. The tract *De honore ecclesiae* is edited in MGH. LdL., ii. 568 ff.

expression *Regalia* when speaking of the "temporalities" of the bishop. For him these kingly rights do not exist, and hence he cannot even use the term. The material possession and the episcopal office are one: they are inseparable, just as body and soul are.[1] With the installation of the bishop he automatically obtains possession of the material goods attached to his bishopric. In his enumeration of these goods Placidus leans heavily on the definition of the *Regalia* in the papal-imperial document. The underlying reason for Placidus's rejection of the idea as well as of the notion of *Regalia* is the old unitary principle rationalized in the view that what was once donated to an individual church, remains the property of the whole Church:

> Quod semel ecclesiae datum est, in perpetuum Christi est.[2]

In a way one might see in this view the old proprietary church principle turned upside down.[3]

Nevertheless, despite the hierocratic condemnation of the division of the episcopal sphere into an "office" and "possessions," and despite the theoretical untidiness and practical difficulties which the division introduced, the idea appeared to appeal to writers with a strong practical bent of mind. This applies in particular to the Upper Austrian monk Gerhoh of Reichersberg writing in the thirties of the twelfth century.[4] Whilst earlier writers, such as Wido of Ferrara, had distinguished between the office and the possessions of the bishop, Gerhoh accepts this division, but, and this is the important point, adds a distinction as regards the king himself. According to Gerhoh a distinction should be drawn between donations which the king made as a private person, and the donations which he made in his function as a king.

---

[1] "Si enim saecularia, quae ecclesia possidet, per saeculares obtinere episcopus debet et spiritualia per spirituales, ergo quoddammodo dividitur ecclesia. Sicut autem qui corpus ab anima dividit, destruit hominem, ita qui corporalia ecclesiae a spiritualibus dividit, destruit ecclesiam," p. 586 B, lines 25 ff. This is a state of affairs "omnes catholici abhorrentes."

[2] p. 577, lines 31 ff. He continues: "Nec aliquo modo alienari a possessione ecclesiae potest in tantum, ut etiam ipse fabricator ecclesiae, postquam eam Deo voverit et consecrari fecerit, in ea deinceps nullum jus habere possit."

[3] We may recall that the question of secular jurisdiction concerning a cleric's feudal matter, was of considerable importance later. Here again the same unitary principle was invoked to demand that no cleric must be judged before the king's justices in a matter of lay fee. This is summed up by Bishop Grosseteste, *Ep.* lxxii\*, Rolls Series, p. 222: "Quilibet singularis homo etiam cum omnibus actibus suis unus et unum est; nec alius nec aliud est Petrus agens et Petrus simpliciter, licet alter sit vel alteratus . . . et ideo si persona sit ecclesiastica, non subest judicio potestatis laicalis (scil. super laico feudo)."

[4] His tract is called *Opusculum de edificio Dei*, ed. MGH. LdL., iii. 136 ff., and was written between 1126 and 1132 and in a second redaction issued in 1138.

The distinction which he tries to draw is that between the person and the office or that between the king and the crown.[1] The important point is that *Regalia* are rights which are inalienable and which are neither at the disposal of the individual king nor at that of the individual church. They are, if we were to employ Roman law or modern terminology, issues of public law.

Neither Gerhoh himself[2] nor, as far as can be seen, any other writer of the period, attached any significance to this very important distinction.[3] And yet, it is the conception of *Regalia*, assuredly only a side-

---

[1] Cap. 21, p. 152: "Sicut enim cuilibet fideli non dubitamus licere, ut sive de hereditate sua sive de alia legitime acquisita possessione oblationem faciat ecclesiis: sic idipsum regibus nemo est qui dubitet. Nemo qui tales oblationes ab ecclesia recusandus putet. De regni autem facultate, quae est res publica, non debet a rege fieri donatio privata. Est enim aut regibus in posterum successuris integre conservanda, aut communicato principum consilio donanda. De re autem privata tam a regibus quam a ceteris principibus potest fieri donatio privata."

[2] See Ott, art. cit., pp. 263–4. It is not easy to construct a system from the various and long tracts of Gerhoh. If any particular trend is noticeable it is his opposition to the essence of the hierocratic scheme, namely that the priests govern and that they lay down binding rules of action. Although attributing to the pope the vicariate of Christ and the successorship of St Peter (*De Inv. Antichristi*, MGH. LdL. iii. 325, cap. 19: "Christus per suum vicarium Petri successorem, Gregorium VII"), he nevertheless inveighs against the worldliness of the Roman curia to which he contemptuously refers as the "Romani" (ibid., p. 372, cap. 58): they claim to judge everything and everyone, but on the other hand, claim that they may not be judged by anyone; nor may anyone ask them "why do you do this?" (ibid., lines 12 ff.: "Cur ita facitis?"). If they had their way, all old law would vanish and they would make a new society, wiping out all distinctions, so that there would be "solum unum ovile et unus pastor, solus Romanus pontifex" (ibid., lines 25 ff.). It is certainly a "jocundum spectaculum" to watch the pope proceed on feast days, riding on the imperial horse, clad with the purple "et aliis regalibus insigniis" (*De Quarta Vigilia Noctis*, p. 511, cap. 12) and playing the role of the caesars and super-caesars (*De Inv. Antichr.*, p. 183, line 18; cf. also his scathing remarks about the "conduct" of the priests, ibid., p. 315, cap. 5). It was bad enough when once kings had added to their royal functions also priestly ones, but it is "more abominable" to witness the same thing "in sede beati Petri": the pope should not claim more than one sword, since this is not warranted by reason, authority or the Fathers (ibid., p. 392). The evil began with Gregory VII (*De Quarta Vig. Noctis*, p. 509, cap. 11, lines 32 f.); from then onwards the pontiffs began to amass gold and silver—"argentum et aurum colligere." The cause of the evil is the claim to unlimited power to bind and to loose. St Peter had not been given limitless powers: "Sed nec ipsam solvendi et ligandi potestatem indifferenter et pro libitu exercendam accepisse arbitrandus est" (*De Inv. Antichr.*, p. 355, cap. 47). This power was restricted: "Ut solveret quae solvenda essent et liganda ligaret," ibid., lines 22 ff. Christ, Gerhoh holds, "*determinate* tradit, sub *eadem determinatione* se accepisse patenter (Petrus) innuit," ibid., lines 31–2. Like the author of *De unitate ecclesiae conservanda*, Gerhoh can arrive at a dualism only by restricting the power to bind and to loose.

[3] D. Knowles, *Episcopal colleagues of Archbishop Thomas Becket*, Cambridge,

issue of the great ideological conflict, which forms one of the embryos out of which the theory of sovereign-public rights will grow and herewith the theory of the modern State.

---

1951, pp. 82–3, was the first to draw attention to the influence of Gerhoh of Reichersberg on Gilbert Foliot during the Becket controversy. But it seems that Gerhoh's influence may even have been greater, particularly concerning the possible distinction between king and crown. Cf., for instance, Henry II's Assize of Northampton, W. Stubbs, *Charters*, p. 180, cap. 7: "Justitiae faciant omnes justitias et rectitudines spectantes ad dominum *regem* et ad *coronam* suam." Cf. on this C. McIlwain, *Growth of political thought in the West*, London, repr. 1949, pp. 379–80, and about the possible inclusion of the respective duties in the coronation oath, see F. M. Powicke, *Henry III and the Lord Edward*, Oxford, 1948, ii. 725, note 1. About the "proprietary theory of kingship" see especially Maitland in Pollock & Maitland, *History of English Law*, Cambridge, 2nd ed., 1923, i. 511 ff., especially 521 ff. Attention should also be drawn to the early thirteenth-century *Leges Anglorum* which contain a title headed "De jure et appendiciis *coronae* regni Britanniae et quod sit officium *regis*" (cf. F. Schulz, "Bracton on Kingship" in EHR. lx (1945), p. 149). The reply of Henry III to Grosseteste is worth quoting, as it also shows the auxiliary role allotted to the pope and the priesthood within the framework of a government built on this principle. In 1245 Grosseteste pleaded with the king for "obedience, fidelity and devotion" towards the Roman Church and the pope, and the reply Henry gave was this: "Domine episcope, quae pertinent ad *coronam et regalitatem* nostram, intendimus, sicut et debemus, *conservare illaesa*; et desideramus, quod dominus papa et ecclesia sint nobis in hac parte *in adjutorium*," but apart from this he promises obedience and devotion; the reply was forwarded to Innocent IV without any comment by Grosseteste; cf. *Ep.* cxvii, Rolls Series, p. 338.

# CHAPTER XIII

# The Final Exposition
## of the Hierocratic Theme

IT cannot reasonably be maintained that the antagonists of the hierocratic theme had presented unanswerable theoretical arguments. The anti-hierocratic arguments especially when fortified by the Aristotelian armoury, no doubt made an impression in later times, but, as the facts proved, made virtually none at the turn of the eleventh and twelfth centuries. One might indeed wonder whether, in the circumstances, there was an effective reply to hierocratic arguments.

When society was conceived to be Christian, the argument that it was to be governed by those functionally qualified, namely those who constitute the "sors Domini," could hardly be countermanded: government consists of giving orders, issuing the law, making decisions, in short directing a given entity. The path to be taken by that entity, the *corpus* of the *congregatio fidelium* was determined by its substance, that is, the Christian faith. This alone was the exclusive criterion by which the *societas christiana* was to be governed and directed. From the governmental point of view the tenet of the primacy of the Roman Church in matters of religion—the *primatus magisterii*—included the *primatus jurisdictionis*. This side of the primatial power is of necessity complementary to the magisterial primacy; or seen from a different angle, the jurisdictional primacy makes real the magisterial one. If we wish to employ more familiar terminology, the monarchic principle —the *principatus*—was the political expression of the jurisdictional primacy.[1] The pope as the monarch directs and governs Christendom conceived as constituting a corporate and organic and juristic entity. In the execution of this government the papal monarch used certain agencies, which functioned in an auxiliary capacity. In course of time this will lead to the theory of the so-called *potestas indirecta*, but the

---

[1] *Matt.* xvi. 18 f.; *John* xxi. 16 f. The "Pasce oves meas" was sometimes also connected with *Ez.* xxxiv. 16 ("Ego pascam oves meas") and 17 ("Ego *judico* inter pecus et pecus, arietem et hircorum"), hence the interpretation that "pascere" means in fact judgment or jurisdiction.

essential hierocratic point is that the pope has the right to give orders to be executed, always provided that there is a corporate and juristic *congregatio fidelium.*[1] He, and through him the *sacerdotium,* are the only organs functionally qualified to govern this corporate body politic.

To these fundamental axioms of the hierocratic theme its opponents did not address themselves, with the exception of the author of the *York Tracts.* They failed to grasp the teleological principle which was to be put into operation. Considering the atmosphere of the time, the hierocratic theme was virtually unassailable, precisely because of the consistency of its structure and the loftiness of its underlying premises. The writings of some twelfth-century authors allow us to obtain a good insight into the maturest manifestations of the hierocratic point of view. The selection of the literary products of Honorius of Canterbury, Bernard of Clairvaux, John of Salisbury and Hugh of St Victor, is justified by several considerations: they set forth the hierocratic scheme in its fully developed form; their writings were influential; they were men of affairs; they approached the theme from different angles.[2]

# I

Hic libellus ad honorem veri regis et sacerdotis, Iesu Christi edatur. Et quia de regno et sacerdotio eius est materia, sit nomen eius Summa Gloria.[3]

These opening words of Honorius's work[4] set the tone and tenor of his thesis. The principle of unity is axiomatic for Honorius. This unitary principle shows itself in his main themes, namely (1) that the universal Church, or the "populus christianus" is one unit and consists of the *sacerdotium* and the *regnum;*[5] (2) that, by virtue of its being the corporate congregation of the faithful, this body must be ruled by

---

[1] Whether the pope has *potestas directa* or *indirecta* is irrelevant. What is relevant from the hierocratic point of view is that he has *potestas,* and this follows from his monarchic position.

[2] We do not adhere to the strict chronological order according to which Honorius should be followed by Hugh of St Victor, Bernard and John of Salisbury. But from the point of view of presenting their themes it seemed to us advisable to disregard strict chronology: and in any case the main works of the three last authors are little more than twenty years apart, so that they all can be counted as contemporaries.   [3] *Summa Gloria,* ed. MGH. LdL., iii. 63 ff.

[4] It has been shown that Honorius came from St Augustine, Canterbury, and not from Autun or Augsburg, see R. Bauerreiss, "Zur Herkunft des Honorius Augustodunensis" in *Studien und Mitteilungen zur Geschichte des Benediktinerordens,* liii (1935), pp. 24–36.

[5] See especially the preface of his work speaking of the *machina universitatis.*

the *sacerdotium* and that, consequently, the king functions in the capacity of an "adjutor," a lieutenant, who is appointed by the "caput sacerdotii";[1] (3) that the pope combines sacerdotal and regal powers and therefore is authorized to appoint the king. What gives the work a particular attraction is the tidy notional differentiation between the *sacerdotium* and the *ecclesia*.[2]

His argumentation is biblical-historical: at the same time it projects the teleological point of view into history. The principle of unity, the principle, that is, that there is but one society, manifests itself in the Old Testament as well as in the New Testament. In the Old Testament the "populus Dei" pre-figures the "ecclesia universalis" of the New Testament. Both societies are composed of the two integral sections, the "clerus" and the "populus." Ideologically, Adam was the "figura Christi," and symbolized the principle of unity, whence *sacerdotium* and *regnum* take their origin.[3] When Moses led the Jews out of Egypt, he did not appoint kings to govern them, but priests[4] who ruled the "populus Dei" until by God's order, Samuel, as a "propheta et sacerdos" anointed Saul as king who was thus instituted by a priest.[5]

The "ecclesia Dei" chronologically and ideologically followed the

---

[1] This is somewhat reminiscent of Ivo of Chartres's designation of the king (Henry I) as a "protector, non possessor"; cf. *Ep.* cxvi to Henry I (PL. clxii. 125): "Regnum terrenum coelesti regno, quod ecclesiae commissum est, subditum esse semper cogitatis; sicut enim sensus animalis subditus debet esse rationi, ita *potestas terrena subdita* esse debet *ecclesiastico regimini*; et quantum valet corpus nisi regatur ab anima, tantum valet terrena potestas, nisi informetur et regatur ecclesiastica disciplina . . . hoc cogitando servum servorum Dei vos esse intelligite, non dominum; *protectorem*, non possessorem." About the different interpretations of the idea of protection cf. supra pp. 69 ff., 230, 295.

[2] Cf. his terminology: "sacerdotium populi Dei"; "sacerdotium ecclesiae"; "princeps sacerdotum ecclesiae"; and so forth.

[3] Abel: *sacerdotium*, and Cain: *regnum*. The same holds true of Noah, also "figura Christi" and his two sons pre-portrayed the *sacerdotium* (Shem) and the *regnum* (Japheth), p. 67: "Romanum quippe regnum a Jafeth descendens quamquam in toto orbe dilatatum, tamen habitat in tabernaculis Sem, in ecclesiis sacerdotum." Honorius also refers to the saying of the Lord to Rebecca, Isaac's wife (*Gen.* xxv. 23) that there are two nations in her womb and that two manner of people will be born: the one will be stronger than the other and the elder shall serve the younger. Naturally, Esau typified the king and the lay population, Honorius writes: "Quis demens contraibit divinae auctoritati? En, aperta voce praecipitur numerositati laicorum, ut serviat devotioni clericorum," cap. 8, p. 69, lines 25–6.

[4] "Hic (scil. Moses) populum Dei de Egypto educens legem et jura statuit et ad hunc gubernandum non regem, sed sacerdotium constituit," cap. 10, p. 69. lines 21–2.

[5] Cap. 11, p. 69: "Samuel propheta et sacerdos jussu divino unxit eis regem regnique mox conscripsit legem." Cf. I *Kgs.* x. 25.

"populus Dei." Christ, "verus rex et sacerdos secundum ordinem Melchisedek"[1] had given His Church its laws and constitution—"ecclesiae leges et jura statuit"—but did not consider that the government of the Church necessitated the institution of a king.[2] There is a parallelism between the Old and the New Testaments: the time from the Egyptian exodus down to Samuel is paralleled by the time from the advent of Christ down to Silvester I.[3] The Emperor Constantine abdicated as a result of his conversion and placed the crown upon Silvester's head, stipulating at the same time that no one should hold the Roman empire without the pontiff's consent.[4]

Hoc privilegium Silvester a Constantino accepit, hoc successoribus reliquit.

Through the constitutional grant of Constantine, Silvester was entitled to dispose of the Roman empire.

Moreover, Silvester realized, Honorius argued, that he could not govern with the "sword of God" alone, since repressive and coercive measures would be called to quell rebellion and to defend the universal Church against internal and external enemies. In other words, Silvester realized that a specific organ was necessary, if the whole Christian body was to be effectively governed. Therefore, Honorius goes on to say, Silvester appointed the emperor an "adjutor" for the purpose of governing the universal Church. And he appointed him thus by conceding to Constantine the sword for the purpose of physical suppression of evil and by conferring on him the imperial crown.[5] The metamorphosis which the Donation of Constantine underwent at the hands of Honorius, need not detain us. It suffices to observe that the transaction appeared now entirely in the light of functionalist and teleological speculations—the function of the emperor, according to Honorius's

---

[1] Cap. 15, p. 71, line 4.

[2] "Ad hanc (scil. ecclesiam) gubernandam non regnum, sed sacerdotium instituit, in quo Petrum apostolum praefecit, cui dixit 'Tu es Petrus . . .'"

[3] "Sicut ergo a tempore Moysi usque ad Samuelem sacerdotes populo Dei praefuerunt, ita a tempore Christi usque ad Silvestrum soli sacerdotes ecclesiam rexerunt," ibid., lines 11 ff.

[4] Cap. 15, p. 71, line 4: "Qui Constantinus Romano pontifici coronam regni imposuit, et ut nullus deinceps Romanum imperium absque consensu apostolici subiret, imperiali auctoritate censuit."

[5] "Cumque sacerdotii cura et regni summa in Silvestri arbitrio penderet, vir Deo plenius intelligens rebelles sacerdotibus non posse gladio verbi Dei, sed gladio materiali coerceri, eundem Constantinum ascivit sibi *in agriculturam Dei adjutorem* ac contra paganos, Judaeos, haereticos ecclesiae defensorem. Cui etiam *concessit gladium* ad vindictam malefactorum, coronam quoque regni imposuit ad laudem bonorum."

interpretation of the Donation, was that of an "adjutor" to the pope, because the pope needed an agency whose sole purpose and *raison d'être* was the eradication of evil and the quelling of rebellions. In brief, the Pauline-Isidorian idea of kingship is clad in the garb of the Donation.[1]

Consequently, the papal *auctoritas* appears in a threefold capacity, namely, as a "dominica auctoritas," as an "apostolica auctoritas" and lastly as an "imperialis auctoritas." It is by virtue of the latter that the Roman Church elects and establishes the emperor.[2] Or expressed in simpler terms:

Imperator Romanus debet ab apostolico eligi.[3]

The same holds true of the other kings: according to Honorius, the king should be elected by the priests and the people should give their consent to the priestly election.[4] That two swords were necessary for the government of the universal Church, Christ Himself declared; and the one, the physical sword, wielded for the suppression of evil, is handed over by the pope.[5]

Sacerdotium jure regnum constituit.[6]

The *universitas fidelium* is divided into two component parts, clergy and people: the accent lies on the "fidelium"; it is they who form that "universitas" and hence it is the spiritual element which is constitutive of this body. Faith alone has brought this body into existence, and faith alone is the criterion by which this body is ruled. The function

---

[1] It is well known that in the thirteenth century, after the devaluation of the Donation by Innocent III, the transaction was considered a mere restitution of rights which belonged to the pope in any case. The Donation then had merely a declaratory character. This is only a logical extension of the functionalist-teleological speculation.

[2] C. 19, p. 72, lines 15 ff.: "Apostolicus a Romanis cardinalibus est eligendus consensu episcoporum et totius urbis cleri et populi acclamatione in caput ecclesiae constituendus. Ad huius providentiam *dominica auctoritate* pertinet cura universalis ecclesiae, scilicet totius populi et cleri, *apostolica auctoritate* sollicitudo omnium ecclesiarum, *imperiali auctoritate* Romani regni electio vel constitutio."

[3] C. 21, p. 73, line 1.

[4] C. 22, p. 73, lines 14–15: "Rex a Christi sacerdotibus, qui vere ecclesiae principes sunt, est constituendus; consensus tantum laicorum requirendus."

[5] C. 22, p. 73, line 16; c. 26, p. 75, lines 15–16: "Ad regimen ecclesiae in praesenti vita duos gladios necessarios praemonstravit (scil. Dominus)."

[6] There may be an echo of Honorius's view in Herbert of Bosham's biography of Thomas Becket: clerics, he says, "terrenis regibus non subsunt, sed praesunt, utpote qui *reges constituunt*, a quo et rex militiae cingulum et gladii materialis accipit potestatem," *Materials . . . Thomas Becket*, Rolls Series, iii. 268.

which an individual member fulfils in society depends upon the character of society. This one, being a body composed of all the believers in Christ, is to be ruled by those who are functionally qualified to rule it, namely the "sacerdotes," hence "jure regnum sacerdotio subjacebit," because the "sacerdotes" alone are entitled to direct the path of the *universitas fidelium*. It is therefore perfectly logical from this point of view for Honorius to say: "Equidem quilibet sacerdos, licet ultimi gradus in sacro ordine, dignior est quovis rege."[1] And the further consequence is equally conclusive: "Justissime, rex qui utique de numero laicorum est, subjectus erit apostolico."[2] From the point of view of contemporary society, his assertion that the priests are the princes of the Church is only an application of the functionalist idea.[3]

In our survey of Humbert's and Gregory VII's thoughts we noted the principle of functional order. Its essence is that each member of society should fulfil the functions which are allotted to him; or negatively expressed, no one should intervene in the sphere of competency which is not assigned to him: this intervention would be an interference. Within the *sacerdotium*, for instance, no bishop should arrogate to himself powers and functions which are assigned to the archdeacon; no metropolitan should usurp functions allotted to a bishop; and so on. If this principle of functional order is disregarded, the result is confusion, and government would eventually become impossible.

If we keep this principle in mind, and if we furthermore recall the substance of contemporary society and the manner and purpose of making a king (or an emperor), it will be easier to understand its application by Honorius. Within the sphere of functions assigned to the king, functions, that is to say, for which he has been specifically created, he must be obeyed: so long as he fulfils this function allotted to him, he is a legitimate ruler. His power in the allotted sphere is a trust, a *beneficium*, conferred in the last resort by the pope. The direction and orientation of the *universitas fidelium* lies in the hands of the qualified members of the *fideles*. But this does not mean that they them-

---

[1] Cap. 9, p. 69; cap. 23, p. 73. Cf. Gregory VII supra p. 286.
[2] Cap. 8, p. 68.
[3] Cf. also cap. 1, pp. 64–5: "Cum universitas fidelium in clerum et populum distribuatur, et clerus quidem speculative, populus autem negotiative vitae ascribatur, et saepe haec pars spiritualis, haec vero saecularis nominatur, et ista sacerdotali, illa autem regali virga gubernetur, solet plerumque apud plerosque queri, utrum sacerdotium regno, an regnum sacerdotio jure debeat in dignitate praeferri. Ad quod quidem breviter possem respondere, quod sicut spiritualis praefertur saeculari, vel clerus praecellit populum ordine, sic sacerdotium transcenderet regnum dignitate."

selves should undertake the specific functions of a king. For he was created to deal with specific matters essential to the wellbeing of the *universitas fidelium*, namely with the "saecularia"; if therefore the priests were to do what he has been appointed to do, what in actual fact is his *raison d'être*, they would upset the principle of functional order. Differently expressed: the "What is to be done" must lie in the hands of the *sacerdotium*; the "How it is to be done," the execution of the "What," lies in the hands of the *regnum*, namely the taking of coercive and repressive measures against rebels, evildoers, pagans, Jews, heretics, schismatics, apostates and so forth.[1] As long therefore as the king functions as a protector and defender of the *universitas fidelium*, he must be obeyed. And he functions as a protector and defender if he wields the sword for the purposes for which it was first given to him by Pope Silvester I. Should the king transgress the functions assigned to him, should he himself become a heretic or a schismatic, or a rebel against the Roman Church—"quam Rex regum et Dominus dominantium caput ecclesiae esse voluit"—he is then no longer an "imperator, sed tyrannus."[2] The essential point is that the *auctoritas* of government rests securely with the "caput ecclesiae," the pope. In the principle of functional order—always keeping the premisses in mind, namely the pope as the emperor-making agency— certain well-known biblical texts can find their concrete manifestations[3] and the secular power within the Church can be allotted an honourable place.

[1] Cf. cap. 9, p. 69; cap. 21, p. 73; also cap. 11, p. 69 and cap. 24, p. 74. The essence of this principle is the old Pauline-Isidorian view on the *raison d'être* of the secular ruler who functions as an auxiliary organ. It is the principle which makes the papal orders to secular rulers understandable, particularly papal orders concerning confiscation of property, expulsion of heretics, occupation and annexation of countries, war against allies of infidels and against infidels themselves, and so forth. Cf. *IV Lateranum*, cap. iii; Innocent III in *Reg.* ii. 270 and 271; *Reg.* iii. 3 (to the king of Hungary); *Reg.* vii. 79 and ix. 28 (to the king of France); x. 141 (to Sicily) and in many other places. Cf. also Lucius III's *Ad abolendam* (*Extra*: V. vii. 9). As regards the latter aspects see the official documents assembled by G. B. Pallieri and G. Vismara, *Acta pontificia juris gentium*, Milan, 1946, pp. 249 ff., 259 ff., 534 ff., 571 ff., 581 ff., all in the thirteenth century.

[2] "Hic inquam talis patienter quidem est tolerandus, sed in communione per omnia declinandus, quia non est imperator, sed est tyrannus. Huiusmodi imperium Martinus renuit dicens 'Christi miles sum, pugnare mihi non licet.'" The "patienter tolerandus" means, as the context makes clear, that no active steps should be taken against the tyrant, such as regicide.

[3] In cap. 24, for instance, he quotes "Render unto Caesar . . ." (*Matt.* xxii. 21) or "Submit yourselves to every ordinance of man for the Lord's sake, whether it be to the king as supreme . . ." (I *Pet.* ii. 13–14) or "Fear God, honour the king" (ibid., 17). Our author comments: "In quibus verbis considerandum est,

## II

John of Salisbury presents the hierocratic theme with all the accomplished elegance and facility of exposition which is characteristic of his writings. Unlike his compatriot, Honorius of Canterbury, John does not need to resort to the Donation of Constantine to support his ideology. Soaked as he was in the ancient Roman cultural elements he operates with the concept of the all-embracing, comprehensive *Respublica* consisting of all the Christians acknowledging the primacy of the Church of Rome. This *Respublica* is not an ideal State, but a living organism: it is the *orbis Latinus*, the congregation of the faithful in its corporate nature. It is axiomatic for John that the human organism is guided, orientated and directed by the soul.[1] And just as this is the function of the soul in the individual human body, so it is the function of the spirit to move the inert body politic. The spirit, that is the Christian faith, is the agency[2] which moves the universal Christian body:

Sicut anima totius corporis habet principatum, ita et hi, quos ille (Plutarchus) religionis praefectos vocat, toti corpori praesunt.[3]

The priests function as the transmitters of the divine mandates as expounded by the head of the Roman Church. The priests themselves therefore "vicem animae in corpore reipublicae obtinent."[4] John explains both the teleological and the functionalist tenets effortlessly setting out as he does from the definition that the *Respublica* is an "animate corpus":

Corpus quoddam, quod divini muneris beneficio animatur.[5]

The body receives its life—"animatur"—through the infusion of the Christian faith: this body becomes then meaningful, because purpose-

---

quod reges et judicies *ob solam vindictam* malorum constituuntur, qui laudem ferre bonis dicuntur."

[1] *Policraticus*, iii. 1: "Deus animam perfecte viventem totam occupat, totam possidet, regnat et vivit in tota."

[2] *Metalogicon*, iv. 13: "Fides autem, tam in humanis quam in divinis rebus, maxime necessaria est: cum nec contractus sine ea celebrari inter homines possent, ut aliqua exerceri commercia, quinimo inter homines quoque meritorum praemiorumque nequit esse commercium, fide substracta."

[3] *Policraticus*, v. 2. On this source cf. C. C. J. Webb, *John of Salisbury*, London, 1932, p. 39; idem, in the Introduction to the edition; and J. Dickinson, *The Statesman's book of John of Salisbury*, Introduct.

[4] *Policr.*, loc. cit.    [5] *Policr.*, loc. cit.

ful, and thereby fulfils the divine purpose of creation. And since the Christian faith is the leaven of society, the vital role which John allots to the priests is understandable.

The basic feature of this corporate body of Christians is its unity: the unitary principle being represented in the pope, the "vicarius crucifixi."[1] The pope alone is set by the Lord over nations and kingdoms—"a domino constitutus super gentes et regna"[2]—and is therefore the Ruler of the whole Christian body.[3] Consequently, he is the judge of all the faithful—"fidelium omnium judex est a Domino constitutus,"[4] and from sacerdotal judgment neither cause nor person is exempted.[5] This unity is achieved by unconditional obedience to the Roman Church, the epitome of the universal Church, or as he terms it, the "praesidium" of all the faithful.[6] Disobedience is schism and heresy, precisely the offence committed by Frederick I.[7] John realizes what the aims of Frederick are—"scio quod Teutonicus moliatur"—namely the subjection of the "world" to imperial rule: in the scheme devised by Frederick the pope would have to play the role which by right was the emperor's.[8] The vehement denunciation by John of Frederick's aims is understandable, realizing as he did that they violated one of his basic axioms, namely the functionalist and unitary

---

[1] *Ep.* cxcviii (PL. cxcix. 217); cf. also *Ep.* cccvi, PL. cit., col. 362. A new edition of John's letters is in preparation; for the dates of his letters cf., in the meantime, R. L. Poole, "The early correspondence of John of Salisbury" in *Proc. Brit. Acad.*, xi (1924–25), pp. 27–53; and H. G. Richardson, under the same title in EHR. liv (1939), pp. 471–3.

[2] *Ep.* ccxxviii, col. 242: *Jer.* i. 10.

[3] *Ep.* lxxxiii, col. 70: "ecclesiam regit, corrigit, et dirigit, universam."

[4] *Ep.* cxciii, col. 210.

[5] *Ep.* cxciii, col. 210: "Ecce quod a judicio sacerdotum nec causam excipit, nec personam, licet alias per seipsos, alias per ministros vicarios ecclesiae decidant sacerdotes. Nonne in persona sacerdotum, sicut ecclesiae decores fideliter tradunt, Jeremiae dictum est: 'Ecce constitui te hodie super gentes et regna.'" About the application of this principle of functional order by Grosseteste see infra 424 n. 6; cf. also Innocent III infra 445 n. 3.

[6] *Ep.* cxxv, col. 105.

[7] Who was an equal of Frederick, John exclaims, having turned "ex catholico principe schismaticus et haereticus? *Non* dico, quod *in articulis fidei*, ne recte credatur, inducat errorem, sed quia in sinceritate ecclesiastici ordinis procedere non sinat veritatem. Ille sacerdotium scidit adversus Dominum et a Domino scissuram sentit imperii," *Ep.* clxxxv, col. 194. Cf. also *Ep.* lix cols. 38–43; *Ep.* cxlv, cols. 133–4. About Henry IV as a heretic see supra 305 n. 2, and Henry II infra p. 422 n. 1.

[8] Epp. cit. About this topic cf. also J. Spörl, "Rainald von Dassel und sein Verhältnis zu Johannes von Salisbury" in *Festschrift f. Eichmann*, Munich, 1940, pp. 249 ff. Cf. also *Studi in memoria di Paolo Koschaker*, Milan, 1953, i. 109–10.

theses: the *Respublica* is a Christian corpus and can therefore be governed only by those qualified to do so, and not by a mere emperor.[1] The task of the secular ruler is to issue such laws as conform to the divine law: hence the priests must be given a hearing in the making of the laws,[2] because it is through them that the body of the Christians is directed and ruled.[3]

It is through the laws which the secular ruler issues that he can properly function. The laws constitute for John one of the chief means by which the purpose of society is realized, hence the contents of the laws is derived from the purpose and aim of society. For the laws, within the Christian *Respublica*, are wholly religious laws: John does not divorce the law from the purpose of society, nor does he separate "politics" from "religion": functionally the laws are the vehicles of government, and government is the direction of a body politic in consonance with the purpose for which this body politic exists. Government is simply the practical realization of the aim underlying society: and John's society was Christian. It is therefore only from the teleological point of view that one can understand the meaning of his statement:

For the whole function of the laws is religious and holy.[4]

[1] And exactly the same must be said of Henry II: *Ep.* cci, col. 223. In a kingdom one only can rule, and if it is the king alone, then the *sacerdotium* must obey him which means its end in a very short time. John is perfectly aware of the true meaning of monarchy: he would have nothing to do with a diarchy or a dualism. "Si pastorale officium non nisi *ad nutum principis* liceat exercere, et procul dubio nec crimina punientur, nec tyrannorum arguetur immanitas, nec reipsa diu stabit ecclesia." Whoever obeys Henry is a heretic: "Haereticum esse non dubito et praeambulum anti-christi, si ipse non sit personaliter anti-christus." Frederick's and Henry's aims are incompatible with the nature of contemporary society; cf. about Henry: *Ep.* ccxxxix, col. 271: Henry thinks that he has the pope and the cardinals "in his pocket"—"in bursa sua"—and glories in obtaining the position of his grandfather "qui in terra sua erat rex, legatus apostolicus, patriarcha, imperator et omnia quae volebat."

[2] *Policr.* iv. 3: "Omnium legum inanis est censura si non divinae legis imaginem gerat; et inutilis est constitutio principis, si non ecclesiasticae disciplinae sit conformis . . . sic enim legitimi *sacerdotes audiendi sunt*, ut reprobis et ascendentibus ex adverso, omnem vir justus claudat auditum."

[3] Only from the functionalist point of view can the biting remarks of John about some clerics be understood. Cf. *Ep.* cl, col. 144: "Numquid enim clerus institutus est ut comedens, bibens, stertens, mortem expectet et variis luxuriae incitamentis inflammet gehennam?" Cf. also John's advice to Roger of Worcester, *Ep.* ccxvii, col. 241. About the extraordinary state of affairs at St Augustine's, Canterbury, see the report of Bartholomew of Exeter and Roger of Worcester to Alexander III, *Ep.* cccx, cols. 366–7.

[4] *Policr.* iv. 3: "Sacrarum namque legum omne officium religiosum et pium

This statement expresses in classic form teleological ideas. In a Christian community all activity is directed by the Christian idea, hence each and every individual law is "religious" and "holy." The law is, John states in consonance with ancient doctrine, "regula recte vivendi."[1]

The civil laws deal with that part of the administration of the Christian commonwealth which is unworthy of being directly dealt with by the priests: for the secular ruler's function is the physical suppression of evil, and he may therefore be likened, in a way, to a "slaughterer": "Quandam carnificis representare (scil. princeps) videtur imaginem."[2] And it is for this purpose that he receives the material sword. The prince is a minister of the priesthood. The priesthood although possessing both swords, does not use both directly, but uses the physical sword through the instrumentality of the secular ruler.[3] The *raison d'être* of the secular ruler is the suppression of evil, and for this he was instituted by the priesthood which gave him the physical-material sword for this purpose. There would never have been any kingdoms at all, John declares, if there had not been iniquity or if human wickedness had not forced God to institute royal power.[4] All this, as we know, is Isidorian, Humbertine and Gregorian thought.

---

est." The "sacrae leges" are the civil laws, the term used by Justinian and also by Frederick I himself; also by Peter Crassus and by Benzo. About the *ordinabilitas* of the laws of Nicholas I, cf. supra p. 207.

[1] *Policr.* viii. 17. Cf. Pseudo-Isidore and the *Hispana,* supra p. 188 n. 5.

[2] *Policr.* iv. 3.

[3] *Policr.* iv. 3: "Hunc ergo gladium de manu ecclesiae accipit princeps, cum ipsa tamen gladium sanguinis omnino non habeat. Habet tamen et istum, sed eo utitur per principis manum, cui coercendorum corporum *contulit potestatem,* spiritualium sibi in pontificibus *auctoritate reservata.* Est ergo princeps sacerdotii quidem minister, et qui sacrorum officiorum illam partem exercet, quae sacerdotii manibus videtur indigna. Sacrarum namque legum . . ." There is an ingenious bracketing of John's views and the famous Bernardine passage (about which see infra 431) by Robert Grosseteste who after quoting John says: "Debent quoque principes saeculi nosse quod uterque gladius, tam materialis videlicet quam spiritualis, gladius est Petri, sed spirituali gladio utuntur principes ecclesiae qui vicem Petri et locum Petri tenent, per semetipsos; materiali autem gladio utuntur principes per manum et ministerium principum saecularium, qui ad nutum et dispositionem principum ecclesiae gladium quem portant, debent evaginare et in locum suum remittere" (with a reference to *Rom.* xiii. 4): *Ep.* xxiii, pp. 90–1, ed. cit.

[4] *Policr.* viii. 17: "Omnino regna non essent quae, sicut ab antiquis liquet historiis, iniquitas per se aut praesumpsit, aut extorsit a Domino." The "extorquere" appeared later with Innocent III as "humana extorsio," cf. the quotation from RNI. 18 supra 285, Cf. furthermore John in *Policr.* viii. 18, saying that the Jewish people "a Deo quem contempserat, sibi regem extorsit." And: "In furore Domini dati sunt reges" (to the Jews). Cf. Augustine, *Civ. Dei,* xi. 1; xiv. 28; xv. 5 and 17; xvi. 3 and 4; xvii. 6; xviii. 2, etc.

Considering thus the creation of the (Christian) ruler, John has indeed no difficulty in saying, on the one hand, that the ruler is the "imago divinitatis" and that he will fulfil his functions properly if he is mindful of his own creation as a ruler,[1] and, on the other hand, that if he should misuse the trust put in him, he may be deprived of his power by him who created him a ruler: this is merely the application of an old legal maxim.[2] Moreover, the contents of the laws are the criterion which distinguishes the tyrant from the true ruler: the latter will always keep in mind the function which he is to fulfil; and, within the sphere allotted to him, his laws will realize the function for which he himself is created. Hence "omnium legum inanis est censura, si non divinae legis imaginem gerat."[3] Or seen from a different angle: "Voluntas regentis de lege Dei pendet et non praejudicat libertati."[4] True law, being a "gift of God"—"donum Dei"—must therefore embody the "norma justitiae" and will consequently be the "image of the divine will." The tyrant's laws are in every respect the opposite: he acts in precisely the way that is opposed to his function which is to suppress evil and iniquity. But the tyrant creates evil and iniquity through his laws.[5] The very term *rex* is derived from *rectum*, but what is, and what is not, right (*rectum*), that to fix is the business of those who are qualified to pronounce upon it. In brief in the making of the laws for the Christian *Respublica*, the "sacerdotes audiendi sunt." They alone know the *norma justitiae*; they alone know what the norm of right conduct is in a Christian community.[6] The prince who acts thus,

---

[1] *Policr.* iv. 3: "Gerit autem (scil. princeps) ministerium fideliter, cum suae conditionis memor." Cf. also ibid., v. 6.

[2] *Policr.* iv. 3: "Porro de ratione juris eius est nolle, cuius est velle, et *eius* est *aufferre*, qui de *jure conferre* potest." Theobald of Canterbury tells Henry II, *Ep.* xliv, col. 28: "Ipsa (scil. ecclesia Cantuariensis) est enim caput regni vestri et vobis et toti regno, fidei parens in Christo." Cf. also *Ep.* liv, col. 34: "Commendo vobis sanctam Cantuariensem ecclesiam, de cuius manu per ministerium meum regni gubernaculum accepistis, ut eam, si placet, ab incursu pravorum hominum tueamini." See also John's *Ep.* ccciv, col. 356. According to Eadmer the see of Canterbury was "totius regni caput," *Hist. novorum*, PL. clix. 402.

[3] *Policr.* iv. 6.

[4] *Policr.* viii. 22.

[5] *Policr.* viii. 17: "Tyrannus pravitatis imago, plerumque occidendus. Origo tyranni iniquitas est et de radice toxicata mala et pestifera germinat." The tyrant is "Luciferianae pravitatis imago."

[6] With specific reference to the jurisdictional powers of secular and ecclesiastical tribunals, exactly the same point of view is expressed by Bishop Grosseteste. He says that properly speaking all judgments (within contemporary society) are those of the priesthood: "*Omne igitur judicium proprie per auctoritatem est sacerdotii et cleri*" (*Ep.* lxxii*, p. 217 ed. cit.); but the priesthood exercises direct jurisdiction in ecclesiastical matters, whilst jurisdiction in temporal matters the

is the "image of deity" and as such "amandus, venerandus est et colendus."[1]

There can be few medieval thinkers and writers who set forth such a closely reasoned and consistent view as did John of Salisbury. To him the universal Church is the corporation of all living Christians; it is the *Respublica*, a truly living organism. It is one body and as such must be ruled by one, by one who is functionally qualified to govern this body. The *Respublica* is indeed a body or an organism in which the individual parts function on the model of the human body. From the head down to the feet each part of the human body fulfils a certain function—and all these parts of the human body can be found in the body politic. Head, heart, eyes, ears, tongue, hands, stomach, and so forth, all find their functional complement in the Christian body politic. And just as the human body is governed by the soul, so as to become a comprehensible, integrated whole, in the same way the body politic is governed by those who "vicem animae obtinent," namely the ordained members of the Church. The one body just as the other constitutes a whole: and this whole is orientated, guided and governed by the purpose for which it exists. The body politic is the human body writ large. Neither can realize its inherent purpose: each must be governed so that its purpose is realized. All individual parts of the *Respublica* must function with a view to the whole body: all their activities must be related to, and orientated by, the "finis" or "telos" of the whole body, or as John has it:

> Ad publicam utilitatem omnia referantur,[2]

---

priesthood hands over to the secular princes (on the principle of the priesthood possessing both swords): "Principibus vero saeculi tradidit . . ." Hence it is that "potestas judiciaria judicis ecclesiastici extendat se etiam in saecularia, cum, ut supra dictum est, omne judicium per auctoritatem et per doctrinam sit ecclesiae, licet non omne per ministerium," p. 220. For John see supra 422, and Innocent III infra 436. Because the priesthood alone has, what Grosseteste calls *sapientia*, they alone rule: "Sapientia in omnibus regit, gubernat, et moderatur, ac per hoc dijudicat potentiam: potentia autem numquam in aliquo potest dijudicare sapientiam; igitur nec populus clerum, nec regnum sacerdotium," ibid., p. 217. The principle of functional qualification could hardly be better expressed. Cf. also John, *Policr.* iv. 6: "Impossibile enim est, ut salubriter disponat principatum, qui non agit consilio sapientum."

[1] *Policr.* viii. 17. For the influence of John's idea of a tyrant on Bracton see F. Schulz, in EHR., lx (1945), p. 153, although it may perhaps be open to doubt whether Bracton accepted all John's premisses.

[2] *Policr.* vi. 20. About the principle of *publica utilitas* cf. also supra 287 n. 2 and Innocent III in *Reg.* i. 409: "Utilitas totius populi christiani," hence preference of "communis utilitas" to "privata utilitas," *Reg.* i. 481; cf. also *Reg.* vi. 138. About *publica utilitas* in Roman law see the important article by A. Steinwenter,

15

for only in this way can the purpose of the whole body be realized. The functions of all the members and their activities must be dovetailed,[1] so as to make the body an integrated whole. This is what John calls *cohaerentia*,[2] a principle which when adhered to, will alone produce *unitas*. In a theocentric world teleological conceptions can produce no other doctrine but the hierocratic one: the *sacerdotium* directs and leads the corporate Church which is geographically the *Orbis Latinus*.[3]

## III

The exposition of the hierocratic theme by St Bernard of Clairvaux is embedded in the vehicles which he employed for his "triumphant propaganda"[4]—in the numerous letters, tracts and sermons, all of which denote the fiery enthusiast with whom the hierocratic theme finds one of its greatest and profoundest exponents. To rank him amongst the "political" writers would be some sort of degradation of Bernard's objectives, and yet the tract which he wrote for the consideration of

---

*    "Utilitas publica—utilitas singulorum" in *Festschrift f. Paul Koschaker*, Leipzig, 1939, i. 84–102: the idea was of Greek origin and adopted by Cicero through whose influence it gained currency in Rome. See now also the fine study by J. Gaudemet, "Utilitas publica" in *Rev. hist. de droit français et étranger*, xxix (1951), pp. 465–99, who shows the development of the notion in Roman law (Papinian, Paul and Ulpian) and in imperial legislation (*utilitas reipublicae*): the meanings attributable to it, were virtually inexhaustible (cf. pp. 485–93). The concept of *raison d'état* is an offspring of this idea. From the hierocratic point of view, the principle of *publica utilitas* is extraordinarily fruitful. Primarily of teleological contents, the notion belongs to the sphere of government and developed partly out of the "cura et sollicitudo" which the pope has for the whole of Christendom, and partly out of the equally old principle of usefulness. In all its maturity this principle was expressed by Guido de Baysio (the Archdeacon) in the following century: "Dominus papa cuius est cognoscere quod utile reipublicae et quod non," *Rosarium* ad XV. vi. 3. Under this heading may come the papal claims to confirm or annul treaties made between secular rulers, to incite rebellion in a country, to depose rulers, etc.; the relevant papal documents are conveniently assembled by Pallieri and Vismara, *Acta pontificia*, cit., pp. 115 ff., 146 ff., 149 ff.

[1] *Policr.*, loc. cit.: "Tunc autem totius reipublicae salus incolumis praeclaraque erit, si superiora membra se impendant inferioribus, et inferiora superioribus pari jure respondeant, ut singuli sint quasi aliorum ad invicem membra, et in eo sibi quisque maxime credat esse consultum, in quo aliis utilius noverit esse prospectum."

[2] *Policr.* vi. 25; cf. also ibid., v. 7.

[3] The whole *Orbis Latinus* has heard with horror of the violent death of Thomas Becket, *Ep.* ccciv, col. 355.

[4] D. Knowles, *Monastic Order in England*, p. 218.

the pope has indeed all the makings of a *speculum paparum* on the model of the *speculum regum*.[1] There is perhaps no other writer in the medieval period who because he was so much a theologian, was so eminently "political." But this cannot cause any surprise. Bernard's outlook, philosophy and therefore theology, was one, was cast into one consistent and integrated whole. With him a separation of the various categories of thinking could not possibly exist: Bernard was indeed the most consequent exponent of Christian cosmology. The overpowering role which he attributed to faith, could not lead to any other "political" doctrine but the hierocratic one.

Unity of the body of Christians presupposes unity of leadership. Unity and monarchy are for Bernard one and the same principle, though seen from two different angles. The corporate body of all Christians, that is, the "multitudo credentium" form the "corpus ipsum Christi,"[2] or the "domus Dei."[3] The nature of this society presupposes that it can have one head only, him who has the "plenitudo potestatis"[4] and who is the vicar of Christ. The function of the pope as the true monarch of this "corpus Christi" is the necessary guarantee of the unity of this "corpus." Those who adhere to Anacletus II— Innocent II's anti-pope—are "enemies of unity";[5] are not Christians, but follow anti-christ.[6] The subject of the papal monarchy is something that concerns the whole Church, and not merely a single individual,[7] such as that man of Jewish extraction, Anacletus, who had occupied the see of Peter to the detriment of Christ.[8] For it is through

---

[1] Cf. also E. Caspar, in *Meister der Politik*, Berlin, 1926, i. 576. The concrete influence of this tract upon the popes in the twelfth and thirteenth centuries would be worth detailed study. That above all Innocent III had studied the tract carefully, becomes clear when one peruses this pope's correspondence. Even the allegedly scholastic triad ("quid liceat; quid deceat; quid expediat") in the *Deliberatio* (RNI. 29) is Bernardine; cf. *De consideratione*, III. iv. 15 (PL. clxxxii).

[2] *De consideratione*, III. i, PL. cit., col. 760; cf. also his *Sermo XII in Cant. cant.*, no. 7 (PL. clxxxiii. 831).

[3] *Ep.* ccxxii. 5 (PL. clxxxii. 389); *Ep.* ccxxxvi. 1, col. 424.

[4] *De cons.*, II. viii, col. 752: "Ergo juxta canones tuos, alii in partem sollicitudinis, tu in plenitudinem potestatis vocatus es. Aliorum potestas certis arctatur limitibus, tua extenditur et in ipsos qui potestatem super alios acceperunt." Cf. also *Ep.* ccxxxix, col. 431. For some interpretative details of Bernard's "plenitudo potestatis" cf. now B. Jacqueline in *Bernard de Clairvaux*, Paris, 1953, pp. 346–7.

[5] *Ep.* cxxvi. 8, col. 276: "Hostes unitatis."

[6] *Ep.* cit., col. 275: "Probaret sese non christianum, sed anti-christum." Cf. with this John of Salisbury's view about Henry II, supra p. 422 n. 1.

[7] *Ep.* cit., no. 11, col. 279: "Universae quippe ecclesiae negotium est, non unius causa personae."

[8] *Ep.* cxxxix. 1, col. 294: "Constat Judaicam sobolem sedem Petri in Christi occupasse injuriam." Anacletus belonged to the family of the Pierleoni.

the instrumentality of the one Roman Church, and therefore of the one pope, that this "corpus Christi" is alive, that what it is, it has become through the papal monarch. Moreover, the papal plenitude of power, that singularly monarchic distinction, is not of human origin, but is divinely derived: he who resists it, therefore resists God's ordinance.[1] The "corpus" thus presided over by the papal monarch, embraces all kingdoms and the empire: this "corpus" is a *State* which is holy—"civitas sancta"—because it is the corporate universal Church of the living God.[2] Unity can be preserved only by the monarchic rule of the one pope.[3]

The pope, in St Bernard's mind, is no longer a vicar of St Peter, but of Christ.[4] The papal plenitude of power was considered to constitute a vicariate of Christ; the crucial words "Tu es Petrus . . ." were understood to mean a vicariate of Christ; the binding and loosening powers of the pope were taken as expressing the mediatory role of the pope, the role of the mediator between God and man. The Pauline declaration that "there is one mediator between God and man, the man Christ Jesus"[5] is now directly applicable to the pope, as the vicar of Christ. Even etymologically, the term "pontifex" demonstrates the function of a bridge-builder—"pontem facere inter Deum et proximum"—of a good mediator, who offers the prayers and the requests

[1] *Ep.* cxxxi. 2, col. 287: "Plenitudo potestatis super universas orbis ecclesias, singulari prerogativa apostolicae sedis donata est: qui igitur huic potestati resistit, Dei ordinationi resistit."

[2] *Ep.* cxxiv. 2, col. 269: ". . . civitatem sanctam, quae est ecclesia Dei viventis." Cf. also Bernard's *Liber ad Milites*, cap. 5 (11), PL. cit., col. 928: "Civitas sancta . . . Regis magna." Cf. also Anselm, *Homil. I* (PL. clviii. 587–8). It may be recalled that St Augustine considered the State a "societas" or a "multitudo hominum" (*Civ. Dei*, ii. 21; xix. 21, 24; also *Ep.* cxxxviii. 10, etc.). This conception of the State is Ciceronian, cf. supra p. 271 n. 2.

[3] Cf. also *Ep.* cxxv. 2, col. 270: "Alemanniae, Franciae, Angliae, Scotiae, Hispaniarum et Jerosolymorum reges, cum universis populis et clero, favent et adhaerent domino Innocentio, tamquam filii patri, tamquam capiti membra."

[4] *Ep.* ccli, col. 451; *De consideratione*, ii. 8, col. 752, and iv. 7, col. 788; cf. also *De moribus*, viii (31), PL. cit., col. 829, and ix (36), col. 832. The popes began slowly to adopt the title "vicarius Christi" as a result of Bernard's influence (cf. Eugenius III supra 342), until with Innocent III this became the official and usual title. Bernard it should be noted, does not seem the inventor of the title "vicarius Christi" as a title exclusively applicable to the pope alone. The immediate predecessor was St Peter Damian, see M. Maccarrone, "Il papa 'vicarius Christi' " in *Miscellanea Pio Paschini*, Rome, 1949, i. 429–31; here also other twelfth-century testimonies, but all coming from non-papal sources, pp. 432–43; they are rather reminiscent of Anastasius Bibliothecarius, see supra 192. About the appellation of Gelasius I by the synodists assembled in Rome, see supra 26 n. 4 and about Gerhoh supra p. 411 n. 2.

[5] I *Tim.* ii. 5.

of the peoples to God and, on the other hand, gives them God's benediction.[1] Indeed, the pope's position on earth approaches that of God.[2] The pope is "os de ossibus suis (scil. Christi)"; he is flesh from His flesh, spirit from His spirit.[3] And Bernard tells the pope that he has no equal on earth: "parem super terram non habes."[4] It is rather self-evident, on this basis, that by virtue of the Petrine commission, the pope as Christ's vicar was given the government of the world (*saeculum*), and not merely the government of the *sacerdotium*.[5] Self-evident also, because if the "corpus unum" is considered a *civitas*, the vicar of Christ must be able to rule, to govern it, otherwise this "corpus" may not fulfil the purpose and aim for which it is established.

Unicum se Christi vicarium designavit,[6] qui non uno populo, sed cunctis praeesse deberet.

It is in his function as vicar of Christ that all Christians show their liveliest interest in the pope: the stupid and the wise, the freeman and the serf, rich and poor, man and woman, young and old, cleric and

[1] *De moribus*, iii. 10, col. 817; cf. also ibid: "Pertingit pons iste usque ad Deum ea fiducia, qua non suam, sed illius gloriam quaerit. Pertingit usque ad proximum illa pietate, qua et ipsi, non sibi prodesse desiderat. Offert Deo bonus mediator praeces et vota populorum, reportans illis a Deo benedictionem et gratiam." Cf. in this context again St Anselm, *Homil.* I, PL. clviii. 588.

[2] *Ep.* cxcvi. 2, col. 364: "Domino papae contradicere est et etiam Domino Deo." Cf. also *Ep.* cxxxi, col. 286: "Bene vobiscum facit Deus; bene vobiscum facit Romana ecclesia; facit ille quod pater, facit illa quod mater." This was written to the Milanese.

[3] *Ep.* cxxvi. 6, col. 275: "Carnem de carne sua, spiritum de spiritu suo." This was frequently quoted in later canonistic doctrine. About Benzo of Alba's description of the emperor, see supra 391. Innocent III's well known expression may be modelled on Bernard: the pope is "inter Deum et hominem *medius* constitutus, citra Deum, sed ultra hominem; minor Deo, sed major homine," *Sermo iii in consecr. pontificis*, PL. ccxvii. 658. *Reg.* i. 335: the pope "non puri hominis, sed veri Dei vicem gerit in terris." According to Peter of Blois, St Peter "regnat, et imperat et *in medio constitutus* est," PL. ccvi. 1270.

[4] *De consideratione*, II. ii. 4, col. 744.

[5] *De consideratione*, II. ii. 8, col. 752: "Nempe signum singularis pontificii Petri, per quod non navem unam, ut caeteri quique suam, sed *saeculum ipsum susceperit gubernandum*. Mare enim saeculum est, naves ecclesiae." With this should be compared Innocent III, *Reg.* ii. 209: "Petro non solum universam ecclesiam, sed totum saeculum gubernandum reliquit . . . per hoc quod Petrus se misit in mare, privilegium expressit pontificii singularis, per quod universum orbem susceperat gubernandum." Cf. also before him Alexander III, *Ep.* 762 (PL. cc. 699): "In hoc mari magno et spatioso (*Ps.* ciii. 25) . . . ubi non tam corporum et corporalium mercium, quam animarum et spiritualium virtutum pericula formidantur, ei qui navem regit ecclesiae . . ."; furthermore Innocent III in *Reg.* vii. 1, obviously borrowing from St Bernard.

[6] These words too are copied by Innocent III in *Reg.* ii. 209, and in other places.

layman, the just and the impious—they all drink from the public fount, the pope's breast: "Omnes de fonte publico bibunt pectore tuo."[1] The pope is the king of the earth, the lord of the heavens,[2] because the apostolic see is "singularly distinguished by divine and royal privileges."[3] Christ Himself was supreme priest and king—"summus et sacerdos et rex"[4]—and consequently *regnum* and *sacerdotium* were united in Him.[5] The pope is His vicar;[6] and hence as the supreme monarch of this universal *civitas sancta* he disposes of kingdoms and empires and presides over the princes, nations and peoples.[7] In short, the pope is "vicarius Christi, christus Domini, deus Pharaonis."[8] His voice as vicar of Christ rings out over the entire world: "Ipsius vox est hodie per universum mundum."[9]

Thrown against such a background and set against the attribution of such functions to the pope, it is something like an anticlimax when St Bernard descends to allegorical language and states that the pope alone possesses both swords. As vicar of Him who was both king and priest,

---

[1] *De consideratione*, i. 5, col. 735. Cf. Eugenius III's expression which may be an echo of Bernard: "Ab ea (scil. Romana ecclesia) sicut a fonte ad universos ecclesiae filios sit religio derivata" (PL. clxxx. 1541).    [2] *Ep.* ccxliii, col. 439.

[3] *Ep.* cit.: "Sacram et apostolicam sedem, divinis regalibusque privilegiis singulariter sublimatam."

[4] *Ep.* ccxliv, col. 441.    [5] *Ep.* ccxliv, col. 441.

[6] That the old conception of the vicariate of Christ was not yet dead in the late twelfth century, is shown by the *Summa Reginensis* in which we read: "Presbiter ... personam Christi habet, argumentum contra illos qui dicunt solum papam esse vicarium Christi. Nam quilibet sacerdos est vicarius Christi et Petri ... Dicebat cardinalis sanctorum Johannis et Pauli quod inde dominus papa dicitur Christi vicarius, quia Iesus Christus toto orbi preest ita et papa," ed. A. M. Stickler, *Salesianum*, xiv (1952), p. 489. About the cardinal mentioned here, cf. ibid., note 68.

[7] See, for instance, his reproach to the cardinals who had elected his pupil pope (Eugenius III). *Ep.* ccxxxvii, col. 426: "Was there not a sensible man amongst you?" he asks them: "Ridiculum profecto videtur, pannosum homuncionem assumi ad praesidendum principibus, ad imperandum episcopis, ad regna et imperia disponenda." And before: "Quid igitur rationis seu consilii habuit ... irruere in hominem rusticanum, latenti injicere manus, et excussa e manibus securi et ascia vel ligone, in palatium trahere, levare in cathedram, induere purpura et bysso, accingere gladio ad faciendam vindictam in nationibus, increpationes in populis, ad alligandos reges eorum in compedibus, et nobiles eorum in manicis ferreis?" Cf. *Ps.* cxlix. 8.

[8] *De consideratione*, iv. 7, col. 788. On the expression "deus Pharaonis" (*Ex.* vii. 1) see J. Rivière, "Sur l'expression Papa-Deus au moyen âge" in *Miscellanea Francesco Ehrle*, Rome, 1926, ii. 278, who also shows that later "deus Pharaonis" was changed into "Papa est Deus imperatoris" (p. 285: Alvarus Pelagius). It should be noted that Innocent III has the same expressions as Bernard in his *Sermo iii in consecr. pont.*, PL. ccxvii. 658.

[9] *Ep.* ccvliii. 2, col. 438.

the pope in the allegorical language of the time, must needs possess both swords, the spiritual as well as the physical-material sword. For the pope is the monarch of this *civitas*. The one sword he possesses and uses, the other he hands over to the secular prince to be wielded at the bidding of the priests: "Is (scil. materialis gladius) *pro* ecclesia, ille (scil. spiritualis gladius) *ab* ecclesia exserendus: ille sacerdotis, is militis manu, sed sane ad nutum sacerdotis et jussum imperatoris."[1] And in order to leave no doubt in the mind of his papal addressee, the Saint tells him: "The material sword is yours and is to be used at your bidding, though it is not to be drawn out of the sheath by your own hand."[2] In his pleading to Eugenius III for the crusade, Bernard urges the pope to wait no longer, but to draw both swords: "Exserendus est

---

[1] *De consideratione*, iv. 3, col. 776. There may be a further echo of Bernard in Innocent III, *Reg.* ii. 259 (to the Armenian king): "Cum . . . materialem acceperis gladium, non in domesticos fidei, sed hostes crucis potius *exerendum*"; see also *Reg.* iii. 24, and several other places. Cf. also the echo of Bernard in Gregory IX's combination of the Two-Sword theory with the theory of the translation of the empire: MGH. *Epp. sel. XIII s.*, i. no. 672, p. 568: "Ecclesia gladii spiritualis et materialis obtinens a Domino potestatem, ut alteram ipsa *exerat*, et ut alter *exeratur* indicat, imperium eidem Carolo . . . contulit." An almost literal borrowing of St Bernard in Gregory's letter to the patriarch of Constantinople: "Uterque igitur gladius ecclesiae traditur, sed ab ecclesia exercetur unus; alius pro ecclesia, manu saecularis principis est eximendus, unus a sacerdote, alius ad nutum sacerdotis *administrandus* a milite," Mansi, xxiii. 60. Gregory omits the Bernardine "ad jussum imperatoris." Cf. also *Epp.* cit. no. 553, p. 448: " 'Ecce gladii duo hic,' id est, non hic unus, et alius alibi sunt, sed hic in uno loco." Innocent IV expressed the allegory in an original manner. The power symbolized by the physical sword is with the pope *potentialis*, and through handing the sword to the emperor this power becomes *actualis*. The coronation ceremony brings this out visibly according to Innocent IV: the pope hands the sheathed sword to the emperor who unsheathes it and brandishes it in the air as a sign that he now has the exercise of physical-material power. "Hoc nempe ille ritus ostendit, quo summus pontifex Caesari, quem coronat, exhibet gladium vagina contentum, quem acceptum princeps *exerit* et *vibrando* innuit se illius exercitium accepisse," F. Winkelmann, *Acta imperii inedita*, ii. 698, no. 1035. This realistic symbolism was indicated already by Gregory IX addressing Frederick II: "(Gladium) de corpore b. Petri sumptum et de manu susceptum vicarii Iesu Christi imperialis *vibravit dextera* ad vindictam malefactorum," *Epp.* cit., i. 392, no. 488; see also Innocent IV after the deposition of Frederick II, ibid., ii. 247, no. 184. Bernard's formula was also incorporated in *Unam Sanctam*, though in accentuated form, cf. now also W. Levison in *Deutsches Archiv*, ix (1952), p. 36. It will be recalled that the pope sent to Henry VII of England (and also to Henry VIII) the sword, cf. J. W. Legg in *Archaeolog. Journ.*, lvii (1900), pp. 183–98; the liturgy, pp. 199–201, may be modelled on the *Ordo* composed by Durantis.(*ob.* 1296).

[2] St Bernard, loc. cit.: "Tuus ergo et ipse, tuo forsitan nutu, etsi non tua manu evaginandus." He continues: "Alioquin si nullo modo ad te pertineret et is, dicentibus apostolis 'ecce gladii duo' non respondisset dominus 'satis est,' sed 'nimis est.' " (*Luke* xxii. 38). On the linguistic dependence of Bernard on the

uterque gladius."[1] "Who else but you can do this?"—"per quem autem nisi per vos"—because both swords are St Peter's: "Petri uterque est," the one to be used at his bidding, the other by his own hand: "alter suo nutu, alter sua manu, quoties necesse est, evaginandus."[2] Any other view would have been inconsistent: the unity of Bernard's outlook demanded unity of government, and this unity of government could be found only in the proper monarchic rule.

St Bernard's thesis is, moreover, entirely consistent with the old tenet of the function which the prince has to fulfil in a Christian society: his *raison d'être* is the suppression of evil.[3] He has to execute what the spiritual sword is incapable of achieving; his function therefore is auxiliary and complementary. He is therefore bidden by the *sacerdotium* to act and to use force for the good of the whole Christian body politic. What the good of this body politic is, must necessarily be left to the pope (or the *sacerdotes*).[4] The decision to act lies in sacerdotal hands: *ad nutum* expresses the binding signal of the pope to the prince to use the sword; *ad jussum imperatoris* expresses the legitimate exercise of physical power. The authority as to when this physical power is to be legitimately exercised always remains with the pope: the prince is the "patronus, advocatus, defensor ecclesiae." In short, he is the protector of the Christian people, and as a protector in the Roman-papal sense he is controlled by those who in the symbolic transfer of the sword hand him his power.[5] The vicar of Christ as successor of St

---

Scriptures in general see V. Lossky, "Études sur la terminologie de s. Bernard" in *Bulletin du Cange*, xvi (1942), pp. 82–6. For Bernard's quotations from profane writers, see now *Bernard de Clairvaux*, 1953, app. iv, pp. 549–54.

[1] *Ep.* cclvi. 1, col. 463.

[2] *Ep.* cclvi. 1, col. 464.

[3] Cf. his *Liber ad Milites Templi*, cap. 3 (PL. clxxxii. 925): In killing the pagans by the sword "Christus glorificatur," for the swords are used "ad destruendam omnem altitudinem extollentem se adversus scientiam Dei, quae est christianorum fides." See also *Ep.* cxxxix. 1, col. 294 (to Lothar): "Non est meum hortari ad pugnam; est tamen (securus dico) *advocati ecclesiae* arcere ab ecclesiae infestatione schismaticorum rabiem . . ." Here Bernard merely expresses the old doctrine of the emperor as the advocate; cf. Eugenius III calling the emperor "specialis advocatus" (PL. clxxx. 1638) or Alexander III: "advocatus ac specialis defensor Romanae ecclesiae" (MGH. *Const.* i. no. 185, p. 256).

[4] About *publica utilitas* see supra p. 425 n. 2

[5] About the two conceptions of protection cf. supra 69 ff. In many ways the ideology of this Two-Sword theory is exactly the same as that underlying the Donation of Constantine, according to which the pope possessed the imperial crown, but left its use to the emperor, cf. supra p. 82. This fact and time-tied ideology was now expressed in biblical-allegorical terms. Common to both was the ideology of the function of the secular ruler in a Christian society.

Peter and therefore as possessor of both swords appoints a suitable actual bearer of the physical sword for the express purpose of protection. The pope appears as, and is, the true monarch. The development of the Pauline-Gelasian-Isidorian thesis was concluded.[1] As the true monarch of the *civitas sancta*, of the corporate congregation of the faithful, the pope exercises a supervisory function over everything occurring in this body: he is the "speculator super omnia."[2] For he is set over the nations and kingdoms for this purpose by Christ Himself as His vicar.[3]

St Bernard pursues this functionalist theme relentlessly. Dealing with mundane matters is beneath the dignity of the *sacerdotes* and all the more so of the vicar of Christ. Of course, if the priests insisted, they could deal with mundane matters directly, and so naturally could the pope. This right is unquestionable. What is questionable is whether it is expedient and advisable for the pope and the priests to act thus. Parcelling out of lands, settling all sorts of disputes concerning the "terrena possessiuncula hominum"[4] or acting as a "divisor terminorum aut distributor terrarum" are activities which are unbecoming to

---

[1] Cf. Bernard himself in his *Lib. ad Milites Templi*, c. 3, PL. cit., col. 824–5.

[2] *De consideratione*, II. vi. 10, col. 748. The term "speculator" is biblical, *Ez.* iii. 17: "Fili hominis, speculatorem dedi te domui Israel." This Bernardine expression was adopted by Innocent III, *Reg.* ii. 95: "Nos, qui licet indigni, *speculatoris officium* super universam ecclesiam exercemus"; also in *Reg.* ii. 240 and in other places. The term was applied to the bishop by the mid-twelfth century *Summa Codicis* (ascribed to Rogerius by H. Kantorowicz, *Studies*, etc., pp. 149, 154 f.; ed. by H. Fitting, but attributed to Irnerius), p. 8, line 3, saying of the bishop "qui recte *speculator* seu superintendens appellatur." It now turns out that St Bernard was very familiar with this *Summa*, cf. B. Jacqueline, "Bernard et le Droit Romain" in *Bernard de Clairvaux*, Paris, 1953, pp. 430–1.

[3] *Ep.* clxxxix. 5, col. 356 (to Innocent II): "Nonne cum esses parvulus in oculis tuis, ipse te constituit super gentes et regna? Ad quid, nisi ut evellas et destruas et aedifices et plantes?" Also *Ep.* ccxl. 1, col. 432, to Eugenius III: "Unde et de flecto genua mea ad ipsum unici huius vestri primatus auctorem, ut det vobis sic sapere et sic agere semper in evellendo et plantando in destruendo et aedificando." Furthermore, *De moribus*, vii. 26, col. 826; *De cons.* II. vi, col. 747. The biblical reference is to *Jer.* i. 10. Cf. Alexander III, *Ep.* 975, PL. cc. 850: quoting the same Jeremiah passage: "Super gentes et regna, licet immeriti, in apostolica *specula* constituti, pontificalis officii debito pro universis compellimur sollicitudinem gerere . . ."; also *Ep.* 979, col. 854: "Constituti a Domino super gentes et regna . . . compellimur . . . ad universum commissi gregis corpus extendere"; also *Ep.* 624, col. 595; *Ep.* 1173, col. 1017. Innocent III, in *Reg.* ii. 220; vii. 42; and *Sermo II in cons. pont.*, PL. cit. col. 657; also RNI. 2, 18, 46 (applied to the papal legate, also in *Reg.* i. 526: legates are sent "per varia mundi climata" so that they do on behalf of the pope as said in *Jer.* i. 10; also *Reg.* ii. 123, 202, and in numerous other places).

[4] *De consid.*, I. vi, col. 736.

16

apostolic dignity:[1] "non quia indigni vos, sed quia indignum vobis talibus insistere, quippe potioribus occupatis."[2] Not that all this direct intervention is incompatible with the power of the keys, but that this is unworthy of this unique power, is the gist of Bernard's advice to the pope. "What is greater," he asks the pope, "to dismiss sins or to divide estates?"[3] "Ergo in criminibus, non in possessionibus potestas vestra" he tells the pope. The power of the keys refers naturally to the conduct, that is, the mode of living, not to (lifeless) possessions.[4] Of course, if the "possessions" are consequences of "criminal behaviour," papal jurisdiction comes into full play.[5] For the substance of the *civitas sancta*, the corporate entity of the Christians, is the spiritual element of faith, and since this is what gives society its complexion,

---

[1] *De consid.*, I, vi, col. 735: "Derogans apostolicae dignitatis." That is why Bernard inveighs against the noise made by Justinian's laws in the Roman curia: "Quotidie perstrepunt in palatio leges Justiniani, non Domini." That the Saint was quite well versed in Roman law is now shown by B. Jacqueline, art. cit., pp. 429 ff. Anxiety about life in the Roman curia had already been expressed by Peter Damian in his letter to the cardinals, PL. cxliv. 256: "Porro quia ad Lateranense palatium a diversis populis de toto terrarum orbe confluitur, necesse est ut ibi prae ceteris uspiam locis, recta semper vivendi sit forma, districta teneatur assidue sub honestis moribus disciplina." Cf. also the vituperations of Bernard's contemporary, Bernard of Morval, in his *De contemptu mundi*, for which see R. C. Petry, "Medieval eschatology, etc." in *Speculum*, xxiv (1949), p. 214; about Gerhoh see supra 411 and cf. also John of Salisbury's well-known account of the people's feeling towards the Roman curia during his conversation with Adrian IV at Benevento, see *Policr.*, vi. 24 ("Nam pauper aut nullus aut rarus admittitur . . . justitiam non tam veritati quam pretio reddunt . . . sedent in ea scribae et pharisaei . . .").

[2] Bernard, loc. cit., col. 736.

[3] An allusion to *Luke*, v. 23. The basis of this Bernardine opinion is I *Cor*. vi. 4: "Saecularia igitur judicia, si habueritis, contemptibiles qui sunt in ecclesia, illos constituite ad judicandum." The great imitator of Bernard, Robert Grosseteste, quotes the Bernardine passage at length in his letter remonstrating against the royal appointments of abbots as itinerant justices. Commenting on the "contemptibiles" he says (*Ep.* lxxii*, ed. cit., pp. 206–7): "Contemptibiles scilicet, non imperitia judicandi, sed vitae inferioris merito et dignitatis gradu et impotentia percipiendi spiritualia. Sed numquid viri contemplativi sunt de contemptibilibus in ecclesia? . . . Liquet quod ad potestates saeculares et non ad dignitates ecclesiasticas pertinent causarum saecularium discussio et decisio; personae namque in gradibus et dignitatibus ecclesiasticis constitutae sunt velut stellae, quas posuit Deus in firmamento coeli (*Gen*. i. 17) et tamquam elementa mundi superiora." The principle applies to all ecclesiastical persons, p. 210.

[4] *De consideratione*, I. vi, col. 736: "Propter illa (scil. crimina), et non propter has (scil. possessiones) accepistis claves regni coelorum."

[5] This is, as we may recall, the theme of Innocent III's *Novit ille*: "Non enim intendimus judicare de feudo . . . sed decernere de peccato, cuius ad nos pertinet sine dubitatione censura, quam in quemlibet exercere possumus et debere . . . super quolibet *criminali peccato*."

meaning and purpose, the pope's jurisdiction in matters affecting the substance of this society, that is, the "crimina," cannot be denied. Priestly and papal authority is directive; it is the regulative authority of the corporate body; it governs by issuing orders as to what is and what is not to be done, so as to realize the purpose of this society; the doing itself is not the proper function of the priests; for this there are special organs, above all the secular princes who are instituted precisely for this purpose.

What Bernard wishes to express in his criticisms of the direct handling of disputes by the clerics, is the danger to which this activity exposes them. Engulfed as they become in the myriads of quibbles,[1] they consequently tend to neglect their proper functions, with the result that they are bound to lose their freedom.[2] Too many have succumbed to this temptation: too many have become victims of what a Gelasius had once called "human frailty." What is necessary, is the implementation of the principle of functional order, or what Bernard calls *discretio*.[3] Functionally the prince exists to do all these numerous terrestrial matters; that is why he has been instituted by the *sacerdotium*, and that is why he has been given the physical sword. Hence strict adherence to the functional ordering within the Christian *civitas* is imperative, if this *civitas* is to be a workable entity, otherwise confusion will prevail[4] instead of unity based upon order:

Dum sibi *assignato officio* nemo *contentus* erit, sed omnes omnia indiscreta administratione pariter attentabunt, non plene unitas erit, sed magis *confusio*.[5]

*Discretio* or order and fulfilling the function assigned to each member of the *civitas* is what Bernard is anxious to see applied.[6] The opposite

[1] Cf. *Ep.* lxxviii. 11, cols. 193, 197, 198.

[2] This theme is strongly re-echoed in Grosseteste's letter, loc. cit., pp. 214–15.

[3] Cf. Bernard's *Sermo xlix in Cant.*, PL. cit., col. 1018: "*Discretio* quippe omni virtuti *ordinem ponit: ordo modum tribuit* et decorem . . . est ergo discretio non tam virtus quam quaedam moderatrix . . . tolle hanc et virtus vitium erit."

[4] Cf. also his observations on clerical soldiers who are neither soldiers nor clerics: "Nempe habitu milites, quaestu clericos, actu *neutrum* exhibent. Nam neque pugnant ut milites, neque ut clerici evangelizant. *Cuius ordinis* sunt? Cum utriusque esse cupiunt, *utrumque deserunt, utrumque confundunt,*" *De cons.*, IV. v. 20, col. 772.     [5] *Sermo* cit., col. 1019.

[6] It will be recalled that Gelasius also said that Christ *discrevit* the two offices. It is not without interest to note that Bernard who to all seeming was not acquainted with Gelasius's writings, uses the same term *discretio* to express the same thought as Gelasius. Cf. Gelasius laying down the principle of functional order, supra p. 25, and also St Augustine, supra p. 290 n. 1. We should not that Bernard's pope was the "vicarius Christi," a position which the pope did not have in Gelasius's thought.

is *confundere ordinem, perturbare terminos*.[1] This *civitas* is one body "fitly joined together" which can realize its purpose only when each member performs the functions due to him—"secundum operationem in mensuram uniuscuiusque membri"[2]—when in other words everyone works towards the same end within his allotted sphere of activity.

The pope, then, in Bernard's conception, is Christ on earth. In this function he is the monarch directing the *civitas*.[3] For the mundane matters he appoints a prince by the symbolic handing over of the physical sword; he appoints a *potestas*, not because he has no right to do what he bids the prince to do, but because the thing itself is unworthy of being dealt with by the "vicarius Christi." But next to this *potestas*, the vicar of Christ should also appoint a chief minister, an "oeconomus," in the curia itself, who is to have *auctoritas* for sacerdotal matters. True, the vicar of Christ will still have to do some things personally, but there is a good deal of ordinary curial business— exchange of bishops; their translation; litigations, and so forth—with the handling of which the chief minister should be entrusted: "Procurandus quem implices, qui pro te molat."[4] This minister toiling for the pope, should be loyal and prudent, but he must also have *auctoritas* in these sacerdotal matters.[5] And the *auctoritas* must indeed be a full

---

[1] *De cons.*, III. iv. 17, col. 768.　　[2] *De cons.*, III. iv. 17, col. 768; *Ephes.* iv. 16.
[3] In IV. i, col. 759, he applies *Matt.* xxiv. 45 to the pope: "Quem constituit super familiam suam"; cf. also *Jer.* i. 10. This Matthew passage was later made the subject of Innocent III's second consecration sermon (PL. ccxvii. 653 ff.) in which the pope combines it with his responsibility as the monarch for all his subjects: "Redditurus Deo rationem, non solum pro se, sed pro omnibus qui sunt suae curae commissi. At omnes omnino qui sunt de familia Domini, sub eius cura constituti sunt; non enim distinguit inter hanc atque illam familiam, nec pluraliter dicitur, super familias, tamquam multas, sed singulariter dicitur."
[4] *De cons.*, IV. vi, col. 785. The general rule should be: "Quaedam per temet facies; quaedam per te et alios simul; quaedam per alios ac absque te." This, too, may be a source of Innocentian thought, *Reg.* v. 128: "Porro saecularis officium potestatis interdum et in quibusdam per se, nonumquam autem et in nonnullis per alios exsequi consuevit (scil. papa)"; cf. also *Reg.* ii. 202.
[5] Loc cit.: "Quaerendus proinde fidelis et prudens, quem constitues super familiam tuam. Adhuc inutilis est, si tertium desit. Quaeris quid hoc? *Auctoritas*." One might perhaps see in the comprehensive powers and authority of the later chamberlain a partial realization of Bernard's idea. On the chamberlain in the thirteenth century see B. Rusch, *Die Behörden und Beamten der päpstlichen Kurie des 13. Jahrhunderts*, Koenigsberg, 1936, pp. 23 f., 54 ff. There can be little doubt that the later papal tribunal, the *Rota*, staffed by the "capellani" and in this function called "capellani auditores" was an implementation of Bernard's advice, I. xi. 14, col. 742: "Quaedam, ut dixi, negotia nec audiendo, quaedam aliis committendo, quae tua digna putaveris *audientia*, fideli quodam et accomodo ipsi causae compendio terminando." Cf. also N. del Re, *La Curia Romana*, Rome, 1952, p. 217.

one, so that nobody can say to this chief minister: "Why did you do this?"—"cur fecisti sic?"—nor shall he suffer any contradiction: "subdendi igitur omnes."[1] All the routine sacerdotal business should be concentrated in this minister's hands.[2] All this is the consistent application of the idea that Christ is head of the Christian *civitas*: it is Christ's vicar who in actual fact fulfils this role of the "caput."[3]

This brief survey of St Bernard's ideas will have shown that within their scope it is not the mystical visionary who speaks to us; rather an author who logically pursues the unitary and monarchic principle; his *civitas* is the Christian body politic ruled by Christ through His vicar: the pope is the vicar of Him Who was "verus rex et pontifex." As the Saint's disciple, Pope Eugenius III, said: the *universa christianitas* knows that St Peter had been entrusted by Christ with the *jura terreni simul et coelestis imperii*.[4]

## IV

Whilst the accent in Bernard's ecclesiastical-political writings lies on the function of the pope as vicar of Christ within the *civitas*, Hugh of St Victor concentrates on the concept of *ecclesia*. It is, we think, no

---

[1] *De cons.*, IV. vi, col. 785: "Praesit omnibus, ut omnibus prosit."

[2] *De cons.*, IV. vi, col. 785: "Potestatem habeat excludere et admittere quos voluerit, mutare ministros, transferre ministeria ad quos et quando voluerit. Ita timore sit omnibus, ut sit utilitati."

[3] This idea leads to the formulation of Christ's visible vicariate in the pope cf. infra pp. 444, 449.

[4] See *Ep.* 232 of 12 October 1147 (PL. clxxx. 1285). The phrase is no more than the Petrine commission expressed in the easily available juristic terminology. It is of course very likely that Eugenius was familiar with Gratian's *Decretum*, cf. R. Gleber, *Papst Eugen III* (in *Beiträge zur mittelalterlichen und neueren Geschichte*, vol. vi, 1936), pp. 74–5. The canonists shortly afterwards coined the significant term of the *claves juris* possessed by the pope (*Summa Coloniensis*). The phrase itself came from St Peter Damian, *Disceptatio synodalis*, MGH. LdL. i. 78, lines 7–8. Cf. also Peter Damian's poem no. LXXII, PL. cxlv. 941: "Tibi, Petre, sunt traditae (claves) tuisque patent legibus terrena cum coelestibus." The phrase was capable of infinite expansion and variation. Cf. Honorius III, MGH. *Epp. sel. XIII s.*, i. no. 234, p. 163; Gregory IX, ibid., no. 672, p. 568; Innocent IV, ibid., ii, no. 71, p. 52, linking the idea of Peter Damian with the conception of true monarchy: "Dominus Iesus Christus, Dei filius . . . in apostolica sede non solum pontificalem, sed et regalem constituit *monarchatum*, b. Petro eiusque successoribus terreni simul ac coelestis imperii commissis habenis, quod in pluralitate clavium competenter innuitur, ut per unam, quam in temporalibus super terram, per reliquam quam in spiritualibus super coelos accepimus, intelligatur Christi vicarius judicii potentiam accepisse," E. Winkelmann, *Acta imperii inedita*, ii. 698, no. 1035. The phrase is quoted as late as the fourteenth century by John XXII (*Extrav.*, V. un.).

exaggeration to maintain that with Hugh the idea of the universal Church as a corporate and autonomous entity which has to be governed according to its own underlying principles, reaches its full maturity.[1]

Hugh of St Victor sharply distinguishes between the Church and the priesthood: the "Church" is by no means the sacerdotal hierarchy, but a living organism composed of the two orders, the laical and sacerdotal. "Quid est ergo ecclesia nisi multitudo fidelium, universitas christianorum?"[2] This organic body is Christian: in so far as every one of its members whether or not ordained, is a Christian, he is an essential part of the body.[3] It is held together solely by the element of Christ's spirit and as such transcends all natural, biological, linguistic or racial frontiers. The element vivifying this body is the faith in Christ:

> Per fidem membra efficimur ... per fidem accipimus unionem.

Nevertheless, this corporate union is also earthy: it must live; it consists of living human beings; it must be guided; it must, above all, be organized so that it may be adequately administered. Hence different functions are allotted to the different parts composing this entity. The character of this *unum corpus* as an organic entity—spiritual in substance, earthy in appearance—presupposes in other words a differentiation of the functions so as to make this body an integrated whole. It is of course true that "omnes unum corpus," but this does not mean that all have the same functions within this *unum corpus*. This body may very well be compared with the human body. The latter's parts are parts of the whole; each part functions for the sake of the whole, and thereby integration of the human personality is achieved. All parts of the human body have, in Hugh's words, "propria et *discreta officia*."[4] The

---

[1] One of the first to draw attention to the importance of Hugh's concept of *ecclesia* was A. Hauck, "Die Rezeption und Umbildung der allgemeinen Synode" in *Hist. Viertel jahrschrift*, x (1907), pp. 467 f.

[2] *De sacramentis*, ii. 2 (PL. clxxvi. 417). Shortly afterwards the chancellor of Lincoln, Richard Wethershet, was to express the same idea: "Credo populum christianum esse sanctam ecclesiam," *Speculum ecclesiae*, Univ. Libr., Cambridge, Add. MS. 3471, fol. 126 rb.

[3] *De sacramentis*, ii. 1, col. 415: "Caput enim est Christus, membrum christianus. Caput unum, membra multa, et constat unum corpus *ex capite* et membris et in uno corpore spiritus unus."

[4] *De sacramentis*, cap. 2, col. 416: there is absolutely no indication that Hugh was acquainted with Gelasius's writings, and yet the identical thought in him and Gelasius produces the identical terminology. Hugh: "discreta officia"; Gelasius: "Christus ... officia discrevit." For Bernard's identical terminology see supra 435 n. 3. In his *De off. eccl.*, i. 43 (PL. clxxvii. 402) Hugh says: 'Papa vicem et locum Christi tenet."

eyes do not see for themselves, but for the whole body, although they are the only part of the body which can see; the same applies to the ears, feet, and so forth. All parts of the human body therefore function for the sake of the whole body, not for their own sakes.[1]

The direction of the human body as well as of the Christian body corporate and politic, the *universitas christianorum*, must accord with the purpose and aim, for which each exists. The logical deduction is that the direction of the *universitas* must lie in the hands of those who are properly qualified. The direction of the human body is the work and function of the soul, the "anima," which operates through the human body and is its prime agent. The direction of the *universitas christianorum* must necessarily be the work and the function of the personified "anima," that is, the "spiritualis potestas."[2] The spiritual power, that is, the sacerdotal order in the Church, is the "anima" of the whole "corpus christianorum."

> Corpus vivit ex anima . . . anima vivit ex Deo.

In the *universitas christianorum*, the *ecclesia*, the lay order corresponds to the human body, because its members busy themselves with the "terrena" only, the physical needs of this life. To the soul of the human being corresponds the sacerdotal order, because its members are engaged in spiritual pursuits. Just therefore as the human being is formed of body and soul, in the same way the universal Church is made up of these two orders:[3]

[1] Loc. cit., cap. 2: "Soli enim oculi vident, et tamen sibi solummodo non vident, sed toti corpori. Solae aures audiunt nec tamen sibi solummodo audiunt, sed toti corpori. Soli pedes ambulant et non sibi tamen solummodo ambulant, sed toti corpori. Et ad hunc modum unumquodque quod habet solum in se non habet solummodo propter se quatenus secundum dispositionem optimi largitoris et distributoris sapientissimi, singuli sint omnium, et omnia singularorum." There may be a direct echo of Hugh's theme in Alexander III's statement, *Ep.* 260, PL. cc. 301–2: "Sicut in humano corpore pro varietate officiorum diversa ornata sunt membra, ita in structura ecclesiae . . . diversae personae in diversis sunt ordinibus constitutae." For the thirteenth century see, for instance, Thomas Aquinas, operating with the same anthromorphic comparisons as Hugh: see his *Ad Romanos*, xii, lectio 2, ending with this statement: "Non potest dicere oculus manui, opera tua non indigeo." Cf. also infra p. 443 n. 2.

[2] Cap. 3, col. 418. Cf. also Thomas, *Summa Theol.*, III qu. viii, art. 2: "Inquantum vero anima est *motor corporis*, corpus instrumentaliter servit animae."

[3] See also in this context Hugh's explanation of why water and wine are mixed in the chalice at the Consecration: "Quaeritur, cur aqua cum vino ponatur in calice Domini? Aqua populum significat: unde nec vinum, qua significatur Christus, debet offerri sine aqua, quia Christus non est passus nisi pro populo, nec aqua sine vino ullo modo: quia populus non est redemptus nisi per Christum," *Quaestiones in Epistolam I ad Corinthios*, qu. 91, PL. clxxv. 531.

Constat his duabus partibus totum corpus Christi quod est universalis ecclesia.

And just as it is the function of the soul to direct the human body, so it is the function of the personified soul, the sacerdotal order, to direct the lay power in the Church. This body being a Christian body, must necessarily be guided, ruled and orientated by those qualified, that is to say, the *sors Domini*: only he belongs to the *sors* who is "electus a Deo ad servitium Dei." For its member has *per se* also regal powers, as is evidenced and signified by the clerical crown which is a royal distinction: "Corona quippe regale decus significat."[1] Hence for the sake of actual government, the sacerdotal order in the Church must needs institute the secular power. And, arising out of this, the sacerdotal power must needs judge whether the lay power performs its functions adequately. The secular power is brought into being by, and kept under the constant controlling supervision of, the sacerdotal power.

Nam spiritualis potestas terrenam potestatem et *instituere* habet, ut sit, et *judicare* habet si bona non fuerit.[2]

On the other hand, and for understandable reasons, the sacerdotal power—which in effect means the pope—is not subject to any judgment: sacerdotal power is directly instituted by God and therefore "a solo Deo judicari potest,"[3] whilst on the other hand, the terrestrial power is instituted by the spiritual power and therefore subjected to the latter's control. In obvious dependence on Honorius of Canterbury, Hugh declares that the sacerdotal power, instituted by God Himself, precedes the temporal-laical power not only in time, but also in dignity.[4] Only later, and by the explicit order of God, the sacerdotal power

---

[1] *De sacr.*, iii. 1, col. 421, with a reference to I *Pet.* ii. 9: "regale sacerdotium." This view may lead to the narrow application of this biblical expression to the *sacerdotium* only.

[2] *De sacr.* ii. 3, col. 417. This was literally copied by Alexander of Hales, *Summa Theol.*, IV, qu. x, membr. 4, art. 2; by Egidius Romanus, *De ecclesiastica potestate*, i. 4 (ed. R. Scholz, pp. 11–12) and ii. 5 (p. 59): "Bene itaque dictum est, quod terrena potestas est per ecclesiasticam et ab ecclesiastica et in opus ecclesiastice constituta"; by Boniface VIII's *Unam Sanctam*; by Hostiensis, *Lectura*, I. xv; Alvarus Pelagius, *De planctu ecclesiae*, i. 36–7; and many others.

[3] *De sacr.* ii. 3, col. 418, with a reference to I *Cor.* ii. 15.

[4] *De sacr.* ii, cap. 4, col. 418: "Quod autem spiritualis potestas (quantum ad divinam institutionem spectat) et prior sit tempore; et major dignitate; in illo antiquo veteris instrumenti populo manifeste declaratur, ubi primum a Deo sacerdotium institutum est." Cf. also ibid.: "Quanto autem vita spiritualis dignior est quam terrena, et spiritus quam corpus, tanto spiritualis potestas terrenam sive saecularem potestatem honore ac dignitate praecedit."

instituted royal power: "Postea vero *per sacerdotium* (jubente Deo) regalis potestas ordinata." In other words, the lay power does not become a truly regal power in the Church, unless it is sanctified by the *sacerdotium*: no legitimate regal power without the sanctification by the priesthood.

Unde in ecclesia adhuc sacerdotalis dignitas potestatem regalem consecrat, et sanctificans per benedictionem et formans per institutionem.[1]

The biblical justification for the royal power's being "jure inferior" is St Paul's statement "The less is blessed by the better."[2]

From the point of view of the character of the *universitas christianorum* this thesis of Hugh of St Victor was the only acceptable and logical one. But priority of the *sacerdotium* in time, its superiority in law, its creation of kingly power, and its control of the king's governmental actions, do not as yet say anything about the administration and the functions within the *universitas christianorum*. It is the function of the king to act for the sake of the whole Christian body politic, that is, it is his function to procure and to protect the necessaries of life— the *terrena*—and the people; he is the *sustentamentum populi*: through his governmental actions he literally sustains the Christian people.[3] And in so far the king or prince must be obeyed: considering the establishment of royal power and the purpose of this creation, Hugh can say:

Reges et principes, quibus obediendum est in omnibus quae *ad potestatem* pertinent,[4]

which is the same point of view which we have met with Honorius of Canterbury and others.

[1] Attention should be drawn to Hugh's discussing the legality of the death penalty in the case of theft (the usual punishment at that time). Could the prince's sword be used for this purpose, since this does not tally with the New Testament? He answers: "Haec nullo modo justitia evangelii est, ut homo pro equo vel bove occidatur, nec in toto evangelio hoc praeceptum invenitur, nec id facit, sed tantum permittit ecclesia," *Quaestiones ad Ep. ad Romanos*, qu. 295, PL. clxxv. 504).

[2] *Hebr.* vii. 7. For a concrete application of this view cf., e.g. Innocent III in RNI. 18, where all the arguments of Hugh are marshalled in Innocentian lucidity and incisiveness. For other applications by the canonists in the thirteenth century see *Medieval Papalism*.

[3] *De sacr.*, ii. 3, col. 417: "Laicus interpretatur popularis; Graece enim λάος, Latine dicitur populus. Unde et βασιλεύς basileus rex dictus putatur; quasi βασιλαοῦ, id est sustentamentum populi." This etymological consideration was of course also applicable to the opposite point of view, cf. e.g., EHR. (lxi), 1946, p. 193.

[4] *Quaest. in Ep. ad Rom.*, qu. 300, PL. cit., col. 505 continuing: "Si autem aliquid percipiunt quod si contra Deum, non sunt audiendi." Of course, what is "contra Deum" must be decided by the agency that sanctifies the king.

16*

Naturally, just as there are different grades and functions—*discreta officia*—in the royal hierarchy, so there are various grades and functions within the sacerdotal hierarchy. Each part and grade has to fulfil the function assigned, so as to make the *corpus* an integrated whole.[1] The presupposition for all this is, however, that there is a directive principle at work, that there is guidance towards a definite object, pursued as a result of the working of that regulative principle: in the individual human being it is the soul, the place of which is taken in the collective organic body of all Christians by the priesthood. For the purposes of the administration of this Christian body politic the functions are allocated by the priesthood, because its members alone have the proper qualification to direct the whole body. Each part to which a specific function is allocated, should confine itself to this specific function. Then the principle of order, or harmonious working together, will be applied to the good of the whole *universitas christianorum*.

From the samples which we have selected in order to present the hierocratic thesis at its most mature, it will have become sufficiently clear that the writers were dominated by the concept of the universal Church as constituting an organic entity, composed of both the lay and sacerdotal orders. The operation of the teleological principle with its functionalist adjunct in the *societas christiana* was explained by a comparison of the Christian body corporate and politic with the human body. Both bodies, the individual and the collective, were considered organic entities: what applied to the one, applied automatically to the other.

In the eleventh century there were some beginnings of this allegorical comparison between the two bodies.[2] But with the further penetration into the texture of hierocratic doctrine, the comparison became a fully fledged theory which thus expressed the profound teleological principle in symbols. This comparison was all the easier as the famous Pauline statements had allegorically suggested this treatment: "We, being many, are one body in Christ": "Unum corpus sumus in Christo."[3] The point which we wish to make is that the teleological principle was transposed onto the plane of allegory. The functions which the members of the "one body in Christ" fulfil, could then be explained by a recourse to the functions which the parts of the human body perform. This again was facilitated by other Pauline statements,

[1] See *De sacr.*, cols. 418–19.
[2] Cf. Gregory VII, *Reg.* i. 19, to the Conqueror.     [3] *Rom.* xii. 5.

which depict the human body as a basis of comparison for demonstrating the various functions within the "one body in Christ."[1] All parts
therefore of an organic unit fulfil certain purposes to which they are
directed. These Pauline expressions setting forth the teleological and
functionalist theme in all its profundity, were now in the twelfth century given practical and political significance.[2]

Now the *unum corpus Christi* was headed by Christ.[3] This one body
was the congregation of all the faithful, the *societas christiana* or the
*universitas christianorum*: in brief, this body was the Church universal.
Again, on the analogy of the human body, this body corporate was
held to have been such that it could have one head only: a human body
with two heads was a monstrosity, and so was this body corporate.
"Est enim unum corpus ecclesia, ergo unum caput debet habere." The
headship of the visible, concrete, Christian society, the *ecclesia*, was
ascribed to the pope as the vicar of Christ. The mediatory role of the
pope thereby obtained practical and political significance:[4] he is the
earthly vicar of Christ—"qui vices Dei gerit in terris"[5]—and as such

---

[1] See especially I *Cor.* xii. 4 ff.: There are diversities of gifts, but the same
spirit; there are *differences of ministries,* but the same Lord; there are *diversities
of operations* . . . for the body is not one member, but many; if the foot shall say
"because I am not the hand, I am not of the body," is it therefore not the body?
. . . and the eye cannot say of the hand, I have no need of thee, nor again the head
to the feet, I have no need . . .; also ibid., 11, 26, 27, etc. *Eph.* i. 23, iv. 10–11, 16,
and again *Rom.* xii. 4: For as we have many members in one body, and all members have not the same *office.*

[2] It should by no means be assumed that these anthropomorphic comparisons
were characteristic of the twelfth century only. Cf. e.g., Thomas Aquinas,
supra 439, and *Ad Corinthios II,* lectio ii, cap. xi: "Dominus papa pro necessitate
unius patriae potest accipere subsidium ab aliis partibus mundi. Ratio est, quia
ecclesia est sicut unum corpus. Videmus autem in corpore naturali, quando
natura deficit virtus in uno membro, subministrat humores virtutem accipiens
ab aliis membris."

[3] See the Pauline statements, supra n. 1, and especially *Eph.* v. 23–4.

[4] Later expressed by Grosseteste in the view that the bishops receive their
power from Christ "per domini papae *mediationem*" (*Ep.* cxxvii, p. 369, ed. cit.;
cf. also ibid., 365, 367). In more general terms this principle was expressed later
by Augustinus Triumphus: "Omnem potestatem, tam spiritualem quam tempora-
lem, a Christo in praelatos et principes saeculares derivatam esse *mediante Petro*
eius successore cuius personam Romanus pontifex representat," ed. by J. Rivière,
in *Revue des sciences religieuses,* xviii (1938), p. 153.

[5] Or as Innocent III expressed it: "Dei, cuius locum, licet indigni, tenemus in
terris," *Reg.* i. 485; also 447, 502, 526, and in many others places; in *Reg.* iii. 44:
"Coelestis patris familias, licet insufficientes penitus et indigni, vicem gerentes
in terris"; *Reg.* v. 128: "eius vicarius, qui est sacerdos in aeternum secundum
ordinem Melchisedek constitutus a Deo judex vivorum et mortuorum" (an
application of the principle that the pope has the "claves juris"). Cf. also *Reg.*
vii. 1 ("Expresse notatur, quod Petro non specialiter aliqua specialis ecclesia, sed

he is the monarch of the Christian body corporate.[1] Moreover, since the *sacerdotium* symbolized the *anima* of the Christian *corpus*, the functions of the personified and institutionalized *anima* were the direction and government of that body. And this direction and government was carried out by means of the law which rested upon the Christian idea of justice. Since the Roman Church and its head, the vicar of Christ, was considered the repository of *justitia*, or the *fundamentum legis totius Christianitatis*, the canon law emanating from this source, appeared as the practical application of a further Pauline idea.[2] Living in society can be regulated by the law only. The canon law was the legalization of the faith.[3] "Materia juris canonici est fides

---

\*  totus mundus commissus fuerit et ecclesia generalis."); *Reg.* xvi. 131 ("Ut in unam vicarii Christi personam quasi corpus et anima, regnum et sacerdotium uniantur ad magnum utriusque commodum et augmentum"); also *Reg.* ii. 209; i. 401; RNI. 2, and Rainer's collection, ii. 2 (PL. ccxvi. 1182: allegory of sun and moon), and *Sermo iii* (PL. ccxvii. 665): he received "spiritualium plenitudinem et latitudinem temporalium, magnitudinem et multitudinem utrorumque." The Roman Church "non solum terrena, sed coelestia quoque dijudicat," Suppl. Reg. 89 *bis*.

[1] As is well known, Thomas Aquinas in the following century built around the theme of monarchy the visible vicariate of Christ in the person of the pope, see his *Summa contra gentiles*, iv. 76, nos. 3–4: "Pax enim et unitas subditorum est *finis regentis*. Unitatis autem congruentior causa est unus quam multi. Manifestum est igitur regimen ecclesiae sic esse dispositum, ut unus toti ecclesiae praesit . . . quia *praesentiam corporalem* erat ecclesiae subtracturus, oportuit, ut alicui committeret, qui loco sui universalis ecclesiae gereret curam." As the late Father Eichmann observed (*Acht & Bann*, p. 37), "Die hierokratische Theorie ist also die konsequente Durchführung der mittelalterlichen Idee der ecclesia universalis, die eines *sichtbaren* Monarchen zu bedürfen schien," referring to St Thomas, loc. cit.: "Si quis autem dicat, quod unum caput et unus pastor est Christus, qui est unus unius ecclesiae sponsus, non sufficienter respondet." It should be pointed out, however, that the term *corporalis presentia* was used before St Thomas by Innocent IV, MGH. *Epp. sel. XIII s.*, ii. 224, no. 301; p. 476, no. 665, etc. Cf. furthermore Thomas, *Summa Theol.*, III qu. viii, a. 2; his lectio ii ad *Romanos XII*; hence the visible monarch, the pope, combines like Christ, according to St Thomas, both powers: ". . . papa, qui utriusque potestatis apicem tenet, scilicet spiritualis et saecularis, hoc disponente, qui est sacerdos et rex in aeternum secundum ordinem Melchisedek," *In libr. II Sententiarum*, Dist. xliv, qu. 2, ad 4 in fine. Because the pope is the visible monarch, it is necessary to salvation to be subject to him, St Thomas declares in a memorable passage which is better known through *Unam Sanctam*: "Ostenditur quod subesse Romano pontifici sit de necessitate salutis," Thomas, *Opusc. contra errores Graecorum ad Urbanum IV*, ed. Venice, 1593, fol. 9b. (All our statements of Thomas are taken from this edition.)

[2] *Rom.* i. 17; *Gal.* iii. 11; *Hebr.* x. 38. Cf. also Innocent III, *Reg.* ii. 220; the faithful receive from the Roman Church "non tantum vivendi normam et morum . . . disciplinam, sed et fidei etiam catholicae documenta."

[3] Cf. e.g., the enumeration of the species of canon law by the Anglo-Norman glossator of the late twelfth century, who says: "Juris canonici species (sunt)

catholica . . . immo et omne jus comprehendit," Hostiensis was to declare in the following century. By virtue of the pope's vicariate of Christ, his verdict was God's verdict.[1] "Omnia de jure potest ut Deus."[2]

On this basis the principle which we have termed the principle of functional order, assumes its true significance. This organic body corporate is one whole, and in order to be an integrated, efficiently functioning whole, its parts must play the role assigned to them in accordance with the purpose for which they are assumed to exist. Again Pauline declarations were to show the necessity of dividing various functions.[3] The pope as Christ's vicar possesses both powers: the symbolic possession of the two swords expresses the principle of unity[4] only to be found in a true monarch. It is not, however, necessary that the monarch uses both swords. The symbolic possession of the swords also expresses the principle that the "vicarius Christi" as the vicar of "the true king and priest," uses certain agencies, so as to make the whole *corpus* function properly; and these agencies within the framework of the *corpus* have to fulfil those functions which are allotted to them. Thereby the principle of functional ordering is given practical realization and shape.

This principle of functional order may explain the often misunderstood hierocratic principle of subordination. This *unum corpus* can work and function adequately only if every member confines himself to the sphere assigned to him. But since it is the *corpus Christi*, since in other words, it is the body headed by Christ's vicar, everyone of its members should recognize not only the value, but also the limitations of his

---

dogma, id est statutum de fide promulgatum . . . mandatum . . . decretum . . ." (MS. 676 of Caius College, Cambridge; I owe this passage to my pupil Mr C. Duggan).

[1] "Sententia igitur papae et sententia Dei una sententia est," Augustinus Triumphus, ed. cit., p. 159.

[2] Hostiensis, *Lectura* ad I. vii. 3, adding: "Consistorium Dei et papae unum et idem censendum."

[3] Cf. the passages supra 443 and I *Cor.* xiv. 40: "Omnia autem honeste et *secundum ordinem* fiant." Cf. again Innocent III, *Reg.* ii. 20: "Superna providentia quae populum humanum per diversa rectorum officia statuit in rectitudine gubernandum"; also *Reg.* iii. 38: "Unum corpus . . . ecclesia tamen non solum propter varietatem virtutum et operum, sed etiam propter diversitatem officiorum et ordinum, dicitur ut castrorum acies ordinata, in qua videlicet diversi ordines militant ordinati." Cf. also *Reg.* ii. 131, and similar statements in many other places.

[4] Cf. of later writers Augustinus Triumphus: "Tota machina mundialis non est nisi unus principatus: ideo non debet esse nisi unus princeps," ed. cit., p. 172.

office, that is, of his function.[1] This principle of subordination of the temporal-material to the sacerdotal-spiritual was a commonplace enough axiom of Christian cosmology; transposed to society at large this principle[2] means that the temporal-secular ruler should subordinate himself to the rulings of those who represent the spiritual-sacerdotal, namely the "sacerdotes." It is this principle which Gregory VII called *humilitas*. And it is this principle which means that there can be no room for autonomous (lay) rulership: there can be no room for lay monarchy.[3] The principle expresses the view that the working of the *unum corpus* demands that the secular ruler shall take, within the framework of the whole *corpus*, the place and function accorded to him. By taking his place within this framework, the secular ruler recognizes the inferiority of the terrestrial and material: and then, according to the hierocratic point of view, the whole organic entity will function smoothly; then there will be harmony and concord; then confusion will be prevented.[4] The principle of functional ordering and consequently the principle of subordination is nothing else but the political formula for the teleological principle, operative only in a society that was viewed as *unum corpus Christi*.[5]

---

[1] As Innocent III expressed it: *Reg.* i. 471: "Unusquisque maneat in ea vocatione, in qua dignoscitur esse vocatus."

[2] In juristic terminology and as regards the relations of pope to emperor the former was said to have the *jus auctoritatis* and the latter the *jus administrandi*: Rufinus, *Summa Decretorum* (about 1157–9), ed. H. Singer, p. 47. True governmental authority remained with the pope; the execution (*administratio*) of papal authoritative rulings was the emperor's task. Cf. on this also the late Mochi Onory, *Fonti Canonistiche*, Milan, 1951, p. 87.

[3] So it was also later expressed: "Nulla terrena potestas potest esse suprema simpliciter," Egidius Romanus *De potestate ecclesiastica*, ed. R. Scholz, iii. 4, p. 165.

[4] As Humbert expressed it in the eleventh century and as Egidius Romanus was to express it in the fourteenth century: "Quia potestas terrena immediate se intromittit de temporalibus, ne sit *confusio* in potestatibus, et ut hee potestates, terrena videlicet et ecclesiastica, non sint *confusae*, sed sint ad invicem ordinate, regulariter et generaliter de temporalibus ecclesia non se intromittit, sed solum se intromittet immediate et per se ipsam ex aliquo casu contingente vel propter aliquid speciale, non quod hoc sit ex ecclesiae impotentia, sed ex eius decencia et excellentia (cf. Bernard p. 434). Nam qui spiritualia judicat, multa magis potest temporalia et saecularia judicare," ed. cit., iii. 4, p. 163.

[5] These conceptions, we believe, were further reasons of why Aristotle fell on such fertile ground in the thirteenth century. The teleological principle could then be stated in terms such as these: "Corpus ordinatur ad animam etiam secundum gentiles philosophos, et temporalia ordinantur ad spiritualia" (Durandus de S. Porciano, cf. *Medieval Papalism*, p. 85, note 4, and 86, note 1). Cf. also Thomas Aquinas, *De regimine principum*, i. 14: "Sic enim ei, ad quem *finis* ultimi cura pertinet, subdi debent illi, ad quod pertinet cura antecedentium finium,

CHAPTER XIV

# *Conclusion*

## I

THE mid-twelfth century provides a convenient terminating point in the presentation of the growth of papal-hierocratic doctrine. Little new ideological substance was added afterwards. What however gives the period from Gratian onwards its complexion is the scientific making and developing of the law—that law which expresses a theme in binding terms. The canon law as it came to be rapidly shaped from Gratian onwards, supplied the *norma recte vivendi* for the members of the *universitas christianorum*. Like any other law, it was compulsory; unlike any other law, it was universal and binding upon all the members of this *universitas*, emanating as it did from the Roman Church, the "communis patria" of all Christians.[1] Being universal, every other law and legal system was considered subsidiary and auxiliary: the auxiliary function of the prince was paralleled above

---

et eius imperio *dirigi*"; hence "reges debent sacerdotibus esse subjecti"; also
cap. 15: "Rex, sicut dominio et regimini quod administratur per sacerdotis
officium, subdi debet, ita prae esse debet omnibus humanis officiis." Idem, *Summa
Theol.*, I, qu. cxvi, a. 4: "Quandoque multa ordinantur ad unum, semper invenitur unum ut principale et *dirigens*"; ibid., III, qu. viii, a. 4: "Unum autem corpus
similitudinarie dicitur una multitudo *ordinata in unum*, secundum actus sive
*officia*." It is therefore perfectly logical for Thomas to say, *De reg. princ.*, i. 14:
"Romano pontifici, cui omnes reges populi christiani oportet esse subditos, sicut
Domino Iesu Christo." In all its maturity this principle is expressed by Egidius
Romanus, op. cit., ed. cit., iii. 4, p. 166: "Tota corporalis substantia per spiritualem gubernatur et regitur et est sibi supposita"; hence: "Sicut Deus sic adminis-
trat istas res corporales, ut eas proprios motus agere sinat, sic Dei vicarius sic
debet administrare potestates terrenas et temporales, ut eas permittat propria
officia exercere." And lastly, see the gloss of Cardinal Johannes Monachus on
Boniface's bull of granting the indulgence for 1300: "Oportet quod multitudo
hominum reducatur ad unum et in genere hominum sit reperire unum hominem
primum, qui sit supremum in illo genere, qui sit mensura et regula aliorum;
huiusmodi autem est Romanus pontifex qui est inter omnes homines supremus
existens mensura et *regula directiva* omnium aliorum."
[1] Johannes de Petesella, *Summa* ad *Extra*: II. ii, fol. 161ra, of MS. Vat. Lat.
2343. For the designation of Rome as the "communis patria" by second-century
Roman jurists, see supra p. 6 n. 1.

all by the auxiliary function of the Roman law which, in Hostiensis's memorable words, was the "ancilla juris canonici."[1]

The papal-hierocratic scheme is a gigantic attempt to translate scriptural and quite especially Pauline doctrine into terms of government. The means by which this government was to be carried out were those of the law, "Roman" as it was in every sense of the term. The *claves regni coelorum*—"the keys of the kingdom of heaven"—were transformed into *claves juris*, the "keys of the law." Perhaps at no other time had the notion of law been raised to so lofty a level as at the time when the papal monarch aimed at ruling the world by his law.[2] This papal-hierocratic government was a government *sui generis*: it was an attempt to direct Europe, that Caroline entity, by means of an idea enshrined in a universally binding law. It was a government that had not at its beck and call the usual paraphernalia of governments (army, police force, etc.), but employed these through the medium of the secular ruler, the *advocatus*, whose control by the papal monarch was therefore essential to this kind of government: without the *advocatus* the papal-hierocratic scheme falls to the ground.

The idea of such a government could only exist, let alone function, in a world that was fundamentally different from ours. And it is this difference which makes it on the one hand so difficult to capture the ideological ingredients, and on the other hand gives rise to some facile generalizations about the "airy" character of medieval doctrines. Whilst faith and religion are nowadays matters of private opinion, at that time they were issues of public law, of public concern and public interest. We have but to recall the public effects of excommunication to appreciate this truism. Moreover, the medieval mind was addicted to what may be termed the charm of sensual concreteness: the most abstract ideas were to be explained by, compared with, and likened to, concrete, tangible objects; whilst on the other hand, the most profound

---

[1] Hostiensis, *Lectura* ad V. xxxiii. 28.

[2] Even in its incipient stages the canon law was the main target of the anti-hierocratic party. Cf. supra ch. xii on Peter Crassus, Gerhoh of Reichersberg, and so forth. (Gottschalk's?) *Liber de unitate ecclesiae conservanda* which, we recall propounded a dualist form of government, was in fact first published by Ulrich van Hutten who delighted in this apology of Henry IV—before Luther made a bonfire of the *Corpus Juris Canonici* on 10 December 1520. This *incendium decretalium*, as Erasmus termed it, was a symbolic challenge to the jurisdictional and legislative authority of the Roman Church. Henry VIII's prohibition of canon law studies (1536) was based on the monarchic view that "the whole realm, clergy as well as laity, hath acknowledged the King to be the supreme head of the Church."

ideas were not expressed in linguistic terms, but in those of objective symbolism. This is a way of arguing, thinking and acting that is a very serious stumbling block to a proper appreciation of medieval doctrines, and quite particularly of the papal-hierocratic theme. In so far then, the criteria of explaining, understanding and judging medieval society are different from our own.

It is superficial to maintain that the actual or attempted exercise of monarchic power by the medieval popes demonstrates their insatiable lust for power. Every *regimen* in whatever sphere is exercise of authority and power. The real problem does not start until the purpose, the "finis" or "telos" of the *regimen* is examined. Considered from their own point of view, the medieval popes regarded it as their duty and office to rule, for they claimed that the "cura et sollicitudo" for the whole of Christendom was in their hands.[1] They believed that since the whole *universitas christianorum*, that juristic, corporate and organic entity, was entrusted to them, they had to govern it so as to lead it to its eventual destination. The mediatory role of the pope (and herewith of the *sacerdotium*) obtained in this scheme of things practical and "political" importance. Hence the logical necessity of considering the Petrine commission to constitute a vicariate of Christ, so that the pope in the most concrete, sensual terms appeared as the "vicarius Dei"— the vicar of the "one mediator between God and men, the man Christ Jesus" (I *Tim*. ii. 5).[2] The visible vicariate of Christ makes the pope the *ostium Dei*.[3] And since at least in an ideational sense Christian

---

[1] The popes considered themselves responsible to God for the government of the whole Christian people entrusted to their care. Cf., for instance, Innocent III in his third consecration sermon (PL. ccxvii. 658): "Redditurus (papa) Deo rationem non solum pro se, sed pro omnibus qui sunt suae curae commissi. At omnes omnino, qui sunt de familia Domini, sub eius cura constituti sunt." Cf. also col. 655 and again Bernard's *De consideratione*, III. i. 2.

[2] Cf. Innocent III in *Reg*. i. 335: "Non enim homo, sed Deus separat, quod Romanus pontifex . . . non humana, sed divina potius auctoritate dissolvit"; and in many other places. It is not without interest to note that in the thirteenth century a litigant who appeared personally before the pope, had to address him in these words: "Mediator Dei et hominum, coram quo loqui praesumo, non considerabit meae scientiae parvitatem," Aegidius Fuscararius, *Ordo judiciarius*, ed. L. Wahrmund, Innsbruck, 1916, iii. 259, under the heading: "Exordium coram domino papa." (I owe this to my pupil Mr J. A. Watt.) In the sixteenth century the Spanish Dominican, Mathias de Paz, in his tract "De dominio regum Hispaniae super Indos," said: "Ergo absurdum videretur dicere quod Christus, rex regum et dominus dominantium, dimiserit orbem terrarum absque judice competenti in omnibus et per omnia, cum ipse vere esset monarcha totius universi," ed. in *Arch. Fratrum Praedicatorum*, iii (1934), at p. 161, lines 28 ff.

[3] As regards Innocent III I could find only one reference to *Prov*. viii. 15, but the statement was not made by him, but addressed to him by Peter of Aragon, see

society was viewed as universal, the pope claimed to be the universal monarch, the world's monarch.[1] And just as this claim as regards the extent was comprehensive, in the same way it was comprehensive as regards the substance: for the Petrine commission was all-embracing —"nihil excipiens": neither cause nor person was excepted. It was a conception of monarchy raised to perhaps the highest possible level.

Seen from yet another angle, this papal world monarchy was also the bridge builder between Roman and modern times. All the characteristic Roman features had impressed themselves upon the physiognomy of the papacy, the Roman Church. Not only the law; also the conception of the universality of government.[2] It was as universal monarchs that the popes partly applied Roman principles, partly developed them, and partly created new ones, which have since gained universal recognition in International Law. The protection of legates; safe conduct of ambassadors; secrecy in diplomatic negotiations; insistence on the adherence to treaties made between secular rulers; condemnation of treaty violations; papal annulment and rescission of treaties and compacts; fixation of treaty conditions; excommunication and deposition of rulers; orders for the release of prisoners, for their humane treatment and that of hostages; protection of exiles, aliens and Jews; condemnation of "unjust" wars and piracy; confirmation of peace treaties; orders for the free passage of troops engaged in a "just" campaign; orders to rulers to enter into alliances; ascription of occupied territories to a victorious belligerent party, and so forth.[3] Being the repository of justice, the *sedes justitiae*, the Roman Church and herewith the popes claimed that they had a right to do and enact all those items. And in the case of a default of justice by a secular tribunal or in the case of a vacancy of the imperial throne, the papal monarch filled the gap by assuming the role of the judge himself or

---

*Reg.* vii. 229: "Romanus pontifex, qui est beati Petri successor, vicarius sit illius per quem reges regnant et principes principantur." This is also incorporated in his *Gesta*, cap. cxx. The passage from *Prov.* is however applied in a vicarious sense by Boniface VIII, MGH. *Const.* iv. no. 105, p. 80: "Apostolica sedes divinitus constituta super reges et regna . . . per quam principes imperant et potentes decernunt justitiam ac reges regnant."

[1] For some development of these views by the canonists see *Medieval Papalism*, ch. 5.

[2] For some challenging views on Roman, medieval and modern universalism, see R. Dekkers, "Deux universalismes" in *Mélanges G. Smets*, Brussels, 1952, pp. 183 ff.

[3] Most of the relevant official documents for the thirteenth century are now conveniently assembled in the work already quoted, G. B. Pallieri and G. Vismara, *Acta pontificia juris gentium*, Milan, 1946.

by taking over the government (so-called imperial vicariate of the papacy).

In view of these claims, the question is legitimate, What other steps should the medieval popes have taken to assert themselves as universal monarchs? At the same time the other question is legitimate, How far were all these measures and actions ordered by the popes effective? Or were these orders and decrees and so forth little more than claims raised on a stupendous scale? The answers to these questions can only be given on the basis of a detailed analysis[1] and a necessary preliminary must be the examination of the legal system itself, that is, of that system which grew up from the mid-twelfth century onwards. What we can usefully do here is to indicate in the briefest possible manner the obstacles to the full realization of the papal-hierocratic system.

## II

Perhaps the most effective obstacle to the full manifestation of the papal-hierocratic system was the role allotted to the king and, to a larger extent, to the lay population. As we have had ample opportunity of pointing out, the king in hierocratic thought, could not, for the reasons stated, be conceived on the monarchic level. Underneath all the numerous conflicts between the *sacerdotium* and the *regnum*, between the papacy and the kingdoms, including the empire, is detectable one and the same current: the battle for the exercise of monarchic functions. The hierocratic denial of monarchic power to the kings accounts for their resistance to the role allotted to them. It is this point, we think, which characterizes the whole medieval scene as far as it is related to this central theme. One might well say, however, that this royal resistance is not exclusively to be explained by "political" considerations, but by considerations belonging to an order outside the historian's purview. The monarchic instincts of a king—the *honor imperii*—could not then be permanently suppressed. The battle and

---

[1] With regard to Innocent III cf. the pertinent observations of C. R. Cheney in *Bulletin of the John Rylands Library*, xxxv (1952), pp. 41–2. See also P. Rassow, "Zum Kampf um das Eherecht im 12. Jahrhundert" in *Festschrift f. Santifaller* (MIOG), lviii, 1950), p. 311, pointing out (with regard to marriage and divorce) the danger to the historical picture accruing from relying on one group of sources only. A further problem is the continued application of the royal coronation *ordines* which retained the features of the tenth century sacral lay monarchy (anointing on the head with chrism, conferment of the ring, etc.) and were followed throughout the medieval period in England, France, Germany, Hungary and Spain.

the nomenclatures take on different shapes at different times, but they are essentially the same. From the time of the Eastern emperor styling himself the *Autokrator* or the *Pontifex inclytus* or the *Rex-Sacerdos*, to Charlemagne, the Ottonians and Salians—the *Monokrator* or the *Christus Domini* or the *Servus servorum Christi* or the *vicarius Christi*— down to the "New Monarchy," it is always the same assertion of true monarchic functions on the part of kings and emperors. Perhaps at no other time had the Sermon on the Mount such practical application as in the medieval period: "No man can serve two masters."

This hierocratic axiom of functional qualification, according to which only the ordained members of the Church are entitled to guide, to orientate, to direct, in brief to govern the whole *corpus* of Christians, met with resistance also on the lower lay spheres. To all intents and purposes the lay members of the Church were excluded from important determinative matters. It was not one of the least results of the twelfth-century Renascence that, for practical purposes, it entailed far greater range of activity for the laymen. Education and scholarship had hitherto been almost exclusively the domain of the clerics. Now the lay section of the *populus christianus* came equally to the fore. Prevailing practices and ways of living of the higher clergy kindled the critical-liberal spirit of laymen and the lower sacerdotal strata. Hence the call to a return to primitive conditions: the call addressed to the higher clergy to divest themselves of their wealth—it is the emergence of the battle cry "evangelical poverty." And the critical spirit now generally abroad, became inquisitive, hence amongst other things translations of the Bible into the vernacular (French), but inquisitiveness on the one side led to inquisition on the other. And inquisitiveness was the fertile ground upon which the element of doubt could arise. Doubt in the mediatory role of the pope and the priesthood was fatal to a system to which this role was vital.

The concept of *ecclesia* as the corporate, juristic entity of all Christians, which had proved such a signal source of strength to hierocratic thought, was, paradoxically enough, to prove a source of weakness. Again, a number of factors combined. The canonists as befitted lawyers, were great constitutionalists. There is observable a certain dichotomy amongst the canonists, particularly those who were cardinals.[1] On the one hand, they were the staunchest upholders of a rigid papalism; on the other hand, they were very insistent on the constitutional limitations of the pope, controlled as he was to be by the College of Cardinals.

[1] Cf. our observations in *Studi Gregoriani*, iv. 127.

They developed as regards the Roman Church the corporation theory according to which the pope and the cardinals were constitutionally on the same level as a cathedral chapter and the bishop. It needed no particular efforts to apply these "Roman Church" principles to the whole *corpus* of believers and to make the whole union of believers the bearers of true power, with the consequence that the pope instead of being the head, became the representative, of the "congregatio fidelium." This was to lead straight on to the Conciliar Movement.[1] The so strongly entrenched idea of the *corpus* was to show itself of extraordinary value to the conciliarists, turning as they did the whole papal-hierocratic system upside down, with the help of the same fundamental concept, the *corpus* idea of the Church.[2] Naturally, the episcopal quarter took a lively interest in these theories—was not the bishop "apostolicae sedis gratia episcopus"?—and the sternly increased centralization of ecclesiastical government together with the virtual exclusion of electoral bodies and the (logically defensible) institutions of expectancies, provisions of benefices and so forth,[3] were bound to play into the hands of the anti-hierocrat and to rekindle the never extinct episcopal ambition of freedom.

The lay opposition to the hierocratic scheme was above all governmentally concentrated in the emperors. The imperial thesis, as far as it was capable of formulating an independent theory of its own, naturally became the focal point of anti-hierocratic opposition, behind which a good many incompatible and diversified strains and equally diverse motives could safely shelter. We do not wish to say that the imperial thesis played any conspicuous part in the weakening of the hierocratic scheme. But what we would maintain is that hierocratic doctrine,

[1] Cf. my *Origins of the Great Schism*, London, 1948, pp. 183 ff.; and B. Tierney, in his as yet unpublished dissertation "The authority of Pope and Council in the Writings of the medieval canonists." Cf. now also E. F. Jacob, *Essays in the Conciliar Epoch*, second edition, Manchester, 1953, pp. 240–1.

[2] The logical consequence of the pope being the representative of the *congregatio fidelium*, from whom in fact he derived his power, was that the *congregatio* could also withdraw the powers from him: the master of the Church was turned into its servant. The *corpus* was founded by Christ—"petra enim erat Christus" (I *Cor*. x. 4)—and its members conferred certain powers on the pope. This was the conciliarist point of view, greatly valued as it was because it provided a possibility of ending the Schism, cf. *Origins of the Great Schism*, pp. 176 ff., 201 ff., 214 ff.

[3] The increasingly heavy taxes imposed together with the numerous subsidies and fees exacted for an incredibly great variety of causes, the sale of all sorts of offices, including the highest curial posts, must also be taken into account. Cf. the documentation in W. E. Lunt, *Papal revenues*, cit., especially vol. ii; also idem, *Financial relations of the papacy with England*, cit.

particularly as practised in the thirteenth century towards the Staufen empire, substantially contributed to its own weakening. There can be no doubt that the lessons of history as well as the maxims of hierocratic theory were not heeded by those who applied it. The specifically created protector and defender and advocate gone—the consequences were inevitable.

Moreover, the hierocratic conception was, as it may have become sufficiently clear, thoroughly Roman in every respect. The whole idea concerning the emperor was Roman. And the execution of hierocratic doctrine was determined by these Roman elements which in practice meant that papal-hierocratic thought manifested clear signs of lack of flexibility and adjustment. Again, traditionalism and conservatism which had been so great a source of strength to the hierocratic scheme, were to prove themselves sources of weakness. This showed itself in papal-imperial relations during the thirteenth century. The emperor, though a "unicus filius" of the Roman Church, admittedly behaved himself sometimes like a troublesome son. Yet, the papal-imperial contests absorbed so much energy to the detriment of the papacy. Apparently unable to free itself from its Roman fetters, the papacy, for the sake of the Roman empire, nurtured the kings, especially those of France and partly also of England. Many issues in these countries which provoked the papal wrath against the emperors, were over-looked. It faintly begins with Gregory VII; it is continued with Alexander III and it becomes quite plain with Innocent III. The empire, in modern parlance, provided an ideological buffer-state for these kings. And the consequences were clear: the heir of the Staufens became France. It was not Boniface VIII, but Innocent III and his successors who reaped at Anagni what they had sown from Rome. The inability of hierocratic doctrine to adjust itself to new circumstances showed itself not only in that the whole Roman-conditioned set of ideas could make but little impression on the French—and they were only too quick to point this out—but it also failed to take into account rising and influential classes, particularly in the cities.

Could above all, in the late thirteenth century, the attractively simple hierocratic arguments make much impression on the Aristotelian trained minds of the age? The impact of Aristotle[1] on the late medieval world is not only, as we are incessantly told, of importance to mere

---

[1] For the actual reasons of papal resistance to the New Aristotle see especially M. Grabmann, *I divieti ecclesiastici di Aristotele sotto Innocenzo III e Gregorio IX* (Misc. Hist. Pont., vol. v, 1941).

philosophic enquiries, but also, and we venture to say, of greater importance in the field of political science. There are indeed two different worlds, that before and that after the Aristotelian absorption. True, Aristotle could be, and was, adduced to buttress hierocratic principles. But it was also the same Aristotle who demonstrated the very human, very natural origin of society.

The impact of Aristotle came at a time which was ready for him. He †
provided what anti-hierocratic thinkers had been groping for so long to find. He had shown, not in any way polemical and quite independent of thirteenth-century actuality, therefore of all the greater topical interest, that there was a *societas humana*, the aim of which was the satisfaction of human needs. This *societas humana* is something fundamentally different from the *societas christiana*. It grows from below, from the household, the village and larger entities into a self-sufficing community formed by the natural impulse of men to live in it; it is therefore a creation of nature. The *societas christiana* comes, so to speak, from above; it is founded or instituted; it has therefore its origin outside nature. The one descends from above, from a unifying principle, from Christ Himself; the other ascends from below, from the natural union of male and female. Into the one *societas* man comes through the working of the social instinct; into the other *societas* man comes through the sacramental act of baptism. Consequently, aim and purpose of these two societies are quite different.

The *societas humana* aims at providing human, earthly felicity; it aims at a perfect, honourable and self-sufficing life. This is an end in itself. The values, criteria and functions of this human society are determined by its character and aim. It is a this-worldly community and on its own showing restricts itself to the satisfaction of human needs. Hence all social, political and cultural activity within this human society is to be orientated by this end which alone is the directive or regulative principle. Wedded to the already formidable awareness of nationhood, this Aristotelian conception of the *societas humana* provided the early fourteenth-century challenge to hierocratic thought, provided the framework out of which the modern nation-state could arise. Aristotle supplied the roof under which anti-hierocratic thought found a shelter.

In fact, then, there were, conceptually, two distinct societies, the one a "Church," the other a "State." Partly foreshadowed by the earlier anti-hierocrats, partly expressed also in religious terms by some heretical sects, this dualism was now given concrete political shape.

None sensed the danger to the hierocratic system more clearly than Boniface VIII, desperately trying to stem the tide. As a canonist he realized that in this scheme of things the "Church" was to be a "mystical body" with the inevitable consequence that ecclesiastical jurisdiction was not *ex se* and *per se* to produce effects in public and social life: ecclesiastical jurisdiction was to be restricted to issues which were pertinent to this mystical body, that is, to spiritual issues.[1] But in the opinion of the curialists this was no longer government in the sense in which they understood the term: curialist opinion perceived the impending reduction of law to morals. *Unam sanctam* was a magnificent swan song of the papal-hierocratic system, pontifically synthesizing Hugh's, Bernard's, Alan's and Thomas's ideas.[2] "Duo principia ponere, haereticum est."

The State as a human and natural community, as the *universitas civium* in Marsiglian terminology, confines itself to human ends; it is human and so is its power; wherefrom the claim arises that jurisdiction, that is, coercive governmental power rests with those who constitute the State, the *universitas civium*. It is they who have sovereign power; it is the "self-sufficing" sovereignty of the people which is the hallmark of the State. And it is this sovereign power that has to institute the various organs who are to operate their own human body politic. Governmental power comes from below, no longer from above through the mediation of the priests. In order to be a *civis*, it is not necessary to be a *christianus*. The State—the *universitas civium* or *civitas* or *civilitas* —concentrates on civil needs. The State is autonomous and sovereign. "Omne regnum," says Ockham, "omnis communitas debet habere

---

[1] Cf. the observations of J. Leclerq, *Jean de Paris et l'ecclésiologie du xiii siècle*, Paris, 1942, p. 109: "Contre ce dualisme menaçant, il (Boniface VIII) insistait sur l'unité de l'église. Affirmer l'independance du pouvoir temporel, c'était imiter à la fois les manichéens et les Grecs schismatiques, et introduire la division dans le monde et l'église. Devant le danger créé par Philippe le Bel et ses partisans, Boniface VIII, Jean le Moine, Mathieu d'Aquasparata et Gilles de Rome appliquaient aux adversaires du pouvoir pontifical la réfutation opposée jadis aux manichéens." Against this was set the thesis: "Le pape était le chef visible de l'église, mais l'église n'était plus seulement pour eux un 'corps mystique' uni par la même foi et les mêmes sacrements, elle était aussi une organization politique temporelle. Revendiquant pour le pape le droit de commander aux hommes en tous les domaines, ils croyaient sauvegarder l'unité du monde: la theocratie pontificale leur semblait être l'un des moyens de soumettre toute créature à l'unique empire de Dieu."

[2] It is not without a certain historical irony that on the very eve of the return to medieval-laical conditions (the Reformation), Leo X in the Council of Rome, 1517, re-issued *Unam sanctam* in the bull *Pastor aeternus*, Mansi, xxxii. 968–9.

unum judicem simpliciter supremum."[1] The State was given a positive
function and purpose; it was also shown to have an origin accessible
to human self-sufficing explanation.[2] In a way, it is the return to the
old monarchic lay principle which the anti-hierocrats had asserted often
enough, but which they never could establish on a satisfactory basis,
bound as they were to the same ways of reasoning as their opponents.
Aristotle gave late medieval man the scientific tools and it is these tools
which eventually will create modern Europe.[3] It is this modern Europe
that will call for the necessary re-adjustment of theories relating to
Church and State. And it will be Aristotle again, though in the
Thomistic metamorphosis, which will adjust the ideological framework.

The debt which medieval Europe owed to the papal-hierocratic
scheme of things is in no need of emphasis. Based upon the view of
the individual's and therefore of society's oneness, this theory made a
positive and constructive contribution to the medieval world, sharply
opposing a divisibility of the individual and therefore of society. It is an
impressive conception which aimed at giving medieval Europe a sense
of unity, order, direction and purpose; it is a doctrine that engaged and
fructified and energized the best contemporary brains; it is a theme which
could produce these fertilizing effects only in a period that is not in-
appropriately called the "Christian Middle Ages." The papal-hierocratic
idea of government is a historical phenomenon and explicable only by
historical criteria: it is a classic demonstration of the evolution of an idea.

[1] With this statement should be compared those supra 446. Due weight should
also be given to medieval representative institutions and electoral procedures
which, opposed to hierocratic ideology, must have, alongside with certain Roman
law principles, facilitated the Aristotelian advance.

[2] The great importance of French publicist literature in the early fourteenth
century becomes all the clearer if set against this background. For instance, the
anonymous *Antequam essent clerici* expresses not only the denial of the mediatory
role of the priesthood, but also symptomatically shows that the teleological view
of history was withering away. This somewhat realistic approach to political
problems is also evidenced by John of Paris, a very able Aristotelian anti-papalist
of the very early fourteenth century. Arguing against a universal body politic—
and re-echoing Pierre de Flotte's famous retort to Boniface VIII—he states the
case for diversities of governments because of the different modes of living,
different climatic conditions and geographical situations of peoples (ed. cit.,
p. 181). The pope is concerned with a mystical body, hence works with no more
than the "verbum," but the king must govern in the proper sense of the term;
his power is "manualis: facilius enim est extendere verbum quam manum," ibid.
Pierre de Flotte had said to the pope: "Vestra (potestas) est verbalis, nostra autem
est realis" (EHR. lxi, 1946, p. 181).

[3] Once the full implications of the concept "societas *humana*" are grasped, the
further development seems clear: humanism, individualism, liberalism and the
doctrine of the Rights of Man.                                                    †

# APPENDIX A

## List of Popes

### (from the beginning of the fifth century)

Compiled on the basis of the corrected list by A. Mercati in *Annuario Pontificio* (1947 et seq.) = idem in *Medieval Studies*, ix (1947), pp. 72 ff. For full details of the popes' Christian names, of their place of origin, of the day and month of their election, consecration, coronation and death, see Mercati, loc. cit. The anti-popes are given in brackets.

| | | | |
|---|---|---|---|
| Innocent I | 401–417 | Boniface III | 607 |
| Zosimus | 417–418 | Boniface IV | 608–615 |
| Boniface I | 418–422 | Deusdedit I | 615–618 |
| (Eulalius 418–419) | | Boniface V | 619–625 |
| Celestine I | 422–432 | Honorius I | 625–638 |
| Sixtus III | 432–440 | Severinus | 640 |
| Leo I | 440–461 | John IV | 640–642 |
| Hilarus | 461–468 | Theodore I | 642–649 |
| Simplicius | 468–483 | Martin I | 649–655 |
| Felix III | 483–492 | Eugenius I | 654–657 |
| Gelasius I | 492–496 | Vitalian | 657–672 |
| Anastasius II | 496–498 | Deusdedit II | 672–676 |
| Symmachus | 498–514 | Donus | 676–678 |
| (Laurentius, 498; 501–505) | | Agatho | 678–681 |
| Hormisdas | 514–523 | Leo II | 682–683 |
| John I | 523–526 | Benedict II | 684–685 |
| Felix IV | 526–530 | John V | 685–686 |
| Boniface II | 530–532 | Cono | 686–687 |
| (Dioscorus, 530) | | (Theodore, 687; | |
| John II | 533–535 | Paschal, 687) | |
| Agapitus I | 535–536 | Sergius I | 687–701 |
| Silverius | 536–537 | John VI | 701–705 |
| Vigilius | 537–555 | John VII | 705–707 |
| Pelagius I | 556–561 | Sisinnius | 708 |
| John III | 561–574 | Constantine | 708–715 |
| Benedict I | 575–579 | Gregory II | 715–731 |
| Pelagius II | 579–590 | Gregory III | 731–741 |
| Gregory I | 590–604 | Zachary | 741–752 |
| Sabinianus | 604–606 | Stephen II (III) | 752–757 |

| | | | |
|---|---|---|---|
| Paul I | 757–767 | Leo VIII | 963–965 |
| (Constantine, 767–769; | | Benedict V | 964–966 |
| Philip, 768) | | John XIII | 965–972 |
| Stephen III (IV) | 768–772 | Benedict VI | 973–974 |
| Adrian I | 772–795 | (Boniface VII, 974; 984–985) | |
| Leo III | 795–816 | Benedict VII | 974–983 |
| Stephen IV (V) | 816–817 | John XIV | 983–984 |
| Paschal I | 817–824 | John XV | 985–996 |
| Eugenius II | 824–827 | Gregory V | 996–999 |
| Valentine | 827 | (John XVI, 997–998) | |
| Gregory IV | 827–844 | Silvester II | 999–1003 |
| (John, 844) | | John XVII | 1003 |
| Sergius II | 844–847 | John XVIII | 1004–1009 |
| Leo IV | 847–855 | Sergius IV | 1009–1012 |
| Benedict III | 855–858 | Benedict VIII | 1012–1024 |
| (Anastasius 855; died c. 880) | | John XIX | 1024–1032 |
| Nicholas I | 858–867 | Benedict IX | 1032–1044 |
| Adrian II | 867–872 | Silvester III | 1044–1045 |
| John VIII | 872–882 | Benedict IX (second | |
| Marinus I | 882–884 | time) | 1045 |
| Adrian III | 884–885 | Gregory VI | 1045–1046 |
| Stephen V (VI) | 885–891 | Clement II | 1046–1047 |
| Formosus | 891–896 | Benedict IX (third | |
| Boniface VI | 896 | time) | 1047–1048 |
| Stephen VI (VII) | 896–897 | Damasus II | 1048 |
| Romanus | 897 | Leo IX | 1049–1054 |
| Theodore II | 897 | Victor II | 1055–1057 |
| John IX | 898–900 | Stephen IX (X) | 1057–1058 |
| Benedict IV | 900–903 | (Benedict X, 1058–1059) | |
| Leo V | 903 | Nicholas II | 1059–1061 |
| (Christopher, 903–904) | | Alexander II | 1061–1073 |
| Sergius III | 904–911 | (Honorius II, 1061–1072) | |
| Anastasius III | 911–913 | Gregory VII | 1073–1085 |
| Lando | 913–914 | (Clement III, 1080–1100) | |
| John X | 914–928 | Victor III | 1086–1087 |
| Leo VI | 928 | Urban II | 1088–1099 |
| Stephen VII (VIII) | 928–931 | Paschal II | 1099–1118 |
| John XI | 931–935 | (Theodoric, 1100; | |
| Leo VII | 936–939 | Albert, 1102; | |
| Stephen VIII (IX) | 939–942 | Silvester IV, 1105–1111) | |
| Marinus II | 942–946 | Gelasius II | 1118–1119 |
| Agapitus II | 946–955 | (Gregory VIII, 1118–1121) | |
| John XII | 955–964 | Calixtus II | 1119–1124 |

| | | | |
|---|---|---|---|
| Honorius II | 1124–1130 | Celestine III | 1191–1198 |
| (Celestine II, 1124) | | Innocent III | 1198–1216 |
| Innocent II | 1130–1143 | Honorius III | 1216–1227 |
| (Anacletus II, 1130–1138; | | Gregory IX | 1227–1241 |
| Victor IV, 1138) | | Celestine IV | 1241 |
| Celestine II | 1143–1144 | Innocent IV | 1243–1254 |
| Lucius II | 1144–1145 | Alexander IV | 1254–1261 |
| Eugenius III | 1145–1153 | Urban IV | 1261–1264 |
| Anastasius IV | 1153–1154 | Clement IV | 1265–1268 |
| Adrian IV | 1154–1159 | Gregory X | 1272–1276 |
| Alexander III | 1159–1181 | Innocent V | 1276 |
| (Victor IV, 1159–1164; | | Adrian V | 1276 |
| Paschal III, 1164–1168; | | John XXI | 1276–1277 |
| Calixtus III, 1168–1178; | | Nicholas III | 1277–1280 |
| Innocent III, 1179–1180) | | Martin IV | 1281–1285 |
| Lucius III | 1181–1185 | Honorius IV | 1285–1287 |
| Urban III | 1185–1187 | Nicholas IV | 1288–1292 |
| Gregory VIII | 1187 | Celestine V | 1294 |
| Clement III | 1187–1191 | Boniface VIII | 1294–1303 |

# APPENDIX B

**1, line 7 from foot:** For this concept of baptism as a legal act see O. Heggelbacher, *Die christl. Taufe als Rechtsakt nach dem Zeugnis der frühen Christenheit* (Freiburg, Switzerland, 1953).

**2, n. 1:** This will become a standing phrase throughout the M.A. and will therefore also be applied to the pope who functions on behalf of Christ. Cf., e.g., Innocent IV in E. Winkelmann, *Acta imperii inedita* (Innsbruck, 1880), ii. 697: "Generali namque legatione in terris fungimur regis regum."

**2, n. 2:** On the intimate connexion between monotheism and monarchy see especially E. Peterson, *Theologische Traktate* (Munich, 1951), i. 60 ff.

**3, n. 1:** Cf. also L. Cerfaux, *La théologie de l'église suivant s. Paul*, 2nd ed. (Paris, 1948), p. 301; cf. also p. 173.

**3, n. 2:** See already the (genuine) *Prima Clementis*, cc. 37–8, employing the Pauline allegory of body and head. For Pauline conceptions cf. also O. Karrer, "Apsotolische Nachfolge und Primat" in *Z. f. kath. Theol.* lxxvii (1955), pp. 131 ff.; O. Kuss, "Jesus und die Kirche" in *Theol. Quartalschrift*, cxxxv (1955), pp. 150 ff.

**4, n. 1:** Cf. also Kuss, art. cit., pp. 168 ff.

**4, n. 2:** For the influence of Tertullian's concept of *monarchia*—an influence that deserves detailed examination—see E. Peterson, op. cit. pp. 68 ff. For the oath of the Roman legionaries (the *sacramentum*) and baptism see A. Ehrhardt in *Festschrift f. Guido Kisch* (Stuttgart, 1955), pp. 147 ff.

**4, n. 3:** About the alleged concrete transmission of Petrine powers by St Peter himself to Clement I, cf. W. Ullmann in *J.T.S.*, xi (1960), pp. 295 ff.

**5, n. 3:** It should be noted that this argumentation was still employed in the fourteenth century by Clement VI who in his jubilee decree (*Extrav. comm.*, V. iv. 2) said that Christ "*uni*, scil. apostolorum principi, sicut bono dispensatori, claves regni coelorum commisit, *alteri* tamquam idoneo doctori magisterium ecclesiasticae eruditionis injunxit;" here also : "per quos (Petrum et Paulum) ecclesia religionis sumpsit exordium." See also following note.

**6, n. 3:** The metaphorical use of a source of a river for the Roman Church suggested itself. Cf. Innocent I, *Ep.* 29 (in *P.L.*, xx. 583): "velut de natali fonte" all other churches received their "life" from the Roman Church. Hence also the designation of the Roman Church as "mater et caput omnium ecclesiarum."

**6, n. 4:** On the influence of the Ambrosiaster and St Jerome, cf. H. Vogel in *Rev. Bénédictine*, lxvi (1956), pp. 14 ff.; cf. also P. Courcelle in *Vigiliae Christianae*, xiii (1959), pp. 133 ff. On Ambrosiaster and the work itself see G. Bardy in *Rev. Biblique*, xli (1932), pp. 343 ff. The Ambrosiaster is edited by A. Souter in *C.S.E.L.*, l (1908).

**7, n. 6:** For an analysis of Leo I's theme of primacy cf. now W. Ullmann in *J.T.S.*, xi (1960), pp. 25 ff. The Leonine primatial thesis has stood the test of time and was especially useful in establishing the relationship between the pope and the bishops. Cf., e.g., in the fifteenth century Johannes de Turrecremata, *De pontif. . . . auctoritate* (ed. Venice, 1563), p. 16 v, no. 22: "Ceteri

# 462 *The Growth of Papal Government in the Middle Ages*

apostoli non immediate a Christo jurisdictionem acceperunt, sed *mediante Petro.*" See furthermore, infra p. 443 n. 4 (Grosseteste, Augustinus Triumphus), and about the modern view cf. the statement of Pius XII, quoted in W. Ullmann, *The medieval Papacy, St Thomas and Beyond* (Aquinas Lecture, London, 1960), p. 12 n. 24.

**8, n. 1:** Through the process of monopolisation the view emerged later that this passage proved the dependence of the prelates' jurisdictional powers on the pope.

**8, n. 4:** For an analysis of heirship see *J.T.S.*, xi (1960), pp. 30 ff. With Leo I's expressions should be compared also a statement made as late as in the early fourteenth century by Clement V (anno 1308): "Christus est nobis via, vita et veritas. Quis ergo potest ipsum negare, *per quem et in quo subsistimus?*" cited from C. Wenck, *Clemens V und Heinrich VII* (Halle, 1882), p. 99. About recent literature on the primatial question cf. also O. Karrer, art. cit. (p. 3, n. 2*), pp. 148 f. at note 13, and A. Rimoldi, *L'apostolo San Pietro* (Rome, 1958).

**10, n. 1:** The prevailing thought in antiquity made the Christian emperor a God on earth. A. Ehrhardt, *Die altchristl. Kirchen* (Bonn, 1937), p. 10, speaks on this context of the poison, according to which the Roman Caesars had become Christian, but not the Roman idea of emperorship.

**10, n. 3:** For the authority of the four ecumenical councils and the hallowing of the number Four, see Y. Congar, *Le concile et les conciles* (Paris, 1960), who refers (p. 101 ff.) to biblical and literary models suggesting the *quaternité* (four empires; four gospels, four virtues; four seasons; four elements; four doctors; four letters of *Deus*; see furthermore, *Roma quadrata, lapis quadrata,* etc.). In the eighth century Egbert of York said: "ex omni parte quadratus numerus perfectus dignoscitur", cit. ibid., p. 105 n. 132.

**10, n. 4:** For the meaning of the Byzantine coronation see now esp. A. Michel, *Die Kaisermacht in der Ostkirche* (Darmstadt, 1959) pp. 132 ff.

**12, n. 1:** See also Y. M. Duvel, "Quelques emprunts de s. Léon à s. Augustin" in *Mélanges de science religieuse*, xv (1958), pp. 85 ff.; on Leo I cf. now P. Brezzi in *Studi Romani*, ix (1961), pp. 614 ff.

**13, n. 2:** This notional juxtaposition of *imperium* and *potestas* reappears also in the Introit for 6 January in the *Miss. Rom.*: "ecce advenit dominator dominus, et regnum in manu eius et *potestas et imperium.*" See further on the intimate link of the two concepts in the acclamations: B. Opfermann, *Die liturg. Herrscherakklamationen* (Weimar, 1953), p. 36: "Ipsi soli *imperium*, gloria, et *potestas.*" Cf. also E. Peterson, op. cit., pp. 148 ff. on the analogy between the Roman emperor and *Christus imperator* in the Revelations of St John; for some observations see also A. Ehrhardt in *Studi P. de Francisci* (Milan, 1955), iv. 428 ff. It is well known that Justinian ascribed to himself the possession of *imperium* and *potestas*. For Christ depicted as Roman emperor see E. Stauffer, *Die Theologie des Neuen Testaments*, 4th ed. (Stuttgart, 1948), Table 71.

**14, n. 1:** It is therefore proved that the concept of *potestas regia* was introduced by Leo I, and not, as it is always maintained, by Gelasius I.

**16, n. 5:** A. Michel, op. cit. (p. 10 n. 4*), p. 78, remarks rightly that the emperor who had been so often proved a heretic, rose to the zenith of infallibility.

**17, n. 4:** For the influence of Eusebius' ideas on the principle of monarchy, cf. H. Eger in *Z. f. neutestamentl. Wiss.*, xxxviii (1939), pp. 97–115; E. Peterson, op. cit., pp. 86–101; G. Bardy in *R.H.E.*, l (1955), pp. 5 ff.

**21, n. 3:** The contrast between "imperialis *potestas*" and "*auctoritas* sacerdotalis" had already been made by Leo I, in his *Ep.* 118; cf. also *Ep.* 117 and *Ep.* 120, also *Ep.* 156. In his *Sermo* 3, after designating Christ as Melchisedek, Leo I however refers both *potestas* and *auctoritas* to the chair of St Peter.

**21, n. 4**: Cf. also H. Siber, *Römisches Verfassungsrecht* (Lahr, 1952), pp. 375 ff. See now also the excellent exposition of *auctoritas* in F. Wieacker, *Vom Römischen Recht* (Stuttgart, 1961), pp. 31, 39, ff.; J. Gaudemet, "Le régime imperial" in *Studia et Documenta Historiae et Juris*, xxvi (1960), pp. 282–322, esp. pp. 309 ff.; E. Meyer, *Römischer Staat und Staatsgedanke*, 2nd ed. (Darmstadt, 1961), pp. 362–8.

**21, n. 7**: In general the monarchic principle is very well expressed by E. Peterson, op. cit., p. 53: "Wenn Gott die Voraussetzung dafür ist, dass es eine *potestas* gibt, dann wird der Eine Gott zum Träger der *auctoritas*. Dann wird der Monotheismus zum Prinzip der politischen *auctoritas*.

**22, n. 1**: The immediate model for this statement is *Hebr.* xiii. 17.

**22, n. 2**: It may very well be, as W. Ensslin in *Hist. Jb.*, lxxiv (1955), pp. 661 ff. stresses, that Gelasius was not consistent in his terminology—a statement that is not quite new—but the significance of the very carefully chosen terms in *Ep.* 12 leaves nothing to be desired in regard to clarity.

**23, ctd from 22, n. 6**: In the twelfth century Frederick I also designated himself as *pater patriae*, *MGH. Const.*, i. 191, no. 137.

**23, n. 3**: For modern literature on the figure of Melchisedek see F. Merzbacher in *Sav. Z., Kan. Abt.*, xlii (1956), p. 61 n. 23a.

**24, n. 3**: The notion of the *humana fragilitas* seems to originate with Theodosius II, see H. Fichtenau, *Arenga* (Vienna, 1957), p. 126; cf. also Leo I in his *Sermo* 36 (in *P.L.*, liv. 256).

**25, n. 1**: For an almost identical diction in St Bernard see below, p. 435 n. 3.

**25, n. 3**: See in this context the statement of E. Peterson, supra p. 21 n. 7*.

**26, line 4**: In the numerous discussions on Gelasian doctrines it is usually overlooked that the power to bind and to loose refers exclusively to the conduct of the Christian on this earth and that the binding and loosing in the other world is, according to Gelasius and the undisputed medieval doctrine, an automatic consequence of the effects of binding and loosing on earth. Hence, it is exclusively the Christian's conduct on this earth which furnishes the criterion. Seen thus, life on earth is considered the only essential criterion, for life hereafter is based on it. The comprehensiveness of the Petrine powers and the resultant view on the Christian's totality—his *Ganzheit*—makes the effects of the Petrine powers understandable and at the same time also explains why there could not be anything approaching a negation of earthly life: on the contrary, earthly life was thereby given its full meaning.

**26, n. 4**: About the statement of Pope Anastasius that the emperor was vicar of God, see especially A. Michel, op. cit., p. 80 n. 562, who emphasizes that such statements should not be taken too seriously, "for the papal chancery is far too much inclined to play with such expressions in order to influence the attitude of the emperor."

**29, n. 1**: For a textual analysis of Isidore, cf. now J. Fontaine in *Vigiliae Christianae*, xiv (1960), pp. 65–101.

**29, n. 9**: As a matter of fact, the edict of King Guntram (anno 585) had already promised the help of the royal power, if ecclesiastical admonition should prove insufficient; see R. Schröder, *Lehrb. d. deutschen Rechtsgesch.*, 7th ed. (Leipzig, 1932), p. 192 n. 96.

**30, n. 4**: Here the statement of St Jerome in *C.S.E.L.*, liv. 421, should be adduced. The examples chosen by L. Hardick, "Gedanken zu Sinn und Tragweite des

Begriffs 'clerici' " in *Arch. Franc. Hist.*, l (1957), pp. 7–26, belong to a later period.

**32, line 11, after note 3**: Here the idea of Justinian as the vicar of Christ on earth plays its important role: since he is the earthly *basileus kai auto-krator* he reflects the heavenly *panbasileus kai pantokrator*.

**32, n. 1**: In this context it should be noted that in the fourth and fifth centuries the term *theios* meant not only "divine", but also—and probably more often than not—"imperial", see A. H. M. Jones in *Harvard Theol. Rev.*, xlvi (1953), p. 172.

**32, n. 3**: The laws, says Justinian, originate in "our divine mouth" (*Cod.* I xvii. 1 (6). In his *Nov.* xiii, Epil., he calls his law a divine precept (*preceptio divina*).

**32, n. 4**: On this point cf. also E. H. Kaden, *Justinien législateur* (in Mémoires publ. par la Faculté de droit de Génève, no. 6, 1952), pp. 58–65; and now B. Rubin, *Das Zeitalter Justinians* (Berlin, 1960), pp. 125 ff., and p. 394 notes 210 ff. Hence also Justinian's attempt to reconstitute the old classical Roman law, cf. E. Levy, *West Roman Vulgar Law* (Philadelphia, 1951), pp. 12 ff. See now also the fine observations of F. Wieacker, *Vom römischen Recht* (Stuttgart, 1961), pp. 224 ff., 242 ff.

**33, n. 1**: See now also A. Michel, op. cit., pp. 101 ff., and B. Rubin, op. cit., pp. 146 ff.

**34, ctd from 33, n. 4**: For the Eastern doctrines relating to this point, cf. further H. G. Beck, *Kirche und Theolog. Literatur im byzantin. Reich* (Munich, 1959), pp. 36 ff., and H. S. Alivisatos in *Akten des XI Internat. Byzant. Kongr.* (Munich, 1960), pp. 15 ff. Cf. also J. Gaudemet, *L'église dans l'empire romain* (Paris, 1958), and R. Tanin, "L'empereur dans l'église byzantine" in *Nouvelle Rev. théologique*, lxxvii (1955), pp. 49 ff. A. Michel, op. cit., p. 124, n. 886, spoke of a "sacral absolutism" practised by the Eastern emperors; here also rich literature and source material about the emperor as king and priest. In his *Nov.* iii. pr. Justinian designated the Church of Constantinople as the "mother of our Empire".

**34, n. 1**: About the interchangeability of *lex* and *canon* see L. Wenger in *S.B. Vienna*, ccxx (1943), esp. pp. 88 ff., 170 f.

**35, ctd from 34, n. 4**: For the curious development of this phrase in the M.A., see H. M. Jolowicz, "The stone that the builders rejected" in *Seminar*, xii (1954), pp. 40–1.

**35, n. 1**: For a practical application of ideological symbolism in medallions see Ph. Grierson in *Dumbarton Oaks Papers*, xv (1960), pp. 221 ff. What is particularly important is that the pictorial representation of Christ becomes adapted to the pictures of the emperor himself and that the pagan imperial cult is simply continued in the Christian empire. Hence the despatch of the imperial portraits to the provinces was to signify the omnipresence of the emperor and the solemn reception of the imperial portrait with incense and torches was to underline the sacral status of the imperial majesty. Hence also Melchisedek in imperial vestments. For all this see A. Michel, op. cit., p. 132, notes 933 ff.

**36, n. 5**: About the gulf existing between East and West see H. Steinacker, "Die römische Kirche u. die griechischen Sprachkenntnisse des Frühmittelalters" in *MIOG.*, lxii (1954), at p. 40; also H. Biedermann, "Zur Frage nach der inneren Entwicklung der Ostkirche" in *Ostkirchl. Studien*, i (1952), esp. pp. 110 ff.

**37, n. 3**: That the title "ecumenical patriarch" existed certainly since 518, has been proved (Fichtenau, art. cit., p. 99, n. 348). Moreover, Gregory's statement in *Reg.* v. 45 that John the Faster had called himself ecumenical patriarch in nearly every line, is incorrect, for the document that gave rise to the whole dispute was merely a *synodica*, and John did not call himself in the way Gregory alleged. Caspar, ii. 455, remarked very correctly that John probably could not understand what had enraged his Roman friend, the pope, so much, but Caspar did not appear to have recognized the link between the English mission and the protest.

**37, n. 4:** Apart from these points there were particularly strongly at work Eastern influences in Irish liturgy, cf. E. Bishop, *Liturgica Historica* (Oxford, 1917), pp. 161–3. Private penance was first practised in the West in Ireland and appears to have come from the East, cf. Bishop, pp. 162 f., and also H. Zimmer, *The Celtic Church in Britain and Ireland* (London, 1902), pp. 115 ff., 129 ff.; P. Finsterwalder in *Z. f. Kirchengesch.*, xlvii (1928), p. 210. The Irish tonsure and Easter reckoning were modelled on Eastern practices, cf. A. Silva-Tarouca, *Humanistische Tradition und östl. Geisteshaltung im M.A.* (Innsbruck, 1947), pp. 9 f. Under John IV the abbot of Iona resisted attempts at Romanization, cf. E. Bruck, *Kirchenväter u. soziales Erbrecht* (Berlin, 1956), p. 199.

**37, n. 5:** Justinian called himself "ultimus servus minimus" (*Cod.* I. xvii. 1). Leo I had used *servitus* for the papal office, *Ep.* 108. See further St Augustine in *P.L.* xxxiii. 494.

**38, n. 2:** For an instructive sidelight on Gregory's handling of papal patrimonies in Gaul see Ph. Grierson in *Rev. Belge de Numismatique*, cv (1959), pp. 95 ff. (striking of pseudo-imperial coins in papal patrimony).

**40, ctd from 39, n. 6:** See further J. Straub in *Studia Patristica* (Berlin, 1957), i. 678; also W. Ullmann in *J.T.S.*, xi (1960), pp. 312 ff.

**40, n. 3:** For the difference between Eastern and Western monasticism cf. D. C. Lialine in *Irénikon*, xxxiii (1960), pp. 435 ff. (posthumously published).

**41, n. 1:** About the application of Gregory I's statement see also H. Fuhrmann in *Sav. Z., Kan. Abt.*, xl (1954), p. 65 and notes 192, 193.

**41, n. 3:** About the alleged "Responsiones" of Gregory I cf. on the one hand M. Deanesly and P. Grosjean in *J. Eccl. Hist.*, x (1959), pp. 1 ff., and on the other hand M., Meyvaert in *R.H.E.* liv (1959), pp. 879 ff. See now again M. Deanesly in *J. Eccl. Hist.*, xii (1961), pp. 231 ff.

**46, n. 4:** For the genuineness of this letter see furthermore H. Bresslau, *Handb. d. Urkundenlehre*, 2nd ed. (Leipzig, 1912), i. 154 and note 1; O. Bertolini in *Riv. di storia della chiesa*, ix (1955), p. 37 n. 63, and A. Michel, *Die Kaisermacht in der Ostkirche* (Darmstadt, 1959), p. 7 and n. 38.

**49, n. 3:** For the background see E. Griffe, "La Gaule chrétienne à l'époque romaine" in *Rev. d'hist. de l'eglise de France*, xxxvii (1951), pp. 40–52; and especially J.-R. Palanque, "La Gaule chrétienne à l'époque franque" ibid., xxxviii (1952), pp. 52 ff.; P. Vaccari, "La Gallia pre-carolingia" in *Studi . . . in onore di Ettore Rota* (Rome, 1958), pp. 31 ff.

**51, line 6 from foot:** We should do well to bear in mind that Gregory II's threat to leave the city of Rome for regions inhabited by "savages and barbarians" clearly indicated the one alternative with which the papacy in the twenties of the eighth century toyed, that is, the physical removal of the pope outside the confines of the empire. Although at first sight this plan to remove the pope bodily, had certainly some attraction, it was not executed, and this for excellent reasons. When we consider that the Roman-Petrine tenor of the papal programme gave the papacy the

17

strongest possible support which, as the most recent history had sufficiently proved, made a correspondingly strong appeal to the Franks, we can well understand why this alternative was not pursued by the papacy: one has but to visualize the pope sitting in Rheims or St Denis and putting forward the Petrine and Roman claims, and it becomes at once understandable how vitally necessary the physical connexion between the pope and Rome was.[a] There remained only the other alternative: not to take the pope bodily out of the empire, but to take part of the imperial territory out of the empire. It was to the execution of this plan that the papacy gradually turned.

[a] The observations of C. Erdmann (infra, p. 96 n. 2) apply here with still greater force: how much more damage would have been inflicted upon the Roman Church in the eighth century by physically removing the pope and thus severing the link between him and Rome, when the papacy was still a very tender plant, in comparison with the damage suffered by the removal of the papacy to Avignon, in the fourteenth century, when the institution could still look back to a past in which it virtually controlled Europe.

**52, n. 1**: For details cf. also O. Bertolini in *Riv. di storia della chiesa*, vi (1952), pp. 1 ff. (turn of the sixth and seventh centuries) and ibid., viii (1954), pp. 1 ff. (seventh century).

**53, n. 1**: The statement of Gregory III should be quoted in this context: "Attendite, vobis et universo gregi, in quo vos spiritus sanctus posuit episcopos regere ecclesiam Dei . . ." (*MGH. Epp.*, iii. 703, no. 13).

**55, n. 1**: The oblique opinion of O. Bertolini (cited infra, p. 59 n. 1) is rightly rejected by F. L. Ganshof in *Annuaire de l'institut de philologie et d'histoires orientales*, x (1950), pp. 276–7.

**56, n. 3**: According to F. L. Ganshof, art. cit., p. 262, the anointing and creation of Pippin as *patricius Romanorum* took place on 28 July 754.

**59, line 13**: To this consideration comes another one. Upon what legal title-deed could the pope base himself, when he conferred on Pippin the office of a *patricius Romanorum?* Where was the pope given the right to nominate this kind of officer? The only plausible explanation is afforded by the Donation of Constantine, for in it we read that Constantine had laid down that the pope should have the right to create patricians (and consuls).[a] The papal title-deed for the appointment of a patrician of the Romans lay in the idea, upon which also the creation of the Emperor of the Romans rested, that is, in the Donation of Constantine.

[a] This is convincingly demonstrated by F. L. Ganshof, art. cit. (supra, p. 55, n. 1*), where also the untenable opinions of Bertolini are rejected. E. Ewig, art. cit., slides over the difficulties.

**59, n. 1**: Cf. in this context also the feeble and unconvincing argumentation of E. Ewig, "Das Bild Constantin d. Gr. in den ersten Jahrhunderten des abendl. M.A." in *Hist. Jb.*, lxxv (1955), pp. 29–31.

**62, n. 2**: Cf. also St Boniface in *MGH. Epp.* iii. 341, no. 73, lines 19 f.: "Apud Graecos et Romanos." For some observations in this respect cf. also W. Ullmann in *Studia Patristica* (Berlin, 1957), ii. 155 ff., esp. on St Patrick. The Visigoths called the Gallic Catholics "Romans" as so to be distinguished from them, see J. M. Wallace-Hadrill in *Bull. J. Rylands Library*, xliv (1961), at p. 225.

**64, n. 4:** It should furthermore be borne in mind that down to the fourteenth century the medieval empire was called the *respublica Romanorum*, see Gierke, iii. 358. Cf. also A. Roselli in his *Monarchia* (in Goldast, ed. Frankfurt, 1612), p. 279, and Cardinal Bellarmin in Mirbt, p. 361, no. 502: "Romanus etiam ante 1100 annos idem erat quod catholicus."

**69, n. 2:** See now also *Reallexikon f. Antike und Christentum*, iii (1956), cols. 651 ff.

**70, n. 3:** This letter is now newly edited by P. M. Gassó and C. M. Batlle, *Pelagii I Papae Epp.* (Montserrat, 1956), no. 27, p. 82, where the editors stress the importance of this letter.

**70, n. 4:** See further *Reallexikon* (cit. supra, p.p. 69 n.2*), col. 656: "beamteter Anwalt für die Vertretung der Kirche vor den staatlichen Gerichten."

**71, n. 1:** For the underlying conceptions cf. now also W. Ullmann, *Principles of Government and Politics in the M.A.* (London, 1961), part II.

**73, n. 1:** Our interpretation of *commendare* is borne out by the use which, for instance, Pelagius I made of it, see *MGH. Epp.* iii. 77 no. 53, lines 17 f. = new ed. (supra p. 70, n. 3*), p. 29, no. 9: "Preterea *commendamus* specialiter tuae dilectioni Romanos, qui . . . confugerunt."

**75, ctd from 74, n. 2:** About Christophorus, the possible author of the Donation and his great influence on the popes, see O. Bertolini, "La caduta del primicerio Cristoforo" in *Riv. di storia della chiesa*, i (1947), pp. 227 ff., esp. 364 ff. For the Donation cf. also R. Buchner in Wattenbach-Levison (Beiheft: *Die Rechtsquellen*, p. 72) ("made probably between 750 and 760"); Ohnsorge's view is rightly rejected in Wattenbach-Levison, p. 211 n. 136. On the other hand, E. Griffe, "Aux origines de l'état pontifical" in *Bulletin de littérature ecclésiastique*, iv (1958), pp. 194 ff., at pp. 206 ff. still pleads for a Frankish origin of the forgery made in the early ninth century. M. Pacaut, *La théocratie* (Paris, 1957), p. 37, states that the forgery was "composé justement à Rome dans les années 750–760." About the unfortunate thesis of W. Gericke in *Sav. Z., Kan. Abt.*, xliii (1957), pp. 1 ff.; xliv (1958), pp. 343 ff., see H. Fuhrmann in *Deutsches Archiv*, xv (1959), pp. 523–40. About the utilisation of the forgery by the medieval jurists see the forthcoming work by D. Maffei, and in the meantime see idem in *Annali della Università di Macerata*, xxiii (1959), pp. 207–32, with copious literature.

**77, ctd from 76, n. 4:** We have already seen that a good deal of this teleology of history goes back to St Augustine. In this context the observations of J. Straub, "Augustinus' Sorge um die Regeneratio imperii" in *Hist. Jb.*, lxxiv (1954), p. 39, should be noted: under the influence of the prevailing doctrines "Christianitas und Romanitas waren so eng miteinander verklammert und verflochten worden, dass die politische Existenz in die gefährliche Nähe der Identifikation mit der religiösen Existenz gerückt war." The tract *De vocatione omnium gentium* is now attributed to Prosper of Aquitaine, see P. de Letter, *St Prosper of Aquitaine: The Call of all Nations* (in Ancient Christian Writers, vol. xiv, 1952). Cf. also the prayer of Milanese stock in the sixth century: "Pro pace ecclesiarum, *vocatione omnium gentium* et quiete populorum," see D. B. Capelle in *Rev. Bénédictine*, xlvi (1934), col. 1, sub no. 7. The same teleological and historical thought is still contained in the *Römisches Messbuch*, ed. A. Schott, in the post-communio where this prayer text for the emperor of the Romans will be found (ed. 1934, p. [134]).

**77, n. 2:** Cf. in this context the stimulating observations of M. Seidlmayer, "Rom und Romgedanke im M.A." in *Saeculum*, vii (1956), pp. 395 ff., at pp. 402–3.

**79, n. 2:** But the Donation speaks in the relevant places only of "sancimus"; there is no evidence of an imperial conferment of primatial powers, as M.

Maccarone, *Vicarius Christi* (Rome, 1952), p. 73, n. 75 erroneously states. What Constantine conferred on the pope was imperial power. On the other hand, the Donation represents progress, in so far as St Peter (cap. xi) is called "vicarius filii Dei", see on this Maccarone, op. cit., pp. 72–3.

**79, n. 5**: About the papal *f*:*rula*, see also P. Salmon in *Rev. des sciences religieuses*, xxx (1956), pp. 313–37, who knows however nothing of modern literature and disregards Byzantium.

**82, n. 1**: From this it is quite clear that the later doctrine of the translation of the empire could indeed be deduced from the Donation. P. A. van den Baar, *Die kirchl. Lehre der Translatio imperii Romani* (Rome, 1956), is quite unsatisfactory, cf. *E.H.R.*, lxxii (1957), pp. 522 ff. Far more satisfactory is W. Goez, *Translatio imperii* (Tübingen, 1958), cf. *E.H.R.*, lxxv (1960), pp. 332 f.

**82, n. 2**: See on this now also R. Bork in *Festschrift f. A. Hofmeister* (Halle, 1955), pp. 39–56.

**88, line 9**: This exposition should now be supplemented by W. Ohnsorge, "Der Patricius-Titel Karls d. Gr." in *Byzantin. Z.*, liii (1960), pp. 300 ff., though we cannot agree with all the statements of this savant.

**89, n. 3**: For some details cf. also E. Delaruelle, in *Rev. d'hist. de l'église de France*, xxxviii (1952), pp. 64 ff.

**95, n. 3**: Cf. now also the important article by H. Beumann in *Hist. Z.*, clxxxv (1958), pp. 518 ff.

**97, n. 1**: The *Chronographia* of Theophanes is now easily accessible also in the translation by L. Breyer (Graz, 1957); the marriage plan is mentioned here pp. 136, 137.

**97, n. 2**: See also S. Giet, "Simple remarques sur l'histoire de Charlemagne" in *Rev. des sciences religieuses*, xxix (1955), pp. 45 ff.

**98, n. 1**: Cf. also the significant passages cited by Giet, art. cit. (supra, p. 97, n. 2\*), p. 50 n. 3. This passage from the *Litania Karolina* is newly edited by B. Opfermann, *Die liturg. Herrscherakklamationen im sacrum imperium des M.A.* (Weimar, 1953), p. 101; on the subject itself see ibid., pp. 63–5. This fact of borrowing serves as an important indication for the co-operation of the Franks in the discussions preceding the event itself.

**99, ctd from 98, n. 2**: In this context reference should also be made to the adoption of the *Dei gratia* title by Charlemagne; for further details cf. *Principles of Government*, cit., part II, ch. 1. The addition *a Deo coronatus* is of Byzantine origin, see W. Ensslin, *SB. Munich*, 1943, p. 106.

**101, n. 3**: There were, even in this early period, definite beginnings of the conception of the vicariate of Christ in the pope. Cf., for instance, Paul I expressing his own vicariate in a way which was not materially different from the view of Innocent III: "(Deo) dignante mediator Dei et hominum, speculator animarum, institutus sum" (*Cod. Carol.*, no. 16, p. 513, lines 19 ff.). For the development of some of these ideas see W. Ullmann in *Misc. Hist. Pontif.*, xviii (1954), pp. 107 ff. and idem in *Studi Gregoriani*, vi (1959), pp. 229 ff.

**103, ctd from 102, n. 3**: There is need to clarify the views expressed in the text and in this footnote. No doubt seems possible that the coronation was preceded by talks between Charlemagne and the pope: this emerges clearly from the *Ann. Laur.* (quoted in this note) as well as from the borrowing of the Frankish acclamations. But what is essential is that the pope obviously did not adhere to the arrangement reached before Christmas day, for Charles was acclaimed as *imperator Romanorum*, that is, acclaimed with a *nomen* to which he had not agreed, as his subsequent conduct sufficiently explains. He found himself, so to speak, pushed into the very situation which he had wished to avoid. This *nomen* was inserted into the Frankish acclamations and it was this *nomen* to which he objected so strongly, as Einhard bears witness. We agree therefore with F. L. Ganshof, op. cit., pp. 24, 25, who says: "Leo III had played a crooked game" and that "the pope had taken him (Charles) now by a kind of treachery." It was precisely the *nomen* which Charles wished to have changed and it took five months before his court had found the proper formula. At the same time it was the *nomen* which aroused the indignation of the Byzantines. H. Fichtenau in *MIOG.*, lxi (1953), pp. 259 ff. stresses the dependence of Einhard on Suetonius, but this fact alone does not diminish the credibility of his report. Einhard's dependence on Suetonius "ne prouve pas que le passage ne révèle rien historique," Giet, art. cit., p. 46, n. 4. See now also H. Beumann in *Hist. Z.*, clxxxv (1958), pp. 515 ff., esp. 521–5 (Einhard) and 525 ff. (*Ann. Laur.*). Cf. now also R. Folz, *Le couronnement impérial de Charlemagne* (Paris, 1964).

**104, ctd from 103, n. 2:** See now also the penetrating observations of M. Seidlmayer in *Saeculum*, vi (1956), pp. 404 ff.

**104, n. 1:** Cf. on this D. Hay, *Europa: the emergence of an idea* (Edinburgh, 1957) and J. Fischer, *Oriens-Occidens-Europa* (Wiesbaden, 1957), pp. 78 ff.

**105, n. 1:** Here it should be noted that just as in Byzantium it was the emperor (and not the patriarch) who crowned the co-emperor, so here too in the West it was Charles who crowned Louis I his co-emperor. Charles himself therefore was the "Spender der Krönung", cf. on this A. Michel, *Die Kaisermacht in der Ostkirche*, cit., p. 172.

**106, n. 3:** For the fertility of contemporary discussions cf. W. Dürig, "Der theolog. Ausgangspunkt der ma. Auffassung vom Herrscher als vicarius Dei" in *Hist. Jb.*, lxxvii (1958), pp. 174 ff.

**109, n. 2:** Cf. also D. Delaruelle in *Rev. d'hist. de l'église de France*, xxxix (1953), pp. 165–200.

**113, n. 1:** Here some consideration should be given to the idea that this *Renovatio* was modelled on the baptismal *Regeneratio* or *Renovatio*, that is, the re-birth of natural man effected through baptism. Cf. II *Cor.* v. 17; *Gal.* v. 6; vi. 15; *Eph.* ii. 8 and *Tit.* iii. 5: "per lavacrum regenerationis et renovationis spiritus sancti."

**114, line 5, after note 1:** The title is not merely a frill or an embellishment, but expresses in a succinct manner the inner substance, the qualification and being of him who bears the title.[a] That is why the change of title effected by Charlemagne has particularly great significance. At the same time a title had to be found which was to express his equality with the Eastern emperor and also his function as the monarch of the Roman-Christian *imperium*.

aFor this see esp. H. Fichtenau in *MIOG.*, lxi (1953), pp. 259 ff.,

**115, n. 2:** See now in particular W. Schlesinger in *Festgabe f. F. Hartung* (Weimar, 1958), pp. 17 ff. (imperial title of 806 from the Donation) and p. 22 (no universal dominion).

**117, n. 1:** See now again E. E. Stengel, "Imperator und Imperium bei den Angelsachsen" in *Deutsches Archiv*, xvi (1960), pp. 15–72, against the unfortunate thesis of Drögereit.

**118, n. 2:** This oath of Leo III has now been proved a forgery of the ninth century, see L. Wallach in *Harvard Theol. Rev.*, xlix (1956), pp. 123 f. and idem im *Traditio*, xi (1955), pp. 37 ff., at p. 62: "The document hitherto known as the oath purgation sworn by Leo III on 23 December 800 is a forgery of the middle of the ninth century." In agreement with this is H. Fichtenau in *MIOG.*, lxiv (1956), p. 380. It should also be stressed that the principle of papal immunity (contained in the *Constitutum Silvestri*) had already been stated by Pope Zosimus, see his *Ep.* 12 (in *P.L.* xx. 677 = *Avellana, C.S.E.L.,* xxxv, p. 116): " . . ut nullus de nostra possit retractare sententia."

**119, n. 1:** For the points made here cf. also H. Löwe, "Von den Grenzen des Kaisergedankens in der Karolingerzeit" in *Deutsches Archiv,* xiv (1958), pp. 345–74.

**125, n. 1:** Cf. also the outspokenly anti-royalist views expressed in glosses of this time, especially in connexion with the Council of Paris (829), see F. Maassen in *SB. Vienna,* lxxxiv (1876), pp. 235–98.

**126, ctd from 125, n. 2:** For some remarks about the monastic revival see also J. Choux, "Décadence et réforme monastique dans la province de Trèves" in *Rev. Bénédictine,* lxx (1960), pp. 204 ff.

**148, n. 2:** It should be recalled that in Constantinople the imperial palace was also called *sacrum palacium,* and that Justinian addressed his ordinances to the *Quaestor sacri palacii.*

**154, n. 4:** For this see the important study by E. Kantorowicz in *Harvard Theol. Rev.,* xlv (1953), pp. 253 ff. The argumentation of Peter Damian in the eleventh century was substantially the same, see his *Liber gratissimus* in *MGH.L.d.L.,* i. 19, lines 9–11.

**178, n. 1:** About the difficult genesis of the prologue and especially about its incorrect beginning in the Hinschius-edition see E. Seckel-H. Fuhrmann, "Die erste Zeile Pseudo-Isidors" in *SB. Berlin,* 1959, which is also an important contribution to the history of the diplomatic formula of invocation.

**181, n. 1:** On the influence see now Ch. de Clercq, "La législation religieuse franque dépuis les fausses décrétales jusqu'à la fin du ix siècle" in *Rev. du droit canonique,* viii (1957), pp. 113 ff., 255 ff.; ix (1958), pp. 122 ff.

**183, ctd from 182, n. 8:** But see now H. M. Klinkenberg, "Der römische Primat im 10. Jahrhundert" in *Sav. Z., Kan. Abt.,* xli (1955), p. 10.

**184, n. 7:** See furthermore H. Fuhrmann, "Pseudo-Isidor und die Abbreviatio Ansegisi et Benedicti Levitae" in *Z. f. Kirchengesch.,* lxix (1958), pp. 309 ff.

**192, n. 3:** The biblical model might have been: *Is.* xxii. 22.

**195, n. 2:** This statement of Nicholas I is actually a practical application of *Ps.* xliv. 17. Cf. also *Miss. Rom.,* 29 June, in the *Graduale* and *Offertorium.*

**198, n. 4:** The allegory of the *maxima luminaria Dei* was later also used by Eugenius III in *Bull. Romanum,* ii. 588.

**199, n. 2:** For Photius cf. also P. L'Huillier, "Le saint patriarche Photius et l'unité chrétienne" in *Messager de l'exarchat du patriarchat russe en Europe occidentale,* no. 22 (June 1955, offprint).

**202, n. 2:** Exactly the same argument was used by Egidius Romanus in the early fourteenth century, *De eccles. potestate,* ed. R. Scholz (Weimar, 1929), ii. 9, pp. 81 ff., at p. 85.

**203, n. 5:** For a discussion of this letter see now also G. T. Dennis, "The 'anti-Greek' character of the Responsa ad Bulgaros of Nicholas I" in *Orientalia Christiana Periodica,* xxiv (1958), pp. 165 ff.

**218, n. 3:** For the background of the different conceptions of the Church in the West and in the East, cf. Y. M. Congar in *Istina,* vi (1959), pp. 187 ff., at pp. 201 ff.

**225, n. 3:** The imperial coronation orders are now newly edited by R. Elze, *Ordines coronationis imperialis* (in *Fontes Juris Germanici Antiqui,* Hanover, 1960); *Ordo B* is here *Ordo I.*

**228, n. 2:** All the English coronation orders have in fact the designation of the king as *christus* (anointed); see the prayer *Protector noster* in the *Liber regalis*, in *Liber regie capelle*, ed. W. Ullmann (Henry Bradshaw Soc., vol. xcii, 1961, p. 99).

**230, n. 1**: Against this explanation is O. Bertolini in *Studi medievali in onore A. de Stefano* (Palermo, 1956), pp. 43 ff., who is apparently unable to penetrate into the texture of the sources and who quite obviously never understood the main arguments employed in art. cit.

**232, n. 1**: For a detailed account of the *Reichskirchensystem* see L. Santifaller in *SB. Vienna*, ccxxix (1954), pp. 22 ff., at 30 ff.

**233, n. 3**: For Widukind's ideas on the empire see now also J. A. Brundage in *Medieval Studies*, xxii (1960), pp. 15 ff.

**235, n. 1**: What the Byzantines always feared was that the recognition of papal primacy would automatically entail a recognition of the universality of the papally created (Western) emperor. This fear was indeed still very much in the foreground as late as the fifteenth century, cf. C. Beckmann, *Der Kampf Sigismunds gegen die Weltherrschaft* 1397–1437 (Gotha, 1902), p. 62.

**238, n. 7**: For a fine characterization of Otto III see now M. Uhlirz, *Jahrbücher d. deutschen Reiches unter Otto III.* (Berlin, 1954), pp. 411–13; here also the rejection of the view that Otto was an eccentric and unbalanced youth.

**239, n. 2**: On the subject of the lance, cf. J. Déer in *Byzant. Z.*, I (1957), pp. 427 ff. On the Empire itself, cf. W. Ullmann, in *Trans. R. Hist. S.* (1964).

**239, n. 3**: See on this now also M. Uhlirz, op. cit., pp. 417–19.

**239, n. 4**: In parenthesis it may be recalled that in the thirteenth century Innocent IV was designated as the thirteenth apostle by the Sultan of Egypt, Ayob: *MGH. Epp. PP. RR.*, ii. 87, no. 123.

**240, n. 4**: Cf. in this context R. Morghen in *I Problemi communi dell' Europa post-carolingia* (Settimani, Spoleto, 1955), pp. 11–35.

**241, n. 2**: Cf. now also W. Messerer, "Zur byzantinischen Frage in der ottonischen Kunst" in *Byzant. Z.*, lii (1959), pp. 32 ff.

**242, ctd from 241, n. 3**: For Leo of Vercelli and DO. 389, cf. now H. Fichtenau, "Rhetorische Elemente in der ottonisch-salischen Herrscherurkunde" in *MIOG.*, lxviii (1960), pp. 39, at 46 ff. For the deacon John cf. also Mathilde Uhlirz, op. cit., p. 358 n. 41.

**243, n. 2**: The *Wahlprivilegien* for the German Church are conveniently put together by L. Santifaller, op. cit., pp. 41–6. Here also a very useful survey of the papal creations by the emperors in this period, appendix VI, pp. 88–100 (of the 25 popes 12 were appointed by the emperors and 5 deposed). About the depositions of popes, mainly by emperors, cf. now the exhaustive study of H. Zimmermann in *MIOG.*, lxix (1961), pp. 1–84.

**250, n. 1**: The statement in the text had by the fourteenth century become *vulgare*, see Bartolus in his Commentaries on *Cod.* VIII. 52. 2 (ed. Turin, 1577, fol. 114).

**251, n. 1**: Henry III is called *caput ecclesiae* by Egbert of Tegernsee in *MGH. Epp. sell.* (ed. K. Strecker, 1925), iii. 142, and *vicarius (Christi) in ecclesia* by Siegfried of Tegernsee, ibid., p. 143.

**253, n. 1**: In the new edition by R. Elze (see supra p. 225 n. 3\*) this imperial *ordo* is now *Ordo XIV*, pp. 35 ff.

**253, n. 2**: R. Elze has in preparation a study of the imperial orders which will clarify the validity of *Ordo C*. In the meantime cf. idem in *Sav. Z., Kan. Abt.*, lxxi (1954), p. 218, maintaining however that this *ordo* originated "around 1100", but according to J. Ramackers in *Quellen u. Forschungen aus ital. Arch. und Bibl.*, xxxvii (1956), pp. 16–54, this *ordo* was composed for the coronation of 1111. But Ramackers gives no satisfactory explanation for the absence of the *Credo* in this *ordo* nor can he explain why at this late date the coronation was still built into the structure of the mass—a feature that is after Gregory VII highly unlikely; the term *canonice intrantes* had been used long before this time (cf. E. Eichmann in *Hist. Jb.*, lii (1932), pp. 284–92, and op. cit., ii. 170 f.); further the designation of *Rex et futurus imperator* in the oath to be taken has been used in the election decree of 1059 (cap. 6) and in Gregory's own correspondence: *Reg.* i. 20.

**255, ctd from 254, n. 3**: For an excellent discussion of the symbolic detail in the imperial ceremonial see J. Déer, "Byzanz und die Herrschaftszeichen des Abendlandes" in *Byzant. Z.*, l (1957), pp. 405 ff.; P. E. Schramm, *Sphaira, Globus, Reichsapgel: Wanderung und Wandlung eines Herrschaftszeichens von Caesar bis Elisabeth II.* (Stuttgart, 1958); cf. also A. Grabar in *Hist. Z.*, cxci (1960), pp. 336 ff.

**255, n. 3**: Part of the explanation may also be supplied by the papal doctrine concerning the function of the emperor. What sense should there have been to enthrone an officer who is charged with specific functions! Cf. on this also W. Ullmann in *Cambridge Hist. J.*, xi (1955), p. 242.

**257, n. 2**: For the concept of *canonice intrans* cf. W. Ullmann in *Studi Gregoriani*, vi (1959), at pp. 246 f.

**259, n. 5**: In the fourteenth century Durantis in his *Rationale divin. offic.* (ed. Lyons, 1612), iii. 13 (p. 75 v, no. 2) applies very much the same argument to the mitre which symbolizes "scientiam utriusque testamenti per duo cornua, per anterius designans testamentum novum, per posterius vetus."

**264, n. 2**: The secular point of view relied on history, tradition and custom, and in these elements lay indeed the strength of the royalist standpoint. The conduct of Henry IV is in fact nothing else but the constant appeal to history and custom. The classic reply to this was made by Gregory VII in his memorable statement: "Dominus non dixit 'Ego sum consuetudo', sed dixit' 'Ego sum Veritas et Vita.' " For this and the Cyprianic and Augustinian origin see G. Ladner in *Studi Gregoriani* v (1956), pp. 225 ff. In other words, what is right and law, cannot be determined by history and custom, but by truth alone.

**267, n. 5**: J. J. Ryan in *Medieval Studies*, xx (1958), pp. 206 ff. unsuccessfully tries to make out that Humbert's piece was a product of Roman-Byzantine relations.

**269, n. 6**: The contrast between *dias* and *monas* was still used by Cardinal Johannes Monachus in the early fourteenth century in his commentary on the bull of indulgence for 1300 by Boniface VIII, in order to demonstrate the true monarchic principle at work in Christendom. Cf. further Francis de Meyronis, *De princ. temp.*, ed. P. de Lapparant in *Arch. d'hist. doctrinale et littéraire du M.A.*, xiii (1942), p. 60 (kind information by my former pupil, Dr M. J. Wilks).

**273, n. 3**: The Gregorian antithesis of *superbia* and *humilitas* may have originated in I *Pet.* v. 5.

**275, n. 1**: For Gregory VII himself cf. also his *Reg.* iii. 7, p. 257: "Desideramus . . . jus suum unicuique observare."

**276, n. 2**: For Gregory's Register cf. now also F. Bock in *Studi Gregoriani*, v (1956), pp. 243 ff., and G. B. Borino, ibid., pp. 391 ff.

**276, n. 7**: Cf. also *Reg.* ix. 2, p. 571, where this society is also called *Romana respublica*.

**277, n. 5**: This was a theme already enunciated by Alexander II, *Ep.* 31 in *Bull. Romanum*, ii. 51.

**277, n. 11**: See further *Reg.* ii. 51, p. 193 and iii. 10, p. 263. The former is particularly interesting.

**278, n. 6**: The background of these strongly Petrine passages (cf. also *Reg.* ii. 9:

"Per Petrum servus et per servum Petrus") is the petrinological idea, about which see *Principles of Government*, pp. 94 f. It is interesting to see that this Petrine function of the pope is faithfully reflected in the composition and poetry of the hymns which mirror the papal-monarchic function in the occident; cf. on this latter aspect J. Szöverffy, "Der Investiturstreit u. die Petrushymnen des M.A." in *Deutsches Archiv*, xiii (1957), pp. 228 ff.

**285, n. 3**: The views here expressed can already be found in Theodoret's *De providentia* (in *P.G.*, lxxxiii. 671 f.).

**287, n. 1**: Another significant statement of Innocent III may be found in X: III. xxx. 33: "Cum autem in *signum universalis dominii . . .* sibi Dominus decimas reservaverit . . ."; for the root of Innocent III's statement in R.N.I. 18 see *Principles of Government*, p. 93. For an ingenious combination of Leonine with Johannine views (St John, i. 16) by Innocent III, see his *Reg.* i. 320.

**289, n. 3**: The same application of this Pauline principle by Eugenius III, *Ep.* 27, in *Bull. Rom.*, ii. 550.

**292, n. 2**: For details of D.P. 23, see W. Ullmann in *Studi Gregoriani*, vi (1959), pp. 229 ff. The statement of Ennodius of Pavia (*ob.* 521) is very similar to that of D.P. 11 and may not have been unknown to Gregory; cf. Ennodius in *C.S.E.L.*, vi. 295.

**295, n. 1**: For the proprietary church system see furthermore G. Schreiber, *Gemeinschaften des M.A.* (Regensburg, 1948), pp. 81, 300–6, 322–30; F. J. Schmale, "Kanonie, Seelsorge, Eigenkirche" in *Hist. Jb.*, lxxviii (1959), pp. 36 ff. For the numerous benefactions and conferments of privileges by kings and emperors in the eleventh century, see the informative account in L. Santifaller, *SB. Vienna*, 1954, appendix II, pp. 46–71.

**302, n. 3**: Cf. as an additional source Gregory in his *Reg.* iv. 3, p. 298 (3 Sept. 1076): "Intelligitur, cur sit (Heinricus) anathematis vinculo alligatus et a regia dignitate depositus."

**305, n. 2**: The terminology of *absolutio omnium peccatorum* appears already in the Privilege of Gregory VII (1074–75), see L. Santifaller, *Quellen und Forschungen zum Urkunden- und Kanzleiwesen Gregors VII* ( = *Studi e Testi*, cxc (1957) ), no. 58, p. 38.

**305, n. 3**: Cf. also E. Dupré, *Introduzione alle eresie medievali* (Bologna, 1955).

**306, n. 4**: For Gregory VII's conception of the crusade see also his *Reg.* i. 46, p. 70, lines 30–1. The split between East and West was always clearly understood as a schism in the proper meaning of the term. Cf., e.g., Adrian IV in *Ep.* 198 (in *P.L.*, clxxxviii) and Gregory IX in *MGH. Epp. PP. RR.*, i. 622, no. 724, lines 31 ff.; p. 623, no. 725, lines 30 ff.

**307, ctd from 306, n. 5**: About the depth of impression which the crusades made, see P. Alphandéry, *La chrétiente et l'idée de croisade* (Paris, 1954).

**313, ctd from 312, n. 5**: On the subject of *mitra-tiara*, cf. the excellent pages of J. Déer in *Byzantin. Z.*, l (1957), pp. 420 ff.

**315, ctd from 314, n. 7**: For this whole question see now M. Andrieu, *Les ordines Romani du haut M.A.* (Louvain, 1956), iv. 168–84.

**316, n. 1**: See also R. Elze in *Sav. Z., Kan. Abt.*, xl (1954), pp. 201 ff.

**321, n. 2**: See also *Cod. Just.*, IX. viii. 5, here also the designation of the imperial senate as *consistorium.*

**322, n. 1**: See also W. Ullmann in *Ephemerides Juris Canonici*, xii (1956), pp. 246 ff., and idem in the *Essays presented to A. Gwynn* (Dublin, 1961), pp. 359 ff.

**323, n. 3**: For a historical survey of papal elections see H. Fuhrmann "Die Wahl des Papstes" in *Geschichte in Wissenschaft und Unterricht*, ix (1958), pp. 762 ff.

**326, ctd from 325, n. 6**: Cf. also J. Sydow, "Untersuchungen zur kurialen

17 *

Verwaltungsgeschichte im Zeitalter des Reformpapsttums" in *Deutsches Archiv*, xi (1955), pp. 18–73.

**330, n. 2:** For some details on papal financial administration, in particular under Albinus and Cencius, cf. V. Pfaff in *MIOG.*, lxiv (1956), pp. 1–24.

**336, n. 6:** About the concept of *tuitio* in Gregory I, cf. H. Appelt in *MIOG.*, lxii (1954), pp. 105 ff.

**336, n. 8:** See also *Reg.* ii. 59, p. 213.

**343, n. 1:** On this passage cf. now also W. Ullmann, "Ueber eine kanonistische Vorlage Friedrichs I." in *Sav. Z., Kan. Abt.*, xlvi (1960), pp. 430 ff. and on the meaning of *beneficium* see idem in *Cambridge Hist. J.*, xi (1955), pp. 242–5, with which interpretation is in agreement Th. Mayer in *Hist. Z.*, clxxxvii (1959), pp. 28 f. Despite the overwhelming evidence against the old interpretation of *beneficium* in the sense of a fief, M. Maccarone, *Papato e Impero* (Lateranum, xxv (1960) ), pp. 180 ff. still appears to prefer this explanation now discarded. For the idea underlying the conception of *beneficium*, cf. now also *Principles of Government*, pp. 57 ff. The thesis that the secular-public power of the State was a divine gift and good deed is still maintained by the modern papacy, cf. Leo XIII in *Acta Sanctae Sedis*, xiv (1881), p. 7: the "potestas rectorum civitatis" as a "donum quodam" and as a *divinum beneficium*.

**343, n. 2:** The same principle was still upheld in the fourteenth century. When in 1346 Clement VI reviewed the double election of 1314 he said: "Ob hoc Romana ecclesia per longa tempora suo caruerat et carebat *speciali advocato* et *legitimo defensore*." Recognizing Charles IV's election, Clement VI said: "Tibi nostrum *favorem et gratias* concedentes . . . to *nominamus*, denuntiamus, declaramus et assumpsimus in regem Romanorum promovendum in imperatorem," Raynaldus, *Ann. eccles.* (ed. Col. Agr., 1618), xiv. 984, 985. Of course, the imperial standpoint never accepted this, maintaining that through election alone and without any intervention by the pope the emperor had received his empire *a solo Deo* (Frederick I). The same principle was expressed in 1237, see *MGH. Const.*, ii. 441, no. 329, and in *Licet juris* of Louis the Bavarian (1338).

**344, ctd from 343, n. 3:** For a neat statement of the imperial (anti-papal) dualist standpoint see also Frederick II in his letter to King Henry III in Huillard-Bréholles, *Hist. dipl. Fred. II*, v. 1125. And yet, there is nowadays the one or the other writer who tries to make out that the dualism was the official papal programme. Only lack of knowledge of the sources or a culpable lack of understanding can give rise to this unhistoric view. On this kind of historiography cf. W. Ullmann in *Hist. Z.*, cxci (1960), pp. 620 ff., and idem in *Archivio storico Pugliese*, xiii (1960), pp. 349 ff., at p. 364 n. 27.

**346, n. 2:** Henry IV is addressed by Hazilo of Hildesheim as "*regis regum* insignis *vicarius* in futuro regnaturus cum eo, cuius vicem executus es strenue" (*Briefsammlung aus der Zeit Heinrichs IV.*, ed. C. Erdmann and N. Fickermann, no. 53, p. 99, line 16).

**348, n. 2:** Cf. in this context also *Reg.* iv. 3, p. 298, lines 20 f.

**349, n. 1:** The concern for the German kingdom is one that belongs to the "majora ecclesiarum *negotia*", *Reg.* iv. 23, p. 335.

**356, n. 6:** It is most instructive to see that the author of these forgeries cannot construct a proper theocratic theme for the king, but has to operate with the opposed theme, that is, the populist thesis. The emphasis on the *voluntas populi*, within this context, reveals in fact the weakness of the royal-theocratic theme and demonstrates how the author realized that on this basis he could not make a reasoned reply to the Gregorian-hierocratic attack. Henry IV himself, however, never, as far as could be ascertained, invoked the populist principle.

**359, n. 1:** The relation between faith and law is neatly expressed by Gregory VII in his *Reg.* ii. 75, p. 237, to King Sven of Denmark telling him that the popes were always anxious "omnes reges et principes ad aeternam beatitudinem cunctos *invitare legalibus disciplinis.*"

**360, n. 1:** The overriding value attributed to an authority makes understandable the prevalence of the deductive method in the M.A., and hence the aversion from induction and empiricism. Hence also the prevalence of thinking in purely abstract terms from which particular ideas could be deduced.

**361, n. 2:** The model for this statement of Gratian seems to have been Justinian: "ex nobis eis (scil. the works of the Roman jurisconsults) *impertietur auctoritas*", *Cod.* I. xvii. 1 (6).

**365, n. 2:** For the general theme of historical jurisprudence and legal history cf. B. Paradisi, "Droit et Histoire" in *Archives de Philosophie et du Droit*, 1959, pp. 23 ff., and W. Ullmann in his *Rapport* to the XI International Congress of Historical Sciences (Stockholm, 1960), fasc. iii, pp. 34 ff.

**366, n. 1:** On Hildebert of Lavardin see also J. Szövérffy, "Hildebert of Lavardin and a Westminster sequence" in *Rev. Bénédictine*, lxvii (1957), pp. 98 ff. In general see also A. M. Landgraf, *Einführung . . . Frühscholastik* (Regensburg, 1948), pp. 12–33.

**367, ctd from 366, n. 2:** For further details see now M. D. Chenu, *La théologie au douzième siècle* (Paris, 1957), and A. M. Landgraf, "Zum Werden der Theologie des 12. Jahrhunderts in *Z. f. kath. Theol.*, lxxix (1957), pp. 417–33.

**367, n. 4:** For Cremona see U. Gualazzini, *Lo studio di Cremona* (Cremona, 1956); also idem in *Studi in onore di Arrigo Solmi* (Milan, 1941), i. 5–52 (twelfth century).

**369, n. 3:** For additional material concerning the early Romanists cf. U. Gualazzini in *Studi Parmensi*, iii (1953), pp. 363, at p. 374 and notes 48 ff. For Bologna see G. de Vergottini, *Lo studio di Bologna* (Bologna, 1954), esp. p. 20, and F. Wieacker, *Vom röm. Recht* (Stuttgart, 1961), pp. 288 ff.

**371, n. 4:** A possible model for this advice of Urban II may be found in Justinian's constitution *Tanta*, cap. 15: "diversitas rationum."

**374, ctd from 373, n. 3:** Concerning the qualities of the popes, Caspar, i. 83, remarked: "Es waren fast zu allen Zeiten andere Qualitäten als die theologische Gelehrsamkeit, welche die Männer auf Petri Stuhl bewährt haben." For an assessment of the canonists cf. also G. Le Bras, "Velut splendor firmamenti" in *Mélanges E. Gilson* (Paris, 1959), pp. 373 ff.

**374, n. 3:** For the historical background cf. now also J. d'Ercole in *Apollinaris*, xxxii (1959), pp. 273 ff.

**381, n. 1:** The subject of the *Summae Confessorum* is now examined afresh by P. Michaud-Quentin, "A propos des premières summae confessorum: théologie et droit canonique" in *Rech. de théol. ancienne et médiévale*, xxvi (1959), pp. 264 ff.

**390, n. 1:** The influence of Benzo of Alba seems to be greater than has hitherto been assumed, cf. W. Ullmann in *Misc. Hist. Pont.*, xviii (1954), p. 110 n. 13; idem in *Sav. Z., Kan. Abt.*, xlvi (1960), p. 433 n. 13. Cf., furthermore, the archbishop of Milan addressing Frederick I at Roncaglia as "orbis et urbis imperator" (Rahewin, *Gesta*, iv. 5, p. 238). For Frederick I himself, cf. *MGH. Const.* i. 271, no. 191; no. 270, p. 372; no. 240, p. 335; no. 161, p. 224.

**393, n. 1:** The term *reguli* (kinglings) had already been used by Gregory VII in his *Reg.* ii. 70, p. 230, though its meaning here does not seem to be the same as Benzo's.

**394, n. 1:** With unconvincing reasons N. F. Cantor, *Church, Kingship and Lay Investiture in England* 1089–1135 (Princeton, 1958) tries to ascribe these tracts to Gerard of York, cf. my review in *J. Eccl. Hist.*, x (1959), pp. 234 ff. For the fundamental importance of these tracts see E. Kantorowicz, *The King's Two Bodies* (Princeton, 1957), cf. my review in *MIOG.*, lxvi (1958), pp. 364 ff.

**399, n. 4:** The same standpoint is found in Gregory of Catina, *Orthodoxa Defensio* in *MGH. L. d. L.*, ii. 358: because kings were *christi*, they too combined both royal and sacerdotal powers.

**406, n. 2:** Hence also the frequent invocation of *St John*, viii. 36 (My kingdom is not of this world) by the anti-hierocrats (dualists), cf. *Hist. Z.*, cxci (1960), p. 621 n. 1.

**411, n. 2:** For Gerhoh of Reichersberg see now D. van den Eynde, *L'oeuvre littéraire de Gerhoch de Reichersberg* (Rome, 1957); E. Meuthen, *Kirche und Heilsgeschichte bei Gerhoh von Reichersberg* (in Studien u. Texte zur Geistesgeschichte des M.A., vi (1959) ); P. Classen, *Gerhoch von Reichersberg: eine Biographie* (Wiesbaden, 1960).

**413, n. 1:** About the juristic tenor of the Matthean passage cf. also *J.T.S.*, xi (1960), pp. 41–2; about the Johannean passage (xxi. 15 f.) see P. Gaechter in *Z. f. kath. Theol.*, lxix (1947), pp. 328 ff., esp. 338, 344.

**414, n. 4:** Whilst there is now doubt about Honorius as a member of St Augustine, Canterbury, there seems certainty that he stayed there at the convent, cf. H. Fichtenau in *MIOG.*, lxvii (1959), p. 406.

**415, n. 2:** Cf. also in this context Ivo of Chartres and his view that *regnum* and *sacerdotium* should work together for the good of the *ecclesia*, *Ep.* 238 (in *P.L.* clxii. 246), and for the implications of this view in a "political" context see M. J. Wilks in *Misc. Hist. Eccles. Stockholm* 1960 (Louvain, 1961), pp. 32 ff.

**420, n. 3:** For recent literature on John of Salisbury cf. H. Hohenleutner in *Hist. Jb.*, lxxvii (1958), pp. 493 ff.

**426, ctd from 425, n. 2:** Other statements on the preference of *utilitas publica* are in Innocent III, *Reg.* ii. 253: "communem causam privatae praeponens" and in Innocent IV, *MGH. Epp. PP. RR.*, ii. 257, no. 344 and ii. 309, no. 425 (dispensation from the impediment of consanguinity (fourth degree) in the interests of *utilitas evidens*).

**427, n. 1:** The same triad is repeated by St Bernard in his *De gratia et libero arbitrio (P.L.* cit., col. 1007).

**429, n. 5:** Another instance of borrowing from St Bernard by Innocent III in X: I. xxiii. 6; cf. *De cons.*, II. viii, cols. 751–2: "Nihil excipitur, ubi distinguitur nihil."

**431, n. 1:** Mention should be made of Innocent IV's view expressed in 1245: "Nec curabimus de cetero *uti gladio materiali*, sed tantum spirituali contra Fredericum", Huillard-Bréholles, *Hist. dipl. Fred. II*, vi. 347.

**433, n. 3:** The application of *Jer.* i. 10 by the papacy could be seen already in the pontificate of Leo IX, *Ep.* 72 (in *P.L.*, cxliii. 692) and see also Gregory VII in his *Reg.* v. 2, p. 350; vi. 13, p. 415. The passage was also incorporated in the speech before the conclave on 25 October 1958, see *Acta Ap. Sedis*, l (1958), p. 858.

**437, n. 4:** For Peter Damian cf. F. Dressler, *Petrus Damiani: Leben und Werk* (in *Studia Anselmiana*, xxxiv (1954) ); J. J. Ryan, *St Peter Damiani and his canonical sources* (Toronto, 1956); J. Goussette, *Pierre Damien et la culture profane* (Louvain, 1956); J. Leclercq, *S. Pierre Damien, ermite et homme de l'église* (Rome, 1960).

**438, n. 1:** For Hugh of St Victor see now also F. W. Witte, "Die Staats und Rechtsphilosophie des Hugo von St Viktor" in *Arch. f. Rechts- und Sozialphilosophie*, xliii (1957), pp. 555 ff.; F. Merzbacher, "Recht und Gewaltenlehre bei Hugo von St Viktor" in *Sav. Z., Kan. Abt.*, xliv (1958), pp. 181 ff.

**438, n. 2:** In the fifteenth century, too, this was still the view: "Clerus et populus sunt nomina collectiva significantia totum populum christianum, qui in duo genera hominum dividitur, videlicet clerum et populum," Petrus de Monte, *De pot. pont.* in I. T. Rocaberti, *Bibl. Max. Pont.* (Rome, 1698), xviii. 122. And yet, despite this currency of the concept in the M.A., there is the one or the other writer on historical subjects who tries to make out that by *ecclesia* only the *sacerdotium* was understood. According to this ill-informed view Christ would have established merely the *sacerdotium* in Matt. xvi. 18 f. About this fundamental mistake in a recent book cf. my review in *J. Eccl. Hist.* vi (1955), pp. 233 ff.

**439, n. 3:** For a similar view on the symbolic interpretation of water see already Alcuin in *MGH. Epp.*, iv. 212, no. 137, lines 14 f. ("in aqua populus intelligitur credentium.").

**443, n. 2:** Cf., furthermore, Innocent III in *Reg.* i. 117, 192, 345. For the influence of the Bible on principles of government, see W. Ullmann in *Settimana Spoleto*, x (1963), 189 ff.

**443, n. 3:** For the whole question of Christ as King see the synthesis of J. Leclercq, "L'idée de la seigneurie du Christ au M.A." in *R.H.E.*, liii (1958), pp. 57 ff.

**443, n. 4:** The same in Johannes de Turrecremata, *Summa de ecclesia* (ed. Venice, 1561), fol. 19r, no. 28, and in the sixteenth century Cardinal Dominicus Jacobazzi in his *De conciliis* in *Tractatus illustr. jurisconsultorum*, xiii–1, fol. 189vb, no. 91.

**444, ctd from 443, n. 5:** See also Innocent III in his *Reg.* ix. 73. Before him the same views were expressed by Alexander III, *Ep.* 150 (in *P.L.* cc. 211) and by Celestine III, *Ep.* 235 (in *P.L.* ccvi. 1127).

**447, ctd from 446, n. 5:** The view of Johannes Monachus on monarchy as the *mensura et regula* seems to be of Thomist origin. Thomas' view on the law was that it provided a *mensura et regula*, see his *S. Theol.*, II–ii. 95, art. 3. Marsiglio of Padua too applies this Thomist view to the government, see his *Def. Pacis*, i. 18. 2. Cf. now also M. J. Wilks, *The Problem of Sovereignty in the M.A.* (Cambridge, 1963).

**449, n. 2:** Another significant statement is in Innocent III's *Reg.* i. 326.

**453, n. 1:** In this context the so-called electoral pacts (*Wahlkapitulationen*) deserve attention, because they were designed to check the constitutional freedom of the pope. For this see W. Ullmann in *Ephem. Juris Can.*, xii (1956), pp. 246 ff.

**456, n. 2:** But it should be noted that this bull changed the original "omnis humana creatura" into "omnes Christi fideles."

# APPENDIX C

**7, n. 6:** See now also V. Monachino in *Arch. Hist. Pont.*, v (1967), 325 ff. (book review).

**22, n. 1:** For the possibility that the Roman *actio noxalis* explains this basic Gelasian standpoint, see the suggestive paper by J. L. Nelson, "Gelasius I's doctrine of responsibility" in *JTS*, xviii (1967), 78 ff.

**37, n. 3:** For the view that Gregory I pursued a policy of bifurcation—one particular line toward the East which differed materially from that pursued toward the West, see W. Ullmann, *A Hist. of Pol. Ideas in the MA* (London, 2nd impr. 1968), 49 f.

**38, n. 4:** In this context see the excellent study by M. J. Wilks, "Roman empire and Christian State in the *De Civ. Dei*" in *Augustinus* (1967), 489 ff., esp. 503 ff. See, further, R. A. Markus, "Two concepts of pol. authority . . ." in *JTS*, xvi (1965), 68 ff.

**58:** According to H. Fuhrmann, "Konstantinische Schenkung u. abendl. Kaisertum" in *DA*, xxii (1966), 63 ff., the story of the Donation begins with Ps. Isidore. Despite the great acumen displayed by the author, the connoisseur misses all reference to the incontrovertible use made of the fabrication from the fifties of the eighth century onwards (see also above 466); the compelling arguments of Levillain, Halphen, Ganshof and others as well as the textual agreements (cf. e.g., the telling instance above 73, n. 2 at the end, which passage is not in the *Legenda s. Silvestri*, but appears in the Donation only) are mentioned neither here in this study by Fuhrmann nor in the introduction to his excellent edition of the forgery (in *MGH, Fontes iuris Germanici antiqui*, x (1968); however diligent, Fuhrmann cannot, as far as the arguments go, convince; nor does he make any reference to "the many copies preserved in the archives of Gallic churches" in the sixties of the ninth century nor to the utilization of the concoction by Aeneas of Paris and others (cf. art. cit., 121–2).

**88:** See further J. Deér, "Der Patrizius-Titel Karls d. Gr." in *Arch. Hist. Pont.*, iii (1965), 31 ff., with some questionable evidential conclusions.

**95, n. 2:** See on this L. Falkenstein, *Der Lateran d. karol. Pfalz zu Aachen* (=Kölner hist. Abh., xiii) (Cologne, 1966).

**161 f.:** See now P. E. Schramm, *Kaiser, Könige und Päpste*, ii (Stuttgart, 1968), 119 ff.; esp. important for the *regnum italicum* of Charles the Bald, ibid., 127 at n. 29 and 128. I am somewhat hesitant to subscribe to Schramm's view that *tuitio* was a rare term at the time (n. 32). For *advocatus* and *protector*, see above 71 ff., 85 f., and below 231 f.

**163:** For details concerning the *Rex Romanorum* as a preliminary to the fully fledged Emperor of the Romans, cf. W. Ullmann, "Dies ortus imperii" in *Atti del convegno internazionale di studi Accursiani* (Milan, 1968), 662–96.

**180 ff.:** For supplementary matter concerning Ps. Isidore and the primacy of the Roman Church, see now Y. Congar, *L'ecclésiologie du haut MA* (Paris, 1968), 226 ff. Cf. also H. Fuhrmann, "Ps. Idisore in Rome . . ." in *Z. f. Kirchgesch.* (1967), 16 ff.

**193:** For a survey of Nicholas I's position in regard to the primatial question cf. Y. Congar, *L'ecclésiologie*, cit., 206 ff.

**229 ff.:** See now esp. R. Folz, *La naissance du saint empire* (Paris, 1968), 108 ff., and for the *Ottonianum* ibid., 269 ff. (with facsimile). Here also very valuable extracts from tenth-century sources. For the *Ottonianum* see also E. E. Stengel, *Abhandlungen & Untersuchungen zur ma. Gesch.* (Cologne, 1960), 245 ff., who (223 n. 31) has altogether misunderstood my argumentation in *Cambridge Hist. J.*, cit. In the already mentioned study by H. Fuhrmann, in *DA*, xxii (1966), 63 ff., at 128 ff. the point is made that the *Ottonianum* was falsified by the deacon without fingers, though it is difficult to accept the arguments: above all, the reasons which made this deacon falsify the Donation whilst still in the service of the pope, John XII, remain quite obscure; in any case, the statement in DO. III. 389 (which contains the reference to this deacon (see above, 242 n. o)), can hardly furnish incontrovertible support for Fuhrmann's thesis, for this diploma was issued 40 years after the event.

**230:** For the deposition of John XII, see now H. Zimmermann, *Papstabsetzungen des MA*, (Cologne, 1968), 77 ff.

**232, n. 1:** For a survey of the Ottonian system of *Reichskirchen*, see now O. Köhler, "Die ottonische Reichskirche: ein Forschungsbericht" in *Adel & Kirche: Festschrift f. Gerd Tellenbach* (Freiburg, 1968), 141 ff.

**237, n. 1:** It should be noted, however, that Otto I styled himself on a number of occasions "imperator *Romanorum* et Francorum", cf., e.g., DO. I. 318; 322; 324; 329; 346.

**238, n. 6:** See now also R. Folz, *La naissance*, cit., 130ff.

**239, n. 1:** For the wider implications of Western imperial policy and its repercussions on the East, see W. Ullmann, "Reflexions on the medieval empire" in *Trans. R. Hist. S.*, xiv (1964), 89 ff.; D. M. Nicol, "The Byzantine view of Western Europe" in *Greek, Roman & Byzantine Studies*, viii (1967), 315 ff.; see also W. Ohnsorge, *Konstantinopel & der Okzident* (Darmstadt, 1966), esp. 49 ff., 176 ff., 287 ff., 294 ff.

**253, n. 1:** For a detailed description of the symbolism and liturgy in Ordo C (=Ordo XIV in R. Elze, *Ordines coronationis imperialis* (Hannover)), 1960, see R. Elze in *Adel & Kirche*, cit., 365 ff., who, however, dates this ordo "around 1200."

**277, n. 1:** The book by L. F. J. Meulenberg, *Der Primat d. röm. Kirche im Denken u. Handeln Gregors VII.* (s'Gravenhage, 1965), deals only with one particular segment of Gregory's primatial expressions; cf. my review in *J.E.H.*, xvii (1968), 101 ff.

**292, n. 2:** See now on *DP*. 23 also D. Lindner, "Die Erbheiligkeit des Papstes" in *Savi Z., Kan. Abt.*, liii (1967), 15 ff., who contributes little to the understanding of the passage, because he is unaware of the Leonine distinction between office and person; but the author brings many interesting passages from the canonistic literature of the twelfth century.

**295, n. 1:** Cf. now *Neue Forschungen über Cluny u. die Cluniazenser*, ed. G. Tellenbach (Freiburg, 1959) with contributions by J. Wollasch, H.-E. Mager, H. Diener, etc.;

also N. Hunt, *Cluny under s. Hugh* (London, 1967).

**302, n. 4:** It should be kept in mind that King Henry was excommunicated and (not deposed, but) suspended from kingship: Gregory put Henry on the same level as a bishop who was suspended (and not deposed) from episcopal functions. He was therefore entitled to refer to Henry as *rex*, until the latter was finally deposed in 1080. This point should always be borne in mind when considering the relations between Henry IV and Gregory VII in the intervening years, though frequently enough the point is missed, so, e.g., by G. Miccoli, *Chiesa Gregoriana* (Florence, 1966), 203 ff.

**305, n. 3:** For heresy conceived as treason by Innocent III, cf W. Ullmann, "The significance of Innocent III's decretal *Vergentis*" in *Etudes d'hist. du droit canonique dédiées à Gabriel Le Bras* (Paris, 1965), 729 ff.

**320, n. 1:** Further C. G. Fürst, *Cardinalis* (Munich, 1967), a highly competent study on the history of the cardinalate.

**323, n. 1:** The decree is now newly ed. by H. G. Krause in *Studi Gregoriani*, vii (1962), 271 ff. Here the author gives a most competent survey of the developments leading to the election decree itself. Krause has considerably clarified the hitherto obscure terms of the *debitus honor et reverentia* in cap. 6.

**328, n. 4:** Cf. in this context W. Ullmann, "On the heuristic value of medieval chancery products with special reference to papal documents" in *Annali della fondazione italiana per la storia amministrativa*, i (1964), 117 ff.; also C. R. Cheney, *The study of the medieval papal chancery* (Glasgow, 1966), esp. 24–29.

**341 f.:** For Frederick I's policy cf. the refurbished work by E. E. Stengel, "Exercitus facit imperatorem" in *Abh. u. Unters. zur Gesch. des Kaisergedankens im MA* (Cologne, 1965), 1 ff., whose mode of argumentation and thought-processes are reminiscent of the Victorian-Wilhelminian era; cf. my review in *Rev. Belge de phil. et d'histoire*, 1967, 531 ff. According to Stengel it was "the armed might of the Germans upon which they based their right to imperial power" adding: "with their arms they (the Germans) have acquired this right, and with their arms they knew how to keep it" (p. 94). It is somewhat baffling to read this sort of thing in the sixties of the twentieth century.

**341, n. 4:** The paper by F. Kempf, "Der favor apostolicus bei der Wahl Friedrich Barbarossas u. im deutschen Thronstreit" in *Speculum Historiale*, ed. Cl. Bauer et al. (Freiburg, 1965), 469 ff. ignores vital matters; cf. my remarks in *Papst & König* (Salzburger Universitätsschriften, no. 3, 1967), 33 no. 52.

**343, n. 2:** For Innocent III's imperial policy see now the observations of W. Ullmann in *Atti . . . Accursiani*, cit., 662–96.

**348, n. 4:** For the points treated here see now also J. Fleckenstein, "Heinrich IV. und der deutsche Episkopat" in *Adel & Kirche*, cit., 221 ff.

**361, n. 2:** For the conception of law by Gratian see now also the exposition by L. de Luca, "Nocion de ley en el decreto de Graciano: legalidad o absolutismo" in *Ius canonicum*, vii (1967), 65 ff.

**363, n. 1:** On the intimate connexion between theology and law in the eleventh century, cf. *Principles of Government & Politics in the MA*, 2nd ed. (London, 1966), 71 f., 209.

**366, n. 1:** For the eleventh-century humanism cf. W. von den Steinen, *Menschen im MA*, ed. P. von Moos (Berne, 1968), 196 ff.

**366, n. 2:** The link between law and theology continued to exist far beyond the period treated in this volume: this has recently been shown by B. Tierney, "Hermeneutics and History . . ." in *Essays in honor of Bertie Wilkinson* (Toronto, 1969), 354 ff. For the connexion between law, faith and governmental principles, cf. W. Ullmann in *La* *storia del diritto nel quadro delle scienze storiche* (Florence, 1966), 195 ff.

**370:** For the influence of Gratian in England resulting in an outburst of canon law collections, see Ch. Duggan, *Twelfth-century decretal collections* (London, 1963), supplemented by his contributions to *Studies in Church History*, i (1964), 132 ff., ii (1965), 179 ff.; see also id., in *Studia Gratiana*, xiv (1967), 53 ff.

**370, n. 2:** Cf. further J. C. Russell, "Gratian, Irnerius and the early schools of Bologna" in *Mississippi Quarterly*, xii (1959), 168 ff.

**373, n. 1:** In this context the profound study by L. Buisson, "Die Entstehung d. Kirchenrechts" in *Sav. Z., Kan. Abt.*, lii (1966) should be consulted, esp. in regard to the need for a law within ecclesiological premisses, already postulated in the early patristic period. See further L. de Luca, "Fonti del diritto canonico" in *Enciclopedia del diritto*, xvii (1968), 1 ff., which is an excellent survey and contains a rich bibliography.

**373, n. 2:** For a detailed examination of the points here indicated cf. the masterly exposition by B. Paradisi, *Diritto canonico e tendenze di scuola nei glossatori da Irnerio ad Accursio* (Spoleto, 1965), also in *Studi Medievali*, 3rd ser., vi-2, 1965. Cf. also Ch. Munier, "Droit canonique et droit romain d'après Gratien et les décrétistes" in *Etudes . . . Gabriel Le Bras*, cit., 943 ff.

**381, n. 1:** The *Summa confessorum* by Thomas of Chobham is now edited in full by F. Broomfield, *Thomae de Chobham Summa Confessorum* (Louvain-Paris, 1968) =*Analecta Medievalia Namurcensia*, vol. xxv.

**394, n. 1:** For the wholly unsatisfactory edition of the York Tracts by K. Pellens, *Die Texte des normannischen Anonymous* (Wiesbaden, 1966), see my review in *Hist. Z.*, ccvi (1968), 696 ff.

**431, n. 1:** A recent exposition of the Two-Sword theory will be found in H. Hoffmann, "Die beiden Schwerter im hohen MA" in *DA*, xx (1964), 78 ff.

**448:** For the role of the Bible and the resultant continuity of papal doctrine, cf. W. Ullmann, "The papacy as an institution of government" in *Studies in Church History*, ed. G. J. Cuming, ii (London, 1965), 78 ff.

**455:** The points here made are elaborated at greater length in my *Principles of Government*, 2nd ed., cit., 231 ff. and *Hist. of pol. ideas in the MA* cit., 167 ff.

**457, n. 3:** For the background of this development and the resultant implications, cf. W. Ullmann, *Individual & Society in the MA* (London, 1967).

# Index

483